HAND BOOK OF MEDICINAL AND AROMATIC PLANTS

(Cultivation, Utilisation and Extraction Processes)

AF632276

New Publications from EIRI

1. HAND BOOK OF EXPORT ORIENTED INDUSTRIES
2. HAND BOOK OF PLASTIC PROJECTS (HI-TECH PLASTIC PROJECTS)
3. AGRO BASED & FOOD PROCESSING WITH EXPORT ORIENTED INDUSTRIES
4. HAND BOOK OF PACKAGING INDUSTRIES
5. ALL CHEMICALS AND ALLIED INDUSTRIES
6. HAND BOOK OF HOSIERY READYMADE GARMENTS & TEXTILE PROJECTS
7. AGRO BASED INDUSTRIES HAND BOOK (PLANTATION & FARMING)
8. REAL ESTATE PLAZAS, HOTEL, MOTEL, HOSPITAL & COMMERCIAL COMPLEXES
9. WORLD IMPORTERS DIRECTORY OF AGRO BASED & FOOD PROCESSING
10. WORLD IMPORTERS YELLOW PAGES (ALL TRADE BUYERS DIRECTORY)
11. HAND BOOK OF PRINTING PROCESSES TECHNOLOGIES & INDUSTRIES
12. SMALL MEDIUM & LARGE SCALE CHEMICAL INDUSTRES
13. DAIRY FORMULATIONS, PROCESSES & MILK PACKAGING INDUSTRIES
14. PLASTIC PROCESSING AND PACKAGING INDUSTRIES
15. STATIONERY, PAPER CONVERTING & PACKAGING INDUSTRIES
16. INDUSTRIAL DIRECTORY (ALL INDIA TRADE DIRECTORY)
17. FOOD PROCESSING AND AGRO BASED INDUSTRIES
18. AGRO BASED PLANTATION CULTIVATION & FARMING HAND-BOOK
19. RUBBER CHEMICALS AND PROCESSING INDUSTRIES
20. PAINT PIGMENT VARNISH AND LACQUER MANUFACTURING
21. MODERN INKS FORMULAES AND MANUFACTURING INDUSTRIES
22. HAND BOOK OF BAKERY INDUSTRIES
23. MODERN TECHNOLOGY OF ESSENTIAL OILS
24. START YOUR OWN COLD STORAGE UNIT
25. TECHNOLOGY OF GUMS, ASHESIVES AND SEALANTS WITH FORMULATIONS
26. MOULDS DESIGN AND PROCESSING HAND BOOK
27. PROFITABLE SMALL SCALE MANUFACTURE OF SOAPS & DETERGENTS
28. PET PRE-FORM AND ITS PRODUCTS (BOTTLES ETC.) MFG.
29. INDIAN INDUSTRIAL AND BUSINESS DIRECTORY
30. ESSENTIAL OILS MANUFACTURING & AROMATIC PLANTS
31. MODERN PACKAGING TECHNOLOGY FOR PROCESSED FOOD, BAKERY, SPICE & ALLIED FOOD INDUSTRIES
32. AGRO BASED HAND BOOK ON CULTIVATION, PLANTATION & FARMING
33. HAND BOOK OF PERFUMES & FLAVOURS
34. HAND BOOK OF SPICES & PACKAGING WITH FORMULAES
35. HAND BOOK OF HERBAL & SYNTHETIC COSMETICS
36. HAND BOOK OF ADHESIVES WITH THEIR FORMULAES
37. HAND BOOK OF ELECTROPLATING ANODIZING & SURFACE TREATMENT TECHNOLOGY
38. HAND BOOK OF AYURVEDIC & HERBAL MEDICINES WITH FORMULAES
39. FRUITS & VEGETABLES PROCESSING HAND BOOK
40. HAND BOOK OF HERBS, MEDICINAL & AROMATIC PLANTS CULTIVATION
41. HAND BOOK OF CONFECTIONERY WITH & FORMULATIONS
42. MANUFACTURE OF SNACKS FOOD, NAMKEEN, PAPPAD & POTATO PRODUCTS
43. ESSENTIAL OIL PROCESSES AND FORMULATIONS HAND BOOK
44. SYNTHETIC RESINS TECHNOLOGY WITH FORMULATIONS
45. HAND BOOK OF PERFUMES WITH FORMULATIONS
46. COSMETICS PROCESSES AND FORMULATIONS HAND BOOK
47. PAINT VARNISH SOLVENTS & COATING TECHNOLOGY
48. HAND BOOK OF SYNTHETIC DETERGENTS WITH FORMULATIONS
49. TECHNOLOGY OF SYNTHETIC DYES, PIGMENTS & INTERMEDIATES
50. HAND BOOK OF AGRO CHEMICAL INSECTICIDES & PESTICIDES
51. PLASTIC COMPOUNDING MASTERBATCHES, PET AND OTHER PLASTIC PROCESSING INDUSTRIES
52. PRESERVATION & CANNING OF FRUITS AND VEGETABLES
53. PHARMACEUTICALS AND DRUGS TECHNOLOGY WITH FORMULATIONS
54. MILK PROCESSING & DAIRY PRODUCTS INDUSTRIES
55. TECHNOLOGYOF BUILDING MATERIALS AND CHEMICALSWITHPROCESSES
56. SMALL AND COTTAGE SCALE INDUSTRIES (LAGHU UDYOG)-IN HINDI LANGUAGE
57. MANUFACTURE OF HOUSEHOLD SOAPS, TOILET SOAPS AND OTHER SOAPS WITH FORMULATIONS.

...........contd.

ENGINEERS INDIA RESEARCH INSTITUTE

Regd. Off : 4449, Nai Sarak, Main Road, Delhi - 110 006 (India)

*** Ph: 91-11- 23918117, 23916431, 23840361, 9811437895 * Fax: 91-11- 23916431**

*** E-Mail : eirisidi@bol.net.in * Website: www.eiriindia.org**

HAND BOOK OF MEDICINAL AND AROMATIC PLANTS

(Cultivation, Utilisation and Extraction Processes)

Written By

EIRI BOARD OF CONSULTANTS & ENGINEERS

ENGINEERS INDIA RESEARCH INSTITUTE

4449, Nai Sarak, Main Road, Delhi - 110006 (India)
Ph: 91-11-23918117, 23916431, 23840361
Fax: 91-11- 2391 6431, 2391 8117
*** E-Mail: eirisidi@bol.net.in**
***Website: www.eiriindia.org**

Sole Distributor :

INDIAN INSTITUTE OF CONSULTANTS, 4/27 ROOP NAGAR, DELHI -110007

PRINTED & PUBLISHED BY

ENGINEERS INDIA RESEARCH INSTITUTE

4449, Nai Sarak, Main Road, Delhi - 110006 (India)

Ph: 91-11-23918117, 23916431, 23840361

Fax: 91-11- 2391 6431, 2391 8117

* E-Mail: eirisidi@bol.net.in

*Website: www.eiriindia.org

DISTRIBUTED BY

SMALL INDUSTRY RESEARCH INSTITUTE (SIRI)
INDIAN INSTITUTE OF CONSULTANTS

© Copy Reserved by Sudhir Gupta, Delhi

ISBN: 81-86732-68-3

Printed in New Delhi (INDIA)

The book is sold subject to the condition that it shall not, by way or trade or otherwise, be lent, resold, hired out, or otherwise circulated without the publishers's prior written cinsenbt, in any form of binding or cover other than in which it is published/complied and without a similar consent including this condition being imposed on the subsequent purchaser and without limiting the rights under copy rights reserved above, no part of this publication may be reproduced, stored in or introduced into a retrieval system, or transmitted in any form or by any means (electronic, mechanical, photocopying or otherwise), without the written prior permission of both the copyright owner and above mentioned published of this book. While the book has been prepared carefully, yet the publisher's, printer and compiler do not hold any responsibility on the subject of the book. All disputes regarding this book are Subject to Delhi Jurisdiction only

Rs. 875/-

Printed & Published by Sudhir Gupta for "Engineers India Research Institute" 4499 Nai Sarak, Main Road, New Delhi -110006

Preface

*The book **Hand Book of Medicinal and Aromatic Plants** covers almost all the basic and advanced details of medicinal and aromatic plants. The new edition of the book is covering madicinal and aromatic palnts which include Medicinal Plants – Priorities in Indian Medicines Diverse Studies and Implications, Dioscorea deltoidea Hook. Distribution and Agrotechnology, Cultivation of Dioscorea composita Hemsl: A Potential Source of Diosgenin, Production of Ergot Alkaloids by Submerged Fermentation, Ajmalicine (Raubasine): A Medicinally Important Alkaloids from Catharanthus roseus (Vinca rosea), Production of Colchicine from Gloriosa Superba Seeds, Studies on Commercial Indian Aconites: Atis, Cultivation of Ammi majus Linn. in India, Cultivation of Rutin Bearing Eucalyptus Species, Aloe, Technology of Podophyllotoxins, Yew (Taxus spp.) (Barhmi), Ginseng, Annatto – The Natural Colour, Neem (Azadirachta indica A. Juss.), Some Endangered Medicinal Plants, Nomenclatural Ambiguity of medicinal Plants used in Indigenous Systems of Medicine, Biotechnology and Genetic Improvement of Medicinal Plants, Improvement on Medicinal Plants Cultivation, Safed Musli, Cinchona, Glory Lily, Henbane, Holy Thistle, Ipecac, Opium Poppy, Ambrette, Bursora Celery, Chamomile, Citronella, Clocimum, Davana, Dill, Fennel, French Basil, Kewda, Khus, Lavender, Lemon Grass, Lemon Scented Gum, Palmarosa, Patchouli, Rosemary, Sacred Basil, Sandalwood, Sweet Marjoram, Thyme, Annatto, Camphor Basil, Spirulina, Stevia, Mushrooms and others.*

The book has been written for the benefit and to prove an asset and a handy reference guide in the hands of new entrepreneurs and well established industrialists.

Director
ENGINEERS INDIA RESEARCH INSTITUTE
Nai Sarak, New Delhi (INDIA)
E-Mail: eirisidi@bol.net.in

New Publications from EIRI

58. HAND BOOK OF OILS FATS AND DERIVATIVES WITH REFINING AND PACKAGING TECHNOLOGY
59. START YOUR OWN EXPORT BUSINESS (HOW TO EXPORT)
60. HERBAL COSMETICS & BEAUTY PRODUCTS WITH FORMULATIONS
61. TECHNOLOGY OFTEXTILES
62. TECHNOLOGY OF PETROCHEMICALS, LUBRICANTS,GREASES AND PETROLEUM REFINING
63. TECHNOLOGY OF RUBBER AND RUBBER GOODS INDUSTRIES
64. HAND BOOK OF MODERN BAKERY PRODUCTS
65. CANDLE MAKING PROCESSES & FORMULATIONS HAND BOOK
66. HAND BOOK OF SCREEN PRINTING WITH PROCESSES & TECHNOLOGY
67. TECHNOLOGY OF COATINGS,RESINS, PIGMENTS & INKS INDUSTRIES
68. HAND BOOK OF FOOD DEHYDRATION & DRYING
69. MEAT PROCESSING AND MEAT PRODUCTS HAND BOOK
70. HAND BOOK OF DAIRY FARMING
71. HAND BOOK OF PACKAGING TECHNOLOGY
72. TECHNOLOGYOFMODERN RICE MILLING & BASMATIRICE
73. HAND BOOK OF ICE CREAM TECHNOLOGY & FORMULAE
74. TEXTILE AUXILIARIES AND CHEMICALS WITH PROCESSES AND FORMULATIONS
75. MODERN SMALL AND COTTAGE SCALE INDUSTRIES
76. TECHNOLOGY OF PVC COMPOUNDING AND ITS APPLICATIONS
77. PROFITABLE BUSINESSES TO START FOR ENTREPRENEURS
78. START YOUR OWN SMALL BUSINESS AND INDUSTRY
79. HAND BOOK OF BIO TECHNOLOGY
80. HAND BOOK OF PRINTING TECHNOLOGY (OFFSET, SCREEN, FLEXO, GRAVURE, INKJET & DIGITAL)
81. FLORICULTURE HAND BOOK
82. HAND BOOK OF MEDICINAL AND AROMATIC PLANTS (CULTIVATION, UTILISATION AND EXTRACTION PROCESSES)
83. PROFITABLE SMALL COTTAGE TINY AND HOME INDUSTRIES
84. INDUSTRIAL CHEMICALS TECHNOLOGY HAND BOOK

PROJECT REPORTS IN CD-ROM

- LUCRATIVE 92 PROJECT REPORTS IN CD
- 43 INFOTECH/ HOSPITALITY, HOSPITAL,COLLEGE, SCHOOL & CLUB PROJECTS
- PROFITABLE CONSTRUCTION PROJECTS IN CD-ROM (23 PROJECT REPORTS)
- PROFITABLE FOOD AND ALLIED 52 PROJECT REPORTS
- PROFITBALE PLASTIC AND ALLIED 29 PROJECTS
- 45 PROFITABLE CHEMICALS AND ALLIED PRODUCTS
- 44 TEXTILE, GARMENTS, HOSIERY AND ALLIED PRODUCTS
- 21 DAIRY FARMING, MILK PROCESSING & OTHER MILK PRODUCTS PROJECT REPORTS
- 29 PAPER, PULP & PAPER CONVERTING PRODUCTS
- 31 ESSENTIAL OILS, PERFUMES, FLAVOURS & AROMATIC PERFUMERY COMPOUNDS

ENGINEERS INDIA RESEARCH INSTITUTE

Regd. Off : 4449, Nai Sarak, Main Road, Delhi - 110 006 (India)

*** Ph: 91-11- 23918117, 23916431, 23840361, 9811437895 * Fax: 91-11- 23916431**

*** E-Mail : eirisidi@bol.net.in * Website: www.eiriindia.org**

Contents

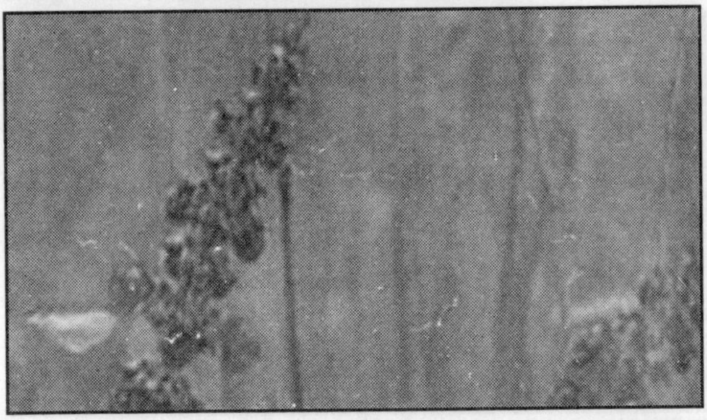

पत्थरचूर - Patharchur

सर्पगंधा - Sarpagandha

बेल - Bael

ब्राह्मी - Brahmi

ईसबगोल - Isabgol

वाय विडंग - Vaividang

जटामांसी - Jatamansi

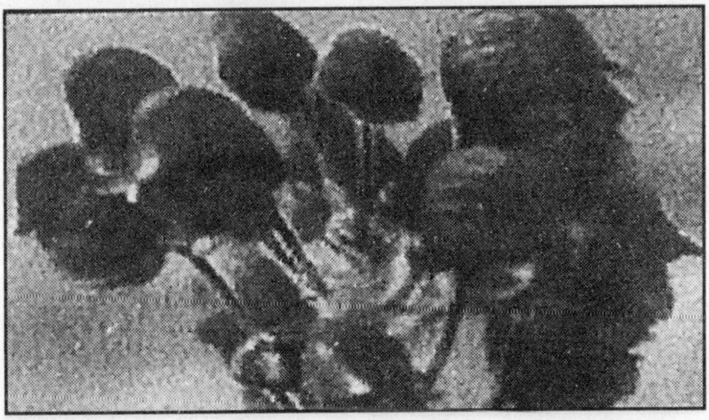

अतीस - Atees

कुटकी - Kutki

गुग्गल - Guggal

मकोय - Makoy

पीप्पली - Pippali

भूमि अमलाकी - **Bhumi amlaki**

चिरेता - **Chireta**

कलिहारी - **Kalihari**

कालमेघ - Kalmegh

अश्वगंधा - Ashawagandha

तुलसी - Tulsi

अशोक - Ashok

गुड़मार - Gudmar

दारूहल्दी - Daruhaldi

चंदन - Chandan

सफेद मुसली - Safaid Musali

केसर - Kesar

आंवला - Amla

वत्सनाभ - Vatsnabh

सना - Senna

शतावरी - Shatavari

कुठ - Kuth

मुलेठी - Mulethi

1

Medicinal Plants – Priorities in Indian Medicines Diverse Studies and Implications

It has been estimated that from 250,000 to 750,000 species of higher (flowering plants) exist on earth; some of these have not yet been botanically described. Although there is no way to determine accurately how many of these species have been used in traditional medicine, a reasonable estimate would be about 10% or from 25,000 to 75,000 species. However, perhaps only about 1% of these are acknowledgement through scientific studies to have real therapeutic value when used in extract form by humans. Virtually all such plants have been discovered and put to wide spread use in traditional medical systems through information derived from their use in folk medicine, ethnomedicine or traditional medicine.

World population is nearing 5 billion today and with this rate of growth it is likely to touch 7.5 billion by the year 2020. Global estimates indicate that over 3/4th of the five billion world population cannot afford the products of the western pharmaceutical industry and have to rely upon the use of traditional medicines, which are mainly derived from plants. This fact is well compiled by W.H.O. in an inventory of medicinal plants list in over 20,000 species. As a part of strategy to reduce financial burden on developing countries which spend 40-50% of their total health budget on drugs, W.H.O. currently encourages, recommends and promotes the inclusion of herbal drugs in national health care programmes because such drugs are easily available at a price within the reach of a common man and as such are time tested and thus considered to be much safer than the modern synthetic drugs. Resurgence of interest is herbal drugs in the western European countries is evident from the fact that two volumes of British Herbal Pharmacopoeia have been published and $33 million worth literature on herbal products was sold in the USA in 1990. The “green wave” in the utilization of medicinal plants resulted in higher consumption.

MEDICINAL PLANTS BASED DRUG INDUSTRY

Medicinal plants based drug industry has four major segments namely, (i) plant drugs for Indian systems of medicine covering Ayurvedic, Unani and Sidha systems, (ii) over the counter, non-prescription items involving plant parts, extracts and galenicals, (iii) essential oils, and (iv) phyto-pharmaceuticals.

MEDICINAL PLANTS BASED DRUG INDUSTRIES IN INDIAN SYSTEMS OF MEDICINE

There are at present 6,780 pharmacies in India Systems of Medicine of which 551 are on loan licence and the remaining 6,229 are on form D. Besides, there are many small manufacturing units using medicinal plants and thousands of *Vaidyas* preparing their own drugs from various plants. Annual herbal drug production has been estimated at around Rs. 800 crores and is expected to reach Rs. 4,000 crores by the year 2010. Various bottlenecks in the Indian herbal drug industry have been discussed elsewhere.

PLANT PARTS EXTRACT AND GALENICALS

The direct utilization of plant material is a feature of traditional medicines not only in the developing world but also in Europe and the U.S.A., e.g., herbal formulations on health food shops. Preparations of decoctions, tinctures, galeniclas and total extracts of plants also form a part of many pharmacopoeias of the world. The current trend of medicinal plants based drug industry is to procure standardized extracts of plants as raw material.

ESSENTIAL OILS FROM PLANTS

The essential oil industry was traditionally a cottage industry in India. Since, 1947, a number of industrial companies have been established for large scale production of essential oils, oleoresins and perfumes. The essential oils from plants being produced in India include ajowain oil, cedarwood oil, celery oil, citronella oil, davana oil, eucalyptus oil, geranium oil, lavender oil, lemongrass oil, *Mentha* oil, palmarosa oil, patchouli oil, rose oil, sandalwood oil, turpentine oil and vetiver oil. The manufacutre of turpentine oil, and resin from pines is a sizable and well established industry in India having 10,000-25,000 tonness annual production of the oil. α-pinene and δ-3 carene are the two vital component produced from the oil. α-Ionone from lemongrass oil for perfumery and β-ionone for Vitamin A synthesis are produced in India. Before 1960, menthol was not produced in India but the introduction of Japanese mint, *Mentha arvensis* and subsequent improvements thereupon enabled India to produce over 500 tonnes of menthol and now tops the world market in export of natural menthol.

Annual world production of limonene is 50,000 tonnes and Brazil is the biggest producer in the world market. It is a by-product of citrus industry.

Though turpentine oil and eucalyptus oil also yield limonene but the best economically cheap raw material is the discarded orange and lemon peel which is being used by Brazilian phytochemical industry. India has not yet tapped this source for limonene production.

PHYTOPHARMACEUTICALS

Before 1947, the production of plant based modern drugs in India was confined to quinine from *Cinchona* in three state owned factories and the very first phytochemical industry for quinine was established by the then British Government at Mungpoo in Darjeeling. During the past three and half decades' bulk production of plant-based modern drugs has become an important segment of Indian pharmaceutical industry. Some of the phytopharmaceuticals which are produced in India at present include morphine, codeine, papaverine, thebaine, emetine, quinine, quinidine, digoxin, caffeine, hyoscine, hyoscyamine, xanthotoxin, psoralen, colchicine, rutin, berberine, vinblastine, vincristine, nicotine, strychnine, brucine, ergot alkaloids, senna glycosides, pyrethroids and podophyllotoxin resin.

Phytopharmaceuticals for which technology has been developed for undertaking large scale production include L-dopa from *Mucuna* beans, ajmaline and ajmalicine from *Rauvolfia serpentina* and *Catharanthus* roots, respectively, and 18 β-acetyl glycyrrhetic acid from *Glycyrrhiza glabra*.

Indian Institute of Chemical Technology (I.I.C.T.), Hyderabad has developed methods for etoposide and tenoposide production and CIPLA is now producing it on commercial basis. At present 100 mg of etoposide is sold at Rs. 400 per vial. National Chemical Laboratory, Punc, developed the method of vincristine (VCR) and vinblastine (VLB) production. CIPLA have further improved the process and now they are third largest manufacturer of VCR and VLB in the world.

Medicinal plants based drug industry in progressing very fast in India, but it is beset with a number of problems. Most alarming problem the industry has started facing and will face in futurc is the dwindling supply of plant material from natural resources. A national policy on medicinal plants with a view to preserve endangered species and promoting cultivation of plants which are being extensively used by industry will help in solving the major problem of the industry. Special attention is required on medicinal plants on which significant research leads have been obtained (Table 1), medicinal plants which are being imported (Table 2), medicinal plants having export potential and the threatened medicinal plants (Table 3).

Trade in medicinal plants in largely unorganised and uncertain, both in demand and price structures. There is a need to have Marketing and Development Board for Medicinal and Aromatic Plants and Phytopharmaceuticals. Such a Board could interact with the growers and user industry to bring stability in their production, demand, price, quality and also to help in fostering international trade.

Table 1: Medicinal Plants on which Significant Research Leads have been obtained

Commphora mukul	Antihypercholesterlaemic
Boswellia serrata	Antiarthiritic
Picrorrhiza kurroa	Antihepatotoxic
Phyllanthus amarus	Antihepatotoxic
Centella asiatica	Brain tonic
Curcuma longa	Antiinflammatory
Abdrographis paniculata	Antihepatotoxic
Withania somnifera	Adaptogen
Coleus forskholi	Cardiotonic
Acorus calamus	Tranquillizer
Sida rhombifolia	Anabolic
Albizzia lebeck	Immunomodulator
Valeriana wallichii	Tranquillizer

Table 2: Medicinal Plants being Imported

Glycyrrhiza glabra	Mullathi
Pimpinella anisum	Anise fruit
Thymus vulgaris	Hasha
Operculina turpenthum	Turbud
Cuscuta epithymum	Aftimum vilaiyti
Smilax ornata	Ushba
S. China	Chobchini
Lavandula stoechas	Ustukhudus

INDIA'S STRENGTH IN MEDICINAL PLANT WEALTH

If we dwell for a moment on our hoary past, *Rigveda*, one of the oldest repositories of human knowledge written between 4500-1500 BC mentions the use of 67 plants for therapeutic use and Yajurveda enlists 81 plants whereas *Atharveda* written during 1200 BC describes 290 plants of medicinal values. *Chakra Samhita* (~900 BC) describes 341 medicinal plants and the next land mark in Ayurveda *Sushruta Samhita* (~600 BC) mentions 395 medicinal plants. India unquestionable occupies the top position in the use of herbal drugs. It is one of the foremost countries exporting plant drugs and their derivatives, and excels in home-consumptions too and this is not all surprising because of the following:

- great biodiversity and abundance of flora
- variety of geographical climate conditions most exotic medicinal plants can be grown here
- Indian systems of medicine dwell heavily on medicinal plants
- long tradition of phytochemical research and scientific cultivation of medicinal plants
- well developed pharmeceutical industry
- rapidly growing phytochemical and herbal drug industry

Table 3: Threatened (Endangered) Medicinal Plants

Name	*Present status*
Aconitum deinorrhizum	Almost extinct
A. heterophyllum	Greatly threatened
Angelica glauca	Threatened
Arnebia benthemii	Threatened
Artemisia brevifolia	Likely to be threatened
A. maritima	Likely to be threatened
Atropa accuminata	Threatened
Berberis aristata	Threatened
Bunium persicum	Greatly threatened
Colchicum luteum	Threatened
Corydalis govaniana	Likely to be threatened
Dactylorhiza hatagirea (orchis)	Threatened
Dioscorea deltoidea	Threatened
Ephedra gerardiana	Likely to be threatened
Ferula jaeschkeana	Threatened
Gentiana kurroa	Threatened
Hedychium spicatum	Likely to be threatened
Jurinea dolomiaea (Dhoop)	Likely to be threatened
Nardostachys jatamansi	Threatened
Orchis latifolia	Threatened
Picrorrhiza kurroa	Likely to be threatened
Podophyllum emodi	Threatened
Rheum emodi	Threatened
Swertia chirata	Threatened
Valerian wallichii	Likely to be threatened
Zanthoxylum alatum	Likely to be threatened

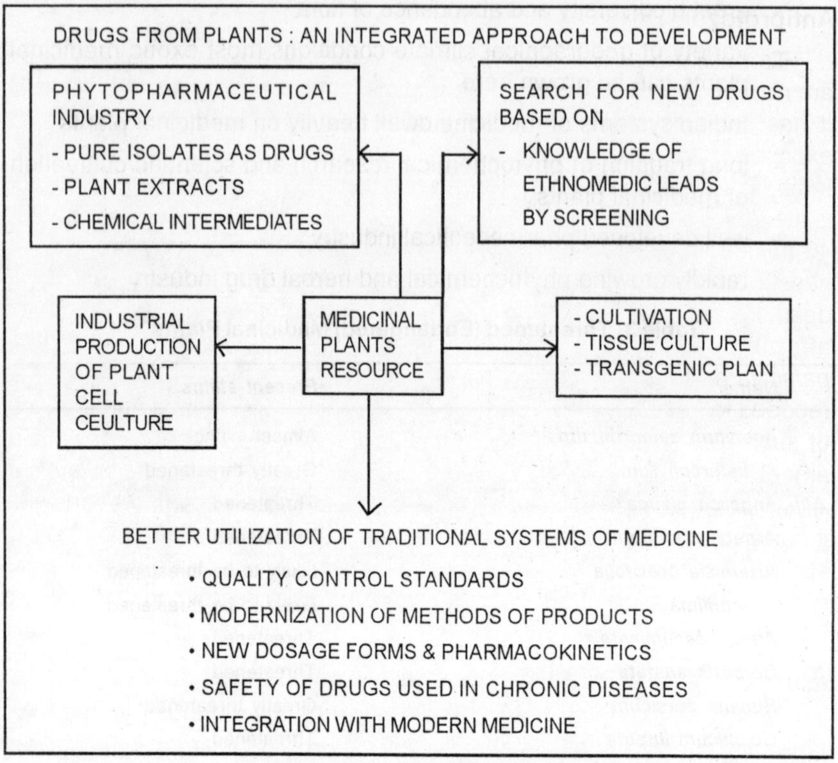

Fig. A. Medicinal Plants Resource

India is thus in a vantage position to exploit this source both for meeting the domestic demand for drugs as also for export.

Medicinal pants continue to be an important resource material for therapeutic agents both in developed and developing countries. The Figure A shows the medicinal plants resource and better utilization of traditional systems of medicine.

PRIORITIES IN RESEARCH ON MEDICINAL PLANTS AND DIVERSE STUDIES

It is desirable to have a "need based" approach to research on medicinal plants including screening of plants for biological activity. This was the objective of a W.H.O. Regional Group which met in 1980. Research efforts could thus be directed for a number of diseases for which suitable drugs are not available in the modern system of medicine and where herbal drugs have a possibility of offering new drugs, some such conditions include the following where new drugs are urgently needed and the medicinal plants have already provided some leads:

Antiprotozoal Drugs from Plants

Tropical diseases including malaria where tissue schizontocidal drugs are needed and drugs for multi-drug resistant blood schizonts are required. It has been estimated that one third of the world's population may be exposed to the risk of malarial infection. Most hard hit areas include Africa, India, China and East Asia. Amoebiasis caused by *Entamoeba histolytica* is the major cause of dysentery in the developing world where an estimated 42 million cases occur annually and untreated disease may progress to hepatic amobiasis and other complications which are responsible for 75,000 deaths each year. Filaria and leishmania are two other protozoal diseases affecting our population. Many plants like *Peganun harmala, Celastrus paniculata, Artemisia annua, Berberis aristata, Tilicora triandra* have been reported to have activities against various species of protozoa and a variety of such plants have been well illustrated in several recent reviews. For amoebicidal drugs plants like *Holarrhena antidysenterica, Berberis aristata, Allium sativum* and *Terminalia balerica* need serious attention. Worldwide it has been estimated that 20 million people are infected with *Leishmania* species and that 400,000 new cases occur each year. The plants which have given leads include *Plumbago zeylanica, Diospyros montana, Ricinus communis* and *Phytolacca* species.

Antiulcer Drugs from Plants

Important plants for the treatment of gastrointestinal ulcers that have. promising prospectus as useful drugs include *Prosopis glandulosa, Calendula* species, *Artocarpus integra, Musa ferrea* (pulp) and deglycyrrhizinated *Glycyrrhiza glabra* and many others which have been reviewed by researchers.

Antirheumatic Plants

Inflammatory diseases including different types of rheumatic diseases are very common throughout the world. Although rheumatism is one of the oldest known diseases of mankind and affects a large population of the world, no substantial progress has been so far achieved for permanent cure. Our recent review reveals that plant species of ninety six genera belonging to fifty six families have exhibited anti-inflammatory activity. Most significant plants include *Aesculus hippocastanum, Azadirachta indica, Boswellia serrata, Commiphora mukul, Curcuma longa, Ochrocarpus longifolia, Pluchea lanceolata* and *Vitex negundo.*

Antidiabetic Plants

15.2 Million people are suffering from diabetes in our country and the number is increasing every year. About 148 plants of 50 families reported to have hypoglycaemic activity have been reviewed by us. The most important hypoglycaemic plants which need serious clinical trials include

Pterocarpus marsupium, Momordica charantia, Trigonella foenum-graecum, Salacia prinoides, Gymnema sylvestris and *Cyamompis tetragonolobus*.

Anti-asthmatic Plants

In the lack of any permanent cure in the modern system of medicine for bronchial *asthma*, plants like *Albizzia lebeck* which have immunomodulatory action need serious attention. Other poly-herbal Ayurvedic formulations like Yastiadivati and Shereeshadi Kashaya may prove to be efficacious.

Anti-viral Plants

Experimental work on a number of plants having antiviral activity has been done. A lyophilized infusion from flowers of *Sambucus nigra,* aerial parts of *Hypericum perforatun* and roots of *Saponaria officinalis* exhibited antiviral effect inhibiting reproduction of different strains of influenza virus types A & B, both *in vitro* and *in vivo* and herpes simplex virus type 1 *in vitro*. These plants need to be carefully examined.

Plant adaptogens: The notion of "resistance" to disease and the idea that such resistance can be modified by life experience and by emotional states, forms one of the basic tenets of Ayurveda thus avoiding the cartesian dichotomization of mind and body. Concept of *Rasaayana* and *Rasaayana* plants have been reviewed by the author. Plant of interest in this area include. *Withania somnifera, Ocimum sanctum, Picrorhiza kurroa, Asparagus racemosus, Pueraria tuberosa, Sida cordifolia, Desmodium gangeticum, Boerhaavia diffusa* and *Cissampelos pareira*. We need to develop suitable models for testing such vital plants of Ayurveda.

Hepatoprotective Plants

A global estimate indicates that there are about 18,000 deaths every year because of the liver cirrhosis mainly caused by hepatitis. Hepatocellular carcinoma is one of the ten most common tumours in the world with over 2,50,000 new cases each year. Although viruses are the main cause of liver diseases, the liver lesions arising from xenobiotics, excessive drug therapy, environmental pollution and alcoholic intoxication are not uncommon. Modern drugs have very little to offer for alleviation of hepatic ailments, whereas, most important representatives of phytoconstituents used for liver diseases, chiefly on regional basis, include drugs like silymarin (*Silybum marianum*), catechin (*Anacardium occidentalis* and others) in Europe, gycyrrhizin (*Glycyrrhgiza glabra*) in Japan and schizandrins (*Schizandra chinensis*) in China. In India, we have over 40 polyherbal commercial formulations reputed to have hepatoprotective action. A review published on the subject from our laboratory indicates that 160 phytoconstituents from 101 plants belonging to 52 families have anti-hepatotoxic activity. Our laboratory has worked extensively on *Andrographis paniculata* and hepatoprotective activity has been established due to the presence of andrographolide. Kutkoside from *Picroshiza kurroa* is a potential hepatoprotectant reported by CDRI. *Phyllanthus amarus* is another most important plant selected for clinical trials. Our future work in this area is bound to give fruitful dividends. Antihepatotoxic activity of *Boerhavia diffusa* and *B. repanda* has been also reported from our laboratory. Kolaviron, a mixture of *Garcinia kola* (Guttiferae) biflavonoids at a dose of 100 mg/kg i.p. prevented thiocetamide induced hepatotoxicity. *Withania fruitescens* (Solanceae) leaves exhibited protective and curative action against carbontetrachloride induced liver toxicity. Plant kingdom appears to be a fruitful ground for the discovery of effective hepatoprotective drugs which we currently lack in the modern system of medicine.

Fertility Control by Plants

The successful introduction of three plants into modern therapeutics and family planning in the last forty years indicates that there are other discoveries waiting to be made. Many indigenous plant preparations are prescribed by Ayurvedic physicians in India from time immemorial for the prevention of conception. Clinical evaluation of such plant preparation is called for on priority basis.

Anti-cancer Drugs from Plants

Cancer is a insidious disease affecting mankind in every country. Work on periwinkle plant, *Catharanthus roseus* (L.) G. Don was independently taken up in two different laboratories for its alleged hypoglycaemic activity as per Jamaican falklore. Though non of the groups could substantiate hypoglycaemic activity, the Canadian group of Nobel Beer and Cutts succeeded in isolating vinblastine while Eli Lilly group headed by Svoboda could isolate vinblastine and vincristine along with two other active dimeric alkaloids. These alkaloids are present in exceedingly low concentrations in a complex mixture of 50 alkaloids. Vinblastine was introduced (Velban Eli Lilly) in 1961 and vincristine (Oncovin, Eli Lilly) in 1963 as anticancer drugs. CIPLA has improved upon the process of isolating vinbalstine and vincristine from *Catharanthus roseus* as developed by NCL, Pune. Today we are the third largest manufacturer of vinblastine and vincristine in the world and we are exporting these alkaloids to European countries and the demand is steadily increasing.

Screening of plant extracts for anticancer activity started in 1961 by National Cancer Institute of the U.S.A., and up to 1981 (20 years) about 1,14,045 plants had been screened, of which only 3.4% (representing about 3,400) different species have been observed to be active in one or more bioassay systems. The promising phytoconstituents which are likely candidates for drug development include in-dicine N-oxide (a pyrrolizidine alkaloid) from *Heliotropium indicum,* ellipticine (a monomeric indole alkaloid) from several *Ochrosia* species, homoharringtonine (a cephalotaxine alkaloid) from *Cephalotaxus* species, taxol from *Taxus* species and camptothecine (quinoline alkaloid) from *Camptotheca acuminata* a Chinese tree). The author has been successful in discovering a number of anticancer agents from plants like *Ostodes paniculata*, *Feddiea fischeri, Soulamea soulameoides, Dirca occidentalis,* and *Passerina vulgaris*. The anticancer principles of podophyllum are contained in the resin, podophyllum resin or podophyllin. American podophyllum yields 2-8% and Indian podophyllum about 6-12% of the resin. It is not only the higher amount of the resin present in Indian podophyllum (*P. emodi* var. *hexandrum*) but there are not peltatins present in contrast to American podophyllum (*P. peltatum*) which contains α- and β-peltatins. Thus, the Indian podophyllum has higher amount of podophyllotoxin. In certain cases Indian podophyllum has yielded 20% resin. The highest amount is in May when the plant produces flowers. Thus the Indian podophyllum, when collected at the proper seaons not only contains 2-1/2 times or even more of the resin compared to American podophyllum, but this resin has double the amount of podophyllotoxin which is the active principle used by pharmaceutical industry for structural modifications to produce anticancer drugs tenoposide and etoposide being marketed by Sandoz. Major problem with the cultivation of this plant is that the seeds take very long time to germinate. We need to concentrate on cultivation of this plant either by propagation or by reducing the period of seed germination. Use of Taxol from *Taxus brevifolia* or *Taxus baccata* is the latest addition of anticancer drug especially in ovarian cancer.

Plants for Urinary Stones

The very first mention of '*Pashanbhed*' in Ayurvedic literature is in *Charak Samhita*, and is recommended for painful micturition and for breaking calculi. *Sushrut Samhita* mentions the drug under various synonyms – *Pashanbhed* for uric acid calculi and *Ashnibhed* for biliary calculi. *Sushrut Samhita* mentions decoction of *Pashanbhed, Astimantaka, Satvari, Vrihati, Bhalluka, Varuna* (*Crataeva nervula*), *Kultha* (*Dolichos biflorus*), *kola* and *katak* seeds for patients of *Vataja Ashmari* while *Kusa, Ashmabhed, Patala, Trikanthaka, Sirisha, Punarnava* (*Boerhavia diffusa*) and *shilajit* are for *Pittaja Ashmari.* About 4000 plants have been mentioned to be useful for dissolving stones in the urinary system in a review published seven years ago. Cystone of Himalaya Drug Co. and Calcury of Charak Pharmaceuticals are already in the market. *Crataeva nervula* bark and *Tribulus terrestris* fruits have been put under clinical trials by Indian Council of Medical Research. *Cucumis trigonus* (curcurbitaceae) has been investigated for its diuretic activity.

Plants as Sedatives/Tranquillizers

Indian valerian (*Valeriana wallichii*) contains 2% valepotriates and is thus four times more potent than European valerian (*V. officinalis*) which contains 0.5% valepotriates. These are triesters of polyhydroxy cyclopentanopyran esterified with isovaleric, acetic and β-acetoxy valeric acid. Compared to known iridoids, valtrats (valepotriates) are neither glycosides nor lectones and are considered original or primary products present in the drug responsible for activity. Valtrates are used as tranquillizers and sedatives, and the action is comparable to meprobmate. Additional advantage is that these can be prescribed to alcoholic patients. Valerian also contains valernic acid having spasmolytic action. Valeranone is found is *jatamansi* (*Nardostachys jatamansi*) possessing sedative property. It will be worthwhile to produce valepotriates in India. A Peruvian plant *Valeriana thalictroides* has been found to contain 14.5% total valepotriate content in the roots and thus yields the highest known concentration of valepotriates in plants to date. The high yield of valepotraites in *V. thalictroides* roots cannot be directly used to overcome shortage of velepotraites for therapeutic use, as the roots have very small diameter (2 cm) and a length of about 5 cm. *V. edulis* spp. Procera (HBK) F.G. Mey, although having a smaller valepotriate content (7%), is a much better source for velepotriates because of its higher drug yield. However, such high yielding plants could be used to establish high yielding tissue culture for the *in vitro* production of valepotriates. Relation between valepotriate content and differentiation level in various tissues from valerianaceae has been studied. Isolation and evaluation of valepotriaites from Indian valerian are well known.

Plant Laxatives

Constipation is a common problem of Western and European countries because of protein rich diet. In the U.S.A., 1000 patents of vegetable origin are there which involves an annual trade of $ 500 million. On an average we export 15,000 tonnes of plantago, 7000 tonnes of senna and 1000 tonnes of rhubarb annually. Trade in plant laxatives increases by over 10% every year. India is the sole supplier of *Plantago ovata* seeds and husk (psyllium) in the international market. India's export of Psyllium seeds in 1980-81 were to the extent 25,743 metric tonnes values at Rs. 85.93 million. Indian Institute of Management, Ahmedabad has published recently a survey on the psyllium production and marketing in India.

PITFALLS IN PLANT-DRUG RESEARCH AND IMPLICATIONS

Medicinal plant research is beset with a number of problems and the major stumbling blocks encountered in plant drug research are listed below:

(a) Medicinal plants being used by traditional practitioners in India not only bear different names in different geographical areas and in different languages, but it is also not uncommon that different plants are known by the same name which add to the confusion and has resulted in controversial identity of many plants.

(b) Major causes of inconsistency in plant drugs include ontogenetic, ecotypic, genotypic and chemotypic besides variations due to harvesting period, method of drying and storage conditions.

(c) Ayurvedic, Unani practitioners invariably use polyherbal formulations, whereas, for obvious reasons, it is easier for the modern scientists to investigate single plant drug.

(d) Appropriate experimental models are not available for validating claims of some very important and useful plant drugs like "Rasaayana" enjoying esteemed repute in Ayurveda and termed in modern terminology as vitalizers, rejuvenators, adaptogens, immunomodulators etc.

(e) Major national laboratories resorted to more broad based screening of plants by including, apart from plants which are well known and time tested by traditional systems of medicine, those which are not mentioned by these systems. Others undertook studies largely on individual initiatives. Inspite of all these efforts, however, the ultimate goal of producing inexpensive, safe and efficacious drugs for most diseases encountered in our country remains to be achieved.

(f) The major bottleneck, however, is the lack of scientifically planned clinical trials on traditionally used medicinal plants. Though research work on medicinal plants has been carried out in Indian research establishments since long but not much has been achieved. The beneficial phase of multidisciplinary integrated approach to the evaluation of plants initiated by the Composite Drug Research Scheme seems to have been almost lost in the pages of history. Recently, however, Indian Council of Medical Research has adopted new strategy of disease oriented approach of carrying out clinical trials on medicinal plants selecting certain 'refractory diseases' i.e. those for which modern medicine has not been able to offer, so far, a satisfactory or a lasting remedy.

(g) The novelty and popular trend on the part of the phytochemists and pharmacologists to continue efforts to find out an "active principle" responsible for the pharmacological action and therapeutic efficacy of a plant, in many instances, has also led to frustrating results. Pharmacologists and phytochemists engaged in medicinal plant research may have to change their approach to wholistic plant material or with semi pure principles or even crude extracts. Gum guggul (*Commiphora mukul*) is a classic example.

(h) Except for Central Drug Research Institute, Lucknow, little facilities exist elsewhere in India for carrying out pre-clinical evaluation including toxicity tests on medicinal plants.

(i) Clinical evaluation of plant drugs is an area which is handicapped with lack of facilities and proper orientation of scientists of different disciplines. At present, for lack of such facilities even the leads obtained so far are being lost to follow-up.

HERBAL DRUG/INTELLECTUAL PROPERTY RIGHTS (IPR)

Medicinal plant research has been and continues to be considered as a fruitful approach for the search of new drugs. The highly respected magazine *Science* calls attention in its editorial of February, 1990 to the potential to medicinal plants in the search of new drugs and expresses concern about the consequences that loss of biodiversity might have in this context. Since most of the chemically unknown flora and associated medicinal lore exist in the developing and underdeveloped countries, especially those which still possess extensive tropical forests, the rapid loss of biodiversity does indeed become an issue for the future of medicinal plant research. The traditional role of developing countries in plant drug production has been as suppliers of raw material. Most of the pharmacological and chemical studies reported in several journals start by quoting the traditional use of a given plant species promising enough to stimulate further research. It is, therefore, reasonable to assume that the indigenous knowledge did play an important role in medicinal plant research and will continue to do so. Posey calls for legislation to secure Intellectual Property Right for indigenous people.

HERBAL DRUG TRADE

The extent of herbal drug usage is hard to quantify the traditional systems of medicine in India as by tradition many of the practitioner manufacture and formulate their own prescription, although there are now about ten well organized large scale herbal drug manufacturers whose individual annual production is of about $ 112 million (June 1998). Their total annual turnover in about $ 350 million. In U.K. there are about 5,500 herbal products involving 1,600 herbal ingredients. It is estimated that some 6,000-7,000 tons of herbs are extracted annually for the ingredients in U.K. medicine. Like India, China is another country which is noted for its adherence to herbal medicines for a number of therapies like in the treatment of abdominal conditions (appendicitis, perforated ulcers, pancreatitis), arthritic disease and some neurological disease. There are about 248 herbal drugs used for a number of reasons e.g., analgesic sedative, diuretic, antitussive antirehumatic and antiashmatics.

Herbs and the literature about them are big business in America. In 1985 the sales of all forms of herbs exceeded $ 190 million. Unfortunately, most of the literature prepared with a single purpose in mind-to sell a product, since to do so most effectively, it is necessary to promote or advocate all of the good features of the herb while minimizing, or even omitting, any negative aspects, such writings are generally referred to as advocacy literature.

Current federal laws do not permit the sale of herbs as drugs, that is, with claims of efficacy appearing on their labels. If such claims are made, the efficacy must be proven to the satisfaction of the Federal Food & Drug Administration, a process as much as $ 100 million per drug. Since no one is willing to spend this amount of money on a product for which patent protection is not available, herbs are sold labeled only with the name of the product, primarily in 'health food' stores. Literature purporting to explain the uses of herbs is also available in such establishments. Because the laws and regulations applied to food naturally do not require any proof of efficacy prior to sale, some manufacturers attempt to market herbal products as nutrients or food supplements, by combining a variety of herbs with standard multivitamin mineral preparation and often make extravagant claim for products based on their herbal contents.

HERBAL MEDICINES – MEDICINAL MARVEL OR MONEY SPINNING MALARKEY

Ayurveda, with many centuries of experience and cultural support has strengths which should be used only through the experts and vaidyas in Ayurveda or by modern physicians, who have undergone practical training and experience in Ayurveda. But gross and rampant commercialization of Ayurvedic herbal remedies, by all and sundry, has to be criticized and even condemned. With the onslaught of media television, radio and press several herbal formulations are promoted, often indiscriminately. Consumer associations are very quick and rightly so, when unscientific claims are made by ethical modern drugs. Should they not take up issue with very tall claims by the so-called herbal drugs by commercial interests? There is an urgent need to create an ethical code for advertising and promotion of Ayurvedic drugs.

SOCIOPOLITICAL, ECONOMICAL AND ETHICAL ISSUES IN MEDICINAL PLANTS RESEARCH

Due to enormous difference of wealth generated by supplying crude medicinal plant material versus the purified isolated phytoconstituent, the developing countries remain the worst sufferers. It therefore, calls for legislation to secure Intellectual Property Right (IPR) for indigenous people. What are the ethics behind utilizing traditional knowledge without adequate compensation to the societies from which it originates.

HERBAL DRUG DEVELOPMENT

One many propose a development procedure trailor made for herbal drugs. Traditional medicine usually consists of a mixture of herbal drugs.

In the first step the therapeutic efficacy of the traditional medicine has to be confirmed. Of course, the composition of the recipe has to be affirmed and authenticated by Pharmacognostic methods which means that we have got to be sure which plant, identified by botanical nomenclature, and which part of the plant to which percentage is used. Only in the country where the recipe has been used traditionally clinical trials can be performed. These trials have to be carried out as scientifically as possible. Well defined clinical parameters have to be evaluated in a population of patients with well defined diagnosis. In India such clinical trials on traditional medicines have been initiated by the Indian Council of Medical Research adopting disease oriented approach.

In the positive outcome of such studies we proceed to second step. We have to select one, perhaps in some cases two or three plants as the active ingredients. This can be done by animal pharmacology or clinical pharmacology. At this stage we have to attempt standardization employing all possible means like finger printing, TLC, HPLC or other related techniques. The clinical trials are performed against a placebo. In each case we have to use as much well defined clinical parameters as possible in order to establish the efficacy of the drug. If the results are positive, we can proceed to the next step where we use purified extract being standardized for the reprocessed extract, we can establish mode of action and also carry out toxicological studies in animals which become mandatory since we now use much higher concentration of the drug than used in the original recipe. With this standardized extract we can perform placebo controlled clinical trials which still should be performed in the country of origin. Nevertheless, we make our first attempt to submit something like Investigational New Drug (IND) in order to be allowed to perform phase I or even phase II clinical studies outside the country of origin. If the results are positive we can proceed to internationalization of the product. There are some countries in the world where the health authorities have a positive attitude to herbal drugs. In these countries facilitated approval may be possible. They can be fore runners for other countries where the developmental requirement would be the same as the synthetic compounds.

STANDARDIZATION OF HERBAL DRUGS

The single and most important factor which stands in the way of wider acceptance of traditional herbal medicines is the non-availability or inadequacy of standards for checking their quality by chemical or bioassay methods. This also prevents modernization or modification of the methods of their preparation or production, as there is no way to establish the equivalence of the product made by the modified method with the original product. Thus standardized drugs of well defined consistent quality are needed for reliable clinical trials and therapeutic use. The major reason advanced for the difficulty in developing quality control standards is that these products use whole plant or parts of plants or their total extracts, and in some cases even a mixture of a number of plants, it is thus challenging to develop suitable standards because a vegetable drug or a preparation thereof is regarded as one active ingredient in its entity, whether or not the constituent with therapeutic activity are known. Standardization of a herbal drug and of a preparation thereof is not just an analytical operation, it does not end with the identification and assay of an active principle rather it embodies total information and controls which are necessary to guarantee constancy of composition. Standardization of plant drugs has been stressed by the World Health Organization.

2

Dioscorea deltoidea Hook. Distribution and Agrotechnology

INTRODUCTION

Plants of genus *Dioscorea* (Family *Dioscoreaceae*) are perennial climbers with tuberous roots. Approximately 600 species of *Dioscorea* occur rather abundantly in tropical area, sub tropical regions with a few species in the temperate regions. Only 15 species are reported to contain steroidal sapongenin chiefly diosgenin. Most of the world production of diosgenin is met with central American species *D. floribunda* and *D. composita* both growing wild in Central America. In India *D. deltoidea* and *D. prazeri* occurring wild in North West and North East Himalayas respectively are the natural sources of diosgerin. *Dioscorea deltoidea* is found in India, Pakistan, Nepal and Bhutan extending to South Western China while *D. prazeri* occurs in Eastern India, Myanmar and northern parts of Malaysia. Mexico, Gautmala, Costa Rica, India, China and some countries in Europe and Africa are the major *Dioscorea* producing countries.

Diosgenin is the major raw material used in the synthesis of corticosteroids, sex harmones and antifertility compounds. Out of the steroid drug precursors diosgenin accounts for 50% of the total steroidal products of the World. Present requirement of steroidal drugs in terms of Diosgenin in the world is approximately 3000 tonnes. The total annual requirement of diosgenin by the pharmaceutical industry of our Country is 150 tonnes, while the total production of diosgenin in India is about 30 tonnes annually. The rest of the requirement is met through imports in the form of diosgenin and drug intermediates. The total estimated demand of cortiocosteroids is 9253 kg, whereas the actual production is 3941 kg. The synthesis of diosgenin not being commercially feasible for production of steroidal drugs, makes it necessary, rather obligatory, for the pharmaceutical industry to resort to natural source for the procurement of this raw material. While *D. prazeri* yields impure diosgenin, it has been reported that diosgenin percentage of *D. deltoidea* varies from 0.6 to 10.3. Hence, *D. deltoidea* seems to be the best natural source of diosgenin.

Cultivation of *Dioscorea* in India became necessary in view of the growing demand of the pharmaceutical industry coupled with the indiscriminate extraction of *D. deltoidea* from the forests which resulted in fast depletion of this species so much so that it has been declared a threatened species. Attempts to domesticate *D. deltoidea* in India were started during fifties, but only partial or little success was obtained. Attempts by a number of pharmaceutical concerns to cultivate this species was not encouraging. After finding it difficult to grow *D. deltoidea* on commercially viable basis, *D. composita* and *D. floribunda* were imported from central America. A collaborative programme was launched by ICAR, CSIR and Ford Foundation during 1967 to 1969 to explore the possibility of domesticating this species by vegetative propagation in Srinagar, Delhi, Bangalore and Lucknow. The studies showed that *Dioscorea deltoidea* contained the highest amount of pure diosgenin, but was too slow growing for adoption as a commercial crop. Most of their work has been reported in the field of propagation, cultivation and agronomy of *Dioscorea deltoidea*. The present paper highlights the detailed agro-technological studies carried out under Kashmir conditions and also its distribution pattern and availability in North-West Himalayas.

DISTRIBUTION

Dioscorea deltoideai grows wild throughout North Western Himalayas and extends from Kashmir, Himachal Pradesh, Darjeeling to Sikkim, Nepal and Bhutan at an altitude ranging from 1000-3500 metres. In J & K it is widely distributed in the forests of Bhadarwah, Kishtwar and Doda (Jammu) and forests of Ovra (Pahalgam), Shikargarh, Kangan and Pirpanchal in Kashmir. In Himachal Pradesh it is widely distributed in Catchment areas of the rivers of Ravi and Beas in Chamba and Kulu Valley. It is fairly common in upland regions of Kangra valley and Kinnaur. In Uttar Pradesh, it is available in upper reaches of Tons and Jamuna valley, dry temperate regions of Uttar Kashi and Chamoli in Garhwal and in Kumaon Hills. In Sikkim the plant occurs in Chughthang Singhik regions of Sikkim. Detailed survey by abrol *et al* in the mountainous regions of J & K, H.P., and Punjab has shown that *D. deltoidea* grows better in area where annual rainfall varies between 100 to 200 cm and minimum temperature in winter goes below freezing point and the maximum temperature in summer does not go up to 32°C. It has also been observed that *Dioscorea deltoidea* grows generally on the northern and eastern slopes in shady but well drained conditions. The tubers of Poonch area of J & K and H.P. contain poor quality of diosgenin content whereas the tubers from Pahalgam, Bhadarwah, Katra, Batote and Kalu contain about 4 per cent diosgenin. The annual availability/out turn of *Dioscorea deltoidea* collected from various forests of H.P. and J & K is given in Tables 1 and Table 2.

Table 1: Annual availability of *Dioscorea deltoidea* from various forest devisions of HP.

Forest Division	*Quantity (q)*
Kinnaur	800
Kulu	700
Seraj	600
Rohru	250
Mandi	160
Nachan	200
Kolgash	250
Kanjora	180
Dalhonsa	150
Chamba	600
Pangi	1000

Table 2: Average out turn of *Dioscorea deltoidea* from the forest division of HP.

Forest Division	*Quantity (q)*
Kinnaur	853
Kulu	1390
Seroj	200
Rohru	156
Nachan	200
Kotgara	1129
Dalhonsic	125
Chamba	200
Simla	26

COLLECTION OF RHIZOMES

The time of collection of rhizomes is important since its diosgenin content varies from season to season. The rhizome starts sprouting in the month of May and vines bear flowers in September and the seeds are ripe by November-December. Abrol *et al.*, 1963 observed that the best time of collection of rhizomes is in the months of January to March when the plants are dormant. It is now advisable to collect the rhizomes in December because the fields are covered with snow. The percentage of diosgenin was reported to vary from 3.8 to 4.6 at the time of sprouting (May), 3.8 at the flowering stage (September), 4.0 during fruiting stage (November), 4.1/4.2 at seed set (December) and 4.6 dormancy (January-March).

AGROTECHNOLOGY OF *DIOSCOREA DELTOIDEA*

Climate

It is a temperature plant and requires an annual rainfall varying between 100 to 200 cm. •Minimum temperature below freezing point during winter helps in release of gibberellins and, thereby, breaking dormancy of the tubers. Even when Srinagar maximum temperature goes upto 34°C we have observed good growth of *D. deltoidea*. Frequent irrigation can avert the transpiration losses during summer and in case Sprinkler irrigation is practised, wilting of the leaves can be avoided.

Soil

A well drained loose textured soil rich in humus with a pH 6.8 to 7.2 results in healthy growth of the tubers.

Propagation

Dioscorea deltoidea can be propagated from seed, leaf node cutting or from rhizomes cuttings.

From Seeds: According to Martin and Gaskin propagation from seed is considered the most reliable method under Peurto Recan condition though asexual propagation may be used profitably. Under certain conditions Khakazi *et al.*, propagated *Dioscorea deltoidea* by sowing seed in nursery and the two years old plants were transplanted in the field. After 4 years of growth the fresh weight of rhizomes/plant was 216 gm. Our observations did not show encouraging results, as the seed propagation trail in a growing season gave an average 12 gm of root mass which was highly disappointing. In India, however, propagation is mostly done vegetatively.

From Rhizomes: The plant can be easily propagated from rhizomes. Tubers (75 gm) planted and harvested after 32 months gave optimum tuber yield of 20.79 g/ha with 2.08 percent of diosgenin. It was observed at Peshawar that tuber pieces with 5 cm diameter having one or two buds gave higher total number of plants Khan *et. al.*, and Bhat and Bindroo, reported that dormancy in tubers can be broken by chilling tubers at 2°C to 0.5°C for 60 days resulting in 95% sprouting and such chilling could save time at the start of fresh cultivation observed that rhizome pieces 3 cm in length and having one bud are quite suitable for raising plantation and early spring is the optimum time for planting the cuttings where 100% sprouting is expected. Our observation on 1162 plants drawn out from the field randomly indicated a positive correlation of r =0.67 between bud number and tuber weight. Based on this finding we planted rhizome cuttings having 3 to 4 buds weighing around 50 gms in the month of November and observed maximum yield or rhizomes after 3 years of growth (Fig. 1).

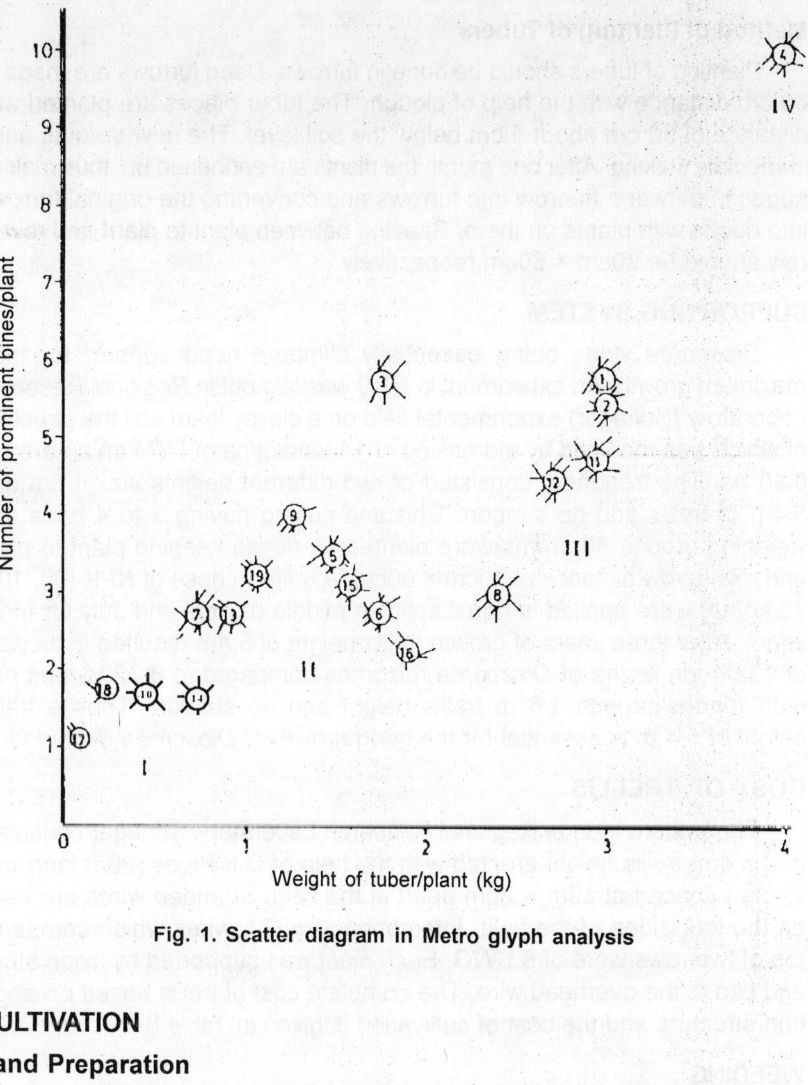

Fig. 1. Scatter diagram in Metro glyph analysis

CULTIVATION

Land Preparation

Land should be prepared thoroughly 4-5 times with a mould board plough. It should be thoroughly mixed with farm yard manure or forest humus. 14 tonnes/ha of FYM should be applied at the time of field preparation.

Pretreatment of Tubers before Plantation

The tubers are susceptble to a number of soil borne diseases, unless treated with proper fungicide. After trying different fungicides it was found that tubers dipped in 0.2% of brassicol for 10 minutes before plantation gave better results.

Method of Planting of Tubers

Planting of tubers should be done in furrows. Deep furrows are made at 60 cm distance with the help of plough. The tuber pieces are planted at a distance of 30 cm about 5 cm below the soil level. The new sprouts need immediate staking. After one month the plants are earthened up, thus making ridges in between the row into furrows and converting the original furrows into ridges with plants on them. Spacing between plant to plant and row to row should be 30cm × 60cm respectively.

SUPPORTING SYSTEM

Dioscorea vines being essentially climbers need support for their maximum growth. An experiment in RBD was laid out in Regional Research Laboratory (Srinagar) experimental field on a clayey loam soil the structure of which was modified by a dressing of 14 tonnes/ha of FYM on an area of 0.10 ha. The treatment consisted of two different heights viz., 1.8m and 5.4m of trellis and no support. Rhizome cutting having 3 to 4 buds and weighing around 50 grams were planted on ridges keeping plant to plant and row to row distance of 30cm × 60cm. A uniform dose of NPK (50, 100, 75 kg/ha) were applied in equal splits in middle of April and July for three years. After three years of growth trellis height of 5.4m resulted in an yield of 13.04 tonnes/ha of *Diosocrea* rhizomes compared to 8.72 tonnes and 6.63 tonnes/ha with 1.8 m trellis height and no support. Thus a trellis height of 5.4 m is essential for the good growth of *Dioscroea deltoidea*.

COST OF TRELLIS

The system tried at Regional Research Laboratory, Srinagar consisted of a 5.4 m trellis height erected with the help of G.I. Pipes (20 ft long with 2" dia.) spaced at 10m × 20m apart in the field. Stranded wires are used on the four sides of the field. Interconnecting G.I. wires which comes on top of two rows were of 8 SWG. Each plant was supported by nylon string and tied to the overhead wire. The complete cost of trellis based on angle iron structure and the cost of cultivation is given in Table 3.

WEEDING

Initially the vines are weak and tender. They can not compete efficiently with the surrounding weeds. Weeding is essential for the first year as and when required. In remaining two years the weeds are reduced due to shade provided by the prolific growth of *Diosocrea* plant with the results that the plants can compete with the weeds, more successfully, thereby, reducing weeding operations.

IRRIGATION

Under Kashmir conditions *Diosocrea deltoidea* does not need much irrigation. However, during months of June to August, it should be irrigated once every fortnight. The newly planted crop of *Dioscorea deltoidea* has to be irrigated when needed during the first year.

Table 3: The cost of Cultivation of Selected clones of *Dioscorea deltoideal* Economics of Cultivation/ha Harvest after every 3 years.

Duration of the crops 3 years

		Quantity	Amount (Rs.)
A.	*Capital cost of Trellis (once only)*		
	1. Angle iron fixture 18'×2"×2"	(70 Nos)	20,790
	2. G.I. wire 8 SWG	15 q.	27,000
	3. Fixation of wire work & Stranded wire etc.		10,000
		Total	57,790
B.	*Recurring expenditure*		
	Items		Expenditure in Rupees
	1. Land Preparation		7,000
	2. Planting material & plantation		28,000
	3. Purchase of Fertilizers, manure and its application		20,000
	4. Weeding & hoeing		15,000
	5. Irrigation		6,000
	6. String (Nylon Yarn)		9,000
	7. Stringing charges		5,000
	8. Harvesting Cleaning & Post drying of tubers		20,000
	9. Miscellaneous		6,000
	10. Land Rent		24,000
		Total	1,40,000
C.	*Return after three years*		
	(i) Yield of tuber/ha		23.0 tons
	(ii) Gross returns/ha at the rate of Rs. 10/kg		2,30,000
	Profit		
	Net return in three years		90,000
	Net return per year/ha		30,000

FERTILIZERS REQUIREMENT

Dioscorea species responds well to organic manure and nitrogenous fertilizers. In case of *Dioscorea deltoidea*, 14 tonnes of FYM/ha is recommended before plantation. Fertilizer trial with 135 kg each of N&P/ha in Kagan Valley of Pakistan gave poor yield of 1.27 tonnes/ha rhizomes. A field experiment in RBD was laid during 1981-84 with six levels of Nitrogen (0, 40, 80, 120, 160, 200 kg/ha) to investigate the optimum does of Nitrogen.

A basal dose of 100 kg P_2O_2 and K_2O each were applied at plantation time. Nitrogen was applied in the form of urea in two equals plits in mid-April and mid-June. The tubers were harvested in November, 1984. The investigation revealed that nitrogen fertilization up to a particular level increased tuber yield/ha and marginally enhanced diosgenin percentage in the tubers of three year crop. The diosgenin percentage showed a decrease above the applied level of 80 kg/ha although the yield, length and girth of tubers along with the yield of diosgenin showed continuous increase (Tables 4 and 5). The optimum economic dose of nitrogen from the quadratic equation worked out 95.12 kg/ha with the estimated tuber yield of 16 tonnes/ha.

Table 4: Effect of Nitrogen levels on the tuber yield, length, girth, diosgenin percentage and diosgenin yield of tubers in *Dioscorea deltoidea*

Levles of Nitrogen	*Tuber yield/ ha (tonnes)*	*Tuber length/ plant (cm)*	*Tuber girth/ plant (cm)*	*Diosgein %*	*Diosgenin yield kg/ha*
0	10.114	14.30	29.20	3.50	353
40	13.834	16.40	33.10	3.75	510
80	15.892	18.20	36.50	4.32	686
120	16.140	19.10	38.30	3.87	625
160	17.080	19.30	38.70	3.76	641
200	17.429	19.30	38.90	3.70	644
LSD 5%	00.080	01.737	01.07	0.34	55

Table 5: Effect of N, P, K on the growth of *Dioscorea deltoidea*

Treatment	*Tuber yield/ Plant (kg)*	*Tuber length/ plant (cm)*	*Tuber girth/ plant (cm)*	*Diosgenin %*
N_1	0.4215	14.40	34.72	3.75
N_2	0.4132	14.20	33.78	3.70
N_3	0.4461	15.10	36.69	3.61
CD at 5%	N.S.	N.S.	N.S.	0.07
P_1	0.4162	14.53	34.50	3.71
P_2	0.4224	14.70	34.82	3.73
P_3	0.4221	14.68	34.67	3.72
CD at 5%	N.S.	0.09	0.12	0.03
K_1	0.4113	13.97	32.97	3.70
K_2	0.4238	14.50	34.20	3.68
K_3	0.4457	14.82	35.76	3.67
CD at 5%	N.S.	N.S.	N.S.	0.02

Diosocrea floribunda and *D. composita* respond well to nitrogen (300 kg/ha) application. Keeping in view the above facts a fertilizers trial of NPK was carried out during 1986-89 at RRL, Experimental field, Srinagar. The experiment was carried out on a loamy soil in a split plot design with three levels of Potash 75(K_1), 100(K_2) and 125 (K_3) kg/ha in main plot, three levels of Phosphorus 100(P_1), 150(P_2) and 200 (P_3) kg/ha in sub-plot and three levels of nitrogen 150(N_1), 200(N_2) and 250(N_3) kg/ha is sub-plot respectively replicated four times. After three years of growth the data was recorded on tuber yield/plant, tuber length/plant and tuber girth/plant analysed statistically.

The results indicated that neither main treatment, nor the sub-treatment nor the sub-treatment recorded any significant effect on the tuber yield/ plant. However, all the treatments were found to be significant for diosgenin percentage (Table 5). The interaction K×N, N ×P, K×N×P were significant and the maximum tuber yield (23.5 tonnes) and diosgenin yield (8.81 q) was obtained with low level of nitrogen and high level of potash and phorphorus viz. 125 (K_3) 200(P_3) 150(N_1) kg/ha and is recorded. Thus *Dioscorea deltoidea* does not need high doses of nitrogen/ha as has been observed in *Dioscorea composita* and *Dioscorea floribunda.*

3

Cultivation of *Dioscorea composita* Hemsl: A Potential Source of Diosgenin

Genus *Dioscorea*, a monocot of family Dioscoreaceae with over 600 species is widely distributed in tropical world, a few species are temperate. About 15 species are known to contain steroidal sapogenins chifly diosgenin in their underground tubers. Diosgenin is a versatile precursor for synthesis of a large number of steriod products such as Corticosteroids, sex hormones and anti-fertility compounds. *Dioscorea composita, D. floribunda* and *D. nipponica* are the most important commercially exploited source of diosgenin. They are central American and Chinese in origin. In India *D. deltiodea* and *D. prazeri*, occurring wild in North West and North East Himalays respectively are the natural sources of diosgenin. According to one estimate the annual requirement of diosgenin in India is approximately 200 tonnes. The total production in the country is 25-30 tonnes annually and rest of the demand is met through imports in the form of finished products from abroad. Recently other precursors like stigmasterol from soyabean oil and sitosterol from other plant sources have also contributed towards synthesis of these drugs in the world market. Inspite of this diosgenin still remains an important source particularly for production of corticosteroids.

Cultivation of exotic *Dioscorea*, in India became necessary in view of the depletion of wild material due to excessive collection by pharmaceutical companies, lack of efforts to regenerate it and also to help establish the Indian steroid industry based on indigenous raw material. As a result of collective efforts under "All India *Dioscorea* improvement project", *Dioscorea floribunda* is being successfully cultivated as commercial crop around Banglore, Goa, Andamans and Assam, and *D. composita* in West Bengal, Tamil Nadu and Assam. During the last 25 years or so many advances have been made in the field of propagation, agronomy, tissue culture and physiology of these species. This paper gives a resume of the work done in this direction on *Dioscorea composita* introduced at RRL, Jammu.

PROPAGATION

Propagation of *D. composita* can be done by seeds, tubers or leaf node cuttings. In its original home (Mexico) it grows wild and is also raised in commercial plantations either by seeds or tubers. Propagation by leaf node cuttings is not practiced on commercial scale because of high cost and labour.

PROPAGATION BY SEEDS

The seeds are sown in seed pansor polythene bags containing soil sand and farm yard manure in suitable proportions or coarse washed sand only. In either case the upper 1-2 cm layer is covered with vermiculite. Before sowing, the seeds are soaked in cold water for 3-4 hrs. The seed containers are kept in a glass house under diffused light. They start germinating in 2-3 weeks time and maximum germination is obtained after a month. Three to four months old seedlings are transplanted during rains i.e. July-August in well prepared ridges at 60 × 75 cm spacing. A mixture of farm yard manure at 30-40 tonnes/ha and phosphorous at 150 kg/ha as superphosphate is applied as basic doze prior to transplanting. Nitrogen as urea at 300 kg/ha is applied in 2 split dozes. First application is made after a month of transplanting is September and second is given 6 months later. Potash is supplied at 150 kg/ha as muriate of potash alongwith urea.

Studies on seed germination (Table 1) have shown that seeds can germinate fairly well under Jammu conditions, during different times of the year. Maximum germination is obtained at 30°C March-April is the best season for sowing because this period is most suitable for further growth of seedlings in the field. Germination percentage is equally good from August – November but for large scale sowing this period is not recommended because of high rate of seedling mortality during winter which follows immediately.

PROPAGATION FROM TUBERS

Population raised from seeds showed great variation with regard to tuber growth and diosgenin content. In order to obtain higher yields clonal multiplication of high yielding plants was very important. The clones were selected on the basis of good diosgenin percentage and high tuber yield.

Tuber Dormancy

Dioscorea composita tubers show strong dormancy which lasts from December to February and is a great handicap in large scale cultivation of this species. Under normal conditions tubers take 2-3 months to sprout and sprouting process is erratic and prolonged. At RRL a study was undertaken to find out various genetical and physiological factors responsible for causing dormancy. Involvement of endogenous inhibitor and its dynamics during different growth phases was investigated. The inhibitor has been identified as abscisin-II like compound. The crown portion of the tuber with preformed buds had a very low inhibitor content as compared to medians and tips. A correlation has been observed between concentration of inhibitor and dormancy. During dormant phase (Dec. – Feb.) inhibitor content is highest in tuber i.e. 2.5 μg dry wt. It starts declining from April onwards with the advent of new sprouts and active growth, completely disappears in July and remains absent till November. Big tubers have higher inhibitor concentration compared to small ones. Temperature and humidity play a key role in breaking dormancy. Chilling, light and dark treatment were found ineffective. Several growth regulators like gibberellins, auxin, Ethrel, cycocel and morphactins were tried at various concentrations and different durations for breaking dormancy out of these only Ehtrel has been found consistently effective. It has given increase in sprouting percentage over control and has also reduced the sprouting period.

Table 1: Relative germination performance of *D. composita* Hemsl. seed during different times of the year

Source	*Date of sowing*	*Media Soil/ petridishes*	*Time taken to germinate*	*% Germination*
P.i.	Aug.-Sept., 1969	Petridishes	8 days	70
201783	Aug.-Sept., 1969	Soil	2-3 weeks	40
E.C.	Sept., 1970	Petridishes	8-10 days	65
87659	Sept., 1972	Soil	2-3 weeks	40
P.i.	Sept., 1972	Petridishes	8 days	60
201783	Sept., 1972	Soil	2-3 weeks	40
Wyeth	Oct., 1975	Petridishes	10 days	75
Laboratories	March-April, 1976	Petridishes	8 days	65
	March-April, 1976	Soil	4 weeks	40
	Aug., 1976	Petridishes	8 days	57

Clonal variation in sprouting *of D. composita* tubers was found after studying sprouting behaviour in a number of clones over a period of 3-4 years. Although the age, time of harvest and environmental conditions at the time of experiment were similar it was found that some clones sprout earlier high sprouting percentage and shorter sprouting period as compared to others. Effect of storage date on sprouting of tubers was also noted. Under Jammu conditions tuber pieces can be stored from March to June. March-April storage is best as the miniplants so raised are right in time for field transplanting in July-August. Based on our studies a technique has been developed for mass production of *D. composita* from tuber pieces. It has given 70-80% sprouting in large scale experiments and has also shortened the time taken for complete sprouting. The technique is being practised till date for regeneration of this species.

Transplanting and After Care

Plants raised from tuber setts are transplanted in ridges either in March-April or during the rains i.e. July-August. They get established within a week. Plants need to be irrigated frequently when young, afterwards they should be irrigated once a week in summer and in winter as and when required. It is hardy plant and can withstand drought conditions to some extent. During summer months Sprinkler irrigation was also used at Jammu.

Tissue Culture Method

For rapid clonal propagation of *Dioscorea* species, tissue culture technique has also been recommended. A number of workers have reported to obtain complete plantlets in *D. floribunda* and *D. deltiodea* through tissue culture of various excised parts. Regeneration of *D. composita* plants from stem callus and nodal explants was reported by Datta. However this method is not adopted commercially in view of the high costs involved.

Inter-specific Hybridisation

Dioscorea is a dioecious plant. Female plants do not set seed unless male plants are in close physical proximity. Hand pollination or intertwining of male and female spikes has resulted in very good seed set a Bengalore in case of *D. floribunda* and *D. composita*. The latter also flowers profusely from September-January under Jammu conditions, but there is no viable seed formation. A number of factors may be responsible for this. It was observed that though pollen is 60% viable, pollen germination is low. Pollen tubes are very short and too slow to grow or reach the ovule. In order to stimulate germination and elongation of pollen tube, a number of *in vitro* systems were tried. Good pollen germination and tube elongation was achieved when pollen was germinated in a medium containing 0.15% sucrose solution in combination with 25 ppm cycocel followed by incubation at 28-30°C for 3-4 hrs. But there was post fertilization ovular break down, in some cases embryo formation was observed but it could not proceed further beyond a few celled stage. Low temperature prevalent during this period (January) may be another factor responsible for seed sterility under Jammu conditions.

Work done at IIHR, Bangalore has indicated that species within the new world group and within the old world group are cross compatible and between the groups the crosses are incompatible. In crosses between species of the new world group also, four levels of crossability were observed, which ranged from complete crossability to early break down of embryo to complete failure. Some promising hybrids between *D. composita* and *D. floribunda* have been made at IIHR, Bangalore.

Spacing

Effect of population density on tuber yield and diosgenin content was studied under field conditions. Four inter and intra row spacings were tried ie. 60 × 90 cm with plant population 18000/ha, 60 × 75 cm having 22,000 plants per hectare, 45 × 60 cm and 30 × 45 cm with 30,5000 and 46,000 plants/ha. respectively. The crop was harvested after 2 years and diosgenin content analysed (Table 2). It was found that with increase in spacing individual tuber/plant was increased but total yield/ha decreased. Highest tuber yield of 94.5 tonnes/ha (fresh) was found at 30 × 45 cm, but per plant yield was low i.e. 2.1 kg. Tuber yield per plant was maximum at 60 × 90 cm spacing i.e. 3.4 kg but total yield/ha was low in this case i.e. 57.8 tonnes. Diosgenin content was not affected by increase or decrease in spacing. This study has shown that 30 × 45 cm spacing is optimum for 2 year crop. But considering from diosgenin point of view, a 3 year crop with 45 × 60 cm spacing is recommended. Effect of population pressure on yield of *D. floribunda* has been studied by Sarma.

Table 2: Effect of population density on the yield and diosgenin content of *Dioscorea composita*

Sl. No.	*Treatment (spacings) (cm)*	*Plant population/ha*	*Fr. Tuber yield/ plant (kg)*	*Total tuber yield/ha Tons (fr)*	*Total tuber yield/ha Tons (Dry)*	*Diosgenin content% (DWB)*
1.	T_1 (60 × 90)	18,000	3.4±.22	57.8	20	1.8±0.20
2.	T_2 (60 × 75)	22,000	2.7±0.19	56.7	18.2	1.4±0.13
3.	T_3 (45 × 60)	30,500	2.4±0.13	70.8	24	2.0±0.15
4.	T_4 (30 × 45)	46,000	2.1±0.10	94.5	30	1.8±0.17

SUPPORTING SYSTEM

Dioscorea vines need support for their maximum growth. The system tried successfully at Bangalore in case of *D. floribunda* consists of stone pillars 3 m high spaced 6 m apart in the field. G.I. wire No. 6 or 8 is used on the four sides of the field interconnecting wires can be of 12 guage. Each plant is supported by a gunny twine and tied to the over head wire. In case of *D. composita* stone pillars are replaced by G.I. pipes, rest of the structure is similar. Both of these supporting systems are cost heavy. Singh,

R.S. tried different methods of staking D. floribunda vines, they reported higher yields of dry tuber and diosgenin under the plants trained on rope fencing as compared to other method such as bamboo, pigeon pea or castorbean staking. Similarly Konnard and Norris noted significantly higher yields in case of *D. floribunda* grown on the chicken wire Trellis pillar system than that grown on poles only or on dwarf castor been or without support. In search of a cheaper substitute for training *D. composita* plants at RRL, jammu, three different supporting systems were tried. They were (i) the Wire-Trellis G.I. pipe system, Eucalyptus poles system and *Leucaena leucophylla* as live support, incase of control the vines were left trailing on surface and were pruned at 50 cm height periodically. Details of first two systems are similar to those described for *D. floribunda* except that stone pillars were replaced by G.I. pipes or Eucalyptus poles as the case may be. In *Leucaena leucophylla* type of support, seedlings of this species were grown in between *D. composita* plants and served as live supports, *Leucaena leucophylla* gets easily established and is periodically chopped, side branches are pruned, since it grows very fast and its roots fix atmospheric nitrogen also. This experiment was conducted at field station Chatha in 1.4 acre area in RBD with 2 replications. A perusal of the data shows that when *D. composita* is grown as a two year old crop on these systems, fresh tuber yield per acre in three systems viz. G.I. poles, Eucalyptus and *Leucaena leucophylla* is, 196, 147 and 115 qtls respectively. Plants without support gave very low yield. The study indicates that the wire trellis-G.I. pole system has higher yield potential as compared to *Leucaena* or Eucalyptus type. But the cost of construction of this system has become formidable in view of the rising prices. Our experience at farm plantations of *Dioscorea composita* has shown that Eucalyptus pole – wire Trellis support system should be recommended for commercial cultivation of this species in order to reduce the cost. Economics of cultivation using this type of support have been worked out. Leucaena type of support is useful for short term plantings only, since it competes with the crop and outgrows it with passage of time.

NUTRIENT REQUIREMENT

Dioscorea in general have high requirement of Nitrogen. A field experiment was conducted to study the effect of different levels of Nitrogen, phosphorous and potash on yield and diosgenin content of *D. composita*. Results showed there was a significant and linear increase in tuber yield with Nitrogen upto 400 kg/ha. Phosphorous and potash were required in moderate quantity i.e. 150 kg/ha each, for optimum growth. The recommended fertilizer schedule for the crop is that phosphorous and potash should be applied in single doze at the rate of 150 kg/ha each at the time of transplanting in pits along with Farm yard manure at the rate of 40 kg/

ha. Nitrogen at 400 kg/ha has to be supplied in 2 splits coinciding with the active growth period of the crop i.e. first dose in April–May and second in Sept.–Oct. of the same year

WEED CONTROL

During first and second years of growth the vines are weak and need great care. Periodic hand weeding as and when required is essential during this period. From third year onwards the overhead vines make a thick cover and provide shade as a result, weed population is considerably reduced and less weeding is required. Chemical weedicides such as Senecer at 3 kg/ha and Lasso at 3 kg plus Diuron at 3 kg/ha have been recommended in case of *D. floribunda*. Chemical weed control has not been reported in *D. composita*.

PESTS AND DISEASES

No Major pests or disease attack has been observed in case of *D. composita* under Jammu conditions. Some times cutworms and aphids were found to infest growing vines either in nursery or in the field. They can be controlled by 2% foliar spray of Sevin. Rarely fungus attack was seen on foliage but it did not cause any harm to the crop.

INTERCROPPING

In case of *D. floribunda* intercropping with legumes like cowpea, horse gram, French bean and Mexican bean was found profitable. No such studies have been done in case of *D. composita*.

HARVESTING

D. composita should be allowed to grow for a minimum period of three years. Though some high yielding clones selected at RRL, Jammu can also be grown as a two year crop economically. The diosgenin content also increases with age and is maximum during the third year. The tubers are deep and can be harvested by pick axes on deep ploughing.

4

Production of Ergot Alkaloids by Submerged Fermentation

INTRODUCTION

Ergot alkaloids have long history of toxic manifestations and medicinal uses to mankind. These tetracyclic indole derivatives are primarily found in the sclerotia of various species of *Claviceps* which parasitize a large number of species of family poaceae. Based on their chemical structures, the alkaloids of ergot can be divided into two classes: clavines and lysergic acid derivatives. Both contain the tetracyclic ergoline ring system in which the substituent at C-8 has the oxidation state of methyl or hydroxymethyl group, and C-8 and C-9 may carry an additional oxygen. The lysergic acid derivatives are of prime interest to pharmacologists due to their effects on uterine and vascular smooth muscles and sympathetic nervous system. During the recent past, new aspects of the pharmacology of the ergot derivatives have been very interesting. Certain ergot derivatives act as inhibitors of prolactine secretion, produce stimulation of dopaminergic receptors and certain newer ergot derivatives have been implicated as potential therapeutic agents in diseases such as parkinsonian suppression of postpartum lactation, treatment of breast cancer and cancer of the prostrate. The clavines have until recently been of little importance from the medicinal point of view. Some of them are, however, intermediate in the formation of lysergic acid derivatives. The first group, the amide derivatives of lysergic acid, shows the broad spectrum of pharmacological effects and that has led to the wide spread medicinal uses of ergot alkaloids and their semi-synthetic derivatives. The current medicinal uses are – (1) Treatment of postpartum haemorrhage; (2) Migrainic headache; and (3) Psychotherapy. Some of the compounds prepared from clavine type of alkaloids were found to be prolactin inhibitor. One of the compounds prepared i.e. 6-methyl-8 ergolenylacetamide was very potent comparing favourably in activity to the best prolactin inhibitors reported to date. Mantle confirmed this antilactating effect of clavine type of alkaloid. Two groups of clavine alkaloids namely elymoclavine and agroclavine may be coupled with each other and each couple with dihydro-d-lysergic acid. This gives us an idea of the interrelationship of the clavine ergot alkaloids among themselves and with those of classic type. As for the structure, it was found that agroclavine was not derivative for lysergic acid. As it contains no carboxyl group, no double bond at position 9 and 10 and no peptide portion, it is just a new alkaloid – an ergotine-8- derivative. It has CH_3 at position 8 instead of a carboxyl group. Thus, we know that its structure is similar to though not the same as that of the lysergic acid portion of the ergot of rye alkaloids.

SOURCES OF ERGOT ALKALOIDS

Ergot alkaloids are obtained by the extraction of ergot sclerotia produced on different grasses of family poaceae under natural conditions. Secondly the ergot sclerotia are obtained from the artificial cultivation of ergot of rye. Thirdly by the exploitation of saprophytic culture of different species of *Claviceps* by using chemical strains of ergot fungi and lastly by partial of total synthesis of ergot alkaloids. The different group of alkaloids namely ergotamine, ergometrine, ergokriptine, ergocristine, ergocarnine, simple lysergic acid derivatives, lysergic acid and phospalic acid are produced by various pharmaceutical companies.

Though the exact statistics are not available from individual countries about the correct requirement of the ergot alkaloids and their derivatives, the total annual requirement of the entire world is approximately estimated at 4,000 kg of the peptide type and more than 12,000 kg of simple lysergic acid derivatives. The approximate cost of the lysergic acid in the international market varies from Rs. 25,000 to 32,000 per kg.

FACTORS AFFECTING THE PRODUCTION OF ERGOT ALKALOIDS UNDER SUBMERGED CULTURE CONDITION

Production of ergot sclerotia by parasitic method depends upon mainly climatic conditions which may be fevourable or may not be every year during crop season. Secondly growing population requires sufficient land for the production of food grains to meet the requirement of the country. The only alternative is to produce the ergot alkaloids by submerged culture conditions. Two strains numbering A6 and B14 of *Claviceps paspali* Stevens and Hall were taken for LAD under submerged culture conditions. The strain P921 of *Claviceps* spp. was employed for the production of clavine type of alkaloids.

Maintenance of Cultures

The stock cultures of all the three strains namely A6, B 14 and P921 were maintained on potato dextrose agar slants at 5°C±1 in screw cap culture tubes. Active cultures were employed in the experimental trials.

First they were transferred on PDA poured plates and then after 7 days the cultures were sub-cultured on PDA slants. Ten days old culture tubes were used in each experiment. Seed and production media were employed for both types of alkaloids with different concentrations of ingredients (Table 3). The factors like sources of carbon, nitrogen, phosphate, sulphate and trace elements, were optimized. The other factors affecting the yield of ergot alkaloids like improvement of strains, stage of seed culture, size of inoclum, storage of inoculum etc. were studied to find out the optimum conditions other than said factors, pure chemicals of A R grade and double distilled water was employed in seed and production media.

Table 1: Selection of Isolates for the production of LAD after the treatment of γ–rays

Sl. No.	*Isolate No.*	*Doses of γ-rays In Krads*	*alkaloid content in mg/L.*	*Incubation period*
1.	A-1	50 Krads	669.6	10 days
2.	A-2	50 Krads	734.4	10 days
3.	A-5	50 Krads	669.6	10 days
4.	A-96	50 Krads	669.6	10 days
5.	A-1-13	50 Krads	554.0	10 days
6.	A-1-4	100 Krads	712.6	10 days
7.	A-1-19	100 Krads	756.0	10 days
8.	A-20-1	100 Krads	885.6	10 days
9.	A-22-7	100 Krads	842.4	10 days
10.	B-8-1	50 Krads	1026.0	10 days
11.	B-8-2	50 Krads	1080.0	10 days
12.	B-3-11	50 Krads	691.1	10 days
13.	B-4-3	50 Krads	669.6	10 days
14.	B-88-3	50 Krads	669.6	10 days
15.	B-123-1	50 Krads	779.6	10 days
16.	B-123-2	50 Krads	680.4	10 days
17.	B-123-8	50 Krads	723.6	10 days
18.	B-123-3-1	100 Krads	1188.0	10 days
19.	B-127-1	100 Krads	771.2	10 days
20.	B-127-2	100 Krads	864.0	10 days
21.	B-127-8	100 Krads	777.6	10 days
22.	B-127-2-1	100 Krads	734.4	10 days
23.	B-127-7-11	100 Krads	907.2	10 days
24.	B-132-17	100 Krads	896.0	10 days
25.	B-132-18	100 Krads	756.0	10 days

Table 2: Effect of age of inoculum on the production of alkaloids

Type of inoculum	*Incubation period for the production of alkaloids content in mg/L.* *6 days*	*8 days*	*10 days*
Fresh incolum	594.0	831.6	896.4
7 days old	562.0	734.4	658.8
14 days old	615.0	461.0	378.0

Table 3: Medium for the production of ergot alkaloids in submerged culture

Ingredients	*Seed Medium*	*Production Medium*
Succinic acid	10 gm	30 gm
Mannitol	40 gm	50 gm
KH_2PO_4	0.1	0.1
$MgSO_4$	0.6	0.6
$NaNO_3$	0.1	0.1
$Ca(NO_3)_2$	0.2	0.3
$FeSO_4$	0.01	0.01
$ZnSO_4$	0.01	0.01
$MnSO_4$	0.08	0.08
$CuSo_4$	0.01	0.01

Fermentation Procedure

Commonly three stage fermentation procedure was followed throughout the investigation. Ten days old, one square centimeter of the mycelial bit was taken for the 1st stage seed culture. It was mixed with nutrient liquid medium and homogenized for 20 seconds in an omnimix; After homegenization the homoginate was taken back into the same sterile conical flask of 500 ml. It was incubated for 6-8 days on rotary shaker operating at 230 rpm. The temperature of the incubation room was maintained at 24°C±1, when the full growth was visible, the entire content of the mycelial growth of stage one, seed culture flask was again homogenized for 10-15 seconds for stage second. Ten ml of homogenized myclial suspension was added to 500 ml flask containing 100 ml of seed medium for the stage second (Table 4). After inoculation, the flasks were incubated for stage second under similar condition mentioned for stage first for 72 hrs. To begin with stage three, ten ml of mycelial suspension from stage second seed culture was transferred into 500 ml of flasks containing 100 ml of the production medium. The production medium was containing various types of sucrose and mannitol, nitrogen sources, phosphate, sulphate and trace elements (Copper sulphate, zinc sulphate, iron sulphate and manganese sulphate).

The flask containing production medium were incubated for 10-12 days under similar conditions after inoculation with 10 per cent of inoculum of 2nd stage seed culture. All the experiments were repeated three times in three replications.

Table 4: Selection of isolates for the production of Clavine type of alkaloids

Isolates	*Yield in Mg/L*	*Incubation period in days*
Mother culture 921	812	10
2A	712	10
2C	1052	10
4	698	10
12	756	10
43	797	10
48	663	10

Sampling and Analysis Procedure

About 10 ml of fermented broth was taken out each time from each treatment under aspectic conditions with the help of separate sterile pipette for the analysis of alkaloid content. The sampling was made at the interval of 6,8,10 and 12 days of inoculation of production media. The mycelia were separated from the broth of each sample by suction filtration through double layer of Whatman No. 1 filter paper disc placed in Buckner funnel. The mycelial free broth thus obtained was used individually for recording pH and optical density. The pH of each individual sample was recorded separately and the quantity of lysergic acid derivatives (LAD) present in the filtrate was estimated by recording colorimetric readings obtained at 590 nm in Elico spectro Model-CI-23. The total alkaloid present was calculated from the calibration curve prepared from an authentic sample of ergotamine maliate. The result are express in mg/L. The colour development was done with the help of van urk reagent (para dimethyl amino benzaldehyde) in 65 per cent sulphuric acid of A R grade. All the glass wares and the appliances used in the experiments were washed thoroughly in the detergent solution and cleaned five times with hot water. They were again washed with HCl and distilled water and finally with double distilled water before drying in oven.

Improvement of Strains

Three strains numbering A6, B14 and P921 were selected for the improvement of their alkaloid contents. They were given the exposure of 12 doses of γ-rays. The treated tubes (5 tubes in each case) were mixed with distilled sterile water and homogenized them in sterile container for 30 seconds. The mycelial suspension were diluted upto the extent to get the single colony from one mycelial bit. They were transferred into PDA tubes and used to test them for the production of alkaloid content. In each case 100 colonies were screened out of twelve doses and the fungal cultures of both strains survived upto 100 Krads. Only two doses 50 and 100 Krads were found to be effective and yielded the higher alkaloid content of 25 isolates than the original mother strains A6 and B14 (Table 1). Out of 25 isolates only one isolate numbering B-123-3-1 yielded the maximum of 1188 mg/L of LAD. It was taken for the further optimization of physical and chemical parameters for the improvement of the yield of alkaloid content (LAD).

Table 5: Effect of mannitol and sucrose in the yield of clavine type of alkaloids producing isolates.

Isolates	*Yield in Mg/L*		*Incubation period in days*
	Manntol	*Sucrose AR*	
921	856	1080	10
2A	1080	1620	10
2C	1296	1620	10
4	872	1196	10
12	929	1026	10
43	1090	1572	10
48	907	1404	10

FACTORS AFFECTING THE YIELD OF ERGOT ALKALOIDS

Age of the Initial Culture

Age of the culture for the production of ergot alkaloids plays an important part in the study of the physical and chemical factors under sub-merged culture conditions. A mycelial bit of fungal culture should be taken from a fully grown young active colony. Five different age group cultures selected were 10, 15, 20, 25 and 30 days old grown at 25°C±1 on PDA agar slants. The alkaloids content obtained revealed that the initial cultures of the age group of 10-15 days old were found to be better than the older colonies for both type of cultures producing LAD and clavine alkaloids. In ergot alkaloid fermentation, generally three stage method is followed by majority of workers. Stage first and second may vary and depends upon the growth of the particular fungal culture but the production period is generally completed within 10-12 days on incubation. Under the trail of concentration of inoculum for the production medium, five concentrations of 5, 10, 15, 20 and 25 per cent of the total volume of the production medium were used. The results obtained indicated that increase or decrease in the concentration of inoculum beyond ten per cent could not improve the yield of alkaloid content. This concentration of inoculum was equally good for the clavine type of alkaloids.

Table 6: Effect of automization of inoculum before inoculation of production medium

Isolates	*Yield in mg/L*		
	Homogenized	*Non-homogenized*	*Incubation in days*
2A	1512	1080	10
2C	1620	1080	10
4	995	856	10
12	1296	993	10
43	1512	1088	10
48	1512	929	10

Table 7: Effect of different grades of mannitol on the yield of alkaloids (LAD)

Grades	*Yield in mg/L*	*Incubation period of days*
B.P. Grade	824.8	10
B.P. Grade further purified	894.0	10
Extra pure	972.0	10
Extra pure further purified	1025.0	10
IDPL	1025.0	10
IDPL further purified	1496.0	10

Table 8: Effect of different carbon sources on the yield of alkaloids (LAD)

Sources of carbon	*Yield in mg/L*	*Incubation period in days*
Mannitol B.P.	712.8	10
Mannitol B.P. purified	734.4	10
Mannitol Extra pure	734.4	10
Mannitol Extra pure purified	771.2	10
IDPL	669.0	10
IDPL purified	972.0	10
Glucose	518.4	10
Galactose	529.4	10
Lactose	302.4	10
Sucrose	1101.8	10

Duration of Fermentation in Production Medium

To find out the duration of incubation period for the production of ergot alkaloids under submerged culture condition, it is an important factor to decide the duration period for the maximum yield of the alkaloids. Four duration periods were taken into consideration. They samples were taken aseptically at the end of 6, 8, 10, 12 and 14 days after inoculation of production medium. It was observed that the maximum yield of LAD and clavine alkaloid was found on 10th day. Shorter and longer period of production could not increase the yield of alkaloid content.

Storage of Inoculum

To find out the effect of storage of inoculum three durations of fresh, one and two weeks were undertaken. The pure inoculum of second stage seed culture was stored at 5°C±1. The production medium was inoculated with 10 per cent of each group of stored inoculum and allowed them for the fermentation for 10 days at 25°±1 at 230 rpm of rotary shaker. All the four samples were analysed and found that freshly prepared inoculum was better for the production of biomass as well as for the alkaloids content in comparison to older and stored inoculum. The stored inoculum was found to decrease the yield of ergot alkaloids of both types. The results are presented in Table 2. The results show that the fresh inoculum used for the inoculation of production medium increases yield upto 10 days and stored inoculum used were observed to decrease the yield. The study reveals that fresh inoculum fir the inoculation of production medium is better. Older inoculum starts lysis earlier and declines the yield of the alkaloids also.

Buffering of the seed and production media with sodium dihydrogen phosphate does not increase the yield of alkaloid content of any one of alkaloids under test. To check the foaming in production period, three concentrations of groundnut and sunflower oils were employed. There was no change in the yield of any one of the alkaloids. In the separate trials, four concentrations of potassium dihydrogen phosphate were used separately for each of two alkaloids by keeping the other parameters the same. The results showed that lg/L was more suitable concentration than below or above concentration for the production of both types of alkaloids. In the application of magnesium sulphate, ten concentrations were employed but the data indicated that 0.6g/L was better than any increase or decrease for production of clavine type of alkaloid (Table 11). The same thing was observed for the LAD production. Six concentrations of calcium nitrate were employed in the production as well as seed media for the improvement of the yield of alkaloid contents. The data presented in (Table 12) indicated that 0.2 to 0.3 g/L was more effective than any other concentration under test. Similar finding was recorded for the production of LAD under submerged culture conditions.

Table 9: Effect of different conc. of sucrose for the production of calvine alkaloid

Conc. of Sugar in per cent	*Yield of alkaloids in mg/L*	*Incubation period in days*
Mannitol	1583.2	10
Sucrose 1	1771.2	10
Sucrose 2.5	1712.8	10
Sucrose 5.0	1742.8	10
Sucrose 7.5	1712.8	10
Sucrose 10.0	1669.6	10
Sucrose 12.5	1669.6	10
Sucrose 15.0	1669.6	10
Common sugar 5	1712.8	10
Common sugar 7.5	1734.4	10

Table 10: Effect of acids of carboxylic group on the yield of clavine alkaloid

Acid 3 per cent	*Yield in mg/L*	*Incubation in days*
Succinic acid	986.6	10
Citric acid	183.6	10
Acetic acid	54.0	10
Fumaric acid	172.8	10
Maleic acid	334.4	10
Oxalic acid	712.8	10
Tartaric acid BDH	432.0	10
Tartaric acid IDPL	205.2	10
Benzoic acid	75.9	10
No acid	340.4	10

Table 11: Effect of magnesium sulphate on the yield of alkaloids (LAD)

Conc. in g/L	*Yield mg/l*	*Incubation in days*
0.2	1069.2	10
0.4	1512.0	10
0.6	1620.0	10
0.8	1512.0	10
1.0	1512.0	10
1.2	1512.0	10
1.4	1432.0	10
1.6	1296.0	10
1.8	1188.0	10
2.0	1080.0	10

REQUIREMENT OF CARBON SOURCES

According to the literature available, it was observed that mannitol as a carbon source and succinic acid for organic nitrogen was recorded by Abe. However, in the present study it was observed that there was a lot of variation in the yield by the use of different grade of mannitol and other sources of carbohydrates (Table 8). Mannitol of IDPL purified was found to be superior than other sources of mannitol for the production of LAD (Table 7). But in the case of clavine alkaloids sucrose 5 per cent AR grade was found to be better than any other source of carbohydrate (Table 9). This indicated that sources of carbohydrates are not the same for all types of strains of alkaloid producing species of *Claviceps*. It was also found that addition of tryptophane does not play any significant role for the production of any type of ergot alkaloids under submerged cultured conditions. Taking into consideration all the factors of physical and nutritional requirements for the production of ergot alkaloids under submerged culture conditions, it is also one of the important factors to homogenize the first and second stages of seed cultures before inoculating the production medium. The results indicated that the homogenized culture increased the yield of alkaloids of all the six isolates of *Claviceps* spp. under test (Table 6). However, some of the factors directly affecting the yield of clavine type of alkaloids were optimized. A strain P921 of *Claviceps* spp. was treates with 12 doses of γ-rays. None of the culture tubes under test could survive beyond 100 Krads. One hundred colonies from each of two doses (50 and 100 Krads) were tested for the production of clavine alkaloids. An isolate no. 2c producing the maximum yield of this alkaloid was further selected for the optimization of some factors affecting the yield of clavine alkaloids (Table 4). The fungal colonies grew comparatively better at 25°±1 and pH 5.2. For the optimization of carbon sources sucrose AR and mannitol were tried and results obtained have shown that sucrose AR was better than mannitol for all the isolates under test (Table 5). Similarly for organic source of nitrogen, succinic acid 30g/L was found better than any other concentration for this alkaloids. For the optimisation of source and concentration of phosphate, potassium dihydrogen phosphate 100 mg/L was detemined to be the better source than any other concentration. However, dipotassium monohydrogen phosphate (K_2HPO_4) could not yield the higher alkaloid with its four contractions. It is well known fact that production of any pure type of ergot alkaloid is very sensitive and particularly chemical have significant role in the production under submerged cultured conditions. The maximum yield was obtained by the use of purified mannitol IDPL grade which was 1101 mg/L in comparison to nine sources of carbohydrates (Table 8). It was further confirmed by a separate trial of different concentrations of sucrose that 5% sucrose of AR grade was superior than any grade of sucrose (Table 9). However, different concentrations of inorganic nitrogen of calcium nitrate and sodium nitrate were tried and the results obtained indicated that

0.2 to 0.3% of calcium nitrate was better than any other source and concentration of nitrate (Table 12). A trial with four trace elements namely ferrous sulphate, zinc sulphate, copper sulphate and manganese sulphate was conducted and the results obtained indicated that deletion of any one of the four trace elements adversely affects the yield of LAD. More over, clavine types requires only two viz. Ferrous sulphate and Manganese sulphate and the remaining two were found to be inhibator for the production of clavine type under submerged culture conditions (Table 13). Incubation period for the stationary culture was attempted and the result showed that the clavine alkaloids increased the yield upto 42 days and started to decline after 48 days (Table 14). However, it does not appear to be economical as it takes long time of incubation to complete the circle of clavine type alkaloids production. Secondly it requires space under aseptic condition for the growth and production of calvine alkaloids. In another set of experiment, seven carboxylic group of acids were tried and the results showed that succinic acid was the better source of organic nitrogen. The optimum concentration of succinic acid used for the production of LAD was again implemented for the production of clavine type of alkaloids in the same concentration. All the acids under test were found to be inferior for the clavine alkaloid production (Table 10) in comparison to succinic acid.

Table 12: Effect of calcium nitrate on the yield of calvine alkaloid

Conc. mg/L	*Yield in mg/L*	*Incubation in days*
0.0	1058.4	10
0.1	1512.0	10
0.2	1620.0	10
0.3	1620.0	10
0.4	1296.0	10
0.5	1188.0	10
1.0	902.6	10

Table 13: Effect of trace elements on the yield of calvine type of ergot alkaloids

Isolates	*Trace elements*	*yield in mg/L*	*Incubation period in days*
2C	No trace elements	486	10
2C	Only $FeSO_4$	907	10
2C	$FeSO_4$ ± $MnSO_4$	1512	10
2C	$FeSO_4$ ± $MnSO_4$ ± $ZnSO_4$	1296	10
2C	$FeSO_4$ ± $MnSO_4$ $ZnSO_4$ ± $CuSO_4$	1026	10

Table 14: Effect of incubation period in stationary surface culture for production of calvine type alkaloid

Isolates	*Yield in mg/L*		
	Incubation period in days		
	30	42	48
2A	1404	1728	1620
2C	1512	1836	1672

SUMMARY

Ergot alkaloids based on chemical structure are mainly divided into two classes: lysergic acid derivatives and clavine type. Both are obtained from ergot sclerotia grown either naturally or by artificial cultivation. It is possible to produce them under submerged culture conditions by optimising physical and nutritional requirements. Any deviation in optimum factors directly affects the yield of alkaloids. Constant temperature of 25°C±1 and pH between 5.2 to 5.5 are the ideal factors. Purified mannitol 4 per cent and 5 per cent of sucrose AR grade are the best source of carbon of LAD and clavine types of alkaloids respectively. Fresh inoculum in comparison to older ones proved to be better. Potassium dihydrogen phosphate 0.1 per cent is superior than potassium monohydrogen phosphate for the alkloids production. Mangnesium sulphate (0.6%) is better for both types of alkloids. In comparison to calcium nitrate and sodium nitrate as the inorganic nitrogen source 0.2-0.3 per cent calcium nitrate is better suited for both types of alkaloids under submerged culture conditions. In a comparative study of eight carboxylic acids for the organic source of nitrogen, succinic acid (0.3%) is more suitable for the production of both types of alkaloids. The combination of two trace elements namely, Manganese sulphate and Ferrous sulphate are proved to be better than individual or any other combination for the production of calvine type of alkaloids. Moreover, a combination of all the four trace elements are required for production of lysergic acid derivatives.

5

Ajmalicine (Raubasine): A Medicinally Important Alkaloids from *Catharanthus roseus* (*Vinca rosea*)

INTRODUCTION

Catharanthus roseus (L.) G.Don is often referred as *Vinca rosea* (Family: Apocyanaceae). In different parts of India it is known as Sadabahar, Sadaphul, Nayantara, Rattanjot, Bilagaanneru, Gul Feringhi, Ainskati and Sudukadu Mallikai. It is pantropical in its occurrence and is widely cultivated as ornamental in the gardens throughout the world. It has been found that the alkaloidal content of *C. roseus* varies considerably in various parts of the plant from different localities and the total alkaloidal content reported in the roots ranges from 0.15-1.34% and even upto 1.7948% in some strains. The plant contains more than 100 alkaloids of the indole group out of which about 25 are dimeric in nature. Two of the dimeric alkaloids vinblastine and vincristine have found extensive application in the treatment of human neoplasms. Among the monomeric alkaloids ajmalicine (raubasine) has been found to have a broad application in the treatment of circulatory diseases, especially in the relief of obstruction of normal cerebral blood flow. In combination with the Rauvolfia alkaloids it has been used to lower high blood pressure. It is reported by Jagdev Singh that 3500 kg of ajmalicine is isolated from natural sources by pharmaceutical industries the world over. Recommended doses for ajmalicine vary widely from 1-20 mg (3 or 4 times daily) by oral or parentral route. The various proprietary products of ajmalicine marketed in European countries are Circolene, Isoarteril, Raubasil, Sarpan (Italy), Hydrosarpan, Raubaserp (Canada), Hydrosarpan Fort (Canada, France), Lamuran (Germany, Italy) and Melanex (S. Africa). Due to the clinical importance of the oncolytic dimeric alkaloids present in the leaves and hypotensive monomeric alkaloids present in the roots, *C. roseus* has attained a high place both in medicine and commerce. The bulk of the leaves which were earlier exported to USA and Hungary are now being processed by M/s Southern Herbals, Bangalore for the production of vinblastine and vincristine based on the process of NCL, Pune. The firm has for the first time dispatched a first consignment of vincristine (330 g) to Germany fetching about Rs. 3.5 crores. The same firm has also taken up the process know-how from RRL, Jammu for the production of ajmalicine from roots. The roots are also exported to Australia, France, Germany and U.K. and during April-March, 1992 (270, 770 kg) fetched Rs.9,147,653 where they are possibly used for the extraction of serpentine and ajmalicine. In order to maintain the supply, the plant is now being cultivated in about 1,500 hectares, mainly in Tamil Nadu and other South Indian States.

CHEMISTRY OF AJMALICINE

It has been found to occur as a natural product in 20 species of the genus *Rauvolfia*, 4 of *Catharanthus*, 2 of *Mitragyne*, in *Pausinystalia yohimbe* and *Stemmandenia obovata*. The yield of ajmalicine reported in *Catharanthus* varies from 0.034-0.1%. It was first isolated by Siddiqui and Siddiqui from *Rauvolfia serpentina*. Ajmalicine belongs to the group of ring E oxygen heterocyclic alkaloids bearing the structure (7). Other alkaloids of E ring oxygen heterocycles include the anhydronium bases, such as serpentine (8) present in *C. roseus* in a yield ranging from 0.02-0.1%. Ajmalicine on dehydrogenation with lead tetra acetate affords the naturally occurring serpentine that in turn can be reconverted by catalystic reduction to the starting substance. The principal difference between the two being in configuration i.e. a trans D/E ring juncture to the ajmalicine group and a *cis* one to the serpentine group. Ajmalicine has also been synthesized as a dl mixture and as (-) ajmalicine.

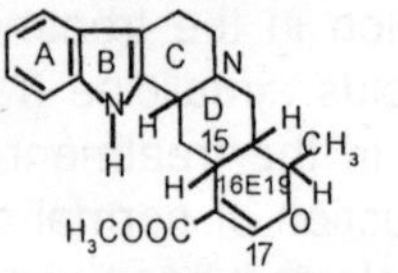

I Ajmalicine

II Ring C-Aromatic-Serpentine

PRODUCTION OF AJMALICINE

Till recently some Indian firms were marketing only the roots of *C. roseus* or their total alkaloidal concentrates to European countries where these are possibly used for the production of ajmalicine (raubasine). It is commercially useful to export a high value low volume product ajmalicine instead of low value high volume thing like roots. Thus Regional Research Laboratory, Jammu took up investigations in this direction and has successfully developed a process on pilot plant scale for the extraction of ajmalicine and serpentine from *C. roseus* and conversion of serpentine to

Flow Sheet Showing Isolation of Ajmalicine (Raubasine) and Conversion to Serpentine of Ajmalicine

Powdered *Catharanthus roses* dry roots
↓ Extract with alcohol
Rasidue
↓ Extract with aq. tartaric acid
Aq. acid extract
Extract with ethylene dichloride

↓ Residue (A)
(i) Extract aq. tartaric acid
(ii) Extract $CHCL_3$
Residue
Ajmalicine (0.025%)

↓ Aq. acid extract
(i) Make weakly alkaline
(ii) Extract with ethylene dichloride

↓ Residue (B) (discard)

↓ Aq. alkaline extract
(i) Make strongly alkaline
(ii) Extract with $CHCl_3$

↓ Residue (C) containing mainly serpentine
Residue (D)↓
Reduce with $NaBH_4$

↓ Aq. alkaline ext. (discard)
chromatograph over acid alumina using $CHCl_3$.MeOH
→ Ajmalacine (0.20%)

ajmalicine and giving an overall yield of 0.15-0.2% depending upon the percentage of total alkaloids in the roots. The consultancy know-how of the process has been released to six Indian firms (Kothari Chemicals, Madurai, Indo-German Alkaloids, Bombay; Mehta Pharmaceuticals, Amritsar; Cipla Laboratories Mumbai; Malabar Phytochemicals, Kerala and Southern Herbals, Bangalore).

The extraction process as reported (Flow Sheet) by us earlier is based on the methodology of selective gradient *p*H extraction technique.

Powdered *C. roseus* roots are extracted in a soxhlet with alcohol. The alcohol from the extract is removed and the residue obtained is extracted with tartaric acid solution. The aqueous acid extract is fractioned into strongly acid, weakly basic and strongly basic fractions. The strongly acid fraction on purification gives ajmalicine in a yield upto 0.025%.

The strongly basic fraction after extraction with $CHCl_3$, removal of the $CHCl_3$ and chromatography of the residue over acid alumina gives crude serpentine in $CHCl_3$: MeOH eluates. The crude serpentine so obtained is reduced with $NaBH_4$ to give ajmalicine (raubasine) in quantitative yield.

The main equipment required for the process includes hot extractor, liquid extractor, pH meter, heating mantle, stirrer, water-bath, distillation assembly and refrigerator.

Purity Parameters:

i.	Mol. Formula	:	$C_{21}H_{24}N_2O_3$
ii.	Mol. Wt.	:	352.42
iii.	m.p.	:	250-52° (prisms from MeOH).
iv.	[α]D	:	-60° (C = 0.5 $CHCl_3$) -45° (C = 0.5 pyridine) -39° (C = 0.025 MeOH)
		:	6.31 (67%DMF in H_2O)
v.	pka	:	23.5
vi.	Rate of methodide formation × 10^{-4} sec^{-1} MeOH		
vii.	Max	:	227,292 nm (log S 4.61, 3.79)
viii.	Cd curves	:	Observed between 250 & 280 nm.
ix.	Infrared spectrum cm^{-1}	:	2850-2750 (Bohlman bands), 1700 (C = O), 1620 (C = C).
x.	NMR spectrum ($CDCl_3$)	:	1.12 (d, 3H, J = 6.5 HZ, CH_3), 3.66 (s, 3H, OCH_3), 4.33 (m, 1H, largest J = 6.5 Hz, $OCHCH_3$), 7.0-7.6 (4 Aromatics), 7.48 (d, 1H, J 1Hz; OCH =), 8.21 (b, 1, NH).
xi.	C NMR spectrum (ppm upfiled from CS_2)		C_2(58.1), C_3(132.5), C_5(139.3), C_6(170.7), C_7(84.6), C_8(65.3), C_9(74.5), C_{10}(71.2), C_{11}(73.27), C_{12}(81.7), C_{13}(56.6), C_{14}(159.7), C_{15}(161.9), C_{16}(85.8), C_{17}(37.9) C_{19} (118.8), C_{20} (151.6), C_{21}(135.7), C_{22}(25.0), C_{23}(141.7).
xii.	Mass spectrum	:	m/e 352 (M+), 351 (M-1), 184, 169, 156 (b.p.)
xiii.	Derivatives a. Ajmalicine HCl	:	$C_{21}H_{25}ClN_2O_3$, leaflets from ethanol, m.p. 290° (dec.) $[\alpha]D^{20}$ – 17 (C = 0.5 in MeOH) sparingly soluble in water or dil. HCl.
	b. Ajmalicine HBr	:	$C_{21}H_{25}BrN_2O_3$, diamond shaped platelets from MeOH, m.p. 295-96°.

PLANT TISSUE CULTURE AND BIOSYNTHESIS

The alkaloids serpentine and ajmalicine have been produced in cell suspension cultures of *C. roseus* in various laboratories and studied extensively in terms of production and/or biosynthesis. For large scale production Zenk's alkaloid production medium was employed. The alkaloid production varied with the cell line and age of the subculture and ranged from 0.1-1.5% of cell dry wt. All subculture of cell lines were grown in 7.5 L Microferm bioreactors over a period of 8 weeks. Most cell lines showed a maximum of accumulation in 3rd or 5th week of culture. For processing for alkaloids water is removed by freeze drying and the alkaloids are extracted in the conventional manner. The studies show that the percentage of alkaloids ajmalicine and yohimbin per gram of cell weight increases with time with optimum production of 3-4 weeks.

Formerly pathways of indole alkaloids formation in higher plants were elucidated *in vivo* only by tracer methods. However, the rapid development of cell suspension culture techniques in recent years has provided the basis for the reinvestigation of alkaloid biosynthesis at the cell free level. Thus, in combination with radio-immunoassy technique, it was possible to establish cell suspension cultures of *C. roseus* which were capable of synthesising substantial amounts of *corynanthe* alkaloids ajmalicine and serpentine. Using cell strains selected for higher content of ajmalicine as an enzyme source, the precursor role of tryptamine (1) and secologanin (2) in the biosynthesis of ajmalicine and related alkaloids was confirmed *in vitro*. The reaction (Fig. 1) is catalysed by enzyme strictosidine synthase, which specifically controls the C-ring closure mechanism. By the action of a second enzyme, a glucosidase, strictosidine (3) is converted via highly reactive intermediates to 4, 21-dehydrocorynantheine aldehyde (4, D-ring closure). This aldehyde in turn cyclises (E-ring formation) probably after isomerisation (5) to the next stable intermediate cathanamine (6) 20, 21-didehydro ajmalicine.

Finally, the NADPH dependent cathenamine reductase catalyses the synthesis of corynanthe type alkaloid ajmalicine (7) which finally oxidises to serpentine (8).

Zenk *et al.* have indicated the l-tryptophan can be incorporated directly and probably enters the cells more easily than tryptamine.

Lee *et al.* showed that several carotenoid inducers were effective in promoting indole alkaloid formation in *C. roseus* cell cultures with a maximum increase of 20% in ajmalicine and cathranthine. Findings by Kutney *et al.*, have further supported that bioregulators dimethyl piperidium chloride (DPC) and 2- (3, 4-dimethyl phenoxy-triethylamine) (DMPTA) caused a significant increase of both alkaloids in *C. roseus* strain.

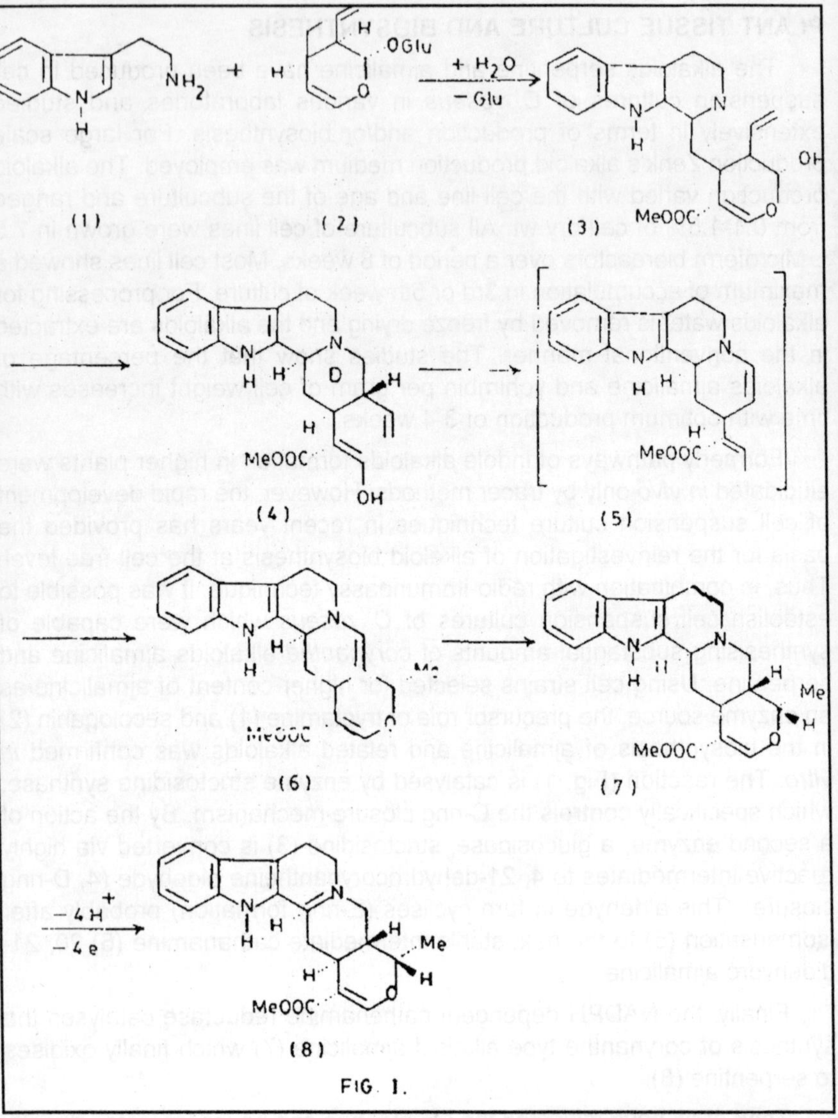

Fig. 1

Kutchan *et al.* have obtained cDNA for strictosidine synthase from *Rauvolfia serpentina* cloned and expressed in *E. coli* and this achievement esents a major break through in plant biotechnology.

ANALYTICAL METHODS

Sarin *et al.* have reported a spectrophotometric method for the estimation of ajmalicine in *C. roseus* roots and stems. The method is based on the quantitative separation of weak bases followed by isolation of ajmalicine by TLC and its determination spectrophotometrically with a recovery of 99 ± 3%.

Rao *et al.* have further reported a spectrophotometric method for the estimation of serpentine in *C. roseus* roots and stems. The method involves the quantitative separation of serpentine by preparative TLC and its estimation at 310 nm. It also involves conversion of serpentine to ajmalicine and its estimation as ajmalicine at 283 nm.

Zenk and co-workers developed a semiautomatic RIA method for the quantitative determination of serpentine and ajmalicine detecting in the range of 0.1-50 mg/01 ml sample meaning thereby that average alkaloid content of about 1 root cell of *C. roseus* could be quantitatively determined.

Kutney *et al.* used HPLC (High Performance Liquid Chromatography) for monitoring subculture development of the target compound in the range of 10-20 mg and has reported it to be the method of choice over radio-active assays. HPLC affords information about the number and concentration of components formed within a given series of fermentation studies.

6

Production of Colchicine from *Gloriosa Superba* Seeds

INTRODUCTION

Colchicine, the principal alkaloid of *Colchicum autumnale* L. (N.O. Liliaceae) is a biologically active molecule, possessing anti-inflammatory, antimiotic and tumour-inhibiting activities. Several reviews on chemistry and pharmacological properties are available. The term Colchicine is derived from the area known as 'Colchis' near the Black Sea. The use of Colchicum in gout was recorded in 560 A.D. and it was so employed until 13th century. In 1873 the re-employment of colchicum in medicine under the preparation "Medicinals" became very popular for the treatment of gout. Early idea of action of Colchicum in gout treatment were pronounced by Thomson and others. In the 19th century it was realized that gout and uric acid metabolism were in some way linked and colchicum might act on this. Gout is caused by deposition of microcrystals of uric acid in joints and may be due to a defective regulatory mechanism for endogenous purine synthesis, but conflicting results for the action of colchicine on synthesis and excretion of urates have been recorded. Colchicine interrupts the cycle of new crystal deposition which seems to be essential for the continuance of acute gout. Distressing side effects have been recorded occasionally but colchicine remains the drug of choice for acute gout. Modification of the side chains of the rings does not abolish anti-gout activity as long as the configuration of C-ring conforms to that of colchicine.

Colchicine may offer a lease of hope to the patients with liver cirrhosis. Experiments, carried by Kershenobich *et al.*, showed that oral colchicine, which inhibits collagen synthesis and secretion and enhances collagenase activity, decreased fibrosis and liver malfunction in rats with carbon tetrachloride induced cirrhosis. The results of the study by Kershenobich *et al.*, raised hope for the treatment of cirrhosis at hand. They are not conclusive because of serious flaws in survival analysis and screening process. Colchicine has also been advocated in many other diseases like cholera, typhus, Bright's disease, colic and skin complaints.

Colchicine acts on mitotically active cell producing metaphasic arrest, the 'c-mitotic' action often results in doubling of chromosome number and giving rise to polyploids. This was discovered first by Pernice in 1899 who did not realize its significance. This action was rediscovered in 1930's and was followed by considerable work on the action of colchicine on plant and animal cell and utility of this phenomenon in biology and medicine.

PLANT SOURCE

Since 1930 the demand of Colchicine has increased which stimulated great interest in plant sources. In this direction much work on resources and extraction of colchicine have been reviewed by Santary *et al.* Different genera studied include: *Androcymbium* (Africa), *Colchicum* (Europe, Russia and India), *Gloriosa* (India, Ceylon and Africa), *Iphigenia* (India and Africa), and *Merendera* (Europe and India). It is quite interesting to know that *Colchicum cornigerum*, a species native to Egypt, has provided the only example which contains colchicine related alkaloid but no colchicine as such. Colchicine is manufactured from *Colchicum autumnale*, a plant indigenous to and widely met within the European continent. A worldwide search for alternative plant sources have been under way. Amongst the Indian plants the corms of *Colchicum luteum* and seeds of *Iphigenia stellata* reported to be rich in colchicine content, are not available in sufficient quantities to warrant any commercial utilization. *Gloriosa superba* L. is another plant containing Colchicine. Many workers have isolated colchicine, colchicine related alkaloids and non-alkaloidal contents from the various parts of this plant. In continuation to our work on indigenous sources of colchicine, extensive analytical studies on the various parts of this plant revealed that the percentage of colchicine in seeds is ten times more than that in the tubers. This prompted us to explore the large scale isolation of colchicine in India.

DESCRIPTION OF PLANT

Gloriosa superba Linn. (N.O. Liliaceae) is a perennial herbaceous climber occurring among scrub forests throughout India upto an altitude of 1800 m. It is native of tropical Asia and Africa and is commonly known as Glory Lily or Malabar glory Lily. The plant flowers during July and August while the capsules (5-6 cm long) containing ripe seeds can be harvested by the end of September. Propagation is effected by tuber cuttings which are planted in the month of May and sprout in July. The fruits with ripe seeds are ready for harvest in the first week of October. The high colchicine content of the seeds accompanied by prospects of their good availability from both wild and cultivated sources, make the material a potential commercial source of colchicine in India.

Exploitation of seeds as source of colchicine has following advantages over the Colchicine extraction from tubers:

1. Perennial natue of the plant ensures sustained supply of the raw material over a number of years.
2. Colchicine content of the seed is ten times more than that in the tubers.
3. The process developed from the seeds is very facile as eliminates the use of column chromatography completely.
4. The recovery of the colchicine content from the seeds is higher than that from the tubers.

EXTRACTION METHOD

Toxic principle of *Colchicum autumnale* was first isolated by Pelletier and Caventou in the year 1819 which believed it to be veratrine. The extraction method of colchicine alkaloids developed by Santavy *et al.*, has given poor yield of colchicine when tried on tubers of *Gloriosa superba*.

A process for the extraction of Colchicine ex. *G. superba* tubers was developed based on high solubility of Colchicine in water. The total alkaloids, thus obtained by water extraction, were further purified through partition with Chlorinated solvent followed by column chromatography over neutral alumina to yield pure colchicine and related alkaloids. Since the seeds of *G. superba* are rich source of Colchicine, attempts were made to develop an economically viable method for the production of colchicine by using various solvents and other parameters such as temperature, time etc. Aqueous ethanol was found to be the solvent of choice for the extraction of the alkaloid from the de-fatted seeds. The crude colchicine thus obtained was purified by using mixtures of solvents instead of column chromatography. The process was found to be successful on large scale trials. The detailed process is given below:

The de-fatted moderately powdered seeds are extracted with continuous stirring using aqueous ethanol as solvent till last drops of the extract do not give positive tests for the alkaloids. The total extract is combined and filtered to remove the sediments. The clear filtrate thus obtained, is concentrated under reduced pressure to 1/6th of the total volume. The concentrated golden yellow solution, thus obtained, is further extracted with chloroform with the help of liquid-liquid extractor. The total chloroform extract is dried over anhydrous calcium chloride, filtered and distilled under reduced pressure to yield yellowish green semi-solid mass (1.5%) as neutral-phenolics. The resinous mass from the netural-phenolics is removed by treatment with a mixture of chloroform and petrol and colchicine crystallized from ethyl acetate to yield 0.70% creamish yellow crystalline material which is highly soluble in methanol, ethanol and water, m.p. 150-3°.

CHEMISTRY AND STRUCTURAL RELATIONSHIP OF COLCHICINE WITH OTHER RELATED ALKALOIDS

Chemically, colchicine is named as methyl ether of colchicine. Furthermore colchicine, N-formyl-N-desacetyl colchicine and 3-demethyl colchicine designated as substance A,B and C respectively have been reported to occur in various plants of liliaceae family (Fig. 1). Chemical studies on these alkaloids indicated the presence of a methoxyl group in colchicine possessing only asymmetric carbon at position C-7. This seems

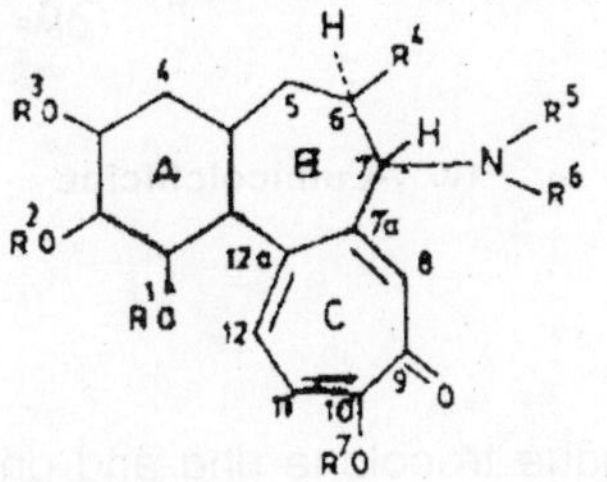

	COMPOUND	R^1	R^2	R^3	R^4	R^5	R^6	R^7
I.	COLCHINE (A)	CH_3	CH_3	CH_3	H	CH_3CO	H	CH_3
II.	N-FORMAL-N-DEACETYL COLCHICINE (B)	CH_3	CH_3	CH_3	H	CHO	H	CH_3
III.	3-DEMETHYLCOLCHINE (C)	CH_3	CH_3	H	H	CH_3CO	H	CH_3

Fig. 1

exceptionally simple when compared with complex alkaloids such as morphine and strychnine yet structural studies spanned more than 100 years. The total synthesis of colchicine was not achieved until 1959. The structure of colchicine does posses some unusual feature of which seven membered ring B and more particularly the troponoid ring C, deserve special mention. The structure of colchicine has attracted widespread attention as a challenging synthetic problem [Schreiber *et al.*, Tamelen *et al.*, Nakamura *et al.*, Scott *et al.*, Woodward, Kotani *et al.*, Evans *et al.*, Boger *et al.* Ik and Brossi *et al.*]. When Colchicine is irradiated by light, photoisomerization occurs and α–β and γ-lumi-derivatives are formed. Santavy isolated compounds designated as I- and J-substances from the natural sources along with the colchicine. The physical properties of compounds I- and J- cirrespond to β- and γ- lumicolchicine respectively. NMR studies of colchicines and its photoisomers, β - and α - lumicolchicines have been obtained using a combination of 1D- and 2D-nmr spectroscopic techniques. The study revealed that γ-lumicolchicine is a steroisomer of β -lumicolchicine shown in Figure 2.

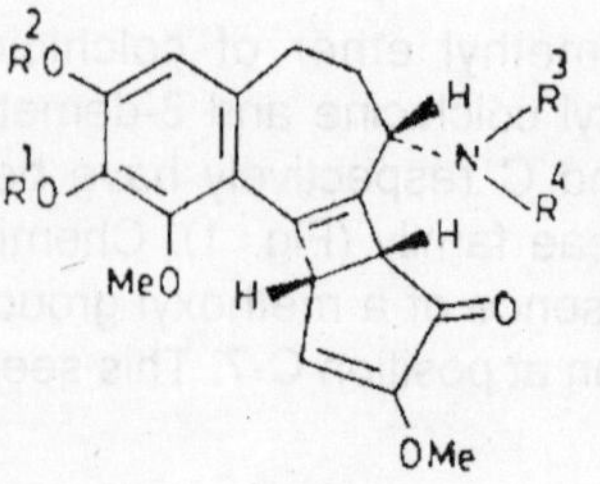

Where
$R^1 = R^2 = Me$
$R^3 = H$
$R^4 = COCH_3$

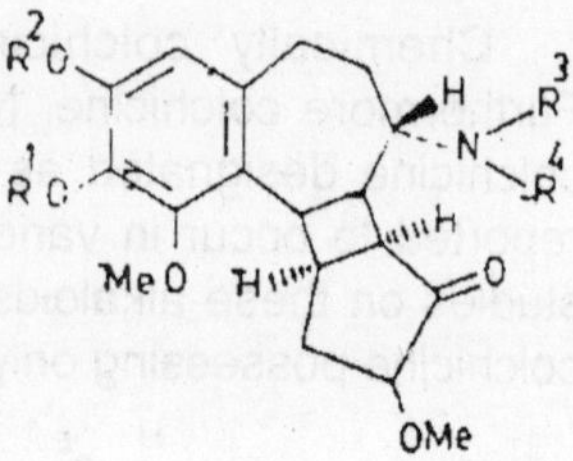

IV. β-Lumicolchicine **IV. γ-Lumicolchicine**

Fig. 2

Biosynthesis of colchicine

Colchicine (I) is an alkaloid with a unique tropolone ring and on the face of it appears to be quite unrelated to any other alkaloid. A pioneer work on the biosynthesis of this alkaloid was carried out by Battersby *et al.*, and Leete *et al.*, on the different species of *Colchicum* and accordingly acetate was the precursor of the N-acetylgroup. Phenylalanine by way of Cinnamic acid serves in *Colchicum* species as the source of right A plus carbons 5,6 and 7. The seven Carbons of the tropolone ring arise from tyrosine which loses C-1 and C-2 from the side chain labels from [4'-^{14}C] and [3-^{14}C] labelled amino acid appear at C-9 and C-12 of colchicine respectively. It follows that the tropolone ring arises by expansion of the tyrosine benzene ring with inclusion of the benzylic carbon but through what series of intermediates.

The answer came from the elucidation of the structure of androcymbine an alkaloid isolated from a relative of *Colchicum*. The dienone structure (VIII) was assigned to androcymbine. Androcymbine could then be thought of as arising from the phenethylisoquinoline skeleton [VI] which was quite unknown at the time. A similar biogenesis for colchicine followed. Plausibly the transformation of the androcymbine skeleton [VIII] to that of colchicine could occur by hydroxylation to give [IX]. Homoallylic ring expansion would lead to colchicine (shown in Figure 3).

A crucial test for the hypothesis lay in the examination of compounds to types [VI] and [VIII] as Colchicine precursors. In the event, O-methyl androcymbine [VII] was a spectacularly good precursor for colchicine. The

BIOSYNTHESIS OF COLCHINE

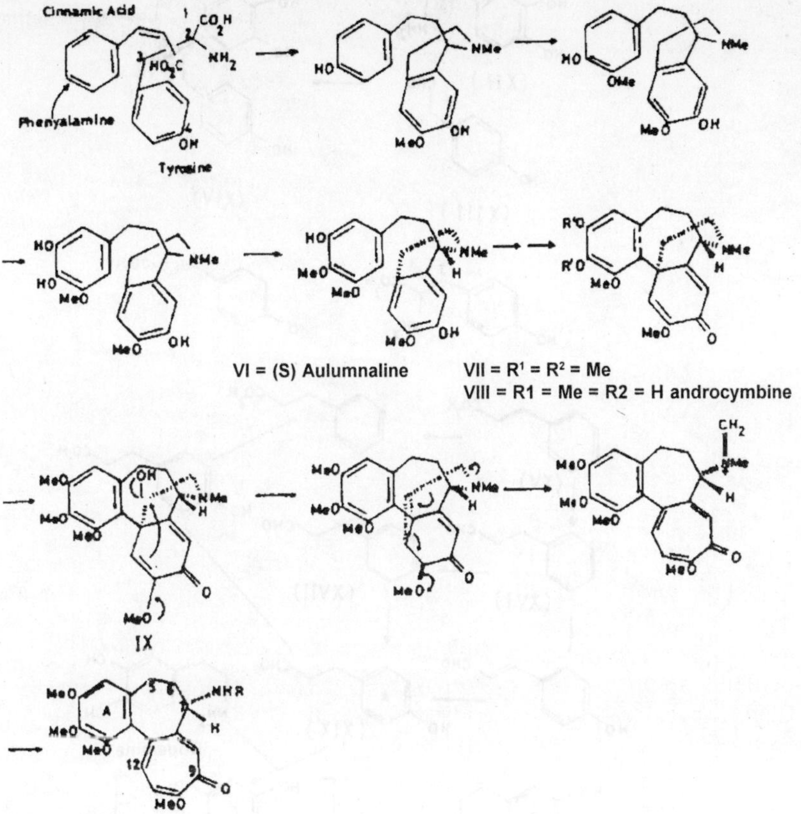

VI = (S) Aulumnaline

VII = $R^1 = R^2 = Me$

VIII = R1 = Me = R2 = H androcymbine

X = R = Me

XI = R = H

I = R = Ac, Colchicine

Fig. 3

phenethylisoquinoline [VI] called autumnaline, was also clearly implicated in biosynthesis, only the (S)-isomer of autumnaline with the same absolute configuration as colchicine is involved, and oxidative coupling of this base occurs in a *para-para* sense rather than the alternative of *ortho-para*. Results of other experiments together with those discussed here, led to the Pathway illustrated in Figure 3. Examination of the final stages of Colchicine biosynthesis showed that demecolcine [X] and deacetyl colchicine [XI] were involved.

BIOSYNTHESIS OF PHENTHYLISOQUINOLINE

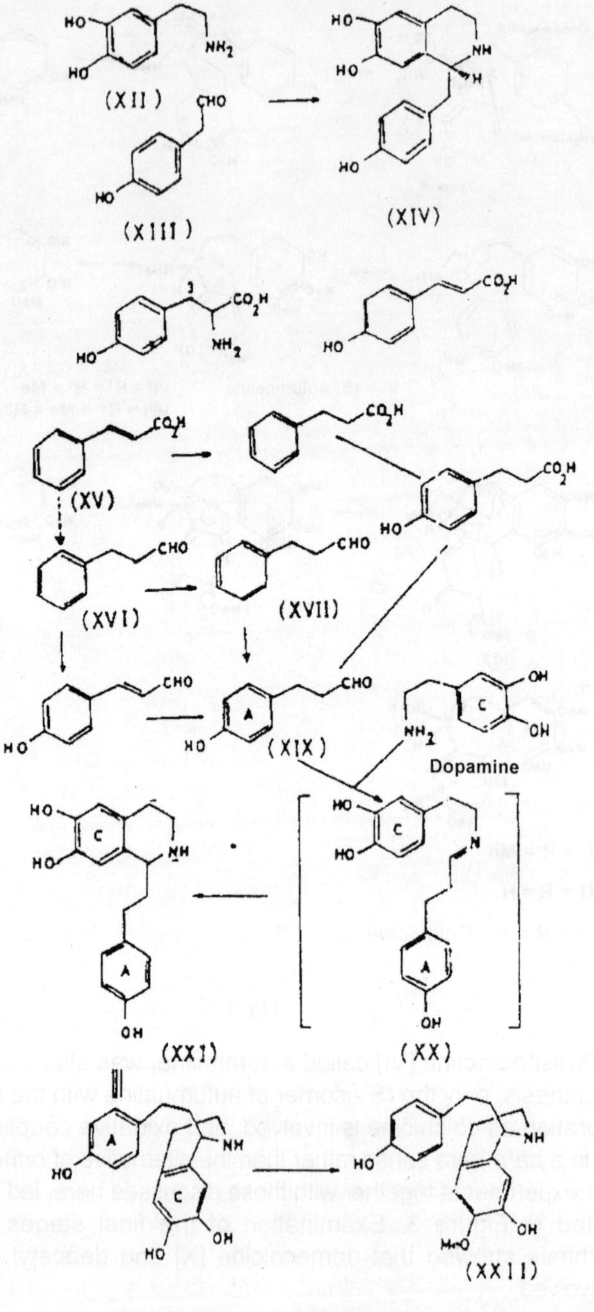

Fig. 4: Biosynthesis of Phenthylisoquinoline

It is with exceptions, now a common observation for the biosynthesis of very many different alkaloids that a key step involves condensation of an aldehyde with an amine, e.g.; biosynthesis of benzyl isoquinoline alkaloids involve the enzyme-catalysed condensation of dopamine [XII] with 4-hydroxy-phenylacetaldehyde [XIII] yielding (S)-nor Coclaurine [XIV] which is the precursor then for the whole family of benzylisoquinoline alkaloids. Keeping in view this observation Herbert *et al.*, recently conducted feeding experiments with mixtures of precursors where one compound bore C-label and the other H- label. The combined results indicate the course of biosynthesis for colchicine [I], demecolcine [X] in *Colchicum* sp. (Liliaceae) illustrated in Figure 4.

In analogy to (S)-nor-Coclaurine, a precursor for benzylisoquinoline alkaloid, from cinnamic acid [XV] via cinnamaldehyde [XVI] arises dihydrocinnamic aldehyde [XVII] which generates an important intermediate as a precursor identified as 3-(4-hydroxphenyl) propanal [XIX]. This precursor allows to build upon the pathway for the biosynthesis of colchicine illustrated in Figure 4. The condensation of the aldehyde [XIX] with dopamine [XII] affords unstable Compound [XXI] Via [XX] which was identified as trihydroxy isoquinoline. The cinnamyl double-bond is reduced before the formation of phenethylisoquinoline skeleton [XXII] similar to structure [VI] shown in Fig. 3 which was not known earlier. The results reported indicate that n-methylation need not occur straight after the formation of [XXII] i.e. may occur after aromatic hydroxylation and O-methylation. Thus it is established that phenethyl isoquinoline is an intact precursor for demecolcine and colchicine.

Herbert *et al.*, observed that *Sceletium* alkaloids belonging to the Aizoaceae family are formed in the early stages in a similar pathway to the *Colchicum* alkaloids, i.e. 3-(4-hydroxyphenyl) propanal [XIX] is involved as precursor as it likely combines with dopamine to form a Schiff's base which acts as an intermediates (XX) in *Colchicum* biosynthesis. It seems as if there is lack of aryl hydroxy group in *Sceletium* biosynthesis which prevents isoquinoline ring formation. This indicated that colchicine has no structural relation with other alkaloids.

7

Studies on Commercial Indian Aconites: Atis

INTRODUCTION

Atis roots constitute one of the major items of crude drug trade in the country and are extensively used in indigenous system of medicines. Inspite of a good amount of work on the taxonomy and identity of the drug as well as the whole plant a great amount of confusion still persists. Studies revealed that neither there are proper estimates of the raw material nor there are any standards for the drug. Similarly the drug was found to be much confused by a number of misnomers and is frequently adulterated by other cheaper roots. A detailed investigation on the plant, the root drug and its trade revealed a number of facts and the same are being discussed in the chapter.

Pharmacognostic studies of the roots of *Aconitum heterophyllum* have previously been done by Datta *et al.* But no work on adulterants or anatomical comparison of different plants has been done. The genus *Aconitum* has been subjected to a great taxonomical confusion. Stapf investigated in detail the Indian species of *Aconites* and separated tham into 3 groups viz., Napellus type, Anthora type and Deinorrhizum type. *Aconitum* species yielding the non poisonous Aconite roots are included under Anthora type. His classification is based on purely anatomical characters of the roots.

USES AND CHEMICAL CONSTITUENTS

In the indigenous system of medicine the drug is considered a valuable febrifuge and a bitter tonic especially in combating debility after malaria or other fevers. The drug in combination with certain other ingredients is also used as antiperiodic. The roots have been reported to contain the alkaloids viz., Atisin, hetratisine, hetisine and heterophyllin Bose, all of which are non-toxic. Almost whole of the produce is consumed by manufactures of Ayurvedic medicines, Vaids and Hakims. Due to the great demand of drug it is sold in the market at a very high price.

PLANT DESCRIPTION, OCCURRENCE AND DISTRIBUTION

Atis of commerce is mainly constituted by the roots of a perennial herb *Aconitum heterophyllum* wall. The roots of yet another species *Aconitum kashmericum* Stapf ex Coventry a closely allied species are also harvested as Atis are sold in the market as frequent adulterant or as a cheap substitute by the name of Atis Kashmiri or Kala Atis or *Aconitum spicatum*.

Aconitum heterophyllum

It is an erect, herb, reaching upto 75 cm. in height with purple marked pale green flowers in terminal racemes which frequently branch to a panicle, the lower leaves are long petioled while the upper are stem clasping and acute (Fig.1).

Aconitum kashmericum

Seldom reaches a height of more than 30 cm. and has deep blue flowers. Leaves few, long, petioled, orbicular, cordate to ovate cordate, incised and toothed (Fig.2).

Fig. 1 Sketch diagram of a plant of *Aconitum heterophyllum*

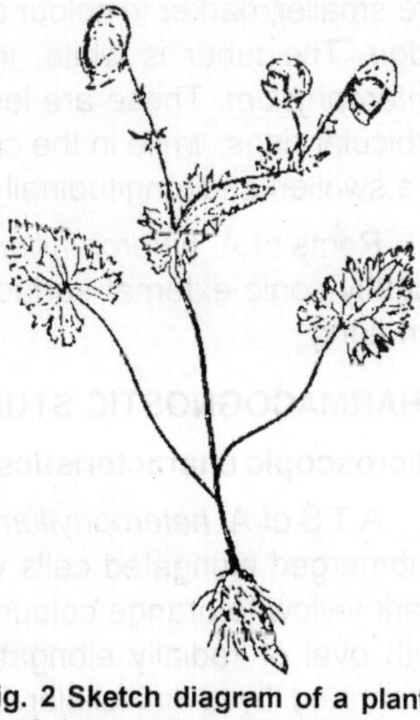

Fig. 2 Sketch diagram of a plant of *Aconitum kashmericum*

Aconitum heterophyllum

Aconitum heterophyllum occurs mostly under the 'banks and mixed conferous forests and also on the moist banks of nallahas at about 3000 m. and extends well above the tree limit beyond 4000 m. On the other hand *Aconitum kashmericum* is exclusively found among the alpine meadows and boulders where sometimes dense formations are noticed. The two simultaneously flower during the pre-autumn months from August to first week of October.

Aconitum kashmericum

Aconitum kashmericum is mainly distributed among the alpine localities of Kashmir, Jammu, Chamba and Kinnaur Himalayas, while the former grows extensively throughout N.W. Himalayas extending from Jammu and Kashmir and in the Western part of Nepal. In *Aconitum kashmericum* the upper sepals of the flowers form a hood over the other sepals, sub-orbicular carpels with long yellowish hairs, limb of nectary narrowed to a point at the top. In *Aconitum heterophyllum* sepals 5, petal like, erect, the upper one (helmet) pointed in front, top rounded, lateral sepals as long as the helmet. In form of leaf it varies considerably.

THE DRUG

The fresh fully grown roots derived from *Aconitum heterophyllum* is of ash grey colour about 1-15 inch and about 0.5 inch thick at its upper edge. Roots of good quality break with a short starchy fracture presenting a uniform milky white surface. The taste is purely bitter and no tingling sensation is produced. The roots derived from *Aconitum kashmericum* on the other hand are smaller, darker in colour and between 5-8 mm. in thickness at its upper edge. The tuber is white, inside fracture is similar to that in *Aconitum heterophyllum*. These are less shriveled and have rounded root scars, in orbicular rings, while in the case of *Aconitum heterophyllum* the root scars are swollen and longitudinally extended.

Roots of *A. heterophyllum* are biennial and paired, cylinderic oblong or slightly conic external surface. The buds at the crown are short, 0.3-0.8 cm. long.

PHARMACOGNOSTIC STUDIES

Microscopic characteristics

A T.S of *A. heterophyllum* shows 3-5 layered epidermis or metaderm of submerged elongated cells which are generally crushed in the old roots. Bark yellow to orange colour. Primary cortex in young roots is 5-6 layered with oval or radially elongated cells (Fig. 3 a-c). The primary cortex is separated by a unicellular endodermis composed of elongated spindle shaped cells from the inner bark which is a uniform tissue having cells full of starch grains. Secondary phloem elements are scattered in this tissue both inside as well as outside the cambium strands. The cambium is broken into 6 triangular steles arranged in the form of a concentric ring. Thus, the whole of central cylinder practically consists of secondary phloem plus a narrow pith whose cells are circular or oval in outline and have got starch grains. The cambium of the isolated xylem stands or the scattered "steles" is very delicate and usually gets crushed in T.S. Xylem tissue inside it is more or less V-shaped, meeting in the center with or without cavities formed by the disintegration of the cells of xylem parenchyma.

Measurements of the cells in T.S. are:- parenchyma cells of secondary cortex containing starch α 9-19-27 μ, b 14-27-53 μ endodermis cells α 4-8 μ, β 4-6 μ; xylem vessels measure of α 41-71-282 μ x b 8-16-21 μ.

T.S. root of *A. kashmericum* shows the metaderm consists of one or more layers of suberised cells with brown or yellowish walls and is often cast off in mature roots. In very young roots primary cortex is clearly observed being composed of 6 or more layers of cells; cells very much elongated, endodermis demarcates between primary and secondary cortex, endodermal cells in T.S. measure α 5.7-9.5-13.3 μ, β 9.5-17-24 μ. Secondary cortex is a uniform tissue of parenchymatous cells and full of starch grains. In this tissue are embedded 4-5 isolated cylindric strands of xylem or steles arranged in the form of ring, each one having its own circular rings of cambium. Cambium is very well differentiated into 3-4 layers of cells, more or less of isodiametric type. Stone cells as in *A. heterophyllum* are absent in this case. Groups of secondary phloem or sieve tissue are found scattered throughout the central cylinder. Xylem is star like in shape enclosing xylem parenchyma which is unoblitelateral (Fig. 4 a, b). Pith is very sma'! practically unidentified.

Parenchyma cells of secondary cortex in T.S. measure α 17-21-36 μ, β 17-27-59-μ; xylum vessels measure α 58-116-191 μ and β 6-8-16 μ. These have got narrow lumen.

Anatomical Characteristics of Powder

In powder form no apparent distinction between two species is found. Root powder of the two species (90-100 mesh) was studied with a view to find out:

1. Structure of starch grains.
2. Presence or absence of calcium oxalate crystals covering trichomes and
3. Lignified vessels, fibres, tricheids, parenchyma and stone cells.

Under the microscope the powder from the two species show very little or no difference at all. The common features of the two species in powder form are:

1. Abundance of starch grains in both types. They vary in size and are from rounded, oval to lunar in shape with central hilum, found in groups of 2, 3, 4 or even more.
2. Fragments of xylem vessels, masses of starchy parenchyma. Vesseis have got spiral, annular and reticulated pittings. Tracheids and fibre tracheids found the later have got simple pits. Calcium oxalate crystals and epidermal trichomes with phloroglucinal and HCl xylem vessels show little lignification.

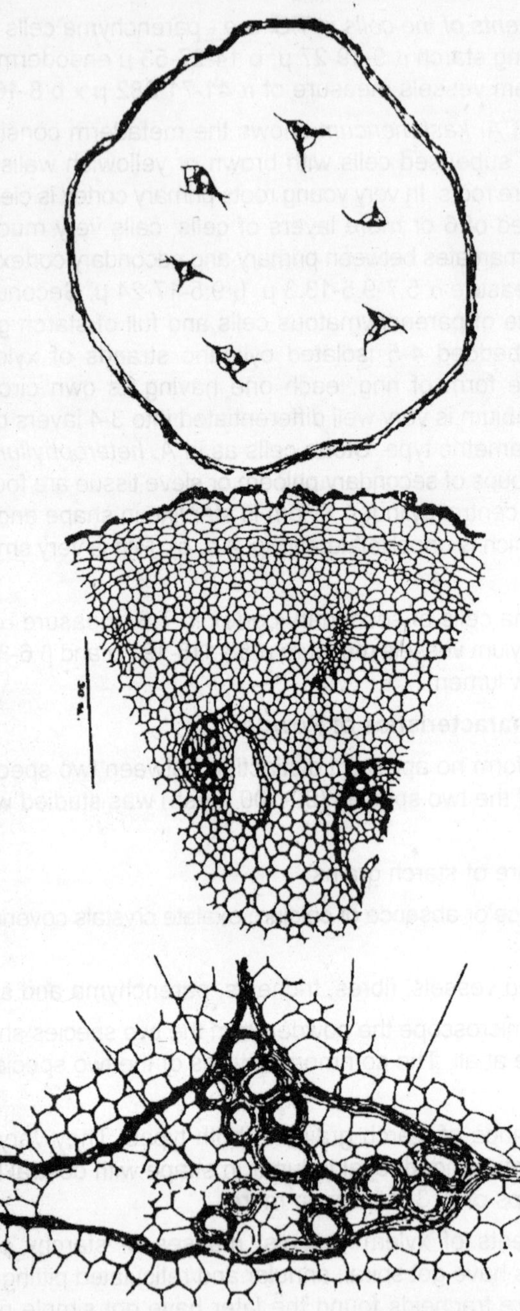

a. T.S. root of A. heterophyllum showing 6 vascular bundles
b. T.S. of a mature root of *A. heterophyllum*
c. Enlarged meristele of *A. heterophyllum*

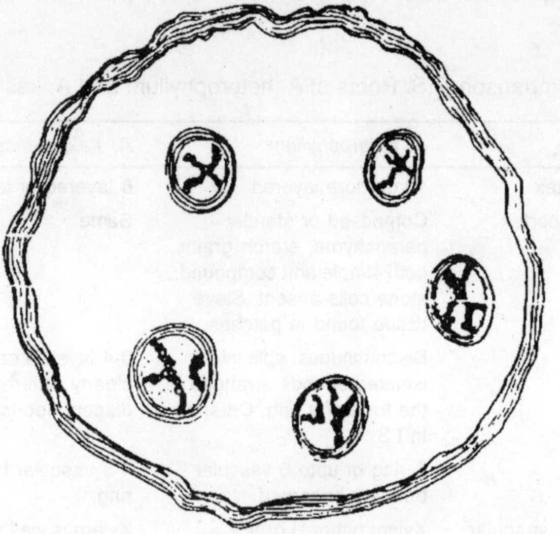

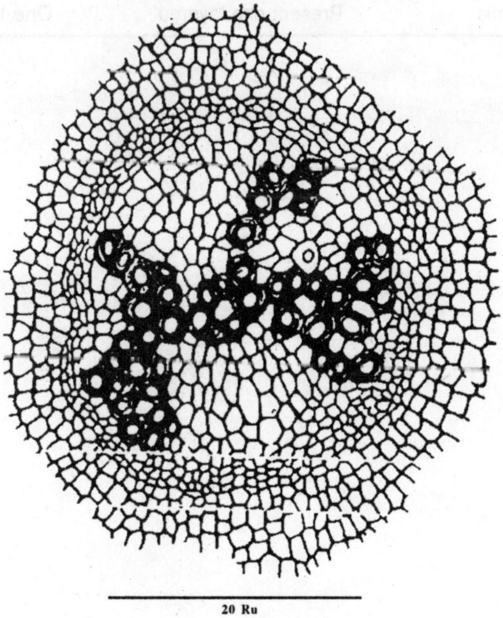

a. T.S. root of *A. kashmericum.*, showing 5 vascular bundles

b. T.S. root of *A. kashmericum*

The various chemical tests performed with the powder are tabulated in Table 1.

Table 1: Comparison: T.S. Roots of A. heterophyllum and A. kashmericum.

T.S. Root	*A. heterophyllum*	*A. kashmericum*
1. Primary cortex	10 or more layered	6 layered or less.
2. Secondary cortex	Composed or starchy parenchyma, starch grains both simple and compound, stone cells absent. Sieve tissue found in patches.	Same
3. Cambium	Discontinuous, split into isolated strands arranged in the form of a ring, Crushed In T.S.	3-4 layered cambium, very clearly differentiated, discontinuous.
4. Stele	A ring of upto 6 vascular bundles observed	4-5 vascular bundles in a ring.
5. Structure of vascular bundle	Xylem either U or V shaped or tangentially flattened with or without Cavities in the tissue.	Xylem is well marked stellate shape with no cavities.
6. Endodermis	Present one layered	One layered.

8

Cultivation of *Ammi majus* Linn. in India

INTRODUCTION

Ammi majus Linn. (Apiaceae) is an important medicinal herb, occurring worldwide in both the hemispheres. The plant is indigenous to Egypt and widely distributed in Mediterranean region, Abyssinia, Europe and West Africa. It constitutes principal commercial source of xanthotoxin, which is commonly used in the treatment of vitilago or leucoderma and also in formulating sun-tan lotions. In India, the plant was first introduced from Egypt at Forest Research Institute, Dehradun. Since then its experimental cultivation has been tried in several parts of the country. Its experimental cultivation in Chakrata Forest Division, Dehradun gave an average fruit yield of 375 kg/ha, and its low yield was suggested to be due to excessive rainfall. France, Switzerland and Federal Republic of Germany required about 400 tonnes of *Ammi majus* fruit annually, part of the requirement met from Indian export. There has been steady increase in the cultivation of *Ammi majus* crop in India and as a result the country meets the demand for internal consumption of the drug and export the finished product as well. Mac Laboratories, Mumbai and Himalaya Drugs Ltd., Delhi were pioneers in the drug production and mainly met the Country's export demand.

In view of the low yield reported in Dehradun, Bradu and Atal undertook its first experimental cultivation in Jammu and later at Palampur and Baijnath (H.P.) registering its success and proved the economic viability of the crop. This finding led to its commercial growing in various parts of north India.

The exotic species was biennial, but behaved as annual under cultivation in India. The plants, also called as Greater *Ammi* or Bishop's weed, is an erect branching herb, upto 1.5-2 m in height, leaves broad ternate or pinnate, leaflets lanceolate, flowers white in loose compound umbels, fruits oblong, 1.5-2.0 mm long and 1mm or less broad. Under large scale cultivation in various parts of India, the growth remained vigorous, prolific in flowering and fruiting. When cultivated at CIMAP drug farm, Chakrohi (Jammu), Duhan *et al.*, reported that crop should be grown in the second fortnight of October with 90 kg N/ha for obtaining good quality seed yield. Gupta and Shah also reported October sowing of the crop with higher xanthotoxin content. Randhawa *et al.*, found that fruit yield was not affected statistically with increase in nitrogen level from 50 to 100 kg N/ha. Adam *et al.* and Shehab *et al.*, reported respectively, the cytological effects of water extracts of *Ammi majus* on the mitosis and meiosis of *Vicia faba*. The extract caused a delay in the completion of the mitotic cycle. While the interphase stages remained unaffected, but prophase and metaphase stages were most influenced. The dominant abnormalities were stickiness, irregular prophase, bridges with low frequency lagging prophase metaphase and despiralization. In meiosis the anomalies in the first division were higher than in second. The induced irregularities were stickiness, bridges, spindle, disturbance, lagging chromosome, breaks, fragments and multinucleate cell. The plant extract caused a decrease in pollen grain length and slightly increased pollen viability.

Greater Ammi contained 0.4% xanthotoxin and additional quantities of xanthotoxin can be prepared by converting imperatorin present in the fruit to xanthotoxin by chemical means. *Wealth of India, Raw Materials*, Vol I: A (revised) quoted that xanthotoxin was effective in the treatment of leucoderma when given orally in doses of 50 mg, three times daily or applied externally as one percent liniment followed by exposure of affected areas to sunlight or ultraviolet light for 2-4 hours. It further added that xanthotoxin (ammoidin) was the Chief active principle in the fruit. It was a furocoumarin marked under the trade mark 'oxsoralen'. Other furocoumarins present were ammidin (imperatorin), majudin (bergapten), marmesin, isopimpinellin, majurin, ammajin (marmesinin), isoimperatorin, ammirin, and 8-isopropenyl 1-8,9-dihydroangelicin (probably angenomalin). The presence of a non-furocumarin umbelli-prenin (mp 60-61°), glycosides of quercetin and luteolin and two artifacts 7-isopropyl-psoralene and dihydro-oroselone. Fruits contained protein (13.8%) and fat (12.9%). The presence of xanthosine (mp 144.47°) was reported in the seed. The leaves contained xanthotoxin and isopimpinellin. A method claimed to be economical was developed at Regional Centre of CIMAP at Jammu. In this method, the seed was cleaned, powdered and extracted with solvent oil (80-100°). The coumarins recovered from the extract by chilling and liquid-liquid extraction, was subjected to chromatographic separation after treatment with alcoholic hydrochloric acid. Bergapten, xanthotoxin and xanthotoxol were separated and the xanthotoxol fraction methylated, and the total xanthotoxin (also known as methoxsalen) obtained was purified by charcoal treatment in acetone or alcohol. Ashraf *et al.*, examined the seed essential oil of Pakistani *Ammi majus* for its quality and chemical composition. He reported the percentage essential oil constituents which comprised high boiling hydrocarbons (1.34%), dl-piperitone (10%) unsaturated cyclic terpene alcohol (15%) and a mixture of furocoumarins (60%). He found that furocoumarins fraction was composed of xanthotoxin, bergaptene, imperatorin, iso-imperatorin and iso-primpinellin of which xanthotoxin was the major component. Wayne reported twelve linear furocoumarrins (psoralens) isolated from the ripened seed of Texas (USA) collection of the photosensitizing Bishop's weed. Four of the compounds i.e. xanthotoxin, bergapten, isopimpinellin and iso-imperatorin had already been isolated, but isolation of six of the eight other psoralens, which were known plant products, but not obtained earlier from *A. majus*. The rest of the two psoralens i.e. 8-(2- (3-methyl-butyroxy)-3-hydroxy-3-methyl butoxy) psoralen, and 5-(2-(acetoxy)-3-methyl butoxy) psoralen, not reported earlier from any plant source, were isolated from *A. majus*. The author further reported that most of the major psoralens from *A. majus* were potent photosensitizers, based on bioassays against chick skin and the presence of these compounds in seed and other parts of the species accounts for high photosensitizing activity towards cattle and sheep, besides reporting their use in the treatment of psoriasis. Witazel *et al.*, also reported occurrence of *A. majus* on the coastal region of Southern USA and in other parts of world, causing severe photosensitization in livestock and contributing to its outbreaks in Texas (U.S.A.) Experimental trials conducted by him on sheep fed with finely ground seed of *A. majus* at dose rates of 1-8g/kg of body weight and exposed in sunlight. A single dose of 8g/kg produced severe clinical signs in 24-28 hours, resulting in corneal edema, conjunctivo-keratitis, photophobia and edema of the muzzle, ears and vulva. Such severe long term photosensitization effects were reported by various other authors. Mendez *et al.*, also reported an outbreak of primary photosensitization in cattle grazing on pasture in Southern Brazil invaded by *A. majus* weed, showing clinical signs characterized by dermatitis in the Udder of the cows and kerato conjunctivitis in the calves.

In the heterotrophic cell suspension initiated from hypocotyls of young *Ammi majus* seedlings, Hamerski *et al.*, reported *A majus* cells suitable for biosynthetic studies on various coumarins as well as for regulatory studies of the inhibition of coumarins phytoalexin accumulation.

CULTURAL PRACTICES

Ammi majus could be grown in a variety of soils but does well in a loamy soil. The soil is ploughed twice and brought to a fine tilth. The seed being very fine is mixed with fine soil or sand before sowing in shallow furrows 90 cm apart. After sowing, the seed should be covered with a fine layer of soil. The seed rate is 2.5 kg per hectare. The seed can be sown from Ist of October to middle of November, but the seed sown at the end of November generally fail to germinate. A dose of superphosphate at 25 kg/ha mixed with liberal quantity of farm yard manure is applied in the furrows before sowing the seed. If it does not rain within a week after sowing, a liberal irrigation is given. The seed starts germinating after a fortnight and takes about a month to complete the germination. When the seedlings develop true leaves and are 8-10 cm in height, thinning is done so that plant to plant distance within the row is 60-90cm. Two hoeings are given to keep the soil mellow and free from weeds. Irrigation is given after a weak or ten days during the dry season. Water should not be allowed to stand in the field as the plants are sensitive to water logging.

HARVESTING

The best stage for harvesting the fruit when xanthotoxin was maximum. Mature brown fruit contained 0.4%, mature but green fruit 0.72% and immature green fruit 1% of xanthotoxin. This suggested the best stage of harvesting the fruit. The highest yield of xanthotoxin, imperatorin and bergapten from the air-dried mature unripe fruits from Cairo (Egypt) was reported to be 1.06, 0.8 and 0.33% respectively. Bradu and Atal found that delay in harvesting caused considerable loss in fruit yield due to shattering. Sobti *et al.*, studied the problem of shattering of fruit in *A. majus*. Planofix (active ingredient NAA) at concentration of 5 ppm was applied at 2 stages, one at the initiation of flowering and second at the time of formation of fruit, in an area of 0.48 hectare. The fruit yield of 1500 kg/ha was obtained as against 900-1000 kg/ha under control, an increase of 50% over control. Uniformity in flowering and maturity of umbels was obtained to a considerable extent, resulting in easy harvesting.

The flowering starts in the beginning of March and fruiting by end of April. The primary umbels fruit first and are hand picked towards end of April or early May when majority of remaining umbels (secondary and tertiary) are about to mature (at mature green stage), the crop is harvested, cut at middle level, and stacked in loose bundles till fruits dry up. The fruit is separated by thrashing and winnowing. A yield of over 1375 kg/ha was obtained under experimental conditions and 900-1000 kg/ha in large scale cultivation under Jammu conditions. In Palampur-Baijnath area, the fruit yield was 600 kg/ha, but the low yield was compensated by hgier xanthotoxin content (1% and above).

ROTATION

A cultural trial of *Heracleum candicans* was also tried at Palampur. The seed was sown in nursery beds in March and seedings were transplanted towards end of April or beginning of May in those field where *A. majus* was grown. The growth became vigorus during rainy season and crop started flowering in July. The crop was harvested after 21 months. Being a root crop, the roots were extracted out in December following year. The fresh weight of root on an average was 1.2 kg per plant having a total coumarin content of 8.5%.

9

Cultivation of Rutin Bearing Eucalyptus Species

Rutin, 3,5,7,3',4' pentahydroxy flavone-3-rhamnoglucose is known as 'P' factor or a substance possessing vitamin P like activity. Rutin was first isolated from *Ruta graveolens*.

Rutin is an important pharmaceutical product. It exerts a wide range of pharmacological effects. It is reported to be useful in the treatment of capillary fragility, and possibly rheumatic fever of haemorrhagic conditions. Generally, capillary fragility occurs in a significant number of cases of high blood pressure, diabetes and other conditions. It is reported to be effective in restoring to normalacy such capillaries in many cases. It is also useful as aid in the prevention of apoplexy and retinal haemorrhage in those cases where capillary fragility is concerned. It is used in the case of coronary thrombosis and purification of blood. Rutin has also been shown to provide protection against harmful effects of X-rays, indicating that it may be of use to the persons exposed to dangerous atomic radiations. The effect of rutin on the cardiovascular system was studied and it was reported that the compound increased the stroke volume of both intact and isolated frog's heart. Under certain conditions, rutin can afford animals protection against histamine shock. Rutin has been shown to be of value in protecting rabbits from frost bite. Rutin can also exhibit the properties of hyaluronidase, especially with ascorbic acid, like hesperidin which incidentally works as an oral contraceptive. It is found that only rutin prevented sexual reproduction, which they attributed to the existence of a sugar molecule at position 3, because quercertin did not influence fertility. But this fact has not been substantiated by other workers. Rutin can also be used as an analytical reagent and quercetin can be prepared from it in a high state of purity by simple acid hydrolysis. Rutin has been used clinically in treating certain types of hereditary hemorrhagic disorders, hemophilia symptoms, bleeding gums, migrainic headache, oedema, hydro-cele, hematuria, toxaemia in pregnancy. The fat anti-oxidant properties of these flavonoids have also been described. Hence, its hydrolysed product can be very useful for preventing oxidation in milk, butterfat, ghee etc. Recently, some preparations incorporating Rutin have claimed improvement in patients testing +ve for HIV and showing the symptoms of AIDS and AIDS-related syndromes.

Number of investigators have since found rutin, usually in small quantities, in a considerable number of plant species. A list of only those plants having more than 5 percent rutin is given in Table 1.

Table 1: Plants containing more than 5 per cent rutin

Family	*Species*	*Rutin (%)*	*Parts of plant*
Myrtaceae	*Eucalyptus macrorhyncha*	10.00-24.0	Leaves
	E. youmanii	6.8-11.0	Leaves
	E. delegatennsis	4.0-6.0	Leaves
Leguminosae	*Acacia dealbata*	5.2-5.9	Flowers
	Sophora japonica	13.0-30.0	Flowers
Caprifoliaceae	*Sambucus canadensis*	5.2	Immature Flowers
Papaveraceae	*Escholtzia californica*	5.0	Flowers
	Hypecoum pendulum	5.0	Flowers
Polygonaceae	*Fagopyrum cymosum*	4.0-8.5	Leaves and
	F. esculentum	0.11-6.37	Flowers
Rutaceae	*Boronia serrulata*	6.80	Leaves
	B. thujona	5.00	Leaves
Violaceae	*Viola lutea*	16.6	Flowers
	V. tricolor	18.3-21.2	Flowers
	Var. maxima		
	V. odorata		
Anacardiaceae	*Mangifera indica*	5.2	Leaves
Rubiaceae	*Uncaria elliptica*	20	Leaves

The important pharmaceutical product is not produced indigenously in sufficient quantity and is imported to meet the internal requirements of the industry. The total annual demand is about twenty tones of rutin and the present market rate is around Rs. 1200-00 per kg. The total world annual requirement is approximately of the order of 37-40 tonnes about a decade ago which must have risen considerably over the years.

Two important rutin enriched plant species of *Eucalyptus, youmanii* and *E. macrorhyncha* have been introduced and domesticated successfully in Kangra valley region of Himachal Pradesh. The leaves of these plant species are rich in rutin content. The trial planting of *E. macrorhyncha* was undertaken in the year 1963-64 in the Nilgiri and Palani hills in South India *E. youmantii* has been introduced in H.P. from Australia by this group for the first time. The preliminary trials made at Palampur (H.P.) have indicated that these species are very promising and valuable crops for this region (76.3° longitude and 32.6° latitude, altitude 1350-1400 meters above M.S.L.)

E. youmanii is moderate sized tree, commonly 12-20 metre in height, and diameter of 0.45 to 0.90 metre. It is usually heavily branched form about 1/3 height and has a moderately large to large, dense crown and grown on the low hills of northern tablelands of NSW in Australia in sclerophyllous Eucalyptus forests. The adult leaves are alternate, stalked, tending to narrow lanceolate, oblique, slightly falcate, lateral veins visible on one side, faint on the other, moderately thick, coriaceous, green in colour and concolorous. It has stringly bark; thick on the lower part of the trunk, grey to reddish-brown in colour, and persistent to the smaller branches.

E. macrorhyncha is commonly known as red stringy bark and sometimes mountain stringy bark. It is medium-sized tree maintaining a height of 21-30 metre; 0.45-105 metre diameter, with bark, as its common name implies that it is dark reddish to brown, persistent and stringly. The plant is indigenous to the sclerophyll forest of the central and south western slopes of N.S.W.; Victoria and in South Austrialia. These regions are subject to hot spells and droughts. It grows there between 300-900 m above MSL in Australia. The leaves of the mature tree are typical of the genus. They have a very thick cuticle and the laminae are borne vertically downwards. The leaves are alternate, petiolate, narrow, lanceolate and somewhat venulose. The leaves contains oil glands and tannin cells. This tree carries a moderately less dense crown than *E. youmanii*. The life of span of *E. macrorhyncha* leaves is short, compared with evergreen trees of other genera. Leaf fall from E. macrorhyncha tree is a constant process and is greatest at the commencement of periods of fresh growth and when the fruit is forming. The mean life of the leaves is about 18 months. It varies with their position on the tree as on vigorous branches, many leaves fall during the first year and most of the remainder leaves fall when the next burst of growth commences.

E. youmanii and *E. macrorhyncha* were raised from seeds by first raising a nursery followed by transplanting the seedlings. Nursery sowing is generally preferred as the tiny plants require intensive care to protect them from frost, severe cold and winter rains. It takes about six months for the plants to gain a height of 15-25 cm when they are transplanted in the field. Seeds of *E. macrorhyncha* are smaller (720 seeds/g). They normally lose viability on ageing and fresh seeds are used for raising nursery. Germination percentage of *E. macrorhyncha* is almost double than *E. youmanii* under Palampur conditions. The germination percentage of both of species is, however, lesser than that in Australia.

Seeds were obtained from several agencies in Australia in successive years and their performance noted under local conditions. The best time of sowing the seed in Jan-Feb.

Table 2

Plant	*No. of seeds Per 10 gm*	*Seed Viability*			
		Palampur (India)		*Australia*	
		per seed lot of 10 gm	*No. of seed lots tested*	*per seed lot of 10 gm*	*No. of seed lots tested*
E. macrorhyncha	7200	450	4	600	-
E. youmanii	4250	215	6	240	-

Table 3: Relative Germination Performance (uncontrolled Conditions)

Period/Month	*E. macrorhyncha Time of Germination*	*% Germination*	*E. youmanii Time of Germination*	*% Germination*
Sept.-Oct.	24	-	35	-
Nov.-Dec.	30	4.30	36	2.25
January	24	4.85	27	3.25
February	25	5.55	25	3.15
March	10	3.55	29	3.50
April-May	11	3.00	14	4.00
June-Aug.	7	4.00	10	3.85

Seedlings raised during this period were healthy, less prone to diseases and could attain considerable height before their transplantation during mid-monsoon period. During the hot summer months of April-May, the seed germination is poor and the seedlings which emerge suffer heavy mortality due to damping off, stunted growth and chlorosis. The germination is fairly good during June-August; but plant growth is stunted in pre-nursery stage, during the long severe winter in this region.

Seeds were sown shallow in alkathene bags, packed with well mixed soil and sand enriched with organic matter in Feb. The seeds, being very small in size, when sown deeper than 1 cm did not germinate. General screening of healthy seeds was done before sowing. Corresponding to the viability figures, an average of 10-12 seeds of *E. macrorhyncha* and 15-18 seeds of *E. youmanii* were sown in each alkethene bag to ensure uniform germination. The extra seedlings were picked and transplanted in separate bags. Alkathene bags were covered with a layer of paddy straw just after sowing the seeds to ensure adequate moisture and heat conservation. The straw layer was removed after the commencement of germination.

The seeds were also sown in wooden or aluminium trays by spreading them on the surface and covering with thin layer of fine soil. The tiny plants, having opposite leaves were picked out with care and transplanted in alkathene bags. The trial was repeated by keeping the trays in small polythene covered air tight chambers to ensure uniform and constant humidity and optimum temperature for quick and better germination. This practice was found to be convenient and successful and is recommended for large scale planting.

Seed of *E. macrorhyncha* germinated within 20-25 days, while those of *E. youmanii* took comparatively more time under controlled conditions.

Regular irrigation of nursery plants in bags, protection from outside cold and frost at night and conservation of moisture was found to be essential. It was done by making bamboo sheds over the nursery beds in the beginning. Regular weeding was also important as the two species are very sensitive to weed during the nursery stage.

In another trial on germination performance, the seeds were treated with varying concentrations of gibberellic acid and kept soaked overnight before sowing. In *E. youmanii*, the period of germination of seeds was reduced considerably whereas germination percentage was increased three times over the control at 50 ppm concentration. Lower concentration of the growth regulator had little effect on the overall performance of *E. macrorhyncha*. Under semi-controlled conditions (Poly chambers) the germination time was reduced to 10-12 days only for the two species.

Evidently, growth was faster in case of *E. macrorhyncha* as compared to *E. youmanii* during the post-nursery stage. The growth of *E. youmanii* was vigorous after transplantation. March to early June is comparatively hot in Palampur and partial protection of plants, still in nursery stage, from the hot weather was made by covering the alkathene bags with bamboo netting. The alkathene sheet was removed during this period. Careful hoeing around the plants to a moderate depth of about 2 cm could help in sufficient weed control. It also helped in improving soil aeration which resulted in better growth of seedlings. But it is desirable to apply this practice when the plants have fully established.

The plant species are very susceptible to termite damage which is increased when the plants lose vigour. To eliminate such attacks, incorporation of prophylactic doses of BHC powder of aldrin dust in soil during the nursery stage was found necessary. Such applications were, at times, needed after transplanting also. Leaf sucker attacked these species during monsoon and spray of 0.05 per cent laby-acid in pre and post-planting stages, controlled the damage.

Pits of 15 × 15 × 15 cm^3 size were made in the field at spacing of 1.5 × 1.5 m^2 for the transplantation of seedlings. The soil was well mixed with adequate quantity of FYM and NPK as basal dose. The transplanting was done towards the end of monsoon in late July-August. Since water logging increased the mortality rate of young seedlings, interchannels were made in the plots to remove excess of water, during rainy season. After planting, the area around each plant was cleaned thoroughly. Coppicing was done to a moderate plant height of 1.5 metre of make a dense crown. An adequate dose of German mixture (NPK 15:15:15) was incorporated in the soil around each plant during the year in split doses *E. youmanii* grew very profusely under Palampur conditions. The leaves were more healthy, dark green in colour and denser than those of *E. macrorhyncha*.

Some experiments were carried out on the different applications of inorganic fertilizers, liquid foliar fertilizers and n-triacontanol. Results indicated that the application of 312 kg N/ha (urea) in two equal split doses resulted in a yield of 446 q/ha of dry leaves. The yield of first harvest was higher as compared to the second harvest. This is attributed to the better growth conditions during the period of February to May in this region. The percent increase in total herb yield over the control was 21.9%. Still higher doses of nitrogen did not produce linear results due to the lack of irrigation.

Various levels of foliar fertilizer when sprayed six times a year resulted in a linear increase of herb yield upto 0.30%. The average dry herb yield per plant with 0.30% treatment was 595.0 g in comparison to 398.0 g/plant under control. Thus on hectare basis, the net leaf biomass increase was 49.6% over the check.

An application of 10 ppm of *n*-triacontanol four times a year resulted in an increase of 51.3% leaf biomass, over the control. Further with the application of 20 ppm dose, there is not significant improvement in the annual herb yield. Earlier reports on the stimulation of growth by this hormone in several field crops are mentioned. The increase in growth (dry weight) after foliar application of *n*-triacontanol is attributed to the factors like increase in chlorophyll concentration and leaf area, its effect on some process which regulates the balance between photosynthesis and photorespiration and reduction in photorespiration, delayed senescence and increased level of photo assimilates.

Two species are grown in Australia in less fertile lands and are reported to improve the texture and fertility of the land *E. macrorhyncha* prefers low altitude between 300-900 m and does not show juvenile growth as compared to *E. youmanii* when planted on higher altitudes. This was noted in the trial plantation undertaken at different heights ranging from 500-1500 m to find out the optimum altitude for large scale cultivation of the two species in the sub- Himalyan region in H.P.

HARVESTING

E. youmanii performed very well at high altitude between 1000-1500 m in the upper Dhaula Dhar range of Himalaya whereas the growth of *E. macrorhyncha* was stunted at this range *E. macrorhyncha* could, however, be grown well below 800 m. height in lower hills to get optimum yields. A record of herbage of the two species from six-year old plantation is given in Table 4 below:

Table 4: Herb Yield from Six Years Old Plantation

	No. of Plants (Ha)	*Dry Leaves (T)*
E. macrorhyncha	4400	4.140
E. youmanii	4400	3.900

Evidently, the yield of *E. youmanii* was less than that of *E. macrorhyncha*. The rutin content in the leaves of two species of three year old plantation was also studied at one month interval.

The maximum rutin content was obtained in the month of July. It was also observed that rutin percentage was more in young leaves near the tip of the twig than in mature leaves Table 6.

EXTRACTION OF RUTIN

Rutin is commercially extracted with hot water at higher temperature. It is fairly soluble in boiling water and starts settling down at about 90°C and adequate care is needed to filter the hot water extract. Fine powdered dry leaves 30-40 mesh are boiled with water (1:20) for about 25-30 minutes In closed vessel at elevated pressure of 15-20 lbs. Excessive heating for long period causes hydrolyses of Rutin into Quercetln. The hot extract is filtered immediately and fine yellow coloured rutin is separated out on cooling. The crystalisation of pure golden yellow coloured rutin is done with methanol. A cost effective extraction unit of moderate capacity has been designed for the extraction of pure rutin on commercial scale.

CONCLUSIONS

Cultivation of Eucalyptus species in mid hills, as a rich source or rutin, is advantageous for the following reasons:

1. Pure rutin of USSRP grade or NF grade can be extracted from Eucalyptus leaves of two Species with less difficulty and low expenditure.

Table 5: Periodic Variation of Rutin Content: Three Years Old Plantation

	Jan.	Feb.	March.	April	May	June	July	Aug.	Sept.	Oct.	Nov.	Dec.
E. youmanii Rutin (%) (MFB)	10.40	10.20	11.05	10.85	11.80	11.20	15.70	13.60	11.35	13.95	12.10	11.80
Moisture	54.50	54.20	53.00	46.00	49.00	55.00	58.00	58.00	50.50	54.50	58.00	51.70
E. macrorhyncha	1.80	8.12	7.40	8.05	8.04	9.60	11.10	9.30	8.45	9.40	9.40	9.10
Rutin (%) MFB moisture	53.40	54.10	50.00	52.00	51.00	50.00	49.50	44.50	48.00	50.40	51.00	49.00

Table 6: Distribution of Rutin Content along the Twig

Distance from tip (cm)	2.5	5.0	7.50	10.0	12.50	15.0
Rutin % in *E. macrorhyncha*	11.50	7.00	6.50	5.50	3.50	2.50
E. youmanii	13.50	9.00	8.50	6.00	3.50	2.00

(Rutin content on moisture free basis)

2. Raw material can be produced in large quantities.
3. It can be a good source of income for marginal growers by utilising their spare land.
4. Return per unit area is comparatively more.
5. The leaves of *E. macrorhyncha* and *E. youmanii* are used exclusively for the extraction of rutin. This is not so in *Sophora japonica* and Buckwheat.
6. *Eucalyptus* species can be grown as high density plantations whereas *Sophora japonica* trees are usually grown scattered.
7. It required regular deployment of labour force to generate farm based employment for harvesting leaves from Eucalyptus plantations. The flower gathering period is only one month in case of *Sophora japonica*. In buckwheat also the harvest is made during a specific period only.
8. Besides rutin, the eucalyptus trees yield wood for fence posts and fuel.
9. These two species do not need good land for growing on commercial scale. Buckwheat on the other hand, should be planted in fertile soil and should receive liberal quantities of mineral fertilizers.
10. Dry leaves of the two Eucalyptus species have a ready market and are sold at ten-twelve thousands rupee per tonne. The leaves can be stored in a dry place in polythene bags for considerable period without any chemical change.

There is vast potential to increase the production of rutin from plant species of *E. youmanii* and *E. macrorhyncha* in the subtropical regions in Himalayan belt. The can be raised to produce rutin of high purity and foreign exchange of about crore of rupees can be saved annually. Small and marginal farmers can take up the cultivation of these exotic plant species in their spare land to generate additional income. Industrial units for extraction of rutin can be set up at central places to utilize the available raw material.

10

Aloe

INTRODUCTION

The term 'Aloe' as described in Pharmacopoeia and used in medicine stands for the dried juice of leaves of *Aloe perryi*, Baker, also known as Socotrine aloes; or of *Aloe barbadensis* Miller (*A. vera* Linn.) known as Curacao aloe or Aloe ferox Miller and hybrids of this species with *Aloe africana* Miller and *Aloe spicata* Baker, known as Cape aloes.

Aloe genus (Family: Liliaceae) comprises about 200 species, indigenous to East and South Africa. A number of species have been introduced into India which grow in varied climates and different types of soils. The fleshy leaves in rosettes are usually prickly at the margin. A yellowing coloured juice flows out from the cut leaves, which is collected and concentrated to make commercial drug aloes. The nature of commercial drug aloes depends upon the species from which it is prepared and the method adopted for concentration. Sun dried aloes and concentrated over low flame makes amorphous, opaque type called hepatic or livery aloes, whereas juice concentrated rapidly over strong fire, gives semi-transparent type called glossy or vitreous aloes. Four types of aloes are official in Indian Pharmacopoeia. These are Curacao or Barbados aloes, Socotrine aloes, Zanzibar aloes and, Cape aloes. These occur as dark brown opaque masses, almost entirely soluble in 60% alcohol.

Aloe is derived from Arabic word *alloeh* or the Hebren *halel* meaning a shining bitter substance. *Vera* is from Latin *Verus* meaning true, Barbadensis refers to the Barbados islands: *ferox* is from the Latin meaning wild or ferocious; Africana refers to the habitat of the plant and Spicata refers to the flowers in spikes.

Aloe vera is a perennial plant with multiple tuberous roots and many fibrous supporting roots penetrating into the soil. The plants do not have true stem but produce bloom stalks. Flowers vary from yellow to rich orange in colour. The plants generally grow close to the ground in typical rosette shape. The plant has strongly cuticularized leaves, having spiny margin with thin walled tubular cells.

Aloe is known by different names in different languages of the country as follows:

Bengali	-	*Ghrit kumari*
English	-	Aloes
Gujarati	-	*Kunvar*
Hindi	-	Ghikanvar
Kannada	-	*Katthaligida, Lolesara, Kumari*
Kashmiri	-	*Musabbar*
Malayalam	-	*Kattavala*
Marathi	-	*Elwa, Korpad, Kunvar pata*
Tamil	-	*Kattazhai, Sirukattashai, Chirukattali*
Telugu	-	*Manjikattali, Chinnakalabanda*
Urdu	-	*Ghiqwara*

USES

In Africa, slukaris in the Congo rub their bodies with mucilage from leaves to reduce perspiration and thereby eliminate human scent. This helps in masking their scent to the prey. The cut leaves of *A. saponaria* are tied on fleshy surface of wounds by some tribes of South Africa for early cure. It has been recorded that Indians used the pulp of *A. barbadensis* mixed with burnt alum for healing country sore eyes. The pulp is also valued as a cooling application on inflammatory joints. To relieve headache, a small piece of sliced leaf is tied to the forehead. Some Africans use the cold infusion of leaves of *A. saponaria* for hair growth. The leaves of *A. variegata*, infused in brandy or liquor is taken to relieve haemmorhoids. During epidemics of cold in Sutos, all people in the village bathe publicly in an infusion of *A. latifolia*.

The parts used in indigenous system of medicine are expressed as dried juice of leaves and pulp. Aloe is reported to be stomachic tonic in small doses whereas in large doses it acts an purgative and indirectly emmenagogue and anthelmintic. It has been a favourite remedy for intestinal worms in children. In the form of a lotion, it is recommended incatarrhal and purulent ophthalmia. Aloe dissolved in spirit, is used as a hair dye to stimulate hair growth. A sweet confection prepared from the pulp of leaves is given in piles. Pulp mixed with honey and turmeric is recommended in coughs and colds. The juice of the leaves is useful in painful inflammations and chronic ulcers.

More recently the use of aloe gel in radiation burns has been advocated for relief from pain and itching and to keep down keratosis and ulceration, thus slowing any possible change towards malignancy.

The Ayurvedic literature describes the actions and uses of aloe as follows:

Bhedinee (Purgation) *netrya* (beneficial to the eyes), *rasayance* (rejuvenator), *balya* (muscular strength), *vrishya* (that which promotes virility), *Gulmaghna* (Indicated in the treatment of tumour like conditions of the abdomen), *vishagna* (antidote for poisons), *pleecharogaghna* (indicated in splenomegaly). *Yakritvriddhihara* (that which cures hepatomegaly), *kaphajwarahara* (that which cures fevers caused by kapha), *grantighna* (that which cures glandular enlargement), *agnidagdhashamanee* (that which relieves the effect of burns), *kushtaghna* (indicated in skin diseases), *shwaasaghna* (antispasmodic, anti-dyspnoic).

Aloe is commonly used as an external application on inflamed painful parts of the body. Aloe was known to the ancients having been cultivated in the island of Socotra as early as at the time of Alexander the Great. It has been employed for eczematous skin conditions in China, India and Tibet. The wounds are quickly cicatrized and healed when covered with a small piece of Aloe. Fresh Aloe leaf gel is also reported to be of value in the treatment of X-ray reactions.

Aloes Powder and aloin are official in I.P. as a purgative. Aloin is a mixture of crystalline compounds obtained from Aloes. It varies in chemical composition and in physical and chemical properties depending on the variety of aloes from which it is obtained. It is generally yellow coloured microcrystalline powder with a faint odour of aloes and intensely bitter taste. On exposure to light and air, it turns dark. Aloin is water soluble as well as alcohol soluble (90%). It is sparingly soluble in chloroform, solvent ether and in benzene.

The United States Dispensary refers to the use of Aloe gel as early as 2,300 years ago. It is repeatedly referred in the Holy Bible and was extensively used in India as long as in 400 B.C.

A large number of research workers have published reports of their findings on the use of Aloe vera leaf in various skin conditions. The healing of abrasions of human skin showed definite improvement by application of fresh *A. vera* leaf. A five week treatment of *A. vera* in patients of severe X-ray dermatitis showed complete regeneration of the skin on the scalp and forehead, new hair growth, restoration of sensation and no scarring 12, 13. *A. vera* gel was found useful in the treatment of sequelae to radiation therapy. Excellent results were obtained on the use of this gel in palmer eczema, ulcers on amputation stumps, ulcers of advanced mammary carinoma, poison ivy and burns. Application of fresh aloe pith relieved pain, burning and itching, had anti-septic action and stimulated rapid granulation and formation of new tissues.

It was suggested that solution of *A. vera* might be incorporated into periodontal dressing. Studies were conducted on the use of *A. vera* gel in the treatment of ulcers and certain other dermatoses in men, like chronic leg ulcers, seborrhea, acne vulgaris, alopecia and alopecia areata. The results showed stimulating effect on the healing of chronic leg ulcers, stimulate hair growth and drying of seborrheic skin. The action is believed to be due to the presence of mucopolysaccharides in the gel which may be aided by enzymatic removal of necrotic tissue.

The therapeutic effect of *Aloe vera* have been examined in preventing progressive dermal ischaemia caused by burns, frostbite, electric injury, distal dying flap and intra-arterial drug abuse. The studies indicated that Aloe has enormous therapeutic potential as it penetrates tissue injury, relieves pain, is anti-inflammatory and dilates capillaries and increase the blood supply to the injured area by inhibiting TxA^2 and maintaining the PGE_2 and PGF_{2a} ratio without causing a collapse of the injured blood vessels.

Extracts of *Aloe vera* possess activities which reverse the degenerative skin changes seen with aging by stimulating the synthesis of collagen and elastic fibers thereby restoring towards normal the regenerative/degenerative equilibrium.

CULTIVATION

The propagation of Aloe is done through root suckers. The plant can be cultivated in dry climatic conditions, in poor soils without much care. The root system of this plant is shallow and does not penetrate deep into the soil. A mixture of nitrogen, potassium and phosphorous should be used as manure and mixed up in soil near the root system gently. Since the plant is not water loving, water should not be allowed to lodge near the plant.

Recently leaf spot disease on *Aloe vera* growing in Bhagalpur and its surrounding areas has been found to be caused by *Alternaria alternata* and *Fusarium solani*.

Studies have indicated that irrigation has the greatest effect on the gel composition of *Aloe vera*. Hence control of irrigation could aid in standardizing the gel composition.

TISSUE CULTURE

Earlier research workers have reported successful callus formation from the root of *Aloe saponaria*, stamen of *Aloe bellatura* and leaf of *Aloe barbadensis* in illuminated conditions. However as tissue culture from *Aloe aborescens* Miller var. natalensis (*Kidachi aloe*) had not been reported, two projects were planned using the same.

1. To determine the culture condition in which callus of Kidachi aloe can synthesize active components of Aloe such as carboxypeptidase or aloin more effectively.
2. To obtain a more useful hybrid plant by cell fusion and regeneration of plants.

The experiments showed that callus was induced when incubated in the dark at 25°C for about 30 days. The frequency of callus formation was in the order of superior stalk > middle stalk > inferior stalk. No callus formation was induced from the leaf. When the Murashige-Skoog (MS) basal agar medium was supplemented with 3% sucrose, 0.1-0.5 μm Kinetin (a plant growth regulator) and 10-50 μm α-naphthalenacetic acid, callus formation occurred at an indicence of 20-52%. When the medium was supplemented with 3% glucose and 10% alpha modification of Eagle's medium, callus formation was promoted, but protein and aloin concentration, and carboxypeptidase activity in the Aloe callus decreased more than those observed in the sucrose-containing medium.

PHARMACOGNOSTIC STUDIES

The plants bear rosettes of large succulent, subulate leaves, flat or slightly concave on the upper surface and strongly rounded on the lower, sessile with a strong spine at the apex and smaller ones along the margins. They bear spikes of yellow to red flowers.

The vascular bundles in the leaf are isolated and form a line parallel with epidermis within the mesophyll. Each bundle has a pericycle formed of large thin walled cells filled with yellowish fluid. These cells are slightly elongated.

Socotrine aloe has a pasty, semi-liquid consistency, opaque with brownish yellow colour. It is dried at a gentle heat to remove moisture when it turns to hard, dark brown mass. It has a characteristic unpleasant odour and extremely bitter nauseous taste. It is entirely soluble in alcohol.

Zanzibar aloe is usually hard in liver-brown colour with characteristic but not disagreeable odour and bitter taste.

Cape aloe occurs in dark reddish-brown or nearly black coloured mass which has a clean glossy fracture. It has a distinct sour odour.

Curacao aloe occurs as yellowish to reddish-brown or chocolate-brown and breaks with a dull waxy even fracture.

The above four kinds of aloes can be distinguished, when in powder form, by microscopical examination mounted in lactophenol. Lactophenol has an advantags over any other oil or liquid paraffin or glycerine in that it brings about a gradual solution of the particles and the crystals become rapidly and clearly evident. Cape aloe appears as transparent, brown, irregular and angular fragments; Curacao aloe shows fragments composed of innumerable minute slender prisms or needles; Zanzibar aloe shows irregular lumps with embedded nodular mass; whereas Socotrine aloe consists of fragments of fairly large prisms grouped irregularly into mass.

Commercial aloes occur both in crystalline and amorphous forms. The crystalline aloes respond to test for Curacao aloe and the amorphous ones to tests for Cape aloe. The two varieties are easily distinguishable under the microscope by mounting in cresol and using polarized light. The crystalline aloin is insoluble in cresol and shines brightly on a polarized light against dark field. The amorphous alin dissolves rapidly and is invisible under polarized light against dark field. The amorphous aloin has one third the cathartic potency of crystalline aloin.

CHEMICAL STUDIES

Aloin is the principal active constituent of aloes which is a mixture of glucosides. Barbaloin is the main glucoside in aloin which is water soluble. Besides this, aloin contains isobarbaloin, β-barbaloin, aloe-emodin resins, etc.

The percentage of barbaloin present in different types of aloes varies to a great extent. Estimation of barbaloin in Indian aloes obtained from *Aloe vera* var. officinalis shows that the Indian species contained less quantity (3.8%) as compared to Curacao aloe which contains 22.1%.

The following chemical constituents have been reported to be present in different proportions: aloin, aloe-emodin, aloetic acid, homonatalion, aloesln, aloesone, emodin, chrysamminic acid, chrysophanic acid, apoise, galacturonic acid, calcium oxalate, choline, choline salicylate, saponins, uronic acid, sugars, mucopolysaccharides, 7-hydroxy chromone, coniferyl alcohol, glucosamines, hexuronic acid, amylse, aliinasse, etc. Many of the above constituents have been isolated in pure form.

The lyophilized *A. vera* juice on neutron activation analysis was found to contain calcium (4.7%), sodium (1.43%) potassium (6.6%), chloride (12.2%) and manganese (0.01%).

The main constituent of all the varieties of aloes is the crystalline substance, barbaloin (aloe-emodin anthrone C-10 glucoside). In *Curacao aloe*, barbaloin is accompanied by isobarbaloin. Socotrine and Zanzibar aloes do not contain isobarbaloin whereas Cape aloe contains traces only. The crystalline aloin is accompanied by an amorphous aloin, beta barbaloin. The latter is particularly abundant in Cape aloe. The other main constituents of aloes are resin and aloe-emodin, a hydrolytic decomposition product of barbaloin.

Studies on the leaves of *A. vera* grown in Egypt showed the presence of free combined anthraquinones, carbohydrates and/or glycosides.

Barbaloin, chrysophanol glycoside and aloe-emodin were isolated and identified. The mucilaginous parts of the leaves were found to contain sugars glucose, galalactose, mannose and galacturonic acid.

The rhizomes of *A. saponaria* yielded phenolic constituents. From the leaves of *A. barbadensis*, free amino acids, free monosaccharides and total saccharides released upon hydrolysis, sterols and triterpenoids have been isolated.

An analysis of the *A. arborescens* leaves during different seasons of the year revealed the presence of highest content of total nitrogen (1.47%), protein nitrogen (1.22%), total protein (9.54%) and real protein (7.63%) in leaves sampled in April; the highest content of aloin (4.31%) and free amino acids (798.17 mg per 100g leaves) in July. Samples collected in January had the lowest amount of components. The leaves of upper regions were comparatively poor in chemical constituents.

Analysis of the dry mass obtained from aqueous extract of fresh leaves of three years old *A. arborscens* showed 6.3% total protein, 3.47% non-protein substance containing nitrogen and 0.6% free amino acids.

A carboxypeptidase was partially purified *Aloe arborescens* Miller var. *natalensis* Berger on a scale suitable for pharmacological studies. The enzyme had a broad specificity against various synthetic peptides, being capable to splitting C-termnal proline. Its activity was inhibited almost completely by di-isopro-pylfluorophosphate, strongly by transition metals, such as Fe^{3+}, Hg^{2+} and Cu^{2+}, and moderately by sulphydryl reagents. These results indicate that Aloe enzyme is a serious carboxypeptidase and appears to contain a sulphydryl group that may be involved in its inactivation.

PHARMACOLOGICAL AND CLINICAL STUDIES

A. indica showed a significant increase in the fertility rate of experimental rabbits receving 60 mg/kg or more of aloe. There was a significant increase in the litter size of these animals.

The aqueous extract *A. littoralis* inhibited the growth of Staphylococcus and *Escherichia coli*, while alcoholic extract of the same did not show any measurable inhibition.

A. vera, according to all available data does not cause or contribute to toxicity in humans or higher animals in gel from or its various extracts. Aloin, however, can be irritating to the skin in higher concentrations.

A number of cosmetic preparations containing aloe extracts in varying proportions are available in the market. Safety data on the various aloe extracts are also available. *A. vera* extracts have been considered safe when used near the eye, on the skin or when ingested in a single dose.

A. vera juice in the form of an ointment in vaseline has been found to hasten healing of wounds of thermal burns and radiation injury in albino rats. In addition to this, hydroxyproline and mucopolysaccharide contents were increase significantly in *A. vera* treated animals.

The antifertility effect of various extracts of leaves of *A. barbadensis* has been studied in rats. Alcoholic and water extracts showed 85% reduction in fertility while benzene and petroleum ether extracts showed significant reduction. The chloroform extract showed much less reduction in the number of young ones produced by each female rats.

Intravenous injection of extract of *Aloe barbadensis* was found to increase hepatic bile flow in anaesthetized dog.

Aloctin A was isolated and purified from *Aloe arborescens*. It showed many biological and pharmacological activities, i.e. *Haemagglutinating* activity. Cyto-agglutinating activity, Mitogenic activity of lymphocytes, Precipitate forming reactivity with alpha$_2$-macroglobulin, Complement C3 activating activity.

Inhibition of heat-induced haemolysis of rat erythrocytes, Antitumour effect, Anti-inflammatory effect and inhibition of gastric secretion and gastric lesions.

The effect of Aloctin A treatment derived from *Aloe arborescens in vivo* and *in vitro* on the immune response of murine and human lymphoid cells has been studied.

Lectins isolated from the gel portion of leaves of *Aloe barbodensis* were found to have strong haemagglutination and mitogenic activities.

Carbopeptidase was partially purified from Kidachi aloe (*Aloe arborescens* Miller *var natalensis* Berger) by an FPLC system, and was administered intravenously to female ICR mice with inflammation. The enzyme preparation exhibited significant analgesic effects and inhibited vascular permeability in the abdominal region. It also revealed an anti-thermal burn action on the hind paw, when administered to female Wistar rats intravenously.

The juice of *Aloe arborescens* was found to have both suppressive and healing substances and is useful in the treatment of gastric ulcer.

Two different components were separated from *Aloe arborescens* and these were found to exhibit hypoglycaemic activity in spontaneously diabetic and normal mice.

Inhibitory effects of freeze-dried *Aloe arborescens* whole leaf powder on induction of preneoplastic glutathione S-transferase positive hepatocyte foci GST P$^+$ were studied in male rats. It was found that 30% Aloe exerted inhibition of the promotion and possibly of initiation stage of hepato-carcinogenesis.

11

Technology of Podophyllotoxins

INTRODUCTION

Podophyllotoxin since long has been known to possess medicinal properties and it is obtained from *P. emodi* Wall. This crystalline substance was first isolated by Podwyssotzki. The alcohol soluble and water insoluble portion of podophyllum is a complex mixture containing most of biological activity of original root. It is usually called podophyllin but has also been named as podophyllum resin. The research on this drug was done on many fronts like pharmacology, biochemistry, cytology and clinical medicine by Kelly. The drug was studied in many clinical conditions including diseases of skin due to infectious agents, non-specific dermatoses, metabolic disease, benign growth and malignant new growths. Podophyllin has been used in the treatment of cancer by private practitioners in US prior to 1897. It was reported by Hartwell for the first time that podophyllin has destructive effect on cancer cells of experimental animals. It was demonstrated by King, L. that podophyllin produced its therapeutic effect by acting like colchicines as a mitotic poison. Podophyllin was so popular in the earlier days of last century as a cathartic and cholagogue that it was included in the first U.S. Pharmacopoeia and was listed until the twelfth revision published in 1942. Both American and Indian podophyllum were included in British Pharmacopoeia of 1948 but were dropped later from 1953 edition. American podophyllum has been listed at one time or other in most European, South American and Asian Pharmacopoeia.

The chemistry and antineoplastic activity of many constituents of podophyllin were actively investigated at National Cancer Institute, USA by Hartwell J.L. in the 1940's. A superb review of this later history, chemistry and pharmacology of podophyllum and its constituents was prepared by Hartwell and Schrecker. Its structure was proposed independently by Boarche and was later revised by Hartwell.

Podophyllin in an amorphous powder light brown to greenish yellow in colour. It has a characteristic odour, a bitter taste and is irritating to eyes and mucous membrane. Besides podophyllotoxin (I) and 4'-demethylpodophyllotoxin (II) podophyllin has other constituents e.g. kaempferol, quercetin, podophyllotoxin-1-O-β-glucopyranoside (XVI), 4'-demethylpodophyllotoxin-1-O-β-D-glucopyranoside, (XVII) and tannins. Extraction of podophyllin with chloroform yields a residue which upon recrystallisation from benzene: methanol and hexane gives a 9:1 mixture of podophyllotoxin and 4'-demethylpodophyllotoxin (30 to 40% based upon resin). The remaining chloroform insoluble portion is called the Marc which consists of quercetin, kampferol, tannins, podophyllotoxin-1-O-β-D-glucopyranoside (XVI) and 4'-demethylpodophyllotoxin-1-O-β-D-glucopyranoside (XVII).

The introduction of anticancer drug Etoposide (XII) the Teniposide (XIII) has created a demand for podophyllotoxin, the natural tetralin lignan (podophyllotoxin) is used for the semi-synthesis of these drugs. Since the total synthesis of podophyllotoxin is still uneconomic, future production of these drugs will depend upon either systematic cultivation of Podophyllum plants or the use of tissue culture techniques to obtain podophyllotxins. Alternatively improvement in extraction techniques of new sources of these compounds need to be exploited.

The lignans of podophyllum can be divided into: Podophyllum aglycones and Podophyllum glycosides.

PODOPHYLLUM AGLYCONES

Podophyllotoxin (I), isolated as early as 1880 by Podwyssotzki, represents the main compound of Podophyllum species. Picropodophyllotoxin (XI) is easily formed by base catalyzed rearrangement of podophyllotoxin and was presumed to be an artefact generated in the course of the isolation procedures. Desoxypodophyllotoxin (III) was isolated from all the Podophyllum species, it was known earlier also from the roots

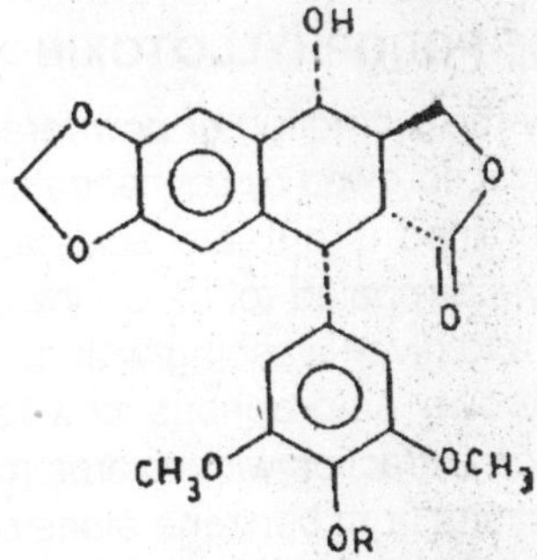

I, R = CH_3. Podophyllotoxin
II, R = H 4'-Demethylpodophyllotoxin

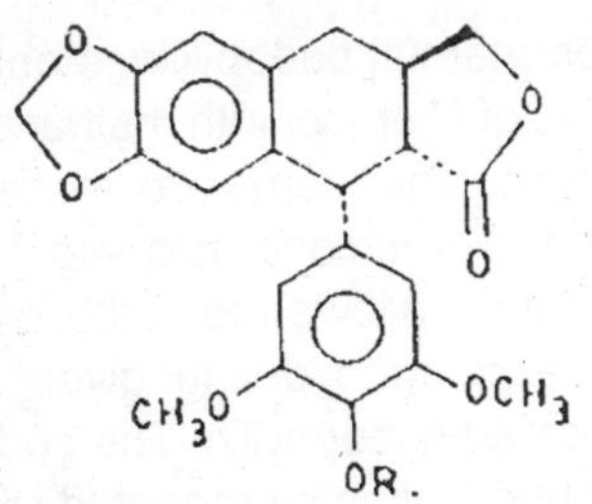

III, R = CH_3. Deoxypodophyllotoxin
IV, R = H 4'-Demethyldeoxypodophyllotoxin

from all the Podophyllum species, it was known earlier also from the roots of *Anthriscus sylvestris* (Family Umbelliferae) by Kawanami and was named "anthricin".

The earlier methods of isolation of natural production like extraction, fractional precipitation, crystallization have failed to yield pure compounds from *Podophyllum emodi* other than the two discovered by Podsyssotzki in 1880 namely podophyllotoxin and quercetin. In the span of ten years (1947-1955) the modern techniques of separation and purification such as column chromatography and thin layer chromatography yielded considerable number

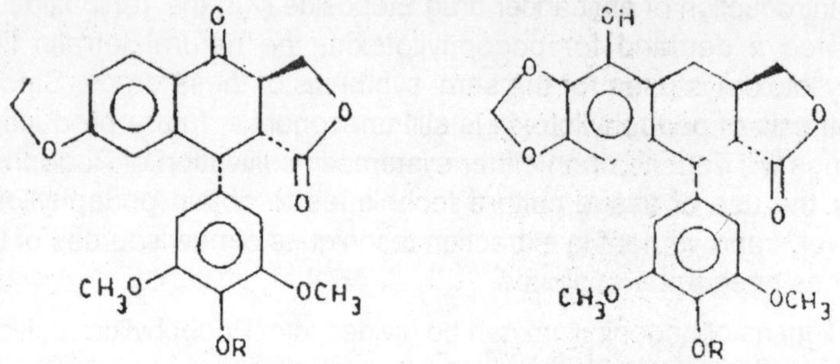

V, R = CH_3. Podophyllotoxone
VI, R = H 4'-demethylpodophyllotoxone

VII, R = CH_3. β-Peltatin
VIII, R = H α-Peltatin

of additional substances such as α-peltain (VIII), β-peltain (VIII), 4'-demethyl podophyllotoxin (II). The solvent partition, and paper chromatography led to the separation of desoxypodophyllotoxin (III) and glycosides of podophyllotxin and 4'-demethylpodophyllotoxin, β-peltain and α-peltatin.

COMMERCIAL METHOD OF ISOLATION OF PODOPHYLLOTOXIN

The commercial podopyllin is obtained by the extraction of powdered rhizome/roots of *P. emodi* with methanol or ethanol, followed by concentration under vaccum. This semisolid mass thus obtained is put into acidulate water (10ml) hydrochloric acid into 1000 ml water cooled to 10°C slowly. The precipitate is allowed to settle, decanted and given washing with cold water.The resin upon drying gives a dark brown amorophous powder commonly called podophyllin. The podophyllin on extraction with chloroform and further purification by repeated recrystallistions from benzene alone or alcohol benzene mixture followed by thorough washing with petroleum ether/ hexane yield the commercial podophyllotoxin. The podophyllotoxin content of the commercial podophyllin usually ranges between 45-55%. The other compounds mostly presented are identical with podophyllotoxin.

Dunstan and Henry separated podophyllin (from *P. emodi* or *P. peltatum*) into three main fractions.

(A) Soluble in chloroform

(B) Insoluble in chloroform but soluble in ether

(C) Insoluble in chloroform and ether also called as podophylloresin.

The chloroform soluble fraction was treated with boiling benzene and the solution cooled slightly, decanted from dark resin and allowed to stand for several days, during which podophyllotoxin separated slowly. Borsche and Niemann employed same method to obtain podophyllotoxin which was then purified by recrystallization from aqueous ethanol. Later on Spath improved the procedure by dissolving the chloroform soluble fraction in ethanol and adding benzene: this made prior removal of the dark resin unnecessary. A recent preparative method by D-Ambressi is based essentially on Spath's procedure. It is noteworthy that most of these preparations were carried out with Indian podophyllin which contains a much larger amount of podophyllotoxin and much smaller proportion of other lignans than American podophyllin.

In our laboratory we have further simplified and improved the method of extraction of pure podophyllotoxin by dissolving the chloroform soluble fraction in alcohol and refluxing it with neutral aluminium oxide so that the solution becomes light yellow in colour. To the alcohol solution added benzene which yielded podophyllotoxin of 95-98% purity. The function of the neutral aluminium oxide is to remove the polyphenolics such as kaempferol, quercetin and isorhamnetin and other minor polyphenolics present in the chloroform extract. Desoxypodophyllotoxin and other minor lignans could be removed by this method. We have experimentally proved that podophyllotoxin on refluxing with neutral aluminium oxide does not form picropodophyllotoxin (XI).

The commercial method of isolating podophyllotoxin from *P. emodi* roots/ rhizomes earlier developed in this laboratory has also been modified. The improved method of isolation of podophyllotoxin from commercial podophyllin/ crude podophyllotoxin (the purity of which is 35 to 90%) involves extraction over a bed of neutral alumina with solvents such as benzene, toluene, xylene, dichloromethane etc. The length of the bed of neutral aluminium oxide is the key factor of the process. The function of aluminium oxide is to absorb the polyphenolics and tannins and also to act as a stationary phase to separate podophyllotoxin from other compounds present as impurities. The extraction may be done for a period ranging from half an hour to 4 hours. The extract upon concentration and recrystallization from organic solvent such as hot benzene/toluene yields pure podophyllotoxin (95 to 97%).

We have further developed method of isolation of podophyllotoxin and 4'-demethylpodophyllotoxin from the chloroform and ether insoluble part also called marc which is a waste material of podophyllotoxin extraction process. The main constituents of the marc are the glycosides of podophyllotxin and 4'-de-methylpodophyllotoxin. The process consists of dissolving the marc in hot methanol and filtration. The filtrate is poured in water and emulsion (β-glycosidase) enzyme added to it. The mixture is kept at room temperature (30-37°C) with stirring and the resulting slurry is repeatedly extracted with chloroform at room temperature which upon concentration and recrystallisation yields a mixture of podophyllotoxin and 4'-demethylpodophyllotoxin in the ratio of 4:1 (total yield 0.6%) of Podophyllum roots/rhizomes. The process of the present invention increase the overall yield of the mixture of podophyllotoxin and 4'-demethylpodophyllotoxin.

The present observation provides a process for the isolation of a mixture of podophyllotoxin and 4'-demethylpodophyllotoxin which comprises treating powdered rhizomes with polar solvents, extracting with chlorinated solvents, separating the residue (marc) by known methods, hydrolysing the marc so obtained with enzyme emulsin in presence of polar solvents at a pH in the range of 5 to 7 at a temperature in the range of 30° to 37°C for 4 to 6 hours; extracting the mixture with chlorinated hydrocarbons treating with neutral alumina to get a mixture of podophyllotoxin and 4'-demethylpodophyllotoxin. The methods developed and described for the isolation of podophyllotoxin is either from the podophyllin, marc or resin of the podophyllum emodi roots, Keeping in view the lengthy and tedious steps, we further simplified the method of extraction of podophyllotoxin directly from the roots/rhizome of *P. emodi.*

It is a single step process for the extraction of podopyllotoxin from the roots/rhizome of *P. emodi.* According to this method of isolation of Podophyllotoxin, the dry powdered roots/rhizomes of *P. emodi* are extracted with an organic solvent at a temperature in the range of 40-70°C over a bed neutral aliminium oxide. The organic solvent used could be aromatic hydrocarbons such as benzene, toluene, xylene or chlorinated hydrocarbon such as dichloromethane, chloroform, 1,2-dichloroethane, carbon tetrachloride etc. The length of neutral aluminium oxide in the bed may depend upon the polarity of the organic solvent used and also on the type of polyphonolic content of *P. emodi.* The function of aluminium oxide is to absorb the polyphenolics and also act as the stationary phase to isolate the podophyllotoxin and 4'-demethylpodophyllotoxin and other aglycone compounds. The extraction is done for a period ranging from 16-36 hr. The extract upon concentration and recrystallization from solvent such as hot benzene/toluene yields podophyllotoxin (2.5-3.5%). The purity of the podophyllotoxin has been determined by HPLC and found to be 97-98%.

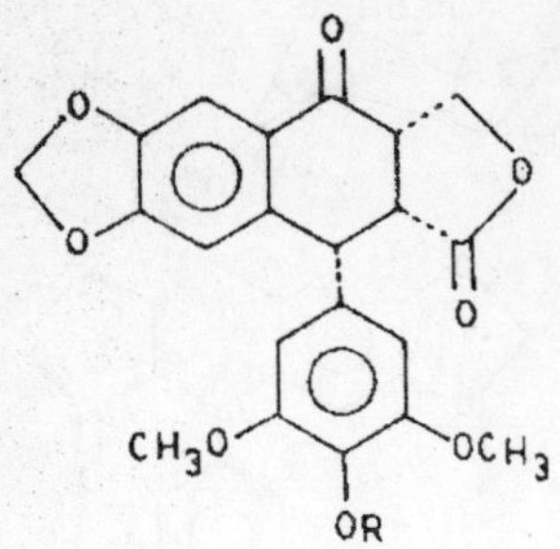

IX. R=CH, Isopteropodo-phyllone
X. R=H 4'-Demethyllsopicro-podophyllone

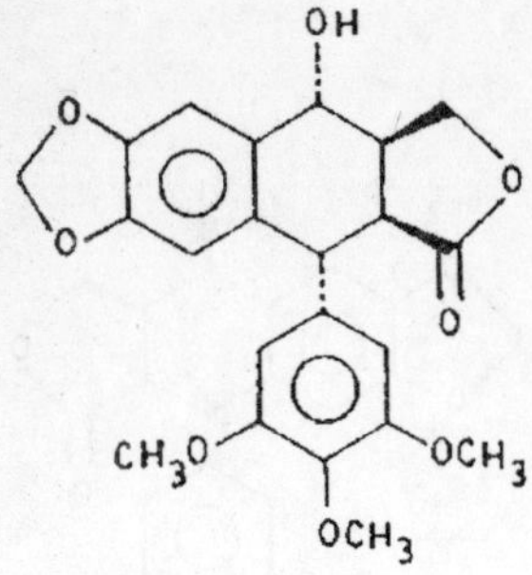

XI. Picropodophyllotoxin

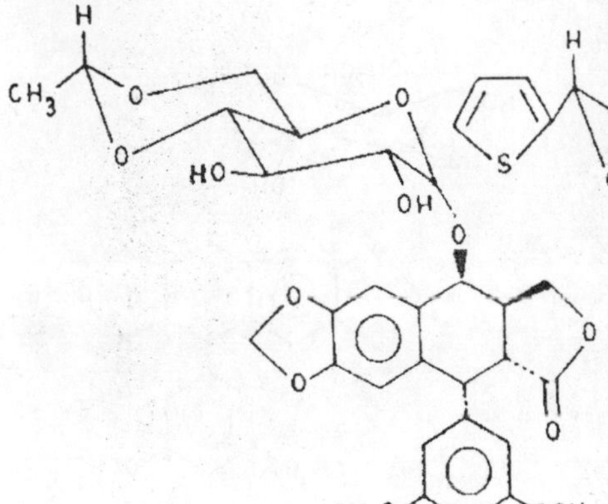

XII. Etoposide

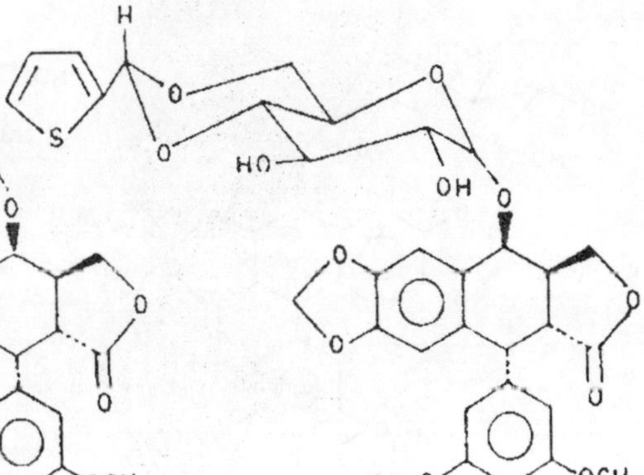

XIII. Teniposide

The method of isolation of podophyllotoxin developed in this laboratory is quite simple and involves isolation of required compound from the dry powdered roots in a single step without involving extraction with methanol/ ethanol; concentration, treatment with water followed by drying in air and subsequent extraction with chloroform and concentration followed by repeated recrystallizations with benzene/methanol mixture.

PODOPHYLLUM GLYCOSIDES

In 1951 the isolation of picropodophyllotoxin-1-O-β-D-glucoside (XVIII) from Indian podophyllin was first reported . Later on isolated four new water soluble lignan glucosides from Podophyllum rhizomes. In this method

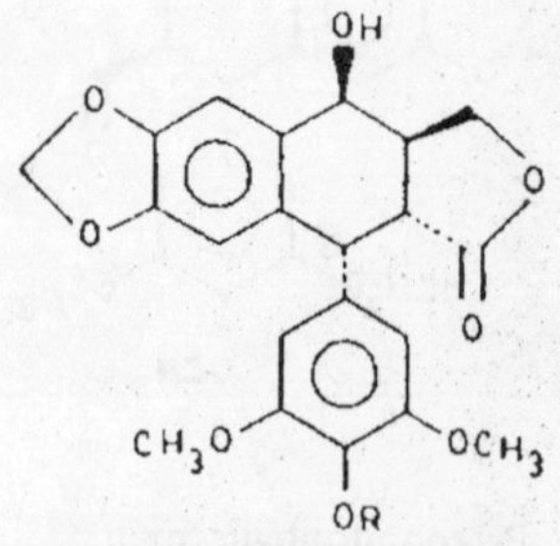

XIV. R=CH, Eplodophyllotoxin
XV. R=H, 5'-Demethyleplpodo-phyllotoxin

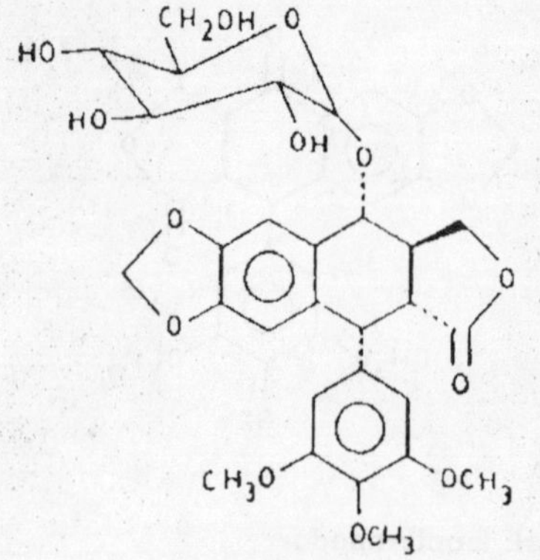

XVI. Podophyllotoxin-1-O-β-D-glocopyranodde

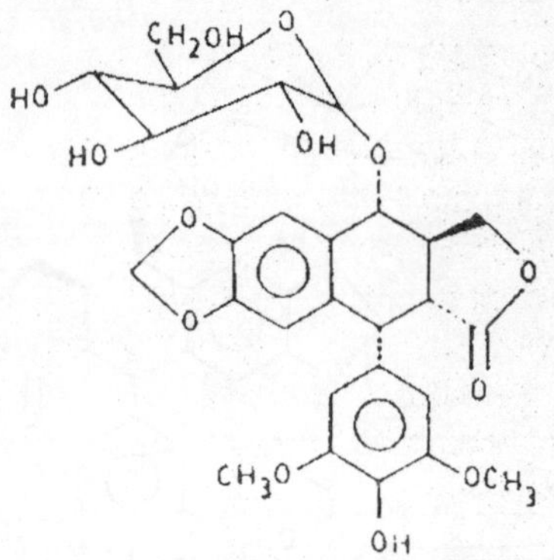

XVII. 4'-Demethylpodophyllotoxin-β-d-glocopyranodde

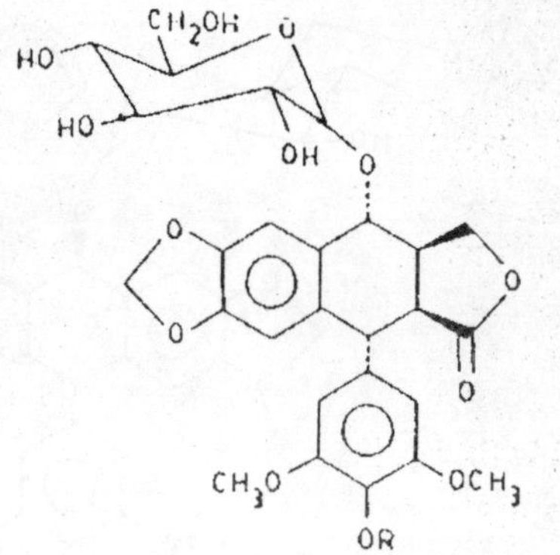

XVII. R=CH, Picropodophyllo-toxin-O-β-d-glocopyranodde

XIX. 4'-Demethylpodophyllotoxin-β-d-glocopyranodde

the dried roots/rhizomes of *Podophyllum peltatum* were extracted with 90% methanol, and the solution was concentrated, diluted with water and extracted with chloroform. After precipitation of tannins with lead acetate; it was re-extracted with chloroform and chloroform butanol (9:1 then 7:3) . The various extracts were placed on column of dry or water saturated diatomaceous earth in the order of decreasing partition coefficient (ethyl acetate / water); the following fraction were eluted with moist ethyl acetate

(a) aglycones (b) the glucosides of podophyllotoxin (XVI) and β-peltatin (XXII, partial separation) (c) the glucosides of 4'-demethylpodophyllotoxin (XVII) and α-peltatin (XXIII). Complete separation of the glucosides was then accomplished by chromatography on silica gel and fractional elution with moist isopropyl acetate containing 0.5 to 2% methanol. By essentially the same procedure, the glucosides of podophyllotoxin (XVI) and 4'-demethylpodophyllotoxin (XVII) were separated from *P. emodi*.

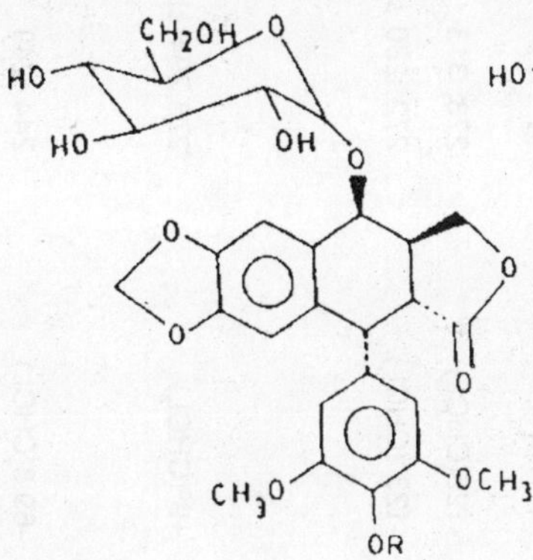

XX. R=CH, Demethylpodophyllotoxin-β-d-glocopyranodde

XVII. 4'-Demethylpodophyllotoxin-1-O-β-d-glocopyranodde

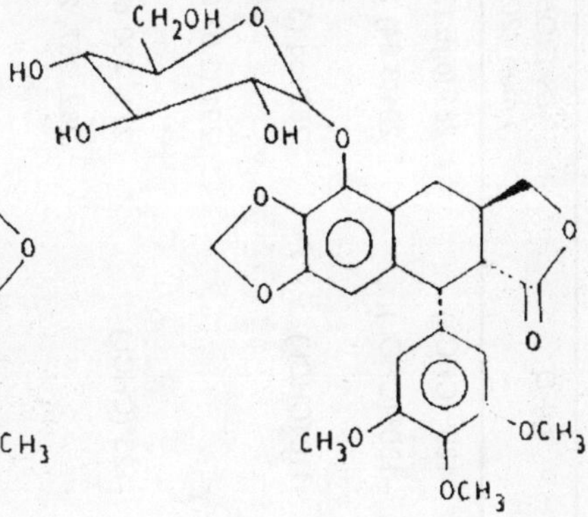

XXII. β-Peltatin-β-d-glocopyranodde

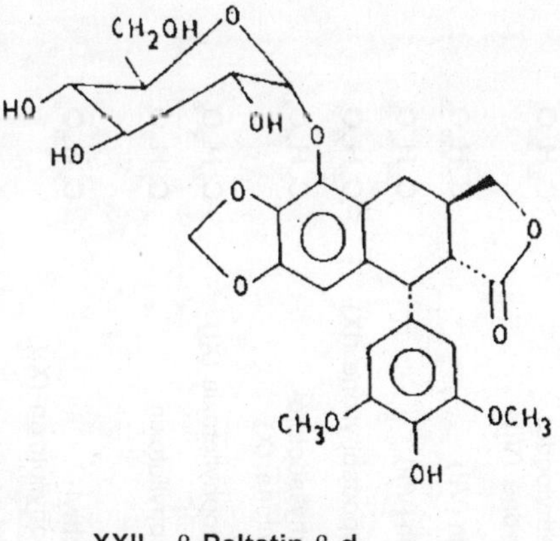

XXII. β-Peltatin-β-d-glocopyranodde

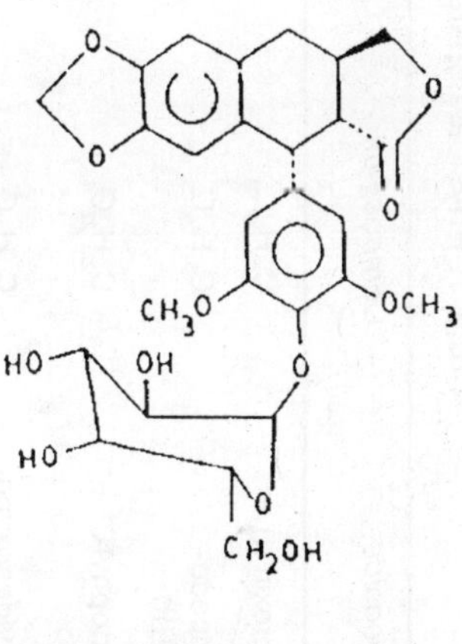

XXIV. 4'-Demethylpodophyllotoxin-4'-β-d-glocopyranodde

Table 1: Physical constant and LD_{50} of Podophyllotoxin lignans & their glycosides

Lignan/glycoside	*Composition*	*m.p.*	*{a} D*	*Uv EtOH men (20)*	*LD-50* mouse mg/kg*
Podophyllotoxin (I)	$C_{22}H_{22}O_8$	183-184°	–133° ($CHCl_3$)	281 logE (3.63)	35
4'-Diemthylpodo-phyllotoxin (II)	$C_{21}H_{20}O_8$	250-252°	–130° ($CHCl_3$)	291(3.64) 295 sh	> 120
Desoxypodophyl-lotoxin (III)	$C_{22}H_{22}O_7$	167-168	-116 ($CHCl_3$)	282 log (3.64)	52
4'-Demethyldesoxypo-dophyllotoxin (IV)	$C_{21}H_{20}O_7$	234-237	-	291 (3.61 296 sh	
Podophyllotoxone (V)	$C_{22}H_2O_8$	191-192	-123°($CHCl_3$)	271, 280 sh	
4'-Demethylpodo-phyllotoxone (VI)	$C_{22}H_{20}O_8$	173-185	-	282, 287, 293, 297 sh	-
β-Peltatin (VII)	$C_{21}H_{20}O_8$	232-235	-125($CHCl_3$)	273, 313	
α-Peltatin (VIII)	$C_{22}H_{22}O_8$	230-232	-123°($CHCl_3$)	272, 280 sh	
Iso-picropodophyllone (IX)	$C_{22}H_{22}O_8$	-	-	-	-
4'Demethylisopicro-podophyllone (X)	$C_{21}H_{20}O_8$	-	-	-	-
Picropodophyllotoxin (XI)	$C_{22}H_{20}O_8$	225-227	+9°($CHCl_3$)	278,294 sh	
Epipodophyllotoxin (XIV)	$C_{22}H_{22}O_8$				
4'-Demethyl-epipodophyllotoxin (XV)	$C_{21}H_{20}O_8$	228-30°C	-69.8($CHCl_3$)	244, 249	

Contd.

Podophyllotoxin-β-D glucopyranoside (XVI)	$C_{28}H_{32}O_{13}$	152-154°	-76°(MeOH) 297	
4'-Demthylpodo-phyllotoxin-β-D-Glucopyranoside (XVII)	$C_{27}H_{30}O_{13}$	165-170°	-81°(MeOH)	
Picropodophyllotoxin -α-Dglucopyranoside (XVIII)	$C_{28}H_{32}O_{13}$	237-238°	-11° (Pyridince)	
β-Peltatin-β-D glucopyranoside (XXII)	$C_{28}H_{32}O_{13}$	154-156	-123°(MeOH)	200
α-Peltatin-β-D glucopyranoside (XXIII)	$C_{27}H_{30}O_{13}$	168-171	-129° (MeOH)	200
4'-Demethyldesoxy-podophyllotoxin-4'-β-D glucoside (XXIV)	$C_{27}H_{30}O_{12}$	-	-	400

*LD_{50} dose killing 50% of animals upon single administration; application was i.v. or i.p.; no major difference being between these two routes where both were tested.

We have observed that the Indian *P. emodi* in addition to the podophyllotoxin 1-O-β-glucopyranoside (XVI) and 4'-demethyl-podophyllotoxin-1-O-β-D-glucopyranoside (XVIII) also contains the Picropodophyllotoxin-β-D-glucopyranoside (XVIII) and 4'-demethylpicropodophyllotoxin-D-glucopyranoside (XIX). In the American species *P. peltatum*, *Linium flavum* and *Linium capitatum* β-peltatin-β-D-glycopyranoside (XXII) and α-peltatin-β-D-glucopyranoside (XXIII) are present.

Our laboratory has developed a process for the extraction of glucoside of podophyllotoxins from the marc (material left after the extraction of podophyllo-toxin and 4'-demethyl-podophyllotoxin from the resin) or insoluble part in chloroform and ether. The marc which comprises of kaempferol, quercetin, podophyllotoxin-l-O-β-D-glucopyranoside (XVI) and 4'-demethylpodo-phyllotoxin-1-O-β-D-glucopyranoside (XVII) was dissolve in hot methanol which gave a dark brown solution decolourised by refluxing the solution with neutral aluminium oxide repeatedly to yield a light yellow solution. This solution upon concentration under vacuum gave light yellow amorphous solid, HPLC analysis of solid indicated it to be a mixture of podophyllotoxin-1-O-β-D-glucopyranoside (XVI) and 4'-demethyl-podophyllotoxin-1-O-β-D-glucopyranoside (XVII) in the ratio of 9:1. The total yield of podophyllotoxin 1-O-β-D-glucopyranoside and 4-demethyl-podophyllotoxin-1-O-β-D-glucopyranosid varies from 0.8-1.2% in *P. emodi* marc. The method of extraction of the mixture of glucosides of podophyllotoxin is quite simple and does not involve the extraction with lead acetate (in order to precipitate tannins). The process reported in literature claims that the glucosides are water soluble. The observation has been verified by extracting water (in which alcoholic extract has been poured) with n-butanol. It showed the presence of trace amounts of these glucosides upon HPLC analysis showing that the major amount of these glucosides remained in marc only. The identity of glycosides was established both by hydrolysis with emulsion as well as by running standard samples of podophyllotoxin-1-O-β-D-glucopyranoside and 4'-demethylpodophyllotoxin-1-O-β-D-glucopyranoside on HPCL.

Accordingly, the present improved process developed by us for the isolation of a mixture of podophyllotoxin-1-O-β-D-glucopyranoside and 4'-demethylpodophyllotoxin-1-O-β-D-glucopyranoside from *Podophyllum emodi* comprises dissolving powdered rhizomes of *P. emodi* in polar solvents to get extract, concentrating the extract and mixing with ice cold water and isolating the resin (residue) so obtained, drying of the resin, extracting with an organic solvent, separating the marc left as residue by known methods, treating the said marc with polar solvent, separating the filtrate and refluxing repeatedly with neutral alumina, removing the solvent by known method to get a mixture of podophyllotoxin-1-O-β-D-glucopyranoside and 4'-

demethylpodophyllotoxin-1-O-β-D-glucopyranoside.The polar solvent used is selected from methanol, ethanol, propanol, isopropanol etc. The concentration of extract is effected under vacuum. The chlorinated solvent used is selected from dichloromethane, chloroform, carbon tetrachloride, dichloroethane etc. An example of the process is given as follows.

Air dried powdered roots/rhizomes of *P. emodi* (100 g) were extracted with methanol (500 ml) in a soxhlet for 15 hr. at a temperature in the range of 50-55°C. The extract concentrated under vacuum and poured in ice cold water (500 ml) with constant stirring. The water removed by decantation. The resin was washed with water (3 × 200 ml) and dried at room temp. when it gave light brown coloured powder (9.5 g). It was extracted with chloroform (7 × 50 ml) which on concentration and repeated crystallization with benzene: methanol gave a mixture consisting of podophyllotoxin and 4'-demethylpodophyllotoxin in the ratio of 9:1 (3.5 to 4 g) and light brown coloured marc (4.0 g). The composition of the marc is kaempferol, quercetin, podophyllotoxin-1-O-β-D-glucopyranoside and 4'-demethylpodophyllotoxin-1-O-β-D-glucopyranoside. The colouring matter like polyphenolics were removed by dissolving the marc in methanol (25 ml) and filtration. The filtrate refluxed repeatedly with neutral alumina (5 ×4 g). The methanol extract on removal of solvent gave a solid which was recrystallised from aqueous methanol to give amorphous powder (0.8 g-1.2 g). The HPLC analysis of the product showed it to be a mixture of two compounds namely (a) podophyllotoxin-1-O-β-D-glucopyranoside and (b) 4'-demethylpodophyllo toxin-1-O-β-D-glucopyranoside in the ratio of 9:1.

The methods developed by Wartburg and other are very lengthy, tedious and involve mixture of solvents. The methods developed by us from the total extract and marc also involve number of steps. In order to improve upon these methods we have further modified the method of isolation of glycosides of podophyllotoxin from the roots/rhizome directly.

The method developed is very simple and economical for the isolation of the podophyllotoxin glucosides and 4'-demethylpodophyllotoxin glucoside from the roots/rhizome of *Podophyllum emodi*. In this method first of all the aglycones of podophyllotoxin and 4'-demethylpodophyllotoxin and other minor lignans such as podophyllotoxone, desoxypodophyllotoxin, 4'-demethylpodophyllotoxin etc. are removed by the extraction with organic solvents such as benzene, chloroform, dichloromethane, hexane etc. The plant material left after the removal of these aglycones is extracted with polar solvents like ethyl acetate, acetone or alcohols. The polar solvent extract is treated with neutral metal oxide such as neutral aluminium oxide. The neutral aluminium oxide absorbs most of the polyphenolics. The glucosides of the lignan are filtered and concentrated in vacuum. This extract generally contains trace amount of aglycones of podophyllotoxins whereas generally contains trace amount of aglycones of podophyllotoxins whereas podophyllotoxin glycoside in major quantity and 4'-demethylpodophyllotoxin glycoside in minor quantity along with the trace amount of the picro-podophyllotoxin-1-O-β-D-glucopyranoside (XIV) and 4'-demethyl-picropodophyllotoxin-1-O-β-D-glucopyranoside (XV). The separation-purification of these glycosides are done on silica gel column to yield the pure podophyllotoxin-1-O-β-D-glucoside and 4'-demethylpodophylloxin-1-O-β-D-glucoside. The column was eluted with chloroform: methanol (95:5).

Fraction A: yields the mixture of aglycones of podophyllotoxin, 4'-demethylpodophyllotoxin and podophyllotoxone.

Fraction B: on elution with chloroform: methanol (9:1) yields mainly podophyllotoxin-1-O-β-D-glucoside.

Fraction C: on elution with chloroform: methanol (85:15) yields 4'-demethylpodophyllotoxin-1-O-β-D-glucoside.

On technological side the earlier methods were tedious, cumbersome and lengthy involving number of steps. The methods developed by us for the isolation of podophyllotoxin are performed in single step and subsequent crystallization processes yields pure compound. However the glycosides are also extracted from the plant in a single step. The separation and purification has been done on column chromatography. The products are quite pure and the process is economical.

Podophyllotoxin is a relatively rare natural product and is presently extracted from the roots/rhizome of two species of Podophyllum (Berberidaceae) *P. emodi* Wallich/*P. hexandrum* (Indian podophyllum) and *P. peltatum* (American podophyllum). The former species is much richer source of podophyllotoxin containing upto 4.0% with *P. pellatum* yielding near of 0.25%. The Chinese species *P. versipelle* and two species of Diphyllcia, *D. cymosa* and *D. grayi,* classified in family berberidaceae sub family podophylloideae; contain podophyllotoxin ranging from 0.2 to 1 per cent.

12

Yew (Taxus spp.) (Barhmi)

INTRODUCTION

Yew, locally known in India as 'Barhmi', 'Rakhala', 'Thuner', has been used in herbal medicine for centuries. The traditional interaction of *Taxus* species with mankind has been varied in different parts of the world. However, it has been much known for childhood and animal poisoning. Except for the red aril of the seeds, all parts of the plant are toxic. The bark was used for treatment of rheumatism, liver and urinary tract affections. In Western Himalayas, a dilute decoction of the bark is taken during winters by nomadic people to increase body resistance to extreme cold. Due to highly tensile properties its wood was used to make bows and implements. Its wood has high calorific value and was used in ignite kilns to make a specific pottery in Kashmir. In Europe, yew is valued for making excellent hedges. The dried leaves are used in 'Havan', the Hindu sacrificial rites and incense materials.

The recent interest in screening plant based drug sources based on ethnobiology and bioassay directed analysis, has thrown *Taxus* as potent source of a new group of diterpenoid compound grouped together as taxanes. Taxol (Fig. 1.I), first isolated from *T. brevifolia*, by Wani *et al.* amongst this group has opened an entirely new approach in treating cancers by its effect on microtubule assembly in dividing cells. The taxanes are now known to be present in most of the *Taxus* spp. growing around the world. The Himalayan yew *Taxus wallichiana* also contains taxanes in appreciable quantities. It has attracted attention particularly on account of high levels of baccatin-III (Fig. 1.II), a precursor of taxanes in its leaves.

Though other varieties of *Taxus* growing in America and Europe have been worked upon in detail with respect of silviculture, ecology, site requirements, reproductive biology, regeneration and genetics, negligible information is available on the Himalayan yew. This article addresses to some of the recent developments in *Taxus* biology and need for conservation of Himalayan yew.

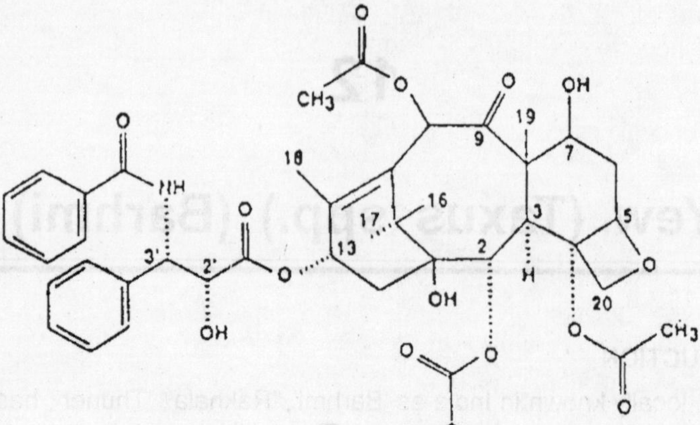

I. Taxol

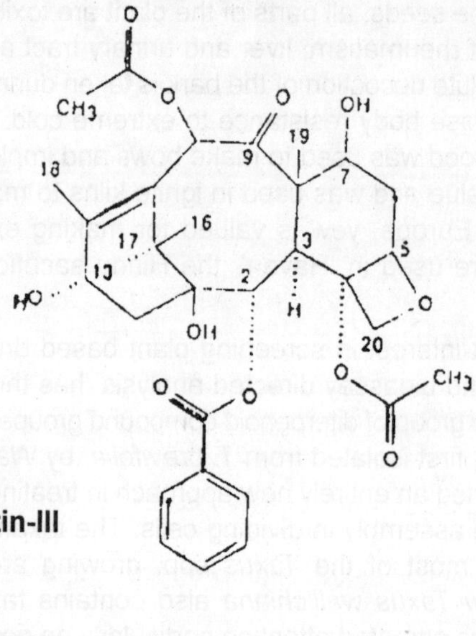

II. Baccatin-III

CURRENT IMPORTANCE

The current importance is mainly due to the demonstration of taxol on murine lukaemia system. Later it was found to be effective against lung cancer, breast and colon cancers and other leukaemias, ovarian cancers. The structure activity relationships have been described in detail by Kingeston *et al.*, and Guenard *et al.*, The C-13 acyl side chain, oxetane rings, a free 2-hydroxyl group, 3-amino group and absolute configuration at C_2 and C_3 contribute to the activity of taxanes to microtubule assay. Besides anticancer activity certain fractions from *Taxus* show antifungal activity and insecticidal and metamorphosis disrupting effects on *Epilachea varivestris*. While screening plants for silk enhancers in our laboratory, extracts from *Taxus* caused incomplete metamorphosis into pupa, when applied topically to 5th instar larvae.

BOTANY AND DISTRIBUTION

Genus *Taxus* belongs to taxales (related to coniferales) and is distributed around the globe in the north temperate areas of world. The plants usually exist in the undestroyed of mixed temperate forests as small evergreen trees and large shrubs, with a dense branch system with dark green long and narrow shiny leaves. Plants are dioecious. Fruits are solitary consisting a single dark ovoid seed surrounded by a red fleshy covering called the aril.

Flowering occurs in March-April. Many species and varieties, exist distinguished on the basis of bud scales, colour of leaves, leaf apices. However, finer distinctions are based on (i) number of stomata rows (ii) papillosity (iii) shape of epidermal cells (iv) curvature of lower midrib and stomatal regions. The main species of interest are:

T. baccata (European yew)

T. cuspidata (Japanese yew)

T. chinensis (Chinese yew)

T. brevifolia (Western or Pacific yew)

T. wallichiana (Himalayan yew)

T. canadensis (Canadian yew)

A large number of horticulared yews are also available. T. *media* cv. 'Hicksii' is a hybrid of *T. baccata* and *T. cuspidata* and *T. x hunnewelliana* is a hybrid of *T. cuspidata* and *T. canadensis*. Recently an electrophoretic characterization of *Taxus* cultivars has been conducted by Greet *et al.*

The Himalayan yew *T. wallichiana* was earlier grouped with *T. baccata*. It is found at an elevation of 7,000 to 11,000 ft. (Fig. 2) above m.s.l., however it is found at lower altitudes also in North Eastern hills of Himalaya. The variety growing in Western Himalayas (Himachal and J&K) is somewhat distinct from one growing in North East (Arunachal Pradesh, Meghalaya, Darjeeling, etc.) The former is more akin to *T. baccata* and the latter is more closer to *T. chinensis* in morphological characters. Cephalomannine, a diterpenoid isolated from a plant originally identified as *Cephalotaxus manni* was later shown to be *T. wallichiana*. Difference also exists in the concentration of Taxane components between the two races (Kapil *et al.*, - unpublished data). Natural populations of Himalayan yew are found in mixed fir and cedrus forests in association with oaks and rhododendrons as understorey scattered plants. Usually the plants are found in the northern steep ridges.

Figure 2: Distribution of *Taxus wallichiana* in different forest divisions of Himachal Pradesh

NEED FOR CONSERVATION

The emergence of taxanes as new generation anticancer agents has resulted in sudden demand and supply crisis. Although the primary source of taxol has been the bark of *T. brevifolia*, it was later found that foliage of most of species also contain extractable quantities of taxol and related compounds. The drug is present in miniscule quantities in the plant tissues. About 2.5 g. of this is required to treat an ovarian or breast cancer patient and conservative projections of the world demand are 700 kg/year. The present production level of taxol is about 350 kg due to non-availablity of raw material. In order to produce 1 kg. of taxol about 7,272 kg of bark is required and the amount of leaf clippings required is multifold. Consequently a drug supply crisis has emerged, resulting is blatant exploitation of *Taxus* flora. The Himalayan yew being no exception.

MANAGEMENT STRATEGIES

Regional Research Laboratory, Jammu initiated a programme for conservation of the Himalayan yew on the following lines:

(a) Survey of *Taxus* growing area and status of regeneration in such pockets.

(b) Standardisation of macropropagation techniques and

(c) Devise a sustainable raw material system without affecting the natural habitat of *Taxus*.

Our survey in Himachal Pradesh and parts of Northeast revealed that the plants are restricted to steep, mostly inaccessible slopes on the northern ridges of mountains. The plants are heavily debarked and lopped; and most of the damage is recent. The regeneration is almost absent except in a few inaccessible areas. The potential areas of *Taxus* which sustained it a few decades ago are now devoid of this plant. Little is known about its genetic diversity. It has been a plant of insignificance to forest departments so far. For its long term health and sustainable utilization, work on; selection and cultivition of elite desirable clones and conservation of natural stands assumes immediate priority. The availability of taxanes on sustainable basis can be assured by harvesting clippings from close density plantations maintained in bush form. The clippings of Himalayan yew contain small amounts of taxol, but higher levels of its precursor baccatin III besides other taxanes. As taxol is no more a drug of choice and many other semisynthetic taxanes like taxotere show better patient acceptance, the availability of baccatin III becomes all the more pertinent than taxol, as it can be converted to such acceptable taxanes with lesser side effects, by esterification reaction or other alternatives. The overall recovery of baccatin III can further be enhanced by chemical process of other taxanes in the crude extracts of the clippings.

REGENERATION AND VEGETATIVE PROPAGATION

Keeping the aforesaid in view work was initiated by Regional Research Laboratory, Jammu at its Extension Centre, Palampur (HP) on mass macro-propagation. Based on survey and screening, the elite plants from natural stands are being clonally propagated with the aim to grow *T. wallichiana* plants in field conditions in close density bush type plantations. The clippings obtained from such plantations can be harvested on sustainable basis without affecting the natural reserves in the forests. The following techniques are being employed for mass propagation after proper optimization:

(i) Propagation through Cuttings

The maximal rooting in *T. wallichiana* depends on (a) type of cuttings (b) health of the mother plant (c) season and (d) rooting conditions e.g., rooting medium, light, temperature, etc. Though induction of rooting was achieved in all types of cuttings (age groups), the maximum rooting was obtained in terminal cuttings (main axis) 80.90%, followed by 2nd year growth 65% and 3rd year growth about 40-50% after IBA treatments. The main axis cuttings are preferred for induction of rooting due to their excellent subsequent shoot extension growth. The cuttings are treated with 100-200 ppm IBA for 18 hrs or a quick dip in 1000-2000 ppm solution and planted in previously prepared plastic tubes or field beds under partial shade. As reported in other species of *Taxus* IBA only helps in enhancing rooting process in *T. wallichiana* also. The root growth is best obtained by making the rooting medium light by mixing thermocol granules and sand. The best season for intduction of rooting was found to be November to February. The plants are ready for transplantation with 120 to 180 days depending upon the time of planting. Rooting response was drastically reduced after April under long day conditions.

Some workers have suggested bottom heat for better results. However, the high cost technique was circumvented by planting the cuttings during winter at lower altitudes. Effective soil sterilization, drainage and use of Bavistin soil drenching is essential to avoid root rot and other infections.

(ii) Air-layering

Through this technique plants can be prepared in about 90 days for transplantation. The air layering is conducted on selected elite plants using green moss and IBA. The number of plants produced through this technique is limited, nevertheless, the plants produced are comparable to 3-5 years old plants raised from seeds. This technique can be gainfully used for producing mother stocks from elite trees with high taxane content.

(iii) Seeds

The propagation through seeds is time consuming due to their double dormancy and slow growth of plants to reach clipping stage. The seeds of *Taxus* required stratification and GA_3 treatments to achieve maximal and earlier germination. Usually it takes one year for the seeds to germinate. Propagation through seeds is being mainly adopted in our laboratory for introduction of exotic cultivars and species for their evaluation under local conditions. So far we have introduced *T. baccata* (European yew), *T. brevifolia, T. cuspidata,* and *T. chinensis.*

CULTIVATION

Taxus can grow in very poor soils one established and does not require nutrient inputs. It is however highly susceptible to water logging and is best planted in sloppy areas. We have adopted a 40 cm x 40 cm spacing for close density cultivation. The plants are susceptible to transfer shock and the transplantation is carried with minimum damage to roots. It grows well in shady areas and can establish in all types of soils from limy to acid. A model of cultivation based on mixed plantation with other tree species like Mulberry has been initiated for creating a two tier canopy model for commercial cultivation in lower Himalayas. Preplant chilling and post-plant enhanced light duration has been reported to have positive effect on the subsequent growth of *Taxus x media* cv. Hicksii.

CHEMICAL CONSIDERATIONS

The work on taxanes in *Taxus* spp. received active attention only after the discovery of anticancer activity in taxol. The chemistry of taxanes is out of purview of this article, however articles by Blechert and Guenard Suffness and Cordel. Kingston, Guenard *et al.,* give excellent details. Thoguh some synthetic approaches have been developed and till such approaches are perfected to economic viability, it is essential to understand the environmental and genetic factors which influence the composition and concentration of taxanes for proper cultivation and management of yew, towards a sustained supply of raw material.

(i) Environmental Effects

Most of the variations in taxane contents within different populations have been attributed to environmental factors. The major factor is that of light. Trees growing in shade have higher taxol content in bark, whereas the reverse is true of cephalomannine, when compared with trees growing in open. Similiarly, baccatin III also behaves differently. Our studies on *T. wallichiana* from Himachal Pradesh reveal higher concentrations of cephalomannine and baccatin-III as compared to taxol. The plants growing in cool and moist sites have overall higher taxane contents in contrast to plants growing on warmer and dry slopes. The total taxane contents also vary with altitude and season. The optimum time of collection was found to be June-July for both bark and needles. Large variations in taxane profile have also been reported in *T. brevifolia.*

(ii) Genetic Factors

Though almost all the species grown around the globe contain taxol and other taxanes or derivatives in their leaf and bark, they show typical differences in their taxane profiles pointing to the inherent genetic differences. Significant differences in taxol concentrations among plants of same species growing under identical conditions, notwithstanding the differences due to season and other factors, also point to genetic variations. However, the amount of genetic variations and heretability of relevant traits are yet to be defined in *Taxus* species. A genetic test based on screening of plants raised through seeds obtained from thirty different populations of pacific yew and grown under identical conditions has been reported by Wheeler *et. al.* Significant differences were found in height, growing points, time of bud burst and bud set, between polulations and among trees within populations.

Working on the allozyme variation based on 24 enzymatic loci in *T. brevifolia* and other plants, Hamrick and Godt reported lower degree of variation as compared in other gymnosperms, but comparable to other angiosperms.

The genetic selection is, however, complicated by changes in taxane contents in different seasons. In view of the lack of a reliable heirarchy in taxane levels, the selection based on maximal biomass accumultion and phonological traits, besides the overall taxane contents seems more attractive proposition. We have already initiated a study in which different *Taxus* species obtained from different parts of the globe are being introduced to evaluate their performance under local conditions. Since taxane biosynthesis involves a dozen or more enzymes or genes, poulation and phenotypic correlation studies in carefully controlled environments would enhance the selection pressure. Such a study on Himalayan yew, with diverse ecological situations through the whole length of Himalayas would be fruitful. In view of the importance of baccatin III as precursor, selection pressure for higher baccatin-III yield needs priority.

POST HARVEST TECHNOLOGY

In view of the limited resource availability, optimization of post harvest operations from harvest to extraction of clippings is receiving attention of late now. The taxol yields are most sensitive to drying protocol. A thin layer drying system has been suggested. The loss of taxane yields on long term storage of clippings is not worked out yet. Recently, Elsohly *et al.* have elucidated taxol content variations in fresh, stored and dried *Taxus* clippings. It is interesting to note the findings of Schulzter *et al.*, who reported enhancement in the yield of taxol and cephalomannine on storage for nine days, regardless of storage temperature. Similarly the extraction procedures also affect the overall taxane yields. A comparison of the values of the taxol and other related compounds by different workers show 2-10 fold differences in the overall values. Notwithstanding the differences due to environmental and genetic factors, these differences have a third component attributed to post harvest procedures, storage and extraction protocol, tissue particle size, type of solvent, temperature and length of extraction which may effect the final yield.

CELL CULTURE AND BIOTECHNOLOGY

Taxol production through cell cultures has been suggested as an alternate source of taxanes. Though may patents have also appeared in this respect, the yields fail to compete with yields and economy of clippings as a source. Christen *et al.*, (US Patent No.501, 9504) obtained callus on Gamborg's B_5 medium supplemented with casamino acids (2g/L) obtained a yield of 1-3 mg/L after 2-4 weeks. The growth of *T. cuspidata* and *T. canadensis* callus and cell suspension cultures have been optimized on Gamborg's B_5 salts supplemented with 1.5% (W/V) soluble polyvinylpyrrolidone 0.3% (W/V) sucrose and 4 mg/L 2, 4-D. Work on growth optimization, characterization and taxol production kinetics have been done by Wickremesinhe and Arteca, Fett-Neto *et al.* Most of such reports are based on the basis of addition of some additives (amino acids) and or elicitors. For example certain amino acids like phenylalanine can increase taxol yields as it serves as a precursor for N-benzyl phenylisoserine side chain of taxol. An increase of taxol from 2 $\mu g/g^{-1}$ to 10 $\mu g/g^{-1}$ of extracted dry weight at stationary phase can be achieved in presence of phenyl alanine and benzoic acid. The stimulation of taxol production in callous cultures by endophytic fungi and even growth retardants has prompted some to suggest a phytoalexin role for taxanes.

DISEASES

Taxus serves as a host to a diversity of micro-organisms some of which are highly pathogenic and pose threat to its cultivation. The Himalayan yew is yet to be investigated in this respect. In *T. brevifolia* a highly destructive root rot is caused by *Phytopthora lateralis*. A lack of self-sown regeneration is caused in *T. baccata* populations infested with *Phellinus hartiqii* and *P. pini* These pathogens along with *Cylindrocarpon radicalis* and *Mycelium radicisatrovirens* cause decay of wood. The yew leaf blight due to *Macrophoma taxi* which cause small black perithecia under the surface of leaves is prevalent in Himalayan yew also. Removal of branches and spray of Bordeaux mixture help in controlling it. Another disease, yew leaf scorch due to *Sphaerulina taxi* causes browning of leaves.

CONCLUSION

The blatant exploitation of Himalayan yew in recent years has created serious concern about its long term health in the already diminishing natural populations. There is a need for developing effective strategies in management of Himalayan yew in light of its recently found utility. The harvest of leaf clippings obtained from close density bush type plantations of genetically elite plants (clonal populations) offers a sustainable and non-environmental impacting system, till some other source through biotechnology or chemical synthesis is perfected to comparative economic viability. The effective conservation and utilization of Himalayan yew requires a comprehensive study on its regeneration potential, reproductive biology, environmental impacts and genetic diversity.

SUMMARY

The disvoery of anticancer agent taxol and its related compounds in different species of *Yew* (*Taxus* spp.) has evoked worldwide interest in development of strategies for a sustainable supply of taxol. As taxol is present in miniscule quantities, its extraction from needles and bark has already resulted in a blatant exploitation of the *Taxus* from its receding natural habitats, Himalayn yew being no exception. The biology, cultivation, conservation, utilization of *Taxus* including its post harvest aspects are discussed here in view of its newly found importance and world demand. The need for exploiting genetic variation to build a strong selection base for enhanced biomass and taxane yields, coupled with recent developments in its agrotechnology are emphasized. It is suggested that besides selection of *Taxus* genotypes from natural habits in India, germplasm from different sources be collected and potential high yields be vegetatively propagated through cuttings, seed and tissue culture on a mass scale both for reforestation and bush type plantation, notwithstanding biotechnological approaches being pursued at the moment for taxol production.

13

Ginseng

INTRODUCTION

Ginseng belongs to genus *Panax* (Araliaceae), has been recognized for centuries as an important plant used in oriental medicines. The name *Panax* is drived from Greek words "Pan" meaning 'all' and "axos" meaning 'cure' to mean Panacea or all curing and its properties have been no less touted. It is perhaps the most widely recognized plant used in traditional medicine and now plays a major role in the ever increasing herbal health care market of the world. Eight species are ascribed to this genus, out of these, the roots and rhizomes of *P. ginseng, P. japonicum, P. pseudoginseng* and its varieties namely, var. *notoginseng* and var, *major* which are native to Asia and *P. quinquefolium* and *P. trifolium,* native to N. America are used medicinally.

Earlier it was used in the treatment of asthenia, atherosclerosis, blood and bleeding disorders, colitis and to relieve symptoms of aging, cancer and senility. Now evidence has emerged that root possesses a general strengthening effect, raises mental and physical capacity, exerts a protectant effect against experimental disbetes, neurosis, radiation sickness and some cancers. Moreover, with the discovery of adaptogenic effect of its saponin content, its popularity has increased many folds. It is popular ingredient in herbal teas, shampoos and cosmetics, and its extract, capsules or tablets are widely used as medicine. Interestingly, all the products of ginseng are not usually associated with any seriour adverse reactions.

COMPONENTS AND IMPORTANCE OF INDIAN GINSENG

Panax ginseng, P. quinquefolium and P. japanicus are the main sources of Korean, American and Japanese ginseng, respectively. Whereas *P. pseudoginseng* provides Chinese wonder drug "*Sanchi*" used to cure all diseases, even cancer. Among these. Korean ginseng is widely used and more accepted in pharmaceutical industry. At present Korean ginseng worth more than 5 million rupees is being annually imported by India. However, Himalayan species of *Panax* are often referred as Indian ginseng. It is least understood of all ginsengs, and is a conglomerate of 5 different species of *Panax* namely, *P. seudoginseng, P. sikkimensis, P. bipinnatifidus, P. burkillianus* and *P. schinseng.* The importance of Indian ginseng to pharmaceutical industry has increased many fold after the recent studies by Dua *et. al.,* who have found it to be comparable and in some tests even better than Korean ginseng. Also Shukla and Thakur have established that almost all the active sapoinins of Korean ginseng are present in Indian pseudoginseng. These reports have generated a lot of scientific and commercial interest in Indian ginseng, which has resulted in a blatant exploitation of its roots and rhizomes from natural habitants. This necessitates a need for the development of strategies for getting the sustainable supply of its roots by bringing in under cultivation. This will not only help us in protecting rich germplasm of Indian ginseng, but will also help in saving the valuable foreign exchange being spent in importance Korean ginseng.

Keeping this in mind, studies were initiated in 1990 on Indian ginseng. Surveys were conducted in N.E. states of Meghalaya, Arunchal Pradesh and Nagaland to record the availability of germplasm, study its natural habitant and biology and to initiate work on its domestication in the experimental fields of Regional Research Laboratory, Extension Centre, Palampur.

In the following pages, botany, distribution, utilization and cultivation efforts on Indian ginseng are presented. Necessity to conserve Indian species of *Panax* has also been emphasised.

BOTANY

Taxonomy of *Pana* species continues to be controversial. There is a lot of confusion about the number of *Panax* species falling under Indian ginseng. Hara attributes all the ginseng collections from Eastern Himalayas to only one species, namely, *P. pseudoginseng* Wall. subsp. *Himalicus* Hara and its two varieties viz. var. *angustifolius* (Burkill) Li and var. *bipinnatifida* (Seem) Li. Later Banerjee recognized 4 species (*P. fruitcosus* L., *pseudoginseng* Wall., *P. sikkimensis* Ban. And *P. assamicus* Ban.) and one variety (*P. pseudonginseng* var, *bipinnatifida* (Seem) Li from India. All these except *P. fruticosus* are associated with the name Indian ginseng and are growing in E. Himalayas, Cannon treated *P. sikkimensis* and *P. assamicus* as synonyms of *P. pseudoginseng* var. *angustifolius* (Burkill) Lt. Whereas, Bennet and Sharma on the basis of leaf and rhizome morphology treated both *P. bipinnatifidus* Seem and *P. sikkimensis,* specially distinct from *P. pseudpgoinseng* and attributed atleast these 3 species to Indian ginseng. Bennet and Viswanathan on the basis of their field studies from Shillong found that the most commonly available ginseng plants, on the basis of rhizome and leaf characters are specifically distinct from *P.*

pseudoginseng var. *angustifolius* of Li should be raised to specific rank as *P. burkillianus* Benn. & Visw.

With the record of *P. schinseng* Nees, (*P. ginseng* C.A. Meyer) from Nagaland by Changkija and Kumar and from our field studies in north eastern states, we believe that the Indian ginseng is a conglomerate of 5 species of *Panax* namely, *P. sikkimensis* Ban., *P. burkillianus* Benn. & View., *P. bipinnatifidus* Seem., *P. schinseng* Nees, and *P. pseudoginseng* Wall.

The Indian ginsengs are small perennial deciduous herbs. The aerial vegetative shoot of mature plant is 25-150 cm tall and is composed of single hollow, weak, green to reddish green, glabrous erect stem, which is arising subapically from rhizome and terminating is whorl of 3-10 palmately compound leaves. The growth of aerial shoots is determinant. A single shoot primordium is differentiated subapically on a sub-terranean rhizome, the year prior to expression and the growth of aerial shoot in any year is limited to the expansion of the performed primordium. The vegetative growth and flowering takes place during May to June and the fruits ripen during October. The rhizome with root system is underground and is variable morphclogically in different *Panax* species (Table 1). The flowers are creamy yellow to greenish white and hermaphrodite, styles 3, free or united at the base. Fruits small, globose berries with 1-3 seeds.

There is difference of opinion regarding the colour of mature fruits. Earlier authors, depending upon their time of collection have given colour of fruits as crimson red in *P. schinseng*, red of half red, half black, red in *P. pseudoginseng*, lower 2/3 red and upper 1/3 black in P. *bipinnatifidus*, red and black in *P. sikkimensis* and crimson red in *P. burkillianus*. During field surveys by the present authors, it was observed that in all the *Panax* species falling under Indian ginseng ripe fruits are initially red and then berries gradually start turning black from upper end. So depending upon maturity, one can fully red or both black and red berries. Thus we disagree with Bennet and Sharma in considering colour of fruits in genus *Panax* of any taxonomic significance.

DISTRIBUTION

International range of Indian ginseng is in the interior temperate mountainous regions of north east India, northern Burma, Nepal, China and Southern Tibet. In India, it is predominantly Himalayan in distribution. It extends from Uttaranchal (W. Himalayas) to Arunachal Pradesh (E. Himalayas) between altitudes of 1500-3000 m. Details of distribution sites (latitude 23°80'-29°70'N; longitude 79°50'-98°2'. E) is given in Map 1. Its distribution is restricted to the areas with annual rainfall of 800 to 2500 mm, temperature range of 4 to 25°C and soil pH of 5-6.5. It thrives well in localities with well drained moist forest soil, rich in organic matter and leaf

Table 1: Distinguishing features of 5 Indian *Panax* species

S. No.	*Characters*	*P. pseudoginseng*	*P. burkillianus*	*P. schinseng*	*P. sikkimensis*	*P. bipinnatifidus*
1.	Rhizome and root stock	Tuber fasicled, fusiform, hard, base of stem swollen with fleshy deciduous scales	Creeping, horizontal ginger like with conspicuous annual abscission scars	Short, mortar shaped attached to stout roots which are less branched and thick	Single, horizontal knotted with ring like persistent scales with a globose tuber at distal end	Same as *P. sikkimensis*
2.	Leaves	3-5 foliate	5-7 foliate	5-6 foliate	5-7 foliate	3-5 foliate
3.	Leaflets	Lancaeolate to oblong lanceolate, serrate, acuminate	Narrow lanceolate, serrate, caudate	Ovate or obovate, dentate, acuminate	Oblong lanceolate serrate, acuminate	Lanceolate, bippinatified lobes serrated, accuminated

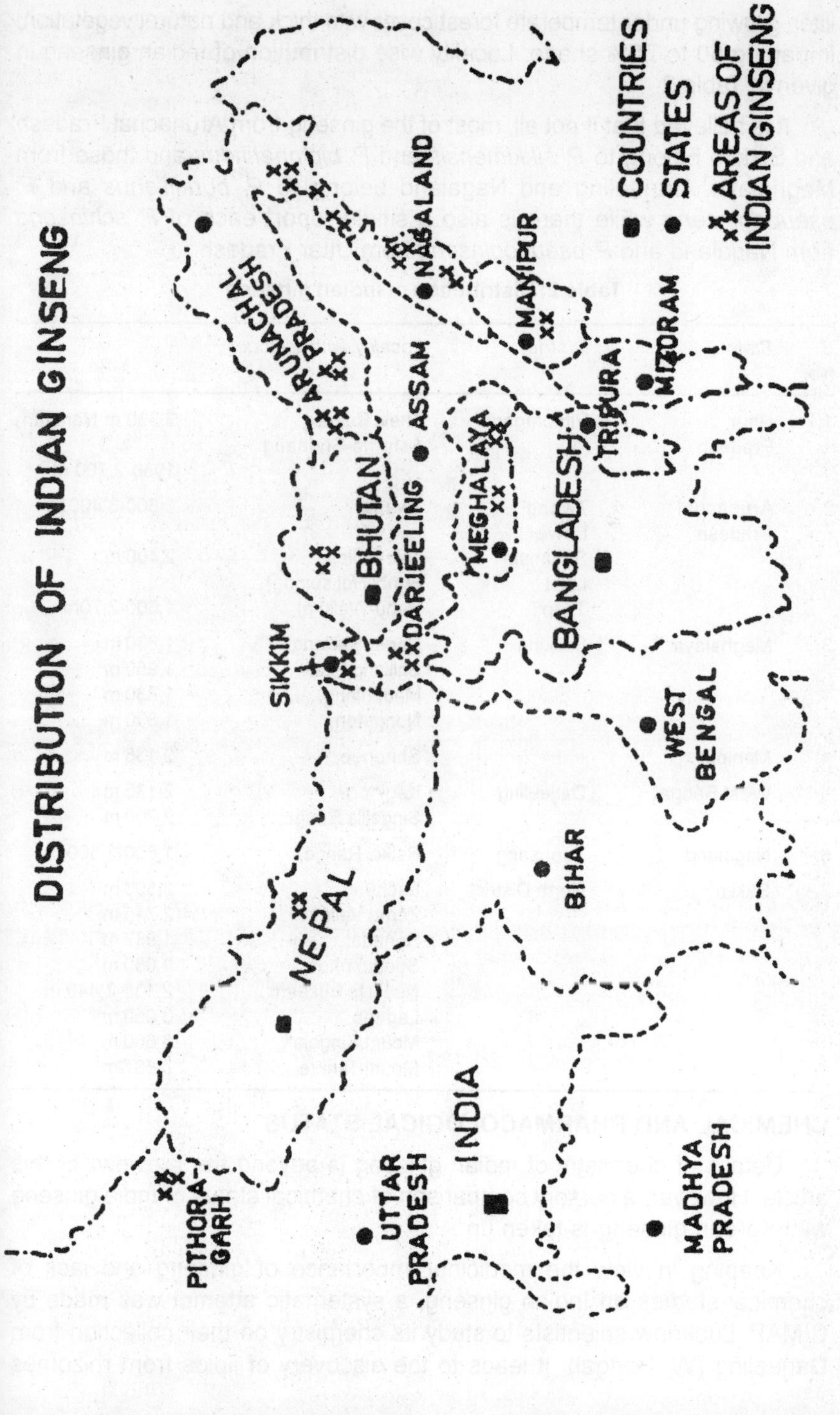
DISTRIBUTION OF INDIAN GINSENG
COUNTRIES
STATES
AREAS OF INDIAN GINSENG
NEPAL
BHUTAN
BANGLADESH
INDIA
SIKKIM
DARJEELING
ARUNACHAL PRADESH
ASSAM
NAGALAND
MANIPUR
MEGHALAYA
TRIPURA
MIZORAM
WEST BENGAL
BIHAR
UTTAR PRADESH
MADHYA PRADESH
PITHORA-GARH

litter, growing under temperate forest cover with thick and natural vegetation, imparting 50 to 75% shade. Locality wise distribution of Indian ginseng in given in Table 2.

It is believed that if not all, most of the ginseng from Arunachal Pradesh and Sikkim belong to *P. sikkimensis* and *P. bipinnatifidus* and those from Meghalaya, Darjeeling and Nagaland belong to *P. burkillianus* and *P. pseudoginseng* while there is also a single report each of *P. schinseng* from Nagaland and *P. pseudoginseng* from Uttar Pradesh.

Table 2: Distribution of Indian ginseng

S. No.	*State*	*District*	*Locality with altitude**	
1.	Utter Pradesh	Pithoragarh	Thala Ruigair, Ashrma-Sridhang	3,330 m Narayan
				1950-2,700 m
2.	Arunachal Pradesh	Twang	Twang,	2,800-3,400 m
		Lower Subansiri	Tale Valley,	2,400 m
		Lohit	Simbi Hot spiring}	
		Tirap	Rahu-Walkka}	1,600-2,70m
3.	Meghalaya	Shillong	Upper Shillong,	1,830 m
			Shillong Peak,	1,950 m
			Mauphlang,	1,830 m
			Nongston,	1,830 m
4.	Manipur	–	Shirohee,	2,135 m
5.	West Bengal	Darjeeling	Kagjhora,	2,135 m
			Singalila Range,	2,700 m
6.	Nagaland	Tuensang	Patkoi Range,	1,800-2,500 m
7.	Sikkim	North District	Lachung,	2,593 m
			Zemu Valley,	2,745 m
			Sonada,	1,982 m
			Sundukphoo,	3,050 m
			Neebi to Bukeem,	2,135-2,440 m
			Lagheb,	3,050 m
			Mount Singolah,	3,660 m
			Mount Tankre,	3,507 m

CHEMICAL AND PHARMACOLOGICAL STATUS

Details of chemistry of Indian ginseng is beyond the preview of this article. However, a cursory comparison of chemical status of India ginseng with Korean ginseng is taken up.

Keeping in view the medicinal importance of ginseng and lack of chemical studies on Indian ginseng, a systematic attempt was made by CIMAP, Lucknow scientists to study its chemistry on their collection from Darjeeling (W. Bengal). It leads to the discovery of lipids from rhizomes and leaves. Also it has been found to be a rich source of oleanolic acid saponins while dammarane saponins are present in minor amounts. From rhizomes of Indian ginseng, ginsenosides, Rb_1, - Rb_2, - Rb_3, - Rc, - Rd, - Re, - Rg_1 and –Ro; pseudoginsenosides, F_{11}, RI_1, RI_2, RP_1, and RT_1; and chikusetusaponins IVa and IV are isolated, while the leaves (Shukla and Thakur, 1990 b) yielded all these saponins, except for pseudoginsenosides RI_1 and RI_2 which were present only in the rhizomes of *P. burkillianus* (= *P. pseudoginseng* var. *angustifolius*). It is interesting to mention that the active saponins of Korean ginseng like, -Rb_1, -Rb_2, -Rd, -Re, -Rg_1 and Ro and chikusetsusaponin VI are also present in Indian ginseng.

Diverse activities are attributed to the roots of ginseng which range from CNS depression or stimulation, variable effects on systemic blood pressure, analgesic and anti-inflammatory protection against the stress induced ulcers, and adaptogenic activity. Due *et al.*, compared the crude extract and saponins of Indian ginseng for adaptogenic, anti-inflammatory and immunostimulant activities using a battery of pharmacological tests and compared with Korean ginseng saponins. The found that the swimming performance of rats markedly increased with Indian ginseng than the Korean ginseng saponins. However, gastric ulceration induced by swimming stress as well as immobilization stress was inhibited equally by both types of saponins. Crude Indian ginseng as well as its saponins has weak anti-inflammatory activity in acute as well as subacute models of inflammation. As immunostimulant, saponins from Indian ginseng were found to be more effective than the saponins of the Korean ginseng.

Since the earlier chemical and pharmacological studies on Indian ginseng are confined only to Darjeeling area, it is suggested that such studies are to be extended to the collection from other areas of the Himalayas, for proper evaluation of germplasm of Indian ginseng, so that strains with higher biomass yield as well as higher activity be selected for bringing under cultivation and future breeding programmes.

UTILIZATION AND CONSERVATION

Ginseng is the most precious drug with cure all properties. Unfortunately due to lakc of proper understanding and knowledge, there has been no serious and consistent organized scientific effort for collection of Indian ginseng, its utilization and to ascertain cultivation prospects. The short life span of aerial shoot during monsoon, is the plus point with ginseng to evade the onslaught of plant collector and also its habitat during monsoon is not easily accessible.

However, massive deforestation, specially in the states of Nagaland and Meghalaya has lead to the habitat destruction and disturbance, which inturn has adversely effected natural regeneration. Further, indiscriminate collection and smuggling of rhizomes and root stocks of this wonder drug to China and Burma has lead to almost depletion of the species from Nagaland. In north eastern states of Maghalaya, Arunachal Pradesh and Nagaland, now natural populations of Indian ginseng are only available in either sacred grooves or inaccessible remote regions of these states. Like *P. quinquefolium*, where in natural populations death rate is 14 times higher than regeneration rate, Indian ginseng is also being depleted at an alarming rate due to higher death rate. But keeping in view the great genetic diversity of species of *Panax* falling under Indian ginseng, it is advisable to protect this rich germplasm for future breeding programmes, of incorporating desirable characteristics to already commercialized American and Korean ginsengs.

Thus to protect the surviving natural populations and to increase the productivity, an augmentaitive plantation and aided natural regeneration are the only answer. So far only Joshi *et al.*, have done some preliminary cultivation trials of Indian ginseng under laboratory conditions, but as such our knowledge if fragmentary.

CULTIVATION

Based on the our own experience on cultivation trials of Indian ginseng at Palampur (Himachal Pradesh) from rhizomes and also available information, cultivation details of Indian ginseng are discussed as under:

Climate and Soil

Ginseng has typical climatic and soil requirements for its proper growth. It can be profitably cultivated in temperature areas, with temperature range of 4-25°C, soil pH of 5-6.5 and annual rainfall of 800-2,500 mm. It prefers well drained, peaty, sandy loam soil with a thick cover of humus, derived from broad leaf species and rich in potassium.

Collection of Planting Material

Crop of ginseng can be raised either from seed or rhizomes. Fruits mature in the month of September and October. After collection, the seeds are extracted from fruits, washed and then shade dried for proper storage, and are sown on the onset of winters next year. During this period the full embryonic development of seed is achieved.

Rhizomes can also be collected during September-October, but are sown the same year. From our field observations, it has been found that due to difference in rhizome morphology, *P. bipinnatifidus* and *P. sikkimensis* produce lesser biomass or rhizomes (3-5 gm/plant), whereas it is higher in *P. schinseng*, *P. pseudoginseng* and *P. burkillianus* (20-30 gms/plant). Thus it seems probable that the latter three species should be brought under cultivation for higher yield, but such inference is yet to be supported by chemical/pharmacological studies.

RAISING OF NURSERY

(i) From Seeds

Before sowing, stratification of seeds is required due to hard seed coat. For stratification, healthy seeds are mixed with fine sand in 1:5 ratio for about three months. Selected seeds with partially opened seed coats are sown in prepared raised nursery beds, prepared in land which is lying fallow for atleast two years, after turning soil to greater depths for alteast fifteen times. To improve soil taxture; sand, leaf and grass mould is added. It has been observed that mixing of ash from leaves and grasses also adds to the quality of soil. For healthy and even growth of seedlings line sowing is recommended. Seed germinate in April next, and continue to grow till early October, when the aerial parts wither off. At this stage mulching of nursery beds is required to avoid frost damage to underground parts. In next March-April the seedlings are drug out and transplanted in the fields.

(ii) From Rhizomes

Nursery plants can also be raised form rhizomes by splitting them into smaller segments with atleast two nodes. Thus from a single healthy rhizome, 10-20 plantlets can be raised.

Rhizome segments are pretreated with 0.3% bavistin to check any attack of fungal organism and sown in nursery beds at 10 × 10 cm distance in the month of November. Plantlests appear by the end of April next. With this method, during first year sprouting percentage of 60-70% is achieved. Sprouted plants are transplanted to field, same year whereas, unsprouted, healthy rhizomes segments are left in nursery beds for sprouting in the next season. During winters all precautions are taken to protect them from frost.

TRANSPLANTATION

Healthy seedlings/plantlets are sorted for transplantation in the already prepared fields with overhead shade, to maintain 8 to 12% of full sunlight in the field. Plantation is done at 30 × 30 cm spacing with about 10 cm soil humus cover. Field is watered after transplantation operation.

MANAGEMENT OF CROP

Weeding and irrigation operations are carried out as and when required. As the field is rich in organic matter, so the external application of chemical fertilizers is not recommended. Hong (1982) is of the view that in Korean ginseng also application of chemical fertilizers adversely affects the quality of ginseng.

Depending upon the intensity of sun and season, shade is also increased or decreased. For good sprouting and to ensure aeration, in the subsequent years, it is necessary to loosen the bed soil and also to apply leaf mold as top dressing every year. Also the fallen bed sides are repaired with the furrow soil. During winter months the root stock is protected from frost by grass mulch. Harvesting of the crop is usually carried out in sixth year of plantation in the months of September-October.

DISEASES

It is reported that *Alternaria* blight and other fungal diseases discouraged many growers to cultivate ginseng in America. Indian ginseng is also highly susceptible to rhizome rot caused by *Fusarium* during rainy season, which causes an extensive damage to the crop. Also seedling damping off is observed at nursery stage which is caused by *Rhizoctonia*. In addition it is also attacked by rust (*Uromyces* sp.) and downy mildew. Thrumalachar and Chupp recorded leaf spot of ginseng from a natural population, cuased by *Cercospora panacis*.

Rhizome rot and seedling damping off is controlled by drenching of ginseng field with 0.1% bavistin.

CONCLUSION

Perusal of literature reveal that despite the rich potential of promoting ginseng as a cash crop in Himalayan region, not much has been done in this direction, mainly due to lack of knowledge and information about this plant. The present communication is a modest step towards this end. However there is a need to develop agrotechnology for this crop, for which studies are required to be initiated to generate information on the soil and microclimatic requirements, of this plant, its genetic improvement, mass propagation, disease management, harvest and storage technology. In addition chemical and pharmacological studies are required to be undertaken on all the *Panax* species referred to Indian ginseng after bringing them under cultivation under uniform environmental conditions, to evaluate their comparative efficacy, so as to select the most potential species for general cultivation. This will not only help us in saving valuable foreign exchange but will also help in boosting the economic status of farmers from temperate Himalayas.

14

Annatto – The Natural Colour

INTRODUCTION

Annatto is one of the oldest food colourants which has also been used for colouring textiles like cotton and silk and in cosmetics. It has been prescribed as a medicine for a large number of maladies. Annato has served as a colourant for butter and cheese for over hundred years. The interest in annatto and other natural colours has been increasing over the years since many of the coal-tar dyes have been found to be carcinogenic.

Annatto is obtained from the seeds of the tree *Bixa orellana* Linn. It belongs to the family *Bixaceae* which is native to tropical America and the West Indies and is naturalised in India. It is known in India as Latkan, Japhra, Rangamale and Sandri. The pods of the tree on drying burst out throwing away the seeds and the dye is present in the thin resin coating of the seeds. The chief coluring constituent of the dye is a carotenoid type of pigment, bixin.

CULTIVATION

The plant is cultivated in Brazil, Guiana, Mexico and the Antilles. In India it is reported to be cultivated to a small extent. The plants are found in Karnataka, Tamil Nadu, Andhra Pradesh, Orissa and Maharashtra.

Annato can be propagated by seeds or vegetatively through mature wood cuttings. Generally, the seeds are sown in April and it takes about 8 to 10 days to germinate. The seedlings which are about 20 cm tall are planted immediately after the onset of monsoon. The soil has to be mixed with compost and fertilizer, to avoid deficiency of macro and micro nutrients. About 500 plants can be accommodated in a hectare.

The flowers appear in the last week of August and continue upto the middle of October. There are two types, one with white flowers and green capsules, and the other, with pink flowers and red capsules. After about 30 days the trees bear fruits and after 90 days seeds appear in the capsules. The capsules are ready for harvest by January and it is important to harvest them when a crack is found in the stigma end of the capsule. When the capsule is allowed to burst there is heavy loss of seeds. On an average each plant gives about ½ kg of seed/yr in the third year and 1 kg from fourth to tenth year. After harvesting, the seeds with pinnacles are packed in gunny bags and kept closed for some days. Then they are sun-dried, the seeds are separated by beating with sticks which are further dried and packed in gunny bags for transport.

EXTRACTION METHODS

Various methods have been used for extracting the crude colour and bixin. Butter colour is obtained by treating the seeds with a vegetable oil, like castor oil, preferable at 120°. The extract is then diluted to specifications.

A concentrate containing 20% bixin was obtained by mechanical agitation of the seeds in an airflow using a spouted bed reactor of capacity ~ 50 kg. According to a report chloroform ethanol (25 : 75) (V/V) gave the highest yield of annatto dye. At a 1:4 seed/solvent ratio (W/V) the extraction yield was 76.48% for 3 extractions. Supercit (supercritical) carbon dioxide has also been used for the extraction of the pigment using pressures of 3,000-7,000 psi and temperature range of 40-55°. Maximum solubility of pure bixin is 0.003 and annatto seed pigment 0.26 mg/g of CO_2. Efficiency of annatto pigment extraction was increased in the presence of oil.

A flow sheet has been made for extraction of bixin using ehthyl acetate in a soxhlet extractor. Boiling acetone, alcohol and chloroform have also been used. According to one Japanese patent stabilized bixin preparation was obtained by holding bixin in alcoholic solution at pH 4.5 for one hour before spray-drying. In another process the seeds or crude annatto colour were stirred with aqueous alkali or aqueous alcohol, filtered and pH of the filterate was adjusted to 5-6 to give bixin.

In one process the colourant was extracted by counter-current method using water during simultaneous mechanical friction on the surface of the seeds. The suspension was evaporated in vacuum, which on subsequent drying and powdering, can be used for colouring various foods like candies.

The commercial cheese colour is an alkaline solution which contains nor-bixin (II) and is obtained by using sodium or potassium hydroxide. Powdered nor-bixin has been prepared by spray drying of on an 1 to 2%

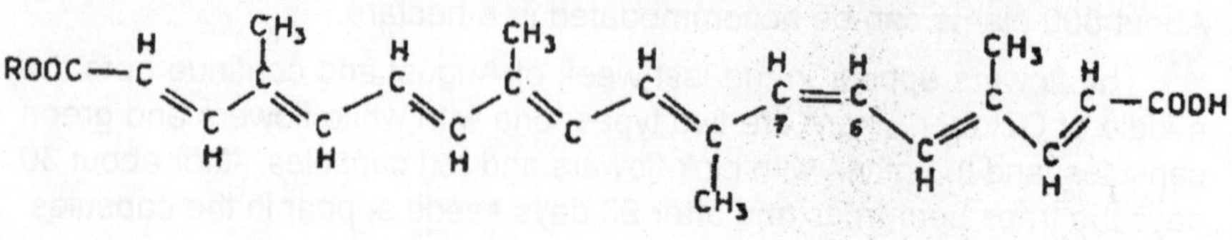

I, R = CH_3 ; II R = H

aqueous alkaline solution using a seed-solution ratio of 1:1 –3 for 10-20 min at ambient temperature (dissolved solid content 10-20° Brix). The spray dryer was operated at an entrance temperature of 150-200° and an exit temperature of 80-100°.

Pigment suitable for use in feed and food was obtained by water extraction after treating the seeds with 1 α-glycosidase.

COMPOSITION AND CHEMISTRY

Bixin (I) is the chief coluring constituent. The proportion of bixin varies from 10-12% of annatto colour. Special grades containing 15-30% are also known. Orellin is a yellow substance. The seeds contain a small amount of fatty oil. The seed coat contains a wax like substance (3%) which is toxic and paralyses intestinal parasites and the embryo. From the oleoresin of *B. orellana* all E-geranylgeraniol has been obtained to the extent of 57% or ~ 1% of the weight of dry seeds, which makes it the richest known source of the important c-20 terpene alcohol. Other compounds isolated include farnesyl acetate, geranylgeranyl octadecanoate, geranyl geranyl formate, δ-tocotrienol and an apocarotenoid. β-carotene, crysptoxanthin, lutein. Zeaxanthin A have been tentatively identified by co-t.l.c. It is claimed that annatto seed is good source of vitamin A because of the presence of β-carotene. The composition of Brazilian annatto seeds is given in Table 1.

Table 1: Composition of annatto seed

Characteristic	*(%)*
Protein	12.13-13.12
Ether solubles	5.22-8.84
Pentosans	11.35-14.97
Pectin	0.23-0.55
Ash	5.44-6.92
Total carotenoids	1.21-2.30
β-Carotene	11.30
Crude fibre	14-40

The vitamin and mineral content, as well as the fibre fraction, are very similar to those determined in cereals but with a high level of carotenoids. The seeds on steam distillation yields a pungent smelling essential oil (0..08%) which gets polymerished quickly. The composition of the essential oil obtained from Indian seeds is given in Table 2.

Isocutellarein was isolated from the hot water extracts of the seeds, which was found to have potent inhibitory activity towards lens aldose reductase. The fatty acid composition was reported to vary depending upon the difference in ecological conditions.

Table 2: Composition of essential oil

Compound	(%)
Ishwarane	30.7
α-Pinene	9.3
β-Pinene	4.8
α-Elemene	3.3
Valencene	2.7
Amorphene	0.2

Natural bixin has a Z-configuration between 6 and 7 carbons. It crystallises as violet prisms and melts at 198°. It is extremely sensitive to iodine, in light, to give all-E-bixin. They differ in their solubilities and form the basis for oil-soluble and water-soluble annatto colour respectively. Ethyl bixin is used for colouring foods such as margarine, whereas methyl bixin has a poor tinctorial value. Esters of bixin with higher alcohols like amyl, octyl, octadecyl, decyl etc. have been prepared to be used as colouring agents.

Bixin has been converted to a yellow colouring material, by heating with acetic acid in the presence of acetic anhydride, for colouring margarine. m-Xylene, a product of degradation of bixin and methyl bixin, has been detected in commercial samples of annatto colour.

Ishwarane and ethyl gallate, leucocyanidin, ellagic acid, 7-bisulphates of apigenin and luteolin and 8-bisulphate of hypolactin (I-OH luteolin) have been isolated from the leaves of the plant whereas tomentosic acid from the root.

Chemotaxonomical studies were made with south Indian Bixaceae and leucoanthocyanidins were found to be present in all the taxa. The distribution patterns of free amino acids phenolic compounds were studied.

STABILITY

Light was found to be the most destructive agent, followed by benzoyl peroxide. Air was much less effective in promoting loss of colour. Ascorbyl palmitate effectively retarded the destructive effect of light.

DETECTION AND ANALYSIS

Bixin was determined by a reproducible spectrophotometric method at 5.50 nm, following chloroform extraction in a tissue homognizer equipped with a porous glass filter to facilitate the separation of the extract. Using a Zorbax ODS column and solvent systems like water/THF AND THF annatto pigments were separated by high performance liquid chromatography. For the effective separation of annatto carotenoids by column chromatography a 1:1 mixture of silica and diatomaceous earth was used with stepwise elution of solvents with increasing polarity.

In column chromatography bixin is strongly absorbed by alumina, even in the presence of fat. Other carotenoids and artificial colours are not retained by the column.

Detection of annatto on paper is done by using antimony trichloride which gives a blue-green colour. If the dye is present in the lipid phase, it is first saponified and filtered from the unsaponified matter. The filtrate is used for running the chromatogram. Bixin can be detected by the green colour in the carr-price reaction using isopropyl alcohol for elution. With alumina-treated paper petroleum ether-chloroform (4:1) was used as solvent system.

Amyl acetate was used as solvent system for t.l.c. To increase polarity 1% HoAC has been added. For the detection of annatto in citrus juices the sample is extracted with petroleum-ether alcohol (20: 10: 13) and the extract was evaporated. The residue was passed on an alumina column and then subjected to t.l.c. using petroleum ether-benzene-acetone-acetic acid (80: 20: 2:1). In the case of margarine the colour was first extracted with acetone and then subjected to t.l.c. using hexaneacetone-ethanol (20: 6: 1). Colour was developed with H_2SO_4, HNO_3, $SbCl_3$ in $CHCl_3$, $SbCl_5$ in $SnCl_2$ in CCl_4 in EtOH (100° for 5-10 min).

UTILIZATION

Annatto is used in India generally for colouring butter. About 1 ml of the commercially available caster oil solution is sufficient for 1 kg of butter. For colouring cheese dilute alkaline solution of annatto, which contains nor-bixin, is used. In other countires annatto or ethyl bixinate in oil medium is used for colouring margarine. It is also used for colouring citrus juices, concentrates, drinks, Vienna sausages, candies, etc. Processes are described for colouring cereal-based products, egg noodles and fish, particularly salmon. A browning composition has been prepared from annatto for uncooked food and which can be used also during cooking. A yellow, transparent water soluble ink, stable to heat, hydrogen peroxide and UV light has been prepared from annatto extracts. A hair dye which has anti-inflammatory and provitamin A properties has been extracted from annatto seeds. This extract has also been used in cosmetic compositions, shampoos etc. A 0.1% solution of bixin in ethanol has been used as an adsorption indicator in argentometric titrations. Coloured coating materials have been made with cellulose acetate-phthalate for tablets, pills, granule, etc. An orange red dye has been prepared for use in Kalamkari painting on cotton and wool textiles. This was found to have good colour fastness in washing, sunlight, perspiration testing and pressing.

15

Neem (*Azadirachta indica* A. Juss.)

INTRODUCTION

Neem (*Azadirachta indica* A. Juss.) is a large evergreen tree which is native to Indian sub-continent. It grows in almost all parts of India except under continuously low temperature conditions as in the upper Himalayas. It is also observed to avoid areas of high rainfall. After revelation of its unique medicinal and other uses over the past century, the neem has been introduced in other south-east Asian countries, tropical Australia, Africa, central and south America, Fiji, Pepua New Guinea, Brunei, Philippines, Mauritius, the Caribbean, Puerto Rico, the Virgin Islands, Sudan, Nigeria etc. Recently it has been introduced in Saudi Arabia.

Use of them to ward off damage by pests is known since antiquity. Ancient Indian folk mixed dried neem leaves with grain meant for storage. Interest in neem research for pest control was triggered after the health hazards and adverse ecological effects of chemical pesticides were recognized. It was 1962 when Pradhan and his associate first time discovered the antifeedant action of neem seed extracts to locusts. Since then lot of literature has been published on its pesticidal properties and other useful attributes for medication and health care. Recent two publications on "Neem Research and Development" and "Botanical Pesticides in Integrated Pest Management" cover various aspects of neem namely, botany, chemistry, genetic diversity, bio-activity, use in health care and medication toxicology etc. This article reports recent advanced in neem research for pest management, neem-based products that have been developed and some promising areas for future research.

CHEMISTRY OF KNOWN PESTICIDAL MOLECULES IN NEEM

Chemistry of neem has been recently dealt by Devakumar and Sukhdev. The bioactive compounds in neem can be classified into 2 categories viz. isoprenoids and others. The latter comprise glycerides, polysaccharides, sulphurous compounds, flavonoids and their glycosides, amino acids etc.

Siddiqui first isolated 3 bitter principles namely, nimbin, nimbidin and nimbinin from its oil. Several new compounds were discovered later. Salamin, a terpenoid possessing feeding deterrent activity. Another compound, Meliantriol, which has similar property. More than 50 compounds with anti-pest activity have been identified from various parts of neem tree and still many more remain unknown.

Among the various compounds known so far, *Azadirachtin* reported by Butterworth and Morgan is the most powerful which possesses not only feeding deterrency but also growth disrupting potential. Moreover, its yield is the highest making it attractive for practical use. The chemical structure of azadirachtin remained controversial till through X-Ray crystallography reported it as given in Fig 1. Future research on identification of bioactive compounds is expected to be rewarding.

PEST CONTROL USES

Neem products have been tested for various properties against more than 300 species of insects, throughout the world In India, it has been evaluated against 106 species of insects, 12 species of nematodes and atleast 9 species of fungi. Among insects the maximum number is from Lepidoptera (32) followed by Cleopatra (28), Hemiptera (23), Diptera (12), Orthoptera (6), Thysanoptera (2), Hymenoptera (1), Siphonaptera (1) and Isoptera (1). Neem products could be used as:

(1) Antifeedant
(2) Repellent
(3) Insecticide
(4) Growth disruptor
(5) Oviposition deterrent
(6) Antifecundity agent
(7) Attractant
(8) Nematicide
(9) Anti-microbial

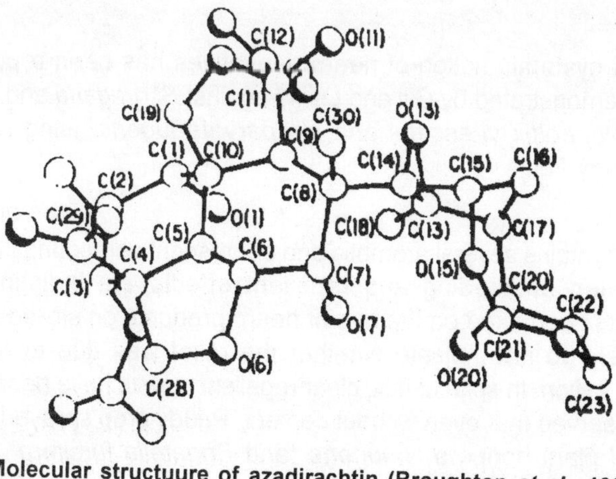

Fig.1–Molecular structuure of azadirachtin (Broughton *et al.*, 1986)

Antifeedant

The most pronounced effect of neem derivatives against insects is their antifeeding effect, which is often indistinguishable from repelling effect. Feeding deterrancy was first recorded by Mann and Burns who observed uniqueness of *Melia azadirachta* not being eaten by locusts (*Schistocerca gregaria*). Clear presence of feeding deterrent in neem was first demonstrated by Pradhan *et al.*, to desert locust (*S. gregaria*) and migratory locusts (*Locusta migratoria*) at the Indian Agricultural Research Institute, New Delhi. As low as 0.1% fresh neem seed powder mixed in water was able to provide complete protection to the treated foliage under field conditions. Since then it forms a standard and most reliable recommendation for protection of agricultural crops from locust invasions.

Antifeeding effect of neem derivatives varies with the insects species, stage of growth of the test insect and the dose. Most insects can be deterred from feeding by less than 0.5% neem seed suspension in water, though some may require as high as 3%. Neem oil has negligible antifeeding effect and hence requires high concentrations. It has been demonstrated that 12% neem oil emulsion when sprayed on paddy suppresses/avoids feeding by brown plant hopper *Nilaparvata lugen* Stal. However, such a high dose makes the findings less exciting.

Based on bio-assay tests, it has been concluded that the active principles can be best extracted in ethanol followed by water. Free solubility in water meant that home made highly effective formulation can be easily prepared with water. This should be reckoned as very valuable observation to take safe plant protection to the poor rural masses with their still crude methods of farming.

Effect of storage on the antifeedant activity is not fully studied. It is, however, known that the activity deteriorates faster in powdered seed than in whole seeds.

Limited systemic action of neem derivatives has been reported. This has been demonstrated by Gill and Lewis against *S. gregaria* and by Saxena *et al.*, on *Nephottix virescens* and *Nilaparvata lugens* using neem seed cake in paddy fields.

Repellent

Neem contains several aromatic and adorescent compounds which repel insects. Often antifeeding and repellent effects are indistinguishable. Experiments conducted on the use of neem products on stored grain or on crops largely do not indicate whether the relief was due to repellent or antifeedant action. In spite of this, clear repellent effects have been observed. Saxena observed that even without contact. Paddy crop sprayed with neem oil repelled plant hoppers *N. lugens* and *Sogatella furcifera*. It has also been observed that white ants (*Microtermes* sp.) and some species of ants do not like the neem scent and move away from the treated vicinity. Neem cake has been used since long in Madhya Pradesh for clearing termite-infested areas. Further studies on this line and on oviposition by insects could be rewarding.

Insecticide

Insecticidal activity as discussed here refers strictly to contact action or immediate stomach toxicity and excludes death of insects due to various other effects of rather latent nature. By and large neem has weak insecticidal activity even in its purified compounds like azadirachtin. Water suspension of NSK was reported toxic to soft bodied insects like aphids.

'Neem oil extractives', a waste from neem oil refining has been found to be effective mosquito larvicide. The material acts as instant killer of the first instar larvae of *Culex fatigans* at 0.04% concentration whereas at lower concentrations it had delayed toxicity. As low as 0.005% neem oil extractive was effective in causing 100% mortality of the Ist stage larvae before they could emerge as adults. Delayed toxicity as described here may be due to mere starvation or some unknown physiological reasons. The efficacy as observed here has opened an outlet for remunerative disposal of this waste product. Incidentally, it has been found to be safe to natural enemies of mosquito larvae like *Gambusia* fish and Tadpoles at normal dosage.

Growth Disruptor

It is said that prevention is better than cure. If we can check the build up of insect population, there would be no need for applying any chemical control methods which often cause adverse ecological effects. Neem derivatives have been demonstrated to possess lethal effects on insects by upsetting the natural hormonal balance causing growth disruption. These effects include prolonging/reducing the normal moulting period in larvae causing death even before pupating or during pupation. Similar effects in nymphal moults as in larval moults in case of those insects which do not pupate, emergence of abnormal forms such as larvae, pupal or pupal adult intermediates or miniature adults with deformed reproductive organs and reduced life span. These latent effects cause progressive decline in insect population leading to its total inhalation in due course of time. In fact, neem should be credited for this silent pest control property.

Growth disrupting activity of neem was first reported by McMillan *et al.*, on *Spodoptera frugiperda* and *Heliothis zea* with chloroform extract of leaves of *Melia azedarach*, a close relative of neem. Growth disrupting effects of extracts of neem seed kernel were later reported on *Pieris brassicae. Epilachna varivestis, Leptinotarsa decemlineata* and *Plutella xylostella, Culex fatigans* and *C. pipiens.* Among other derivatives, neem oil is known to interfere in normal growth processes of insects. Saxena (1987) reported ecdysial failures and other development deformities on rice bug, *Leptocorisa oratorius.*

Neem leaves, seed kernel powder, cake and oil when mixed with stored grains protected them from damage by inhibiting growth, development and emergence of adults.

Precise studies on insect growth regulatory effect have been conducted using azadirachtin. The mode of action of azadirachtin is not yet clear. It is known to reduce and delay titre of morphogenic hormones. It is also suggested to be interfering with neuroendocrine system which controls ecdysone and juvenile harmones. More investigation are required to elucidate the mechanism of its action.

Ovicide

Ovicidal effect of neem derivatives is little known. It was reported that Trialeurodes eggs laid on the leaves of brussel sprouts sprayed with 1% neem and seed suspension either did not hatch or the larvae died in egg shells partially hatched. Similarly eggs of *Stomoxys* incubated on filter paper moisterned with 0.01% azadirachtin did not hatch. These studies indicate that growth disrupting factor penetrated the egg shell and affected the developing embryo. This should be considered as a very valuable observation for the practical pest management and deserves extensive research.

Oviposition Deterrent

Neem contains a variety of chemicals which interfere in normal mating behaviour of insects and may deter them from laying eggs on the treated surface. Disruption of normal courtship signals and mating behaviour has been reported on *N. lugens* when caged on plants sprayed with 3% neem oil emulsion. At higher concentration of oil, the females did not call at all and consequently the males could not locate the females. A few females that emitted signals were not in tune with male calls and the duration of the calls were decreased significantly. Neem oil deterred egg laying by *N. lugens. Amrasca devastans, Bemesia tobaci* and pulse beetle, Callosobruchus sp. Extract of neem seed kernel, caused 90%, oviposition deterrency of *Heliothis armigera* on chick pea under laboratory conditions.

Antifecundity Effect

Neem products are known to reduce fecundity and hatchability of insect eggs. This has been reported in case of rice green hopper, *Nephotettix virescens* cucurbit fruit fly. *Dacus cucurbitae* and *D. dorsalis.* Drastic reduction in the fecundity was observed in *Spodoptera litura* following azadirachtin treatment. Untreated moths laid as many as 7,923 eggs whereas only 705 eggs were laid by 5 pairs of azadirachtin treated moths the reduction being almost 90%. This property has a great role to play in gradual, rather invisible, reduction of insect population in practical pest control.

Attractant

Neem leaves attract the adults of white grub (*Holotrichia* sp.) which are serious leaf defoliators of several species. The grubs damage tubers and roots of several crops. Neem has been successfully utilized for control of this pest. Neem twigs with leaves are inserted in rows in the infested pockets around sunset time at the start of monsoon. At dust, swarms of these beetles which normally come out to feed on foliage of various plants, are attracted to these twigs where these are mechanically killed. The nature of the attractant is not yet known.

Nematicide

The potential of neem for the control of plant parasitic nematodes has been exhaustively reviewed recently by Alam. Only some relevant information is included here.

Utility of neem and its derivatives for nematode control has now been established beyond doubt for management of nematode problem. Among different neem materials, neem cake has proved to be the most effective in controlling various nematode species. In addition, it has several merits over synthetic nematicides, none of which could gain popularity for large scale use. Neem cake is eco-friendly product in true sense. It is biodegradable, plant-based, non-polluting, nutritionally rich manure which improves soil structure and fertility, and is ecologically safe. It is remarkably cheap and easy to apply uniformly in the soil. Hence, neem cake is the finest material known today for practical control of nematodes.

In addition to neem cake, the leaves, the root. The flower, the bark and the gum have also been reported to possess nematicidal properties. The nematicidal effect of neem cake often lasts for 2 cropping seasons.

Effectiveness of neem cake has been found to be better or at least comparable to synthetic nematicides. Seed treatment with synthetic systemic nematicides before sowing in the soil treated with neem cake has proved still more effective. For example, treatment of seeds of mung and lentil with fensulfothion and phorate respectively and then sown in soil amended with neem cake was found to be highly effective method for control of plant parasitic nematodes.

It has been observed that application of N, P and K alone as fertilizer to soil results in marked increase of plant parasitic nematodes. But if applied in combination with neem cake, the population dwindles slowly and steadily.

Neem possesses a variety of chemicals and it is not difficult to imagine that the crude neem derivatives will exert their effect in several ways. Based on these data and theories put up to explain that the mode of action by various scientists are as follows:

1. Change in the physical and chemical properties of soil inimical to nematodes.
2. Release of plant nutrients which accelerate rapid root development and overall plant growth thus helping the plant to escape nematode attack.
3. Induction of resistance/tolerance in plant roots against plant-parasitic nematodes.
4. Nemato-toxic substances present in the amendments are released after dissolving in water.
5. Increase in predaceous and parasitic activity of soil biota.
6. Toxicants are produced during microbial decomposition.
7. Metabolites of microbes which become active during decomposition of organic amendments are toxic to plant-parasitic nematodes.

Anti-pathogen/Anti-microbial

Neem is already well known to possess curing property for skin and viral infections of human beings and animals. This has now been checked on plants. The information available has been reviewed recently by Parveen and Alam. It is now well established that the neem possess some fungicidal and antiviral potential. The growth of *Fusarium oxysporum* f. sp. *Ciceri, Rhizoctonia solanii,* and some other soil-borne fungal pathogens of chickpea (*Cicer arietinum*) was inhibited in the liquid medium containing extracts of leaf, trunk, bark, fruit pulp and oil of neem. Chickpea seeds treated with neem oil sown in soil infested with pathogens produced disease free seedlings, whereas all the seedlings from untreated seeds exhibited disease symptom.

Leaf extract of neem has been reported to successfully control the fruit rot disease of cucurbitaceous plants and fungal diseases of groundnut.

Neem oil 1% and 10% emulsion sprays were able to inhibit the growth of *Alternaria alternata* by 61% and 100%, respectively. Neem seed cake (2%) reduced muskmelon wilt caused by *Fusarium solanii* by 80%. Pant *et al.*, reported that some sulphur compounds present in neem leaves possess the reported fungicidal activity.

Attention is drawn here to our failure in controlling fungal diseases that infest the crops virulently during rainy season. Attempts to control by spraying chemical fungicides are almost infructuous as the chemical ir quickly washed away by repeated rains. Neem oil, if effective, holds great promise under such circumstances. Late potato blight spread by *Phytophthora infestans* and apple scab are cases in view. Both these diseases cost millions of rupees to potato and apple growers and still without much success. Neem oil is worth testing in such cases.

Anti-viral property of some neem derivatives has been reported. The anti-viral effect is either through inhibiting the virus growth or indirectly by killing the insect vector. The nimbidin and nimbin, obtained from neem oil were active against potato virus. Inhibitory effects of extracts of neem were found on spinach mosaic virus on the host *Chenopodium amaranticolor.* There are several reports where use of neem derivatives has reduced the viral infection by controlling the insect vector particularly on rice.

There is practically no information on the use of neem against plant pathogenic bacteria. Nevertheless, there is a great need and scope for work and optimism for success in this line.

Inhibition of pesticide degradation in soil has been reported by Ravi Prasad. This finding provides a clue to develop insecticide granules with regulated release by using neem derivatives or other antimicrobial agents, an entirely new approach.

TOXICOLOGICAL AND ECOLOGICAL EFFECTS

Effects on man

Neem derivatives except neem oil, are practically non-toxic. Alcohol and aqueous extracts of seeds have no oral or dermal toxicity to mammals. Sodium nimbidinate did not produce any local or general side effect on human beings. However, neem oil toxicity has been reported. It produced symptoms like vomiting, diarrhoea, nausea and general discomfort. In Malaysia acute poisoning of over a dozen infants was reported after injestion of 5 ml of neem oil. Another death of a 4 months infant given 12 ml of margosa oil for 2 successive days has been reported. It was, however, suspected that contamination of oil with aflatoxin might have synergised the toxicity. There are reports of renal failure in Ghanians who were drinking leaf tea for malarial treatment. It is hence concluded that neem oil in particular needs to be used with proper care and precautions, though its toxicity and *per se* in negligible as compared to synthetic pesticides.

Ecological Effects

Neem products are ecologically safe at doses much above the normally used. Higher doses have, however, been reported to be toxic in some cases particularly to the aquatic life. Neem oil extractive at 0.005% was non-toxic to insectivorous fish *Gambusia* sp. But caused 100% kill at 0.04% concentration. This concentration (0.04%) was also toxic to tadpoles causing 80% mortality in 24 hours and 100% in 2 days. However, this material was non-toxic at 0.01% concentration. Margosan-0 is also reported to have mild toxicity to rainbow traut and bluegill sun fish but has been reported to be benign to honey bees at well above the recommended doses of 20 ppm foliar spray.

Avian toxicity studies have been carried on poultry birds by feeding them water extract of neem seed kernels. This caused severe hepatitis and mild to severe nephritis. Interestingly, neem barriers are favourite fruit of certain tropical birds in Nigeria and Kenya.

The above studies indicate that neem products need to be used with due care in aquatic bodies whereas these are reasonably safe for use in other ecosystems.

NEEM IN PARTICLE PEST CONTROL

As discussed in preceding section, the neem possesses about a dozen pest control properties and the neem products are ecologically safe. In spite of this, it has not yet been widely adopted for pest control. The main reasons for its low profile are:

(i) Most entomologists have evaluated the success of neem derivatives on the basis of their instant killing ability *vis-à-vis* that of synthetic chemicals. It is well-known that neem is a weak instant killer for most of insect species. It rather acts slowly over long periods by exerting its other effects like deterring the insects from feeding, discouraging egg laying, disrupting normal growth etc. so that ultimately the population declines but steadily. This has not been adequately appreciated. Long-term studies on the, population dynamics with repeated application of the test material are required to assess the real success.

Integrated pest management aims ultimately at saving the crop from pest ravages and increasing the yield. The assessments carried so far did not often go into in-depth cost-benefit analysis which take into account the advantage accrued due to repellency, feeding deterrency, overall reduction in population, enhanced crop growth (due to application of materials like neem cake which serves as nitrogen regulator and excellent manure) plus the ecological benefits. Ignorance of all these factors have put other products at unfair advantage over neem products.

(ii) *Lack of Suitable Commercial Formulations*: This is the age of readymade goods now. People have little patience to collect, process and preserve neem materials and prepare the formulations themselves. There is a need for commercial formulations based on neem derivatives. Recently some formulations have been put up in the market, which are struggling to make a place for themselves. Main problem with these formulations is their short shelf-life. All plant products tend to degrade with time unless properly formulated.

Not only that, the material when applied on the crop is susceptible to thermal and photo degradation and later to microbial degradation. Hence formulation technology assumes special significance.

(iii) *Technology Transfer:* No technology becomes popular unless adequately demonstrated. Hardly any training programme is arranged by the State Agriculture departments or Central Government agencies for repairing simple yet effective formulations from neem at farm level. Publicity and demonstrations on TV are totally ignored Govt. incentives are rare. Under such a scenario, a strong push is required for technology transfer by all the agencies involved.

With all this, environmental problems associated with use of chemical pesticides have created special interest in neem products. Considerable work has been recently done to use neem derivatives either alone or in combination with other methods of control for management of various pests of rice, cotton, groundnut, tobacco and vegetables as well as mosquito in malaria control. These are the cases where significantly large quantities of pesticides are used and still without much success.

On rice, field experiments have demonstrated reasonably good control of gall midge, *Orseolia oryzae* W-M, leaf folder, *Cnaphalocrocis medinalis,* brown leaf hopper *Nilaparvata lugens* and green leaf hopper, *Nephotettix virescens*, earhead bug, *Leptocoriza oratorius*, stem borer, *Scirpophage incertulas*. On cotton, neem oil emulsion and neem seed or neem cake extract have been found to give satisfactory control of cotton while fly, *Bemesia tobaci*, cotton boll worm, *Helicoverpa armigera*. Neem cake/seed extract has been reported to be highly effective against *Spodoptera litura* to protect. Neem seed kernel has been found to be effective against pod borer of gram, *Heliothis armigera*. Methanolic extract deoiled cake or 2% neem seed kernel suspension sprayed at 10 days interval was highly effective in protecting tobacco from caterpillar, *Spodoptera litura*. Neem derivatives have been found to control various pests of vegetables particularly the aphids and fruit borers. Neem cake as the most effective material known today for nematode control has already been discussed.

Malaria control in India is at cross roads due to development of resistance among the mosquito species to DDT and HCH and increasing cost of these chemicals. Neem derivatives provide successful control of larvae. Neem oil has also been shown to break DDT resistance among the mosquitoes. In spite of these merits, it has not been possible to popularize the use of neem products for malaria control. The reason is that malaria control is largely based on chemical control rather than on integrated multi-method approach and this is true in case of all other crop pests.

16

Some Endangered Medicinal Plants

INTRODUCTION

Every year thousands of tonnes of medicinal herbs are collected from forest land and traded to foreign countries. The trade in medicinal herbs is an important source of revenue of the government and a major source of income to the rural people of the country. The medicinal plants in Nepal lists well over 700 species comprising about 10% of the known vascular plant species of the country. Among these, more than 100 species of medicinal herbs are currently exploited for the commercial purpose. Over 60% of the total export of herbs is to India with whom trade links have prevailed since time immemorial. The varied natural resource of medicinal herbs is not only an item of export, these also have been playing an important role in the health care of native people. About 85% of the rural Nepalese population still use traditional herbal remedies utilising the local plant resource. These remedies are fairly well accepted, easily available, bearing a minimum cost and, in most of the cases, are the only available means. Therefore, native herbs play an invaluable role in the health services of the Nepalese population. However, medicinal herbs, Nepal's major export and foreign exchange earner, and the most vital source of folk medicaments, are in deep trouble, most of which are even endangered.

CAUSES OF THREAT

A. Deforestation

Tropical hardwood has dominated the trade based on natural resource in Nepal since more than a century and this trend has very recently declined because of the depletion of timber reserves from the natural forests through logging and conversion of forest land to other uses. Apart from industrial and commercial uses, forests are also destroyed as it is the major source of fuelwood and construction materials. Population pressure and the so-called developmental activities are causing a rapid depletion of forest in every part of the country. As the forests are destroyed, countless plant species face considerable danger of extinction.

B. Forest Fires

Occasionally, forests are subjected to fire to obtain dead tress for fuelwood and construction materials, and also to extend the area of the adjoining agricultural lands. Forests fires, especially those in the high-altitude pine (*Pinus wallichiana*) forest are set to enhance the growth and yield of the high priced morel mushrooms (*Morchella conica*, *Morchella esculenta*, etc.) The Pastures are regularly subjected to fire to produce tender grasses. As a consequence, many valuable herbs flourishing in those open habitats are indiscriminately destroyed. It also destroys the alpine butterfly belonging to the genus *Leptropteris* whose larvae are the host for the highly reputed medicinal fungus *Cordyceps sinensis*, ultimately threatening even the fungus. Mostly the fires are beyond control, resulting in severe loss of the forest, destroying the herbs, roots and rhizomes at ground level and even the clumps. Organic matter of the upper layer of the soil is usually destroyed resulting in the retardation or even the extinction of many valuable plant species in the area.

C. Shifting Cultivation

The shifting cultivation, another form a destruction of forests, called 'Khorea phandne' is identical to the 'Jhumming' system of agriculture practiced in Meghalaya, India. A patch of the climax forest is destroyed, burnt and used for farming for some years after which it is abondoned and the farmers shift to another forest area, cleaning another patch of the climax vegetation. This practice results in the destroying of a large number of biological species and the abandoned land is mostly succeeded by a few number of sporadic species that are quite different from the original vegetal cover.

D. Over-grazing

The livestock population in rural localities exceeds far more the human population and the shortage of fodder and other feeding materials resulting in the over-grazing in the pastures has been contributing not only to the deplition of natural vegetal cover but also to the retardation of plants including the medicinal herbs in the region.

E. Over-exploitation

Medicinal herbs are regarded as a free commodity to be collected from nature. Every year thousands of tones of medicinal herbs including roots and rhizomes are collected from forest land and traded to foreign countries. The trade in non-timber forest products has long been an important source of income to the rural people of the country, estimated in the order of ten million US dollars per year.

The traders provide easy credit to the rural people and are interested in obtaining the largest volume possible. The local collectors therefore find themselves in debt to the traders and to pay the debt must meet the collection demands of the traders. The consequence, raw materials are over-harvested when, for example, immature plants, roots, tubers and rhizomes are taken or overpruning are done. This destroys the region's natural resources and gradually particular species have become more difficult to find in a given locality where once they flourished.

Apart from the commercial purposes, a large number of plants that are regularly harvested for local uses like medicine, food, fodder, fibre, dye, tan, gum, etc., also have severely affected the natural regeneration, habitat destruction and the very existance of many medicinal herbs in many areas.

SOME ENDANGERED MEDICINAL PLANTS

In the following enumeration fourteen medicinal plants, supposed to be most endangered in Nepal due to various factors mentioned earlier, has been dealt in an alphabetical order according to their Latin names. For each species, its common synoname and family are given in succession. It is followed by the common names of the species consisting of English (E), Hindi (H), Nepali (N), and Sanskrit (S) names, where available. A brief account of the habit and habitat of each plant is given, followed by the phytochemical characteristics and a review on medicinal uses with literature sources. The voucher specimens of the considered plants, collected by the author in different parts of the country, can be found in the National Herbarium (KATH), located at Godawari, Lalitpur district, Nepal.

1. *Acorus calamus* L. Araceae

Common names: Sweet flag (E), Batch, Ghobach (H) Bojho (N). Vachara (S).

A semi-aquatic perennial found in the tropical to the temperate regions (200m-300m) in marshy and moist situations.

Chemical Constituents

The rhizome contains glucosides scarin and acorin, and essential oil; the essential oil contains calamen, calamenol, calamenon, ascarone, asaryl aldehyde, eugenol, pinene and camphene.

Medicinal Uses

A piece of the rootstock is chewed to relieve throat infection it is said to act as an expectorant; it is also used to relieve cough and colds; it is also used as mesticatory for toothache.

A paste of the rootstock is considered antiseptic to wounds in man and cattle.

A warm decoction of the rootstock is used to wash the mouth to treal gingivitis, pyorrhoea and scury.

A warm decoction of the rootstock is sipped to exhibit in anthelmintic action; it is also taken to relieve bronchitis. The rhizome is taken to cure fever dysentery, brenditis and asthma; it is also considered useful in abdominal pains inflammations, neck pains and to improve appetite.

The rhizome juice mixed with sesame oil (*Sesamum indicum* L.) is massaged over chest to relieve chest pains.

The rhizome is carminative, emetic, expectorant, tonic and stimulant. It is said to be effective in dysentery and snake bite.

The rootstock is crushed with salt, diluted in water and prescribed to cattle to relieve dyspepsia.

The rootstock is boiled with goat's milk and drunk to relieve infantile diarrhoea.

The rootstock is crushed with honey and orally prescribed to children to improve vocabulary.

The rootstock is crushed with rape oil (*Brassica rapa* L.) and applied on the anus to relieve piles.

The rootstock is crushed with neem leaves (*Azadirachta indica* A. Juss.) and eaten to facilitate expectoration and to relieve sore throats.

A decoction of the rootstock prepared together with neem leaves is said to act as an expectorant. It is said to possess antipyretic property and also used to relieve colic pains.

It is an aromatic bitter tonic and carminative; it possesses emetic and anti-spasmodic properties; it produces beneficial results in case of dyspepsia and chronic diarrhoea.

Powdered rhizome is used as vermifuge.

Alcoholic extract of the plant has sedative and analgesic effects and causes moderate depression in blood pressure.

Rhizome form an ingredient of several Ayurvedic and Unani medicinal preparations.

Other Uses

The powdered rhizome possesses insecticidal properties and useful against bed-bugs., moths, lice, etc.

The crushed plant is used to wash head to kill lice rhizomes are used in flavouring gin, beer, drinks and other foodstuffs; essential oil obtained from the leaves is used by perfumers of hair powder.

2. *Asparagus racemosus* Willd,; Liliaceae

Common names; Asparagus (E), Satavari, Satawar, Satmuli (H), Kurilo, Satawari (N), Shatavari (S).

A woody much branched, spinous climber found in the tropical to temperate regions (200 m – 300 m) in forests and shrubberies.

Chemical Constituents

Plant contains sarsapogenin and glucoside.

Medicinal Uses

The tender shoots are eaten raw as an antipyretic drug.

A decoction of the tender shoots is considered a vital tonic which is prescribed to convalescents and post-natal mothers.

Decoction of the bark is used in amoebic dysentery.

The root paste is eaten as an antipyretic drug; it is also used as an antiseptic to wounds.

The root powder is given to women during labour paints to facilitate delivery.

The root decoction is taken to relieve diarrhoea and dysuria; it is also considered a vital tonic; it is also eaten to relieve stomach complaints.

The semi-roasted root is taken with milk to relieve dysuria.

The root is used medicinally as a refrigerant, demulcent, diuretic, aphrodisiac, antispasmodic, alterative, antidiarrhoeatic and antidysenteric.

The root is used by native physicians as a stimulant and restorative.

The root is said to be tonic and diuretic and useful as a galactagogue.

Roots are used as an ingredient in the preparation for treating impotency; they are used as an aphrodisiac and tonic; it is taken with milk to initiate conception, and also considered an abortifacient.

Roots are used as an aphrodisiac and tonic; they are also used in piles and diseases of eyes.

Root extract is given as a nerve sedative; it is also dropped in the mouth or nose to stop bleeding.

Root is useful in leprosy, rheumatism, gonorrhoea and tuberculosis, and also used as a remedy against amenorrhoea.

A mixture of honey and fresh root is given as a demulcent in dyspepsia.

Root pounded with other plant products is drunk to cure bloody urination and other urinary complaints.

The root is largely used in the preparation of medicated oils, prescribed for nervous and rheumatic complaints. It is also used as an ingredient of many medicines.

The root is used as a demulcent in veterinary medicine.

The fruits are eaten to treat pimples.

Other Uses

Tender shoots are cooked like vegetables; roots are boiled and eaten fresh root is used for the preparation of "Ranu", material used for fermentation.

3. *Cordyceps sinesis* (Berk.) Sacc.,; Hypocreaceae

Common names: Yarsagumba, Jiwanbuti. (N).

A fungus parasitic in a caterpillar (*Lepidopteris* sp.) found in the alpine open slopes (4300 m – 5000 m).

Medicinal Uses

The fruiting bodies are eaten as an aphrodisiac and a tonic; mostly it is eaten with honey or milk.

The fruiting bodies are prescribed to cattle, especially to yaks, as an aphrodisiac.

4. *Dactylorhiza hatagirea* (D. Don) Soo; syn. *Orchis latifolia* L.; Orchidaceae

Common names: Orchis (E), Salap (H), Panchaunle, haslajadi (N).

A perennial ground orchid found in the temperate and sub-alpine Himalaya (2800 m – 4000 m) in shrubberies, open slopes and marshes.

Chemical Constituents

Rhizome contains glucoside

Medicinal Uses

A paste from the rhizome is applied to cuts and wounds for the rapid healing action.

The rhizome are boiled and eaten as a remedy for various types of abdominal pains.

The rhizome is eaten with honey or milk as an aphrodisiac and a tonic.

The tuber is expectorant and astringent.

The tuber is supposed to be nutritious and helpful in diarrhoea, dysentery and chronic fevers.

The tuberous roots, finely powdered and boiled with milk, form a nutritious article of diet and is given in the phthisis, diabetes, chronic diarrhoea and dysentery.

Salep of commerce, consisting of washed, scalded and dried tubers, are used as farinaceous food, nervine tonic and aphrodisiac.

Other Uses

Tubers are eaten raw or boiled.

5. *Daiswa polyphylla* (Sm.) Rafn. Var. *wallichii* Hara; Syn. *Paris polyphylla* J.E. Smith; Liliaceae

Common name: Satuwa (N)

Chemical Constituents

Rhizome contains two glucosides, a-paridin and a-paristyphnin, and sugars.

Medicinal uses

A piece of the root is chewed to heal "internal" wounds below the throat.

The root paste is applied for rapid healing of wounds, boils and carbuncles. It is also applied as an antidote to the bites of poisonous snakes and insects; it is also eaten to alleviate narcotic effects.

The root paste is applied to treat boils and carbuncles; it is also applied to heal open wounds.

The root paste is eaten with honey and milk as a galactagogue and a tonic.

The root powder is taken as an anthelmintic drug; it is also considered useful in fever and diarrhoea.

A decoction of the root is drunk as an anthelmintic can febrifuge.

The glucoside a-paristyphin has a depressant action on carotid, myocardium and respiratory movements.

6. *Fritillaria cirrhosa* D. Don; Liliaceae

Common name: Kakuli (N)

A herbaceous plant found in the temperate to alpine Himalaya (2700 m – 4000 m) in open slopes and shrubberies.

Medicinal Use

The bulbs are made into a paste and applied to wounds as an antiseptic drug; it is also eaten to relieve abdominal pains.

The dried corms are given in asthma, bronchitis, and tuberculosis.

7. *Nardostachys grandiflor* DC.; Syn. *N. jatamansi* DC.; Valerianaceae

Common names: Spikenard (E), Jatamansi, Balchhar (H), Jatamansi, Bhulte (N), Jatamansi (S).

An aromatic perennial herb found in the sub-alpine and alpine regions (3600 m – 4500 m) on screes and rocky slopes.

Chemical Constituents

The rhizome and roots contain volatile essential oil, resin, sugar, starch, bitter extractive matter and gum.

Medicinal uses

The rhizome paste is eaten as a bitter tonic; it is also eaten to treat dysentery.

The rhizome paste is applied to treat piles.

The rhizome is considered tonic, stimulant, antispasmodic, diuretic, deobstruent, emmenagogue, stomachic and laxative.

An infusion of the rhizome is reported to be useful in epilepsy, hysteria, palpitation of heart and cholera.

A itncture of the rhizome is given in intestinal colic and faltulence.

The rhizome is said to have antiseptic and haemostatic properties.

Rhizomes are used as a diuretic, blood purifier, in coughs, ulcers and snake bites; it is considered to be beneficial in low blood pressure. The rhizome is considred to have anthelmintic properties, and also considered useful in cholera and jaundice.

A tincture of the rhizome is used for treating epilepsy, hysteria and convulsions; it is also used as laxative and for improving urination, regulating menstruation and digestion.

The rhizome is used as an aromatic adjunct in the preparation of medicinal oils; it is reported to promote the growth of hair and also impart blackness.

The essential oil possesses antiarrhythmic activity with possible therapeutic usefulness in cases of auricular flutter.

The plant is said to posses all the properties of official valerian (*Valeriana officinalis* L.) and used as a substitute for the same.

Other Uses

The essential oil is largely used in perfumery (48, 81); it is an ingredient of hair washes and hair oils.

The rootstock is used as an auxillary in dyeing along with *Mallotus philippensis* Muell.-Arg.

8. *Picrohiza scrophulariiflora* Penell; Syn. *P. kurroa* Royle ex Benth.; Scrophulariaceae

Common namer: Hellebore (E), Katki, Kuru (H), Kutki, Katuki (N), Katu la, Katuka, Katurohini (S).

A perennial herb found in the sub-alpine and alpine regions (3600 m – 4500 m) on screes and rocky slopes.

Chemical Constituents

Roots contain picrorhizin, kutkin, kurrin, vanillic acid, kutkiol, kutkisterol and picroliv. The constitution of kutkin, the bitter glucoside, has been studied in detail.

Medicinal Uses

The root paste is applied to heal wounds in cattle.

Roots are used in abdominal pains, and as a laxative and purgative. They are said to exhibit anthelmintic properties, and are also used in dyspepsia.

Roots are useful in asthma and jaundice, they are also used in scorpion sting.

The root decoction is drunk as an appetizer, especially to overcome anorexia; it is considered to be a tonic; it is drunk as an antipyretic drug; it is taken to relieve cough and colds, supposed to act as an expectorant.

The root decoction is considered to have galactagogue and anthelmintic properties.

Roots are used as stomachic, tonic and improves appetite and stimulates gastric secretions.

It is considered to be a valuable bitter tonic, almost as efficacious as gentian, *Gentiana kurroo* Royle. Dried rhizomes and roots is used either as an adulterant of or as a substitute for Indian gentian, *Gentiana kurroo*.

It is antiperiodic, cholagogue, stomachic, laxative in small doses and cathartic in large doses; it is reported to have beneficial action in dropsy.

The root decoction is given with salt to febrile cattle as a febrifuge (II); roots are used traditionally in animal treatment.

9. *Podophyllum hexandrum* Royle; Syn. *P. emodi* Wall.; Berberidaceae

Common names: Himalayan May apple (E), Laghupatra (N.S), Papra (H).

A perennial herb found in the temperate to alpine Himalaya (2400 m – 4500 m) in forests, shrubberies and open slopes.

Chemical Constituents

The rhizome contains podophyllin, quercetin, kaempferol, astragalin, as essential oil, wax, and mineral salts. Podophyllin contains podophyllotoxin as the major active constituents. Chemical investigation revealed that the constituents of the rhizomes of Indian podophyllum,

Podophyllum hexandrum, are identical with those of *Podophyllum peltatum*, the American podophyllum.

Medicinal Uses

The ripe fruits considered to be a mild laxative.

Rhizomes and roots are used in fever; they are also considered stimulant and used for increasing bils secretion.

The rhizome paste is applied to treat gynaecological complaints; it is also eaten as a purgative.

The dried rhizomes and roots of *Podophyllum hexandrum* are official in I.P. and B.P. and form the source of a medicinal resin, podophyllin. Podophyllin is listed in various other pharmacopoeias and formulations.

During recent years, the resin podophyllin has acquired special importance for its possible use in controlling some forms of cancer.

Podophyllin is used as stimulant and purgative; it is considered a cholagogue, alterative, emertic and bitter tonic.

Podophyllin is also used in veterinary medicine as a cathartic for dogs and cats; an ointment of podophyllin is employed to remove warts in animals.

Other Uses

The ripe fruits are edible; seeds are used in fermenting a country liquor.

10. *Rauvolfia serpentina* (L.) Benth. Ex Kurz.; Apocynaceae

Common names: Serpentina (E), Chandrabhaga, Sarap gandha, Chota-chand (H), Sarpagandha, Chandmaruwa (N), Sarpagandha, Chandrika (S).

An erect evergreen, small shrub found in the tropical region (upto 1000 m) in forests.

Chemical Constituents

Root contains a large number of alkaloids, oleoresin, starch and calcium oxalate.

Medicinal Uses

The root paste is applied and eaten as an antidote to the bites of poisonous reptiles and stings of insects.

The root paste is eaten to cure malarial fever; it is also considered to be a general febrifuge. It is considered a bitter tonic and narcotic.

Extracts of the root are valued for the treatment of intestinal disorders, particularly diarrhoea, dysentery and also an anthelmintic.

Root extract is used in treatment of mental diseases; it is also given in guiddiness. It is given in high blood pressure.

Decoction of roots and leaves is given to stop vomiting.

Mixed with other plants the roots have been used in the treatment of cholera, colic and fever.

Juice of leaves is used as remedy for opacity of cornea.

In recent years, *Rauvolfia serpentina* and its preparations have become important therapeutic agent, both as antihypertensive and as a sedative; it is employed for relief of various central nervous system disorders associated with psychosis, schizopherenia, insanity, insomnia and epilepsy; extracts of roots are valued for treatment of intestinal disorders; roots are reported to stimulate uterine contraction and is used in child birth.

Rauvolfia serpentina is an official drug in I.P.

11. *Rheum australe* D. Don; Syn. *R. emodi* Wall. Ex Meisn.; Polygonaceae

Common names: Indian rhubarb, Himalayan rhubarb (E), Ravand chini (H), Padamchal, padamchalnu (N), Amlavetasa (s).

Tall perennial found in the sub-alpine and alpine Himalaya (3000 m – 4200 m) on open slopes.

Chemical Constituents

Root contains emodin, a glucoside rhapontien, tannin, resins, mucilage, sugar, starch, pectin, lignin, calcium oxalate and organic salts. Leaves and stem contain oxalic acid, leaves and flowers contain rutin.

Medicinal Uses

The petioles are eaten with salt as an appetizer.

The rhizome paste is used to massage the affected parts to treat rheumatism.

The rhizome paste is used to plaster the affected parts to treat sprains and swellings in man and cattle.

The rhizome paste is eaten with milk as a purgative.

It is used as a purgative, astringent, tonic and also in dyspepsia; it is also used in diarrhoea.

Root powder is sprinkled over ulcers for quick healing; rhizome paste is applied on cuts for the accelerated healing action; it is also used in many veterinary complaints.

Rheum australe is official in I.P.

Other Uses

Powdered roots are used for cleaning teeth.

Roots with madder and potash are used for dyeing fabrics red.

The petioles, leaves, leaf – stocks and flowers are edible.

12. *Rubia manjith* Roxb. Ex Fleming; Syn. *R. cordifolia* L.; Rubiaceae

Common names: Indian madder (E), Manjit, Manjith (H), Majitho (N), Manjistha, Kala-meshika (S).

A herbaceous climbing perennial found in the sub-tropical to temperate Himalaya (1200 m – 2700 m) in forests and marginal lands.

Chemical Constituents

Roots contain resinous and extractive matter, gum, sugar, salts of lime, and colouring matter. Colouring matter consists of purpin, majistin, garanein, alizarin and xanthine. The root also contain small amounts of purpuroxanthin and pseudopurpurin.

Medicinal Uses

The plant is used in rheumatism, pleurisy and other chest complaints.

The root is used as an astringent and tonic; it is also given in urinary troubles.

The roots are useful in eye sores, liver complaints and spleen enlargement; they are also used internally to treat menorrhagia and other menstrual complaints.

Root decoction is used in paralysis and jaundice.

Roots and fruits are used in paralysis, ulcers and skin diseases; the stem is used in cobra bile and scorpion sting; crushed roots are applied for poisonous stings of insects and caterpillars.

The root juice, mixed with ginger, is boiled in milk and drunk warm to relieve menostaxis.

A decoction of the leaves and stem is used as a vermifuge; crushed leaves are applied for ulcers.

Roots form an ingredient of several Ayurvedic preparations.

Other Uses

It is employed for dyeing cotton fabrics, blankets and carpets. The root is also used for colouring medicinal oils.

13. *Swertia chirayita* (Roxb. Ex Fleming) Karsten; Syn. *S. Chirata (Wall.) C.B. Clarke; Gentianaceae*

Common names: Chirata, Chiretta (E), Chireta, Kiryat-charayatah (H), Chitaito (N), Kirata-tikta, Bhunimba (S).

An erect annual herb found in the sub-tropical to temperate Himalaya (1200 m – 3000 m) in shrubberies and open lands.

Chemical Constituents

Plant contains two bitter principles, ophelic acid and chiratogenin, two bitter glucoside, chiratin and amarogentin, gentiopicrin, two yellow crystalline phenols, swerchirin, resin, tannin, and ash.

Medicinal Uses

A decoction of the aerial parts is taken as an antipyretic drug; it is also taken to relieve various types of body aches.

It is considered a tonic, febrifuge, stomachic, laxative, anthelmintic, antidiarrhoeal, useful in anaemia, bronchial asthama and liver disorders.

The plant is used in intermittent fevers and bilious dyspepsia accompanied by fever; it is also used in skin diseases.

The plant is considered stomachic, anthelmintic, appetizer, alterative, antidiarrhoeic, and also considered beneficial in bronchial asthma.

The dried twigs are used as a remedy in malarial fever; it is also used as a blood purifier.

It is an effective substitute for gentian (*Gentiana kurroo*).

It is official in I.P. and was formerly also official in B.P. and U.S.P.

Other Uses

Chiretta is used for dyeing cotton cloth yellow. It is also used in the liquor industry as a bitter ingredient.

14. *Valeriana jatamansi* Jones; Syn. *V. mallichii* DC.; Valerianceae

Common names: Indian valerian (E), Tagar, Mushkbala (H), Sugandhawala, Samayo (N), Tagara (S).

Perennial herb found in the sub-tropical to sub-alpine Himalaya (1500 m – 3600 m) in forests, shrubberies and open slopes.

Chemical Constituents

The rhizome contains tartaric, citric, malic, and succinic acids and a volatile oil.

Medicinal Uses

The root paste is applied on the forehead to relieve severe headache; it is also applied to treat various eye problems.

Roots are stimulant, carminative, antiseptic, effective in epilepsy, neurosis and hysteria, they are also used in diseases of eye, blood, liver, spleen and nervous system; bath of valerian is useful in rheumatism.

The essential oil has tranquilizing properties.

The root juice is used as a nasal drop to overcome nose-bleed; it is also applied to treat gout.

The root juice is diluted in water and used to bath children to relieve "weeping sickness".

It is prescribed as a remedy for hysteria, hypochondriasis, nervous unrest and emotional troubles.

The rhizome is used as a carminative; powdered rhizome, mixed with sugar, is used in urinary troubles; a decoction of the drug is given to mothers after parturition, probably as a sedative.

It forms an ingredient of a number of Ayurvedic recipes.

Valeriana jatamansi is official in I.P.

The plant is said to possess all the properties of official valerian (*Valeriana officinalis* L.), and used as a substitute for the same.

Other Uses

The rhizome is employed for hair oils and perfumes, as incense and as an insect repellant.

17

Nomenclatural Ambiguity of medicinal Plants used in Indigenous Systems of Medicine

Medicinal plants have been used for the treatment of human ailments and suffering since time immemorial. In India, the knowledge of herbal medicine is widespread – ranging from tribal folklore use to age-old practices and closely guarded recipes handed down from generation to generation, to highly evolved systems of medicine like Ayurveda, Siddha and Unani-Tibb.Ayurveda and Siddha have been part of Indian civilization since its inception. The Unani system of medicine was introduced in this country in the 10th century A.D. by Muslim rulers. Later on a number of Ayurvedic plants were adopted by Unani physicians and vice-versa. These systems have served mankind through the centuries and it is certain that for indefinite period more they will continue to be in use.

Of the 20,000 and odd species of plants reported to be growing in India, about 2,500 species have therapeutic value and more than 500 are used in indigenous systems of medicine. A large number of plants listed in pharmacopoeias are not being utilized by the drug industries in the traditional systems of medicine due to lack of correct identity, standardization and quality control of plant material forming the drug on which these systems depend heavily. The lack of exposure of later day physicians and researchers to science of Botany and Pharmacognosy, made them dependent on herb collectors which consequently caused deterioration in the efficacy of preparations. In ancient time, people, particularly the physicians had no problem in identifying medicinal plants as they had very close contact with nature and were able to identify plants whose roots, leaves, bark, flower, fruits, and seed were useful in the preparation of medicines. But gradually in the process of urbanization this contact with nature was cut off and consequently the knowledge about identification of plants also deteriorated to a great extent. The subsequent practitioners of these traditional systems tried to identify drug plants on the basis of morphological characters mentioned in the old treatise of these systems which has resulted in coining of the same name to more than one plant or different names applied to one plant. This has put many plants in the controversial position, and their identity has become doubtful. It can be seen in the available literature on Indian medicinal plants that in many cases quite unrelated plants are given the same name or same plant is given different names. Due to the ambiguity of plant names overlapping of data may occur in chemical or pharmacological information's where the botanical identity of market sample of crude drug taken up for research is not ascertained. The botanical identity of many such controversial plants is yet to be resolved. In the present communication an attempt has been made to compile a list of such plants which are known in the literature on are sold in market by different names and *vice-versa*. The plants are enumerated alphabetically. Synonym has been avoided for the sake of economy of space. Only Sanskrit, Unani, common or trade name of the plants are given. Local names are not given, since they vary from locality due to the existence of several regional languages and innumerable dilects in India.

I. SANSKRIT, UNANI, COMMON OR TRADE NAMES APPLIED TO MORE THAN ONE PLANT

Agnimantha – *Clerodendrum phlomides* L.f.; *Premana obtusifolia* R. Br.

Ajmuda – *Trachyspermum roxburghianum* (DC) Craib; *Apium graveolens* L.

Amlevetta – *Rumex vesicarius* L.; *Garcinia pedunculata.* Roxb. Ar. (a)lu – *Oroxylum indicum* (L.) Vent.; *Orchis latifolia* L. Ar(a)ni – *Clerodendrum phlomides* L.f.; *Premna obtusifolia* R.Br.

Ashoka – *Saraca asoca* (Roxb.) De Wilde; *Polyalthia longifolia* Thw.

Badaward – *Cardus nutans* L.; *Fogonia arabica* L.; *Volutarella ramosa* (Roxb.) Santapau.

Bak(am) – *Sesbania grandiflora* Pers; *Caesalpinia sappan* L.

Bala – *Sida cordifolia* L.; *S. acuta* Burm.f.; *Pavonia odorata* Willd.

B(a)rahikand – *Tacca integrifolia* Ker-Gawl.; *Dioscorea* spp.

Bhumikushmanda	– *Pueraria tuberosa* DC.; *Ipomoea paniculata* R.Br.
Bidarikand	– *Ipomoea digitala* L.; *Pueraria tuberosa* DC.
Brahmdandi	– *Echinops echinata* DC.; *Argemone mexicana* L.; *Tricholepis glaberrima* DC.
Brahmi	– *Bacopa monniera* (L.) Pennell; *Centella asiatica* (L.) Urban
Celery	– *Apium graveolens* L.; *Trachyspermum roxburghianum* (DC.) Craib.
Cha(u)lmoogra	– *Gynocardia odorata* R.Br.; *Hydnocarpus laurifolia* (Denn.) Sleum.
Devdar(u)	– *Cedrus deodra* (Roxb. ex Lamb) G.Don.; *Polyalthea longifolia* Thw.
Dicamali	– *Gardenia lucida Roxb.; Peucedanum grande* Cl.
Gaojaban, Gajawan, Gaozaban, Gayuban	– *Caccinea macranthera* Brand. var. *crassifolia*; *Onosma bracteatum* Wall.
Gokharu, Goksh(u)ru, Gokshura(k)	– *Tribulus terrestris* L.; *Pedalium murex* L.
Indian Gentian	– *Gentiana kurroo* Royle; *Picrorhiza kurroa* Royle ex Benth.
Kadu	– *Gentiana kurroo* Royle; *Picrorhiza kurroa* Royle ex Benth.
Kahu(a)	– *Lactuca sativa* L.; *Terminalia arjuna* (Roxb.) Wt. & Arn.
Kak(a) Jangha	– *Asteracantha longifolia* Ness; *Leea acquata* L.
Kakoli	– *Lillium polyphyllum* Don; *Luvunga scandens* (Roxb.) Buch. – Ham. ex Wight.
Kalijri	– *Vernonia anthelmintica* Willd.; *Nigella sativa* L.
Kanranj(a) Bij	– *Capparis spinosa* L.; *Pongamia pinnata* Pierre.
Khadir (Chhal)	– *Acacia catechu* Willd.; *Uncaria gambier* Roxb.
Khetpapra	– *Oldenlandia aspera* DC.; *Rungia repens* Nees.
Kukti	– *Gentiana kurroo* Royle; *Picrorhiza kukrroa* Royle ex Benth.
Mari	– *Caryota urens* L.; *Piper nigrum* L.
Mayur shikha	– *Celosia argentea* L.; *Actinopteris dichotoma* Bedd. *Adiantum caudatum* L.

Meda	–	*Laptadaenia reticulata* Wt. & Arnn; *Litsea monopetala* (Roxb.) Pers.
Moth(a)	–	*Cyperus rotundus* L.; *Phaseolus aconitifolius* Jacq.
Murva	–	*Clematis triloba* Heyne ex Roth; *Origanum majorina* L.
Pashanbhed	–	*Bergenia ligulata* (Wall.) Engl.; *Coleus aromaticus* Benth.; *Didymocarpus pedicellata* R. Br.
Pitpapada	–	*Fumaria officinalis* L.; *F. indica* (Hsussk.) Pugsley; *Hedyotis corymbosa* (L.) Lamk; *Peristrophe bicalyeulata* (Retz.) Nees.
Priyangu	–	*Aglaia roxburghiana* Mia.; *Prunus mahaleb* L.
Ras(h)na	–	*Alpinia officinarum*; *Hanc e; Pluchea lanceolata* Oliver; *Vanda tessellata* (Roxb.) Hook. ex. G. Don.
Ratanjot	–	*Geranium wallichianum* sw.; *Onosma echioides* L.; *Clausena pentaphylla* D.C. *Potentilla nepalenses* Hook.
Rudanti	–	*Capparis moonii* Wight.; *Cressa cretica* L.
Salam (misri) (panja)	–	*Eulophia campestris* Wall; *Orchis habenarioides* King & Prantl
Sankhpushpi	–	*Canscora decussata* Schult; *Convolvulus microphyllus* Sieb. ex Spreng; *Evolvulus alsinoides* L.; *Clitoria ternatea* L.
Satmuli	–	*Asparagus racomosus* Willd.; *Emilia sonchifolia* DC.
Somlata	–	*Ephedra gerardiana* Wall.; *Sarcostema acidum* (Roxb.) Viogt.
Talispatra	–	*Abies webbiana* Lindl.; *Taxus baccatta* L.; *Rhododendron anthopogon* D.Don.

II. DIFFERENT NAMES (INCLUDING SANSKRIT, UNANI, COMMON OR TRADE NAMES) APPLIED TO THE SAME PLANT

Abroma augusta L.f.	–	Abroma, Olat-Kambal, Ulat-Kambal
Abrus precatorius L.	–	Gumchi, Gunja, Kanchabeej, Ratti
Abutilon indicum G. Don	–	Atibala, Kanghi, Kamkatimoola
Achyranthes aspera L.	–	Apamarga, Apang, Chirchira
Aconitum heterophyllum Wall.	–	Atis, Ativisha, Shringi, Shrigik

Acorus calamus L.	–	Bach, Bock, Buch, Calamus, Vacha
Adhatoda zeylanica Medik	–	Arusa, Vasa(ka)
Alhagi pseudalhagi (Bieb.) Desv.	–	Durlava, Duralabha, Javasa
Aloe barbedensis Mell.	–	Aloes, Eliyak, Elua, Elva, Gheekuar, Ghikanwal, Ghrita Kumari, Kumari, Kuvarpatha, Musabbar.
Alstonia scholasis (L.) R. Br.	–	Chatwan, Chhatim, Dita, Saptaparna
Anethum sowa Roxb.	–	Anethi, Anithi, Satapushpi, Soia, Sowa, Soyak
Anogeissus latifolia (DC.) Wall ex. Bedd.	–	Dhataki, Dhava Dhavdiphool
Apium graveolens L.	–	Ajmod(a), Ajmuda, Randhuni, Chanu.
Argemone mexicana L.	–	Piladhatoora, Satyanasi, Swarnakshiri
Argyreia nervosa (Burm.f.) Boj	–	Samudrapalaka, Bidhara, Samudrasosh(Beej), Vridha daruk, Vrikshamla, Vrudhadaruk, Vrudhhadaur
Artemisia maritime L.	–	Kirmala, Shih, Kirmani
Asparagus racemosus Willd.	–	Satumuli, Satamuli, Satamundi, Shatavari, Satavar(y), Shaqakul-Misri
Bacopa monniera (L.) Pennell	–	Brahmi, Jalbrahmi
Bambusa arundnacea (Retz.) Roxb.	–	Vans(h)a, Bansalochan, Bamboo manna, Vans(h)alochan
Berberis aristata DC.	–	Daruhald(i), Dur(u)hald(e), Rasot, Daruharidra, Darvi, Rasanjan, Berberis, Rasavauti, Rasaunt
Bergenia ligulata (Wall).	–	Engl. Pashanbhed, Patharchati
Bombex ceiba L.	–	Semal, Shalmadi (mool), Musli Senbhal, Mochras *Butea monosperma* (Lam.) Taub, - Palashushpa, Palas(bij), Kamarkas
Caccinia glauca Savi	–	Gaozaban, Gajawan, Gayuban
Caesalpinia bonduc (L.) Roxb. emend. Dandy & Excell	–	Gajga, Kakachia, Karanj, Kuberex, Sagargota, Nata Karanj, Putikaranj

Calotropis gigantea (L.) R. Br. – Ark, Aak, Akanda, Mader, Calotropis,

Capparis moonii Wight– Wagati, Rudanti, Luthikai

Carum carvi L. – Jira siyah, Siajira, Jira, Krishana Jirak, Sankhajiru, Caraway

Cassia angustifolia Vahl – Senna (pod), Sonamukhidoda, Markandi, Sonamukhi, Swarnapartri, Cassia

Cassia fistula L. – Amaltas, Aragdah, Aragvadha, Aragwadi, Cassia, Germala, Garmalo

Cassia occidentalis L.– Kasari, Kasaundi, Kasondi, As(h) and (a)ra.

Cedrus deodara (Roxb. ex Lamb.) G.Don – Deodar, Devdaru, Cedarwood

Centella asiastica (L.) Urban – Brahmi, Mandukparni, Centella, Tholkuri, Thankuni

Cinnamomum tamala Nees ex. Eberm – Tamalpatra, Tejpat(tar), Tuj, Twak

Cinnamomum zeylanicum Breyn – Darchini, cinam, Cinnaman(i)

Cissampelos pareira L.–Kalipat(h), Pahadmool, Katori, Akanadi

Clerodendrum phlomides L.f. – Bharangi, Agnimantha, Ar(a)ni

Crocus sativus L. – Keshar, Saffron, Zafran, Kumkum

Cuminum cyminum L.– Jirak, Jeera, Cumin, Jeevaka, Jira safed, Shwet Jirak.

Curcuma longa L. – Haridra, Cancha haridara, Haldi, Gandhapalasi, Kancha haridra

Cyperus rotundus L. – Nagarmotha, Moth(a) Must(h)a, Mustak, Nut Grass

Didymocarpus pedicellata R. Br. – Patharthodi, Patharphodi, Patharphori, Pashanbhed

Eclipta alba (L.) Hask. – Bhangra, Bharan(a) raja, Bhringaraja

Elettaria cardamomum (L.) Maton – Belchi, Ela(ichi), Ellaichi Khurd, Kagdi Elaichi, Welchi, Sukshma Ela, Cardam(om), Choti Elaichi

Embelia ribes Burm. – Biranga, Vavding, Vidang(a), Babring, Bidang, Wavding

Enicostema hyssopifolium (Wild) Verdoorn – Mamajjak, Mamajwa, Chhota Chirayta

Eulophia campestris Wall. – Mujjatak, Salib Shalabmisri, Salam (panja)

Euphorbia neriifolia L. – Manasa Sij, Euphoribia, Snuhi (Dugdha), Sahund

Evolvulus alsinoides L. – Kali-sankhavli, Sankhapusphi, Vishnugandhi

Ficus racemosa L. – Gular, Fig, Udambar, Udumber, Umbra (Paan Phal)

Foeniculam vulgare . Mill – Saunf, Sounf, S(h)atapushpa, Madhurika, Mouri, Fennel, Foeniculam

Gentiana kurroo Royle – Kadu, Karu, Gentian, Indian Gentian

Glycyrrhiza globra L. – Liquorice, Glycyrhizal, Glycerhiza, Mulethi, Jetimadh, Licorice, Madhueshti, Jyeshthimadh, Yashtimadhu, Yashtri, Jastimadhu, Asius-soos

Gmelina arborea Roxb. – Gambhar(i), Kashmari

Gynocardia odorata R. Br. – Bandrephal, Chau(u)lmoogra

Hemidesmus indicus (L.) Schult – Indian Sarsaparilla, Anantamool(a) Salsa, Hemidesmus

Hibiscus rosasinensis L. – Jaba, Jawakusum, Gudhal, Gul-gudhal

Holarrhena antidysenterica (L.) Wall. ex. DC. – Kutaja, Kadachhal, Kudhachhal, Indrajava, Indrayava, Kurchi

Hydnocarpus laurifolia (Denn.) Sleum – Tu(r)varaka, Cha(u)lmoogra, Hydnocarpus

Hygrophila auriculata (Schum.) Heine – Kokilakshya. Asteracantha, Kulekhara, Kuliakhara, Kakjangha, Gokkasu

Ipomoea mauritiana Jocq. – Bhumikushmanda, Bhuikobola, Bhuipatri, Bidarikanda, Bidhari, Vidarikand

Ipomoea nil (L.) Roth – Krishna til, Kaladana, Krishna beej

Lepidium sativum L. – Asalio, Halim, Ashelia, Chandra, Chandrika

Leptadaenia reticulata (Retz.) Wt. & Arn. – Jivanti, Meda, Dodi, Jeevant(h)i, Dronapushpi

Luffa acutangula (L.) Roxb. - Luffa, Koshataki, Shirola, Turai

Melia azedarach L.	–	Mahanimb, Mahaneem, Bakayan
Mesua ferrea L.	–	Nages(h)war, Nagkes(h)ar, Nagpus(h)p(y)a
Nimusops elengi L.	–	Bakul, Maulsari, Molsari
Moringa oleifera Lam.	–	Sajina, Sigru Shigru (twak) Saragva (Bij), Shajan, Moringa, Saragwa (Chaal)
Mucuna prurita Hook.	–	Banari, Kapicahhu, Benarmul, Kaucha, Kauncha, Alkushi, Atmagupta
Myristica fragrance Hoult	–	Nutmeg, Mace, Jaiphal Jayaphal, Jat(i)patri, Jatiphalam, Javitri, Javantri, Javintiri
Nardostachys grandiflora DC.	–	Jantamansi, Balchad, Balchar, Mansi, Masi
Nigella sativa L.	–	Kalaunji, Jira, Kalijiri, Kalonji, Black cuminum, Upakunchika
Onosma bracteatum Wall.	–	Gajawan, Gaozaban, Gojihivat, Gojiwha, Gayuban
Operculina turpethum (L.) Silva-Manso	–	Turpethum, Trivrit, Truvrit, Nishoth, Nishottar, Trivrut(a).
Orchis habernariodes King and Prantl	–	Panjasalam, Salam (misri) (panja)
Orchis latifolia L.	–	Aralu, Salep, Salap
Oroxylum indicum (L.) Vent.	–	Shyonak, Ar(a)lu, Ardusi, Sheonak
Pavonia odorata Willd.	–	Netravala, Netrabala, Herber, Sugandhbala, Netarmool
Pedalium murex L.	–	Gokshura(k), Gokhru Mota, Mota Gokhru, Goksh(u)ru
Picrorhiza kurroa Royle ex Benth.	–	Kat(u)ki, Kadu, Kutki, Balkadu, Picroh, Kalikutki
Pimpenella anisum L.	–	Badyan, Badian, Anise, Aniseed, Anisi, Saunf, Sounf
Piper cubeba L. f.	–	Kankol, Shitalchini, Kabachini, Cubeb, Chankabad, Chini Kabab
Paper longum L.	–	Long piper, Pipal, Pipul, Pipli (mul), Long pepper, Piper, Pippalimul
Piper nigrum L.	–	Kalimiri, Maricha, Kalimirchi, Black Piper, Mirch Seah, Piper, White Marich, Mari

Polyalthia longifolia Thw. – As(h)ok(a), Devdaru, Debdaru

Premna obtusifolia R. Br. – Karnika, Agetha, Agnimantha, Ganiyar

Pterocarpus marsupium Roxb. – Asan, Vijayasar, Hirdakhan, Bijesar

Pueraria tuberosa DC.– Vidarikanda, Bidarikand, Bhumikushmanda, Bidhari

Rheum emodi Wall. ex Meissn. – Rhubarb, Revandchini, Amlaparni, Ravanchi, Shiro, Revanchu, Lakdu, Rewandchini

Rubia cardifolia L. – Manjistha, Majith, Manjit, Manjistha

Rungia repens (L.) Ness – Kharmor, Khetpapra, Parpat

Saccharum spontaneum Linn. – Kans, Kash, Kansda mool, Sherdi (mool)

Saussurea lappa Clarke – Kusth(a), Kur, Kusta, Saussurea, Uplet, Kut

Semecarpus anacardium L.f. – Bhallatak(a), Bhilawa, Bhela

Sesbania grandiflora (L.) Poir – Agastya, Bak, Rakta Agastya, Agati, Bakam

Sida cardifolia L. – Balapanchanga, Bala, Bare(l)la, Berula, Bariar(a), Khareti, Kharenti, Bariyer

Similex china L. – Chob-Chini, China, Chopchini, Topchini

Solanum indicum L. – Brihati (Kar), Vrihati, Brah(e)ti, Kateri, Brah(u)ti

S. surattense Burm. f.– Kantikari, Kantakari(ka), Kateli, Bhuiringani, Brihati(kar), Brah(u)ti, Brah(e)ti, Kater

Sphaeranthus indicus L. – Munditika, Mundi, Gorak(h)mundi

Sterospermum suaveolens DC. – Patha, Tamarapushpa, Pat(a)la

Strychnos nux-vomica L. – Kuch, Kuch(i)la, Kuchelaka, Nux-vomica, Vishatinduk, Vishamustri

Swertia chirayata (Roxb. ex Flem.) – Karst, Kirata(k), Kirayat, Kirayta, Kariyetu, Chiereta, Chiraita, Bhunimba, Lodhra, Lodh(ar)

Syzygium cuminii (L.) Skeels – Jaman, Jammu Jambool, Jambu(bij)

S. aromaticium (L.) Merille et Perry	– Lavang(a), Laung, Caryoph, Qarananphal, Mehaka, Clove, Qaranfal
Tephrosia purpurea (L.) Pers.	– Sharpankha, Sarapunkha, Shripankha
Terminalia arjuna (Roxb.) Wt & Arn.	– Arjan(a) Kahu(a), Koh
T. bellirica (Gaertn.) Roxb.	– Bibhitak, Bakera, Behda
T. chebula Retz.	– Shiva, Putina, Harde, Hararrh, Haritaki, Hare, Pilihar(i) Piliher Abhaya, Himaj, Harar(a) Bal Harde
Tinospora cordifolia (Willd.) Hook f. & Thoms.	– Gulvel, Guduchi, Guddochi, Giloe, Guducha, Gaduchi, Gulancha, Guruchi, Giloy, Amruta, Amrita
Trachysperumun ammi (L.) Sprague	– Aj(o)wain, Ajovan, Ajma, Ptychotis
Trachyspermum roxburghianum (DC). Craib	– Ajmood(a), Ajmuda, Celery, Yavan(i), Curcuma Ajmoda, Rajani
Uraria logopadioides (L.) Desv. ex. DC.	– Prishnaparni, Prasniparni
Urginea indica (Roxb). Kunth	– Urginea, Squill, Parnabija, Jangil Pyej, Indian squill, Coromandel Squill
Urgenia maritima Babor	– Scilla(c), While squll, European Squil
Vateria indica L.	– Ral, Kaherbam, Pishti, Sarj, Swarjika
Veteveria zizanioides (L.) Nahs	– Khas, Valak, Usheeram, Ushir, Usir
Viburnum prunifolium L.	- Viburni, Viburni pruni (fol), Black Haw, Viburnum Pruni, Viburum
Zingiber officinale Rosh.	– Sunth(i), Adrak, A(rd)arak, Ginger, Indian Ginger, Pulvginges, Sonth, Zanjebeel Zinger, Zingiberis

In the recent years, a great emphasis is being given to analyse the drugs used in traditional systems of medicine for various ailments. Majority of the pharmaceutical industries, herbal practitioners and common people depend largely upon crude drug dealers for the supply of plant materials. These plants are generally collected by the professional collection who may not be a botanist or taxonomist. Sometimes the identity of crude drug purchased from market, which is based on trade or vernacular name, is taken for granted without subjecting the plant material for stringent method of botanical identification. It is equally possible that one may not get the desired plant as the trader may supply other plant having same trade or vernacular name. In addition to nomenclatural ambiguity, bazar drugs are adulterated, sophisticated or substituted by quite unrelated plant materials. Since there is no government control over the sale of adulterated or spurious drugs, the traders take full advantage of this and sell to their customer anything that resemble or may be made to resemble the genuine drug. Thus, authentication of botanical source of plant material taken up for research or medicinal use is necessary to achieve satisfactory results and also to maintain efficacy and therpeutic property of the preparation in which these plants are used.

18

Biotechnology and Genetic Improvement of Medicinal Plants

INTRODUCTION

Development of superior strains/clones/varieties which manifest high degree of performance with respect to the productivity, quality and stability of the economic end-products in plants is the hallmark of crop genetic improvement. Such superior stocks/varieties are indeed the permanent and the cheapest source of changes in crop plants over generations and over the time and space. The genetical processes involved are very many suited to both environmental conditions and the target materials. Out intent, however, is not to elaborate and explicate here genetic principles and diverse breeding procedures and strategies adopted for crop improvement. But we do intend to project in brief its tremendous impact on revolutionarizing the agricultural crop production across the world with the sole objective to draw a corollary that similar revolution can be ushered in medicinal plants as well.

Many countries in the world harvested excessively increased yield of cereals by growing superior crop varieties during the past couple of decades or so resulting into a quantum jump in total production of grains. Such an amazingly phenomenal increase in crop yields caused ushering in an era of 'Green Revolution' in particularly South-East-Asian countries which harbours no illusion. In this backdrop of food plants, what is the state-of-art in medicinal plants? And, why and how can they be genetically manipulated, not only to enhance their end-products quantitatively but also qualitatively as well as adaptively to new areas and to newer agencies? In the next few sections, we would like to capture the flavour of these very aspects and impress upon the gravity and exigency of exploiting the exciting capability of conventional plant breeding and modern biotechnology for genetic upgradation of medicinal plants under the herbal drug development programmes.

NEED FOR GENETIC IMPROVEMENT OF MEDICINAL PLANTS

In contrast to the food crops where yield ceiling is limited by genetic potential coupled with prevailing environment in medicinal plants, the production of raw materials is dependant upon a set of complex but integrated factors, namely genetic, environmental, socio-economic, marketing structures and all that. Direct collection of samples from natural resources and/or domestication of medicinal plants from wild stocks may perhaps maintain a sustained supply of raw materials for pharmaceutical industries for some period of time. But this ostensibly suffers from three grave obstacles : One, the wild resources are not unlimited, hence cannot last for long; two, the production of raw materials through such collections cannot be assured; and three, materials sampled from natural forests are nearly always heterogenous thus adversely affecting the quality of herbal drugs and their efficacy. The simplest way to increase the yield (quantitative production) for assured supply may be to expand the area under cultivation. Crop husbandry too involving improved package of agronomic practices can raise the yield levels to the extent of genetic potential of the commercial bulk (domesticated wild/exotic stocks). However, the poor yield potential and heterogeneity of wild bulks brought under cultivation will not suffice the purpose of both quantitative and qualitative production of raw materials. Moreover, such plants under cultivation will have to compete with other food crops and also have to be cultivated under varying environments. Hence, increase in their production (quantitative yield) ought to be consummated by increase in productivity (yield per unit of area, time and input). But any way, no amount of agronomic maneuvering can help achieve the uniformity of the crop (to attract grower's acceptance) and quality of the yield (to elicit the preference of pharmaceutical concerns) both. This could however be achieved together with quantitative improvement only by expeditious and judicious genetic manipulation of these crops on permanent basis.

Thus, in nutshell, genetic improvement of medicinal plants is exigently necessitated to serve the following objectives:

(a) Fixing a high genetic ceiling by effecting permanent (heritable) improvement in wild/alien medicinal plants for higher productivity per plant, thus reducing the cost of cultivation and making them highly remunerative and cost-effective.

(b) Introducing impressive uniformity of crop under cultivation to attract grower's acceptance.

(c) Promoting the quality and homogeneity of herbal drugs to make them highly priced and saleable.

(d) Conserving the natural resources by restricting indiscriminate destruction by unscrupulus agencies, thus helping escape irreversible genetic erosion.

(e) Developing new crop cultivars well adapted to new areas of cultivation and also to newer agencies for their better exploitation.

(f) Converting them into a viable component of crop diversification under different cropping systems.

(g) Promoting the export potential of raw materials or even finished products and reducing or overstepping the import-gaps through increased production of quality produce.

GENETIC UPGRADATION OF MEDICINAL PLANTS AT CIMAP

It is amazingly unfortunate that while upsurge in yield due to HYV leading to ushering in the era of 'Green Revolution' was witnessed in food crops; virtually no serious attempts were ever made to genetically manipulate the herbal drugs plants. R & D works on medicinal plants commenced some four decades ago but mostly confined to chemistry, introduction and pharmacology. Only during the last one and a half decade or so, intensive work on genetic manipulation of these plants was initiated in right earnest in India, though genetic manipulation of crop adaptation is an age-old process. Despite specific constraints imposed by their natural characteristic features, such as – importance of secondary metabolites more than or equal to that of primary metabolites, seasonal variation in the rate of biosynthesis of active principles, and variable and complex mode of reproduction, etc., some tangible successes have been achieved in developing genetically superior cultivars in some important medicinal plants over the years at CIMAP. Besides, ample progress has also been made with respect to *in vitro* production of secondary metabolites micropropagation of elite lines and endangered species, somatic hybridrization, etc. through biotechnological approaches.

The current status of genetic improvement of medicinal plants through Mendelian and modern techniques both at CIMAP has been succinctly assembled here below.

(a) Genetic Improvement through Conventional Approaches

Six of the economically viable medicinal plants having national priority, namely opium poppy, periwinkle, Indian and Egyptian henbane, pyrethrum and quinghao were genetically manipulated through plant breeding leading to development of superior varieties (see Table 1). Besides, three other important medicinal plants viz., psyllium senna and chamomile were also lately subjected to genetic improvement under the first phase of our crop improvement programme at CIMAP. We may now enumerate successes in each of these crops.

1. RELEASED VARIETIES

Intensive breeding efforts in the former six crops resulted into development of superior varieties which were subsequently released by CIMAP for commercial exploitation in different crops as under:

Table 1: Genetically superior varieties of some medicinal plants released by CIMAP for commercial cultivation

	Crop	*Cultivar released*	*% Superiority over the best check*	*Desirable end-product*
1.	Opium poppy (*Papaver somniferum*)	*Shweta*	+57%	70° Latex (raw opium)
		Shyama	+64%	70° Latex (raw opium)
		Sanchita	+20%	Poppy-straw
			+25%	Seeds
			+50%	Straw-morphine
		Vivek	~	Straw-morphine
2.	Indian henbane (*Hyoscyamus niger*)	*Aela*	+46% +109%	Biomass Crude drug
3.	Egyptian henbane (*H. muticus*)	*HMT-I*	+15% +36%	Biomass Crude drug
		NP-41	~ +35%	Biomass Crude drug
4.	Pyrethrum (*Chrysanthermum cinerariaefolium*)	*Hansa*	+142% +180%	Flowers Pyrethrins
5.	Periwinkle (*Caltharanthus roseus*)	*Nirmal*	+20% +195% +203%	Leaves Roots Crude drug
6.	Quinghao (*Artemisia annua*)	*Asha*	+60% +37%	Biomass Artemisinin

(i) Opium poppy

This plant is a natural source of opium alkaloids, like morphaine, codeine, papaverine and nascopine which are pharmaceutically unique. It is commercially grown mainly in Utter Pradesh, Madhya Pradesh and Rajasthan States under the strict control of Narcotic Commission of India. Unlike the food growers having several improved varieties, opium poppy growers were cultivating age-old land races. They did not have improved variety till 1984 when CIMAP released two improved gum harvest (GH) varieties – *Shweta* (with higher morphine concentration in latex) and *Shyama* (with moderate morphine strength but high latex yield) giving 57% and 64% more yield of raw opium (70°), respectively than the local check.

While our efforts at CIMAP were still afoot to breed new GH varieties excelling *Shweta* and *Shyama*, global concern was shown since late eighties to do away with opium linked with menacing social abuses. One approach was the crop substitution of opium-yielding *P. somniferum* by non-opium species, *P. bracteatum*. However, this was not successful in India as the temperate plant *P. braeteatum* cannot be grown in sub-tropical climate where *P. somniferum* is cultivated. Another approach was to develop concentrated poppy-straw (CPS) varieties of *P. somniferum* with higher concentration of alkaloids in the poppy-straw (1/3 peduncle + capsule husk) where lancing to obtain latex is strictly prohibited. This is much prevalent in Turkey, USSR, France, Netherlands and Australia. Yet another approach – the ideal one – could be the genetic conversion on narcotic *P. somniferum* (latex +) into non-narcotic one (latex$^-$) through massive mutagenesis programme and/or genetic engineering by blocking the pathway of latex-synthesis with the help of anti-sense technique or like. But this is, of course, a swim against the natural course of evolution, hence successes may not be guaranteed. Therefore, pending this last approach, we intensified our genetic improvement programme to develop CPS varieties. As a consequence, two CPS varieties – *Sanchita* and *Vivek* were recently released by CIMAP as a respite measure to combat social abuses associated with opium. Of these two *Sanchita* with 0.76% morphine in straw was found to excel even the world best recovery of 0.70% morphine reported from Tasmania (Australia). It is also a very good straw and seed yielder, hence can be adopted under cultivation. Indeed, the Narcotic Department has taken a lead to initiate its captive farming at appropriate sites in India.

(ii) Indlan/black henbane

An important national source of hyoscine (Scopolamlne) and hyoscyamine – the tropane alkaloids, the Indian henbane is a good supplement to belladonna. It has limited cultivation in India, major part of herb is gathered from wild with poor alkaloid content and heterogenous quality. In order to harvest higher yields of biomass, and tropane alkaloids and to ensure uniform quality of produce under cultivation, the first superior variety – *Aela* was released by CIMAP during 1987, thus replacing the wild bulk for commercial cultivation. This registered 46% superiority in biomass and 109% in crude drug yields over the wild bulk (check). It is highly leafy and bears thin (less woody) branches possessing higher alkaloid content.

(iii) Egyptian henbane

This was introduced in India from Egypt during late seventies. Its biomass contains higher concentration of hyoscyamine than hyoscine (which is several-fold more important than the former in international market) vis-à-vis Indian henbane. However, being a smaller herb its cultivation is easier and more profitable in semi-arid zones than Indian henbane. To make its cultivation successful, CIMAP released two varieties – a tetraploid *HMT – 1* and a line *NP-41* both around 35% superior for crude drug over the bulk check.

(iv) Pyrethrum

This a para-medicinal plant containing pyrethrins which is an eco-friendly biopesticide used as mosquito repellent. This is an introduction from Kenya, grown as commercial bulk under temperate climate of Kashmir valley (J&K) and Palni hills (T.N.). In order to make its cultivation cost-effective, yielding higher amount of dry flowers, with high pyrethrine concentration, per unit area, CIMAP released a superior variety, *Hansa* during 1985. The variety is exceedingly superior over the commercial bulk (check) for both flowers (+142%) and pyrethrine (+180%) yields under Palni hills conditions.

(v) Periwinkle

A wonder drug plant containing vinblastine and vincristine in the leaves and ajmalicine in roots, the leaf alkaloids being potentially effective as anticancer agents (monocrytic leukaemia, lymphosarcoma, carcinoma of breast, lungs and testes), and the root alkaloid as hypotensive agent. It is omnipresent, but prefers tropical and subtropical climate conditions. Its commercial cultivation is however very limited in India, though it has now attracted world-wide attention because of its pharmaceutical significance. Considering the exigency, CIMAP released a genetically improved variety, *Nirmal* for extending its profitable cultivation. Although var. *Nirmal* is at par with local bulk for alkaloid concentration in both leaves and roots, it is 20, 195 and 203% better than bulk for the yields of leaves, roots and crude drug, respectively. It is also tolerant to die-back disease, hence enjoys good establishment in the field.

(vi) Quinghao

A well-known anti-malarial Chinese drug plant, quinghao was recently introduced in India. Its active constituent – arteminisinin has been found to be very effective against chloroquin-resistance strains of malarial parasite, more so against cerebral malaria (brain fever). Its bulk cultivation is now established in Kashmir valley. With a view to improving its biomass yield and artesimnin content, a superior variety – *Asha* was released by CIMAP during 1988 for commercial cultivation. This variety, basically an improved population gives 60% more biomass and 37% more artemisinin content than the introduced bulk material (ckeck). It grows well in subtropical climate also, but does not set seeds.

In addition to these released varieties, under the germplasm enhancement programme, many more promising lines (see Table 2) have also been identified and evaluated over years under initial evaluation trials (IET), bench scale trials (BST), pilot scale trials (PST) and yield optimization trial (YOT) at CIMAP. They are now in pipeline to be graduated shortly for commercial cultivation.

2. ELITE STRAINS IN PIPELINE

Varietal improvement programme was also initiated in three new medicinal plants, viz., psyllium, senna and Geman chamomile, and further intensified in opium poppy and Indian henbane. As a result superior strains were identified in these crops as elaborated below: (see Table 2):

Table 2: Genetically superior elite strains of medicinal plants in pipeline for release by CIMAP

	Crop	*Elite strains*	*% Superiority over the best check*	*Desirable end-product*
1.	Isabol (Psyllium) (*Plantago ovata*)	M-22 (*Niharika*)	+170%	Seeds Pods + Leaves
2.	Senna (*Cassia angustifolia*)	S-121 (*Suphala*)	+70%	Blue oil
3.	German chamomile (*Chamomilla recutita*)	M 70-1 (*Vallary*)	+200% + 60%	Flower heads
4.	Opium poppy (*Papaver somniferum*)	DR-3 (*Shakti*)	+50%	Latex (raw opium)
		Mass-2B (*Sampada*)	+25%	Latex (raw opium)
5.	Indian henbane (*Hyoscyamus niger*)	Rb (Aekla)	+50% +70%	Biomass Crude drug

(i) Psyllium

This plant, which is of Mediterranean origin, is a source of natural laxative – the property present in its seeds and husk. In India, it is cultivated mainly in Gujarat and to a limited extent in adjoining Rajasthan and Haryana States. As the seeds and husk both are of substantial export-potential, the area under this crop must be expanded. With this objective, breeding for improved varieties of psyllium, especially adapted to north Indian plains commenced at CIMAP a few years back. Now we have identified a superior strain – M 22 (*Niharika*) which under north Indian conditions gives seed yield as good, if not more, as harvested in western India. In fact, it registered 170% more seed yield under a pilot scale trail at Lucknow than the check var. Gujarat Isabgol – I (which is perhaps not well suited to north Indian conditions).

(ii) Senna

This is also an exotic plant native to Somalia and South Arabia. It was introduced in India long back by Arab traders. Its leaves and pods contain sennosides which have laxative/purgative property. Its cultivation is confined mainly in Tamil Nadu State. However, next to psyllium, senna (leaves + pods) is the biggest export commodity of India; it is, therefore, imperative to expand its cultivation in newer areas so as to increase its production for export. As such, CIMAP started improvement of genetic stocks by developing superior strains of senna suitable of north Indian plains and now a strain – S-121(*Suphala*) has been identified, which registered 70% superiority over the commercial bulk (check) for leaves + pods yield in pilot scale trial at Lucknow. It is much more rich in sennosides also than the check.

(iii) Chamomile

A native of southern and eastern Europe, chamomile is the natural source of an essential oil, known in commerce as 'Bule Oil' which has wide curative effect and uses (e.g. anti-inflammatory and softening effects on the digestive tract when used internally, and applied externally for treatment of hemorrhoids and inflammations of the ophthalmic mucosa and uterus). Its flower-heads too are used as drug. Its bulk stock/population was introduced in India from Germany, USA and Bulgaria for commercial cultivation. But its yield potential (oil and flower-heads) was poor, hence CIMAP took up its genetic improvement programme through mutation breeding which resulted into identification of a superior strain – M701 (*Vallary*). In a semi-commercial pilot scale trail, it registered 200% superiority over the best check – German Bulk for oil yield and 60% for flower-head yield. Its very deep blue oil is indicative of superior quality. It grows well even in alkaline soil (PH9).

(iv) Opium poppy

Though our emphasis has now shifted from developing GH varieties to CPS varieties, it will perhaps take some time to discontinue cultivation of latex varieties. The simple reason is that opium itself is the biggest foreign exchange earner for India. In view of this, simultaneously armed with CPS varieties (*Sanchia* and *Vivek*) CIMAP continued breeding for still petter GH varieties. As a consequence, we have now identified a dwarf recombinant – DR-3 (*Shakti*) and a downy mildew resistant strain – Mass-2B (*Sampada*) giving 50% and 25%, respectively more latex yield than the best check (*Shyama*) under pilot scale trials.

(v) Indian henbane

Owing to non-condusive plant-type characterized by initial prostrate branching restricting population pressure per unit area and overlapping leaf-arrangement rendering the plant physiologically less efficient, a genetic rectification of plant-type through mutagenesis was initiated during early eighties. A superior mutant variety *Alae* was released earlier. But its plant-frame remained the same, though primary branches become thin and number of leaves and tropane alkaloid content both increased, hence superior on an over all basis. Concurrent with polygenic changes, an unbrached (Ub) mutant was also detected in M_2 generation. It was an unique genotype because a dozen traits were changed at one stroke; it was ubranches (with single main stem, permitting higher population density, hence higher biomass per unit area) with leaves thick, and large, arranged in non-overlapping fashion (hence physiologically most efficient plant-type), thus completely altering the plant-frame to be quite desirable. Higher crude drug content than even *Aela*, provided a premium to this Ub mutant. But seed-seting was very poor (though seeds are not the economic product, they are used essentially for sowing the crop). Hence, selection for high seed-setting began over generations.

While selecting for high seed-setting in Ub progenies, a restricted branching (Rb) segregant with 2-4 erect branches appearing from the top (unlike prostrate braches appearing from the bottom in the original/normal plant) with better seed-setting but quite akin to parental Ub mutant for all other features, was identified in later generation. Further rigorous selection for seed-setting brought this Rb mutant at par with the normal. In view of its physiologically most efficient plant type, high herb yield and high alkaloid concentration, coupled with near-normal seed-setting, the Rb mutant (*Aekla*) in now ready for commercial cultivation.

Thus, from the foregoing statements, it is apparent that tangible successes have been achieved by CIMAP in developing and releasing a number of genetically superior varieties/strains in different medicinal plants through conventional plant breeding approaches.

(b) Genetic Manipulation through Biotechnological Approaches

In addition to conventional plant breeding approaches, since the last nearly one decade, CIMAP has made a distinct headway in genetic manipulation of medicinal plants though biotechnological approaches also, particularly cell/tissue culture techniques (see Table 3) in the following areas:

1. MICROPROPAGATION

Tissue culture is routlnely used for *in vitro* propagation and conservation of various plant species. Such multiplication of medicinal plants has been successfully accomplished in several species. Following aspects of micropropagation have been worked out at experimental level, advancing to the field conditions:

(i) Direct regeneration from explant

In appropriate culture-media (varying protocols) using shoot tip and auxillary bud explant in *Valeriana wallichii*, shoot tip and leaf explant in *Rheum emodi*, shoot tip in *Picrorrhiza kurroa*, and stem-node explant in *Duboisia myoporoides*, high frequency of plant regeneration has been achieved and plantlets were successfully transferred to the field conditions.

Table 3: Genetic manipulation of medicinal plants through biotechnological approaches at CIMAP

Medicinal plant species	*Techniques employed*	*State of success/target Achieved*
1. *Picrohiza kurroa*	Direct regeneration from explants	Plantlets regenerated and transferred to field for micropropagation and conservation of germplasm
2. *Glycyrrhiza glabra*		
3. *Duboisia myoporoides*		
4. *Valariana wallichii*	(i) Direct regeneration from explants	
5. *Rheum emodi*	(ii) Regeneration from calli	
6. *Allium govanianum*	Regeneration from calli	
7. *Aconitum heterophyllum*	Regeneration through somatic embryos	
8. *Solanum sarrachoides*		
9. *Hyoscyamus muticus*		
10. *Withania somnifera*	Agrobacterium mediated genetic transformation	The best strain – A_4 of *Agrobacterium* efficient for transformation identified
11. *Atropa belladonna*		The cheap and indigenously marketed antibiotic-Cephalaxin identified as a substitute for imported cefotaxime
12. *Panax quinquefolium*	*In vitro* production of secondary metabolites	The presence of saponin in callus and medium both recorded
13. *Rauvolfia serpentina*	(i) Direct regeneration from explants (ii) Regeneration from calli	Establishment of complete tetraploid plant from the induced tetraploid plant with 4*n* shoots but 2*n* roots
14. *Hyoscyamus albus*	Somatic hybridization with *H. muticus*	Somatic hybrids with *H. muticus* produced

(ii) Regeneration from calli

Calli were induced from petiole explants in *V. wallichii*, and from segment of flower head explant in *Allium govanianum* wherefrom complete plantlets were regenerated and subsequently transferred to the field following the standard hardening procedures.

(iii) Regeneration through somatic embryos

Somatic embryogenesis was successfully induced from callus culture in *Aconitum heterophyllum* and *Solanum sarrachoides* and from protoplast culture in *Hyoscyamus muticus*. Complete plantlets were formed and established in soil in all the target materials. These results could be important in developmental regulation of morphogenesis in plants.

(iv) Establishment of induced autotetraploid of rauvolfia

Colchiautotetraploid shoots were induced in *R. serpentina*, but the roots (the planting material) stayed diploid. Therefore, propagation and multiplication of complete autotraploid plants was conventionally not possible (seeds were sterile). But complete autotetraploid plantlets were regenerated from the induced tetraploid shoot, following tissue culture technique either through auxillary bud elongation or via multiple shoot formation on supplemented MS medium. This is of considerable consequence for commercial exploitation of tetraploid *Rauvolfia* and other such plants.

(v) Improved Methods for Rapid Micropropagation

Nand Lal and Ahuja demonstrated that use of agar-solidified culture medium for micropropagation is not a cost-effective as the use of liquid medium. This is because of more labour needed, high cost of agar and wastage of nutrients in the medium at the end of subcultures in case of gelled media, besides poor growth and proliferation rates of cultures. With the aim of devising an economical procedure in terms of media, time and space they examined the performance of liquid static and shake cultures vis-à-vis the agar-solidified culture in *Rheum emodi* and found the best results of multiple shoot formation on using the liquid shake culture (120 RPM). This caused at least 50% reduction in medium requirement and 37.5% in time and led to 1.5-2.2 fold increase in growth and multiplication rate in comparison to agar solidified cultures. Besides, liquid culture-raised plantlets also facilitated easy transplantation and ensured 90-95% survival of plantlets on transfer to potting mix in glass house.

Kukreja also suggested an improved method of high frequency of plant regeneration through multiple shoot formation from nodal explant in *Glycyrrhiza glabra*.

2. MORPHOGENESIS

Rapid clonal propagation through tissue culture of elite lines where sexual or asexual propagation is limiting factor, is most frequently exploited either through direct or organogenesis is cultured issues or through an intervening callus phase. The former route, i.e. direct organogenesis is preferred over the latter as it ensures genetic uniformity and retention of morphogenetic potential. Different explants can be used for clonal propagation, but they must possess morphogenetic potential. Kukreja *et al.*, obtained successful plant regeneration via organogenesis from foliar explants of *Duboisia myoprides* – an important source of tropane alkaloids. Based on the success, the process was upscaled and 50 trees were established in field. The procedure outlined by them has the potential for the production of thousands of trees per explant per annum.

Beside the effects of explant, role of antibiotics to supplement the culture media, either for selection of drug-resistant cell lines to serve as 'marker' in the *in vitro* genetic manipulation programme or from overcoming problems of microbial contamination of culture media, has been studied by several workers for better understanding of possible biochemical and molecular events underlying morphogenesis *in vitro*. Some antibiotics are toxic while others are stimulatory for cell growth and enhanced shoot differentiation in callus cultures. Kukreja *et al.*, demonstrated that certain antibiotics, like chloramphenicol exhibited stimulatory effect in shoot-bud organogenesis at levels upto 150 mg/l in *Hyoscyamus muticus* callus. A 6-10 fold increase in shoot-bud primordial-formation was observed at 50 mg/l. Not only this, a two-fold increase in total tropane alkaloid content was also observed at this level which supported optimal shoot morphogenesis. This, obviously highlights the possible role or antibiotics in differentiation and morphogenesis *in vitro* and their potential use for production of secondary metabolites at the callus and cell levels.

3. AGROBACTERIUM MEDIATED GENETIC TRANSFORMATION

Hairy root culture in the most frequently used method for genetic transformation, i.e. transfer and expression of foreign genes (genetic material DNA) in plants. The technique involves co-culture of explants with *Agrobacterium rhizogenes* (with root inducing Ri plasmid) for specified duration followed by transfer to a suitable medium supplemented with antibiotics to eliminate bacteria for plant regeneration. The success of genetic transformation depends largely upon the efficiency of *A. rhizogenes* strain employed and the type and dose of antibiotics used in the culture media.

In an important medicinal plant, *Withania somnifera*, Banerjee *et al.*, analysed the specificity of the bacterium strain and the frequency of transformation events. They found the best transformation ability and growth of the hairy roots of the strain A_4 of *A. rhizogenes*. They also observed the presence of withafrin-A in the media as well as in the hairy roots of 10 weeks old cultures.

Besides, Sultana and Ahuja studied the effect of many bacteriocidal antibiotics used in hairy root culture of *Atropa belladonna* for genetic transformation. They found in indigenously marketed cheap drug –

Cephalexin as a better alternative to the imported *Cefotaxine* heretofore being extensively used in genetic transformation experiments.

4. *IN VTIRO* PRODUCTION OF SECONDARY METABOLITES

The first successful commerical production of Shikonin from cell of the plant, *Lithospermum erythrohizon* by M/s Mitsui Petrochem Ltd. in Japan opened the new possibilities and renewed enthusiam for production of secondary metabolites, like alkaloids, saponins, flavonoides, etc. from cell cultures of medicinal plants. Banerjee *et al.*, in collaboration with Bose Institute, Calcutta identified fruit as the best explant or tissue source of *Solanum sarrachoides* for *in vitro* production of solasodine – a nitrogen analogue of diosgenin. The amount of solasodine so obtained even without optimization studies, was higher than that reported in several other species of the genus *Solanum*.

Besides, Mathur *et al.* also demonstrated *in vitro* production of ginsenoside – an adaptogenic and stimulatory saponin from 25-day old callus and cell suspension cultures of *Panax quinquefolium*. They also observed the typical segmoidal growth pattern of its callus and cell suspension tissues over a 35-day culture cycle modified MS medium.

5. SOMATIC HYBRIDIZATION

Development of parasexual (somatic) hybrids is an exciting possibility of remote hybridization at interspecific and even at integeneric level for *inter se* transfer of novel genes *inter se*. The two species of *Hyoscyamus*, viz. *H. muticus* and *H. albus* are wide apart in chromosome number (2n = 28 and 68, respectively). The former contains more hyoscyamine than hyoscine and is susceptible to aphids and viruses. In contrast, the latter has high scopolamine (hyoscine) in its roots and is resistant to insects and stresses. But owing to pre-zygotic incompatibility, sexual hybridization between these two species was not successful. However, Liaq-ur-Rahman *et al.* were able to develop parasexual hybrids from fused protoplast of these two species and thus combine characters of interest across species. The somatic hybrid plants showed intermediate morphological characters with 82-120 chromosomes (modal number being 96). They produced 33-78% viable pollen grains and set viable seeds upon selfing and backcrossing with either parents.

Thus, a good deal of success has been achieved in genetic manipulation of medicinal plants through biotechnological tools, especially tissue/cell culture techniques at CIMAP. But it would require considerable time and input to reach to commercial scale. Nevertheless, it has shown the path definitively.

Blue Print and the Future Vision

As could be visualized, all these medicinal plants enumerated hitherto have direct bearing in modern system of medicine, because the major/

active chemical constituents and their biological activities in these plants have very well been established. The literature also abounds with numerous reports on basic genetic studies in these crops, which we purposely skipped to save time and space. But this is by no means all that is the need of the hour. An array of herbal drug plants which play unique roles in traditional systems of medicine where not the specialty chemicals but the whole crude drug (the compound mixture) is important, is yet to be subjected to organized cultivation and intensive genetic acceleration. Therefore, our future vision underlies the conservation and genetic amelioration of myriads of untouched or scarcely manipulated herbal flora which nature has so generously bestowed upon us. Fortunately, the recent biotechnological advancement has crumbled all the major bottlenecks, hence rapid successes might be assured. The final product, i.e. an improved cultivar arising from genetic enhancement of germplasm of these plants might confer many advantages:

(1) It is a permanent genetic restructuring (stable/heritable over generations) of the germplasm lines.

(2) It is the cheapest way of germplasm enhancement, hence the most cost-effective component of superior cultivation technology.

(3) The product is not doubt environmentally clean and bio-friendly.

(4) The product may fit into varying cropping systems, such as intercropping, crop-rotation, agro-forestry, etc.

However, a close and adequate monitoring is expeditious while subjecting the target material to genetic manipulation. For instance,

(a) Whether the final product commensurate with the prevailing demand of pharmaceutical market for its qualitative profile.

(b) Whether the new strain/variety matches well with the environment of its cultivation without any loss of quantitative and qualitative performance. In other words, whether the product is appropriately buffered from genotype x environment interaction.

(c) Whether the equilibrium of the biotic and abiotic stresses is properly maintained under cultivation.

These strategies of genetic manipulation of herbal drug plants will set the human health care system on sound scientific footing. Not only this, the conventional/Medelian plant breeding coupled with modern and sophisticated biotechnological tools may soon become the harbinger of 'Green Drug Revolution' (GDR) *vis-à-vis* 'Green Revolution' (GR) in food crops. However, as against the latter (GR) which has often been regarded as an agronomic splendour but societal disaster and is browning/waning fast; the former (GDR) might overcome social imbalances as HYV's evolved in medicinal plants may fit well into both conservative (subsistence) as well as opportunistic (modern) agricultural systems.

19

Improvement on Medicinal Plants Cultivation

INTRODUCTION

The active principles which are found in plants are generally secondary metabolities, the physiological activities of which have rendered them important as potential drugs and for related uses. The biosynthesis of these active compounds, although controlled genetically, is affected strongly by environmental influences. As a result, there are fluctuations in the concentrations and quantities of the secondary metabolites such as alkaloids, glycosides and steroids etc. There are scattered reports on detailed studies regarding the effect of environment on medicinal plants. Poor informations are available regarding the physiological studies in relation to developmental growth of medicinal plants. Systematic studies have been reported by different authors in different crops like *Cinchona*, *Cephaelis*, *Rauvolfia*, *Catharanthus* and *Datura*. Scientific cultivation of *Dioscorea* and extraction of their active principles have been reported by Mehta and Staba and Nandi and Chatterjee. Panda analysed the agronomical aspects of *Costus speciosus* plants. The developmental aspects of *Digitalis* have been analysed by Nandi and Chatterjee and also by others. The present report is an attempt to improve medicinal plants cultivation in West Bengal hills.

MATERIAL AND METHODS

Seedling of alkaloid yielding plants like *Cinchona ledgeriana, Cephaelis ipecacuamha, Solanum khasianum, Rauvolfia serpentina, Catharanthus roseus, Datura innoxia, Datura stramonium, Atropa belladanna* and *Hyoscyamus niger*; steroidal sapogenin yielding plants like *Dioscorea composita, Dioscorea floribunda, Dioscorea prazeri* and *Costus speciosus* and cardiac glycoside yielding plants like *Digitalis lanata* and *Digitalis purpurea* were used as exprimental material. Experiments were conducted in randomized block design in experimental nurseries at different altitudes. Active principles of different plants were assayed following I.P. for *Cinchona* and *Cephaelis*; Nandi and Chatterjee for *Rauvolfia;* Janot *et al*. for

Catharanthus; Scieder for *Hyoscyamus, Datura* and *Atropa*; Selvaraj for *Dioscorea* and *Costus* and A.O.A.C. for *Digitalis*. Nitrogenous fractions viz total nitrogen (TN), protein nitrogen (PN) and soluble nitrogen (SN) contents were estimated following the method of Vogel. Estimation of reducing sugar (R-CHO) and non-reducing sugar (NR-CHO) contents were done according to the method described by Panda. Post harvest incubation and histochemical studies on *Costus* and *Dioscorea* were analysed following the method described by Nandi *et al.*

Quantitative data on stem growth, leaf formation, flower/fruit formation and formation of different active principles were analysed systematically at intervals of 15 – 30 days according different species and percentage increase or decrease of different growth and biochemical functions during some predetermined interval of time, together with the formation of active principles in different plants were worked out. Such data were collected during vegetative, reproductive, and post-reproductive stage for development in all the plants species study.

Experiments were conducted by removing the flower buds (de-budding) and fruits (de-fruiting) to find out the role of reproduction in the synthesis of active principles. In long-day (18L + 8D) experiments, additional light was supplied to the plants being 100 Fc for 15 days and 30 days. In other experimental studies, the plants were grown in different altitudes to find out the best suitability of altitudinal zones for their cultivation. Growth hormones like gibberellic acid (GA_3) and mineral nutrients like Mg and Mn were applied through leaves in different concentrations. The results of effective optimum doses have been included in the report.

EXPERIMENTAL RESULTS

Experimental results from *Cinchona* and *Cephaelis* growing at different elevations revealed that *Cinchona* prefers high range of elevation for maximum bark yield and alkaloid formation. In *Cephaelis*, though the alkaloid synthesis is favoured at higher altitude but the root yield is maximum in lower elevations (Tables 1, 2). *Rauvolfia serpentina* can favourably be cultivated at lower altitude when alkaloid content is also high but in *Catharanthus* the alkaloid content is maximum at medium elevation and the herbage yield at lower elevation (Table 3). Studies on altitudinal effect on Datura revealed that the alkloid formation favoured at lower altitude whereas the formation of the same was favoured at higher altitude in *Atropa*, *Hyoscyamus* and *Solanum* (Table 4). Variations in diosgenin formation in *Dioscorea* and *Costus* have been shown in Table 5. Synthesis of diosgenin was more pronounced in plants cultivated at high altitudes but the production of biomass was generally high in lower elevations. In *Digitalis*, the cultivation of plants at higher altitude favoured the production of biomass as well as the glycoside formation in both the species. Glycoside formation was of lower magnitude at lower elevations (Table 6).

Table 1: Effect of altitude on bark yield and alkaloid content in *C. ledgeriana*.

Altitude (M)	Bark yield kg/plant		% alkaloid	
	Root	Stem	Quinine	Quinidine
100	1.08	0.40	4.21 (2.66)	0.16 (0.06)
500	1.10	0.42	4.32 (2.73)	0.17 (0.06)
1000	1.12	0.48	4.85 (2.97)	0.18 (0.09)
1500	1.25	0.62	4.91 (3.12)	0.18 (0.11)
2000	1.11	0.41	4.65 (2.60)	0.17 (0.06)

Figures within the parenthesis is % alkaloid of stem bark.

Table 2: Effect of altitude on root yield and alkaloid content in *C. ipecacuamha* root

Altitude (M)	Root yield/ plant(gm)	Total alkaloid (%)	Emetine (% of TA)
50	9.1	2.4 to 2.5	45 to 50
100	8.5	2.6 to 2.7	50 to 52
150	8.0	2.9 to 3.2	50 to 55

Table 3: Effect of altitude on root yield and alkaloid content in *Rauvolifa* and *Catharanthus*

Species	Altitude (M)	Root yield/ plant(gm)	Total alkaloid (%)
R. serpentina	100	58.5	2.22
	500	47.2	2.01
	1000	42.3	1.95
C. roseus	100	67.9	0.97
	500	62.5	1.11
	1000	58.3	1.01

Table 4: Altitudinal variations of alkaloid formation in *Datura, Atropa, Hyoscyamus* and *Solanum*

Species	Altitude (M)			
	50	500	1000	1500
A. belladonna	0.13	0.15	0.16	0.18
H. niger	0.76	0.80	0.85	0.88
D. innoxia	0.46	0.32	0.30	0.26
D. stramonium	0.49	0.35	0.32	0.28
S. khasianum	0.92	0.98	1.10	1.15

Table 5: Effect of altitude on diosgenin and biomass production in *Dioscorea* and *Costus*

Species	*Altitude (M)*	*Biomass (Kg/A)*	*Diosgenin (%)*
D. composita	50	5500	3.00
	500	4800	3.50
D. floribunda	50	4550	3.54
	500	4100	3.79
D. prazeri	50	2000	2.00
	500	1100	2.21
C. speciosus	50	2250	1.21
	500	1200	1.85

Table 6: Effect of altitude on biomass and glycoside content in *Digitalis*

Species	*Altitude (M)*	*Yield/ha (Qntl)*	*Total glycoside (%)*
	100	27.5	0.6 to 0.8
D. purpurea	500	52.5	0.7 to 0.9
	1000	75.0	1.0 to 1.5
D. lanata	100	12.0	0.4 to 0.6
	500	21.0	0.5 to 0.6
	1000	30.0	0.8 to 0.9

The assay of alkaloid content in roots of *Rauvolfia* and *Catharanthus* and in leaves of *Datura*, *Hyoscyamus* and *Atropa* was done during vegetative, reproductive and post-reproductive stages of development (Table 7). Developmental stages were distinguished from each other in respect of quantum of flowers and fruits formation per plants. A positive accumulation of alkaloid formation occurred in all stages of development of *Rauvolfia* and *Catharanthus* whereas a negetive accumulation of the same was represented in *Datura, Atropa* and *Hyoscyamus* during post-reproductive stage of development. Maximum accumulation of alkaloid was noted in all the species during reproductive stage of development when there also occurred a maximum rate of flower formation. Rate of formation of total glycoside (TG) in both rosette (R) and axial (A) leaves as well as flower formation during different developmental stages of *Digitalis* have been shown in Table 8. The TG content in A-leaves gradually increased upto initiation of reproductive stage of development i.e. late bolting stage and its rate of formation in these leaves became highest when rate of flower formation was maximum. In R-leaves, though TG formation increased upto initiation of reproductive stage, its rate became highest in these leaves before initiation of flower took place on the bolted axis. Insteroidal sapogenin yielding plants, the diosgenin synthesis in *Dioscorea* occurred during all the stage of development, maximum rate of synthesis being noted during vegetative stage of development. In *Costus*, diosgenin synthesis increased upto reproductive stage of development and there after declines. Maximum rate of synthesis of diosgenin was noted during reproductive stage when the rate of flower formation was also maximum in this plant species (Table 9).

Table 7: Alkaloid formation in relation to reproductive function in alkaloid yielding plants.

Species	*% increase(+) or decrease (-) during*		
	Vegetative	*Reproductive*	*Post-reproductive*
R. serpentina	FL -	+ 70.06	+ 55.66
	TA + 28.62	+ 36.53	+ 29.65
C. roseus	FL -	+ 750.00	+ 60.08
	TA + 12.60	+ 25.51	+ 18.35
D. innoxia	FL -	+ 330.00	+ 51.00
	TA + 13.75	+ 17.90	- 6.97
A. belladonna	FL -	+ 280.00	+ 34.70
	TA + 15.45	+ 22.83	- 7.05
H. niger	FL-	+ 190.50	+ 21.30
	TA + 19.51	+ 31.32	- 4.25

Table 8: Rate of glycoside formation in relation to flowering in *Digitalis*

Species	*Parameters*	*% Increase(+) or decrease (-) during*			
		Vegetative	*Bolting*	*Reproductive*	*Post reproductive*
	Fl formation	0	0	+ 380.45	+ 5.10
D. lanata	TG R-leaf	+ 10.52	+ 15.16	+ 2.43	-5.12
	TG A-leaf	0	+ 8.10	+ 12.28	- 4.31
	Fl formation	0	0	+ 320.51	+ 10.22
D. purpurea	TG R-leaf	+ 17.20	+ 22.55	+ 9.53	- 4.32
	TG A-leaf	0	+ 15.19	+ 19.33	- 4.15

The effect of removal of flower buds (de-budding) and removal of fruits (de-fruiting) on growth and active principle content in different medicinal plants have been shown in Table 10. De-budding and de-fruiting operations accelerated leaf formation in all the species under study except *Rauvolfia* where there is a decrease in laminar area formation. Maximum increase in leaf formation was noted in *Digitalis lanata*. The de-budding operation decreased the linear growth in all the alkaloid yielding plants (except *Rauvolfia*) and cardiac glycoside yielding plants where the active principle synthesis was augmented in all the species by both the operations.

Table 9: Rate of diosgenin formation in relation to flowering in *Dioscorea* and *Costus*

Species	*Parameters*	*% increase(+) or decrease (-) during*		
		Vegetative	*Reproductive*	*Post-reproductive*
	Fl formation	0	+ 1142.85	+ 9.62
D.composita	Diosgenin	+ 2.50	+ 2.25	+ 2.06
	Fl formation	0	+ 62.08	+ 3.61
IC. Speciosus	Diosgenin	+12.46	+ 19.95	- 10.31

Table 10: Effect of removal of reproductive units on growth and active principle formation

	% increase(+) or decrease (-) over control					
	Removal of flower buds			*Removal of fruits*		
Species	*Leaf growth*	*Linear growth*	*Active principles*	*Leaf growth*	*Linear growth*	*Active principles*
D. stramanium	+ 9.9	- 19.2	+ 43.3	+ 4.2	+ 13.4	+ 21.9
A. belladonna	+ 28.1	- 21.3	+ 29.3	+ 15.2	+ 7.3	+ 17.1
H. niger	+ 45.7	- 18.6	+ 33.6	+ 18.2	+ 5.0	+ 19.6
R. serpentina	- 5.9	+ 3.8	+ 17.6	- 3.2	- 4.2	+ 11.5
C. roseus	+ 25.8	- 14.9	+ 19.6	+ 30.1	- 2.3	+ 9.2
C. ledgeriana	+ 15.8	- 6.2	+ 29.5	+ 7.1	- 2.2	+ 21.3
C. ipecacuanha	+ 10.4	- 8.2	+ 17.2	+ 6.3	- 3.6	+ 11.1
D. lanata	+ 98.6	- 50.0	+ 17.2	+ 78.9	+ 30.6	+ 10.3
D. purpurea	+ 38.4	- 29.5	+ 12.6	+ 14.6	+ 22.6	+ 9.3
C. speciosus	+ 26.0	+ 22.6	+ 32.1	+ 14.2	+ 11.2	+ 9.7
D. composita	+ 22.6	+ 18.3	+ 12.5	+ 8.3	+ 11.7	+ 6.2
D. prazeri	+ 12.6	+ 10.1	+ 9.3	+ 6.6	+ 7.1	+ 4.2
D. floribunda	+ 18.6	+ 14.2	+ 11.3	+ 8.5	+ 7.9	+ 5.1

The effect of light an GA_3 on the formation of active principle in different medicinal plants have been shown in Table 11. Long-day treatments and foliar application of GA_3 augmented the biogenesis of active principle in all the plants in a considerable way. Maximum augmentation was noted in *Rauvolfia serpentina* plants treated with 30 long day photoperiodic cycles and in *Datura innoxia* plants treated with 200 ppm gibberellic acid.

Analysis of different physiological and biochemical functions during different developmental stages in *Atropa, Datura* and *Hyoscyamus* has been shown in Table 12. It is revealed that long day exposure to the plants increased the total alkaloid synthesis during vegetative stage of development. Extension growth (EG) was found to be positively correlated with total alkaloid synthesis during vegetative stage. Alkaloid synthesis was also found to be correlated with flower formation during reproductive stage of development of the plants. Analysis of biochemical fractions revealed that during vegetative stage all the biochemical fractions along with the TA content increased when treated with long day photoperiodic cycles, a maximum increase being noted in SN content. During reproductive stage, decrease of TN and PN content remained associated with increase of SN and TA contents. Such study when examined during post reproductive stage revealed that TN and PN contents increased during this stage with the decrease of SN and TA contents. Results of effects of long day on *Dioscorea* have been shown in Table – 13. It is revealed that extension growth gradually decreased with the advancement of stages of growth along with the synthesis diosgenin. Maximum extension growth as well as diosgenin synthesis was revealed during vegetative stage of development. It is also observed that during all the developmental stage, there occurred a positive accumulation of all the biochemical fractions. The rate of diosgenin and R-CHO synthesis was miximum during vegetative stage and then gradually declined whereas the rate of NR-CHO content gradually increased showing maximum increase during post-reproductive stage of development. Table 14 shows the glycoside content in *Digitalis* increased due to application of GA_3 during vegetative stage with the reduction of R-leaf formation. It is to be noted that with the increase of TG content during reproductive stage of development, the rate of extension growth, A-leaf formation and flower formation increased. Thus, during reproductive stage, a positive correlation between the rates of increase of extension growth, A – leaf formation and formation of flowers and TG content could be shown GA_3 treatment increased all the biochemical fractions during vegetative stage. During reproductive stage, TN and NR-CHO contents decreased which was accompanied by an increase of R-CHO and TG contents. During post-reproductive stage, TG and R-CHO contents decreased with the increase of NR-CHO

The results of application of Mg and Mn in different medicinal plants have been shown in Table 15. Both Mg and Mn increased dry weight accumulation and alkaloid synthesis in all the species. A reduction in linear growth was observed in *Rauvolfia* and *Catharanthus*. Plants treated with Mn revealed higher potentialities than Mg in synthesizing alkaloid. Dry weight accumulation and formation of alkaloid were increased in all the treatments and a close relationship could be established between these two biochemical entities. The foliar application of mineral nutrients like Mg, Mn and B showed pronounced effects on augmentation to tuber growth and diosgenin formation in *Dioscorea* and *Costus* (Table 16). All treatments augmented diosgenin formation as well as tuber yield. Maximum tuberisation was noted in plants treated with Mg + Mn + B (10 mg/l) whereas synthesis of diosgenin was favoured in plants treated wtih Mg + Mn (10 mg/l) treatment.

Table 11: Effect of longday and GA_3 on active principle formation

Species	% increase (+) or decrease (-) over control	
	30 LDPPC	GA (200 ppm)
A. belladonna	+ 17.00	+ 8.22
D. innoxia	+ 12.13	+ 22.16
D. stramonium	+ 21.59	+ 9.56
H. niger	+ 19.78	+ 11.58
C. roseus	+ 3.22	+ 6.72
R. serpentina	+ 36.10	+ 11.39
D. lanata	+ 15.67	+ 14.05
D. purpurea	+ 14.85	+ 11.16
D. composita	+ 13.90	+ 13.63
D. floribunda	+ 14.32	+ 12.52
D. prazeri	+ 15.36	+ 11.32
C. speciosus	+ 21.73	+ 16.35

Table 12: Physiological and biochemical correlation in alkaloid yielding plants treated 30 LDPPC

Parameters	% increase(+) or decrease (-) over control		
	Vegetative	Reproductive	Post-reproductive
A. belladonna			
EG	+ 35.22	+ 7.52	+ 2.16
FI	0	+ 69.93	+ 13.11
TN	+ 5.32	- 1.95	+ 2.47
SN	+ 9.84	+ 15.47	- 8.22
PN	+ 8.10	- 15.33	+ 9.53
TA	+ 10.25	+ 17.00	- 3.21
D. stramonium			
EG	+ 28.19	+ 6.52	+ 2.13
FI	0	+ 122.82	+ 12.55
TN	+ 17.16	- 2.84	+ 5.38
SN	+ 30.81	+ 17.00	- 10.69
PN	+ 16.42	- 14.52	+ 11.50
TA	+ 18.84	+ 21.59	- 6.05
H. niger			
EG	+ 41.39	+ 8.22	+ 2.11
FI	0	+ 98.52	+ 7.59
TN	+ 13.19	- 2.15	+ 4.13
SN	+ 23.52	+ 21.88	- 7.89
PN	+ 12.16	- 14.18	+ 7.33
TA	+ 14.53	+ 19.78	- 7.42

Table 13: Effect of 30 LDPPC on the pattern of changes of functional paramerters in *Dioscorea composita*

Parameters	% increase(+) or decrease (-) over control		
	Vegetative	*Reproductive*	*Post-reproductive*
EG	+ 121.11	+ 22.80	+ 8.73
FI	0	+ 1340.00	+ 48.18
TN	+ 8.00	+ 2.25	+ 3.01
R-CHO	+ 10.12	+ 8.33	+ 8.02
NR-CHO	+ 2.31	+ 3.56	+ 5.22
Diosgenin	+ 3.90	+ 3.78	+ 3.14

Table 14: Effect of GA-200 ppm on pattern of changes of functional parameters in *D. purpurea*

Parameters	% increase(+) or decrease (-) over control		
	Vegetative	*Reproductive*	*Post-reproductive*
R-leaf	- 14.31	0	0
A-leaf	0	+ 183.61	- 26.81
EG	0	+ 201.74	+ 15.22
FI	0	+ 109.33	+ 12.75
TN	+ 3.01	- 2.11	+ 1.07
R-CHO	+ 4.20	+ 5.35	- 2.68
NR-CHO	+ 1.19	- 3.69	+ 2.42
TG	+ 8.63	+ 11.15	- 2.81

Table 15: Effect of Mg and Mn on growth and alkaloid formation in alkaloid yielding plants

Species	% increase(+) or decrease (-) over control					
	Linear growth		*Dry weight*		*Total alkaloid*	
	Mg	*Mn*	*Mg*	*Mg*	*Mn*	*Mg*
C. ledgeriana	+ 3.5	+ 3.6	+ 34.2	+ 47.5	+ 44.1	+ 66.2
C. ipecacuanha	+ 12.7	- 11.3	+ 14.8	+ 16.1	+ 20.6	+ 25.3
R. serpentina	- 17.4	- 5.1	+ 18.6	+ 21.6	+ 21.1	+ 30.0
C. roseus	- 29.7	- 12.2	+ 25.3	+ 39.8	+ 22.5	+ 54.1
D. starmonium	+ 14.2	+ 9.7+	+ 9.3	+ 11.5	+ 11.3	+ 22.6
A. belladonna	+ 12.4	+ 7.8	+ 11.5	+ 26.5	+ 17.9	+ 31.2
H. niger	+ 10.6	+ 6.2	+ 19.1	+ 32.4	+ 21.7	+ 29.3

Tables 17 and 18 showed the histochemical analysis of *Costus* and *Dioscorea* respectively. In *Costus speciosus*, there revealed a distinct correlation between the microscopic characters of the starch grains and the corresponding diosgenin content. The starch grains in the older rhizomes with the high diosgenin content were larger and oval, being restricted in number; whereas in younger rhizomes with low diosgenin content, the starch grains were abundant, small and spheriodal in shape. A tendency of accumulation of starch grains surrounding the vascular bundles with the increase of age and diosgenin content could also be established. With the advancement of age of *Dioscorea composita*, the diosgenin synthesis increased along which there occurred a change in the shape and size of starch grains. In one year old plants, the diosgenin content in the tuber is low when the number of very small round starch grains is maximum. The shape of the starch grains passes some transitional stages (triangular and elliptical) and become lens shaped at the age of the 4 year old crop when diosgenin content is also high. A tendency of accumulation of starch grains around vascular bundles with the increase of diosgenin in *Costus speciosus* could also be established. (Table 19) The post-harvested incubation with 2,4-D and Na-acetate established the relationship of starch grain size, number and orientation with diosgenin content. Treatments which induce higher diosgenin content, showed lesser dimension and frequency of starch grains.

Table 16: Effect of mineral nutrients on tuberisation and diosgenin formation in *Dioscorea* and *Costus*

Treatments	*Kg tuber/plant*			*% Diosgenin*		
(10 mg/l)	*DC*	*DF*	*CS*	*DC*	*DF*	*CS*
Mg	0.62	0.55	0.66	4.68	5.46	2.22
Mn	0.61	0.53	0.64	4.60	5.32	2.15
B	0.60	0.51	0.60	4.33	5.06	2.13
Mg + B	0.61	0.53	0.61	4.20	4.49	2.10
Mg + Mn	0.62	0.54	0.65	4.69	5.48	2.25
Mn + B	0.61	0.52	0.60	4.18	4.40	2.06
Mg + Mn + B	0.64	0.58	0.69	4.31	5.00	2.16
Control	0.55	0.50	0.52	3.30	3.70	1.85

DC = *D. composita*, DF = *D. floribunda*; CS = *C. speciosus*.

Table 17: Distribution of starch grains in relation to age and diosgenin content in *Cotus specious*

Age (yr)	*Diosgenin (%)*	*Frequency of starch grains*	*% of starch grain in:* Cortex	Ground	Around vascular bundle
0.5	0.70	96	100	92	26
1.0	1.50	79	90	66	40
1.5	1.80	65	77	53	64
2.0	2.30	58	57	46	75

Table 18: Distribution of starch grains in relation to age and diosgenin in *Dioscorea composita*

Age (yr)	*Diosgenin (%)*	*% occurrence of starch grains/vision field*				
		Very small round	*Small round*	*Large round triangular*	*Large elliptical*	*Large lense shaped*
1.0	2.01	98	2	0	0	0
2.0	2.71	30	65	5	1	0
3.0	2.79	5	8	70	12	5
4.0	3.84	2	5	10	20	83

20

Safed Musli

Safed Musli is being used in various medicinal preparations in India since ages. This is considered to be one such medicines which can be used for any kind of physical weakness of any etiology. Therefore any Ayurvedic medicine, such as *chyavanprash* is considered incomplete without *safed musli*. This plant is so potent, it is often considered equivalent to *Ginseng* and *Shilajit*. Apart from these, the plant can be used in medicines related to diabetes, sterility, post delivery problems, milk increase in mother etc. Owing to these exclusive properties, this plant has immense value in Unani, Ayurvedic and allopathic medicine.

Safed Musli, a tuber plant which grows up to about 1½ ft. The tuberous roots (fingers) grow up to 10 inch deep into the soil. This plant, scientifically, called *Chlorophytum borivillianum* is usually found wildly in forests spread over India.

If this herb is scientifically cultivated it can yield more profits than any conventional crops. So much so that one can make a clean profit of about 2-3 lakh rupees per acre. Currently, the climatic conditions of UP, Maharashtra, Madhya Pradesh, Bihar, Orissa, Andhra Pradesh, Karnataka are quite favourable for its cultivations.

HOW TO CULTIVATE SAFED MUSLI?

- Since this is a tuberous plant, sandy loam soils are best suited.
- Usage of sprinklers is the best method. However, care should be taken to see to it that water would not be stagnant.
- Usually 5 types of fertilizers are used for cultivation of Safed Musli. Cow manure, Chemical manure, Green Manure, Bone Manure, Soil Conditioner etc.
- Since export quality specifies less or no chemicals, avoiding usage of such fertilizers is recommended.
- After harvesting, the weeds such as Datura should be let grown. During May-June, when the field is prepared, these plants should be thoroughly mixed in the soil.

- Bone meal is considered to be very useful to a healthy of crop growth.
- Usage of any soil conditioner was proved to be beneficial to the crop.
- The field should be deeply ploughed. Then the green manure of compost (5-10 troleys/acre) should be applied.
- The roots/fingers/tubers are used as planting material, care should be taken to keep the outer skin intact. Sometimes the whole crown can also be used for germination. The fingers can be separated till no leaves arise from them. For a good crop the tuber should be between 3-10 g weight. For a quality crop; at least the first planting material should be procured from a reputed farm.
- Since musli is a high quality produce, the planting material is expensive. To overcome the initial expenditure, the material can also be procured from wild.
- Growing plants through seeds proved to be difficult. It was found that the plants take more than 2 years to mature through seed plantation.
- The crown-tipped fingers of 5-10 g should be planned at 6 × 6 spacing. Approximately 80,000 fingers are required in one acre.
- The material should be disease free immersed in either badstein or cow urine for about 2 hr prior to planting.
- Harvesting is done after about 90-95 days from planting to the leaves dry and drop. This indicates the time to harvest but, after the leaf drying, the harvest should be postponed for about 2 months with light watering.
- The roots when mature, they exhibit blackish brown colour. At this stage uprooting should be done manually and not by tractors.
- There is nothing to worry if the tubers are left in soil due to any reason. They will grow into new plants during monsoon. However, the productivity of such new plants is markedly low.
- To remove soil on the roots, tubers should be washed under running water.
- Before marketing, the skin of the tubers should be stripped. The stripping is easy but labour intensive. Unskilled labour can be used.
- The stripped material is left under sun for through drying for 2 days.
- The dried material is packed in polythene bags.
- Loss in weight in natural after drying. But the thickness of the tubers will make a difference. Thick tubers lose less weight than

thin ones. Normally about 25% of the uprooted tubers are obtained after dying.

- The smaller tubers are used as plant material while the thicker ones are stripped and dried. Since the tubers are harvested during March-April. They have to be protected till May-June. The storage is best done in chambers with 70-80% humidity. But cold storage is discouraged.
- Musli can be grown in intercrop between teak and other plantations. This method yields good result without extra expenses.

APPARENT PROFITS

- In one acre about 80,000 plants can be planted. Even if 70,000 of them survive, a farmer can get about 2100 kg (@ 30 g/plant) of musli. After stripping and drying about 4 quintals can be obtained.
- Apart from this, the planting material for one acre will also be procured.

MAJOR ADVANTAGE OF *SAFED MUSLI* CULTIVATION

- Most profitable crop in first 6-8 months and the yield in one acre can fetch more than 2 lakh rupees.
- No special processing is required and the activities involved are simple like-uprooting, removing the root coat, drying and selling.
- No need for marketing since the market is always open and demand is high.
- Can be helped by unskilled personnel.
- The crop is climate/weather resistant.

WHAT IS QUALITY MUSLI?

- Which retains whiteness after stripping.
- Which gives more profit after drying.
- Which does not have any stains.

21

Cinchona

PLANT PROFILE

Family	:	*Rubiaceae*
English name	:	Quinine bark, Peruvian bark
Indian name	:	*Sinkona*, *Kunayanah* (Sanskrit) *Kunain* (Hindi), *Cinkona* (Tamil)
Species and varieties	:	*C. succirubra, C. officinalis, C. ledgeriana, C. robusta, C. hybrida*
Distribution	:	India, Andes, Bohemia, Bolivia, Burma, Colombia, Costa Rica, Eucador, Guatemala, Indonesia, Java, Kenya, Panama, Peru, Philippines,

South America, Sri Lanka, Tanganyika, Tanzania, Uganda, Zaire

Uses : Quinine, Anti-malarial drugs

Cinchona Linn. belongs to the genus *Rubiaceae* which has about 65 species. Among these species, *C. succirubra, C. officinalis, C. ledgeriana, C. robusta* and *C. hybrida* are grown commercially for cinchona bark which is the source of quinine and other anti-malarial drugs. In addition, more than twenty other alkaloids have been isolated from *cinchona*, of which cinchonidine, quinidine and cinchonine are the most important. The other alkaloids present are quinamine, quinicine (quinotoxin), cinchonicine (cinchotoxin) hydroquinine, hydroquinidine, hydrocinchonine (Cinchotine), hydrocinchonidine (cinchonidine), cinchonamine, quinamine, conquinamine, poricine, etc. The alkaloids exist chiefly as salts of quinic and cinchotannic acids, and their relative concentrations vary in different species. The leaves contain 1% total alkaloids. In addition to the alkaloids, the bark also contains the bitter glycoside, a-quinovin, cinchofulvic, cinchotannic and quinic acids, a bitterish essential oil possessing the odour of the bark, and a red colouring matter. Quinovin, on hydrolysis, yields quinonic acid and mannitan. In individual plants, the total alkaloid content increases up to the age of 8 to 12 years and then begins to decrease. The alkaloids are formed during the descent of the sap, and their concentration is low in twigs and increases down the stem to a maximum in the root-bark. In *C. ledgerina*, almost 90% of the total alkaloids of the stem bark is quinine, while of the total alkaloids of the root-bark, only 60% is quinine.

Quinine, as a cure for malaria, has been known of for a long time and, even today, expert medical opinion regards quinine as a safe and sure remedy for malaria. Besides, quinine was in use as an anaesthetic as a substitute for cocaine. Its anaesthetic action is prolonged. It has been used as a sclerosing agent in the treatment of internal haemorrhoids and varicose veins. Quinine protects the skin against sunburn. It is a bitter tonic, stomachic and appetizer. In small doses, in the form of a solution, it is a mild irritant and a stimulant of the gastric muscosa and other mucous membranes. It is a weak uterine stimulant. Quinine and other alkaloids have a number of non-medical uses also. Salts of quinine are employed in beverages, as an addition to hair-oils, as a vulcanization accelerator in the rubber industry, for making polarized lenses and has various other uses in photography and optics.

ORIGIN AND DISTRIBUTION

Cinchona is indigenous to South America, and occurs in the Andes, Colombia, Eucador, Costa Rica, Peru and Bolivia between 10°N and 19°S at attitudes ranging from 750 to 2725 m (2500-9000 ft). Some species are also cultivated in Java, Sri Lanka, India, Burma, Tanganyika, Bohemia, Panama, Indonesia, Guatemala, Uganda, Philippines, Tanzania, Kenya, Zaire and Costa Rica. In India, it is confined to some parts of West Bengal, Tamil Nadu (the Anamalais, Naduvattam, Shevaroy Hills, Palani and parts of Tirunelveli) and Karnataka (South Kanara and Coorg) in an area of about 6000 to 8000 ha.

BOTANY AND DESCRIPTION OF THE SPECIES

Cinchona spp. (x=17) are evergreen shrubs or trees. The leaves are opposite, simple, entire; the stipules are interpetiolar and deciduous. The inflorescence is a terminal panicle. The flowers are small and fragrant; the calyx is small, united and has pointed lobes; the corolla is tubular with 5 spreading lobes and a frill of hairs along the margins; it is heterostylous. In microstyles plants, 5 exserted anthers alternate with corolla lobes, while the bifid stigma reaches half the length of the corolla tube. In marcostyled plants, the stamens are half the length of the corolla tube and the stigma is exerted. The fruit is a capsule, dehiscing from the base upwards with 40-50 small, flat, winged seeds.

The following are the commercial species.

a. *C. succirubra* Pav. ex kl. (2n=34)

It attains a height of 40-50 ft or more. This species has a red bark. The quinine content (0.5 to 1.5%) in the bark of this species is very poor. The species is vigorous and grows well between 660 to 1800 m (2000 and 6000 ft) altitude. The species is possibly a variety of *C. pubescens*.

b. *C. officinalis* L. (2n=34)

This species is well suited for the higher altitudes of South India and flourishes well at elevations of 1800 to 2420 m (6000-8000 ft). It is a slender tree, 20-30 ft high. It is the source of 'Crown' or 'Loxa bark'. The quinine content of the bark ranges from 1.5 to 2.0%. The species is indigenous to the mountains of Colombla and Peru.

c. *C. ledgeriana* Moens and tremen (2n=34)

This is a weak but fast growing species, attaining a maximum height of about 20 ft, and it can be grown between 900 to 1800 m (3000-6000 ft) elevations. It is a source of 'Ledger bark' or 'Yellow bark' which is the richest in quinine (4 to 5%); the quinine content is occasionally as high as 14%. This species is considered either a hybrid between high-yielding varieties like *C. calisaya* and *C. succirubra* or a complex hybrid between *C. calisaya*, *C. succirubra* and *C. lancifolia*.

d. *C. robusta*

The origin of this species is uncertain, but it is presumed to be a hybrid between *C. succirubra* and *C. officinalis*. In India, it is grown in the

Darjeeling Hills, West Bengal, and can be grown in places with an elevation of up to 1510 m (5000 ft). The average quinine content of the bark is about 2 per cent.

e. *C. hybrida*

This vigorous growing hybrid is a cross between *C. succirubra* and *C. ledgeriana.* The yield of bark is high and the quinine content varies from 2 to 2.5%.

VARIETIES

Cinchona is a naturally cross-pollinated plant, due to which a great deal of admixture has taken place among the various species and the present stands of cinchona are only crosses between these various species. An outstanding clone - No. 701 - containing over 12% of quinine sulphate in the bark has been spotted by the Tamil Nadu Forest Department and is propagated on a extensive scale in the Nilgiris and Anamalais.

SOIL

Cinchona prefers a light, well drained, virgin forest soil, rich in organic matter with no possibility of subsoil water-logging and with a high moisture holding capacity. It prefers acidic soils (pH 4.6 to 6.5). The calcium requirement of this crop is high.

CLIMATE

C. ledgeriana grows best in tropical climates at altitudes of 1800 m (6000 ft). However, the other species grow well in areas with an average minimum temperature of 13.5°C and a maximum of 21°C with a mean relative humidity of 83%. The growth is very poor at temperatures below 7°C or above 26°C. It grows well in places where the annual rainfall is a little less than 200 mm and is well distributed over at least eight months of the year. *Cinchona* is susceptible to frost and, hence, is not grown on very high hill ranges.

LAND PREPARATION

For raising cinchona plantations, virgin forest soils are best suited. The forest is cleared and the ground is levelled and dug to a depth of 1½ ft to improve the soil structure and to remove stones, if any. About a fortnight prior to planting, pits, of 60 × 60 × 60 cm are dug and filled up with top soil and well decomposed organic matter.

CULTIVATION

Propagation

Cinchona is propagated both by seeds as well as vegetatively by cutting, stooling, layering, cleft-grafting, veneer of side-grafting and patch-budding.

As most of the species of cinchona are highly heterozygous, vegetative propagation is preferred. But, in India, cinchona is propagated by seeds as it is comparatively less expensive.

Propagation by Seeds

Cinchona seeds are small and light and lose viability on storage. The seeds are generally sown during April in sloping beds, 12×4 ft, and covered with a thatched roof. The nursery area is prepared in such a way that the top layer, up to a depth of 2-3 inches, is composed of a mixture of leaf-mould and sand in equal proportions, and is carefully pressed by hand so that it is uniformly firm all over. Cattle manure is usually not applied to the nursery beds.

While sowing, the fresh seeds are scattered thickly on the surface and covered with a thin layer of fine sand. The beds are then lightly watered using a spray can. The seeds germinate in about 20-40 days after sowing. About 50% germination is noticed, out of which only about 10% of the seedlings will be suitable for transplanting after eliminating all the weak, lean and lanky seedlings. The seedlings grown in the nursery can be transplanted in baskets or polythene bags when they are about four months old, with two pairs of leaves. The seedlings will be ready for planting in the main field during mid-May of the succeeding year when they are about 14-18 months old and 30-60 cm in height.

Vegetative Propagation

Among the vegetative methods of propagation, patch-budding, soft terminal cuttings and layering have recorded the best results. A high percentage (85%) of success is obtained in patch-budding in the period from march to the middle of June. Patch-budding is usually done in the nurseries or plantations, *in situ* on plants which are one to two years old. Even the budding on coppices has given a better growth of budded plants. The cuttings are made to root by cincturing and etiolation. During May-June, the shoots are treated, from which cuttings are taken after 50-65 days and planted in the nursery. In layering, the East Malling method with some modifications has given good results, each shoot giving annually about 100-200 shoots in 2 or 3 coppicings. *C. succirubra* is used as stock wherever grafting is done.

PLANTING

Planting is done before the onset of heavy rains. The soil should be sufficiently moist at the time of planting. The planting is done in open pits at a spacing of 120×120 cm or 150×150cm or dense planting of about 8000 plants per hectare is done. The plants are gradually harvested from 3-5 years, until about 800 plants remain in one hectare after 25 years. Young cinchona plants need shade which is provided by planting shade plants like *Alnus nepalenis, Erythrina indica, Albizzia stipulata* and *Grivellea robusta,* 20 ft apart.

Application of Fertilizers

Application of a fertilizer mixture containing N, P and K gives marked results. Liming (dolomite or limestone) is done for the soil if the pH is 5 or lower. Nutrients are supplied @ 115 kg N, 105 kg P_2O and 115 kg K_2O/ha in the form of triple superphosphate, muriate of potash and ammonium sulphate. The quinine content in cinchona is known to increase with the age of the trees, under favourable nutritional conditions.

Weeding

Weeds have to be removed at regular intervals, particularly in young plantations.

Cover Cropping

Besides the native cover, *Crotalaria usaramoenis* or *Leucaena glauca* are grown as cover crops in cinchona plantations. When the plantation becomes older the ground is shaded more heavily, hence the original cover crop must be replaced with shade-tolerant species.

Cultivation Operations

The plants should be staked properly in the first three years to prevent their swaying or leaning.

PESTS AND DISEASES

Pests

The grubs of cockchafer beetles (*Holotrichia repetita, Rhizotrogus refus, Serica nilgiriensis, Popilla chlorion,* etc.) cause serious damage to the seedlings in South Indian plantations. The adults of these beetles come to the surface during summer and should be flushed by irrigating the seed-beds with water mixed with crude oil emulsion. The beetles must be then hand-picked and killed.

Crickets also cut the young seedlings and drag them to their haunts in the seed-beds. The haunts must be searched and the insects killed. The application of tobacco decoction with kerosene or phenyl wards off these insects.

The tea-fly, *Helopeltis antonii* and *H. cinchoni,* infest the leaves in nurseries and also in the main field. These insects cause leaf-curl by sucking the juice from the tender leaves. If heavy damage is noticed, sodium arsenate mixed @ 28 g with 113 g of molasses in 9 litres of water may be sprayed on the plants for controlling these insects. The leaf bug, *Disphinctus humeralis,* is occasionally found on tender foliage.

Diseases

Stem blight caused by *Sporotrichium* and *Verticillium* spp., seedling blight due to *Phytophthora parasitica,* root-rot due to *Phytophthora cinnamomi,* and *Sclerotium rolfsii* and damping-off due to *Pythium vexans* and *Rhizoctonia solani* are some transplant bed-diseases affecting cinchna seedlings. The spread of these diseases can be checked by scooping out the soil in the diseases patches all around, to a depth of 10 cm and throwing it away. The cavity, so formed, may be filled with sterilized, dry soil. The nursery-beds should also be drenched with mercurial fungicide to check the spread of the diseases.

Trunk and branch cankers are plantation diseases which are most prevalent during the rainy season. *C. ledgerina* and its hybrids are more susceptible to this disease. Dark, shrivelled, brittle patches appear on the stems or branches. The pruning of the diseased parts is recommended. Besides, a physiological canker disease has been reported to affect *C. succirubra* and *C. ledgeriana* in Burma. As a result of this canker, the collar of the affected plant swells to about 3 times the normal size and the bark turns dark brown to black. The leaves drop off and those that remain on the plant are much reduced in size. The plants which are badly affected will die, collar canker is said to be caused by too deep planting combined with wind action.

A bark disease and collar rot caused by *Fomes noxius* and *Sclerotium rolfsii,* respectively, have also been reported.

Die-back or pink disease is caused by *Pellicularia salmonicolor.* This organism attacks the tender tips of the stems and branches and gradually spreads. The branches should be pruned to prevent the spread of the disease. Besides, the fungus *Armillaria mellea* causes root rot and *Rosellinia* spp. causes leaf spot diseases.

HARVESTING

By judging the amount of vegetative growth, the trees are coppiced when they are 6 to 8 years old. Coppicing involves pruning the trees at a height of 5 cm (2 inches) from the ground-level. The leftover stump regenerates to produce a large number of shoots, but only two or three of these are retained and allowed to grow further. The rest of the coppices are removed. A second coppicing is done 8-10 years after the first coppicing, where only about 2 to 3 shoots are left to grow further. The plants are uprooted in the 30th year when their vigour declines. The major harvests are obtained at the time of the first two coppicings and only little yield of bark is obtained from the dead and drying trees and prunings. The first set of yields are obtained in the third year after planting. The bark is separated from the coppices by beating it with a mallet and is then peeled by hand or a knife. The peeled bark should be dried immediately to prevent the loss of alkaloids, preferably in the shade. In rainy weather, drying is done in special sheds or by means of artificial heat. In well-established plantations, drying is done in well-regulated ovens. For this purpose, hot air ovens, regulated by 70°C, are employed. The long, strips of bark are cut into small pieces and fed into the upper end of a long, slightly inclined, rotating, cylindrical oven. The dried product contains 10% moisture. The dried bark is then packed in gunny bags. The dried bark is called 'Druggists' bark (quinine content 1.8-2%) in trade.

YIELD OF BARK

During the first two coppicings, a yield of 4000 kg of dry stem bark per hectare is obtained. At the final stage of uprooting the tree, the yield of the bark may be about 6000 kg/ha.

ISOLATION OF QUININE

The alkaloids are extracted from the powdered bark. Quinine is isolated from the total alkaloids of the bark as quinine sulphate. The Commercial preparations contain cinchonidine and dihydroquine also, and the quinine may be purified by recrystallization to constant specific rotation. The crystalline, efflorescent trihydrate, is a white, odourless, intensely bitter, micro-crystalline powder.

22

Glory Lily

PLANT PROFILE

Family	: Wurmbaeoidae of Liliaceae
English name	: Glory Lily
Indian name	: *Langali*, *Visalya* (Sanskrit), *Karihari Languli* (Hindi), *Agnishike*, *Gowrihoo Akatangiballi* (Kannada), *Kalappaikkilanku Nabhikkodi* (Tamil)

Species and varieties : *Gloriosa superba* Linn., *G. lutea, G. plantii, G. carsonii, G. richmondensis, G. virescens, G. latifolia, G. magnifica, G. rothschildiana. G. bayssinica, G. longifolia, G. simplex*

Distribution : India, Africa, Asia, Indo-China Madagascar, Sri Lanka, U.S.A.

Uses : Drugs

Gloriosa superba Linn., belonging to the family *Liliaceae,* subfamily *Wurmbacoidae,* is commonly known as glory lily, gloriosa lily or the lily flower. It is a fascinating genus of great scientific interest. In Kannada, it is called *Agnishike, Akkathangiballi, Karadikannina gadde* or *Nangulika,* while in Hindi, it is called *Karihari.*

The plant has been used in the Indian system of medicine since time immemorial. Its tubers are reported to have been used as a tonic, antiperiodic, anti-helminthic and also against snakebites and scorpion stings. The drug is a gastrointestinal irritant and may cause vomiting and purging. It is sometimes used for promoting labour pains and, coversely, also as an abortifacient. It is considered useful in colic, chronic ulcers, piles and gonorrhoea. It is used in local applications against parasitic skin disease and as a cataplasm in urological pains. The leaves, when applied in the form of a paste to the forehead and neck, are reported to cure *asthma* in children. The leaf-juice is used against head lice.

The medicinal properties of the drug are due to the presence of alkaloids, chiefly colchicine ($C_{22}H_{25}O_6N$;mp 151-52°) and gloriosine ($C_{22}H_{25}O_6N$;mp 248-50°). Colchicine is used in the treatment of gout, a common disorder in the temperate parts of the world. Gout is caused by the deposition of microcrystals of uric acid in the joints, which is attributed to a defective regulatory mechanism for endogenous passive synthesis. It is said that colchicine interrupts the cycle of new crystal deposition which seems to be essential for the continuance of acute gout. In addition, these alkaloids are also used as polyploidizing agents in polyploid breeding in crop research. The colchicine content in *Gloriosa superba* Linn. varies from 0.15 to 0.3% in the tubers, and in the seeds it ranges from 0.7 to 0.9%. Until recently, only the tubers are exploited but, after discovering the fact that the seeds also have a high quantity of alkaloids, the crop is grown mainly for its seeds which are in great demand within the country and in the international market.

ORIGIN AND DISTRIBUTION

Gloriosa is a native of tropical Asia and Africa. The genus derives its name from the Latin word *gloriosus,* referring to the flowers. It is found growing throughout tropical India, from the North-west Himalayas to Assam and the Deccan peninsula, extending up to an elevation of 2120 m. In Karnataka, it is commonly found growing all along the Western Ghats. It is also found growing in Madagascar, Sri Lanka, Indo-China and on the adjacent islands. The area under this crop in India is around 2000 ha.

RELATED SPECIES

The genus *Gloriosa* is comprised of about 10 to 15 known species. The important species found in India are *G. superba* and *G. rothschildiana.* The other species found growing in other parts of the world are *G. carsonii, G. plantii* (USA, Africa) *G. simplex, G. abyssinica* (Africa), *G. richmondensis, G. virescens, G. lutea, G. magnifica, G. longifolia* and *G. latifolia.*

Gloriosa is monobasic with a genetic base x = 11. Out of the 10 elemental species, *G. superba, G. lutea* and *G. plantii* are diploids (2n=22); *G. carsonii,* G. *virescens* and *G. richmondensis* are tetradploids (2n=44) and *G. rothschildiana, G. latifolia* and *g. magnifica* are octoploids (2n=88). In general, octoploid species are comparatively short-statured and constitute a medium group of plants.

DESCRIPTION OF THE PLANT

It is a herbaceous, climbing perennial, growing between 3.5 to 6 m in length, but usually trained at 1.5 m above ground-level. The vines are tall, weak-stemmed with tuberous roots that support themselves by means of cirrhosed tips. The leaves are ovate, lanceolate, acuminate, the tips spirally twisted to serve as tendrils. The flowers are large, solitary or may form a lax-corymbose inflorescence, twisted and crisped with six recurved or reflexed petals, blossoming yellow but changing to yellow-red and deep scarlet. In the bud stage, the petals hang down over the ovary and, on maturity, they assume an erect position, leaving the ovary with its stigma exposed at right angles. There are five, long stamens, each with a long anther that displays profuse orange-yellow pollen. The ovary is 3-celled and it forms an ellipsoidal capsule. There are numerous seeds in a capsule and the seeds are warty and dorsally compressed.

CROP IMPROVEMENT

In the year 1979, a cross-breding programme was attempted involving *G. superba, G. lutea and G. plantii* (diploids), *G. carsonii, G. virescens* and *G. richmondensis* (tetraploids) in several combinations. The only successful hybrids were *G. virescens* × *G. carsonii* and its reciprocal: *G. virescens* × *G. richmondensis* and *G. carsonii* × *G. richmondensis.* Morphological analysis and cytogenetical behaviours of all the hybrids has been worked out. Based on these studies, it was reported that the tetraploid *Gloriosa species* had higher crossability as compared to the diploid species.

Further, *G. superba* has always failed to produce hybrids, although it was involved in numerous hybridization combination.

SOIL

If prefers sandy loam soils of the acidic side, with good drainage, for its successful growth. In Southern India, it is found growing luxuriantly in red and black loamy soils which have a good amount of humus with a medium water-holding capacity. A soil pH range between 6-7 has been found suitable for raising this crop.

CLIMATE

Glory lily is a tropical plant and comes up well in warm, humid regions. Under natural conditions, it is found growing up to an elevation of 600 m from sea-level. An annual rainfall of about 373 cm, well-distributed throughout the year, is ideally suited for this crop. It does not withstand continuous moisture stress and requires frequent irrigations up to the flowering in dry periods. The temperatures favourable for its growth and flowering are 15-20°C during the day and 10-15°C at night. The relative humidity should be high. However, continuous cloudy weather is congenial for the pathogen *Curvularia,* which is a very serious threat, resulting in 75 to 80% mortality of the vines. Suitable prophylactic measures have to be adopted, in case the crop has to be grown under such conditions.

CULTIVATION

Propagation

It is commercially propagated from its underground, V-shaped rhizomes or sexually propagated by seeds. The plants raised from seeds take nearly three to four years to flower. Hence, except for experimental purposes, seed propagation if not favoured by the growers.

Gloriosa produces a biforked tuber during the growing season and each of these forks has only one growing bud. Tubers should be handled carefully, as they are brittle and liable to break easily. If the growing bud is subjected to any kind of damage, the tuber will fail to sprout. Since the vigour of the vine and its flowering and fruiting ability depends on the size of the tubers, it should not weigh less than 50-60 g. The plants raised from smaller tubers do not produce flowers during their first year. Large tubers can be divided into two by breaking them in the middle. The dormant tubers start sprouting from the month of May. Under Bangalore conditions, planting during the months of July and August has been found to favour good growth and yield. About 2.5 to 3.0 t/ha of tubers are required for planting. In order to avoid rotting of the tubers before sprouting, only healthy tubers should be selected for planting. In addition, the selected tubers or tuber pieces should be treated with suitable fungicides, preferably Emisan-6 (methoxy ethyl mercury chloride) @ 0.08%.

FIELD PREPARATION AND PLANTING

The field should be ploughed and harrowed several times until it is brought to a fine tilth. All the grass-stubble and roots should be removed. The field must be levelled properly and drainage arrangements made to avoid water-logging during the rains. The field is then divided into subplots of convenient sizes. About 15-20 t/ha of FYM or compost should be mixed well into the soil. One foot deep furrows are opened at a spacing of 45-60 cm. The treated tubers are planted at a depth of 6-8 cm, keeping a plant-to-plant distance of 30 to 45 cm, depending upon the type of soil. Closer spacing has been reported to favour cross-pollination, thereby improving the fruit set.

MANURES AND FERTILIZERS

Though gloriosa makes satisfactory progress with little manuring and fertilization, the addition of well-decayed manure, bonemeal and fertilizers to the soil ensures a vigorous plant, stronger tubers and better flowering. Experiments carried out on this crop have shown that under Bangalore conditions, a fertilizer dose of 120 kg N, 50 kg P_2O_5 and 75 kg K_2O/ha is required for a good crop. Of the nutrients, the whole P_2O_5 and K_2O and one-third of N is applied as a basal dose and the remaining two-third of N should be given in the first six to eight weeks after planting.

IRRIGATION

Frequent irrigation is required during the sprouting time to keep the surface soft, so that there is no hard-pan formation, in order to facilitate easy sprouting and emergence of the growing tip outside the soil. Irrigation should be withheld until after the flowering is over, to prevent rotting of the tubers. Excess watering is harmful to the plants and causes yellow or brown-coloured patches on the leaves, which fall off prematurely.

CROP MONITORING

The provision of some kind of support is necessary for successfully growing gloriosa. Since the stem is very tender, when the plants are about 30-40 cm tall, they should be staked or tied to wires or allowed to climb on some sort of frame.

WEEDING

In the initial stages, the gloriosa plantation requires frequent weeding to control the weeds which will otherwise complete with plants for moisture and nutrients and will restrict the growth of the plant. While weeding, utmost care should be taken to avoid any damage to the growing tip, as once damaged, it does not sprout again during the season. Chemical weed control is possible only when there is wide spacing between the rows and the plants themselves.

PESTS AND DISEASES

Comparatively speaking, gloriosa has few pests and diseases. However, some pests and diseases pose a serious threat when they get favourable conditions, causing severe damage. Hence, great care has to be taken to control them.

Pests

1. Lily caterpillar (Polytela gloriosae)

The lily caterpillar, marked with bands of red and black colour on its body, attacks almost all parts of the plant. They lay a mass of eggs on the undersurface of a tender leaf or in the crown of the growing shoot. Within a very short time, the newly-hatched caterpillars with their voracious appetites damage the leaves and growing points. This pest can be effectively controlled by spraying Metacid at a concentration of 0.2% at fortnightly intervals.

2. Green caterpillar (Plusia chaleites)

This caterpillar is small and green in colour and attacks the leaves and flowers. It completely eats away the flowers causing severe damage to the crop. The control measures recommended for the lily caterpillar will control this pest also.

In addition to the above two insects, the following twelve new insect pests have been reported from the university of Agricultural Sciences, Bangalore. The new pests are: *Diabolocatantops pinguis, Oxya fuscovittata, Monolepta signata, Curculio* spp., *Myllocerus udecimpunctatus, M. viridanus, Ptochus* spp., *Amsacta lactinea, Utetheisa pulchella, Archips micaceana, Lygaeus hospes* and *Graptostethus servus.*

Diseases

1. Leaf blight

This disease is caused by the fungus *Curvularia lunata.* The spores of the fungus are airborne and attack the foliage. The affected leaves first turn light-yellow and, later, small black spots are seen which ultimately spread to the entire leaf and neighbouring plants. The incidence is higher during cloudy weather coupled with high humidity. The disease can be controlled by spraying 0.3% Dithane M-45.

2. Tuber rot of Basal stem rotting and wilting

The soil-borne *Sclerotium* spp. affects the underground tubers and causes the death of the plant. In the initial stages, infected tubers start becoming soft and the foliage exhibits a yellow appearance and in advanced stages, the whole tuber gets infected giving the appearance of a discoloured mass and the plant dies off. Drenching the soil with Bavistin @ 0.2% or Cuprassol near the root-zone of the plant has been observed to control the disease.

HARVESTING AND PROCESSING

Gloriosa is a crop of 170-180 days duration. When planted in June, it starts bearing flowers after 55 days and continues to flower and fruit till October. The fruit requires about 105-110 days from the set to reach maturity. The right stage of harvest is when this capsule starts turning light-green from dark-green and the skin of the fruit shows a shrunken appearance and becomes light in weight. At this stage, when pressed, the pod gives a crinkling sound. After picking, the capsules should be kept in the shade for 7 to 10 days to facilitate the capsules to open up, displaying deep orange-yellow coloured seeds. The seeds and pericarp are separated manually and dried for a week in the shade, by spreading them uniformly over any clean, dry floor or any platform specially erected for the purpose. At the later stages, the seeds are moved to the sunlight for a week till they dry completely. The dried seeds are then packed in moisture-proof containers and stored until exported or extracted for the alkaloids.

YIELD

The yield of seeds differs greatly, depending upon the vigour and age of the plant which, in turn, depend on the size of the tuber. The yield in the initial year will be low, but it gradually increases in the subsequent years. After three years, from a well-managed field, we may get about 200-250 kg/ha of dried seeds. The yield of pericarp (husk) is about 75% of the seeds.

CHEMICAL ANALYSIS OF SEEDS

Colchicine has been extracted from the corms of *Colchicum automnale,* growing wild in some parts of Europe. Recently, the supplies of colchicine from the conventional sources has not been sufficient to cope with its increasing demand. Among the other Indian plants, the seeds of *Iphigenia stellata* contain 0.90%, the corms of *Colchicum leuteum* contain 0.25% and the seeds of *Gloriosa superba* were found to contain 0.60% of colchicine. The easy availability from both wild and cultivated sources make the seeds of *Gloriosa superba* a potential source of colchicine in India.

In order to extract colchicine, 20 g of powdered seed material is exhaustively extracted in a Soxhlet's apparatus with 150 ml of methanol. The extract is concentrated to about 10 ml, when a white deposit is formed. On TLC, it is found that colchicine is present in the mother liquor and not in the white deposit (0.6 g). The mother liquor is dried in a vacuum to get 3.7 g of extract. One gram of the extract is taken as a preparative for thin-layer chromatography. The extract is spotted on precoated silica gel plates, every time using pure colchicine as a standard on the left-hand side. After detection in the iodine chamber, the band corresponding to colchicine was scraped, extracted with methanol and dried (0.03 g). The colchicine obtained, corresponds to 0.55% of the dry seed material.

DVOVACKOVA'S METHOD

About 20 g of powdered seed is extracted with methanol in a Soxhlet's apparatus. The extract is concentrated and diluted with water and is acidified to pH 4, with citric acid. It is extracted with ether and the ether extract is discarded. Further extraction with chloroform gives the neutral phenolic portion which, on passing through a column of silica gel and drying in a vacuum, gives almost pure colchicine.

23

Henbane

PLANT PROFILE

Family : *Solanaceae*

English name : Henbane, black henbane

Indian name : *Parasikayavani* (Sanskrit) *Khurasani ajavayan*, *Khurassani jamani* (Hindi) *Kurassaniyomam* (Tamil)

Species and varieties : *Hyoscyamus niger* L., *H. muticuls* L., IC-66, Aela

Distribution : India, America, Central Asia, Europe Finland, Greece, Portugal

From Western Punjab through Afghanistan to Egypt

Uses : Drugs

Henbane, comprising of the dried leaves and flowering tops of *Hyoscyamus niger* L., commonly black henbane or common henbane and *H. muticus* L., is an official drug of repute. The herb and seed yield tropane alkaloids (0.03-0.06%), 90% of which are hyoscyamine and hyoscine and the rest are scopolamine, atropine, hyoscipirin, choline, fatty oil, mucilage, albumen and KNO_3. They are used as an anodyne, sedative, tranquillizer, antiseptic antispasmodic, mydriatic, in asthma and whooping cough. Hyoscine is particularly useful in protection against shocks caused by accidents and loud noises.

ORIGIN AND DISTRIBUTION

Hyoscyamus niger is a native of Europe, Central Asia, India and tropical America and is distributed throughout Europe from Portugal and Greece in the South to Norway and Finland in the North. In India, it is mainly found growing in temperate to subtropical regions and is grown largely in Kashmir and Uttar Pradesh. Its successful cultivation at Indore, recently, has indicated that it can also be grown in warmer regions as a winter crop. The plant has been found to grow well under Bangalore conditions also. *H. muticus* is, however, essentially a desert plant attaining a height of 90 cm (and 30 cm spread) and is found growing from Western Punjab through Afghanistan to Egypt.

DESCRIPTION OF THE PLANT

H. niger (2n=34), belonging to the family *Solanaceae,* is an erect, viscidly hairy, biennial plant growing up to 160 cm in height, and is grown as a short duration (90-100 days) winter crop in the Indian plains. The leaves are simple, large, ovate or oblong, coarsely dentate and pinnately lobed. The flowers are yellowish, pale, sessile or subsessile, borne on terminal cymes. The fruit is a berry containing numerous minute seeds. The seeds are small, about 1.5 mm long, 2000/g, brown to black, marked with fine, conspicuous reticulations.

H. muticus Linn (2n=28) is very similar to *H. niger,* but shorter in height (90 cm.) The leaves are small, having a smooth dentate margin with a thick and sticky texture. The seeds are somewhat heavier, covered with a dark brown seed-coat.

VARIETIES

IC-66 is a short duration (100 days) variety of *H., muticus,* developed and released by the National Bureau of Plant Genetic Resources, New Delhi. It is reported to yield 25 q/ha with the total tropane alkaloids varying from 0.05 to 0.10%. Another variety which is a tetraploid and a profusely-seeding polyploid line has been released by the CIMAP, Lucknow. This variety is reported to have a growing period of 200 days and produces 645 q/ha fresh herb or 43.2 q/ha dry herb, in comparison to 511 q/ha and 37.3 q/ha in the diploid parent. The alkaloid content is also high, suggesting that it will be more profitable than the existing varieties. The CIMAP, Lucknow, have released one variety of *H. niger* through mutation breeding. *Aela* is the mutant culture of *H. niger,* selected from irradiated progenies, which have yellow flowers with a slight purple tinge at the base of the petals. It grows vigorously giving a yield of 73 q/ha, which is 109% more than the parent (50 q/ha). It has a high total of alkaloids—0.545% against 0.167% in the parent plant.

SOIL

Henbane, being a foliage crop, requires a level, well-drained fertile, sandy loamy soil, rich in organic matter, for its optimum growth. A soil pH range of 7-8.5 is preferred by the crop. Deep black and water-logged soils are not suitable for its cultivation.

CLIMATE

Henbane is a cool season crop and it does not tolerate very cold temperature, as the growth and development of these plants is appreciably slow below 20°C and becomes almost static if the temperature remains below 10°C. The plants perish under frosty conditions. Low temperature has also been reported to affect the seed germination. Seeds of *H. niger* and *H. muticus* germinate best in 8-10 days if a temperature between 20-30°C is maintained with adequate moisture. In temperature it is cultivated as a winter crop. In any case, the plantation must get bright sunlight which is important for the proper growth and development of this crop. Similarly, regions with high temperature and humidity must be avoided as both are detrimental to plant growth and also to their content of alkaloids.

CULTIVATION

Propagation

The crop can be raised either by sowing the seeds directly in the main field or by raising the seedlings in the nursery and transplanting them.

Successful regeneration of plants from hairy root cultures has been achieved in *H. muticus* through hormonal induction, at the CIMAP, Lucknow.

DIRECT SOWING

The best time for sowing the seeds directly in the field is early October in subtropical regions, while June-July is most appropriate in temperature regions. As henbane seeds are very small, it is important to ensure that the soil is prepared to a fine tilth for sowing. Seeds must be sown not deeper than 2 to 2.5 cm below the soil for good germination. Soaking the seeds overnight and incubating them for 7-8 days at 25ºC for sprouting before sowing, gives a better germination rate. In order to ensure the uniform distribution of seeds all over the field, the seeds should be mixed with dry, powdered earth or sand in a ratio of 1:10 before sowing. About 2-3 kg of seed would suffice to sow an area of one hectare.

The optimum sowing time of *H. niger* at Indore is reported to be the second fortnight of November with 30×30 cm spacing. In Delhi, the first fortnight of November, with 30×15cm was found suitable.

RAISING OF SEEDLINGS

The best time for raising the nursery is September in the plains and April-May in temperate regions. The seeds are mixed with sand and sown by broadcasting in rows of 8 cm, in raised nursery beds. The seeds are then gently covered with a fine mixture of soil and FYM or sand, mulched and immediately watered. About 500 g seeds are required to raise enough seedlings to cover an area of one hectare. Germination takes place in about 8-10 days. At this time, the mulch is removed but watering and weeding are continued as usual. If the temperature is low, the seeds take a longer time to germinate and the growth of the seedlings is also very slow. The seedlings take about two months to reach a suitable stage for transplanting. A foliar spray of 1% urea, when seedlings are about 20 days old, has been found to accelerate their growth.

PLANTING

The seedlings are transplanted at a spacing of 45 cm in rows and 15-30 cm from plant-to-plant in a well-prepared field and followed up with light irrigation. Transplanted seedlings take about a week to establish. Since there is a heavy mortality in the transplanted seedlings, it is recommended that this crop should be grown on a commercial scale only by direct sowing.

MANURES AND FERTILIZERS

At the time of land preparation, well-decomposed FYM at the rate of 15-20 t/ha is added. In addition, a dose of 40-80 kg N, 30-40 kg P and 20-30 kg K/ha, has been recommended to obtain the maximum dry-matter yield. The entire quantities of P and K along with 20 kg N is given as a basal dose. The remaining quantity of nitrogen is given as a top-dressing in two equal split doses during the growing season.

IRRIGATION

The transplanted crop is given the first irrigation immediately after transplanting. Subsequent irrigations are given at 8-10 days' intervals, until it is about a month old and, subsequently, the crop is irrigated at intervals of about 15-20 days. In all, 4-5 irrigations are required. But in the directly sown crop, to secure the proper seed germination, it is necessary that one pre-sowing irrigation is given before ploughing. If the seed germination is sparse, a week after sowing another irrigation is essential. After this, 3-4 more irrigations at an interval of 15-20 days are required for the standing crop.

INTERCULTURE

The crop raised by direct sowing should be thinned after a fortnight of germination and a spacing of 30 cm within the rows should be maintained. Usually, two weeding-cum-hoeing operations are necessary during the entire cropping season.

PESTS AND DISEASES

No serious attack of insect pests and diseases are reported on both the species of henbane. However, the larva of the cotton bug attacks the leaves and capsule of this crop during July-August, causing heavy damage. Aphids also infest the crop. These two insects may be controlled by 2-3 sprayings (at 10-15 days' interval) of Endosulphon (2 ml/l of water) or Methyl Parathion or Metasystox (2 ml/l).

A green mosaic caused by a virus has been reported to affect the crop in India. The nematodes *Meloidogyne incognita* and *M. javanica* cause root-knot disease.

HARVESTING PROCESSING AND STORAGE

The leaves and flower-tops of *H. niger* are collected at the flowering stage of the plant, while the entire aerial part of *H. muticus* may be harvested at a similar stage. In *H. niger,* the older leaves of the lower regions of the plant touching the ground should be picked first and dried separately. The herb is sun-dried for 2-3 days followed by 6-7 days in the shade, with constant raking over with sticks. Approximately, every 100 g of fresh leaves yield 14 g of dry leaves. After drying, the material is stored in gunny bags and kept in a cool, dry place. The produce should not be stored for more than 2 months.

YIELD

The yield of the herb varies greatly with the spacing. By adopting a spacing of 45 × 30 cm, an average yield of 15 q/ha of dry herb may be obtained.

ESTIMATION OF HYOSCYAMINE IN LEAVES

For this purposes, 40 g of leaf-powder is weighed and transferred to a flask containing 200 ml of a mixture of 4 volumes of solvent and 1 volume of ethanol. It is shaken well and allowed to stand for ten minutes. Then 6 ml of dilute ammonia solution is added and it is shaken frequently for one hour. The mixture is then transferred to a percolator plugged with cotton-wool and, when the liquid ceases to flów, packed firmly. Continue the percolation, first with 100 ml of the ether-alcohol mixture and then with solvent ether, until complete extraction of the alkaloids is effected. The total time of percolation should not exceed three hours. The volume of the percolate is reduced to about 20 ml by distilling over a water-bath. The distillate is transferred to a separator, then the flask is washed with chloroform three times taking 10 ml each time and the washings are added to the separator followed by 30 ml of 0.5 N sulphuric acid. The separator should be shaken well, allowed to separate, and the lower layer allowed to run off.

The extraction is continued with successive quantities each of 10 ml of a mixture of 3 volumes of 0.1 N hydrochloric acid and 1 volume of ethanol, until complete extraction of the alkaloids is effected. The mixed acid solution is washed with about 10 ml of chloroform and the latter run-off into a second separator containing 20 ml of 0.1 N hydrochloric acid. It is shaken, allowed to separate and the chloroform is discarded. Repeat the extraction in the first separator with chloroform, twice, taking 5 ml each time, and transfer the liquid to the second separator each time and wash with the same aqueous acid as before. Transfer the acid liquid from the second separator to the first separator. The liquid is made distinctly alkaline with a dilute ammonia solution (25%) and shaken with successive quantities of chloroform, until complete extraction of the alkaloids is effected. Wash the combined chloroform solution with about 3 ml of water. Remove most of the chloroform and transfer the remainder of the chloroform solution to a shallow, open dish. Complete the removal of the chloroform, add 2 ml of ethyl alcohol, evaporate to dryness at 105ºC, and weigh at intervals of one hour until two successive weighings do not differ by more than 1 mg. Dissolve the residue in 20 ml of 0.02 N sulphuric acid, and titrate with 0.02 N sodium hydroxide, using a solution of methyl red as indicator. Each ml of 0.02 N sulphuric acid is equivalent to 0.005787 g of alkaloids, calculated as hyoscyamine.

24

Holy Thistle

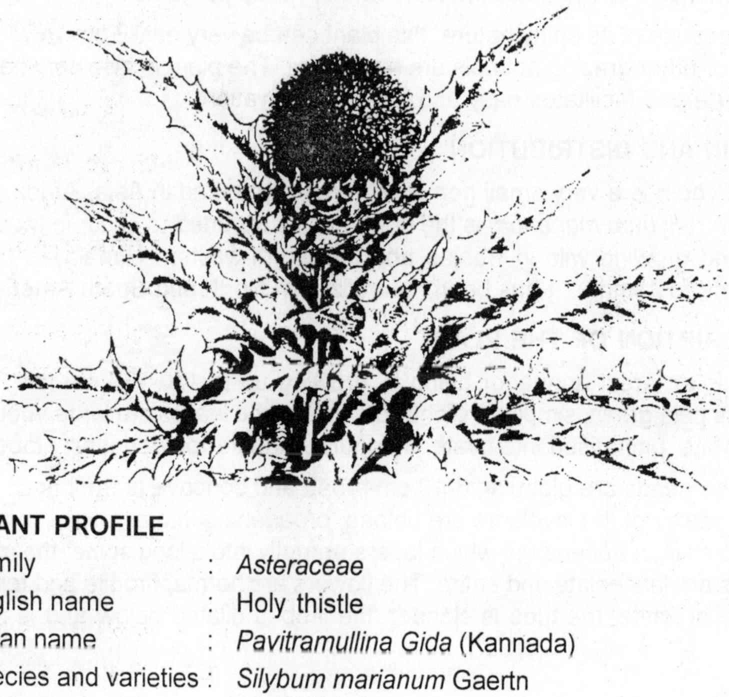

PLANT PROFILE

Family	:	*Asteraceae*
English name	:	Holy thistle
Indian name	:	*Pavitramullina Gida* (Kannada)
Species and varieties	:	*Silybum marianum* Gaertn
Distribution	:	India, Africa, Asia, North and South America, Europe
Uses	:	Drugs

Holy Thistle (*Silybum marianum* Gaertn), belonging to the family *Asteraceae,* is an important medicinal plant used by man from ancient times. According to the great Greek physician, Dioscorides, who accompanied the occupying Roman army in Britain, in the first century AD, they used parts of the holy thistle as a remedy for those who are punished by having their body drawn backwards. It is also mentioned in the writings of the venerable Bede (872-735 BC) as a plant which was cure for all ailments and had supernatural properties.

Its seeds contain the flavonoids silymarin and sylibin which are considered as the main components for the antihepatotoxic (antagonizing liver damage) property of the drug. In Europe, the herb is used against jaundice, intermittent fevers, dropsy and uterine trouble. As a diet or infusion, the leaves are said to be reliable galactagogues. The seeds are pungent, demulscent and antispasmodic. They are used for the treatment of calculi of the liver and gall bladder and in controlling haemorrhage. The flowering heads are good for diabetics. The extract of seeds is reported to increase the peristalsis of the small intestine and is mildly purgative.

Because of its spiny nature, this plant can be very easily grown where cattle or other grazing animals are a problem. The plant is also very hardy in nature and facilitates easy and low-risk cultivation.

ORIGIN AND DISTRIBUTION

Silybum is a very small genus of herbs distributed in Asia, Africa and Europe. *Silybum marianum* is the only species reported τo occur in India. It is found growing wild in Punjab and the North-western Himalayas from Kashmir to Jammu. It has been naturalized in North and South America.

DESCRIPTION OF THE PLANT

It is an erect annual or biennial, growing up to 120-130 cm tall. The stem is pale-green, simple or slightly branching, the leaves are large, mottled with white, pinnatified into ovate, triangular, sinuate-toothed, spiny lobes.

The heads are globular, 6-10 cm broad and concave at the base. The outer scales of the involucre are oblong, broadening into an ovate, prickly, cellate margin appendage which tapers abruptly into a long spine, the inner scales are lanceolate and entire. The flowers are hermaphrodite and fertile, purple or white, the tube is slender, the limb is dilated below and is five-fold.

SOIL

It is a very hardy plant and is found growing on a variety of soils. However, sandy loam soils which have good drainage are ideal. The crop can be grown successfully even on marginal lands by supplementing the nutrients through fertilizer application.

CLIMATE

The holy thistle prefers a moderate type of climate for its successful growth. Places with extreme climates are unsuitable for its cultivation. The plant can be grown up to an altitude of 2400 m from sea-level.

CULTIVATION

Sowing

The crop is raised by using the seeds obtained from the previous season's crop. It is sown during September-October in the plains and March-April in hilly areas. Before sowing the seeds, the field is prepared well, divided into convenient sized plots and thoroughly mixed with organic manure. Then the seeds are either sown by broadcasting them in the rows spaced at 60 cm and later thinned to maintain an approximate spacing of 60 cm between the plants within the row, or they can also be sown at 60×60 cm spacing using a seed-drill. If enough moisture is not available, the field should be irrigated immediately after sowing.

MANURES AND FERTILIZERS

The crop responds well to the application of manure and fertilizers. FYM at the rate of about 8-10 t/ha should be added at the time of land preparation. In addition, a dose of 120 kg N, 100 kg P_2O_5 and 75 kg K_2O/ha, is recommended for obtaining a good yield. Among the fertilizers, a half-dose of N and the whole dose of P and K are applied at the time of planting and the remaining half-dose of N is given as a top-dressing after the seedlings are one month old.

IRRIGATION

It is a sufficiently hardy crop and does not require very frequent irrigations, except during the early stages of growth, when the crop has to be irrigated at weekly intervals. Subsequently, watering once in a fortnight will suffice. In all, about 10-12 irrigations during the entire cropping season will enable the crop to grow luxuriantly.

INTERCULTURE

Weeds are a problem in this crop only during the early stages of growth. Once the crop picks up, it covers the field with its large foliage and the weeds are automatically suppressed. One or two weddings when the plants are young will help to avoid completion from weeds.

INSECT PESTS AND DISEASES

Silybum is practically free from most pests and diseases. However, there is a report of the pest *Tanyameus polliatus* which can be controlled by a spray of 0.03% Methyl Parathion. Among the diseases, root-wilt caused by the *Rhizoctonia* species has been observed under Bangalore conditions, which can be controlled by drenching the soil in fungicides like Captan or Brassicol (0.1%).

HARVESTING AND YIELD

Silybum is a 4 months duration crop. The crop is prickly and hence it is to be harvested carefully by cutting the individual heads with the help of a sharp instrument. Since all the heads do not reach maturity at the same time, harvesting is done 2-3 times. There is also a problem of seed-shattering; therefore, the heads should be harvested when the seeds are just turning brown. If the crop is to be harvested mechanically, is should be harvested when the majority of the heads have reached maturity. The heads are spread in the threshing-yard for 3-4 days for drying. While drying, quite a few of them burst and release the seeds, and the remaining are threshed, separated and stored.

If harvested at the right time, on an average, about 1 t/ha of seeds may be obtained.

25

Ipecac

PLANT PROFILE

Family	:	*Rubiaceae*
English name	:	Ipecac
Species and varieties	:	*Cephaelis ipecacuanha*

C. acuminata Karst.

Distribution : Rio or Brazilian and Cartegena, India, Bolivia, Brazil, Burma

Uses : Drugs

Ipecac [*Cephaelis ipecacuanha* (Brotero) A. Richard] is one of the oldest medicinal plants known to man. It is said to have been used by South American Indians before the beginning of recorded history. Dr. Adrian Helveties of Paris is credited with the introduction of ipecac to Europe. The early Brazilians appear to have applied the term *ipecacuanha* to a number of roots with common emetic properties, until a Portuguese scientist, Berhardino Gomes, collected the authentic plants. These plants were later described by Flex de Aucllor Brotero, in 1803, who named it *Callicocca ipecacuanha.*

A Portuguese priest named Trislasu, travelling in Brazil in the later years of the 15th century, came to know of the curative properties of ipecac from the natives, which they called 'Igpecaya'. By the end of the 17th century a regular trade in this drug commenced, mainly through the efforts of the Dutch. Later, for fear of depletion of its supply from wild sources, many European countries became interested in its cultivation.

The root of ipecac is the source of the important drug 'emetine'. Although the plant is rich in non-phenolic compounds in its stem (0.21-0.54%), leaves (0.58-1.22%) and roots (0.61-1.35%), it is only the root which is being exploited commercially.

Five major alkaloids have been isolated from the drug. Of them, emetine and cephaeline are the more important. The commercial value of the drug depends on its total alkaloid and emetine contents. The principal constituent of the non-phenolic fraction of the total alkaloids is emetine. Cephaeline is a phenolic alkaloid, too toxic for use, and is usually converted into emetine by methylene. Small amounts of psychotrine, methyl-psychotrine, emetamine, and traces of ipecamine and hydroipecamine have also been isolated. These, however, play a relatively unimportant part in any of the therapeutic effects of ipecac. The principal therapeutic use of emetine is in the treatment of amoebiasis. Besides the alkaloids, the roots contain choline, a colourless glycoside (ipecaccanhin), a phytosterol (m.p., 160-162) and a crystalline colouring matter, erythrocephaline. The presence of several glycosides, tannins, malic and citric acids, saponin, resin, fat and a large amount of starch in the roots has been reported.

Ipecac is an important drug being at once an emetic, a diaphoretic, one of the convenient known expectorants, and an excellent remedy for the treatment of amoebic dysentery. A dose smaller than 0.03 g of the dry drug is a stimulant to the stomach, exciting appetite and facilitating digestion. It is used in the form of syrup, powder, tinctures and lozenges. It has become one of the most prominent chemicals used in cancer research. A mixture of ipecac powder and opium was prescribed as a sudontic at the onset of influenza, but this is no longer official. The syrup of ipecac is often given in the early stages of acute bronchitis. It has been used successfully in the treatment of bilharziasis, guinea-worms and oriental sores. The chief adulterant of the drug is the aerial stem of the plant. It can be distinguished from the root by the pith composed of cells with lignified walls and by the surface scars.

When administered in large doses (0.03-0.12 g) it is nauseating, a diaphoretic and expectorant. It acts as an emetic resulting in myositis of the injection site, diarrhoea and vomiting, neuromuscular symptoms, hypertension and heart palpitations and also circulatory failure. Powdered ipecac is a respiratory irritant causing coughing and sneezing. Pharmacists and assistants *scentitized* by repeated exposure may experience rhinitis and asthma.

ORIGIN AND DISTRIBUTION

This plant is a native of the humid forests of Bolivia and Brazil. It has been grown on a commercial scale in Malaysia, and to a small extent in Burma, Brazil and India. It is cultivated in Mungpoo, rongo, Munsong and Latpanchor (Darjeeling District) as a subsidiary crop in cinchona plantations and in the Nilgiris, especially near Kallar. It has been successfully raised at the Rungbee Cinchona Plantation in Sikkim. Jorhat and Srimargal in Assam, Sinduhans and Jalpaiguri in West Bengal and Bilaspur in Orissa are also considered to be suitable localities for its cultivation. The total area under this crop in India is about 100 ha.

DESCRIPTION OF THE PLANT

The species *ipecacuanha* has been placed in several genera. However, the genus *Cephaelis* has been considered as correct, according to the International Code of Botanical Nomenclature. This is the name recognized by the US and British pharmacopoeias. The plant belongs to the family *Rubiaceae* and has the chromosome number 2n=22.

It is a tropical perennial, herbaceous plant, 50-75 cm high, with a slender, cylindrical, corky, sinuate, underground stem (or false rhiozme) from which extend several horizontal roots. When mature, the roots have a brick-red to dark-brown bark, smooth or more or less prominently transversely ridged or ribbed. They possess a musty odour and have a bitter taste. The stem above ground-level is quadrangular, somewhat downy, with few or no branches. The leaves are opposite near the top of plant, alternate below, dark-green on the upper surface and light-green below, rough, hairy with short, downy petioles. The flowers are white, funnel-shaped, sessile, less than 1 cm wide and are borne in dense, globular clusters of 8-20 on a purplish-green stalk. The fruit is oval, purple, becoming nearly black when ripe and contains two hemispherical stones, each enclosing a single white seed.

The rhizome is slender, bearing horizontally-spreading fibrous roots. The latter are smooth, slender and whitish when young and develop, on maturation, into a thick, brownish bark with numerous closely placed transverse furrows, giving the roots an annulated appearance. These constitute the drug of commerce.

TYPES OF VARIETIES

Two types of ipecac, Rio or Brazilian and Cartegenian, are recognized by the pharmacopeias of the U.S.A., U.K. and India. The Rio or Brazilian ipecac is obtained form *Cephaelis ipecacuanha.*

Cartegena ipecac (Syn. Nicaragua, Savanilla and Panama ipecac) is obtained from *C. acuminata* Karst which grows in the moist forests of Columbia. The plant is similar to the preceding one but bears white fruits. The roots are greyish-brown and less distinctly ridged.

There are two varieties of cartagena ipecac, one is a greyish-brown form; the other is reddish-brown, comes largely from Nicaragua and is appropriately called Nicaraguan ipecac. This variety is characterized by numerous transverse ridges on the roots that frequently bear light-coloured abrasions.

Many strains of ipecac exist and several commercial varieties have been distinguished, the more important among them being known by names indicating the country of origin. The Rio, Matto Grosso, Minas and Manaos varieties, all come from Brazil. Indian and Johore ipecac are from Bengal, Burma and the Federation of Malaya. The best commercial drug comes from Matto Grasso in Brazil and is collected from wild plants. Two strains of *C. ipecacuanha* exist at present in Brazil, one of which appears to be the source of the commercial Matto Grasso drug and the other of the Johore drug.

SOIL

The plant requires deep soil with a high humus content. It thrives best in forest areas in sandy loam soils, rich in potash, magnesium and lime. Heavy soils and water-logged conditions, which provide poor aeration for the roots, are not suitable for growing this crop. The ideal soil pH is reported to be around 6.

CLIMATE

Ipecac is a shade-loving plant, sensitive to direct exposure to sun and light, and prefers high humidity and moisture and also protection from winds for its growth and development. It thrives well in a tropical mild, humid climate. An annual rainfall of 150-500 cm well distributed throughout the year and a temperature ranging from a minimum of 18-20°C to a maximum of 36-38°C, are essential for its successful cultivation. Temperature fluctuations should not be great. The plant is sensitive to frost, but can be grown successfully at altitudes of 350-850 m.

CULTIVATION

Propagation

The crop is raised from seeds as well as cuttings from old plants, petioles and adventitious buds produced by roots. The vegetative method of propagation is not favoured, because the root-yield is poor. Commercially, the plant is propagated by seeds.

In seed propagation, it can be raised either by direct sowing or transplanting seedlings grown in nursery beds.

Nursery Raising and Transplanting

The seed-bed and nursery preparation require very thorough soil working, the removing of all weeds, roots and stones from the soil. Terraces are cut off at 3 to 4 m in width and the soil is dug to a depth of about 3.5 m and thoroughly mulched. The soil is mixed with leaf-mould and organic manure and the terraces are levelled, so as to give a slight slope downwards to drain off excess irrigation and rain water. The nursery beds are covered with thatched roofing raised with the help of bamboo poles. In some places, strong polythene sheets instead of thatched roofing are also used. About one-third of the seeds are sterile and so the seeds are sown @ 35 g/sq m. before sowing, the seeds are treated with lime for 48 hr, or with hydrogen peroxide for 96 hours. In the nursery, the seeds are either broad-casted uniformly or, preferably, sown thickly in lines about 5 cm apart. The sowing is done between January and March, depending upon the local climatic conditions. The germination of seeds is slow and erratic, it takes between 3 and 5 months. The small (up to 4 cm height), seedlings are transferred to another nursery-bed at a spacing of 5×5 cm. This is done during August-September, when the monsoon rains are over. The young plants are allowed to remain in this nursery till March-April of the following year. The young growing plants are then transplanted into the main field at a spacing of 10×10 cm or 15×15 cm and allowed to remain there for the next 3 years, till they are dug out upon maturity. Growing the plants under the shade of plants like *Teprosia candida* and *Crotalaria anagryoides* and also inter-cropping with *Cinchona ledgeriana* have given encouraging results.

DIRECT SOWING

In direct sowing, the seeds are either sown at a spacing of 15×15 cm or sometimes also broadcasted.

MANURES AND FERTILIZERS

The use of organic manures, leaf-mould and compost has been recommended to increase the quantity of nutrients in the soil and to improve drainage. There is not much information available on the nutritional requirement of ipecac. In an experiment conducted at Mungapoo, the highest root yield has been reported by the application of castor-cake @ 600 kg/; whereas, superphosphate in combination with nitrogenous fertilizers, augmented the formation of non-phenolic alkaloids.

IRRIGATION

The nursery-beds require very careful irrigation. A watering can with a fine, low nose is used to water the seed beds in order to keep the soil moist and avoid crust formation. The crop in the field is also provided with regular irrigation during the dry period.

WEEDING

A schedule of weeding-cum-hoeing should be followed in such a way that the plantation is kept free of weeds and the soil remains porous. Mulching the nursery beds with coloured polythene sheets (25 gauge in thickness) has been reported to reduce the cost of weeding. The sheet is perforated at the places where the seedlings are transplanted.

PESTS AND DISEASES

The plants are affected by damping-off fungi like *Rhizoctonia* spp. in the nursery. As a control measure, the seeds should be treated with a suitable seed-dressing of fungicide before sowing. *Fusarium moniliforme* is reported to cause wilt disease, for which suitable control measures like field sanitation and drenching the plants with fungicidal solution like copper oxychloride (3 g/l) may be taken up. The other diseases reported on this crop are leaf-blight and rot caused by the fungi, *Alternaria alternata* and *Fusarium* spp., respectively.

HARVESTING AND PROCESSING

The plant is a perennial herb. One-fourth of the planted area is uprooted and replanted annually, to maintain a uniform market supply. It survives for up to 5-6 years. It starts flowering from the second year onwards, and its fruits take 3 months to ripen. The production of fruits peaks during the 3rd to 4th years. The formation of alkaloids increases with the age of the plants and roots and is the most during the 3rd-4th years. Therefore, harvesting should be done after the plant is 3 years old.

At the time of harvesting, the roots are dug out from the soil, cleaned of the adhering soil and exposed to the sun in a thin layer for drying, as quickly as possible. The roots are kept covered during the night to protect them against heavy dew. The drying takes 2-3 days, thereafter the roots are broken into small pieces and sieved to remove the remaining adherent soil. The root pieces, finally packed into bales, are ready for export or transported to extraction plants for the production of emetine alkaloids and other preparations.

YIELD

A 3-years-old crop (4 years from seeds) yields the maximum amount of roots and also contains a high alkaloid content. The ***Indian Pharmacopoeia*** requires that the roots contain not less than 2% of the total alkaloids, of which not less than 50% should be emetine in content.

A 3-years-old plantation, on an average, may yield up to 6.5 t/ha of fresh roots, when managed properly.

26

Opium Poppy

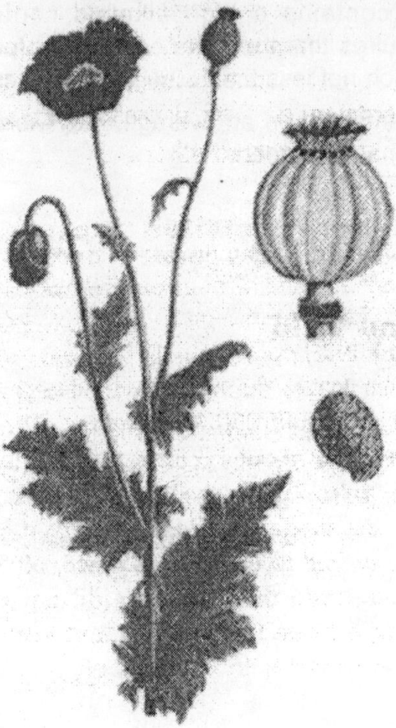

PLANT PROFILE

Family : *Papavaraceae*

English name : Opium poppy, White poppy

Indian name : *Ahiphenam*, *Aphukam* (Sanskrit), *Kas-kas Aphim* (Hindi), *Gasagase* (Kannada) *Kasakasa*, *Posttakkai* (Tamil)

Species and varieties : *Papaver somniferum*

Distribution : India, Argentina, Bulgaria, China, Czechoslovakia, Egypt, Germany, Greece, Holland, Hungary, Iran, Japan, Poland, Portugal, Spain Turkey, USSR, Yugoslavia

Uses : Confectionery, Culinary items, Drugs, Oil

Papaver somniferum (2 n = 22), commonly called opium poppy, is an annual herb belonging to the family *Papavaraceae.* It grows up to a height of 60-120 cm. It is an important medicinal plant, the source of over 40 alkaloids including psychoactive agents, a great boon to psychiatry for the treatment of mental and nervous diseases and to medical research. The commercial product 'Opium' is an addictive narcotic obtained from the seed capsules of the opium poppy, the source of a number of very valuable alkaloids like morphine, codeine, narcotine, papaverine and thebaine. Other minor alkaloids include aporeine, codamine, cryptopne, guoscopine, hydrocotarnine, laudanine, narcotoline, neopine, oxynarcotine and papaveramine. The seeds are also reported to contain a high percentage of linoleic acid which lowers blood cholesterol in the human system. The alkaloids, morphine and codeine, are widely used as sedatives to relieve pain ad induce sleep, in addition to their use against cough. Opium is a very valuable but dangerous drug. It should be used in very limited quantities and under the strict supervision of a physician.

In India, this plant is mainly cultivated for its latex (opium) and the seeds come as a by-product. These seeds are quite a rich source of fatty oil and protein and, in many countries of Europe, employed as a major source of cooking oil. The seed is also an important culinary item in India. It is extensively used in the preparation of native confectionery, pastries and bread. In some places, the young plants are also consumed as a leafy vegetable This is one medicinal plants which is very lucrative. A crop raised properly, in one hectare area, fetches about 1 lakh rupees. But its cultivation has to be done under the strict control of the Central Excise Department and it cannot be cultivated everywhere. It can be grown only in those areas specified by the Government of India.

ORIGIN AND DISTRIBUTION

It is supposed to have originated in the western Mediterranean region and from there it has spread through the Balkan peninsula to Asia Minor and India. Since antiquity, its cultivation has been in vogue in Italy, Greece and Asia Minor. It was during the 15th century that the herb was introduced in India. First, it was cultivated along the sea coast and later penetrated into the interior of the peninsula.

AREA AND PRODUCTION

The 1953, the United Nation's Opium Conference Protocol (still in effect) for limiting and regulating the cultivation of opium poppy plants assets that Bulgaria, Greece, India, Iran, Turkey, the USSR, Egypt, Czechoslovakia, Poland, Germany, Holland, China, Japan, Argentina, Spain, Hungary, Portugal and Yugoslavia are the countries that may legally produce opium. Other countries might grow it for other purposes. The only country where substantial amounts of opium is now produced for export is India which amounts to 1465t annually and forms over 90% of the world production. In India, all the opium of commerce is now grown mainly in the states of Uttar Pradesh, Madhya Pradesh and Rajasthan covering an area of 18000 ha.

The control and regulation of all aspects of the cultivation of poppy and wholesale trade has been under the purview of the Government of the India since 1773. After the partitioning of the Indian subcontinent in 1947, the essentials of the present system of narcotics control, which derived from the system instituted by the British in the 1857 Opium Act, where retained with few changes.

The Government of India is able to effectively licence farmers to grow opium. This is highly organised so as to allow elimination of those growers whose yield of opium is poor.

DESCRIPTION OF THE PLANT

The poppy is a small, erect, scarcely branched (towards the top) herb attaining a height of 120 cm with large, serrated leaves and attractive brightly coloured (white, pink, purple, red and variegated) flowers. The main shoot and branches terminate into large, oblong to globose capsules, filled with small white, flat seeds. The seeds are small, kidney-shaped, whitish-yellow, grey-brown, reddish-brown or black, and rich in oil.

VARIETIES

The most popular varieties grown in the country remain in the field from 140 to 160 days. The following are some of the important varieties of which Talia, Ranghatak and Dhola Chota Gothia are popular varieties recommended for heavy black soils.

(i) Talia

It is sown early and it remains in the field for 140 days. Its flowers are pink and have large petals. The capsule is oblong, ovate, light-green and shiny (waxy).

(ii) Ranghatak

It is a medium-tall variety, maturing for lancing in 125-130 days after sowing. It bears white and light-pink flowers. It produces medium-sized capsules (7.6 cm × 5.0 cm), which are slightly flattened on the top. It yields opium of a comparatively thin consistency that changes to a dark-brown colour on exposure.

(iii) Dhola Chota Gotia

It is a dwarf cultivar (85-90 cm), bearing pure white flowers and light-green capsules which are oblong-ovate in shape. It is ready for lancing after 105-115 days of sowing and matures for seed in 140 days.

(iv) MOP-3

This variety has been developed at the Jawaharlal Nehru Krishi Vishwa Vidyalaya, Mandsaur, recently. It bears pinkish-white flowers comprising of large non-serrated petals. Its capsules are ready for lancing 120 days after sowing and the variety is recommended where adequate irrigation facilities exist in the later part of the season.

(v) MOP-16

This is another promising selection made at the Jawaharlal Nehru Krishi Vishwa Vidyalaya, Mandsaur. The plant bears white flowers with serrated petals and round, flat-topped capsules. This is comparatively drought tolerant and is ready for lancing 105-110 days after sowing. It is recommended where an early maturing crop is preferred.

(vi) Shama

This variety was released by the CIMAP, Lucknow during the year 1983. The main alkaloids like Morphine (14.51-16.75%), Codeine (2.05-3/24%), Thebaine (1.84-2.16%), Papaverine (0.82%) and Narcotine (5.89-6.32%) in this variety are reported to be on higher side than the existing commercially cultivated variety. It yields 39.5 kg of latex and 8.8 kg/ha of seeds.

(vii) Shweta

This variety was also released by the CIMAP, Lucknow, along with Shama. However, it is reported to be superior to Shama in the content of the main alkaloids-morphine (15.75-22.38%), codeine (2.15-2.76%), thebaine (2.04-2.5%), papaverine (0.94-1.1%) and Narcotine (5.94-6.5%). It gives an average yield of 42.5 kg of latex and 7.8 kg/ha of seeds.

(viii) BROP 1 (Botanical Research Opium Poppy-1) (NBRI-3)

It is a synthetic variety developed at the National Botanical Research Institute, Lucknow, by crossing selections from *Kali Dandi*, *Suyapankhi* and *Safaid Dandi*. This variety is highly adaptable to varied agroclimatic conditions and gives a higher yield than national checks. It is moderately resistant to diseases. It yields about 54 kg/ha of opium and 10-13 q/ha of seeds. The morphine content is 13% and above.

(ix) Kirtiman (NOP-4)

It was developed at the Narendra Dev University of Agriculture and Technology, Kumarganj, Faizabad, through selection from local races. The variety is moderately resistant to downy mildew. It yields 35-45 kg/ha of latex and 9-10 q/ha of seeds. The morphine content is up to 12%.

(x) Chetak (U.O. 285)

This variety was developed at the Rajasthan Agriculture University, Udaipur. It is moderately resistant to diseases. The opium yield is up to 54 k/ha and the seed-yield is 10-12 q/ha and contains up to 12% morphine.

(xi) Trishna (IC-42)

This variety was developed at the National Bureau of Plant Genetic Resources, Delhi, through selection and selfing. It yields 49 to 53 kg/ha of latex and 12 to 14.78% morphine. The variety is resistant to frost, root-rot and tolerant to downy mildew disease.

(xii) Jawahar Aphim 16 (JA-16)

It is a pureline selection of local landraces developed at the Jawaharlal Nehru Krishi Vishwa Vidyalay College of Agriculture, Mandsaur (Madhya Pradesh). It is moderately resistant to downy mildew. It gives 45-54 kg/ha of latex, 8-10 q/ha of seeds and contains up to 12% morphine.

Recently, another three varieties: 'NBRI-3' of opium, 'Sujatha' an opium-free poppy for the production of oil and seed and 'Shubhra' for high morphine and seed yield have been released from the NBRI, Lucknow, RRL, Jammu and CIMAP, Lucknow, respectively.

SOIL

The opium crop needs deep clay loam, highly fertile and well-drained soils with a pH range of 6.0 to 7.5. Such soils, containing adequate organic matter, retain moisture and there is not need of irrigation during lancing. However, with adequate manuring and use of fertilizers even light, loam to sandy-loam lateritic soils can give high yields under good management. Heavy clay or fine sandy soils generally pose a problem, since they remain wet during the rains and are too difficult to cultivate in the dry period.

CLIMATE

In general, the crop needs long cold season (20ºC) wit adequate sunshine in the early season for a healthy vegetative growth; heavy rains after sowing cause loss in seed germination. Warm, dry weather with a temperature of 30-35ºC is required during the reproductive period. Cloudy whether, frost, hailstorms and high gusty winds, particularly during lancing, causes immense damage to the growing crop. Dry, warm weather conditions in February-March favour a good flow of latex and results in higher yields.

Cultivation

Land Preparation and Sowing

Poppy seeds should be sown in very well-prepared soil. The field should be given 5-6 cross-ploughings, followed by planking. The land should be divided into small plots to facilitate irrigation. The seed rate is around 8 kg/ha when sown by broadcasting but when sown in lines at 30 cm apart, about 5-6 kg/ha of seeds are sufficient. In addition, this method is reported to result in higher yields, besides promoting inter-culture and lancing operations. Experiments conducted at Mandsaur showed that a plant population of 300,000/ha is conducive to higher yields. Treating 1 kg of seed with 4-5 g of Thiram or Brassicol before sowing, protects the seeds from soil-borne diseases. The seeds are sown between late October and mid November in different parts of the country. After sowing, the seeds are covered by a thin layer of soil followed by a light irrigation.

MANURES AND FERTILIZERS

Usually farmers maintain a rich top layer of humus by adding large amount of FYM to the opium field. It is found that the application of 10-20 t of FYM is enough to maintain the soil in good physical condition and to support good initial growth. In addition, the field is applied with 30-50 kg PO_{25} and, wherever potash is deficient, K_2O should be applied at the rate of 25-30 kg/ha. Both these fertilizers are placed 5-6 cm deep in the rows before sowing. The amount of nitrogen varies from 60 (10 t of FYM) to 90 kg (20 t of FYM/ha). It is applied in three equal split doses, the first dose is given at the time of sowing and the subsequent doses at 30-40 and 60-65 days after sowing. For correcting zinc deficiency, 12-30 kg/ha of zinc sulphate should be added.

IRRIGATION

The first irrigation is given immediately after sowing, if there is not enough moisture available in the soil. For subsequent irrigations, 7-10 days irrigation schedule is the optimum depending upon the weather and soil conditions. A total of 10 to 15 irrigations are required for this crop.

INTERCULTURE AND WEEDING

All cultivation operations are done by hand. When the plants are 5 to 6 cm high with 3-4 leaves, i.e., after 3-4 weeks of sowing, the first weeding is done. The intervals of the other weeding has to be adjusted locally. In all, about 4-5 weedings may be required during the whole cropping season.

FLOWERING AND FRUIT-SET

After about 90 to 100 days of sowing, the plants which are waist-high begin to flower, i.e., flowering will take place during first week of March, if the crop was sown during the second fortnight of November. Usually after 3 days of flowering, the petals fall off and after another 10-14 days the capsules are ready for lancing.

PEST AND DISEASES

Insects

1. Cutworms (*Agrotis suffusa)* do great harm to these plants. They remain burrowed in the soil during day and during the nights they cut and eat the leaves. This insect can be controlled by flooding the field with water and dusting the crop with 2% Carbaryl.
2. Weevils (*Stenocarus fuliginosus*-root weevil and *Ceutorhynchus maculalba*-capsule weevil) attack young seedlings and feed on young leaves. As the plant matures, the insect eats its way up the stem and ultimately bores its way into poppy head and proceeds to destroy the capsule.

A capsule borer (*Heliotis armigerai*) is also reported to damage the capsules.

Diseases

1. The downy mildew (*Peranospora arborescens)* disease may appear any time from the seedling to maturity stage. In primary, infections, the plants develop chlorosis, curling, abnormal plant form with stunted growth or the plant may not even survive. If the plants are attacked in the later stage, the capsules are affected. This disease can be controlled by the application of Dithane Z-78 (0.4%).
2. Powdery mildew (*Erysiphe polygoni*) appears after 90-100 days of sowing as a white mycelial growth on the stem and lower side of the leaves, it grows into large patches of white powdery mass which turn black. The diseased plants in the early stage should be uprooted and burnt. At the later stage, the crop should be sprayed with Sulfex or Microsulf (1 l in 100 l of water). A spray of Dithane Z-78 or Dithane M-45 (2 g/l), beginning at the flowering stage and repeating it 2-3 times at an interval of 15 days also prevents the spread of the disease.

The other diseases reported on this crop include, root-rot caused by *Fusarium semitectum,* leaf-blight caused by *Helminthosporium papaveris* and virus diseases (cabbage-ring spot virus, beet-yellow virus and bean-yellow mosaic virus).

LANCING AND LATEX COLLECTION

The lancing operation is performed by skilled labour (an average of 6 persons to a plot), usually on bright sunny days between noon and 4 p.m. The hottest part of the day is chosen since the pellicle is said to form on the surface of the freshly exuded latex due to the hot sun, resulting in a greater degree of evaporation and quicker thickening. This also helps prevent the latex from falling off the capsule. The lancing operation is started at the edge of the field and the person works backward to avoid contact with the exuding latex. The hand is quickly passed over a capsule and a subjective decision is made as to whether it is ready for incision or not.

The lancing instrument, called "Nastar" or "Naka", comprises of four lines about the dimension of ordinary needles spaced at 1.5 to 2 mm apart and affixed to a holder about 18 cm long. The *nastar* is held carefully, as one holds a pencil while writing and the incision is made by a swift downward stroke starting just below the stigmatic rays. The depth of the incision is controlled by the affixation of the lines to the holder, for if incisions are too deep the latex is exuded to the interior of the capsule and is thus lost. If the cut is too shallow the yield of latex will be low. Usually, an incision with a depth of 0.4 cm is considered ideal. About 150-200 capsules can be lanced per hour by an experienced worker.

Immediately on lancing, the latex exudes, it is initially milky and gets accumulated in the outer wall of the capsule. It quickly darkens and dries during the course of the day and is generally collected the next day before 10 a.m. by scraping with a trowel called the *Seetoah.* The collection may also be delayed for one or two days, depending upon the 'appearance' of the capsules and the vigour after the latex flow. In other words the interval is subjectively determined by the collector. The lancing process is usually repeated twice, making a total of three series of vertical incisions. The spacing of the incisions on the capsule is generally even. If the capsules are exceptionally, large, four to five lancings can be done. The air-dried latex, which has now become blackish in colour, is scraped from the capsules into small earthenware pots which are lined with polythene sheets. Scraping is carried out by grasping the capsule between the thumb and forefinger of the left hand and inclining it gently, the scraper is then drawn upwards. The capsule is finally 'cleaned' with the thumb.

The semi-dry, blackish latex is then transferred to wooden trays and dried further. Upon arrival at the factory, appropriate samples and drawn from each grower's produce and their quality is determined in the laboratory of the Chief Opium Chemist. The material is graded according to morphine content as follows:

A = with morphine content more than 12%,

D_1 = with morphine between 11 and 12%,

B_2 = with morphine between 10 and 11%,

B_3 = with morphine between 8 and 10%.

PROCESSING

The crude opium is transferred to the appropriate storage vats capable of holding 3 to 30 t. The opium of variable consistency contained in these tubs is removed as required and is carefully air-dried in the sun to 70° consistency. The drying generally takes 21 days and is carried out in wooden trays, by turning the latex 3-4 times a day. Sun-drying is considered a critical process, since artificial drying causes a substantial loss in alkaloid content. Each processed tray comprises of 36 kg of opium with 70° consistency. The opium is then packed in polythene bags, each containing 5 kg of the product, which are then shipped in wooden chests: 60 kg chest for air-freight and 50 kg/chest for surface shipment.

In addition to export, a small amount of 90° consistency opium is prepared for domestic quasi-medical purposes. This is called 'Government Excise Opium' and is available in cubical cakes. These are wrapped in 'butter paper' tied and stamped and shipped to various states where the opium is taxed and sold to those who are duly registered as addicts and consumers.

HARVESTING OF SEEDS

The capsules, after the lancing operation and collection of opium latex, are allowed to dry on the plant itself. The drying process takes about 15 days after the lancing is completed. In India, the capsules are plucked by hand and the seeds are separated after breaking the capsules. A dry capsule weigh about 7 g and it contains 11 to 12 thousand seeds weighing about 3.5 to 4 g.

YIELD OF CRUDE OPIUM AND SEED

On an average 25-30 kg/ha of crude opium and 400-500 kg/ha of seeds are obtained in India.

CHEMICAL EVALUATION

(i) Extraction of alkaloids from the poppy husk

For this purpose, 28 ground poppy husks are treated with 20% NaCl solution (10 ml) and stirred for one hour. Then, this is further treated with a solvent mixture of methanol and benzene (1:1) (25 ml). The mixture is shaken for half-an-hour. Later on, it is filtered under suction. The residue is washed three times with a solvent mixture, taking 5 ml each time. The filtrate, thus obtained, is treated with 20 ml of HCl (0.5 N) and is kept in a separating funnel. The pH of the aqueous layer is maintained between 4-6. Now. 5 ml of HCl (1 N) is added and it is made up to 100 ml. This solution is tested by TLC for the presence of major opium alkaloids and used for the estimation of morphine.

(ii) Determination of morphine in poppy capsules

Grind the dry poppy capsule to fine powder with the help of a pestle and mortar. Weight 5 g of this dry powder into a 100 ml beaker and treat it with 25 ml 10% W/V aqueous sodium carbonate solution and keep it for 1 hour. The stirred mixture is then treated with 5 ml of 20% W/V aqueous sodium carbonate solution and shaken for 1 hour with a solvent mixture (45 ml) of 3:1 volumes of chloroform and isopropanol. The proportion of the organic solvent minimizes emulsions formation. The resulting mass is suction-filtered with a 150 ml sintered Buchner Funnel and washed with 5 ml of solvent mixture, four times. The combined filtrate and washings are extracted with 1N HCl (20 ml) and then with distilled water (2 quantities each of 10 ml). The aqueous layer is filtered, adjusting the pH to 5 by treating with 1N HCl (45 ml) and diluted to 200 ml.

Take 20 ml aliquot into a volumetric flask and add 5 ml 1N HCl and make the volume 100 ml.

Take three 10 ml aliquots into three 25 ml volumetric flasks. To one add 5 ml of 0.1 N HCl, and to the other two add 2 ml Iodic acid, each. After exactly 2 minutes add 10 ml ammonium bicarbonate-nickel chloride complex and make up the volume to 25 ml with distilled water. After 90 minutes, the Optical Density (red filter) in a balanced cell colorimeter-102 is measured and the morphine content computed from the calibration curve.

(iii) Extraction procedure for opium by colorimetric analysis

The sample is dried at 65° to 79°C for 24 hours and ground to a fine powder with the help of a pestle and mortar. Of this, 0.5 g (based on availability) of sample is weighed and transferred to a 15 ml centrifuge tube, containing 5 ml of water. The sample is warmed and stirred with a glass rod and kept overnight at 45°C, so that a total dissolution of all the suspension takes place and it becomes a homogeneous mixture.

To the mixture, 400 mg of calcium hydroxide is added and mixed well till a homogeneous paste is formed. It is kept for half-an-hour with intermittent stirring. Further, it is centrifuged for 10 minutes and the supernatant liquid is taken in a 100 ml volumetric flask. It is added with 10 ml distilled water to the residue in the volumetric flask, stirred well again with a glass rod and centrifuged for 10 minutes; the same procedure is repeated 6 times which gives 60 ml of combined filtrate.

It is mixed with 3 to 4 ml of 1N HCl to make the pH 4 to 5 and distilled water is added to make the volume 10 ml. 2 ml aliquot (in case of 1 g opium sample) and 4 ml aliquot (in case of 5 g opium sample) is taken in the 25 ml volumetric flask containing 5 ml 1N HCl (pH 1.6) and the volume is made up to 10 ml with water.

Further, colour development is done similarly by adding Iodic acid and Ammonium bicarbonate nickel chloride complex and the reading is taken at 670 nm in the visible spectrophotometer after 90 minutes.

27

Ambrette

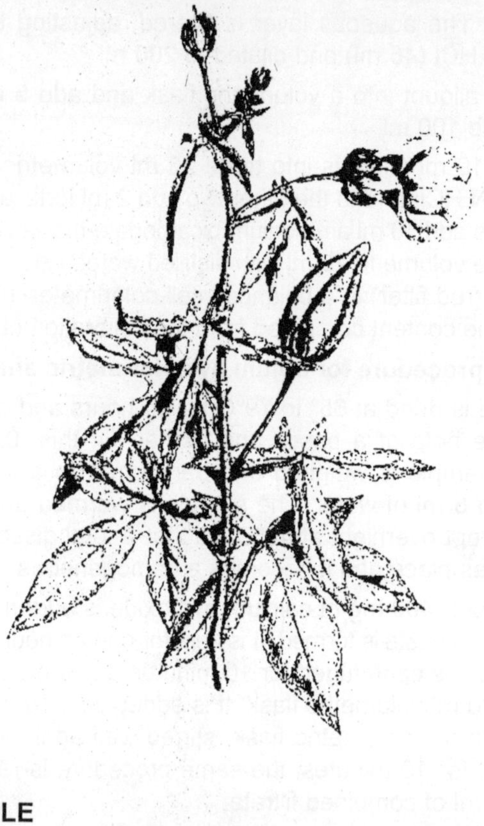

PLANT PROFILE

Family	:	*Malvaceae*
English name	:	Ambrette, Musk plant
Indian name	:	*Lata Kasturika* (Sanskrit), *Mushkdana* (Hindi), *Kasturibende* (Kannada), *Kattu Kasturi*, *Vetrilai Kasturi* (Tamil) *Vetrilai Kasturi* (Tamil)

Species and varieties : *Abelmoschus moschatus* Medic

Distribution : India, Southeast Asia, Northern Australia Brazil, South China, Columbia, Ecuador peninsular Indo-China, Indonesia Madagascar, Southwest Pacific Islands Papua and New Guinea, Seychelles

Uses : Cosmetics, Drugs, Flavouring, Perfumery

Ambrette (*Abelmoschus moschatus* Medic) (2n=72), also known as 'Mushkdana' or 'Kasturi bende', is a native of India. The seeds of this plant are the source of the essential oil which is extensively used in perfumery, flavouring and cosmetic industries. The essential oil is present in the seed-coat. It is a mixture of farnesol and ambrettolide, seed to the extent of 0.12 and 0.03%, respectively. The compounds responsible for its musk-like odour are acetic acid and ambrettolic acid and its lactone - ambrettolid. The seeds also contain a fixed fat and traces of a resinous substance which is noted for its rich, sweet, floral musky, distinctly wine- or brandy-like smell with a incredible tenacity of odour rarely found in any other perfume material. The seeds are used to impart a musky odour to sachets and hair-powder and in the manufacture of indigenous flavoured tobacco (*zarda*). They are powdered with clove and other scented materials for use in body perfumes. It also used as a substitute for *kasluri* or musk, an animal product. The essential oil present in the seeds blend exactly with rose, sandalwood oil, and aliphatic aldehydes. Ambrette restored in the form of extracts is used in perfume, creams, lipsticks, brilliantines, hair oil and in cosmetic products.

The seeds also possess medicinal properties and are employed in the treatment of diseases due to '*kapha*', '*vata*' and in stomach and urinary troubles, gonorrhoea, nervous debility, hysteria and skin diseases. They are a stimulant, antiseptic, stomachic, cooling, tonic, carminative and aphrodisiac.

The plant yields good quality fibre. The leaves are used for cleaning sugar. The tender leaves and shoots are reported to be used in soups and the green pods are sometimes used as vegetables. The seeds are also reported to possess insecticidal properties.

ORIGIN AND DISTRIBUTION

The ancestral home of this species is in India, Southeast Asia, South China, Indonesia, Peninsular Indo-China, Papua and New Guinea, Northern Australia and the Southwest Pacific islands. The species is under cultivation in the Seychelles, Madagascar, the warmer humid regions of Ecuador, Columbia and Brazil. In India, it is found growing wild all over the hilly regions of Deccan and Karnataka and in the foothills of the Himalayas.

DESCRIPTION OF THE PLANT

It belongs to the family *Malvaceae.* It is an erect, hirsute, branching shrub, 0.5 to 1 m in height, with leaves of varying shape, usually palmate, with 5 to 7 lobes. The flowers are large, 7.5 to 10 cm in diameter and yellow coloured with a purple centre. The fruit is a capsule or pod, oblong, lanceolate, 5 to 7.5 cm long, containing a large number of seeds which are scented.

SOIL

Ambrette is a hardy plant and comes up well on a wide range of soils, particularly in sandy loam soils with a pH of 7.0. It also gives a good yield in soils with a pH of 6.0 to 8.6. However, it prefers loose, fertile and well-drained soils.

CLIMATE

The crop is cultivated widely in India up to an elevation of 1000 m under different climatic conditions. It is reported to occur throughout the hotter parts of India. In Karnataka, it can be grown twice a year, once during June-July and again in October-November, as an irrigated crop. Whereas, in the Terai area of Kumaon (Uttar Pradesh) and in Punjab the crop is grown during the rainy season.

CULTIVATION

Propagation

Ambrette is propagated by seeds.

LAND PREPARATION AND SOWING

Before sowing the seeds, the land should be dug deep and worked thoroughly to bring it to a fine tilth. It should be well manured as the plant is a heavy feeder. The seeds can be sown twice during the year, during the months of June-July and again in September-October. The seeds take about 8-10 days for germination. While sowing, 2-4 seeds may be sown on each hill by dibbling to a depth of 1 cm. pre-soaking the seeds for 24 hr in water improves the germination. About 6 kg of seeds are sufficient for sowing a one hectare area. A spacing of 60 cm between rows and 30 cm between plants is recommended. The seedlings are thinned 20 days after sowing.

MANURES AND FERTILIZERS

Well-decomposed FYM is applied to the soil @15 t/ha. Since ambrette is a heavy feeder, it also requires chemical fertilizers in large quantities. Fertilizer trials have shown that an application of N at 120 kg, P_2O_5 at 35 kg and K_2O at 40 kg/ha have resulted in the best yields under Bangalore conditions. Of these, a full dose of P and K and 40 kg N are applied as a basal dose, while the remaining 80 kg N is applied in two equal split doses of 40 kg each at 60 days and 120 days after sowing. The fertilizer mixture is applied about 10 cm away from the plants and mixed well into the soil.

INTERCULTURE

In the early stages, weeding and hoeing are done twice a month. As the plant grows and spreads its branches, the weeds are naturally suppressed.

PESTS AND DISEASES

There are several diseases and pests which infect this crop and result in low yields. The spotted boleworm *Earias insulana* and *E. fabia* are the most severe pests of the plant. These insects attack the plants during the flowering as well as at the fruiting stages. The growing shoots are affected by this pest. The infested shoots above the point of infestation become brown, droop and die. The attack of the pest extends from seedling to harvesting stage. During the fruiting stage, the fruits are attacked; the female worm lays eggs in the fruits. On hatching, the larvae feed on the seeds. Spraying the plant with a 0.15 to 0.2% solution of Thiodon 35 E.C. at 10-15 days' interval from the time the plants are one month old till harvest, reduces the incidence of the pest.

The plants are sometimes seriously infested with red mites (*Tetranychus telarius)*. The mites cover the undersurface of the leaves and suck their juice. In the later stages, the mites make a whitish net and kill the leaves. Spraying the infested plants with 0.1% wettable sulphur solution controls the pest.

Red cotton bugs (*Dysdercus cingulatus*), cotton aphids (*Aphis gossypii*), and green peach aphids (*Myzus persicae),* have also been observed on the plants, but these have not caused much damage to the crop.

Diseases

The young plants sometimes exhibit a mosaic-like appearance on the leaves which is caused by the Hibiscus mosaic virus. Such plants have to be removed immediately.

Collitotrichum hibisci is reported to cause anthracnose. For controlling this disease, the seeds should be treated with Agrosan GN or Cerason before sowing and the crop may be sprayed with Bordeaux mixture. Leaf-spot disease is caused by *Alternaria hibiscicum,* and *Phytophthora* spp. causes leaf blight. *Fusarium* wilt caused by *Fusarium vasinfection* has been reported. On the drying stems and branches, a sooty black fungus (*Pseudotorula verrucosporazi*) has been observed.

HARVESTING AND YIELD

The crop starts flowering after about 2½ months of sowing. The flowers set fruits in nearly 3-4 days. The fruit requires about 2 months from set to maturity. The harvesting stage of the pods is identified when they turns blackish and white strips appear at the angles at the ridges of the fruit. Harvesting is a difficult process if the flowering season is long. The fruit should be harvested carefully as it possess stiff hairs which causes itching. Harvesting must be undertaken regularly at intervals of 7-10 days, depending upon the availability of mature, ripe fruits. It is a 170-180 days' duration crop and in all 20-25 pluckings have to be carried out. The pods have to be shade-dried after harvest. The seeds are separated from the pods by beating the pods with sticks or by splitting the dry pods by hand. The seeds have to be cleaned, shade-dried and stored.

A normal crop may give a yield of 9-10 q/ha of seeds.

28

Bursera

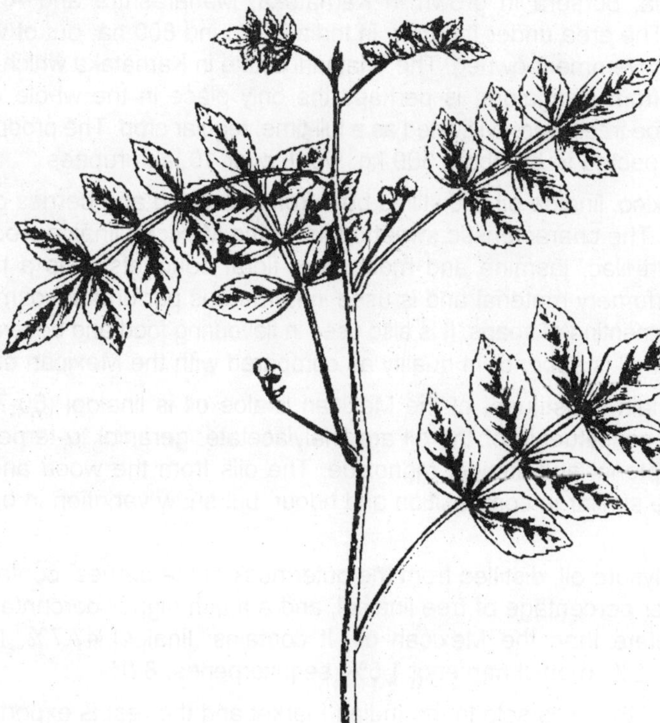

PLANT PROFILE

Family	:	*Burseraceae*
English name	:	Indian Lavender Tree, Linaloe Tree
Indian name	:	*Linelomara* (Kannada)
Species and varieties	:	*Bursera deplechiana, B. gumifera, B. icilarita B. javanica, B. leptopholes, B. serratea*

B. simaruba, B. penicilliata, B. kluggis

Distribution : India, Mexico

Uses : Cosmetics, Flavouring food and beverages Perfumery

Bursera, (*Bursera delphechiana*), belonging to the family *Burseraceae,* is one of the important essential oil-yielding plants introduced into India from Mexico in 1920. The natives of Mexico call this tree linaloe of Indian lavender tree and call the oil, linaloe oil.

In India, bursera in grown in Karnataka, Maharashtra and Andhra Pradesh. The area under the crop in India is around 800 ha, out of which 450 ha is government-owned. The Thatguni estate in Karnataka which is 19 km away from Bangalore, is perhaps the only place in the whole world where linaloe trees were cultivated as a full-time, regular crop. The production of oil is expected to be about 300 kg, worth over 10 lakh rupees.

In Mexico, linaloe oil is distilled both from the wood and berries of the wild trees. The characteristic sweet odour of the Mexican linaloe wood-oil blends with lilac, jasmine and most other floral bouquets. It is a highly valued perfumery material and is used in numerous perfumes, cosmetics and in the scenting of soaps. It is also used in flavouring food and beverages. The Indian oil is superior in quality as compared with the Mexican oil.

The main constituent of the Mexican linaloe oil is linalool (60-70%). The other constituents of the oil are linalylacetate, geraniol, α-terpeneol, methyl heptenol and linalool monoxide. The oils from the wood and the berries are similar in composition and odour, but show variation in optical rotation.

The Mysore oil, distilled from the outer husk of the berries, contains a much lower percentage of free linalool, and a much higher percentage of linalyl acetate than the Mexican oil. It contains: linalool 47.7%, linalyl acetate 40.8%, methyl heptenol 1.5%, sequiterpenes, 8.0%.

Most of the oil is sold in the Indian market and the rest is exported to London. In many parts of Mexico, the wood of the plant is made into toys and furniture. The different parts of the plant from which the oil is extracted with their percentages are: foliage—0.13-0.3%, mature heart-wood—7.9% in India and 2.5-3.0% in Mexico, green fruits—2%, the shade-dried husk of picked berries—10.0-14.0%, the shade-dried husk of fallen berries—14-18% and the roots—0.27%.

DESCRIPTION OF THE PLANT

Bursera is a large deciduous tree. The male tree is medium-sized, has a longer trunk and grows to about 7.5 m. The inflorescence is a paniculate cyme with a pubescent axis up to 10 cm long and contains about 40-50 staminate flowers. The female tree attains about 6 m height and has larger leaves, some of them are 18 cm long. The leaves are imparipinnate, serrate or nearly entire. The inflorescence contains 8-20 pistillate flowers. The flowers are green, pentamerous; the calyx is small, the lobes rounded; the petals are valvate in the bud; the stamens are 10, nearly equal; the ovary is hairy and surrounded by a broad, crenate disc. The fruit is a fleshy berry, a little larger than a pea, about 1 cm in diameter, dark green in colour turning to reddish-brown as it matures and falls off. The pericarp of the fruit contains resiniferous ducts, surrounded by a large layer of thick-walled cells.

SPECIES/VARIETIES

The Linaloe tree belongs to the tropical American genus *Bursera* of the family *Burseraceae,* under the natural order *Geraniales.* The genus has 45 species. The important species are as follows:

1. *Bursera gumifera:* American gum tree or Indian birch or birds tree. An infusion of its leaves is occasionally used as a substitute for tea.
2. *Bursera icilarita:* This tree bears edible, aromatic fruits.
3. *Bursera javanica:* The juice of the leaves and fruits are used.
4. *Bursera leptopholes*: The mature fruits are edible.
5. *Bursera serratea*: The pulp is edible and also yields essential oil.
6. *Bursera simaruba*: Commonly called Rumb or 'West Indian birch'; its leaves are used as a substitute for tea.
7. *Bursera penicilliata*: Every plant part contains essential oil.
8. *Bursera kluggis*: It yields triterpenes, which have anticancer properties.

SOIL

In Mexico, it flourishes even on very rocky soils. The plant makes little demand on the land as it is more or less a xerophytic species. The species comes up well even in stony, gravelly and very shallow soils where other species are not likely to grow well. Well-drained, sandy soils with neutral pH are preferred, since water stagnation appears to be harmful to the tree. Clayey and marshy lands are to be avoided completely.

CLIMATE

Linaloe is a hardy tree which grows in dry tropical climates. It is said to grow well in areas with a rainfall of 500 to 900 mm (about 20-36"). The plant prefers frost-free conditions. The deciduous nature of the tree, the shooting of vegetative growth and the simultaneous flowering during a limited growth period of 7-8 months (April-November), synchronizes with the climatic vagaries of arid, tropical regions. The plant favours dry summer months where the average maximum temperature varies between 36ºC and 38ºC. Blossom rains during April-May increase the incidence of flowering and fruiting. It thrives well at altitudes from 800 m to 1200 m above MSL.

CULTIVATION

Propagation

Natural Regeneration

It is mainly done by seeds, which are carried by birds for a short distance. Natural regeneration is also found underneath the tree, probably due to fallen fruits. The other means of natural regeneration is by coppicing. It coppices well, but it is not encouraged because of the spreading nature of the coppices. It rarely produces suckers.

Other Methods

1. Seeds

The seed germination is very low (5-10%). Hence, the seeds are sown immediately after collection in the months of February to May. The seeds germinate only during June-July. The nursery-raised seedlings, when they are 15 cm in height, have to be picked out and planted in containers for few months till they attain an average height of 45 cm.

2. Vegetative propagation

(a) *Air-layering:* This gives 80-100% success. The best season for air-layering was found to be October-January. In this case, root-initiation was noted in 26 days and the layers were ready for separation in 2 months.

(b) *Cleft-grafting*: This method of grafting was tried with a view to increase the fruit-yield of the species. When male branches are grafted onto a female tree, the pollen produced will in 3-4 weeks. About 60-100% success was obtained using this method.

(c) *Cuttings:* Cuttings are the best means of production of new plants. A mother plant which is above 5 years of age gives good cuttings. Cuttings taken in early February and March have proved the best. Cuttings of 0.5 to 1.0 m length, 1-3 cm in diameter with a clean cut are taken from a well-established mother plant, inverted for 12-24 hours and then planted in polythene bags of 20 cm × 30 cm or earthenware pots of 12 cm diameter and 25 cm height filled with sand, FYM and red earth in a 1:1:1 ratio. Sprouting takes place in 30-40 days, while a healthy root system develops in about 4-6 months. The rooted cuttings are maintained in the nursery till planting time, i.e., August-September.

PLANTING

Pits of 0.5 m^3 are dug at 6m × 6m intervals and the rooted cuttings are planted during the rains. The pits are refilled with a mixture of FYM, red earth and sand in the ratio of 1:2:3 prior to planting. A pinch of Gramaxone is added to the soil to keep off termites. About 300 cuttings can be accommodated in one hectare of land. Planting is done in such a way that a male tree will be surrounded by 6-8 female plants top meet the pollination requirements. The plants are staked and watered after planting.

PRUNNING AND TRAINING

The rooted cuttings get established in the rainy season and continue to grow until about November, when they start shedding leaves. The plants are then completely bare at foliage till about late March or early April when the new flush of leaves appear. In order to train the plant, the first 2 or 3 branches immediately above the ground should be pruned to avoid it becoming bushy. The plant develops a good crown in about 6-8 years.

FERTILIZERS

Not much work on the fertilizer requirement of this crop has been done. However, an *ad hoc* dose of fertilizers at the rate of 80:40:30 g of ammonium sulphate, superphosphate and muriate of potash per plant year is recommended to obtain better results.

IRRIGATION

Bursera requires protective irrigations up to about 2-3 years and after that no regular watering is done. A small bund 3 m away from the plants is built to collect the rain water, which greatly helps the growth during the early stages.

INTERCULTURE

In large-scale forest plantations one scraping and hoeing is given around December, to avoid incidental burning.

INTERCROPPING

In order to obtain some income till the plants come to the bearing stage, intercropping with legumes can be done.

PESTS AND DISEASES

The most serious pest of Bursera is the borer which burrows into the tissue of the young stem with an exudation and the stem dries up with a dirty film on the surface. The growth of the stem is arrested at this point. No control measure has been suggested for this insect. White ants are also reported to cause damage to the plants. To control white ants, Aldrin may be applied to the soil at the rate of 25 kg/ha.

DISEASES

Leaf-blight is a fungal disease reported on this crop and this can be controlled by spraying copper fungicides. Downy mildew is another disease reported and the same can be controlled by spraying Bordeaux mixture (0.5%).

Sometimes die-back, whose symptoms are cracking in the stems of young saplings from which a resinous substance is exuded, has been reported. This ultimately results in the gradual wilting and finally the death of the tree. This can be controlled by removing the dieback affected plant-parts and burning them and spraying the other plants with copper fungicide (0.3%).

NON-INSECT PESTS AND EXTERNAL DAMAGES

Monkeys are the important non-insect pests. The have developed a taste for the tender fruits. Birds are also fond of the ripe fruits.

Fire also causes damage to the plantation. This can be safeguarded against by internal and external fire-lines.

HARVESTING

In India, linaloe oil is mainly extracted from air-dried husks, mature or ripe berries. Whereas in Mexico, it is mostly from heartwood of 50-60 year-old trees. Thus, it is only the ripe berries that the harvested in India. The plant bears its first crop of fruits during the 3rd or 4th year. Occasionally a few fruits set in earlier, but it is better to remove them to allow adequate vegetative development in the first instance. They are allowed to bear crop only after about 5-6 years.

The ripe berries have to be hand-picked, or the ripe fallen fruits have to be collected. On an average, the trees come to the stage of economical bearing after 10 years of planting.

(i) Hand-picking

The ripe fruits are individually picked from the trees with the help of a ladder and then dried. The only advantage of this method is that it can be followed even in adverse climatic conditions, such as during rainy days, also. The disadvantages are: (a) The husks of the fruits require more time for drying (b) It is costly, as a number of labourers have to be engaged, and (c) The quality of the husks, with reference to the oil content, is poor.

(ii) Collection of fallen fruits

The ripe and dehusked fruits fall to the ground. The ground is kept clean so that the dehusked fruits are not lost and are then collected by sweeping the floor of the plantation. The advantages of this method are: (a)

It is very convenient and cheap, (b) the husk requires less time for drying, (c) The quality of the husk, in regard to the oil content, is good.

The disadvantages are: (a) It cannot be followed under adverse climatic conditions, (b) The floor has to be kept clean throughout the season, which requires constant weeding.

The collected berries are dried under the shade and the fruits are split into two halves, exposing the seed kernels. The husk is separated and stored till distillation. The essential oil in the berries is found entirely in the outer pericarp or husk.

EXTRACTION OF ESSENTIAL OIL AND YIELD

The oil is extracted by steam distillation. Care should be taken to see that the steam pressure in the boiler is between 1.0 to 1.5 kg. The period of distillation of fresh fruits is 5 hours. The actual duration varies with the equipment, quantity and steam pressure. The period of distillation is appreciably less when the fresh fruits are crushed and distilled, but there is a risk of mechanical losses of oil while crushing the fruits. The yield of oil, when fresh fruits are distilled, is about 2.5-3.0%. Air-dried husks require more time for distillation, i.e. 20-25 hours and the yield of oil under this method varies from 10-14%.

The Mexican linaloe wood-oil is colourless or pale-yellow, with a characteristic sweet odour. The Mysore oil is a very light-coloured, mobile liquid with a fine lily-rose tone. The oil from the berries is not sold per se, but is added to the oil from the wood which has better storing qualities.

The yield in Mexico is reported to be 2.5-3%, but when distilled in Europe, the wood from the older stems is said to yield 7-9% and sometimes even 10-12%. The low yield in Mexico is due to the crude methods of distillation. In the case of young trees, an attempt is often made to increase the yield by wounding the stem. In this crop also, we notice an alternate bearing tendency. The yield of oil per hectare is dependent on the: (i) locality (ii) age of the trees (iii) number of trees (iv) proportion of male trees (v) cultural operations and (vi) rains during the flushing season.

One hectare area of plantation containing 300 plants (10 years old) yields about 1500 kg of berries. The yield of husk is 18% of the berry weight, accounting for 255 kg/ha The oil content of the husk is 10%, thus yielding about 25 kg/ha of oil.

29

Celery

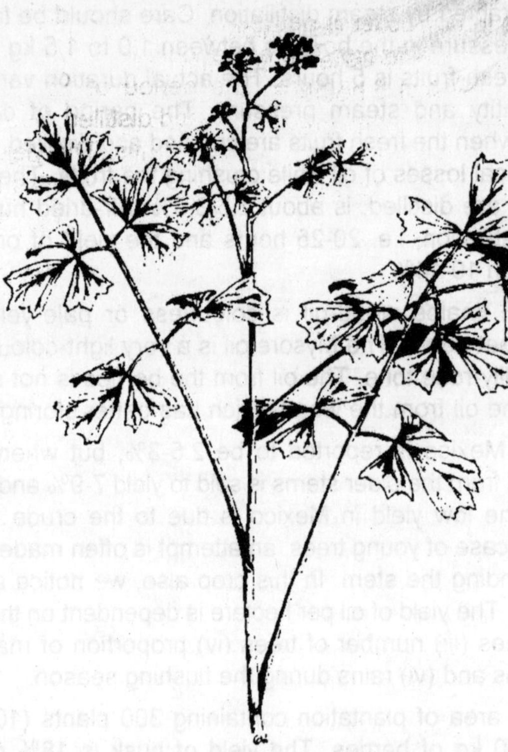

PLANT PROFILE

Family	:	*Apiaceae: Umbelligerae*
English name	:	Celery
Indian name	:	*Ajmoda* (Sanskrit), *Karnauli*, *Shalary Ajmod* (Hindi), *Ajmada* (Tamil)

Species and varieties : *Apium graveolens* Linn., *dulce* (Mill) pers., *rapaceum* (Mill) Gaudic (celeriac), *secalinum smallage*

Distribution : India, Algeria, Asia, Baluchistan, Belgium Caucasus, Egypt, Ethopia, France, Germany Holland, Italy, Sweden, UK, USA

Uses : Culinary, Drugs, Flavouring, Food, Perfumery

The dried fruit of *Apium graveolens* Linn. (2n=22) Family: *Apiaceae; Umbelliferae* is known as celery. It is popularly known as 'Karnauli' or 'Ajmod'.

There are four known horticultural types of celery. *A. graveolens* var. *dulce* (Mill) Pers., whose leaves and stalks are consumed as a salad, appetizer and as a flavouring in soups; and var. *rapaceum* (Mill) Gaudich commonly called celeriac with dark green leaves, cultivated for root tubers which are cooked and eaten. The other two are var. *secalinum* and *smallage*. The main variety cultivated in India is var. *dulce*.

Commercially, celery is available as celery seeds, celery flakes, vegetable, celery seed oil and celery seed oleoresin.

The celery seed has the following constituents. Moisture: 5-11%; volatile oil: 1.5-3; (average 2.4%); non-volatile ether extract: 5.8-14.2% (average 9.4%) cold water extract: 5.9-12.6% (average 8.4%); total ash: 6.9-11.0% (average 8.8%); ash insoluble in acid: 0.5-4.0% (average 2.5%).

Fresh celery leaves and stalks contains moisture: 81.30, 93.5%; protein: 6.0, 0.8%; fat: 0.6, 0.1%; fibre: 1.4, 1.2%; carbohydrates: 8.6, 3.5%; mineral matter; 2.1, 09%; calcium: 0.23, 0.3%; phosphorus: 0.14, 0.4%; Iron: 0.06, 0.05%; Vit A: 5800, 7500 I.U.; Vit B_1 traces Vit C: 62, 6 mg/100 g; calorific value; 64, 18 calories per 100 g respectively.

The seeds, on steam-distillation, yield an oil (1.75%) which contains limonene (80%) as a major constituent. The other constituents of the oil are: α-p-dimethyl styrene, n-petryl benzene, caryophyllene, α-selinene, n-butyl phthalide and sedanolide along with sabinene, β-elemne, trans-1, 2-epoxy limonene, linalool, isovaleric acid, cis-dihydrocarvone, trans-dihydrocarvone, terpinene-4-0l, cis-p-menth-2, 8-dine-1-ol, trans-p-menth-2, 8-dien-1-01, a-terpineol, carvone, transcarveol, cis-carveol, tans-anethole, trans-p-menth-1 (7), 8-dien-2-ol, perillaldehyde and thymol. The seeds are also rich in Vitamin B.

The dried, ripe seeds are used as spice to flavour food and liquids, the seeds are stimulant and carminative and are used as a nerve tonic in domestic medicine. It is also a remedy for rheumatism. The seed-oil is used as a food flavouring, and in the perfumery and pharmaceutical industries. The fatty oil, obtained from the fruit, is used as an antispasmodic and nerve stimulant.

ORIGIN AND DISTRIBUTION

The native habitat of celery is the lowlands of Italy from where it spread to Sweden, Egypt, Algeria and Ethiopia, and in Asia, to India, the Caucasus and Baluchistan. Celery is also claimed to be first mentioned as a cultivated food plant in France as early as 1623. The countries growing it are the USA, France, Germany, the United Kingdom, Italy Belgium and Holland. In India, it is cultivated in the North-western Himalayas, the Punjab, Haryana and Western Uttar Pradesh in an area of about 5000 ha. Punjab produces about 90% of the total Indian production. Celery seed is in great demand both in Indian and abroad. Indian celery seed is exported mostly to the UK and the USA and to a lesser extent to continental countries like France, Italy, the Netherlands, Germany as well as to Australia and New Zealand. India exported celery seeds worth rupees 46 crores during the period 1991-92.

DESCRIPTION OF THE PLANT

Celery is a herbaceous annual or biennial erect herb growing to a height of 60-90 cm. It has a shallow tap-root system. The stem is branched, succulent and ridged. The leaves are reduced, pinnate, large, deeply divided and coarsely-toothed at the apex. The leaflets are ovate to suborbicular, 3-lobed, 2.0-4.5 cm long. The inflorescence is a compound umbel. The flowers are small and white, the calyx teeth are obsolete. There are 5 petals, ovate, acute with inflexed tips. The carpels are semiterete, subpentagonal the primary ridges are distinct and filiform. The fruit is a schizocarp with two mericarps, suborbicular to ellipsoid, 1-2 mm in diameter, aromatic and slightly bitter. Celery is naturally cross-pollinated but not self-incompatible.

VARIETIES

The important high-yielding varieties recommended for cultivation under this crop are EC-99249-1 and PRL-85-1.

SOIL

Celery can be successfully cultivated on all soils except saline, alkaline and water-logged ones; however, the loamy soils which are rich in organic matter and retentive of soil moisture, are the best. This crop is not suited to clayey soils. It cannot withstand water stagnation. Celery is sensitive to the extremes of soil reaction, a soil pH range of 5.0 to 7.0 is suitable for its cultivation.

CLIMATE

In colder climates and on the hills, celery behaves as a biennial, but in the plains it behaves as an annual plant. Celery is a moisture-loving plant, requiring a cold climate. It can be successfully cultivated as a winter crop in areas which are free from severe frost and with low atmospheric humidity during February-March when the crop flowers. Northern and Central India, including the hills, with a cold and dry climate, are the most suited for celery cultivation. A combination of 12° to 15° and 22 to 25°C day-night temperatures gives 80% seed germination within a 2-week period.

CULTIVATION

Propagation

Celery can be grown from seeds, by raising the seedlings in nursery-beds. The seeds are very small. An ounce contains about 70,000 seeds. The germination percentage in seeds is about 50%. A seed rate of 1.5 kg/ha is sufficient. The seeds are sown in boxes and covered with thin layers of soil and FYM mixture. The seedlings are ready for transplanting when they are about 10 cm tall.

Sowing

When grown as a garden crop in the hills, the seeds are sown in March-April. The seedlings are transplanted in May and the crop is ready for harvest in November. In the plains seedlings, preferably brought from the hills, are transplanted in September-October and the crop is ready within three months and the transplanting of seedlings 30 cm apart in rows spaced at 30-45 cm is carried out in January. It is also grown as a directly seeded crop, on a smaller scale, in Amritsar District.

MANURES AND FERTILIZERS

Before planting the seedlings, about 30-50 t/ha of FYM is added. On medium soils about 80-200 kg N, 33-40 kg P and 20 kg K/ha is applied to the crop. A half dose of N, a full dose of P and K are applied in rows at the time of planting and the remaining N is given as a top-dressing after one month.

IRRIGATION AND INTER-CULTIVATION

The crop requires 10-12 irrigations during the crop period. Once established, the crop requires 3 to 4 hoeings to keep down the weeds. The application of chemical weedicides like Basalin (pre-planting) at 2-3.5 l/ha or Stamp at 2 l/ha or TOK-E-25 + Lasso @ 2.5 l/ha or Fluchloralin 0.90 kg/ha and Pendimethalin at 0.60 kg/ha, are reported to control the weeds.

PESTS AND DISEASES

Insects

The leaf-miner (*Liriomyze trifolii*) is found attacking the outer leaves of the celery plants and causes damage to most of the leaves. The insect can be effectively controlled by spraying a systemic insecticide like Quinoilphos (0.1%). The carrot rustfly, tarnished plant bugs, celery leaf tier, celery fly, aphids, caterpillars, flea beetle, mole crickets, spring trails, army worms, wire worms and red spider mites are the other insect pests which causes losses in some areas. Suitable control measures may be taken up as and when they are noticed.

Trichopulsia spp. and *Spodoptera exigua* are two major insect pests of celery in California.

Diseases

Cercospora apii is reported to cause early blight; *Septoria petrosalnii* causes late blight and *Phyllosticta apii* causes leaf-spot diseases to celery crop. These diseases can be controlled by spraying Thiophanate Methyl (0.5%) + Mane (0.1%) or Fenthin hydroxide (0.2%) at 2-week intervals. Petiole rot caused by *Sclerotium* spp., and *Fusarium,* and yellow mosaic are the other diseases reported on this crop.

HARVESTING AND YIELD

In cooler climates and on the hills, celery is a perennial plant and produces seeds only in the second year. It takes about 4-5 months from the time of sowing to seeding. In the plains, the crop matures within about 3 months of transplanting.

The crop is harvested when about 80% of the buds begin to turn light-brown. The harvested crop is stacked in the field for a few days and then threshed to obtain the seeds. Care must be taken to avoid prolonged exposure to sun. The seeds are then cleaned by winnowing.

The average yield of celery is about 1000-1500 kg/ha. Celery seeds yield 2-3% of pale-yellow volatile oil with a persistent odour. The volatile or essential oil contained in the seed is isolated by steam-distillation. The seeds should be crushed and immediately sent for distillation to avoid the loss of oil by evaporation. It is important that the seed be spread evenly on the perforated grids with which a still, serving for seed distillation, should be equipped. The distillation of one batch lasts for about 10-12 hours. The distillation wastes are usually redistilled.

30

Chamomile

PLANT PROFILE

Family	:	*Asteraceae; Compositae*
English name	:	Chamomile
Indian name	:	Babunah, Babuni-ki-Phool (Hindi) *Seemasevanthi poo* (Tamil)
Species and varieties	:	*Matricaria chamomilla* Linn., *Anthemis nobilis* Linn. *Ormenis multicaulis* Braun

Distribution : India

Uses : Beverages, Confectionery, Cosmetics Drugs, Flavouring, Perfumery

The well known old-time drug, chamomile, is ascribed to three species belonging to the family *Asteraceae; Comositae*. The three species are *Matricaria chamomilla* Linn. (2n=18) (German or Hungarian chamomile or Persian chamomile), *Anthemis nobolis* Linn. (English or roman chamomile or Double chamomile) and *Ormenis multicaulis* Braun-Blanquet and Marie (Moroccan chamomile). The German or Hungarian or small chamomile, having a variety of uses also yields an essential oil, commonly known as 'Blue oil', on account of its deep blue colour, which is of medicinal and aromatic importance and is in great demand throughout the world.

The essential oil extracted from the flowers contains azulene (1-15%, average 6%) which determines its quality. Besides, the oil contains pro-chamazulene or matricin, terpene hydrocarbons, sesquiterpene alcohols including bisabolol, and unsaturated ketonic alcohol, bisabolol oxide, methoxy coumarin (Umbelliferone methyl ether), furfural and paraffins. The active constituents of the flower as such are the viscous oil, a bitter principle (3%), apigenin and its glycosides apiin, quercimetritrin, 7-methoxy coumarin, 7-hydroxy coumarin, a doioxy coumarin, salicylic acid, a resin, phytosterol, fatty acids, Vitamin C and nicotinic acid. As a drug, the infusion of chamomile is used as a mild sedative and digestive in Europe. It is used in many medicinal preparations, such as 'Chamomile tea' and in toilet preparations, such as bath preparations and shampoos. The essential oil finds use in alcoholic and non-alcoholic beverages, ice-cream, ice-candy, baked goods, chewing gums and as a flavouring agent. The essential oil, in very small percentage is used in expensive perfumes. Besides, the oil has many therapeutic uses and acts as an anti-spasmodic, expectorant, carminative, anthelmintic anti-inflammatory, sedative and diuretic. The oil is used in infant ailments such as teething trouble and stomach disorders. The oil also possesses anti-bacterial and fungicidal activities.

ORIGIN AND DISTRIBUTION

The German chamomile is indigenous to Europe. Its cultivation is fairly widespread in many European countries, viz., Germany, France, Yogoslavia, Hungary and Russia.

In India, it has been cultivated in Lucknow for about two hundred years and the plant was introduced in Punjab about three hundred years ago, during the Mughal period. It was introduced into Jammu in 1957. It is now grown on a commercial scale in Lucknow (UP), New Delhi, Bombay, Jammu and Punjab.

DESCRIPTION OF THE PLANT

Chamomile is an annual, herbaceous, much-branched, spreading or erect aromatic plant, reaching a height of 60-90 cm. The stems are leafy and hollow. The leaves are doubly pinnate, with narrow linear segments not truly thread-shaped or cylindrical but rather flat or channelled above and convex beneath, all acute, the bristles often pointed and a little hairy. The flower-heads are terminal, solitary, 1.3-2.5 cm diameter, rather longer than a daisy with a convex, yellow disk and turned to one side. The involucre has 2-3 rows with shining, membranous, border scales which are rather downy. The receptacle is obtusely conical. The ray florets are incomplete, zygomorphic, female, epigynous and ligulate; the ligules are white, 3-lobed, reflexed, about 12-30 in number and small; the disc florets are numerous, yellow and tubular; the peduncles are 2.5 cm long, dark-brown or dusky greenish-yellow. The gynoecium is bicarpellary and synacarpous, with a long tubular style and penicillate stigmas; the ovary is inferior and unilocular, with a single ovule. The stamens are 5, syngenesious and epipetalous; the anthers are longer than the filaments and basifixed, the dehiscence is longitudinal. The fruit is a small achene, with 3-5 ridges and a single head will have 40-50 seeds. The seeds are less than 1.0 mm and yellow or light-brownish in colour.

VARIETIES

Recently, a *M. chamomila* variety 'Vallary' has been released by the CIMAP, Lucknow.

SOIL

Chamomile can be grown on any type of soil. Moist, moderately heavy soils, rich in humus are best suited for this crop. The optimum soil pH is 7. But soils having a pH as high as 9.0 also support good growth. In Yogoslavia, it is grown with success on saline soil over fairly large areas. In Hungary also it is cultivated in substandard clayey-alkaline soils, which are considered too poor for other crops.

CLIMATE

In India, chamomile can be grown as a winter crop in the plains and as a summer crop on the hills up to an altitude of 2000 m. The optimum temperature for seed germination is between 10 and 20°C. Temperature and light conditions have a significant effect on essential oil and azulene content.

SEASON

The seeds can be sown in nursery-beds, to raise seedlings, during late September or early October. Transplanting can be done by the last week of November or by early December.

LAND PREPARATION

Chamomile is a shallow-rooted plant, hence, deep ploughing is not necessary. The land is ploughed once followed by four cross-harrowings and levelled properly and flat beds of convenient size are made. At the time of the final harrowing, FYM or compost @ 20-25 t/ha is applied and mixed well into the soil.

CULTIVATION

Propagation

Chamomile is propagated through seeds. About 1 kg of seeds are required to raise seedlings sufficient to plant one hectare of land; sometimes the crop is also grown by direct sowing, for which 3 kg of seeds are required. A thousand seeds weigh just 0.088 to 0.153 g.

Nursery Raising

The nursery area is well prepared by repeated ploughing and brought to a fine tilth. Well-rotted FYM is applied to the soil, and nursery-beds of convenient sizes are prepared. As the seeds are small, the seeds are mixed with sand or fine soil in the ratio of 1:4 and sown in the nursery-beds. The nursery should be watered frequently. The seeds germinate in 15-20 days of sowing and the seedlings are ready for transplanting into the main field when they are 4 to 5 weeks old.

TRANSPLANTING

In order to obtain the maximum flower and essential oil yield, the crop has to be planted at a spacing of 30 cm × 30 cm. For varieties with a spreading habit, a 40 cm × 40 cm spacing is ideal.

APPLICATION OF FERTILIZER

The crop responds well to the application of fertilizers. Hence, a balanced dose of N, P and K is recommended in order to obtain the maximum yield. Application of 60 kg N and 60 kg P_2O_5/ha is recommended for red sandy soils. However, a fertilizer dose of 80 kg N, 40 kg P_2O_5 and 20 kg K_2O/ha is considered optimum for a good crop.

IRRIGATION

When the crop is grown in normal soils, about 3-4 irrigations may be given during the entire crop period, whereas, saline soils need frequent but light irrigation. About 5-7 irrigations are quite sufficient for such soils.

WEEDING AND INTERCULTURE

About 3-4 weedings and hoeings are required for raising a good crop. In the case of crops grown in saline-alkaline soils, only one thorough weeding and hoeing one month after planting, is sufficient. The application of herbicides, 2, 4-D Sodium salt @ 1 to 1.5 kg/ha, 4 weeks after transplating or Oxyflouren @ 0.6 kg/ha are reported to control weeds.

CROPPING SEQUENCE

Chamomile is a winter season crop and its duration is about 5 months (December-April). Hence, it fits well in rotation with paddy for water-logged lowlands. It also forms a good combination with crops like maize and early potato and, on submarginal lands, following a green manure crop it gives better results.

PESTS AND DISEASES

No serious pests or diseases are observed on this crop. However, black bean aphids (*Aphis febae*); and an insect, *Nysius minor,* which attacks flowers and cause their shedding, and a defoliating insect, *Antographis chryson,* are noticed on this crop. The black bean aphid can be controlled by spraying Phosdrin at 0.1% and Brevinyl at 0.5% concentration. *Nysius minor* can be controlled by spraying the crop with Endosulphon (0.2%).

HARVESTING AND YIELD

Flowering starts from the second fortnight of February and it continues till the middle of April. Fully-opened flowers should be picked immediately, as delay in harvesting may result in the shedding of seed. The picking of individual flowers may be done by hand or by means of flower-scoops or skippers. About 4-5 harvests could be taken at 10-15 days' intervals. The harvest of flowers will be maximum in the 3rd or 4th flush of flowering. The last flush of flowers (5th) will be allowed to set seeds on the plant itself.

On normal soils, an average yield of 6000 kg/ha flowers (1000-1500 kg/ha on a dry-weight basis) is obtained. Whereas, in saline-alkaline soils, the yield will be 4000-5000 kg/ha. The seed-yield will be around 150-200 kg/ha.

DRYING AND STORAGE

The freshly harvested flowers have a moisture content of 60 to 85%. Hence, their drying is necessary. For drying, the harvested flowers are spread in thin layers in the shade. The flowers are dried at a temperature ranging between 20°C to 24°C. While drying, the flowers are turned once or twice. Temperature-controlled dryers are used for drying the flowers in European Countries.

The dried flowers are packed in moisture-proof containers and stored under moisture-free conditions, so as to avoid spoilage by insects and fungi.

DISTILLATION OF OIL AND YIELD

The essential oil from the air-dried flowers is extracted through steam distillation. Steam of high pressure viz., 7 atmosphere/sq cm in the steam generator, is used for distillation. The oil deposits on the inner walls of the condenser, the flow of the cooling water is frequently stopped until the temperature of the condenser rises sufficiently. The distillation process takes about 5 hours.

The yield of oil varies from 0.3 to 1.3% and is influenced by the location, strain and the conditions and the fertility status of the soil. The day temperature during the flowering period also influences the oil-content of flowers and the best results are obtained when the temperature ranges from 22ºC to 25ºC. Chamomile oil possesses a deep-blue colour when freshly distilled, and changes to a brown colour when exposed to light and air during storage.

31

Citronella

PLANT PROFILE

Family : *Poaceae*

English name : Citronella

Species and varieties : *Cymbopogan winterianus* Jowitt
C. nardus Rendle
confertiflorus, linnael

Distribution : India, Brazil, Guatemala, Honduras Malaysia, Sri Lanka, Taiwan

Uses : Cosmetics, Flavouring, Perfumery

Citronella (*Cymbopogan winterianus* Jowitt) (2n=20) is an aromatic grass belonging to the *Poaceae* family, which upon steam distillation, gives an essential oil known to the trade, as the oil of Java citronella. This is used extensively as a source of important perfumery chemicals like citronellal, citronellol and geraniol, which finds use in soap, perfumery, cosmetic and flavouring industries throughout the world. Citronella oil is classified in trade into two types, i.e., Ceylon citronella oil obtained from *Cymbopogon nardus* Rendle a rather inferior type, while the Java citronella oil obtained from *Cymbopogon winterianus* is considered a superior type. Java citronella oil has higher alcohol content (90-95%) than the Ceylon type (60-71%). Citronella is used as a starting material for further derivatives. Hydroxy citronellal can be prepared from citronella, which is one of the most frequently used floralizing perfume materials. While, citronellol is used in many perfumery blends of soap and cosmetic industries when rosaceous notes are required. Citronella oil also contains geranyl acetate, citronellyl acetate, limonene, elemol and other sesquiterpene alcohols, β-elemene, r-cadinene and traces of cubebene, calamenene, bourbonene, bissabolene, eugenol, isopulegol, nerol, linalool, methyl heptenone, myrcene, and α-pinene.

ORIGIN AND DISTRIBUTION

Both the Ceylon and Java types of citronella have probably originated from Managrass of Ceylon, which occurs today in two wild forms: *Cymbopogon nardus* var. *linnael (typicus*) and *C. nardus* var. *confertiflorus*. The Java citronella, which is called '*Mahapengeri*' in Ceylon, is the result of a selection from the Ceylon citronella. It is distributed in tropical and sub-tropical countries like India, Taiwan, Guatemala, Honduras, Malaysia and Brazil. The National Botanical Research Institute (NBRI), Lucknow, introduced citronella into India.

AREA AND PRODUCTION

At present, the world production of citronella oil is approximately 2000-2500 t, the bulk of which is produced in Taiwan, Guatemala, the honduras, Malaysia and Brazil. India produces about 120 t oil annually. The important states in our country growing this crop are Assam, Gujarat, Jammu, Kashmir, Karnataka, Maharashtra, Tamil Nadu, West Bengal and Uttar Pradesh.

DESCRIPTION OF THE PLANT

A tufted, aromatic, perennial herb with fibrous roots, it grows in stout clumps. It is erect, over 2 m tall, smooth and shining, leafy and glabrous at the nodes. The leaf-blades are linear, gradually tapering to a long, membranous, acuminate tip, up to 1 m long, 1.5 cm wide, drooping at two-thirds of its length. The leaf-sheaths are smooth and glabrous, yellow or purplish-red in colour. The inflorescence is very large with a decompound panicle spreading loose, over 30 cm long, erect, finally drooping, consisting of a branched and rebranched axis, giving rise to branches of the third and fourth degree which finally end in recemose pairs supported by the proper sheaths. The spathes are 12 mm long, narrow, dull-reddish in colour and membranous on the margins. The racemes are 20 mm long—one sessile or short the other longer pedicelled with two lower spikelets, which are homigamous, male or neuter. The remaining pairs in both racemes are heterogamous. The ovary with 1 carpel is unilocular; the stigma is bifid, lateral, leathery, and superior; the ovule is single and erect.

VARIETIES

Jorhat-C_2, Java-2, CIMAP-Bio-13 are the high-yielding varieties of this crop for southern and eastern India. Whereas, 'Manjusha' and 'Mandakini' are the varieties released by the CIMAP, Lucknow, for the North Indian plains. An elite mutant clone of Manjusha 'M3-8', named Manjari, which has been found to possess 50-90% more oil, high citronellol and low elemol content on an average, over the above varieties, has been developed recently at this institute. 'Manjari' is an erect-growing herb, with yellowish-green leaves and a dark purple stem. It has profuse tillering and rapid growing ability, hence produces a high herb yield.

SOIL

The plant has been found to grown well under varying soil conditions, but sandy loam soil with abundant organic matter is the most suitable. Heavy clay and sandy soils are not conducive to the good growth of this plant. Citronella thrives well in a wide range of soil pH, ranging from 5.8 to 8.0. However, a pH of around 6.0 is the most suitable. The plants are reported to grow well at altitudes between 1000-1500 m.

CLIMATE

Citronella thrives best under tropical and sub-tropical conditions. It requires abundant moisture and sunshine for its good growth. However, the distribution and not the total amount of rainfall is important. Well-distributed rainfall ranging from 200-250 cm and high atmospheric humidity appear to influence the plant's growth, yield and quality of oil favourably. In areas where the rainfall is low, the plant can be grown with supplementary irrigation.

LAND PREPARATION

The land is brought to a fine tilth by ploughing and harrowing and the field is laid out in 6 m × 6 m size beds, providing irrigation channels. Ridges and furrows are made at 60 cm intervals.

CULTIVATION

Propagation

Citronella flowers profusely in South India at higher altitudes and sporadically in the plains of the North and North-eastern regions. Viable seeds, however, are not formed because of irregularities in meiosis and, therefore, the species can be propagated only vegetatively. This is achieved by splitting the clumps into slips. The slips are taken from healthy, vigorously growing young bushes. The bush is gently dug out and separated into a number of slips and each slip contains 1-3 tillers. The fibrous roots and leaves should be trimmed off the slips before planting. It is observed that a 1-year-old clump, on an average, gives about 50 slips.

PLANTING

The slips are planted in May-June when they establish well in this region. Late planting, particularly after July, sometimes results in heavy casualty. The slips are planted at a distance of 60 cm × 60 cm apart. However, in areas where the soil is very fertile and the climatic conditions support luxurious growth, a spacing of 90 cm × 90 cm may be followed. It is better if the slips are planted on ridges to avoid water-logging.

The field should be irrigated immediately after planting, if there are no rains within the next 24 hours.

MANURES AND FERTILIZERS

In the red laterite soil of Karnataka and other southern states where the plant grows throughout the year, 10 t of FYM is applied. A fertilizer dose of 80-120 kg N, 80 kg super phosphate and 40 kg muriate of potash is given. Nitrogen is applied in 4 equal split doses, the first about a month after planting and then after each harvest, at an interval of about 4 months.

The CIMAP, Lucknow, has recommended a spray of 0.5% Fe through $FeSO_4$+Citric acid to check the spread of chlorosis, if noticed.

IRRIGATION

Citronella requires sufficient moisture of good growth and yield of leaves. In the areas where the annual rainfall is about 200-250 cm, well distributed over the year and humidity is high, supplemental irrigation is not necessary. In the drier months, however, irrigation may be provided and this increases the yield. Under Karnataka conditions, about 8-10 irrigations are required in the dry period.

INTERCULTURE

Citronella plantations should be kept weed-free. When the plants have established themselves and grown into bushes, the problem is not that severe. However, in newly-established plantations and after each harvest, weeds spring up in the inter-row spaces and weeding is essential.

PESTS AND DISEASES

Not many diseases and pests have been reported to attack citronella plants. Sometimes the plants are affected by the leaf-blight disease caused by *Curvalaria andropogonis* at the beginning of the monsoons. This disease appears in the form of small, brownish spots, which enlarge into long patches along the tips and margins of the leaves. The disease can be controlled by prophylactic spraying of either Dithane M-45 or Dithane Z-78 (0.3%) at intervals of 10-15 days, during the growing period. A new sheath-rot disease caused by *Rhizoctonia solani* is reported from the Terai region of Utter Pradesh. It can be controlled by spraying hexaconazole 5% EC. Another fungus, *Colletorichum graminicola,* has been found to affect the crop in Karnataka. The CIMAP, Lucknow, has found an isolate of *Trichoderma* spp. completely inhibiting the growth of *Pythium aphanideramatum,* as a biocontrol agent for the lethal yellowing disease that affects this crop.

Among the insects, termites are reported to cause the most damage to the plants. The termite menace can be controlled by the application of 25 kg/ha Aldrin to the soil at the time of planting.

HARVESTING, DISTILLATION AND YIELD

The crop is ready for the first harvest after about 9 months of planting. Harvesting is done by using an ordinary sickle, at about 20-45 cm above the ground. Under Karnataka conditions, the crop is harvested in the months of March, June and September. The crop flowers during October-November and the flowering stalks should be nipped off to discourage flowering. If the flowering stalks are allowed to grow, the plants will tend to age very soon and their life span may be reduced. Generally, the crop once planted yields a profitable income for about 3-4 years and should be replanted after this period. Well-maintained plantations may thrive longer.

The fresh herbage is steam-distilled immediately, never later than 24 hours, to obtain citronella oil. The oil-content of the leaves is affected by various factors, such as the soil, climate, age of plantation and method and efficiency of distillation. On an average, however, the oil-content is about 1% on the basis of the fresh weight of leaves. The yield of leaves may range from 15-20 t/ha in the first year and 20-25 t/ha in the second and third years. The yield of oil obtained during the first year is about 100-150 kg/ha and, in subsequent years, about 200-250 kg/ha oil of may be obtained.

32

Clocimum

PLANT PROFILE

Family : *Labiatae*

English name : Clocimum

Indian name : *Vridhutulsi* (Sanskrit), *Bantulsi* (Hindi) *Lavangatulasi* (Kannada), *Perumtulasi*, *Elumichamtulasi* (Tamil)

Species and varieties : *Ocimum gratissimum* L.

Distribution : India, Africa

Uses : Cosmetics, Drugs, Flavouring, Perfumery

An improved chemotype of *Ocimum gratissimum* L. was evolved as a result of the screening and breeding of *Ocimum* species at the RRL, Jammu in the year 1980. It has been appropriately named as 'Clocimum' because the oil extracted from this plant is clove-scented and possesses a high (70-75%) eugenol content which is the main constituent of clove oil. It also contains 10-15% myrcene. Eugenol is widely used in the perfume, cosmetic, pharmaceutical and confectionery industries. It is also used in the bakery and ice-cream industry.

India is importing eugenol, containing essential oil, to meet the internal demands of perfumery and pharmaceutical industries and losing a lot of money in terms of precious foreign exchange. In order to avoid this, clocimum, which is a perennial herbaceous plant can be used as a substitute to the eugenol-yielding crops like *Cinnamomum zeylanicum* and clove which are very specific in their climatic requirements and cannot be grown everywhere. Besides, clove and cinnamon are very expensive sources of eugenol (Rs. 400/kg), while clocimum (*Ocimum gratissimum* L.) is an alternative and also a cheap source (Rs. 100/kg) and can find a good place in the Indian economy.

DESCRIPTION OF THE PLANT

Clocimum is a tall, many-branched and perennial aromatic shrub belonging to the family *Labiatae.* The stem is erect, green, quadrangular, with short hairs and attains a height of 1.25 to 2 m. The leaves are ovate, coarsely crenate-serrate, pubescent on both surfaces and bilaterally arranged. The oil glands are present on the dorsal surface of the leaves. The leaves are 2.5 to 14.5 cm long. The flowers are white or greenish-to pale-yellow in colour, small, occurring in simple or branched racemes, which are moderately close-whorled. The nutlets are subglobose, rugose, brown in colour with a glandular depression.

SOIL

The crop is sufficiently hardy and can grow on any type of soil except on highly saline, alkaline or water-logged soils. However, sandy loam soils with good organic matter is considered ideal for the growth and development of the plant.

CLIMATE

The wide distribution of the plant shows that it is not very specific in its climatic requirements. It has a wide range of adaptability and can be grown successfully in tropical, sub-tropical and warm temperate regions, as it is capable of withstanding the extremes of drought and frost. However, the growth of the crop is much better in tropical areas than in sub-tropical or temperate areas, where its growth is slow due to low temperatures during winter. Long days and high temperatures have been found favourable for plant growth and higher oil production. It flourishes well under medium to high rainfall (500 to 1200 mm) and humid conditions. The crop is found growing up to an altitude of 900 m.

CULTIVATION

Propagation

Clocimum is propagated through seeds

Nursery Raising

The land required for raising the nursery should be cleared of stubbles and weeds and worked up well up to a 30 cm depth. The soil is brought to fine tilth and well-rotted FYM is applied @ 2 kg/sq m and mixed well. Beds of 3 m length, 1 m width and 15 cm height are laid out, properly levelled and cleared of any clods or pebbles. As the seeds are minute, they are mixed with sand in the ratio of 1:4 and 10 g seeds are used for a nursery-bed of 3 m × 1 m × 0.15 m size. About 300-400 g of seeds are enough to raise the nursery of /ha area. Over the nursery-bed, the seeds are evenly broadcasted and covered with a thin layer of sand and FYM mixture. The beds are uniformly watered immediately after sowing and every day thereafter till germination is over, and later, once in two days. Germination is noticed after a week and continues up to 10 days.

AFTER-CARE OF THE NURSERY

The beds must be kept weed-free and care should be taken to maintain good, healthy and vigorous seedlings. Since the seedlings are slow in their initial growth they are given a 2% urea spray after 30 days of sowing, in order to boost their initial growth.

TRANSPLANTING OF SEEDLINGS

The healthy, vigorous seedlings of about 12-15 cm height, which have 5 to 6 leaves and which are about 50 days old, are carefully removed from the nursery-bed after sufficient watering and digging to avoid any possible damage to the roots. The seedlings are immediately transported and planted in the main field at a distance of 30 cm × 30 cm. Spacings of 40 cm × 50 cm and 50 cm × 50 cm also recommended for this crop.

FERTILIZER APPLICATION

Clocimum is a heavy feeder and responds well to the application of nutrients. A fertilizer dose of 150:75:75 kg/ha has been responsible for maximum herb-yield and essential oil. Of this, the entire dose of P and K are applied at the time of transplanting. Whereas, N is applied in three split doses. A first dose of 50% N is given as a basal dose and the remaining 50% is split into two equal portions and applied after first and second cutting, respectively. Since the crop is a perennial and remains in the field for 4-5 years, the recommended dose of fertilizers should be repeated every year.

IRRIGATION

Irrigation is provided twice a week for a month. Afterwards, the interval between irrigations is increased to once a week, depending upon the rainfall and soil moisture status.

INTERCULTURE

After first and second cuttings, the soil should be stirred and the fertilizer applied and incorporated in the soil. Generally, for a 3-year crop, during the first year one hand-weeding and two hoeings; during the successive years, four hoeings one after each harvest are recommended. Gramaxone @ 3 kg/ha is reported to control the weeds effectively.

PRUNING

The crop should be pruned at least once in a year to maintain the growth and yield at an economic level. It has been observed that pruning done up to 10 cm from ground-level resulted in higher herbage, oil and fresh wood-yield up to 7 years of cultivation. However, the maximum herbage and oil yield was recorded in the 2nd, 3rd, 4th and 5th years crops when pruning was done at ground level or 10 cm above it. The crop should be pruned within 3 days of the second harvest in each year.

PESTS AND DISEASES

The crop is sufficiently hardy and there is no serious incidence of insect pests or diseases observed on this crops. However, sometimes, mealy bugs and termites are reported to cause damage to this crop. Mealy bugs can be controlled by spraying 0.2% Quinalphos or Methyl Parathion on the crop and termites can be controlled by application of 25 kg/ha Aldrex to the soil, followed by irrigation.

HARVESTING AND YIELD

The crop is ready for the first harvest after 90-95 days of transplanting. Further harvests can be made after every 65-75 days', intervals. The number of harvests increase from 2-3 harvests in the first year to 4 harvests in the subsequent years. The time of harvest plays an important role in the quantitative and qualitative production of oil. Harvesting done on bright sunny days yields oil of good quality and higher quantity. The crop should be cut at 15-20 cm above ground-level in the first year, 25-30 cm in the second year and 35-45 cm high in the third year. Since almost all the oil is stored in the leaves, harvesting should not include the woody stem portion just for the sake of a few lower leaves. The oil and eugenol content is maximum at the flower initiation and seed-setting stages. One hectare of clocimum yields 45t of fresh herb in the first year and about 70 t/year in the subsequent years.

DISTILLATION OF OIL AND OIL YIELD

Clocimum oil is distilled immediately after the harvest. However, it can be delayed up to 6-8 hours without any change in the oil quality and its yield, beyond which there will be considerable loss in oil-yield. The essential oil-yield is 200-250 l/ha.

33

Davana

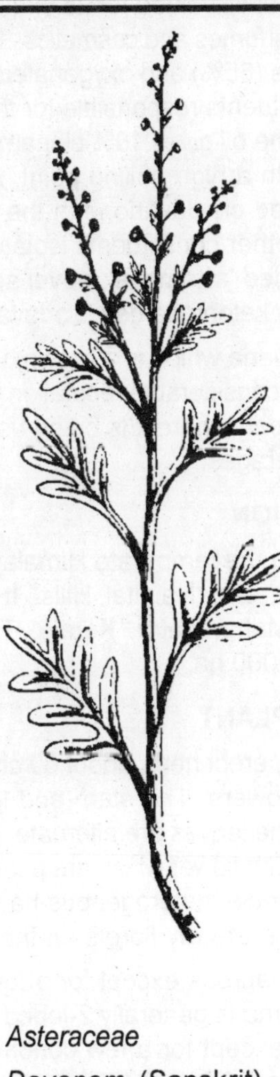

PLANT PROFILE

Family	:	*Asteraceae*
Indian name	:	*Davanam* (Sanskrit), *Davana* (Hindi) *Davana* (Kannada), *Davanam* (Tamil)

Species and varieties : *Artemisia pallens* Wall.

Distribution : India

Uses : Cosmetics, flavouring beverages, confectionery and tobacco, Perfumery

Davana (*Artemisia pallens* Well. (2n=16), belonging to the family *Asteraceae,* is an important annual aromatic herb, much prized in India for its delicate fragrance. The davana springs are commonly used in garlands, bouquets and religious offerings in most parts of the year. The leaves and flowers contain the essential oil valued for its exquisite and delicate aroma and is used in high-grade perfumes and cosmetics. The oil of davana contains hydrocarbons (20%), esters (65%) and oxygenated compounds (15%). The esters are the major constituents responsible for the characteristic smell of davana. Saponification of the oil gives 10% cinnamic acid, while the alcohol part gives a viscous oil with a high boiling point. It is reported that a new sesquiterpene ketone called cis-davanone in the oil is responsible for its characteristic odour. The other constituents isolated from the oil include a sesquiterpene ketone named 'artemone', novel sesquiterpenoids named. 'davanafurans' and another ketone named 'isodavanone'.

The essential oil of davana which is a brown, viscous liquid with a rich, fruity odour has acquired a considerable reputation in the international trade, particularly in USA and Japan where it is being used for flavouring cakes, pastries, tobacco and beverages.

ORIGIN AND DISTRIBUTION

The plant grows wild in the temperate Himalayas. It is common in the Kashmir Valley, the Simla and Nainital Hills. It is being commercially cultivated in Karnataka, Maharashtra, Kerala, Tamil Nadu and Andhra Pradesh in area of about 1000 ha.

DESCRIPTION OF THE PLANT

Davana is an aromatic, erect herb, about 60 cm tall, with much-divided leaves and small yellow flowers. The stem and leaves are covered with greyish-white tomentum. The leaves are alternate, petiolate and lobed. The inflorescence is capitulate with flower which are peduncled to sessile, axillary or forming lax racemes, simple, heterogenous having bisexual disc florets in the centre and a few pistillate ray florets on the periphery.

The outer florets are glabrous except for a few cottony hairs, tubular, generally 3-lobed. The stigma is generally 2-lobed and rarely 3-lobed. The inner florets are glabrous except for a few cottony hairs, tubular, 5-lobed and bisexual; the stamens are 5 in number with free, epipetalous filaments and a dithecous inflorescence; it has syngenesious anthers which are connective, prolonged, tapering-style and bifid.

SOIL

The crop is found growing on various types of soils from sandy loam to medium black. However, a fertile, well-drained, sandy loam soil which is rich in organic matter is ideal.

CLIMATE

Season is an important aspect to be considered when davana is grown for extracting essential oil. The oil content in the plants was observed to be maximum when the crop was grown during the winter season compared to the other seasons. Thus, when the crop is grown for the production of oil, it should be planted during the first week of November. A few light showers with moderate winter conditions and no frost is conducive to the good growth of the plant. High temperature and heavy rains at the time of flowering have not only been found to affect the plant growth adversely, but also reduces the oil content and ultimately the oil yield.

CULTIVATION

Nursery Raising

Davana is propagated by seeds. As the seeds lose viability rapidly, only the seeds from the previous season's crop should only be used for sowing. About 1.5 kg of seed is required to produce enough seedlings to transplant into an area of one hectare.

Usually, nursery-beds 2 m long and 1 m wide are preferred. The surface of the beds should be clod-free. It is then incorporated with finely prepared FYM at the rate of 10 per bed. Sowing of seeds at the rate of 1 g/sq m is desirable. The seeds may be sown either dry or after wetting them along with sand for about 48 hours. In the latter case, the seeds are thoroughly mixed with sand @ 4-5 times their volume. To this mixture, water is added so that the sand is sufficiently wet. It is then tied in a cloth bag and stored in a warm place for 48 hours. This will hasten the sprouting of seeds and the radicle will emerge at the end of 48 hours. The nursery-bed is then flooded with water to make a pool and the sprouting seed and sand mixture is broadcasted all over the bed, homogeneously. This method helps in uniform distribution of seeds. When the seeds have settled down, a thin layer of sand is spread over just enough to cover them. The seeds will germinate within 2-3 days of sowing. Hand-watering is done till the seedlings establish themselves (7-10 days), after which the beds are irrigated directly though the water channels.

While sowing the dry seeds, they are mixed with sand in the ratio of 1:10 and broadcasted homogeneously all over the bed. A thin layer of sand is then spread uniformly to cover the seeds and the beds are hand-watered twice a day. To prevent the ants from carrying away the seeds, an application of 10 kg/ha of Heptachlor to the soil about 10 days prior to sowing has been helpful. Using this method, the germination of seeds is observed in about 4-5 days.

In areas where there are rains at the time of nursery raising, the seedlings may be grown on raised nursery-beds which will also help in reducing the incidence of damping-off disease.

As there is a very slow growth of seedlings initially, foliar sprays of urea (0.1%) at weekly intervals, 3 weeks after sowing, may be given to boost their growth.

TRANSPLANTING

The seedlings will be ready for transplanting in about 6-8 weeks from the date of sowing. At this stage, the seedlings, should be about 10 cm tall.

Before transplanting, the field is thoroughly prepared by bringing the land to a fine tilth with repeated ploughings. It is then laid out into plots of convenient size by laying out bunds and channels. The size of the plot depends on the conditions prevailing locally. However, generally, plots of 3-4 m × 1.5-2.5 m size are preferred as it facilitates irrigation, weeding and other intercultural operations. After the preparation of the plots, the soil is incorporated with 6 t/ha of well-decomposed FYM or compost. The plots are irrigated a day prior to transplanting. The seedlings are then transplanted at a spacing of 15 cm between rows and 7.5 cm between plants. Trials have shown that transplanting davana plants closer together results in higher herbage-yield and, subsequently, higher oil-yield compared to wider spacing, which results in larger plants but lower herbage and oil-yield per unit area.

MANURES AND FERTILIZERS

Davana responds well to the application of manures and fertilizers. Well-decomposed FYM at the rate of 6 t/ha is incorporated into the soil at the time of land preparation. Subsequently, a fertilizer dose of 40 kg P and 40 kg K/ha is given at the time of transplanting. While N is applied at the rate of 120 kg/ha in three equal split doses: the first dose is given at 10 days after transplanting and the subsequent two doses at 15 days' intervals thereafter.

IRRIGATION

After transplanting, the plots are immediately provided with light irrigation. Later, irrigation is provided daily till the seedlings are well established (10-12 days) and, subsequently, once in 3-4 days depending on the weather conditions.

INTERCULTURE

The field is kept weed-free by regular weeding as and when required. In all, about 2-3 hand-weedings during the early period of growth will help to keep the weeds down.

GROWTH REGULATOR APPLICATION

Growth regulators have been used to boost the growth and yield in many crops. In davana also, an application of GA at 200 ppm after five weeks of transplanting has been found to increase the herb and essential oil-yield per unit area.

PESTS AND DISEASES

Insect Pests

No serious attack of insect pests has been reported in davana. However, some insect pests like leaf-eating caterpillars, aphids and termites have been observed to affect the crop.

The application of Aldrex to the plots will control the attack of termites, while the spraying of any systemic insecticide like 0.05% of Monocrotophos or 0.2% of Dimethoate will control the incidence of aphids and the spraying of contact insecticides like 0.2% Metacid will control leaf-eating caterpillars.

Diseases

Damping-off

This disease is caused by fungus belonging to the *Rhizoctinia* spp. It is usually severe at the nursery stage, particularly when there is high humidity and cloudy weather conditions, resulting in the heavy mortality of seedlings.

Controlling the irrigation will reduce the incidence of the disease. Treating the seeds with Emisan @ 0.2% or Ridona MZ at 0.1% before sowing and then drenching the seed-beds with the above chemicals a week after germination, controls the disease.

HARVESTING

The crop starts flowering after 110-115 days of sowing, which will be around the 2nd or 3rd week of February. In order to obtain the maximum essential oil-yield, the plants should be harvested when about 50% of them have come to the flowering state. This is usually at the end of February or in the 1st week of March, about 120-125 days after sowing. Harvesting is done by cutting the plants from the base. Although there are reports about the possibility of obtaining a ratoon crop in davana, it is not practical as the main crop is harvested only during the month of March and the ratoon starts sprouting by the end of March or the beginning of April which, due to the high temperatures prevailing during these period, results in poor growth of the plants and mutilated flower-buds which may even fail to open. The crop, thus obtained, become uneconomical as the flower-heads are the major contributors of oil.

DISTILLATION

The harvested material, before distillation, is dried under the shade for 2 days. It is better to distill this immediately rather than to store it. The dried material is steam-distilled to obtain good quality oil. However, for the estimation of essential oil under laboratory conditions, particularly of a small sample, the shade-dried material is hydro-distilled.

In the case of hydro-distillation, the material is placed in a glass-still and water is added to it, so that around three-fourths of the material is immersed in water and it is then heated. During boiling, the water vapours along with the vapourized oil moves into the condenser, gets condensed and collects in a graduated receiver. Based on the amount of oil collected, the oil content of the material can be determined.

However, for commercial purposes, steam distillation should be used. The distillation equipment consists of: (i) A Boiler, which produces the stem; (ii) A Distillation Still in which the material is filled and steam is passed through; (iii) A Condenser, wherein the vaporized oil gets condensed into a liquid from; and (iv) A Receiver, to collect the oil.

The boiler and the distillation still are made of steel. The boiler is connected to the distillation still by a steel pipe through which the steam passes. A perforated grid (plate) is placed at the bottom of the still on which the plant material is kept. The distillation still is connected to the condenser through a pipe. The condenser consists of many metallic pipes mounted inside a jacket. It is provided with an inlet and an outlet. Water is passed through the gap between the pipes in order to cool the steam and essential oil vapours into liquid form, which then gets collected in the steel receiver. The oil, being lighter than water and insoluble, floats on the surface of the water.

For distillation, the air-dried herbage is chopped into smaller pieces and then charged into the still. While filling, the material should be tightly packed inside the still, as otherwise steam channels may be formed during distillation resulting in poor yields. About 5-6 hours are required to complete the charge.

After decantation of the top, clear layer of oil, the bottom layer which consists of small quantities of water and oil has to be clarified. To separate the oil, a saturated solution of sodium chloride is added to this mixture so that a separated layer of water and oil is formed. The lower water-layer is drained off with the help of a separating funnel and the upper layer of oil is collected.

YIELD AND OIL CONTENT

The yield of fresh herbage, including flower-heads, is around 12-13 t/ha. Though, under laboratory conditions, the oil content in the whole plant after drying it in the shade for 2 days is 0.29%. An average recovery of around 0.2% under large-scale distillation, yielding 12-13 kg/ha of oil may be considered satisfactory.

When oil is extracted from the whole plant, the flower-heads contribute the major portion of the oil. The contribution of the leaves and stems towards the percentage of oil content in a whole plant is very little. The percentage of oil content in different plant parts, worked out under laboratory conditions on V/W basis, is as follows:

Plant part	*Percentage of oil content (2 days air-dried basis)*
Flower-heads	0.53
Herbage (leaves+stem)	0.14
Whole plant	0.29

34

Dill

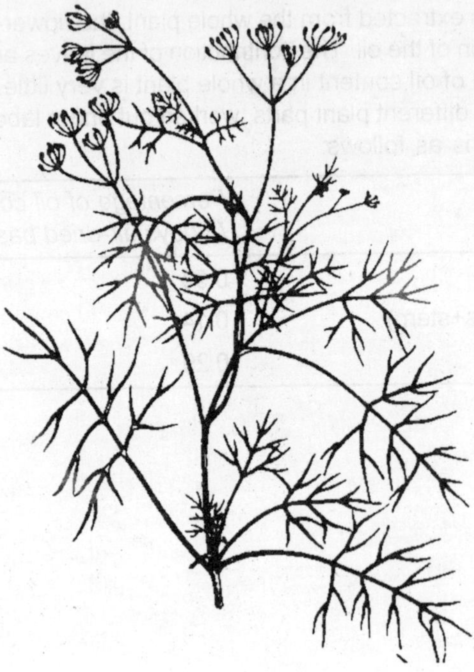

PLANT PROFILE

Family	:	*Umbelliferae*
English name	:	Dill, Garden Dill, Anet
Indian name	:	*Satapuspi* (Sanskrit), Soya (Hindi) *Sabasige* (Kannada), *Satakuppi* (Tamil)
Species and varieties	:	*Anethum graveolens* L., *A. sowa* Roxb English stock, Gribovskii, Haldwani selectio Herkules, K-299, K-253, Lesnogorodsk Mammoth Long Island
Distribution	:	India, Abyssinia, Africa, Asia, Asia Minor, Egyp

England, Europe, Iran, Germany, Holland, Hungary, Orient and Mediterranean countries, Southern Russia, Sweden, USA

Uses : Culinary purposes, Drugs, Flavouring, Perfumery

Dill belongs to the family *Umbelliferae.* It comes under the genera *Anethum,* in which there are two species under cultivation, namely: the European dill, *A. graveolens* L. and another closely related Indian dill, *A. Sowa* Roxb.

The entire dill plant is aromatic, but most of the volatile oil is in the seeds (i.e., the fruit). The herb and fruit oils possess different flavour constituents. The principal constituent of the herb oil is phellandrene and that of the seed oil is carvone. It is said that the quality of fruits present in the harvested material and their state of ripeness determines the oil content of the crop and its flavour. The oil of the herb is a colourless to brownish-yellow, mobile liquid, while the oil of the seed is plain yellow in colour, becoming dark on storage. In addition to phellandrene, the herb oil contains α-pinene, β-pinene, δ-3-carene, a-terpinene, limonene, y-terpinene, cymene, terpinolene, undecane, cis-3-hexanyl acetate, cis-4\3-hexanol, trans-2-hexanol, terpinene-4-ol, α-terpineol, carvone, thymol, carvacrol, myriciticin and apiole. And the seed-oil in addition to carvone contains apiole, carveol, caryophllence, dihydrocarveol, dihydrocarvone, dillapiole, D-limonene, Di-phelliandrene, eugenol, iso eugenol, L-pinene l-terpinene and myristicin.

The oil content of the fresh herbage varies from 0.60 to 2.84%. The oil content in the leaves rises progressively from the roselle stage (0.6%) to the commencement of flowering (1.5%) up to mass flowering (1.7%) only. Thereafter, it declines. It is 1.2% at the milky ripening of fruits, 0.65% at the mid-ripe fruit stage and 0.4%, when the fruits grow to maturity on the plant. The flowers at the bud stage contain 0.8% oil, which rises steeply to 4.8% at the mass-flowering stage.

Dill leaves are used for seasoning soups, sauces and particularly pickles. The seed is used as a condiment in India and also as a carminative, an aromatic, a stimulant and diuretic in *Ayurvedic* and *Unani* medicines. The emulsion of the seed-oil in water is an important constituent of gripe water, useful in flatulence, colic pain, vomiting, diarrhoea and hiccoughs.

The European dill seed-oil is preferred in Pharmacy over that of the Indian dill or sowa, due to the presence of a large percentage of dillopiole, varying from 15.6 to 39.6%, and a lower percentage of carvone in sowa seed oil. Dillopiole is a toxic substance, not found in European dill seed oil.

ORIGIN AND DISTRIBUTION

Anethum graveolens is a native of the Orient and Mediterranean countries, found growing wild in Iran, Egypt, Abyssinia, various parts of

Europe, Southern Russia, Africa and Asia. It is cultivated in the United States, Hungary, Germany, Holland, Sweeden, Asia Minor, North Africa, India and England. In India, it has been successfully cultivated on an experimental scale in Jammu and Kashmir State, Maharashtra, Gujarat, Andhra Pradesh, Madhya Pradesh and Rajasthan.

DESCRIPTION OF THE PLANT

Dill is a hapaxanthic annual or biennial aromatic herb, growing to a height of about 1 to 1.20 m. The leaves are feathery, standing on a sheathing of foot-stalks, with linear and pointed leaflets, compound and light-green in colour. The stem is smooth, shiny and hollow, grows upright and bears flat, terminal compound umbels, with numerous yellow flowers, whose small petals are rolled inwards. The flowers are regular, bisexual, pentamerous and dichogamous. The fruits are flat, dry and groomed (they are commonly, but erroneously, called seeds) and are produced in great quantities. They are very pungent and bitter in taste and very light in weight. It consists of two brown, broadly oval, compressed, indehiscent, one-seeded carpels (mericarps), 3-4 mm long and 2-3 mm broad, with a thickness of 1.0 mm. They have five ridges, the three dorsal ridges being an inconspicuous brown colour and the two lateral ridges are yellowish and wing-like. The chromosome number is 2n=22.

VARIETIES

'Haldwani selection' and 'English stock' are the varieties recommended for cultivation in India. Among the foreign varieties 'Gribovskii', is recommended for early and high herbage and seed yield and 'Lesnogorodski' has the best-flavoured leaves and highest oil content in the leaves and seeds, besides 'K-299', 'K-253', 'Mammoth Long Island', 'daniel' and 'Herkules'.

SOIL

Dill grows well in any good garden soil with high fertility. Sandy loam soils with good drainage are the most suitable. Light sandy or heavy clay soil should be avoided. It can be successfully grown in soils with a pH of up to 8.6.

CLIMATE

Dill is quite a hardy plant and may thrive in much cooler climates, provided it finds a warm location. It is a long day, cold weather crop, growing during the *rabi* season in the Indian plains. Strong winds and heavy rains during the flowering period may be injurious and extreme heat during maturity will reduce the oil yield to practically zero.

CULTIVATION

Propagation

Dill is propagated by seeds.

SOWING

The seeds are usually sown in March-April or in mid-October by drill or broadcast, in well-prepared land, treated with FYM @ 19 t/ha. The recommended seed rate is 3 kg/ha, which is sown in rows 60 cm apart and later thinned to 30 cm apart within the rows, after about 30 days from sowing when they are 13 cm high. The seeds have a viability of about three years and take about 7-9 days for germination, when sown during the month of October, with 96 to 98% germination. If the crop is sown late, the vegetative phase is reduced, which seriously lowers the yield of the seed crop. Spacings of 45 × 20 cm and sowing in lines 30 or 45 cm apart have also been found suitable for this crop.

APPLICATION OF FERTILIZERS

The crop responds well to application of nitrogenous and phosphatic fertilizers. A dose of 40 kg/ha each of N, P and K is recommended for obtaining economical yields in dill.

WEEDING AND IRRIGATION

The plant requires frequent cultivation. The plots should be kept free from weeds. Weedicides like Influtalin and Ethafluralin (1.1 kg/ha), Sethoxydim (4.5 kg/ha), Linuron (1 kg/ha), Chlorbromuron (4.5 kg/ha) and Thiobencarb (6-8 kg/ha), have been recommended for chemical weed control. Since it is a herbaceous crop, regular irrigation at intervals of about 8 to 12 days, depending on the soil and climatic conditions is necessary. Generally, 8-9 irrigations are adequate for the maturity of the crop.

GROWTH REGULATORS

Gibberellic acid (50 ppm) sprayed 15 days after emergence and again 10 days later, increased the yield and improved the flavour. Ascorbic acid (50 ppm) treatment is reported to yield oil with a high concentration of carvone and dihydroxycarvone and the lowest amount of dillapiole.

INTERCROPPING

Dill can be intercropped with *Rauwolfia serpentina* or *Mentha arvensis* or *Salvia sclarea*.

PESTS AND DISEASES

Pests

Aphids: They occasionally cause damage and are generally controlled by spraying Malathion (0.5%) 2 to 3 times during the infestation.

Diseases

Powdery mildew (*Erysiphe umbelliferum*) is the major disease noticed at the flowering and early seedling stages. It can be controlled by spraying wettable sulphur (2%), 2-3 times at weekly intervals. *Fusarium* spp. causes root-rot disease, and this can be controlled by phytosanitory measures, seed treatment with Agrosan @ 3 g/kg of seed and by a foliar spray of Bavistin (0.1%). *Systola albipensis* has been reported to infect the seeds. The plants are also reported to exhibit mottling, leaf necrosis, dwarfing and malformation due to viral infections.

HARVESTING

Harvesting should be properly timed, since the quality of oil depends upon the state of maturity of the herb and the fruits. Plants sown in mid-October will be ready for harvest by the end of April, i.e. the plants take about 5½-6 months to reach maturity. The main axis of the stem ends in a large-sized compound umbel, which is axillary in position or on the branches. The crop continues to produce umbels on tertiary branches and these will be at various stages of maturity at the harvest time for a seed crop. The crop is prone to shedding on maturity and, therefore, should be carefully collected at the right time of maturity. Generally, for obtaining the oil of dill, harvesting is done when the crop is about 3½ months old and is in a milky, ripening seed stage and the fruit is turning brown in the most advanced fruits (seeds). After harvest, the plants are allowed to wilt in the field for 1-2 days and then distilled. When the crop is grown for its fruits, it is harvested, when most of the fruits are fully developed (ripe), but still green in colour. The fruit, at this stage, contains the maximum oil and carvone content and also the shedding of seeds is avoided. In very dry whether, this is preferably done early in the morning, when the plants are damp with overnight dew to avoid shedding. The harvested material is dried in the field, till the fruits can be easily threshed. The threshed fruits should be spread in a thin layer and frequently turned over until they are thoroughly dry.

YIELD

The herbage yield is about 2.5 to 3.0 t/ha, which, on distillation, gives about 18-20 kg of oil containing 30% of carvone, while the seed-yield is about 5 to 7 q/ha.

DISTILLATION

The essential oil is extracted by steam distillation from the herb, including the immature fruits and also from the mature and separated fruits. The two oils, however, differ in composition in odour and flavour. The 'herb oil' (isolated from the aboveground parts, including the unripe seeds) is preferred by the food industry, because of its more typical dill-herb characteristics. The seed-oil, with its high carvone content, resembles the oil of caraway seeds. During recent years, dill herb oil has largely replaced the fruit oil for flavouring and seasoning purposes.

35

Fennel

PLANT PROFILE

Family : *Apiaceae*

English name : Fennel

Indian name : *Misreya*, *Madhurika* (Sanskrit) *Saunf*, *Saumph* (Hindi), *Sompu* (Kannada), *Sompu* (Tamil)

Species and varieties : *Foeniculum vulgare* Miller

Subspecies : *Capillaceum dulce*

Distribution : India, Africa, Asia, Bulgaria, Southern Europe, France, Germany, Hungary, Italy, Morocco, Rumania, Russia, Spain

Uses : Culinary purposes, Drugs, Flavouring, Perfumery

Fennel (*Foeniculum vulgare* Miller), commonly known as '*Saunf*' or '*Badi saunf*', belongs to the family *Apiaceae*. It is cultivated mainly for its seeds, from which the spice oil is obtained. The main constituent of the oil from the fruits of cultivated *F. vulgare is trans-anethole.* Fennel oil of good quality contains 50-60% trans-anethole. The other constituents are: d-2-fenchone, methyl chavicol, α-2-pinene, limonene, 1, 8-cineole, r-terphinene, linalool, cis-anethole, anisic aldehyde, anisic ketone and foenicullin. The presence of a toxic etonic constituent has been recently reported. Indian fennel oil contains over 70% anethole and 6% fenchone. The sweet or Roman fennel fruits contain anethole, α-phallandrene and D-limonene. The high percentage of anethole (up to 905) and absence of fenchone are responsible for its delicate, sweet odour and flavour. Anisaldehyde ad anesic acid are also present.

The fruits, in addition, contain volatile oil. The percentage of oil is lowest in the fruits of Indian origin (0.7-1.2%) and highest in the fruits of Eastern Europe (4-6%). They also contain fixed oil (9-13%), pentosan and pectin. Starch is present in small quantities along with trigonelline and choline. The percentage of ash does not exceed 12%. The fruits also contain iodine (C:88 g/100 g), vitamin-A (139 i.u./100 g), thiamine (36 r/100 g), riboflavin (36 r/100 g), niacin (38 mg/100 g), and ascorbic acid (9.31 mg/100 g). Traces of aluminium, barium, lithium, copper, manganese, silicon and titanium are also present.

The plant is pleasantly aromatic and is used as a pot herb. The leaves are used in fish sauces and for garnishing. The leaf-stalks are used in salads. Medicinally, the leaves are regarded to have diuretic properties while the roots are purgative. The dried fruits are extensively used for flavouring soups, meat dishes and sauces, bread rolls, pastries and confectionery. They are also used for flavouring liquors and pickles. The fruits are aromatic, stimulant and carminative. They are considered useful in diseases of the chest, spleen and kidney. They are also employed as a corrective for less pleasant drugs, particularly senna and rhubarb.

Fennel oil is largely used as a flavouring agent in culinary preparations, confectionery, cordials and liquors. It is useful in infantile colic and flatulence. It also checks griping in purgatives and is used as a germicide against hookworms. It is also used in scenting of soaps in addition to perfumery.

The residue left over after the distillation of essential oil from seed is used as cattle-feed. The seeds contain 14-22% proteins and 12-16% fat.

ORIGIN AND DISTRIBUTION

The plant in a native of Southern Europe, Asia and Africa. It is widely cultivated throughout the temperate and sub-tropical regions of the world; particularly in France, Italy, Bulgaria, Morocco and Spain for its aromatic fruits used as a culinary spice and for the extraction of essential oil. In India, it is grown as a garden crop or as a small-scale crop during winter, mainly in the states of Rajasthan, Maharashtra and Gujarat and also in some parts of Punjab, Uttar Pradesh and Andhra Pradesh. In Karnataka, it is grown on a small scale in Belgaum and Dharwad districts. The area under this crop is reported to be about 13000 ha and the production around 21000 t. In spite of having a number of industrial and medicinal uses and being a good foreign exchange earner, at present the crop is not being exploited commercially.

DESCRIPTION OF THE PLANT

Foeniculum is a small genus of annual, biennial and perennial herbs. The biennials and perennials have firm and round, greenish-blue, finely straightened stems about 150-200 cm in height. The leaves are 2-4, pinnate, the segment is always very narrow and often filiform. The flowers in large numbers, found in the second year of growth, are small and yellow in a compound, terminal umbel. The fruits are at first bluish, then become brownish-gray. All the parts of the plant are aromatic. Different races of fennel exist, with fruits that are sweet or bitter or acidic in taste. The fruits are oblong, cylindrical, 6-7 mm in length, greenish or yellowish-brown in colour, 5-ridged with prominent furrows which have oil glands.

SPECIES/VARIETIES

There are a large number of varieties and races differing in size, odour and taste of the fruits and are barely distinguishable from one another. They are regarded as races, varieties or subspecies of *F. vulgare*. The varieties which yield commercially important volatile oils are generally reduced to the sub-species, *capillaceum,* and placed under two distinct varieties: *vulgare* giving bitter fennel and var. *dulce* producing sweet fennel oil. The variety *dulce* is mainly cultivated in India, while *vulgare* is cultivated in Russia, Rumania, Hungary, Germany, France, Italy and in Southern Europe.

SOIL

Fennel grows in any good soil, but thrives best in rich, well-drained loam or black sandy soil containing sufficient lime. Any soil which has a high salt content and is prone to water-logging is unsuitable for its cultivation.

CLIMATE

It is cultivated throughout India at altitudes up to 2000 m. It requires a fairly mild climate and is cultivated as a cold weather crop in some parts of North India. It does not grow so well in South India except at high elevations.

SEASON

The time of sowing is during October-November in the plains and March-April in the hills. Under Bangalore conditions, the crop can be grown as a winter crop during the months of October-November.

LAND PREPARATION AND SOWING

The field is brought to a fine with tilth by continuous ploughings and laid out into beds of convenient size along with irrigation channels. It is treated with 25 t of FYM along with the basal dose of N, P and K.

The seeds are either broadcasted or drilled in rows at 45 cm spacing and irrigated. About 9-10 kg/ha of seeds are required. When the seedlings are 8-10 cm in height they are thinned at 30 cm in rows.

CULTIVATION

Propagation

It is propagated readily by seeds, but can also be grown by root or by corm division. The seeds are broadcasted or drilled by shallow drills. The seeds can be sown in nursery beds and later the seedlings are transplanted to the field, when they attain 8-10 cm in height.

FERTILIZER APPLICATION

Experiments at Bangalore have revealed that an application of 100 kg of N and 25 kg each of P_2O_5 and K_2O has resulted in good seed and oil-yield. Of this, half the N and the entire quantity of P and K are applied as a basal dose, while the remaining half of N is given as a top-dressing when the crop is about a month old.

IRRIGATION

The field is irrigated immediately after seeding, if there are no rains. Initially, irrigation (up to one month) is given at 3-4 days' intervals and thereafter at weekly intervals. This has been found to improve the yield considerably.

INTERCULTURE

As it is a delicate crop, frequent weedings at the initial stages of growth are essential. Subsequent weedings may vary with the situation. About 3-4 weedings may be enough for the entire life-cycle of the crop.

PESTS AND DISEASES

Not many diseases and pests are reported to attack this crop. The leaf blight (*Cercospora foeniculi*) and mildew (*Levillula taurica*) are among the diseases that do attack this crop, which can be controlled by spraying 0.2% Dithane M-45 and 0.3% wettable sulphur, respectively. The fungi, *Aspergillus* and *Penicillium,* are reported to damage the seeds during storage. Thrips (*Hercothrips indicusi)* are reported to cause considerable damage to the crop, which can be controlled by spraying 0.15% Dimethoate.

HARVESTING AND YIELD

The crop is harvested after 5-6 months of sowing, before the fruits are fully ripe to avoid shattering. While harvesting, the stems are cut with a sickle and spread out in loose bundles to dry in the sun. Dried fruits (after 4-5 days) are threshed and cleaned by winnowing. The yield in fennel ranges from 20-25 q/ha which, in turn, may yield about 35-40 kg/ha of essential oil under irrigated conditions.

Fennel fruits (seeds, as they are known in commerce) are classified for trade purposes according to their place of origin. Some of the well-known types in India are Bombay, Bihar and Uttar Pradesh. Fennel seeds from Lucknow are considered to the best for culinary purposes and are higher priced than those from other areas.

DISTILLATION OF OIL

For obtaining the maximum oil, the fruits are crushed before distillation. The oil, obtained from the fruits by steam-distillation, is a pale yellow-coloured liquid with a characteristic taste and odour. Two types of oil are recognised in commerce: (i) Sweet Fennel oil from the fruits of var. *dulce,* and (ii) Bitter fennel oil from the fruits of var. *vulgare.*

36

French Basil

PLANT PROFILE

Family	:	*Lamiaceae; Labiata*
English name	:	Sweet Basil, Common Basil
Indian name	:	*Barbari* (Sankrit), *Babul*, *Babuyitulsi* (Hindi) *Kama Kasturi*, *Sajjagida* (Kannada), *Tirunittru*, *tiruniruppaccai* (Tamil)
Species and varieties	:	*Ocimum basilicum* Linn. Var. *Majus difforme, purpuroscens, glabratum pilosum, crispa, thyrisiflora, darkopal* *O. basilicum* Linn. Subsp, *minima* Danert *O. americanum* Linn., *O. gratissimum* Linn. *O. kilimandscharicum* Guerke

		O. sanctum Linn., *O. viride* willd RRL-011
Distribution	:	India, Africa, South America (Brazil), Asia
Uses	:	Cosmetics, Culinary purposes, Drugs, Flavouring, Perfumery

Of the 150 species of *Ocimum,* the sweet or French or common or Roman Basil (*O. basilicum* Linn.) belonging to the family *Lamiaceae; Labiata* is the most important species, being utilized as a source of essential oil (Sweet Basil Oil). The volatile oil contains D-linalool and methyl chavicol as the major components, with the former up the 55% and the latter about 70%, depending on the sources. Other components include methyl cinnamate, which has been reported to be the major component (28%) of a variety of sweet basil, 1, 8-cineole, eugenol, borneol, ocimene, geraniol, anethol, 10-cadionals, β-caryophyllene, α-teripenol, camphor, 3-octanone, methyleugenol, safrole, sesquithujene and 1-epibicyclosesqui-phellandrene, among others. There are great variations in the concentration of these components in the volatile oil from different sources. Other constituents present in sweet basil include protein (14%), carbohydrates (61%) and relatively high concentrations of vitamins A and C.

The herb, leaves and seeds are used medicinally in indigenous systems of medicine and homoeopathy. Thus, an infusion of the plant is used for cephalalgia, gouty joints and as a gargle for bad breath. The juice, obtained from the leaves, gives relief in irritations of the throat, earache and ringworm.

The herb is aromatic, diaphoretic, a stimulant, carminative and expectorant. It is also considered by some to be anti-emetic, anti-diarrhoeic and antihelmintic. The seeds are used internally in constipation and piles.

The oil is extensively employed in several European countries and in the USA for flavouring of food stuffs, confectionery goods, condiments and in toiletry products such as mouthwashes and dental creams. It also finds a prominent place in the flavouring of baked goods, such as spiced meats, sausages, tomato pastes, various kinds of sauces, catsups, vinegars, pickles, ketchups and beverages. In the perfumery industry, the oil is used for compounding certain popular perfumes notably jasmine blends.

ORIGIN AND DISTRIBUTION

The genus *Ocimum* is well represented in the warmer parts of both the hemispheres from sea-level to 1800 m elevation. The maximum number of species are from the tropical rain-forests of Africa. The main centres of diversity in this genus are Africa, South America (Brazil) and Asia. In India, the cultivation of French basil is mainly concentrated in Uttar Pradesh in an area of about 500 ha.

TYPES OF FRENCH BASIL

In view of the great diversity, the various species and varieties have been classified, in accordance with their chemical composition and geographical sources, into 4 major types as given below.

1. European sweet basil

The oil obtained from this type consists of mainly methyl chavicol and linalool, but no camphor. This group comprises the French and American sweet basil oils which are in demand because of their high quality and the finest odour. It is distilled in France, Italy, Bulgaria, Egypt, Hungary, South Africa and occasionally, in the United States.

2. Reunion basil

The main constituents of the oil obtained from this type are methyl chavicol and camphor, but no linalool. The oil is of somewhat lower quality. It is distilled in the Reunion Islands, Comoros, Malagasy Republic, Thailand and occasionally in the Seychelles.

3. Methyl cinnamate basil

The oil of this type consists principally methyl chavicol and linalool; methyl cinnamate is present in substantial amounts. It is distilled in tropical countries like India, Haiti, Guatemala and a few African countries.

4. Eugeol basil

Eugenol is the principal constituent of the oil. It is distilled in the USSR and in some North African countries including Egypt and Morocco.

Nine species are recorded in Eugenol basil from India, of which three are exotic The more important of these species are:

(a) *Ocimum basilicum* Linn (2n-48) (English or French Sweet Basil). It has the following subspecies and varieties:

1. *O. basilicum* Linn. Subsp. *minima* Danert (2n=48) (Syn. *O. minima* Linn).
2. *O. basilicum* Var. *majus* Benth
3. *O. basilicum* Var. *difforme* Benth (Curly-leaved basil)
4. *O. basilicum* Var. *purpurascens* Benth (2n=48) (Violet-red basil)
5. *O. basilicum* Var. *glabratum* Benth (Common white basil)
6. *O. basilicum* Var. *Pilosum* Benth (Syn. *O. pilosum* Roxb)
7. *O. basilicum* Var. *crispa*
8. *O. basilicum* Var. *thyrisiflora* (2n=49)
9. *O. basilicum* Var. *darkopal*

(b) *O. americanum* Lin. (Syn. *O. canum* Sims.) (Hoary basil)

(c) *O. gratissium* Linn. (Shrubby basil)
(d) *O. kilimandscharicum* Guerke (Camphor basil)
(e) *O. sanctum* Linn. (Eng. Sacred or Holy basil)
(f) *O. viride* Wild (Fever plant of Sierra Leone).

Of the above species, *O. basilicum* Linn. alone is cultivated in India on a commercial scale.

DESCRIPTION OF THE PLANT

O. basilicum Linn. occurs in nature as a tetraploid (2n=48). It is a large, herbaceous, erect, strongly aromatic, annual herb, about 30-90 cm high. The leaves are opposite, ovate to lanceolate, 3.75-5 cm long; entire or deviate, the surfaces are glabrous, the petioles very slender and usually slightly hairy. The flowers are 0.72-1.25 cm long, borne in long terminal racemose inflorescences, simple or much-branched. The calyx is 5-toothed, the upper tooth is rounded and shorter than the others, the 2-lower teeth are ovate and lanceolate with a brittle point, the 2 laterals shorter than the lower. The corolla is 0.72-.25 cm long, white, pink or pale-purplish 2-lipped tube, short, the upper lip equally 4-lobed, there are 4 protruding stamens. The ovary is bicarpellary, syncarpous and bilocular; the stigma is bifid; the fruits are nutlets and are mucilagenous when wet.

VARIETIES

RRL-011 is an improved strain isolated from the segregating generation. The oil of this strain is sweet smelling and is a better substitute for French Basil oil. It gives a herbage yield of 50 t/ha and an oil recovery of 320 kg/ha. The green herb contains 0.45% oil with linalool (40%) and methyl chavicol (35%) as its main constituents.

'*Vikarsudha*' is a hybrid variety released from the CIMAP, Lucknow. It was developed through hybridization between exotic basil from Australia (EC 331886-CSIRO No. L 6323) and a local adaptive land race referred as Badaun local. The variety breeds true, grows 75-90 cm tall and matures at about 75-90 days after transplantation. The spacing recommended for this varlety is 45 cm × 30 cm. The variety is day neutral (photoinsensitive) and can be cultivated throughout the year except in areas experiencing severe winter, where the growth is retarded. The leaf to steam ratio (t/ha) is 75 and it yields 3.73 t/ha herb, the oil content is 0.7% and the oil yield is 261 kg/ha.

'Kusumohak' is a recently variety from the CIMAP, Lucknow, from seed-aided progeny of the introduced strain from Argentina. The plant has higher linalool (46%) and moderate chavicol (38%) content. The oil yield is 134 kg/ha.

SOIL

Moderately fertile, well-drained loamy or sandy loam soils are considered ideal for its cultivation. Clayey, water-logged soils are unsuitable for cultivation of this crop.

CLIMATE

The plant is susceptible to frost. The crop growth is poor in areas which receive heavy and continuous rainfall. In such areas, the crop could be raised, provided that the plants are well established prior to the onset of the monsoons and that the rainwater does not stagnate in the field.

SEASON

The crop can be grown annually from the middle of February to the end of September and also during the *kharif* season in the plains of North or South India.

LAND PREPARATION

The land is well prepared with 2 or 3 ploughings until a fine tilth of soil is obtained. FYM, if available, may be applied @ 10-12 t/ha before the 2nd or 3rd ploughing.

CULTIVATION

Propagation

The crop is raised through seeds, but direct sowing in the field is not advised. The seedlings are first raised in the nursery and then transplanted into the field. About 125 g seeds are sufficient to raise seedlings for planting one hectare of land.

Nursery Raising

The nursery area should be well-prepared. Well-rotted FYM and leaf-mould, each at the rate of 1 kg/sq m is applied and mixed well into the soil. Beds of 1 m × 4 m, with irrigation channel systems are laid out and the seeds (10-15 g/bed), mixed with fine sand or wood-ash, are sown in lines 6 cm apart of broadcast over the beds. The seeds are then covered with a thin layer of fine soil or FYM. The nursery-beds are watered immediately after sowing and regularly thereafter. In the plains of North India the seeds may be sown in the nursery in the months of April-May or August-September and in the hilly regions, in April. The seeds start germinating 3 days after sowing and the germination will be complete in about 10 days. The nursery should be kept weed-free. The seedlings will be ready for transplanting when they attain a height of 6-10 cm.

PLANTING

The seedlings may be transplanted, preferably in the evening, with an inter-plant spacing of 40 cm in rows 60 cm apart. Cloudly weather and fine drizzle are considered ideal weather conditions for transplanting.

APPLICATION OF FERTILIZERS

In order to raise a good crop, it is advisable to apply 20 kg N, 40 kg P_2O_5 and 40 kg K_2O/ha as a basal dose before planting, Nitrogen @ 40 kg/ha should also be applied as a top-dressing in two equal split doses. In order to get increased herbage (68-84% increase) and almost doubled oil-yield, it is recommended to apply N, P and K @ 120:100:100 kg/ha.

In a study conducted at University of Agricultural Sciences, Gandhi Krishi Vignana Kendra (UAS, GKVK), Bangalore, the maximum herbage and oil yields have been obtained by the application of 160 kg N/ha in two equal split doses along with 80 kg P_2O_5. This crop is tolerant to higher concentrations of Copper and Zinc and is susceptible to Cobalt and Nickle.

IRRIGATION

When raised as a summer crop, irrigation is required once a week. With the onset of the monsoon, the rains meet the water requirements of the crop fully till September. The crop needs irrigation once or twice a month thereafter.

WEEDING

Normally, the seedlings get well established in the field within a month of planting. The first weeding is done at this stage and a second is done 4 weeks after the first. No further weeding is required as the plants become bushy, thereby naturally suppressing the weeds. In large plantations, the expenditure on weeding can be minimized by the use of a tractor-drawn cultivator.

NTERCULTURE

Hoeing is done two months after planting. The crop may also be earthed-up at this stage.

PESTS AND DISEASES

Insect Pests

Among the insects, the larvae of leaf-rollers cause serious damage to the plants by sticking to the undersurface of the leaves, folding them from midrib length-wise and webbing them. Finally, the infected leaves fall off. A spray of Thiodon or Malathion (2 ml/l) with water, reduces this insect menace.

Diseases

Leaf-spot disease in this crop appears as small, water-soaked spots which later turn brown. The disease is caused by *Coynespora cassicola* (Berk and Curt) Wie. Scab disease, caused by *Elsinoe arxii,* causes a little defoliation with a puckering and dipping of the leaves and distortion of the tender twigs.

Blight of basil caused by *Alternaria* spp. is an important disease, which starts with a chlorotic appearance of the leaves which turn purple and finally black. Ultimately, the leaves are shed. *Colletotrichum capsici* also causes leaf-blight. The disease appears as small chlorotic spots on the leaves which enlarge rapidly. Older leaves appear to be more susceptible to the infection. The blight disease can be controlled by spraying the crop with 0.2% Dithane Z-78 or Dithane M-45, once or twice.

Basil wilt is caused by *Fusarium oxysporum* at all stages of growth. The disease is more pronounced in the rainy season. Initially, the leaves wilt but it soon spreads to the whole plant. To control this disease. The seedlings should be dipped in a solution of Tafason or Agallol at the time of planting.

HARVESTING AND YIELD

The crop is harvested 8-12 weeks after planting, at the stage when the plant is in full bloom and the lower leaves start turning yellowish. Harvesting is done with the help of sickles. While harvesting, the whole herb or flowering tops are harvested. Corresponding to the part harvested, two grades of oil are obtained, i.e., herb oil or flower oil. The flower oil has a superior note. For obtaining the highest quality oil, only the flowering tops are harvested. Normally, 3-4 floral harvests are obtained in this crop. The first harvest is taken when the plants are in full bloom, and the subsequent harvests after every 15-20 days. The whole plant is harvested finally about 15 cm from the ground-level leaving enough for regeneration of the crop. The harvested produce will be allowed to wilt in the field for 4-5 hours so as to reduce the moisture and also the bulk.

The floral harvest yields about 3-4 t/ha of flowers and the final harvest of the whole herb is about 13-14 t/ha.

DISTILLATION OF OIL AND ESSENTIAL OIL YIELD

The oil is sweet basil is obtained by hydro-distillation or steam-distillation of the young inflorescence or the whole herb. Extraction of oil through steam-distillation is better than extracting oil by hydro-distillation, as it takes less time and effects better recovery of the oil. While the extraction of oil by hydro-distillation which is carried on in a direct fire-still, is cheaper and more handy for small plantations, steam-distillation is still preferred for large plantations. Steam-distillation takes about 1-1½ hours to exhaust a charge completely.

The inflorescence contains 0.4% oil and the whole herb about 0.10 to 0.25%. The sweet basil oil-yield will be about 30-35 kg from the flower (flower oil) and 18-22 kg from the whole herb. If only the whole herb is harvested and distilled, the oil yield will be about 30 kg/ha.

37

Kewda

PLANT PROFILE

Family : *Pandanaceae*

English name : Screw Pine, Umbrella Tree

Indian name : *Ketaki* (Sanskrit), *Kedgi*, *Kevda* (Hindi), *Kedige* (Kannada), *Thalai*, *Talai* (Tamil)

Species and varieties : *Pandanus fascicularis* Lam
P. odoratissimus Linn, *P. tectoroius* Soland
P. laevis Kunth, *P. variegatus* Miq
P. latifolius Hassk, *P. amarylligolius* Roxb

Distribution : India, Iran, Malaysia, Mauritius, Myanmar

Uses : Baskets, Drugs, Flavouring for food and beverages, Paper, Perfumery, Rope-making, Thatching

Kewda or screw pine (*Pandanus fasciculais* Lam), belonging to the family *Pandanaceae,* is a shrub whose fragrant male spadices yield an oil called *kewda* oil (0.03%). The oil contains methyl ether of phenyl alcohol (66.68%) which gives the characteristic aroma to the spadices, dipentene (16.24%), D-linalool (19.16%), phenylethyl acetate (4.65%), ester of phthalic acid, citral (1.82%) and steropentene. The male flowers are very fragrant and are used for hair decoration and also in the preparation of *kewda attar*, *kewda* water and *kewda* oil which were among the ancient perfumes of India. *Kewda attar* blends with almost all types of perfumes and is used for scenting clothes, *paan masala*, bouquets, lotions, cosmetics, soaps, hair oils, tobacco and *agarbathi*. *Kewda* water is used as a food flavouring in sweets, syrups and soft drinks. The male flowers are sometimes kept in sachets in wardrobes and boxes to impart fragrance to stored garments. Medicinally, *kewda* oil is used as a stimulant, antispasmodic and is reported to relieve headache and rheumatism. Besides, the terminal and tender buds are also eaten raw or in a cooked form.

The leaves are used for covering huts, for making mats, cordage, hats and baskets, and are said to be good for paper making. Apart from this, the leaves are of value in the treatment of leprosy, small-pox, scabies, leucoderma and diseases of the heart and brain. The juice of the inflorescence is useful in rheumatic arthritis in animals. The plant is also considered as a good soil-binder. Fibres from its long aerial roots are very strong and are used in making ropes and baskets.

ORIGIN AND DISTRIBUTION

The plant occurs in the coastal regions of India, Iran, Malaysia, Mauritius and Myanmar. It is distributed in the coastal regions of Andhra Pradesh, Tamil Nadu, Orissa, Gujarat and the Andaman Islands in India. However, the Ganjam district of Orissa which distills over 30 million flowers per year is the major production centre. In this district, it is distributed in the taluks of Chatapur, Gopalpur and Behrampur. *Kewda* plantations are also found in the districts of Balasore, Cuttack and Puri. In Uttar Pradesh, *kewda* is grown on a plantation scale in Badayun, Balia and Ghazipur districts.

In Orissa, the *kewda* perfumery trade is controlled by the distilleries located at Ghazipur, Kannauj, Lucknow and the neighbouring parts of North

India. The other centres of production are Kotabamali in Tamil Nadu; Jaunpur, Ghazipur and Sahaswan in Uttar Pradesh; Alwar and Pushkar in Rajasthan.

DESCRIPTION OF THE PLANT

The genus *Pandanus* includes over 600 species of trees and shrubs extending from Western Africa in the west to the Polynesian Island in the east. The species has been described under several specific names such as *P. odoratissimus* Linn, *P. tectorius* Soland ex Parkinson, *P. laevis* Kunth, *P., variegatus* Mid, *P. latifolius* Hassk and *P. amaryllifolius* Roxb. It is highly polymorphous and includes numerous varieties and forms. In India, about 30 species of *Pandanus* have been recorded. *Kewda* is a densely-branched shrub, growing up to 6 m high. The leaves are glaucous-green, 0.9-1.5 m long, 4 cm wide, acuminate, coriaceous and have thorny spines on the margin and mid-rib. The growing plant is supported by aerial roots. This plant will flower after 5 years and will continue bearing for 40 to 50 years thereafter; flowering will be maximum between 15 and 25 years. The male spadix is 25-50 cm long with numerous subsessile cylindrical spikes, the spike measures 5-10 cm in length and is enclosed in a long, white, fragrant caudate and acuminate spathes. In the female flower the spadix is solitary, 5 cm in diameter, the fruit is a syncarpium, oblong or globose in shape, 15-25 cm in diameter and becomes yellow or red when ripe. The plant bears numerous drupes.

The plants flower during May-June and the flowering is extended up to September-October. The season is the peak flowering period.

SOILS

It is a hardy plant and in nature it is found growing on sandy, saline wastelands and marshy land on the bunds. However, for commercial cultivation, a fertile and well-drained soil is preferred.

CLIMATE

In the wild state, *pandanus* grows along the coasts producing a thick belt of impenetrable vegetation above the high water-mark. The plants are found growing generally on the banks of rivers, canals, fields and ponds. It is a tropical species and cannot withstand frost. The plant requires reasonably high rainfall.

CULTIVATION

Propagation

Kewda is propagated vegetatively by the division of suckers, and cuttings (60-80 cm long and 8-10 cm thick) made from non-flowering branches and old stumps.

PLANTING

Planting is generally done from June to August. The spacing followed is 3 to 7 m.

PESTS AND DISEASES

Generally, the plant is not affected by any pests or diseases of a serious nature. However, leaf-blight caused by *Alternaria tenuis* and *Botrydiplodia theobromae* have been reported.

FLOWER PRODUCTION, FLOWER COLLECTION AND YIELD

The plants start producing flowers when they are 5 years old. A 5-year-old plant attains a average height of 170 cm with a stem circumference of 50 cm and with 20-25 aerial roots and bears 4 flowers. The plant is dioecious. The flower production increases with the age up to 20-25 years (24 flowers/ plant). There are reports of a fully mature tree bearing 20-40 spadices in a year. The flowering depends on the branching of the plant, the rainfall and its nearness to a water source.

The plants start flowering from May and continues up to January, with peak production during July-October. Generally, warm and moist weather is conducive for flower production and plants are harvested by hand after breaking the stalk with the help of a stick fitted with a hook. The flower-bud is damaged if a knife is used for cutting. The best time for the collection of flowers is early morning. The flowers are immediately transported to distillation units by 9.00 a.m. for the distillation of oil.

DISTILLATION OF FLOWERS

Kewda attar, *kewda* water and *kewda* oil are the major perfumery products obtained by the distillation of the flowers. It is estimated that in the Ganjam district of Orissa, in India, nearly 10 million spadices are used for the production of these three products.

Ripe spadices are distilled with water to obtain *kewda attar*. The vapours generated during the distillation process are absorbed in sandalwood oil or refined liquid paraffin (known as white oil). Liquid paraffin is used when cheaper grades are required. Small quantities of palmarosa oil (10 g/kg) is added to the sandalwood oil before distillation, to improve the aroma of the *attar*. At the time of distillation, the green leaves around the spadices are separated and the spadices are cut into 3-4 pieces and distilled. In the distillation process, the ratio of spadices of water is kept at 2:1 by volume. Fully-ripe spadices, creamy in colour, give higher yields of perfume of better quality compared to the immature ones. Depending upon the quantity of spadices consumed per pound of sandalwood oil or liquid paraffin, *kewda attar* is graded into several groups. The prepare 1 kg of *attar* about 1000 to

10000 flowers are distilled. The number depends upon the grade of the *attar.* The spadices are simply distilled with water to obtain kewada water. About 18 litres of *kewda* water is obtained from 1000 flowers. The *kewda attar* and *kewda* water are packed in airtight, galvanized iron drums before they are sent to the perfumery industry.

Kewda oil is not extracted in India on a commercial scale. For the extraction of the oil on a commercial scale, the flowers are treated with a solvent, and then the fatty and waxy matter is precipitated with alcohol to obtain the absolute. The absolute is distilled under reduced pressure and the oil is obtained. Generally, the oil-yield is very low (0.1-03%). The oil obtained is light-yellow in colour with a strong characteristic odour, reminiscent of lilac superimposed on hyacinth and tuberose notes.

38

Khus

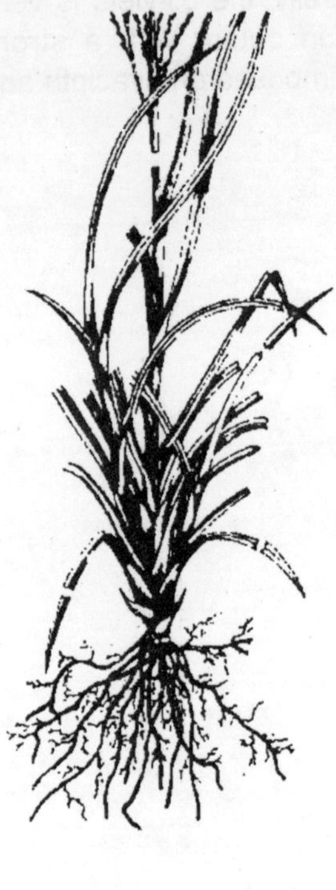

PLANT PROFILE

Family	:	*Poaceae*
English name	:	Vetiver
Indian name	:	*Usirah*, *Sevyah*, *Sugandhimulah* (Sanskrit) *Khas* *Khas-khas* (Hindi), *Lavancha* (Kannada *Vettiver* (Tamil)
Species and varieties	:	*Vetiveria zizanoides* (Linn) Nash.
Distribution	:	India, Tropical Asia, Africa, Australia, Brazil, Congo Haiti, Indonesia, Jamaica, Java, Malaysia

Reunion Islands, Sri Lanka, Seychelles Islands, Vietnam, Zambia, Zaire

Uses : Baskets, Cosmetics, Drugs, Fodder, Screens or blinds, Soil-binders, Perfumery

Vetiver (*Vetiveria zizanoides* (Linn.) Nash). (2n=20) or khus, of the family *Poaceae,* is a densely tufted, perennial grass, found growing on various types of soils. The underground part of the plant consists of numerous fine rootlets of light-yellow or gray to reddish in colour, which contain a viscous essential oil, with a pleasant and persistent odour. The commercial oil of vetiver is obtained by the distillation of the root. In India, the plant is known as 'khus khus', 'khus' meaning aromatic root. The oil obtained from the North Indian type has constituents like Khusol, Khusone, Khusene, etc. whereas, the oil extracted from the plants grown in Haiti, Zambia, Java, Reunion Islands and Congo is reported to have veticelinol, vetivone, and other sequiterpenes.

However, the major constituents are vetivone (vetiverone), vetiverols, vetiverenyl, vetivernate, benzoic acid and palmitic acid.

The commercial part of the plant is the root which possesses a most agreeable aroma and is employed to scent clothes, either by itself or in the form of sachets. From time immemorial, vetiver roots have been employed to make baskets, hand-fans and mats which, when sprinkled with water and hung like curtains in houses, cool the air and emanate a pleasant odour. The oil of vetiver is one of the most valuable and most important perfumer's raw material, widely used in perfumeries, cosmetics, and for the scenting of soaps. It also acts as a natural fixative. The oil of vetiver blends well with other oils particularly with those of sandalwood, patchouli and rose. Medicinally, it is reported to be uses as a carminative in flatulence and colic and as an anthelminthic and possesses stimulant and refrigerant properties. It is locally applied to relive pains on the body.

Young leaves are used as fodder and are a good bedding for horses and cattle, the leaves are also used for thatching purposes; while the stem and inflorescence peduncles are used for making brooms and ornamental baskets. Of late, the plant has also gained recognition as one of the best soil-binders and is being used extensively in arid zones to check soil erosion.

DISTRIBUTION

Vetiver is indigenous to the Indian subcontinent and is widely distributed in tropical Asia, Africa and Australia. It flourishes on the slopes of the Himalayan mountains, and in many parts of India, Sri Lanka and Malaysia. It is cultivated extensively in Java, on Reunion Island, Indonesia, Haiti, Jamaica, Zaire, Vietnam, Brazil and in the Seychelles Islands.

In India, it is found growing wild in the forests of Rajasthan and Uttar Pradesh. It is also found in some parts of Assam, Jammu, Bihar, Orissa, Andhra Pradesh and Karnataka. However, it is systematically cultivated as a crop in Kerala. It is found in a semi-wild state in the East Godavari and Kurnool districts of Andhra Pradesh, Karnataka, and its cultivation is picking up in parts of Madhya Pradesh, Uttar Pradesh and Haryana.

DESCRIPTION OF THE PLANT

It is a perennial grass. The clumps are erect, growing to a height of 1 to 1.8 m. The underground stem is branching with a spongy, aromatic root system having fine rootlets, 10.56 cm long and 1-3 cm in diameter. The aerial stem is tall, smooth, glabrous and the leaf is polished. The leaves are long with the leaf-blade 30 cm to 40 cm long, erect, rigid, firm, narrow, 0.7 cm or less wide and somewhat spongy; usually glabrous, pale-green, and rough along the edges. The panicle is an oblong of many-rayed whorls of slender simple racemes (and is terminal), 5 cm long with pairs of dissimilar spikelets, the pedicel is male and the sessile is hermaphrodite, the spikelets are reddish-brown or purplish. The anthers are 2 mm in size and the stigma is purple in colour. The grain is oblong and oblique at the top. The pedicelled spikelets which are male are smooth, the upper floral glume is entire, acute and 3 mm long. Vetiver is an autogamous plant. Self-pollination does not occur and it is an obligatory cross-pollinated crop.

TYPES AND VARIETIES

The grass growing wild in North India and that cultivated in South India are two different types. Thus, there are two main types namely, flowering or seeding and non-flowering or non-seeding. The one which grows in North India is mainly the flowering type, while that which is cultivated in South India is the non-flowering type.

The North Indian type is poor in oil yield, but its oil quality is superior; whereas the South Indian type yields more oil, but the quality is inferior.

The CIMAP has developed two superior clones, KS-1 and KS-2, from a collection from Baharatpur (North Indian type). These have a yield which is almost comparable to the existing high-yielding material. However, the quality of oil from both the clones was rated the best among all the clones evaluated.

An improved tetraploid strain named 'Sugandha' has also been released by the CIMAP and is reported to be superior in terms of oil-yield over the corresponding diploid parent. This is attained by an enhancement in the root biomass and an increase in the percentage of oil content in the roots. The new strain can yield 1.4% oil content in fresh roots and 21.2 q/ha of roots, against 1.15% oil and 18.5 q/ha of roots in the control.

Pusa hybrid numbers (1-30) have been evolved by the NBPGR, New Delhi. Of these, F_1 hybrids, Hyb-26 gives higher yield of roots (14.58 q/ha) with an oil content of 1.50%. Whereas, hybrids 26, 7 and 16 perform better in saline and alkaline soils with high root-and oil-yield. Under Bangalore conditions, hybrid-8 has been found to be better. Its roots yield 1% essential oil and possess 70-85% vetiverol content. The yield of roots ranged from 12-15 q/ha when harvested at 15 months age. A vetiver clone, ODV-3, developed at the Lemongrass Research Station, Odakkali, is reported to give good root-and oil-yield in Kerala.

SOIL

Vetiver can be grown on almost every kind of soil. Light soil, however, should be avoided as the roots obtained produce a very low percentage of oil. Well-drained, sandy loam and red lateritic soils rich in organic matter are considered to be ideal as the roots produced in such soils are thick and contain more essential oil. It can be grown even in saline and alkaline soils, with a pH range of 8.5 to 10.0.

CLIMATE

The crop prefers tropical and sub-tropical climates for its proper growth, development and essential oil yield. It grows luxuriantly in places with an annual rainfall of about 1000 to 2000 mm, the temperature ranging from 21-44°C and with a moderately humid climate. In the places which are otherwise suitable but have scanty rainfall, it can be grown as an irrigated crop.

LAND PREPARATION

The land is ploughed to a depth of 20-25 cm repeatedly, and the soil is mixed with the recommended dose of manure and fertilizers and made ready for planting.

CULTIVATION

Propagation

Vetiver is propagated from seeds or slips. Seeding is found to be profuse in the crop, in areas where it occurs in the wild, and regeneration takes place from self-sown seeds and by tilling during and after the rains. In South India, where the crop is cultivated on a large scale, the non-seeding type is grown. This is propagated from slips obtained from the uprooted clumps of the previous crop. These clumps, when broken, give a number of slips. Slips that are separated from the clump with the rhizome portion intact and have 15-20 cm of the shoot portion, constitute the material for planting.

PLANTING

Vetiver is planted in rows 45 cm apart with a plant-to-plant distance of 30 cm. Planting is usually done during the months of June-July, at the advent of the rainy season. If irrigation facilities are available, it is better to plant during March-April. However, in that case, frequent irrigation will be required. Two to three slips are planted in each hole of 5-8 cm depth and the soil is pressed around the hole. Late planted plants yield coarse roots which, in turn, yield inferior quality oil. A spacing of 60 × 25 cm is also recommended to allow 60,000 plants/ha.

MANURES AND FERTILIZERS

In order to obtain economic yields, the vetiver crop may be supported with 10 t FYM, 25 kg/ha each of N, P and K. While the entire quantity of FYM, half N and a full dose of P and K are applied at planting, the remaining half of N is given after about 6 months of planting. A fertilizer dose of 60 kg N, 22.5 each of P_2O_5 and K_2O is recommended in Kerala.

IRRIGATION AND INTERCULTURE

In areas where rainfall is good and well distributed throughout the year and humidity is high, supplemental irrigation is not necessary. However, in drier areas, about 8-10 irrigations will be required in order to obtain the optimum yield.

Once the plants have established and grown into bushes, the weed problem is not severe because of the nature of the bushes. However, in the newly-established plantations, 3-4 weedings are necessary until the bushes are formed.

PESTS AND DISEASES

Very few diseases have been reported on vetiver. During the rainy season, the plant is attacked by *Fusarium* spp. It can be effectively controlled by drenching the soil with Creasan or Bordeaux mixture. Leaf-blight, caused by *Curvularia trifolii,* is controlled by repeated spraying of copper fungicides in appropriate doses. Nematode infestation of the roots by *Heterodera zeae* is also reported. Treatment with hot water is also effective in controlling the nematode menace.

There are no serious insect pests which attack this crop. However, sometimes white ants attack the roots. Aldrex @ 25 kg/ha may be incorporated into the soil for effective control of white ants.

HARVESTING AND YIELD

The time of harvesting is very important, as the yield of roots and oil percentage vary with changes in environmental conditions. The plants planted in July should be harvested after 18 months to get the maximum oil-yield.

Harvesting is usually done during the dry season from December to February, by manually digging out the bush along with its roots. The roots are then separated from the leaves, washed and dried under the shade for 1-2 days before distillation. This improves the quality of the essential oil, while prolonged drying in the sun reduces the yield.

The yield of the roots may range from 3-4 t/ha. A recovery of about 1% of essential oil is considered satisfactory. A root-yield of up to 14-18 q/ha has been obtained in North India.

OIL DISTILLATION

The oil is extracted by steam-distillation from both dry and fresh roots. The oil obtained from stored roots is more viscous and possesses a slightly better aroma than that obtained from freshly-harvested roots.

The roots should be distilled when fresh, in order to obtain the maximum yield of oil and to reduce the time of distillation. The distillation of roots is generally done in country stills. In North India, the distillation process is completed in 12-14 hours while in South India, it usually takes 72-96 hours.

The oil-yield of vetiver roots varies considerably and depends on a number of factors such as: the degree of dryness of the roots, the age of the roots, the nature of the land under cultivation, the lifting time, the perfection of the distilling equipment, and so on. The average yield of the North Indian variety is between 0.15 to 0.2%, whereas the average yield of the South Indian variety is 1%.

Ageing for a period of six months improves the odour of the oil substantially. The 'harsh' 'green' and 'earthy odour' character of the freshly-distilled oil disappears and a fuller, heavier and sweeter odour develops.

39

Lavender

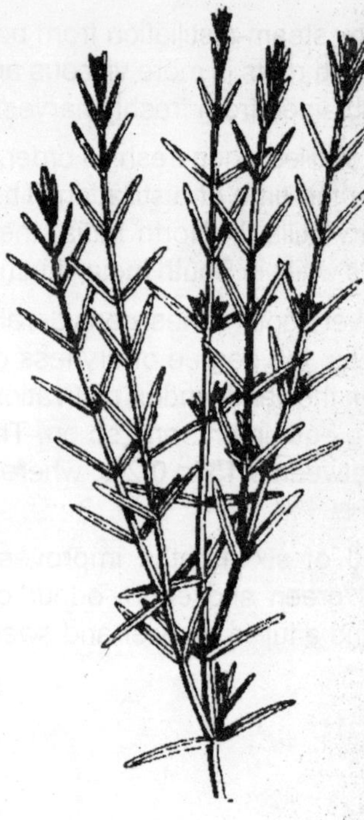

PLANT PROFILE

Family	:	*Labiatae; Lamiaceae*
English name	:	Lavender
Indian name	:	Lavender (Hindi), Lavender (Kannada) Lavender (Tamil)
Species and varieties	:	*Lavendula* Linn *L. angustifolia* Mill, *L. latifolia* Mill *L. spica* DC, *L. intermedia* Emeric Aroma, hemus, Karlovo, Karzanluk, Svezhest, Vanets, French

		Bareme, Goranya, Lambris, Prima, Recor, Stepnaya Shar-E-Kashmir, AM-1, AM-2, AM-3, A-5 A-7, A-8, A-9, B-2, B-11
Distribution	:	India, Bulgaria, Southern France, Italy Mediterranean region
Uses	:	Cosmetics, Disinfectants, Perfumery, Potpourri

Lavender (*Lavendula* Linn.) is a small genus of perennial aromatic herbs, semi-shrubs or shrubs of the *Labiatae or* Lamiaceae family. It includes about 28 species. Three species of *Lavendula* are extensively utilized for extracting essential oils. These are True Lavender, *L. angustifolia* Mill sub. sp. *angustifolia* (Syn *L. officinalis* Chiax, *L. vera* Dc.), Spike lavender, *L. latifolia* Mill., *L. spica* DC and *Laandin, L. intermedia* Emeric; ex Loiset (Syn. *L. hybrida* Revr.). The latter is a hybrid between true lavender and spike lavender. True lavender is one of the most important essential oils used in the perfumery industry. Spike lavender yields an inferior oil, which is less fragrant than that of the true lavender and its odour resembles a mixture of oils of lavender and rosemary. Lavandin possesses the characteristics of both the parents and yields an oil which combines the fragrance of true lavender with the camphoraceous harshness of spike lavender. However, lavandin oil is not as fine as lavender. But because of the relative ease of cultivation, higher yield and reasonable price of the oil, the production of lavandin oil has gone up with a marked fall in the production of lavander oil.

Lavender oil has a delightfully clean, refreshing and sweet odour. Its main constituent is the ester, linalyl acetate, which ranges from 30 to 60% and to which the characteristic lavender odour is attributed. Another compound which is present only in small amounts but plays an important role in the odour is ethyl-n-amyl ketone. Free linalool is also a major component, particularly of the English lavender oil, which has a peculiar heavy and slightly camphoraceous odour. The other compounds present in lavender oil are: α-plnene, camphene, β-pincne, limonene, cineole, cis-oscimene, trans-ocimene, comphor terpinen-4-ol, caryophyllene, lavandulyl acetate, lavandulol, α-terpineol and borneol.

Lavender oil is one of the most popular scents, its delightfully refreshing odour blends well with many other essential oils. Lavender water, a mixture of oil in water and alcohol, is a highly popular *toilette* article in England. The best quality oil (50% esters) is used in the preparation of high-grade perfumes, second quality (38 to 42% esters) for lavender water, *toilette* waters, *eau de cologne,* etc.; and low grade (30 to 35% esters) oil in the scenting of soaps and talcum powders. The oil is also used in medicine as a flavouring agent and sometimes as a carminative. Lavender flowers are used in making sachets and potpourri.

The oil of lavandin is used as a substitute for true lavender oil. It is of considerable value in the soap industry. On account of its microbicidal action, it is nowadays finding increasing use in the form of aerosols, for disinfecting houses, classrooms and public halls in Europe.

ORIGIN AND DISTRIBUTION

Lavender is indigenous to the Mediterranean region, growing wild in the higher hills of Southern France, Italy and Bulgaria. It is also cultivated in several other countries in Europe and elsewhere. In India, it has been successfully cultivated on an experimental scale in the Kashmir Valley. Presently, lavender is also grown in low rainfall areas and on the slopes of hills in Himachal Pradesh and Uttar Pradesh.

DESCRIPTION OF THE PLANT

Lavender (2n=42 or 48) is a perennial, herbaceous, bushy plant with straight, woody branches, the lower of which are leafless, putting out numerous herbaceous stems to a height of 1 m, these are quadrangular, greyish and pubescent. The leaves are opposite, long, narrow, lanceolate and light greyish-green, with a downy appearance. The inflorescence is borne at the end of each slender stem. The flowers are densely packed in layers and seem to be in whorls. The long calyx is tubular, pilosect and 5-lobed; the corolla is tubular and bilabiate, the upper lips are 2- to 3-lobed, and the lower one is 3-lobed. The flower is a mauve to violet shade, tinged with a light blue.

The broad-leaved Lavender (*L. latifolia*) has much better developed tufts. The old ligneous branches are more densely set. The leaves are longer (7-8 cm) and broader (5-6 mm) than those of the common lavender. At their base they are thickly covered with short hairs, giving them a silvery-whitish appearance, while on the top these short hairs are more sparsely set and more greenish. The floriferous stalks are longer and usually branched into three. The floscules are usually compact and, in rare cases, loose.

Lavandin has two forms: Spikevero and Verospike. The former has a general appearance like spike lavender, while the latter is like true lavender. The tufts of the spikevero form are strongly developed, reaching over 1 m in height and 90-11 cm in diameter within rows and 120-170 towards the inter-row spaces, its leaves are broad, shovel-like and grey-green. The floriferous stalks are usually branched. The ear is compact, long, slightly tilted. Its flowers are large and almost always sterile. The verospike forms smaller tufts, has darker green and less smoky leaves. The floriferous stalks are long, but usually not branched. Their floscules are compact, with less florets per node (6-10). The florets are most often sterile.

VARIETIES

In Bulgaria, six new varieties have been evolved through selection programmes. These are Kazanluk, Karlovo, Hemus, Aroma, Svezhest and Vanets, In addition, a few Soviet varieties, i.e., Stepnyay, Goranya, Prima, Record, French Bareme and Lambris are also known. Out of the Bulgarian material introduced in Kashmir Valley, a new variety has been developed and named 'Shar-E-Kashmir' by the CIMAP, Lucknow, which is reported to yield 80 to 100% more oil than the existing Bulgarian varieties. The oil of the present variety is superior to the old Bulgarian variety, 'Karlovo'. Some of the other important high-yielding clones are: AM-1, AM-2, AM-3, A-5, A-7, A-8, A-9, B-2 and B-11.

SOIL

Light, well-aerated, dry and calcareous soils with enough nutrients are best suited for lavender cultivation. Poor carbonate and sandy soils are also suitable, but water-logged soils are unsuitable. The crop is reported to give high herb- and oil-yields in neutral and alkaline soils (pH 7.0 to 8.4).

CLIMATE

Lavender is a temperate, photophilous plant. It does well only in those areas which have cold winters and cool summers. Due to its very deep root-system. Lavender grows very well on sloping lands, thereby checking soil erosion to a great extent. It is resistant to drought and frost. Lavender can be grown successfully on arable lands at very high altitudes.

CULTIVATION

Propagation

Lavender may reproduce itself in two ways: by seeds and vegetatively. Seed reproduction is cheap and quick. However, due to cross-pollination, a great variety of generation forms are observed, which complicates lavender cultivation and harvesting at the most suitable time.

(i) Nursery Raising

The seeds are sown in nursery-beds in autumn (November-December). For 1 sq m area, 0.2-2.5 g seeds are required. The seed-sowing depth is 1-2 cm. The seeds germinate in spring (April) at 14-15°C. The seedlings should be pruned periodically to avoid follicle formation and to achieve regular growth of the young plants.

(ii) Vegetative Means

Vegetatively, lavender is propagated by cuttings. These are obtained from the annual and biennial branches of the mother plantation during October-November in the plains and in February-March on the hills. The cuttings should by 8-10 cm long with intact vegetative tops. The cuttings are treated with 500 ppm IBA to obtain 95% rooting. Beds are made and covered by a 5 cm thick layer of organic manure and sand (1:1), topped by 3-4 cm of clean river sand. The cuttings are struck at 5 × 5 cm or 4 × 5 cm from each other, and in depth: 2/3 of the length of the cutting. The soil around the cuttings should be pressed down and immediately watered. A glass or polythene cover should be used over the beds, as well as mats in places that have severe winters.

TRANSPLANTING

The seedlings or rooted cuttings or slips or suckers are planted at a distance of 1.20-1.40 m between the rows and 3.5-4 cm within the row. About 20,000 plants/ha give the highest yields.

APPLICATION OF FERTILIZERS

Generally, a basal dose of 20 kg N, 40 kg P_2O_5 and 40 kg K_2O is applied before planting, while 80 kg of N/ha is applied in four split doses during each year. The CIMAP centre at Srinagar has obtained the highest spike-yield (100 kg/ha) by 150 kg N/ha in limed plots.

IRRIGATION

During the dry periods, the crop must be irrigated frequently to obtain a good spike-yield.

INTERCULTURE

During the first two years of planting, 2-3 cultivations along the rows and 5-6 cultivations between the rows to a depth of 8-10 cm are required. This keeps the soil loose and free of weeds and helps in the proper development of the plants. Regular weeding and hoeing are also done to keep the field free from weeds.

Lavender plantations which are over three years should be machine hoed, 3-4 times between the rows. One digging is done before the blossoming in the spring.

PESTS AND DISEASES

In the UK, *Coniothyrium lavendulae* is a species of fungus known to cause wilt and die-back of *L. angustifolia*. The alpha mosaic virus causes spots of irregular shape on the leaf margins in *L. officinalis;* besides, five important diseases are reported from Bulgaria which include *Septoria, Phoma, Fusarium* and others. Among the pests, are about fifty kinds of cicadas and four kinds of pests from the order *Orthoptera.* The nematode, *Melodiogyne hapla,* is reported to cause serious damage to the crop.

REGENERATION OF THE OLD PLANTATIONS

Lavender plantations start ageing about 10-12 years after planting and the yield decreases. Its regeneration is therefore necessary, which is achieved when the plants are in a period of rest during November to February. This can be done by cutting the plants 4-5 cm above the ground and by abundant fertilization.

HARVESTING

The first sizeable harvest is obtained 3 years after planting and the plantation remain productive for 3 or 4 years. The flowers are harvested with stem lengths not greater than 12 cm when the plants are in full bloom, after the characteristic blue lavender colour of the flowers has changed to a greyish-blue. Harvesting should begin at 50% blooming and should continue till the flowers have finished blooming. Harvesting should be done only during the day when weather is warm and sunny. Harvesting has been mechanized at present in the erstwhile USSR countries, Australia and Bulgaria.

ESSENTIAL OIL CONTENT AND YIELD

The essential oil content in different varieties varies from 0.5% to over 1.1%, with 0.8% as the average oil content. However, some Bulgarian varieties contain oil from 1.2 to 1.4%. A yield of 50 to 80 kg/ha essential oil is recorded. The Lambris and French Bareme have a lower oil content of 0.82 to 0;91% and the oil-yield is low (46 to 47 kg/ha).

Compared to Lavender, lavindin is capable of rather extraordinary growth and usually the yield of lavendin oil is very high (100 kg/ha).

LAVENDER OIL PRODUCTION

Lavender is made by steam distilled from fresh flowers of flowering tops. Water-distillation has proved unsuitable at it causes ester saponification, which lowers the ester content in the oil and may also change its composition.

40

Lemon Grass

PLANT PROFILE

Family	:	*Poacea; Graminae*
English name	:	Lemon grass
Indian name	:	Lemon grass (Hindi), *Nimbehullu* (Kannada)
Species and varieties	:	*Cymbopogan flexuosus* Nees *C. pendulus, C. citratus* *C. khasianus* Sugandhi, Pragathi, Praman, RRL-16, CKP-25 OD-408, RRL-39, Kaveri, Krishna
Distribution	:	India, Tropical and Sub-tropical parts of Asia, Africa, America, Bangladesh, China, Comoros Islands, Madagascar, Thailand, West Indian Islands
Uses	:	Confectionery Culinary purposes, Drugs Flavouring, Insect repellents, Liquors Perfumery

Lemon grass (*Cymbopogan flexuosus* Nees ex. Steud Wats.) is the source of lemon grass oil obtained from the leaves and shoots of the plant. A GLC analysis of the oil showed the presence of the terpinene (0.5%), beta terpineol (0.40%), alpha terpineol (2.25%), triphenyl acetate (0.90%), bonreol (1.90%), geraniol + nerol (1.50%), citral-b (27.7%), citral-a (46.60%), farnesol (12.80%) and farnesal (3.00%), with the rest being unidentified compounds. Lemon grass oil is mainly used in the manufacture of perfumes for soaps, hair oils, scents and medicines. It also has antibacterial properties. Lonone prepared from the citral present in lemon grass oil is one of the most important raw materials for the preparation of vitamin A. In addition to its use in perfumery, lonone is used in certain kinds of confectionery and liquors. The oil can be used to improve the flavour of some fish and can be used to flavour wines and sauces. It can also be used for headaches, toothaches, baths, fereentations, as a diuretic agent for fever and as an insect repellent.

ORIGIN, DISTRIBUTION AND PRODUCTION

The species is considered to have originated in India. It grows wild in many tropical and sub-tropical parts of Asia, Africa and America. The plant is grown for its oil in the West Indian Islands and also in Central America, South America, Thailand, Bangladesh, the Comoros Islands, Madagascar and China. Although, the oil has been known since very early times in India, the systematic cultivation and distillation of the grass were started in Kerala only about 90 years ago. At present, it is grown commercially in the northern district of Travancore and Cochin, Assam, Maharashtra and parts of Uttar Pradesh. The crop is under cultivation in India in an area of about 200 ha.

AREA AND PRODUCTION

Traditionally, India has been the largest supplier of lemon grass oil to the world market but has ceased to be so any longer. The production of oil which was 1800 t in 1961-62 has declined to about 400 to at present. The Indian monopoly in the lemon grass trade in the world market has been broken due to the entry of Guatemala and a few other Latin American states including Brazil and Mexico, Puerto Rico, Dominica, Haiti and China. Besides this, the introduction *Litsea cubeba* oil as a substitute source for citrol and the expansion of lemon grass cultivation to non-traditional areas in African countries are the other contributing factors for this steady decline. But still, due to the expansion of indigenous perfumery and related industries and the increase in the price of derived aroma-chemicals, the demand for the oil has increased considerably, thereby, creating scope for the expansion of lemon grass cultivation in the country.

DESCRIPTION OF THE PLANT

C. flexuosus var. *flexuosus* grows to a height of about 3 m. The leaves of the plant are linear, lanceolate, 125 cm long and 1.7 cm broad. The panicles are very large, drooping, lax, greyish or greyish-green, rarely purple-tinged, with the raceme pairs in dense masses. The plant is spreading, 100-135 cm tall, slightly hairy, the lower glumes of the sessile spikeletes are 3-4 and rarely 4-5 mm long, 1 mm wide, with 1-3 definite or obscure introcrainal nerves, shallowly concave, with one or two depressions.

TYPES AND VARIETIES

There are two main types of lemon grass namely, the East Indian or true lemon grass (*C. flexuosus* Ness ex. Steud Wats) and the West Indian (South American) lemon grass [*C. citratus* (D.C.) Stapf]. The oil obtained by the distillation of the grass of *C. flexuosus,* called the East Indian oil, is the genuine oil of commercial importance. It is produced in Kerala and is popularly called the Cochin oil, since it is shipped mainly from the port of Cochin. A small quantity of oil is also obtained from *C. pendulus,* popularly known as North Indian lemon grass or Jammu lemon grass, since it is grown mainly in Jammu and other North Indian States. The West Indian (South American) oil of *C. citratus* is extracted in Indo-China, Madagascar, Guatemala, Brazil, Haiti, Tanganyika, Congo and the West Indies. It is found that the East Indian oil, produced in South India, is readily soluble in alcohol. Both the types have practically the same citral content (75-86%), but the West Indian oil along with citral contains other aldehydes which lower the quantity of the oil. In *C. flexuosus,* the red-stemmed plant with chocolate to purple coloured stems, yields the genuine oil, while the white-stemmed grass does not. Recently, a new species *C. khasianus* has been discovered which is important for its geraniol content. Some lemon grass varieties released for cultivation are given below.

Sugandhi (OD-19)

It was released from the Aromatic and Medicinal Plants Research Station, (AMPS) Odakkali, Kerala. This variety is red in colour and is adapted to a wide range of soil and climate conditions. The plant grows from 1-1.75 m height and with profuse tillering yields 80-199 kg/ha of oil with 80-88% citral under rainfed conditions.

Pragathi

It is a clonal selection from OD-19, evolved at the CIMAP, Lucknow. The variety is tall with a dark purple leaf-sheath and is adapted to the North Indian plains and Terai belts of sub-tropical and tropical climates. The average oil content is 0.63% with 86% being the citral content.

Praman

Evolved through clonal selection from *C. pendulus* at the CIMAP, Lucknow, it is a tetraploid plant with a profuse tillering habit. The leaves are erect and medium in size. This variety is reported to yield 227 kg/ha/annum of oil with 82% citral content.

RRL-16

It is evolved from *C. pendulus* and released for cultivation from the RRL, Jammu as Jammu lemon grass. The average yield of the herb is 15-20 t/ha/annum, giving 100-110 kg of oil. The oil content varies from 0.6-08% with 80% citral content.

CKP-25

It is a interspecific hybrid between *C. khasianus* and *C. pendulus,* developed by the RRL, Jammu. The strain gives a herb yield of 80-85 t and

350-400 kg/ha/annum of oil. The citral content in the oil ranges from 80-85%.

In addition to the above, 'OD-408' from the AMPRS, Odakkali, RRL-39 from RRL Jammu and 'Kaveri' and 'Krishna' from the CIMAP, Regional Station, Bangalore, have been recently released as high-yielding varieties for cultivation. The other varieties under cultivation are SD-68 and GRL-1.

SOIL

It flourishes on a wide variety of soils ranging from rich loam to poor laterite. In sandy loam and red soils, it requires good manuring. Calcareous and water-logged soils should be avoided as they are unsuitable for its cultivation.

CLIMATE

It requires a warm, humid climate with plenty of sunshine and a rainfall ranging from about 200-250 cm, well distributed over the year. In areas where the rainfall is poor, it can be grown with supplemental irrigations. It grows well at altitudes between 1000-1200 m.

CULTIVATION

Propagation

Lemon grass in generally propagated through seeds, vegetative propagation and rooted slips. It is reported that both the seedlings and the rooted slips performed equally well, with respect to growth and yield. But, due to the high cost of transplanting, direct seeding is widely practised, especially over the plains and terraced lands in Kerala. For raising the crop by direct seeding, a seed rate of 20 to 25 kg/ha is recommended. While sowing, the seeds must be thoroughly mixed with dry river sand in a ratio of 1:3, to ensure the uniform distribution of seeds during sowing.

Nursery Raising

For raising the seedlings required for planting 1 ha of land, a 1000 m area is required. The area is well prepared and raised beds of 1 to 1.5 m width and of convenient length are made. The recommended seed rate is 3 to 4 kg/ha. The seeds are uniformly broadcasted on the beds and are covered with a thin layer of soil, followed by watering at regular intervals.

The seeds collected during the months of January-February are usually sown in the nursery during April-May.

PLANTING

The land is prepared by repeated ploughing and harrowing, and beds of 1 to 1.5 m width and convenient length are made with a spacing of 30 to 50 cm between beds. The beds are made along the contour of the land slopes.

Three to four-leaved, 50 to 70 day-old seedlings, are planted during the monsoon season (May-June) in Kerala. A spacing of 30 cm × 30 cm with a plant density of 1,11,000/ha is recommended. A wider spacing of 60 cm × 45 cm for seedlings and 90 cm × 60 cm for slips have been recommended for fertile, irrigated land under North Indian conditions.

MANURES AND FERTILIZERS

Lemon grass is an exhaustive crop and it requires 275 kg N, 25 kg P_2O_5 and 175 kg K_2O/ha/annum. In order to promote growth and to obtain a higher oil-yield, the crop is treated with 2 t/ha of compost made from spent grass and 2 t/ha of wood ash at the time of bed-formation. In addition, it has to be supplied with chemical fertilizers. Under Odakkali (Kerala) conditions, it was found that an application of 100 kg N in 3 to 4 split doses was found to be optimum, though a response up to 200 kg was recorded. The response to P and K was found to be erratic. The application of 50 kg/ha each of P_2O_5 and K_2O as a basal dose gave encouraging results in West Bengal. It is recommended to apply 60:45:35 kg/ha N, P_2O_5 and K_2O as a basal dose and 60 kg N in 3 to 4 splits/annum as top-dressing during the growing season as an optimum dose. Lemon grass is also reported to respond well to the application of copper, iron, calcium and sulphur.

It is reported from the CIMAP, Lucknow, that a lower dose of boron (2.5 ppm) in combination with chloride salts (chloride salinity) can be beneficial for the crop.

INTERCULTURE

The earthing-up of the plant after about 4 months of planting and again after every harvest is beneficial, as the root region of lemon grass has a tendency of grow above the soil. The field is kept stubble free. Generally, 2-3 weedings are necessary during the year. Among the herbicides, diuran @ 1.5 kg a.i./ha and Oxyflurofen @ 1.5 kg a.i./ha are effective for weed control. Interculturing can be done by a tractor-drawn cultivator or a hand-held hoe in row-planted crops. Under rainfed conditions, burning the dry grass and stubble of the standing crop prior to the onset of monsoon is practised in Kerala to prevent white ant attack and also to rejuvenate the old clumps.

IRRIGATION

After planting, if there are no rains, the crop should be irrigated every alternate day for about a month. It is recommended that 4 to 6 irrigations are given during the period February to June under North Indian conditions, for an optimum yield.

PESTS AND DISEASES

Insects and Nematodes

Pest infestation is very low for this crop. However, the infestation by the spindle-bug (*Clovia bipunctata*) from Odakkali, and severe damage by the stem-boring caterpillar of *Chilotrea* under North Indian conditions have been reported. Spraying with Malathion (0.2%) can control the insects. Nematodes like *Tylenchorhychus vulgaris, Rotylenchulus reniformis, Helicotylenchus* spp. and *Pratylenchus* spp. have also been found to infect the grass, but the extent of damage to the crop has not been studied.

Diseases

Several disease are reported on lemon grass, but none are serious enough to a cause major reduction in oil-yield. Among these diseases, little-leaf, malformation of the inflorescence caused by the fungus, *Balensia scierotica* (*ppt*) *Hohnel*, is reported to reduce the seed-yield. *Helminthosporium sacchari, H. leucostylum, Drechslera victoriae* and *D. helmi,* all species of fungi, cause leaf-spot diseases on this crop. Two strains of *Curvularia andropogonia,* viz. CLS and CLB, are reported to cause leaf-spot and leaf-blight, respectively. Leaf-spots are also reported to be caused by *C. verruciformis*, *C. trifolii* and *Collitotrichum graminicola.* The other diseases reported on this crop include smut, caused by *Tolyposporium christensenni* and *Ustilago andropogonis,* grey blight caused by *Pestalotiopsis magniferae,* leaf-spot and clump-rot caused by *Fusarium equiseti* and *F. verticillium,* root-rot by *Botrydiplodia theobromae,* leaf-speck by *D. colocasia* and leaf-blight by *Rhizoctonia solani.*

These leaf diseases can be controlled by prophylactic sprays of Dithane M-45 and Dithane-Z-78 @ 3 g/l thrice, at intervals of 15 days.

HARVESTING AND YIELD

The crop is perennial in nature and gives good yields for 5 years. Harvesting is done by cutting the grass 10 cm above the ground level. During the first year of planting, 3 cuttings are obtained and, subsequently, 5-6 cuttings per year are taken subject to weather conditions. The harvesting season begins in May and continues till the end of January. The first harvest is done about 90 days after planting. The interval from sowing to harvest exerts a considerable influence on the yield and the quality of oil. Both immature and over-matured grass give a lower quantity of oil. For the local type of lemon grass, the optimum interval is 40-50 days. The optimum periods of harvesting, when grown on hill-tops and low lying areas is 60 and 50-55 days, respectively. We may obtain a herbage yield of 15 t/ harvest and a recovery of oil about 0.3-0.5% from fresh grass. The oil is obtained by steam-distillation. An oil-yield of about 350-400 kg/ha from the second year onwards is considered satisfactory.

FACTORS INFLUENCING THE OIL-YIELD

The factors influencing the oil production during distillation are: (i) Storage of the plant material, (ii) Treatment of the material, and (iii) The method of distillation.

The major source of loss is by oxidation and resinification of the essential oils. So, if the material is to be stored before processing, it should be kept in a dry atmosphere with limited air circulation. The cut-grass, when stored in the shade, can increase the oil recovery up to 96 hours and storage for a further period will only decrease the oil-yield. The essential oils are enclosed in the oil-glands, oil-sacks and glandular hairs of the plant. Therefore, before distillation, the plant material must be cut into small pieces to enable them to directly expose as many oil-glands as is practically possible. Once the plant material has been reduced in size, it must be distilled immediately. Otherwise, the essential oil, being volatile, will be lost by aerial evaporation. Dipping the chopped lemon grass in sodium chloride solution for 24 hours at 1-2% concentration before distillation has been found to increase the citral content.

UTILIZATION OF SPENT MATERIAL

The residue thrown out after the extraction of the oil is called spent grass. Cattle relish it when it is hot or is converted into silage by adding a dilute solution of molasses. It is also an excellent source of manure. It is applied either after composting or in the form of ash by burning. The waste lemon grass is also used as fuel for distillation after drying and as cheap packing material for glassware or other fragile objects.

41

Lemon Scented Gum

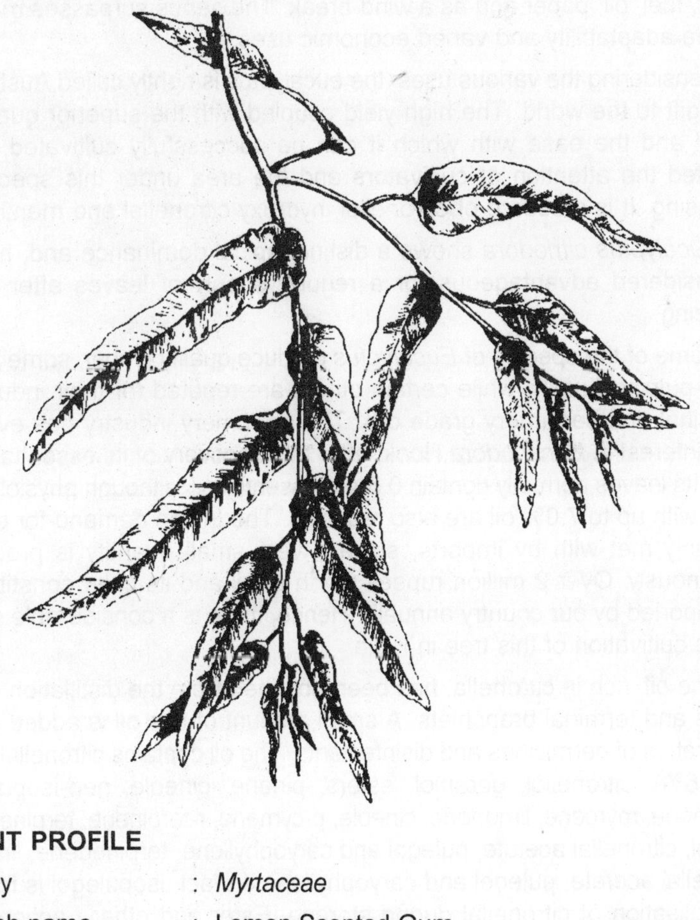

PLANT PROFILE

Family : *Myrtaceae*

English name : Lemon Scented Gum

Indian name : *Nimbevasaneya Neelagiri* (Kannada) *Thaila Maram* (Tamil)

Species and varieties : *Eucalyptus citriodora* Hook
EC-153, EC-261, EC-3315

Distribution : India, South Africa, Australia, Belgian Congo, Brazil, Guatemala, Java, Malaysia, Seychelles Islands

Uses : Cosmetics, Disinfectants, Drugs, Germicides Paper, Perfumery, Timber

Lemon scented gum, also known as spotted gum and citron scented gum is *Eucalyptus citriodora* Hook, belonging to the family *Myrtaceae.* The species has strong lemon scented leaves. It is grown around the world for timber, fuel, oil, paper and as a wind-break. The genus surpasses many in its wide adaptability and varied economic uses.

Considering the various uses, the eucalyptus is rightly called Australia's great gift to the world. The high yield coupled with the superior quality of the oil and the ease with which it can be successfully cultivated, have attracted the attention of cultivators and the area under this species is increasing. It is a source of citronellol, hydroxy citronellal and menthol.

Eucalyptus citriodora shows a distinct apical dominance and, hence, is considered advantageous for a regular supply of leaves after every coppicing.

Some of the species of *Eucalyptus* produce quality timber, some are of paper-pulping quality, while certain others are reputed for their industrial, medicinal and perfumery grade oils. The perfumery industry has evinced great interest in *E. citriodora* Hook, after the discovery of its essential oil in 1882. Its leaves normally contain 0.5-4% essential oil, although physiological races with up to 7.0% oil are also reported. The Indian demand for this oil is mainly met with by imports, since a very small quantity is produced indigenously. Over 2 million rupees worth of oil and its chief constituents are imported by our country annually. Hence, there is a considerable scope for the cultivation of this tree in India.

The oil, rich in citronella, has been obtained from the distillation of the leaves and terminal branchlets. A small amount of this oil is added in the preparation of germicides and disinfectants. The oil contains citronellal (26.7 to 82.6%), citronellol, geraniol, esters, pinene, cineole, neo-isopulegol, camphene, myrcene, limonene, cineole, p-cymene, r-terpinene, terpinedene, linalool, citronellal acetate, pulegol and caryophyllene, terpinedene, linalool, citronellal acetate, pulegol and caryophyllene. In fact, isopulegol is formed by enolisation of citronellal during storage. Ester and other fractions are present only in traces.

The oil is an effective substitute for Java citronella oil and is also used in the soap and cosmetic industry. It is used as an antiseptic, especially in the treatment of infections of the upper respiratory tract and in certain types of skin diseases. Internally, it is found to act as a stimulant in chronic bronchitis. The wood of *E. citriodora* is used to make railway sleepers, in the construction of houses and for making paper pulp.

ORIGIN AND DISTRIBUTION

The species is native to the semi-tropical and warm temperate regions of Australia and Malaysia. It is essential a Queensland tree, being particularly abundant in the north coastal area of that state. It is grown commercially in the Seychelles Islands, Java, South Africa, Guatemala, the Belgian Congo and Brazil.

In India, it is being grown in the plains of North India and in the submontane tracts. The species is also successfully grown in Kerala (Malabar), Tamil Nadu (Nilgiris), Karnataka (Coorg), and Uttar Pradesh (Lucknow).

DESCRIPTION OF THE PLANT

Eucalyptus citriodora Hook, (2n=22) is a tall tree 25 to 40 m high with a crown of branches and leaves at the top. The bark is smooth, white or faintly bluish in colour. If the apical region is damaged, side shoots emerge and grow vertically, but the lateral spread of branches at lower levels is extremely rare. It exhibits a marked heterophylly.

Five distinct types of leaves, (i) Cotyledonary (ii) Seedling (iii) Juveniie (iv) Intermediate (v) Adult leaves, are observed at various stages of the life-cycle of the plant. The young seedlings, after the cotyledonary state, develop 5-10 pairs of seedling leaves of varying shapes and sizes. This is followed by the formation of juvenile leaves which are opposite in disposition up to a certain state, but later become alternate and are quite distinct from mature, adult leaves. In certain cases, the intermediate leaves are very difficult to distinguish. They are larger and coarser than both the juvenlle and adult leaves. The juvenile leaves often differ from the adult leaves in their texture, pubescene and glaucousness. The former are usually dorsiventral and, hence, structurally different on both the surfaces while the latter are almost isobilateral, thus, identical on both surfaces. The juvenile leaves are covered with trichomes and the adult ones are almost naked. The adult leaves are lanceolate, up to 15 cm long and 3 cm broad, acuminate, with finely-marked venation, the lateral veins are numerous, oblique, parallel and mildly spreading, the inter-marginal veins do not reach the margin.

The flowers are numerous and occur in axillary panicles, the calyxtube is hemispherical to cylindrical, the anthers are adnate. The fruits are ovoid, truncate, contracted at the thin edge and the valves open downwards.

E. citriodora is characterized by the presence of three kinds of buds, i.e.: (i) naked, (ii) accessory, and (iii) epicornic. The naked buds are unprotected by any covering and occur in the axil of each leaf. The accessory buds, unlike the naked buds, are resistant to frost and drought. The epicornic buds, also known as provertious or dormant buds, give rise to epicornic shoots. These are pads of tissues accompanying each leaf, but not buried in the stem.

VARIETIES

EC-153, EC-261 and EC-3315 are the three varieties available in this crop.

SOIL

It is usually found on rather poor gravelly soil, podzols or and residual podzols of lateritic origin. It prefers well-drained gravelly soils, where it usually grows with other useful *Eucalyptus* species such as *E. crebra* and *E. acenenoides.* The crop is reported to also grow well in acidic to slightly alkaline soils with a good organic matter content in it.

CLIMATE

E. citriodora thrives well at an altitude of 600 m in tropical and sub-tropical climates. A moderate atmospheric temperature coupled with reasonable humidity and well-distributed rainfall, are essential for development of these plants in the early stages of growth. The seeds do not germinate if the atmospheric temperature is either very high or very low. Germination is best during the periods from mid-February to mid-April, and July to the middle of November, when the temperature oscillates between 15ºC and 30ºC approximately. Desiccating high temperature during May and June, and low temperature during December and January are most unfavourable for germination. Even if the seeds germinate, they do not survive. A moist climate during July to September is also not favourable for the seedlings, because of very high mortality due to the incidence of collar-rot of young plants by heavy rains. At temperatures below 15ºC, the growth of plants is proportionately retarded and at about 0ºC the plants even die.

LAND PREPARATION

Pits of 45 cm^3 are dug at a spacing of 75-90 cm for planting seedlings. They are treated with FYM and 20 g rock phosphate and filled in to receive the seedlings.

CULTIVATION

Propagation

E. citriodora is commercially propagated through seeds. However, vegetative methods of propagation have also been developed.

Vegetative Propagation

Several trails on vegetative propagation by using different parts of the shoot-system with root-promoting hormones were conducted in the past with little success. A breakthrough has been evolved by using the lignotuberous tissues of *E. citriodora* treated with root-promoting hormones. The experiment will ensure both quality and purity of the progeny. Plots can be laid out using the Transverse cut and Longitudinal cut and treating them with IAA, IBA and IPA at concentrations of 50 ppm and 100 ppm. A rapid clonal propagation method by tissue culture has also been developed.

Seed Propagation

The seeds are very small and, approximately 240 seeds weigh 1 g. The seeds germinate in 4-14 days, depending upon atmospheric humidity and temperature. However, cold-stored seeds germinate even in 2-4 days. A commercial cultivation of the crop requires either rasing a nursery or, alternatively, direct sowing in well prepared field in the proper season.

Nursery Preparation

The seeds should be sown as fresh as possible, although they do retain their viability for 1 year.

The nursery is reared between February to September on raised beds of 1.2 m × 1.2 m size or even in polybags or trays filled with soil. Care must be taken while sowing, so that the seeds do not go deeper than 1 cm under the soil. The seedlings, with 2-4 pair of leaves (about 2-3 cm tall), about 4-6 weeks after sowing, are at the proper stage for transplanting into the secondary polybag nursery. Older seedlings develop an extensive root system which is very sensitive to even mild disturbances, resulting in very high mortality. Individual seedlings are picked out on a spatula with a ball of earth attached and 4-5 seedlings are transplanted in each bag, filled with soil and followed by irrigation. The seedlings are allowed to grow for 4-6 months in the bags, depending upon the season. If the plants are raised in polythene bags, they are transplanted when they have attained a height of about 20-30 cm after removal of the bag, without disturbing the soil.

Direct Sowing

The risk of raising a nursery can be overcome by sowing seeds directly in the field. It is better is prepare small ridged, about 10 cm high and 10 cm wide, 90 cm apart and the seeds are sown on the ridges. This method prevents the seeds from drifting away after irrigation. The seeds can be sown in February and September. However, direct sowing cannot be adopted in regions subject to heavy rainfall or frost.

PLANTING

A spacing of 75-90 cm between rows and 75 cm between pits is ideal for raising a commercial crop. Initially, each pit will have 4-5 plants and the population can be thinned subsequently. Transplanting in August or early September in frost-free areas favours the establishment of plants and helps them to withstand the adversities of winter. The regions experiencing frost during winters would not be suited for August-September transplanting. February is the best month for transplanting in such areas.

FERTILIZER APPLICATION

The available data on fertilizer requirements of *Eucalyptus* in general and *E. citriodora* in particular is very scanty. Nitrogenous fertilizers contribute positively towards increased production of leaves, which indirectly increase oil production per unit area. Phosphate and potash fertilizers do not appear to have any effect on the crop and hence are not recommended for regular use unless the soils are very deficient in these ingredients. Hence, a small dose of phosphatic and potash fertilizers should be given to the plantation every year. It is, accordingly, suggested that in irrigated areas about 20 kg N and 30 kg K/ha should be applied at the time of ploughing as a basal dose. Three top-dressings of N in the form of urea or ammonium sulphate should be given @ 20 kg/ha, preferably after every harvest, followed by irrigation. In rainfed areas, fertilizers should be applied during rains. The above dose of fertilizers should be repeated every year. According to another source, the optimum dose of nitrogen for obtaining higher herbage and oil-yield is 120 kg N/ha.

INTERCULTIVATION

To check weed growth, the plantation requires hoeing during the first year. The roots of *E. citriodora* grow quite deep after a year and after that weeds do not pose any threat to the plantation. Moreover, regular intercultural operations keep the weeds under control.

PESTS AND DISEASES

Pests

The important pests of *E. citriodora* are termites, leaf-cutting ants, Eucalyptus snout beetles, weevils, scale insects cicadas, thrips and wood-borers. Certain areas are known for termite menace. If the soil is dry for a considerable period of time, termites eat away the roots and bark on the stem causing plant mortality. It is, therefore, essential to treat the soil with Aldrin or Dieldrin or Aldrex or 1-2% aqueous solution of Tafdrin, besides not allowing the soil to remain dry for more than a fortnight. The hairy caterpillar also feeds on the leaves in the early stages and the same can be controlled by a timely spray of Malathion (0.2%).

Diseases

Some of the pathogens causing diseases are *Pseudophaeolus baudonii, Diaporthe* spp. (canker), *Corticum salmonicolor* (stem-end rot), *Phytophthora nicotinae* (basal stem canker), *Cylindrocladium scoparium* (seedling, leaf and stem blights), *Physalospora latitans* (drying and defoliation of leaves) and *Pestalotiopsis funera* (leaf-spot). Viral diseases which reduce the quality and quantity of oil in the leaves are: tobacco mosaic, little-leaf and leaf-crinkle. Certain other fungal diseases also seriously affect the plants. *Fusarium orthoceros* attacks the seedlings at the hypocotyl level in the rainy season. Excessive humus content in the soil promotes the disease and the entire nursery perishes overnight. The fungus, *Colletotrichum* spp., attacks the leaves, which turn brown and die with the spread of the disease. An aqueous spray of Micop (0.2%) or any other copper fungicide will control the disease. Plants showing virus diseases should be immediately uprooted and destroyed.

HARVESTING, DISTILLATION OF OIL AND YIELD

Care must be taken to harvest the crop when the leaves are rich in oil content and the weather is also quite clear. Cloudly as well as rainy days are unsuitable for harvesting the crop. The first harvest can be taken from 6-8 months-old plantations. At this stage, the yield of the herb as well as the oil is rather negligible, but coppicing the plants is very necessary since it promotes the vigrous sprouting of side branches. Fresh shoots sprout about 4 weeks after coppicing, which are again ready for coppicing after 4-5 months. This process results in the regular increase in the yield of the herb which is almost stabilized after the plants are 3 to 4 years old. The first coppicing is done at about 30-45 cm above the ground and the subsequent ones are done at 75-90 cm above the ground. This level of coppicing is advantageous for subsequent cultivation operations. Usually, three harvests can be taken annually from the irrigated plantations corresponding with the maximum oil content of the leaves. These stages are reached between the middle of February to the middle of March, the middle of July and the end of October to early November. This provides a growing time for the fresh shoots of nearly 4 months, during which period the leaves also reach adulthood—the best stage for maximum oil content. After two years, the plantation can be thinned to one plant per pit so that new shoots get enough space and nourishment to grow normally.

It has repeatedly been observed that, at the above spacing and coppicing, the yield of green herb per hectare during the first year is approximately 7 t, during the second year about 30 t and about 40 t during the third year, in irrigated areas. The yield is almost stabilized after this age and a plantation is expected to remain economical for about ten years, if properly maintained. From unirrigated rainfed areas only two harvests with nearly 37 t/ha/year of green herb is possible. The pronounced shoot potentiality of *E. citriodora* ensures a regular supply of green herb after each coppicing. The harvested material should immediately be separated from the hard, thick wood since only the leaves attached to pencil-thick or thinner branches are suitable for distillation. The herb should immediately be distilled. On storing, the leaves either dry or even decay if not regularly upturned, resulting in a substantial loss of oil. Separating the leaves completely from the branches is not advisable from an economic point of view. The mixture of leaves and thin branches is roughly in the proportion of 7:3. Such a herb-yield from a hectare of irrigated plantation, on an average, yields 200 l of oil; while from unirrigated land, about 150 l of oil is obtained. Besides oil, a hectare of plantation also yields about 11 t of dry wood suitable for the paper-pulp industry and fuel. If the leaves are not distilled soon after harvest, there will be a loss of oil through evaporation.

42

Palmarosa

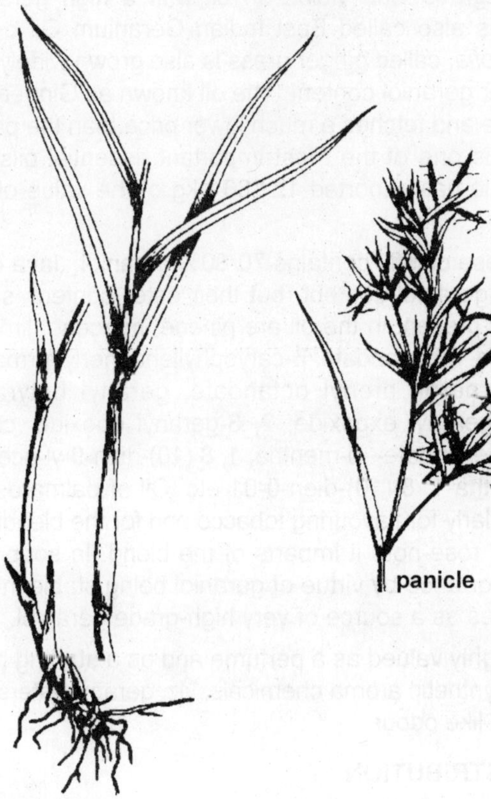

PLANT PROFILE

Family	:	*Poaceae; Graminae*
English name	:	Palmarosa, Rosha grass, Rusa grass
Indian name	:	*Dhyamakah*, *Rohisah* (Sanskrit), *Gandhabel Rusa ghas* (Hindi), *Palmaroshahullu* (Kannada), *Kavattampillu*, *Munkilpu*, *Curaippul* (Tamil)

Species and varieties : *Cymbopogon Martinii* Stapf var. *motia*
C. martinii Stapf var. *sofia*
sel. IW-31243, IW-31245, Trishna, Tripta

Distribution : India, East Africa, Brazil, Cuba, Indonesia

Uses : Perfumery, Flavouring, Tobacco

The oil of Palmarosa is obtained from the floral shoots and the above-ground parts of *Cymbopogon martinii* Stapf. variety *motia* (2n=40), belonging to the family *Poaceae; Graminae.* This variety is also referred as 'Rosha grass' or 'Russa grass' and yields on oil with a high geraniol content (75.90%), which is also called East Indian Geranium Oil or Russa Oil. Another variety, *Sofia*, called ginger grass is also grown widely in India and it yields oil of lower geraniol content. The oil known as Ginger Grass Oil is of an inferior grade and fetches a much lower price than the palmorosa oil. Oil of palmarosa is one of the most important essential oils. During the year 1995-96, India has exported 12.186 t kg of the value of Rs. 49.007 lakhs.

Oil of palmarosa chiefly contains 70-80% geraniol. Java oil also have almost the same geraniol content, but their ester content is higher. The other constituents present in the oil are pinene, myrcene, limonene, 1, 8-cinene, β-terpinene, n-hexanoate, β-caryophyllene, nerly formate, geranial, geranyl acetate, nerol, prenyl octanoate, geranyl butyrate, geranyl isovalerate, 6, 7-geranyl expoxide, 2, 3-geranyl epoxide, caryophyllene epoxide, geranyl hexanoate; -p-mentha, 1, 8 (10)-dien-9-yl-acetate, geranyl octonoate, p-mentha-1, 8 (10)-dien-0-01 etc. Oil of palmarosa is used in perfumery, particularly for flavouring tobacco and for the blending of soaps, due to the lasting rose-note it imparts of the blend. In soap perfumes, it has a special importance by virtue of geraniol being stable in contact with alkali. It also serves as a source of very high-grade geraniol.

Geraniol is highly valued as a perfume and as a starting material for a large number of synthetic aroma chemicals, viz. geranyl esters, which have a permanent rose-like odour.

ORIGIN AND DISTRIBUTION

Russa grass (*C. martini* Stapf var. *motia*) is a native of most parts of sub-tropical India and it grows in warm humid areas. It occurs in patches, in open scrub forests, in parts of Madhya Pradesh, Maharashtra and Andhra Pradesh. It is also found occasionally in Karnataka, Tamil Nadu and parts of Uttar Pradesh. There is now an expansion in the cultivated area, which is spread over in the states of Uttar Pradesh, Andhra Pradesh, Jodhpur (Rajasthan), Karnataka, Maharashtra, Madhya Pradesh and Tamil Nadu, in an area of about 2000 ha. Outside India, the crop is gown commercially in Indonesia, the East African countries, Cuba and Brazil.

Another form called ginger grass (*C. martini* Stapf var. *sofia*) is distributed in more moist regions.

DESCRIPTION OF THE PLANT

Palmarosa is an aromatic, perennial grass, which attains a height of 300 cm. The aerial parts die in the winter. Being very susceptible to frost, its leaves and shoots may dry up even in November when there is early frost, but usually withering starts in December, and by the end of January the plant dries up completely.

The leaves are linear-lanceolate to lanceolate, cordate or amplexicaul, 8-50 cm long, 1-3 cm broad, finely caudate; the panicles are 10-30 cm along, turning reddish, often very bright red when mature; the glumes are 3.3-4 mm long, awns 11.4-14 mm long; the lower glume of the fertile spikelets are deeply channelled. The channel of the glumes in the lower half are very narrow, corresponding to a rib on the inner side, the lowest pedicel is sessile, the racemes slightly swollen and connate to the base of the rachis.

VARIETIES

Some of the high-yielding varieties under this crop are sel. IW-31243 and IW-31245, released under the All India Co-ordinated project on the improvement of Medicinal and Aromatic Plants, and 'Trishna' and 'Tripta' from the CIMAP Lucknow. PRC-1 is another important variety recommended for cultivation.

SOIL

A well-drained loamy soil with a pH of 6 to 7 with irrigation facilities is ideal for the cultivation of palmarosa. A rise in pH above 8.5 is found to decrease the growth and consequently the oil-yield, but has no adverse influence on the quality of oil produced. It also grows well in well-drained clayey loam soils, free from water-logging. If the soil is not well drained or if after heavy irrigation, the water remains standing in the hot weather, the growth of the grass is badly affected.

CLIMATE

Palmarosa is a crop which grows well in a warm tropical climate with an elevation of up to 300 m. Locations with an annual variation in temperature between 10 to 36ºC and rainfall around 150 cm, with ample sunshine are the best suited for its cultivation. Areas which are affected by severe frost are not suitable, as the frost kills the grass and reduces the oil content.

LAND PREPARATION

The field is prepared well before the onset of the monsoon. It is ploughed and harrowed to a fine tilth. All the stubble and roots of weeds are removed.

At the time of the last ploughing, FYM @ 10 t/ha is incorporated into the soil.

Healthy and established seedlings, which are 15 cm high, are carefully removed from the nursery and planted in rows at 60 cm × 60 cm apart. In fertile areas, the spacing should be increased. It has been demonstrated at the CIMAP, Lucknow, that a closer plant spacing of 30 cm × 30 cm improves the palmarosa oil production by 44% over the planting at 60 cm × 30 cm.

CULTIVATION

Propagation

It is best raised by: (i) transplanting the nursery-raised seedlings, (ii) by root-cuttings of healthy plants, and (iii) through slips. For commercial planting, the crop is propagated through seeds.

Nursery Raising

The nursery-beds are prepared in May. Raised beds are preferable as the seeds are not washed off by irrigation. Liberal amounts of FYM should be added to the seed-bed.

As the seeds are small land light, they are mixed with fine soil in the ratio of 1:10 for even distribution and ease in sowing. They are sown in lines at 15-20 cm apart. The seeds should not be sown densely as this will lead to crowding of seedlings, resulting in poor growth of the plants. About 2.5 kg seeds are adequate to give enough seedlings for planting one hectare. The beds are watered lightly and regularly. Germination starts within two weeks. Later on, a weak solution, of urea (0.2-05%) may be given for their good growth. In about 3 to 4 weeks, the seedlings are ready for transplanting.

By Root-cuttings

Plants that give a good yield and high-quality oil should be used for taking root-cuttings. In this way, it is possible to raise plantations yielding high-quality oil, which is not possible when the plantation is raised from seeds, as the seeds give rise to many morphologically indistinguishable but different varieties. However, the rate of establishment of rooted slips is very poor as compared to nursery transplants. Slips can be planted in June-July during the rainy season.

PLANTING

The seedlings are transplanted into the prepared fields as soon as the rainy season sets in (June-July). They can be transplanted even earlier, if the weather is not very warm and irrigation is available.

FERTILIZERS

As the grass is perennial, it is necessary to replenish the soil. In rich soils, manuring may not be required for the first two years. By manuring already rich soils, the vegetative growth is increased and the oil content is reduced. However, for deficient soils, a mixture consisting of 20 kg N, 50 kg P_2O_5 and 40 kg KO_2/ha is used as a basal dose at the time of planting. About 40 kg/ha of N is applied in three split doses after each harvest. The mixture of N, P and K should be repeated at the time of the appearance of fresh leaves each year.

A foliar spray of $FeSO_4$ and $MnSO_4$ has been found to improve the plant growth, herbage and oil-yield of palmarosa. The CIMAP, Lucknow, has also recommended an application of 10 kg/ha of Zn which is reported to significantly increase the number of tillers, herbage and oil-yield without affecting the oil content and quality. Similar results were obtained by the application of 20 kg/ha of sulphur in the form of elemental sulphur or ammonium sulphate.

IRRIGATION

The irrigation required depends upon the climatic conditions. The grass requires irrigation after about 8-10 days during the growing season. With an ample supply of water, growth is luxuriant, but if drought prevails the growth is arrested, the leaves wither and the oil content is reduced. However, before harvesting, irrigation should be discontinued.

WEEDING

Odour is an important factor of the oil quality and it is essential to keep the fields clean of other growing plants, particularly those which impart their own odour. Therefore, the plantation should be kept free from weeds by regular weeding and hoeing. Particular care is required in the initial stage of growth, so that the weeds d not overpower the grass. Diurom (1.5 kg a.i/ha), Isoproturon (0.25 kg a.i/ha) and Oxyfluofen (1.5 kg a.i/ha) are the weedicides recommended to control weeds in palmarosa.

PESTS AND DISEASE

The crop is not attacked by any insect pests or diseases of a serious nature. However, *Curvularia trifolii* and *C. andropogonis* cause leaf-blight and the symptoms are the yellowing of leaves and necrosis. *Dreschlera cymmartinii* is also reported to infect palmarosa. *Collectotrichum caudatum* sometimes causes leaf-spot disease.

HARVESTING

The essential oil is distributed in all the parts of the grass viz. the flower-heads, leaves and stems; the flower-heads containing the major portion. The grass is harvested when it is 4 months old and in full bloom. Usually the grass is cut at a height of 5-8 cm from the ground-level and the whole plant is used for distillation. The maximum yield of oil is obtained when the entire plant is at full flowering stage.

The number of harvests depends upon the climatic conditions. During the first year, usually one crop is obtained during October-November, whereas 2-3 crops are obtained in the subsequent years.

Palmarosa plantations remain productive for about 8 years. However, the yield of grass and oil starts decreasing from the fourth year onwards. It is, therefore, recommended that the plantation is kept only for 4 years.

DISTILLATION

Oil is palmarosa is generally obtained by hydro-distillation. The process is primitive and has remained unchanged over the year. As the quality of oil suffers from this method, it is advisable to use steam-distillation.

The distillation equipment consists of a boiler to produce steam, a still, a condenser and 1-3 separators.

The still is made of mild steel and has a perforated bottom, on which the grass rests. The still has a stream inlet pipe at the bottom. A removable lid is fitted at the top. Charging and discharging can be done in perforated cages with iron chains which can be lowered into the still with the help of a chain-pulley block.

Different types of condensers are available, but tubular condensers are better than the others. The condenser is provided on inlet and outlet which cold water flows through the chamber to cool the pipes for condensing the distillate.

To obtain the maximum yield of oil and to facilitate the release of oil, the grass is chopped into shorter lengths. Chopping the grass has further advantages: that more grass can be charged into the still and even packing is facilitated. The grass should be packed firmly as this prevents formation of steam channels. Steam is allowed to pass into the still with a pressure from 18-32 kg in the boiler. The mixture of the vapours of water and palmarosa oil pass into the condenser. As the distillation proceeds, the distillage collects in the separator. The oil, being lighter than water and insoluble, floats on the top of the separator and is continuously drawn off. The oil is then decanted and filtered.

Small cultivators can use direct-fire stills, but properly designed stills should be used. In such cases, the stills are provided with a boiler at the bottom. Water is poured into the boiler and the grass is charged in the top portion. In the still, the water does not come into contact with the grass.

For economical production of the oil, it is advisable that the harvested material is allowed to wilt for a short time. From the quality point of view, the grass should be distilled as fresh as possible. Oil obtained from dry or fermented grass is of inferior quality. The distillation unit should be clean, rust-free and free of any other odour.

The oil should be free of sediment, suspended matter and moisture before it is stored. The containers should be clean and rust-free.

OIL CONTENT AND YIELD

The content and yield of the oil depend upon many factors, such as the climatic conditions, the time of harvesting, the maturity of the grass, the nature of the material being distilled, i.e., fresh material or wilted material, the method of distillation, etc.

All parts of the plant contain the essential oil, the maximum oil being present in the flowers, with the stalks containing a negligible quantity. On an average, the oil content in the various parts of the plant are:

Plant Part	*% of Oil Content*
Whole plant	0.10 to 0.40%
Stalks	0.01 to 0.03%
Flowering tops	0.45 to 0.52%
Leaves	0.16 to 0.25%

The yield of oil is low in the first year. In increases with the age of the plantation. From an economic point of view, it is advisable to keep the plantation for four years. The yield for the first 4 years from the rainfed crop is given below:

Year	*Yield*
1st year	20 kg/ha.
2nd year	60 kg/ha.
3rd year	70 kg/ha.
4th year	70 kg/ha.

An oil-yield of about 220-250 kg/ha may be obtained from the second year onwards from an irrigated crop. The clumps should be burnt during summer; this increases the yield of grass and oil.

43

Patchouli

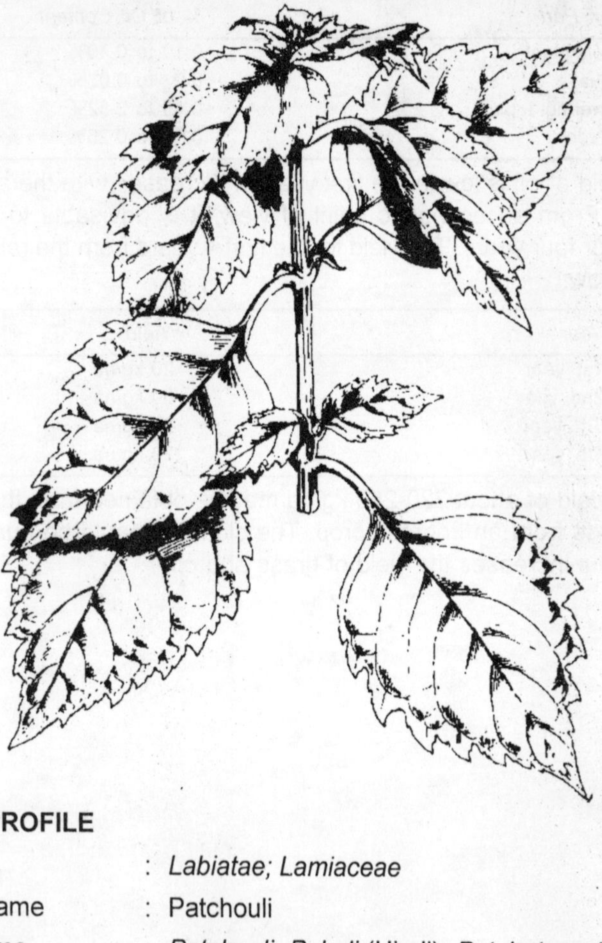

PLANT PROFILE

Family	:	*Labiatae; Lamiaceae*
English name	:	Patchouli
Indian name	:	*Patchouli*, *Peholi* (Hindi), *Patchetene* (Kannada), *Kadir pachai* (Tamil)

Species and varieties : *Pogostemon patchouli* Pellet
Johore, Singapore, Indonesia

Distribution : India, Indonesia, Malaysia, Paraguay Penang, Singapore, West Indies

Uses : Cosmetics, Drugs, Flavouring, Insecticides Perfumery

Patchouli, *Pogostemon patchouli* Pellet (syn. *P. cablin* Benth.) (2n=34) belonging to the family *Labiatae; Lamiaceae* is a native of the Philippines. It is often confused with *Pogostemon heyneaxhus* Benth. which is indigenous to India and is grown in gardens, but has no commercial importance. More than hundred years ago, India used to export fabrics heavily perfumed with dry patchouli leaves, a technique which was later adopted by the French manufacturers to create a typical oriental aroma for their homespun shawls.

It is very difficult to specify the field of application of the oil of patchouli which is obtained by steam-distillation of the dry leaves of this plant. The oil contains about 97% of compounds which have no influence on the aroma. Out of these 40 to 45% belong to the sesquiterpene group and the balance seems to consist of patchouli alcohol. The oil contains small amounts of benzaldehyde, eugenol, cinnamic aldehyde, an alcohol with a rose-like fragrance, a ketone with an orris root-like odour, another ketone, two bases possessing a strong benumbing odour, azulene and a sesquiterpene alcohol, β-patchoulene, gammagauaiente, α-bulonesene, α-terpene, cadinene, benzaldehyde and patchouli alcohol.

Patchouli oil is extensively used as a flavouring ingredient in major food products, including alcoholic and non-alcoholic beverages, frozen dairy desserts, candy, baked goods, gelatine, meat and meat products. It is one of the most important essential oils of the perfumery industry because the oil blends well with other essential oils like vetiver, sandalwood, geranium, lavender, cedarwood derivatives and clove oil. Hence, it is regarded as the best fixative for heavy perfumes which imparts strength, character, alluring notes and lasting qualities. There is not synthetic chemical to replace the oil of patchouli, which further enhances its value and unique position in the perfumery market, and there is great demand for it in soaps, scents, body lotions, pre-shave and after-shave lotions, detergents, tobacco and incense manufacturing factories. The oil also gives one of the finest *attars* when blended with sandalwood oil. The oil of patchouli is used as an ingredient in insect repellent preparations and is said to have antibacterial properties as well.

The fresh leaves of patchouli have medicinal value and are used as a decoction with other drugs to treat nausea diarrhoea, cold and headaches in the Chinese system of medicine. The dried leaves are used for scenting wardrobes, and known for their antirheumatic action. It is also used as a masking agent for alcoholic breath. Tenacity of odour is one of the virtues of patchouli oil and is one of the reasons for its versatile use. The adulteration of patchouli oil is quite common and is done on a large scale. The main adulterant is gurjon balsam oil. The other adulterants include copaiba balsam oil, 8-camphene, methanol, cedarwood oil, castor oil and isobornyl acetate.

DISTRIBUTION

The patchouli plant grows wild in Malaysia, Indonesia and Singapore. Its natural habitat extends across Paraguay, Penang, East and West Indies, the subcortical Himalayas and the Deccan peninsula. This crop was introduced in to India by Tata Oil Mills as early as 1942. However, systematic cultivation was started by the CIMAP regional centre at Bangalore in 1962. Now, it is cultivated in Bangalore and the coastal areas of South India, Bengal and Assam.

The production of patchouli oil in India is very negligible (about 100-150 kg/year). India is importing over 20 t of oil annually from Indonesia, Malaysia and Singapore. The total annual world production is around 700-800 t.

DESCRIPTION OF THE PLANT

Patchouli is an erect, branched, pubescent herb, 0.5 to 1.0 m high and aromatic when crushed. The leaves are ovate to oblong-ovate, coarse, simple or doubly crenate-serrate, on both surfaces more or less densely tomentose, the glands are dotted beneath, up to 12 cm by 10 cm. The petiole is 6-8 cm; the stem is densely tomentose and swollen on the nodes; the spikes are terminal and axillary, panicled, dense sometimes interrupted, 2.5-14 cm long. The calyx is 5-6.5 mm; the corolla lobes are obtuse, 6-9 mm, pink, purple of white-violet blotched on all segments. The filaments are violet, with the bracts as long as the calyx. Flowering takes place from January to February in India, Malaya and Philippines. In Java, it is never found flowering.

VARIETIES

Johore, Singapore and Indonesia are the commonly cultivated varieties of patchouli. Of these, Johore yields the best quality oil in terms of chemical composition and odour value whereas, the other two have high herbage and oil-yield potential, but their oils are of inferior quality.

SOIL AND CLIMATE

The plant is hardy and grows on a wide range of soils and under varied climatic conditions. However, partially shaded, well-drained, fertile soils with evenly distributed rainfall or places with assured irrigation are ideal. A deep, loamy soil rich in humus and nutrients, in the tropics, is said to be the best for optimum oil production. The crop requires a soil pH of 5.5-6.2. Patchouli prefers a warm and humid climate and flourishes well in places with fairly heavy and evenly distributed rainfall, ranging from 150-300 cm/ annum. The crop grows well with irrigation in low rainfall areas. A temperature of 24-28°C and 75% average atmospheric humidity is reported to be ideal. It grows successfully up to an altitude of 800 to 1050 m above sea-level.

LAND PREPARATION

The main field for transplanting is thoroughly disced and tilled. Nematicides like Furadan at the rate of 20 kg/ha (3% a.i.) is mixed well into the soil a few days before transplanting. The plot is then laid out into ridges and furrows. The ridges should be 20-25 cm high and 18-22 cm broad, with 60 cm row-to-row distance. The beds should be irrigated a day before transplanting.

CULTIVATION

Propagation

Patchouli is propagated either through seeds or cuttings. Since crops raised from seeds wide variation in the leaf characters and oil-yields, vegetative propagation through cuttings is preferred. The leaves can also root under intermittent mist and adventitious plantlets can be obtained from these leaves.

Nursery Raising

Since the crop is highly susceptible to nematode attack, it is advisable to adopt phytosanitary measures a the nursery stage itself.

Seed-pans or polythene bags are filled with well-heated sand which can be made by passing steam through it for about one hour. If this is not practicable for a grower, the sand should be treated with a suitable nematicide like Furadan (3% a.i.) at the rate of 20 kg/ha.

Shade is essential for raising a nursery and it can be raised at any time of the year. Stem cuttings from 9-month-old branches of 10-12 cm length, consisting of 4-5 nodes especially with the terminal bud and a crown of 2-3 leaves are quite suitable. The basal end of the cutting should be neatly cut in oblique from just about 1 cm below the node. Treatment with 1500 ppm IBA to the basal end encourages rooting. The cuttings should then be planted in seed-pans, nursery-beds or in polythene bags with the help of a dibbler at a spacing of about 10 cm. Aeration, partial shade and regular watering are essential for early rooting. The plants should be removed from the shade about 10 days before transplanting. The cuttings take about 30-35 days for rooting in the nursery and, in about 8-10 weeks, they are ready for transplanting.

TRANSPLANTING

The rooted cuttings are transplanted to the main field at a spacing of 60 cm × 60 cm. Transplanting in August-October gives about 90% establishment.

Crops can also be raised by direct planting of the cuttings in the main field. For this, 15-20 cm long cuttings are required. In order to have better establishment, 2-3 cuttings are planted per planting point. During the early stages, partial shade and sufficient moisture are essential. Cuttings planted at an angle give better results compared to those planted erect.

When there is a scarcity of cuttings, single-node cuttings can also be raised, but the initial rate of growth of these cuttings is slow and the percentage of success is lower.

MANURES AND FERTILIZERS

Patchouli requires rich soil. If the soil is of low fertility it should be supplemented with suitable doses of fertilizers. About 12 t/ha of FYM is added while preparing the main field and is mixed well. At the time of transplanting, normally a basal dose of 25 kg N, 50 kg P_2O_5 and 50 kg K_2O/ha, is given in the form of urea, super phosphate and muriate of potash. Thereafter nitrogen is applied in 5 split doses after ever harvest, in such a way that the crop receives the first dose just after the harvest and another about 2 months later. In total, 150 kg/ha/yr of N is applied to the crop.

The crop is sensitive to manganese (Mn) deficiency which can be corrected by spraying $MnSO_4$ at 5.5 to 11.0 kg/ha.

IRRIGATION

After transplanting, the plants should be watered every day for 3-4 days and subsequently on alternate days for 10-15 days. By this time, the seedlings will have established well and thereafter irrigation once in every 3 days will suffice. Patchouli needs evenly distributed rainfall and, hence, artificial irrigation is necessary in areas where rainfall is scanty, to obtain good yields.

INTER-CULTURE

The crop may require weeding after about six weeks of transplanting and one hoeing after each harvest. During the first 2 to 3 months, the field should be kept weed-free. Pre-emergence spray of herbicides, Diuron (2 or 3 kg/ha), Linuron or Simazine, effectively control weeds with low phytotoxicity.

GROWTH REGULATORS

Foliar sprays of Triacontanol (0.05%), auxin (0.25%) + cytokinin or phenol compound (3 ppm) at 2-weekly intervals or 2, 4-D (0.5%) at 4-

weekly intervals were found to enhance plant growth and yield with the auxin-cytokinin mixture being the most effective. It is reported that Kinetin treatment (0.5 × 10^{-4}) was effective in improving growth and increasing oil-yield.

INTERCROPPING

Patchouli is a shade-loving plant. It can be grown as an intercrop with coconut, arecanut, rubber, coffee, banana and other plantation crops.

PESTS AND DISEASES

Pests

1. Root-knot Nematode (Meloidogyne incognita and M. hapla)

It is commonly found in tropical and subcortical regions. The nematode is an obligatory parasite which enters into the root by thrusting with the mouth spear, usually in the region of cell elongation or at the base of lateral roots. They reach the cortex, multiply and cause galls which are commonly called root-knots. The diameter of the knots varies from 0.2 cm to 5.0 cm. Heavily infected plants show stunting of top growth and wilting symptoms, otherwise in the beginning there will be hardly and difference between the infected and healthy plants. Typical symptoms of an infested plant become apparent only after 8 months. If left to its fate, the crop dwindles and the whole stand may perish during the next 2 or 3 months.

Treatment with suitable nematicides and proper management practices greatly reduce the incidence of root-knot and provides better scope for commercial cultivation of this crop. For this, the nursery should be raised from healthy mother-stock under nematode-free conditions. The plot should be treated with a proper nematicide like Furadan @ of 20 kg/ha (3% a.i.) of Dasanit @ 150 kg/ha (5% a.i.). The first dose of the nematicide should be given as a preplanting treatment and the second dose can be given one year after transplanting as a packet application to the plants. It is desirable to plant a crop of citronella or other nematode-resistant crops in a nematode infected soil for few years before planting patchouli.

The leaf-eating caterpillar (*Pronomis profusalis*), leaf-roller (*Herpetogramma licarsisalis*), mirid bug (*Pachypeltis* spp.) and leaf webber (*Pachyzanica aegrotalis*) are the insect pests of patchouli. Metacid (0.1%) or Methyl Parathion (0.2% may be sprayed for the control of caterpillar or leaf-webber.

Diseases

Leaf-blight (Cercospora spp.)

The disease is characterized by the appearance of brown spots near the margin or at the apical region of leaves which enlarge irregularly, coalesce, cover the entire lamina and create drying. It is seen in one-year-old plants and is less serious than the root-knot nematode. It can be controlled with two sprays of Dithane Z-78, (0.5%) at a one month interval.

The other diseases reported to this crop include wilt caused by *Rhizoctonia solani, Fusarium solani* and *Pythium aphanidermatum* and virus diseases of which pogostemon virus-1, yellow mosaic virus and tobacco necrosis virus (TNV) are important. Yellow mosaic virus is transmitted by white fly (*Bemisia tabaci*)

HARVESTING, DRYING (CURING) AND YIELD

The stage at which crop has to be harvested is very important for a good yield and better quality of oil. The first harvest of the crop is obtained after about 5 months of transplanting. It is harvested when the foliage becomes pale-green to light-brown and when the stand emits the characteristic patchouli odour which can be easily smelt by a passerby, especially in the morning hours. Subsequent harvests can be done after every 3-4 months, depending much upon the local conditions and management practices. The length of cut-tops ranges from 40-60 cm. It is necessary to leave 4-6 juvenile sprouting buds at the basal region for rapid regeneration. Harvesting is done with the help of a small, sharp shear or secateur. The crop should not be harvested prematurely as it gives less yield and oil of inferior quality. The first 2 or 3 harvests of the new plantation give good yield and high-quality oil. The crop can be maintained for about 3 years.

The harvested material is spread out under the shade in thin layers and is turned periodically to ensure proper drying, which is of great importance for obtaining maximum yield and oil of good quality. Drying normally takes about three days. During the process, the material should be frequently turned over in order to promote even and thorough drying and to prevent fermentation. Later, completely dried material is pressed into bales and stored in a cool, dry place till distilled.

A good crop yields about 2 t/annum of dry leaves and about 50-60 kg/ha of oil.

DISTILLATION OF OIL

The shade-dried patchouli leaves are subjected to steam-distillation for obtaining the oil of patchouli. The dried herb can be immediately distilled or could be stored for some time, according to convenience.

The distillation equipment consists of a boiler, distillation still, condenser and receiver. The herb is loaded into the distillation still which has a perforated metal sheet at the bottom and is made of mild steel. The lid of the still can be swung aside during loading and unloading. It is important that the herb should be evenly packed inside the still, otherwise steam channels may form during the distillation resulting in poor yield. The condenser, made of copper or stainless steel, is provided with an inlet and an outlet for the circulation of cooling water which cools the hot vapours consisting of steam and essential oil vapour which will flow out into the receiver. The oil being lighter than water and insoluble, floats on the top in the receiver which consists preferably of two compartments, and only the water gets drained out. The oil can be drawn off separately at the end of the distillation. An intercharge of 1.4 to 3.5 kg/cm^2 to high and low pressures produces better yield as more cell-walls rupture in this process.

The duration of the distillation varies from 6-8 hours. Prolonged distillation gives higher yield and better quality of oil. But if it is distilled for too long, the oil will have a disagreeable odour. Patchouli resinoid is also prepared occasionally by extracting the leaves with volatile solvents such as benzene. Such extraction gives 4.5 to 5.80% of resinoid which contains 70-89% of alcohol-soluble absolute.

OIL CONTENT AND CHEMICAL CONSTITUENTS

The oil is found mainly in the leaf and a small quantity is present in the tender parts of the stem. The yield of oil varies from 2.5 to 3.5% on shade-dried bags of leaves and an average yield of 2.5% may be considered satisfactory in commercial distillation.

The oil of patchouli is a viscous liquid, yellowish-green to brownish in colour and possesses a warm, powerful, sweet herbaceous, aromatic, spicy fragrance which improves with ageing. It is found that 92% of the oil consists of compounds which have very little influence upon its odour. Sesquiterpene constituents 40-45% of the oil out of which patchouli camphor or patchouli alcohol, called patchoulol, represents 35-40% of the oil, which is also odourless. However, it is found that one or more satellite components of patchouli may be responsible for the characteristic odour.

STORAGE OF OIL

Immediately after distillation, all free water in the oil should be completely removed and the remaining traces of water can be removed by adding anhydrous sodium sulfate @ 20-30 g/l and stirring the contents. This chemical can be left in the oil for 4-5 hours and the oil is filtered to remove this and other sediments which might come during distillation. Untreated oil develops high acid value and low ester value, resulting in deterioration of the oil. The purified oil is stored in clean, dry aluminium containers which are free from any chemical and odour. Oil is filled to the brim of the containers which are airtight, otherwise air can also deteriorate the oil quality. Only metal corks are used for closing the mouth of the containers. The oil containers are then kept a in cool place.

The odour of the oil improves on ageing; oil preserved well for some months possesses a finer and fuller odour than fresh oil, and is highly esteemed by perfumers.

44

Rosemary

PLANT PROFILE

Family	:	*Lamiaceae; Labiatae*
English name	:	Rosemary
Indian name	:	*Rusmari* (Hindi), *Rosemary* (Tamil)

Species and varieties : *Rosmarinus officinalis L.*
French Rosemary, Italian Rosemary

Distribution : India, Algeria, France, Italy, Morocco, Spain, Tunisia, Portugal

Uses : Cosmetics, Culinary purposes, Flavouring Perfumery

Rosemary, botanically known as *Rosmarinus officinalis* L. of the family *Lamiaceae; Labiatae,* is a native of the Mediterranean regions of Europe, Asia Minor and North Africa. The leaves and flowering tops, on steam-distillation, yield the essential oil. The oil has 1,8 cineole (20-50%), borneol (20%), camphor, linalool, α-pinene, camphene, β-pinene, sabinene, myrcene, α-phellandrene, α-terpinene, limonene, α-terpinene, p-cymene, terpinolene, thujone, copaene, terpinene-4-ol, caryophyllene, methyl chavicol, α-terpineol, thymol and carvacrol. The oil is valued for its used in culinary, medicine, perfumery and cosmetic industries. It is an excellent fixative material and the oil also contributes a strong fresh odour, which blends well with various other oil odours and also serves to mask the unpleasant smell of certain other ingredients in any preparation. Rosemary oil is known to have antimicrobial activity against certain gram-positive and gram-negative organisms. It is also used in formulations of compounded oils for flavouring meat, sauces, condiments and other food products. The leaves are used in cooking. A distilled water is obtained from the flowers which is used as a soothing eye-wash.

DISTRIBUTION AND PRODUCTION

Rosemary is grown in Spain, Italy, France, Algeria, Morocco and Portugal for its essential oil. Spain has traditionally been the largest supplier of the oil, but is appears to be rapidly losing ground to Tunisia. The annual world production of the oil has been increasing gradually over the years and now 200-300 t of oil is being produced annually, against the negligible quality produced in India. In India, Rosemary is cultivated to a limited extent in the Nilgiris in South India. Its cultivation in the plains is of recent origin and now it is being cultivated in and around Bangalore on a small scale. The oil is comparable to the Spanish oil in quality and has been well received by the trade.

DESCRIPTION OF THE PLANT

The plant is an hardy, dense, evergreen shrub, growing up to 1 m in height with an erect stem divided into numerous long, slender branches bearing many sessile, opposite leaves which are smooth and green, woody, whitish and glandular beneath. The leaves are 2 to 4 cm long and cylindrical, leathery and green on top, white and hairy below and sticky to touch. The flowers are situated in little clusters towards the end of the branches. The calyx is two-lipped, the upper one with a single broad oval lobe, the lower one with two segmented triangular lobes. The corolla is also two-lipped with two violet stamens and a long style projecting from it. The fruit is an oval, four-sectioned cremocarp.

TYPES AND VARIETIES

There are two types of rosemary under cultivation. They are the 'French rosemary' and the 'Italian rosemary'. The French type produces white-coloured flowers and its oil is superior in quality to that of the Italian type whose flowers are purple coloured.

SOIL

It is a very hardy plant and is found growing on rocky terrains in the temperate parts of the world. In India, the plant comes up well on the light loamy soils of the Nilgiris and the sandy loam soils of Bangalore. The crop requires a soil pH ranging from 6.5-70 for its successful growth.

CLIMATE

Rosemary prefers a Mediterranean type of climate with low humidity, warm winters and mild summers for its successful growth. However, any place where frost occurs frequently should be avoided as the plant is succeptible to it. The climate of the Nilgiris and Bangalore, in India, have been found suitable for its cultivation.

LAND PREPARATION

The land is prepared well by repeated ploughing and harrowing. About 20 t of well-rotted FYM is incorporated into the soil at the time of the final ploughing.

CULTIVATION

Propagation

Vegetative Propagation

It is best propagated vegetatively by stem-cuttings. Cuttings from healthy mother-plants, 10-15 cm in length, are taken. All leaves about half of the length from bottom should be removed. The cuttings are then planted in nursery beds of sandy soil under partial shade at a depth of about 6 to 10 cm. Thereafter, regular watering and weeding is provided to the nursery for about a month; After about 6-8 weeks, the cuttings are ready for transplanting into the main field. They can also be raised in small polybags or seed-pans. This helps in easy transportation of the rooted cuttings.

Seed Propagation

The crop can be propagated by seeds also. The ideal season for raising the nursery is between September and November. The seeds are very small and about 0.2 to 2.5 g seeds are required to cover 1 sq m area and are sown to a depth of 1-2 cm.

After they are sown in well-prepared nursery beds, regular watering and weeding of the nursery is continued. The seeds germinate best at a soil temperature ranging from 14-15ºC. When the seedlings are about 8 to 10 weeks old, they are ready for transplanting into the main field.

PLANTING

Eight to ten weeks-old rooted cuttings or seedlings are planted in the main field at a spacing of 45 cm × 120 cm. About 20,000 plants/ha give the highest yield of oil. It is reported from the CIMAP, Lucknow, that a spacing of 45 cm × 45 cm between plants is optimum and gives the best yield.

MANURES AND FERTILIZERS

Prior to transplanting, 20 to of FYM, along with 40 kg of P_2O_5, 40 kg of K_2O and 20 kg of N is applied to the soil as a basal dose. After each harvest, 80 kg/ha of N is applied in 4 equal split doses as a side-dressing to promote vegetative growth. For obtaining the highest yield, the CIMAP, Lucknow has recommended the application of 300 kg N/ha/year.

IRRIGATION

Initially the crop is irrigated twice a week till the plants establish. Afterwards, once a week is enough. By nature, this crop is drought-resistant and can withstand long drought periods.

INTERCULTIVATION

About 5-6 cultivations between the rows and an equal number of weedings within the rows are required to keep the weeds under control.

PRUNING

After 2 to 3 years, the bushes are cut frequently to keep them from becoming leggy and to promote the formation of numerous shoots, which can be harvested for the oil.

PESTS AND DISEASES

When the crop was introduced, there were no major pest and disease problems for this plant. But of late, blight caused by *Rhizoctonia* spp. a soil-borne fungus, *Phytocoris rosmarini* and *Orthotylus ribesi* have been reported. Maneb (1%) can be sprayed on the crop and drenching may be done at 8-10 days' intervals to keep these diseases under control.

HARVESTING

During the first year, the crop is ready for harvest 8 months after planting and only 2 harvests are obtained. In subsequent years, 3 to 4 harvests at

100 to 120 days intervals can be taken. Depending upon the exposure of the plantation, the plants start flowering earlier in warmer and low altitude areas and later on the high slopes.

Harvesting should begin at the time of 50% blossoming and continue till 75-90% inflorescence emerges and must end when the flowers have finished blossoming. The shoots are cut for distillation when they have reached their maximum size, but have not become woody. The hardwood should not be distilled as it imparts an odour of turpentine.

DISTILLATION

Essential oil is obtained by steam-distillation of the freshly harvested herbage. The most modern method uses steam directly or indirectly, produced at 2-3 atmospheric pressure. The herbage can also be shade-dried, stored and distilled at convenience without any loss of oil.

The time required to distil one charge is 3 hours. Recently, the CIMAP, Bangalore, has recommended that rosemary be distilled for 2 hours for the maximum recovery of oil.

OIL CONTENT AND YIELD

In the laboratory, the fresh rosemary leaves yield 1% and shade-dried leaves yield 3% oil. However, in field-distillation units, a yield of 0.7% is considered satisfactory. About 12 to 15 t/ha/annum of herbage, yielding about 85 to 100 kg/ha/annum of oil, is obtained.

REJUVENATION OF THE OLD PLANTATION

When a 10 to 12-year-old plantation starts ageing and its yield is reduced, its regeneration is necessary. This should be done when the plants are in a period of rest. For this purpose, the plants are cut 4-5 cm above the ground. Quick regeneration of a plantation requires abundant fertilization. A normal yield from an adult plantation is obtained during the second year after regeneration. Regeneration restores the production capacity of the old plantation, after it has been uprooted and replanted.

45

Sacred Basil

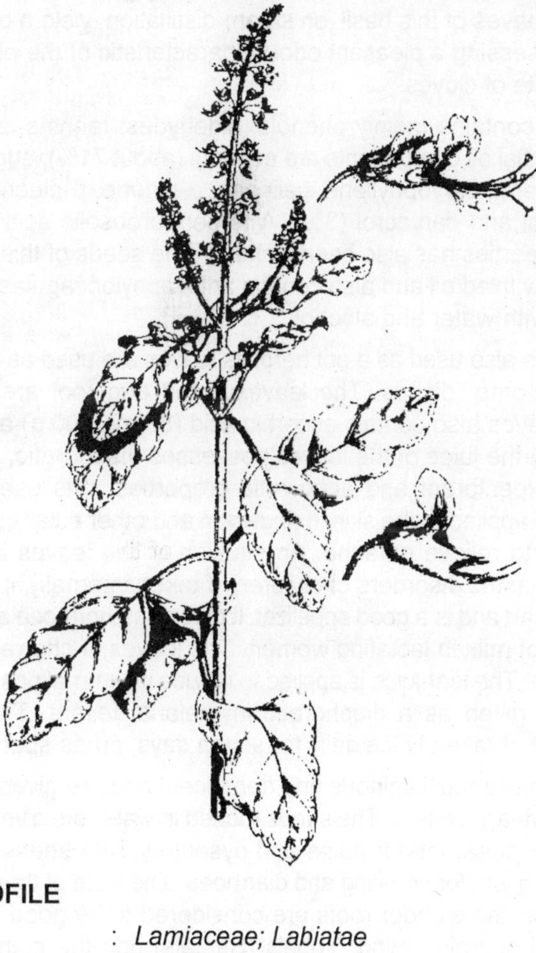

PLANT PROFILE

Family : *Lamiaceae; Labiatae*

English name : Sacred Basil, Holy Basil

Indian name : *Ajaka*, *Manjari* (Sanskrit), *Tulsi* (Hindi), *Pavitra Tulsai* (Kannada), *Thulasi* (Tamil)

Species and varieties : *Ocimum sanctum* Linn
Sri Tulsi, Krishna Tulsi

Distribution : India, Andaman and Nicobar Islands

Uses : Culinary purposes, Drugs, Flavouring Insecticide, Perfumery

The 'Sacred basil' or 'Holy basil', *Ocimum sanctum* Linn. (2n=32), a biennial or triennial shrub belonging to the family *Lamiaceae,* is commonly cultivated in gardens; it is frequently found as an escape. The species is worshipped by the Hindus of India and traditionally grown in courtyards and temples. The leaves of this basil, on steam-distillation, yield a bright yellow, volatile oil possessing a pleasant odour characteristic of the plant, with an appreciable note of cloves.

The plant contains mainly phenols, aldehydes, tannins, saponin and fats. The essential oil components are eugenol (about 71%), eugenol methyl ether (20%), nerol, caryophyllene, selinene, α-pinene, β-pinene, camphor, cineole, linalool and carvacrol (3%). A terpeneurobsolic acid possessing anticancer properties has also been isolated. The seeds of this plant give a greenish-yellow fixed oil and also contain antistaphylocoagulase which can be extracted with water and alcohol.

The plant is also used as a pot herb; its leaves are used as a condiment in salads and other dishes. The leaves, seed and root are medicinally useful. The leaves also contain ascorbic acid (83 mg 100 g) and carotene (2.5 mg/100 g) the juice of the leaves possesses diaphoretic, antiperiodic, stimulating, expectorant and antipyretic properties; it is used in catarrh and bronchitis, applied to the skin in ringworm and other cutaneous diseases and as drops to relieve earache. An infusion of the leaves is used as a stomachic in gastric disorders of children. If taken internally, it strengthens the liver and heart and is a good appetizer. It cures amenorrhoea and promotes the secretion of milk in lactating women. The leaves, if chewed, give relief from toothache. The leaf-juice is applied to reduce inflammations. A decoction of the root is given as a diaphoretic in malarial fevers. The dried and powdered root, if taken twice daily for seven days, cures spermatorrhoea.

The seeds are mucilaginous and demulcent and are given in disorders of the genito-urinary system. The seeds rubbed in water are given for irritating coughs, gonorrhoea, labour pains and dysentery. The seeds rubbed with cow's milk are given for vomiting and diarrhoea. The juice of the fresh leaves, flower-tops and the slender roots are considered to be good antidotes for snakebite and scorpion sting. Tribals (Santals) use the plant in cholera, cough, postnatal complaints, haemorrhagic septicaemia and dog bite. The volatile oil is reported to possess antibacterial and insecticidal properties. It inhibits the *in vitro* growth of *Mycobacterium tuberculosis* and *Micrococcus pyrogenes* var. *aureus.* It has marked insecticidal activity against mosquitoes.

ORIGIN AND DISTRIBUTION

O. sanctum has a wide distribution, covering the entire Indian subcontinent, ascending up to 1800 m in the Himalayas and as far as the Andaman and Nicobar Islands. This plant occupies a wide range of habitats.

DESCRIPTION OF THE PLANT

It is an erect, herbaceous, much-branched, softly hairy, biennial or triennial plant, 30-75 cm high. The leaves are elliptic-oblong, acute or obtuse, entire or serrate, pubescent on both sides, minutely gland-dotted; the flowers are purplish or crimson, in racemes, close-whorled; the nutlets are subglobose or broadly ellipsoid, slightly compressed, nearly smooth, pale-brown or reddish with small, black markings.

TYPES AND VARIETIES

In India, two types of *O. sanctum* are under cultivation; the green type (Sri Tulsi) is the most common, the second type (Krishna Tulsi) bears purple leaves and is preferred in the trade for its higher potency of the drug.

SOIL

It thrives well on a variety of soils. Rich loam to poor laterite, saline and alkaline to moderately acidic soils are all well suited for its cultivation. Well-drained soils aid in better vegetative growth. Water-logged conditions can cause root-rot and result in stunted growth.

CLIMATE

The plant can be grown under partially shaded conditions but it yields less oil. It flourishes well under fairly high rainfall and humid conditions. Long days and high temperatures have been found favourable for the plant growth and oil production. Tropical and sub-tropical climate (at altitudes up to 900 m) are suited for its cultivation. The plant is moderately tolerant to drought and frost.

SEASON

The nursery can be raised in the third week of February and transplanting is generally started in the middle of April. This can be undertaken in the month of March, if the seedlings are raised in beds.

LAND PREPARATION

The land is brought to a fine tilth and laid out into plots of convenient sizes for irrigation. It is preferable to add 15 t/ha of FYM during the preparation of the land.

CULTIVATION

Propagation

The plant is propagated by seeds. The seeds are likely to deteriorate in future generations on account of the highly cross-pollinated nature of the crop. Hence, for fresh plantings, the growers have to take fresh seeds from the pedigree stock.

Nursery Raising

Raised seed-beds of 15' × 4' × 9" size should be thoroughly prepared and well manured by the addition of FYM. About 200-300 g seeds are enough to raise seedlings for planting one hectare of land. The seeds should be sown 2 cm deep in the nursery-beds. After sowing the seeds in the nursery, a mixture of FYM and soil is thinly spread over the seeds and irrigated with a sprinkler-hose. The seeds germinate in 8-12 days and the seedlings are ready for transplanting in about 6 weeks' time, at the 4-5 leaf stage. A spray of 2% urea solution on the nursery plants 15 to 20 days before transplanting helps in raising very healthy plants for transplanting.

TRANSPLANTING

It is recommended to plant the seedlings at a distance of 40 cm × 40 cm, 40 cm × 50 cm and 50 cm × 30 cm to get high herbage and oil-yield per hectare at Lucknow, New Delhi and Indore, respectively. The plots are irrigated immediately after transplanting. The seedlings will establish well by the time of the second irrigation. At this stage, gap planting and replacement of the poor plants is done so that a uniform stand is achieved.

FERTILIZER APPLICATION

The application of 120 kg/ha N, 105 kg/ha each of P_2O_5 and K_2O is recommended for saline and alkaline soils at Lucknow. The optimum fertilizer dose recommended for this crop is 120 kg N and 60 kg P_2O_5/ha. Half the dose of N and the entire dose of P_2O_5 is given as a basal dose. Whereas, the remaining N is applied in two split doses, after the first and second cuttings. The application of the micronutrients Co and Mn at 50 and 100 ppm concentrations, respectively, is reported to increase the oil-yield significantly.

IRRIGATION

Irrigation depends upon the moisture content of the soil. In summer, 3 irrigations per month are necessary whereas, during the remaining period, it should be done as and when required, except in the rainy season when no irrigation is necessary. Altogether, about 12-154 irrigations a year are sufficient.

WEEDING

The first weeding is done one month after planting, and the second 4 weeks after the first. After this, no further weeding is required as the plants become bushy, thereby naturally suppressing the weeds.

INTERCULTURE

One hoeing, two months after planting, is sufficient. The crop may also be earthed-up at this stage.

DISEASES AND PESTS

The plant is susceptible to powdery mildew caused by *Oidium* spp., seedling blight caused by *Rhizoctonia solani* and root-rot caused by *Rhizoctonia bataticola.* Powdery mildew can be controlled by spraying wettable sulphur (4g/l of water), and the latter two diseases are managed by improved phytosanitary measures and by drenching the nursery-beds with a solution of mercurial fungicide.

Among the insects, the larvae of leaf-rollers sticking to the under-surface of the leaves fold them backwards length-wise, thus webbing them. Malathion (0.2%) may be sprayed to control this insect.

HARVESTING AND YIELD

The crop is harvested when it is in full bloom. The first harvest is obtained 90-95 days after planting. Afterwards, it may be harvested at every 65-75 days' intervals. Harvesting should be done on bright, sunny days in order to obtain good quality oil-yield. It is not desirable to harvest the crop if it has rained the previous day.

The crop should be cut 15-20 cm above ground-level. The harvested produce may be allowed to wilt on the field itself for 4-5 hours, to reduce the moisture content and the bulkiness.

About 5 t/ha of fresh herbage can be obtained twice or thrice a year.

DISTILLATION OF OIL

The harvested produce is usually distilled in its fresh form. However, the oil quality and yield do not diminish up to 6-8 hours after harvest, but any further delay may cause considerable loss in yield and quality of oil. Steam-distillation is found to be superior to water distillation. The whole herb contains 0.1 to 0.23% essential oil. The yield of oil varies with the type, season and place of origin. The oil-yield will be approximately 10-23 kg/ha.

46

Sandalwood

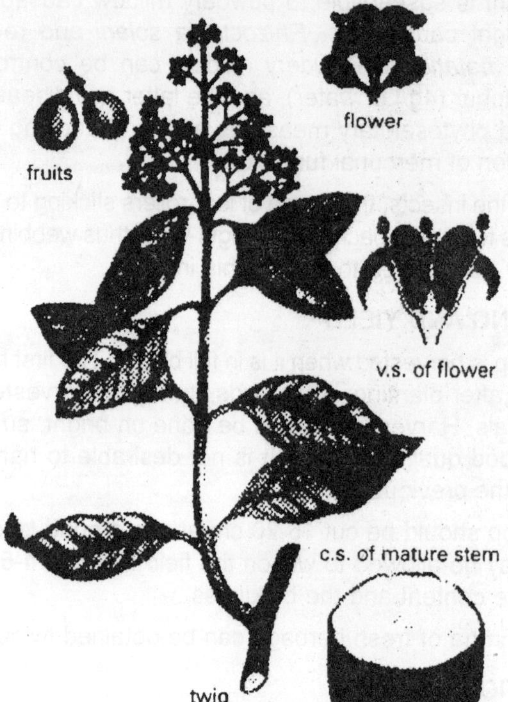

PLANT PROFILE

Family	:	*Santalaceae*
English name	:	Sandal tree, White-sandal tree
Indian name	:	Chandanah, *Srikhandam* (Sanskrit) *Safed Chandan*, *Santal* (Hindi) *Sreegandha* (Kannada), *Chandanam* (Tamil)

Species and varieties : *Santalum album L.*
S. acuminata, *S. lauolata*, *S. spicatum*
S. murrayana, *S. yassi*

Distribution : India, Australia, Indonesia, Malaysia, New Zealand, Polynesia

Uses : Carvings, Cosmetics, Drugs, Incense Perfumery, Soaps

The sandalwood tree belongs to the genus *Santalum* of the family *Santalaceae,* which comprises of shrubs and small trees distributed in South India, Indonesia, parts of Malaysia, Australia, New Zealand and Polynesia, extending up to the Hawaiian archipelago and it has also been introduced elsewhere. The trees are root parasites of grasses, herbs, shrubs or trees. The host specificity is unknown. The genus is represented by *S. album* L. (2n=20). In South India, both the wood and oil obtained from this species are used in increase, perfumes and medicine. Apart from this, it is used in carving. The tree is probably indigenous to India, but some believe it was introduced into India from Timor in Indonesia.

The natural traits of sandal trees are confined to Karnataka (90%) and Tamil Nadu. The most important sandal producing districts of Karnataka are Dharwad, Shimoga, Chickmagalur, Tumkur, Hassan, Coorg, Mysore, Kolar and Bangalore. In Tamil Nadu, this tree is found in Coimbatore, the Nilgiris, Madurai, Ramanathapuram, Kanyakumari, Salem and Vellore and to a small extent in Tirunelveli and Tiruchanapalli. In Kerala, sandal apparently grows wild and in Andhra Pradesh it found in Cudappah, Hyderabad, Kurnool, Chittoor and Ananthapur. It is also grown in Maharashtra and Orissa. Sandal has been naturalized in some parts of Rajasthan, Madhya Pradesh and Uttar Pradesh. It has been introduced in Bihar, Assam, Manipur and West Bengal as well.

The area covered by sandalwood trees in Karnataka is 1,25,000 ha. In Kerala it is negligible, in Andhra Pradesh an area of 1,100 ha is under sandalwood. The present production of sandalwood in our country is about 2,000 t, of which nearly three-fourths comes from Karnataka.

All over the world, sandalwood is used as a bass for the manufacture of perfumes and in cosmetics. The heartwood, found in the stem and the roots of the tree, is the valuable portion of the tree. The sapwood, also called white wood, is utilized only as firewood or, in some cases, for the manufacture of *agarbatthies*. The heartwood is also utilised for the purpose of carving. The heartwood is converted into chips and is used for the distillation of sandalwood oil. The oil content varies from 6-10%, depending on the age of the tree and the locality from where it is obtained. The oil contains about 90 different constituents with varying proportions. It contains sesquiterpenic alcohols (90%), hydrocarbons (6%) and other minor components. The alcohol fraction contains cis-alpha-santalol, cis-beta-santalol, trans-beta-santalaol and dihydro-epi-beta-santalol. Alpha-santalene, beta santalene and epibeta santalene are the hydro-carbons present The minor and trace components are aldehydes (tricyclo-eka-santalol, exonor bicyclo exa santalol, teresantalol), ketones (santalones), phenols, acids and heterocycles. The spicy odour of the oil is due to the minor constituents which include curcumene, fornescene, borneol, dihydro beta santalol, teresantalol, santenone, santalone and teresantalic acid, etc.

Sandalwood is exported to the USA, France, England, Hong Kong, Japan, Singapore, Sri Lanka, Malaysia, the Netherlands and Switzerland. Within the country, the main centres of utilization are Bombay, Calcutta, Delhi, Kannauj, Lucknow and Kanpur.

Sandalwood and its oil form an excellent medicine. In *Ayurveda,* it is treated as a cooling, exhilarating, elexitric, antipyretic, expectorant and stimulant. It is used as an astringent to the bowels and as an aphrodisiac. In *Unani* medicine, sandalwood dissipates the effect of the hot sun and fever and satiates thirst and leaves a cool and refreshing feeling. The wood, ground into paste, gives relief if applied on local inflammations, on boils, on the forehead in fevers and for skin diseases. Sandalwood decoction is given to ease defects of the genito-urinary tract. In migraines, sandal paste or oil (in dilute form) may be applied into the nostrils for relief.

DESCRIPTION OF THE PLANT

A small, erect, glabrous, evergreen tree occurring in fairly large groups. They are semiparasitic on the roots of other kinds of trees and is known as an obligatory root parasite. It can reach up to 16-18 m in height and 2.4 m in girth, with slender drooping branches. The leaves are opposite, 3.5-4 cm, elliptic to ovate, dark-green and exstipulate. The flowers are hermaphrodite, regular, occurring in small axillary or terminal compound cymes. The bracts are usually small, the stamens are four to five in number, the filaments are short, the ovary is semi-inferior, the ovules are 2-3 and pendulous. The style is elongated and the stigma is 2-3-lobed. The fruit is a drupe globose, 1.25 cm in diameter, black when ripe; the seeds retain their viability for about a year.

SPECIES' VARIETIES

The genus *Santalum* has 20 sandalwood-yielding species. Out of these, *S. album* is the most important. Some species furnish fragrant heartwoods, but yield wood and oil of a different kind and quality. The sandalwood from the species *S. album* is known as East Indian sandalwood in commerce and the oil as East Indian sandalwood oil. Some of the other species are: *S. acuminata, S. spicatum, S. lauolata, S. yassi,* and *S. murrayana.*

There are three recognized types of sandalwood in commerce:

1. Indian sandalwood from India.
2. East Indian sandalwood from the East Indies group of islands.
3. Pacific sandalwood from Australia and New Zealand.

SOILS

Sandal trees grow mainly on red ferrugineous loam, overlying metamorphic rocks, chiefly gneiss. They can tolerate shallow, rocky ground and stony or gravelly soils, voiding saline or calcareous soils, and are not exacting about the depth of the soil. It is not found on black soils. The growth is poor on rich and fairly moist soils such as well-drained alluvial soils and the heartwood in such trees will be deficient in oil. The trees grown on poor soils produce sandalwood giving a better yield of oil. However, they cannot withstand water-logging.

CLIMATE

The tree flourishes best between altitudes of 600 and 1050 m, though it may go up to 1350 m and descend as low as 360 m. The important sandal tracts lie in places where rainfall varies from 60-160 cm. The formation of the heartwood will be at its best at an altitude of 600 to 900 m and with a rainfall of 85-135 cm.

In general, the sandal tree flourishes in regions where the climate is cool with moderate rainfall, plentiful sunshine and long periods of dry weather. The ideal temperature for its growth is between 12° and 30°C.

PROPAGATION

Natural Regeneration

Most of the sandalwood is obtained from the natural forests, although small quantities are also obtained from plantations and trees grown in private fields. It reproduces plentifully from seeds dispersed by birds and also, to a certain extent, from suckers and coppices. Germination is profuse in the forests immediately after the monsoons, but the mortality of the seedlings is equally high due to excessive weed growth. The majority of the natural seedlings that come up on private holdings are destroyed during the normal agricultural operations, only a few located on margins, bunds and fencing survive. Some of the important resources for the natural regeneration of sandal trees include: (i) Maintenance of suitable hosts and avoiding undesirable host plants, (ii) Protection of seedlings in dry localities from damage by drought and sun-scorch, (iii) Careful attending of the suppressed trees, and (iv) Facility for free and natural expansion of the growth, right from the planting stage onwards.

Artificial Regeneration

Numerous large-scale plantations of sandal have been tried in Karnataka and Tamil Nadu but there have been many failures because of insufficient understanding of the host-parasite relationship, lack of protection from animals, spike disease, exposure to the sun and vandalism by man. The most favoured method of regeneration is by dibbling seeds. For processing seeds, the fruits are collected during January-March. The usual practice is to sweep the forest floor beneath selected mother-trees (plants over 20 years old) clean, and pack the slate-grey, dry, pebbly fruits in gunny bags. Germination of these seeds is up to 80% and there is no obligatory period of storage prior to germination. The seeds begin to lose viability after about 2 years. Just after the first monsoon showers, the sandal seeds are dibbled 4-5 in a batch under selected bushes, scattered over the entire area. The thorny bushes offer a measure of protection against the grazing of tender plants. It is advisable to coat the seeds with red lead to prevent rodent attack and it is better to mix sandal seeds with host seeds. The seed take about 40-90 days to germinate after sowing. They can remain without any host for haustorial connection for about a year. One kilogram contains 5,000 seeds.

Parasitism

The roots of sandalwood saplings attach themselves to the root of the host plant with the help of haustoria. It obtains its requirements of lime and potash from soil through its roots, while for N and P it depends upon the host. The hosts are classified as 'good' or 'poor' depending upon the number of host parasite connections. There are also instances of sandal parasitising on sandal itself.

Sandal grows well with hosts such as: *Acacia, Albizzia, Bambusa, Cassia, Erythrina, Erythroxylon, Gossypium, Pongamia, Semecarpus, Strychnos, Tectona, Thespesia, Vitex* and *Zixypus* in natural forests. Spike disease has been reported to be transmitted from hosts, such as *Lantana, Acanthaclous, Ocimum, Dedrocalamus, Dodonea, Vinca* and *Eucalyptus.*

CULTIVATION

Nursery Raising and Transplanting

In some areas where the sandal tree has to be raised on a small scale, the seedlings are raised in nursery-beds or in polythene bags (size: 15 cm × 25 cm), and then transplanted into the main field. For this purpose, fresh seeds from the October fruiting are collected and sown in well-prepared nursery-beds. The seedlings can also be raised in polybags by sowing 2-3 each of sandal and host plant seeds. Gibberellic acid has been found to be effective in bringing down the dormancy period and inducing quick and uniform germination. The plants can be thinned out after germination. The optimum stage for planting is when the seedlings are 25-50 cam in height and the basal portion becomes dark. One-month-old sandalwood seedlings are the optimum size for transplanting to obtain a higher percentage of survival. The area for planting is completely cleared. Pits of 30 cm^3 size are dug and the sandal seedlings along with the host seedlings are planted from May to October, at a spacing of 2.5 to 4 m.

AFTER-CARE

Weeding and soil working is done in the first year and, if necessary, in the second year also. In case the sandal seedlings are overtopped by the host plants, the host is tipped to provide enough light to the seedlings; climbers, if any, are cut and removed.

PLANT PROTECTION

Sandal is subject to only a few diseases, of which spike disease is the most destructive. This disease was first noticed in Coorg by Mc Carthy, in 1899. This has attracted attention because of the lethal nature of the disease and the consequent serious losses to the foreign exchange earnings occurring from sandalwood. It has spread over wide areas in the forests of Karnataka and Tamil Nadu. The disease with thought to be due to an unbalanced circulation of sap, due to nutritional deficiency and effect of association of sandal with unfavorable hosts, etc. From the graft transmissibility of the disease it was found to spread more rapidly by insects (jassids) than through haustoria. A considerable lowering of C/N ratio of the diseased leaves, served as an index of infection. The tissues of diseases sandal had high levels of starch and sugar.

The disease is also reported to have been caused by *Mycoplasma*-like organisms (MLO), which are found in the sieve tubes of the spikes of infected leaves and twigs. The most characteristic symptoms of the diseases are the severe reduction in leaf-size and shortening of the internodes of affected branches, accompanied by the suppression of the reproductive phase in the spiked branch. The colour of the leaf turns yellow and finally reddish, shortly before death. The disease causes the death of root-ends and haustorial connections. There is also a reduction in the size of the chromosomes. The disease is transmitted by insect vectors like leaf-hoppers and *Niphotetex virescence.*

An intensive survey has been done on the histological, chemical, physiological and silvicultural aspects of the healthy and diseased sandal plants. Diagnostic characters and modes of disease control measures and curative methods have also been studied. The presence of intracellular bodies associated with the nucleus of cells, the necrosis of phloem, the accumulation of starch and the imbalance of nitrogen metabolite are the features of the diseased cell. No definite cure for sandal spike has been discovered so far. The only control measure suggested, is as follows.

CONTROL

Evidence exists that tetracyclines are effective in the suppression of symptoms, accompanied by the disappearance of the mycoplasma-like organisms from phloem. Unfortunately, the tetracyclines cannot completely eradicate the disease. The application of tetramycin or ledermycine, either along or in combination with Benlate, to diseased sandal plants brought recovery within 25-30 days. However, the recovery lasted only for 120-125 days.

The other diseases of sandal include seedling diseases incited by *Phytophthora* spp. and *Helicotylenchus indicus,* also cause considerable damage to the sandal seedlings. A number of leaf-spot diseases caused by *Ascochyta santali, Microphomina phaseoli, Asterina congesta* and *Sphaecelomia santali* have been reported. The stored logs are also subjected to certain diseases. Deficiency diseases due to trace elements have also been noticed in sandal.

HARVESTING AND YIELD

The tree comes into flush twice in the year, once before the onset of the monsoon and once after. It starts flowering from an early age of 3-4 years, but good seeds can be obtained only when they are 20 years old. The flowering season lasts from February to April, while fruiting takes place between July–September.

In sandal, the sapwood and heartwood are clearly demarcated. The heartwood is the most valuable portion. The roots are also scented. The sandal is, therefore, harvested by uprooting and not by cutting. The formation of heartwood commences when the tree is about 20 years old and it continues for the life of the tree. The heartwood formation is maximum when the trees are between 30 and 69 years old, and have attained a girth of 40-60 cm. The trees with a girth of 60 cm or above are harvested during the post-monsoon period. After uprooting, the trees are cut into billets and dressing and removal or sapwood is done in the depot. Commercial transaction of sandalwood is done by weight and not by volume, and an annual drainage of 2% of the gross weight of the good wood and 5% of the rough wood is allowed.

The yield of heartwood varies from locality to locality and the age of the tree. Trees with a girth of 50-60 cm yield 195 kg/tree of heartwood in North Coimbatore, 38.0 kg in Salem and 217 kg in Karnataka (Sirsi). A tree of 100 cm girth will yield 88 kg in North Coimbatore, 144 kg in Salem and 84.4 kg in Karnataka (Sirsi). The annual production in Karnataka ranges from 200-300 t.

DISTILLATION AND EXTRACTION TECHNIQUES

Sandal oil can be prepared by using different methods of extraction. More than 90% of the present production of oil comes from factories employing the modern steam-distillation method, where the sandalwood is converted into smaller pieces by a motor-driven axe and then fed in to a chipping machine consisting of a rapidly rotating disc on which six knives are mounted. The coarse powder is fed to disintegrators where it is turned into a fine powder (Balloon dust). The powder is sieved to get sandal dust of 12 to 36 mm mesh and then charged into copper or stainless steel stills of 1 t capacity. Steam is bubbled up at the base under a pressure of 30-40 Psi (low-pressure steam) for 100-120 hours. Although the use of high pressure steam helps in obtaining a higher yield of oil, the odour gets affected due to decomposition or polymerization of some constituents. The crude oil floating on the surface of the distillate (collected in florentine receivers) is skimmed off and filtered. This crude oil, as such, is used by attar manufacturers. Further refining of crude oil is done, first by distillation with super-heated steam and then by heating the oil in a steam-jacketed vacuum still; thereby, sandal oil gets decolourized. Distillation is always done in the composite manner of charging both superior class heartwood (root, stem or trunk portions) and inferior class mixed wood (chips, shavings), in order to obtain homogeneity in the final product which is a pale yellow, optically clear oil in yield (4.5 to 25%) and having characteristics conforming to ISI specifications and this ensures the standard quality for export.

In the water-distillation method, which is followed in small production units, sandal powder is soaked in water for 48 hours in a copper vessel and then heated on an open fire. The vapours are conducted through a copper pipe to receivers kept in cold water. The floating oil is ladled off, refined by filtration and decantation methods. The yield of oil by this method is about 4.5% with a finer note (empyreumatic). The acid value and specific gravity were noticed to be slightly higher for this oil.

Important sandal oil distillers are located at Mysore, Shimoga (Karnataka), Kuppam (Andhra Pradesh), Mettur, Salem, Tekkapattu and Tiruvannamalai (Tamil Nadu), Mumbai (Maharashtra), Kannauj and Kanpur (Uttar Pradesh) Several smaller units exits in Kerala.

About 15% of the oil (based on the oil content of samples, is left undistilled in the interstices of the wood, in spite of prolonged distillation. This method actually suffers from losses due to the hydro-solubility of some polar constituents. High boiling fragrant principles need large amounts of stem to volatilize. Also, the close-grained structure of the wood and the low volatility of oil makes the distillation process rather slow. Hence, solvent extraction methods have to be resorted to. Finely comminuted wood can be extracted using a hydrocarbon or oxyenated solvent to secure the concrete, which may be processed further by high vacuum-distillation. For this purpose, the solvent used should be of low cost, high purity and economically recoverable.

By resorting to nardenization (which is a separation of terpenic components by shaking with two immiscile solvents; 95% methanol and hexane), methanol solubles prepared from benzene extract of sandal powder upon decolourization in acetone with activated charcoal, give santalol-rich sandal oil.

Through a rectification process (intended to free the odoriferous components from the by-notes) using the property that one volume of sandal oil goes into solution in five volumes of 70% alcohol, the benzene extract of sandal powder gives a slightly higher yield of sandal oil. The addition of polyethylene glycol 200 (PEG 200) to solvent-extracted concretes of sandal powder before the steam- or vacuum-distillation state, has provided 15% more oil than that obtained from the direct steam-distillation process. Steam-distillation in the presence of PEG 200 of acetone extract is particularly effective in recovering almost all the sandal oil from the sandal material.

A new extraction process has been attempted using liquid and dense carbon-dioxide, recently. It is found tat compressed carbon-dioxide (a clean, cheap, non-reactive, non-toxic, non-pollutant, solvent medium) is quite suitable for the preparation of sandal extract (concrete) from sandal powder.

ADULTERANTS

The oil of *Erythroxylon monogynum,* cedarwood oil, araucaria oil, guaiac wood oil, copaiba balsam oil, gurjan balsam oil, castor oil odourless organic solvents and chemicals such as liquid paraffin, glyceryl acetate, diethylphthalate, benzyl alcohol and benzyl benzoate are used to adulterate sandal oil.

In USA and Europe, a synthetic organic product, a polycyclic alcohol called 'Sandela' is available. The company Firminish et Cie, Geneva, manufactures 'Sandalidol'. These products are cheaper than natural sandalwood oil.

OTHER SOURCES OF SANDALWOOD OIL

In Australia, a substitute oil is extracted from the wood of *fusanus spicatus* and *F. acuminatus.* But this oil does not possess the woody and persistent odour so characteristic of sandalwood oil. Again, in the West Indies, an oil is extracted from a similar wood called *Amyris balsamifera* L. (*Rubiaceae)* and in East Africa from *Osyris tenuifolia* Engl. (*Santalaceae*), which is a bush.

47

Sweet Marjoram

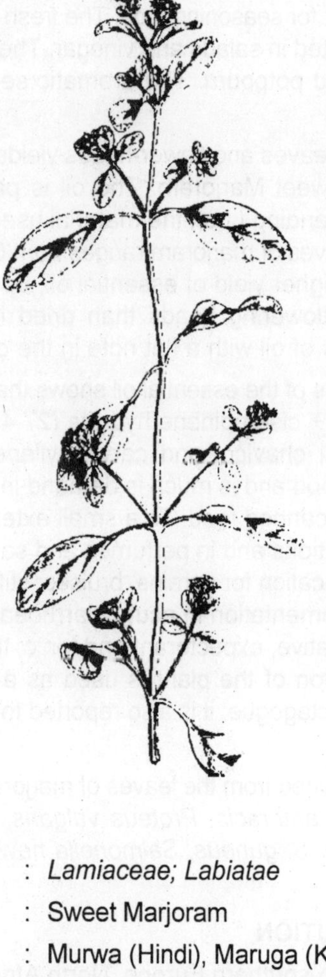

PLANT PROFILE

Family	:	*Lamiaceae; Labiatae*
English name	:	Sweet Marjoram
Indian name	:	Murwa (Hindi), Maruga (Kannada) Maruvu, Marukkolundn (Tamil)

Species and varieties : *Kanorana hortensis* Moench.

Distribution : India, North Africa, North and South America, Asia Minor, Southern Europe, France, Germany

Uses : Confectionery, Cooking, Drugs, Flavouring Perfumery, Potpourri

Marjoram (*Majorana hortensis* Moench.) is an aromatic, perennial, herbaceous plant belonging to the family *Lamiaceae.* The plant has been used as a flavouring and herb spice from time immemorial. Fresh sprigs of this plant are also used to flavour garlands, bouquets and for hair adornment. Traditionally, the leaves of the plant are used fresh or dried and are highly esteemed as a condiment for seasoning food. The fresh leaves are employed as garnish and incorporated in salads and vinegar. The dried flowering-tops are used for sachets and potpourri. The aromatic seeds also find use in confectionery.

Steam-distillation of leaves and flower-heads yields a volatile oil, known in the trade as Oil of Sweet Marjoram. The oil is pale-yellow to yellow-green or colourless, depending upon the material used for distillation. The oil content in the fresh leaves of marjoram ranges from 0.3 to 0.5%. Although the dried plant gives a higher yield of essential oil, up to 1%, it is better to distil fresh leaves and flowering heads than dried herbage as there is possibility of lower yields of oil with a flat note in the case of dried leaves.

The chemical analysis of the essential oil shows that it contains terpene-4-01 (28.973%), linalool + cis-sabinene hydrate (27.404%), linalyl acetate (4.972%), alpha terpinol chavicol and caryophyllene. The oil is mainly employed in flavouring food and is much is demand in the food processing industries for flavouring canned food. To a small extent, it is used in high-grade flavouring preparations and in perfumes and soaps. Medicinally, it is used as an external application for sprains, bruises, stiff and paralytic limbs, toothache, and for hot fomentation in acute diarrhoea. Sweet marjoram is considered to be carminative, expectorant and tonic; the leaves and seeds are astringent. An infusion of the plant is used as a stimulant, sudorific, emmenagogue and galactagogue; it is also reported to be useful in asthma, hysteria and paralysis.

The essential oil obtained from the leaves of marjoram has anti-microbial activity against *Bacillus anthracis, Proteus vulgaris, Salmonella stanley, Streptococus agalactiae, S. guneus, Salmonella newport* and *Aspergillus fumigatus.*

ORIGIN AND DISTRIBUTION

The plant is native to southern Europe, North Africa and Asia Minor. It is an important kitchen herb with a wide range of uses and it is cultivated throughout Europe and the Mediterranean region as Well as North and South America. France and Egypt are the biggest exporters of marjoram oil in the world. The USA alone consumes about 300-400 t/annum of marjoram oil, but France and Germany have larger markets with a requirement of over 500 t/annum. In India, this crop is cultivated only on a small scale in several states. It is being grown in home-gardens in Karnataka, Andhra Pradesh and Tamil Nadu.

DESCRIPTION OF THE PLANT

Sweet marjoram is a perennial plant which is often grown as an annual, because it does not survive well in wet, cold winters. It grows into an upright, compact bush about 20 to 40 cm height, with a woody main stem and many softer branches. The leaves are round, soft, matte green with a marvellous, sweet smell. In the bud, the flower-heads (spicules) are the same grey-green colour as the leaves and are like little, oval knobs. These expand slightly to show the frill of tiny, white flowers only just protruding from their overlapping bracts. The flowers are bracteate, sessile, complete and bisexual; both the calyx and corolla are irregular, zygomorphic and hypogyrnous. The bract is prominent, spatulate, 4 mm in diameter, hairy along the margin and on the abaxial surface it encloses the calyx. The calyx has five sepals, united to form a single spatulate structure, with wide and large (5 mm in diameter), bilobed anterior and narrow, small posterior parts. The corolla has five petals, .is gamopetalous, biolobed with 3 petals (osterior) and 2 petals (anterior) and has imbricate aestivation. The corolla tube is 4 mm long and 5 mm in diameter. It is white in colour, is wider (2 mm) above and narrow (1 mm) below, each limb measuring 1.5 to 2.0 mm. There are 4 stamens which are epipetalous didynamous, the anterior shorter (3 mm) than the posterior (4 mm) ones. The staminode is absent. The anthers are two-celled, dehiscing by a longitudinal slit, hypogynous and the disc is fleshy. The ovary is superior, bicarpellarcy, syncarpous, four-partite by a secondary division, with a single anatropous erect basal ovule attached to an axile placenta in each locule; the style is gynobasic (5 mm long), and simple with a bifid stigma. The fruit has 1-4 seeded nutlets, included within the persistent calyx The seed is brown and oblong 3 mm long and 1 mm wide; the testa is thin; the endosperm is scanty; the embryo has flat cotyledons parallel to the fruit axis and a short, inferior radical.

SOIL

Marjoram prefers a well-drained and nutrient rich soil for its successful growth. Soils which have a tendency to form crusts will retard germination greatly and hence are not suitable for marjoram, unlike most other herbs from the same family. Marjoram has a strong flavour when grown in a rich soil. It is one of the few crops which can be grown even on saline or alkaline soil as well, and can withstand high salinity in the soil. The plants resist drought, but prolonged period of drought are harmful.

CLIMATE

Marjoram is primarily a warm season plant and, as such, rather sensitive to cold. Yet, it is hardy enough to grow in colder region, provided the plants are well mulched with straw or leaves for protection against winter-killing or still better, grown as an annual crop and planted a new each season. It requires a sunny position, though mid-day shade is preferred.

SEASON

The planting time is one of the important factors in obtaining optimum yields from each unit area. Under Bangalore conditions, November planting is found is found to be the best with respect to growth and yield.

CULTIVATION

Propagation

(i) Nursery Raising

Marjoram can be propagated by seeds. The seeds can be sown twice a year, during June-July and September-October. They are sown in well-prepared nursery beds, in rows spaced at about 15 cm apart. About 50 g of seeds give seedlings sufficient to plant one hectare of land. As the seeds are tiny, they are mixed with dry sand in the ratio of 1:10 and broadcasted in rows of neatly prepared nursery-beds. A thin layer of sand is spread uniformly over the seeds to cover them. The seeds germinate after 8-10 days. Sprinkler irrigation and thorough after-care of seedlings must be taken after germination. The seedlings are ready for transplanting when they are about 2 months old.

As this method is rather cumbersome and the initial growth of the seedlings is slow, it is followed only where it is absolutely necessary.

(ii) Vegetative Propagation

Sweet marjoram is commercially propagated through cuttings. The plants, thus propagated, are not only true to type but also grow faster initially. Stem-cuttings obtained from the second ratoon-crop are the best for planting; herbaceous cuttings of 15 cm length are taken from healthy plants. Seed-pans filled with sand may be used for planting the cuttings. After planting, they should be transferred to a mist propagation chamber or into the shade, where they are watered twice a day. The cuttings take about one month to root. Individual polythene bags of small size may also be used to raise the cuttings. In this method, the roots do not get damaged during transplanting. The establishment rate of rooted cuttings in the main field is about 90-95%.

PLANTING

Only healthy seedlings or rooted cuttings with well-developed root-systems are transplanted into the main field, at a spacing of 15 cm × 7.5 cm.

FERTILIZER APPLICATION

In an experiment in Bangalore, it was found that the application of N at 240 kg/ha, P at 40 kg/ha and K at 80 kg/ha in three equal split doses, give the maximum herbage and oil-yield in marjoram.

USE OF GROWTH REGULATORS

Studies conducted at Bangalore revealed that the application of GA_3 at 200 ppm increased the fresh herb recovery, recording the maximum oil-yield (0.39% oil content and 55.54 kg/ha of oil-yield). Although Cycocel at 500 ppm and Triacontanol at 6 ppm increased the fresh herb recovery and oil-yield over the control, it was not as much as GA_3.

IRRIGATION AND INTERCULTURE

After transplanting, the crop is irrigated by a sprinkler for 5-6 days and then a light surface irrigation is given. Subsequently, the crop may be irrigated once in 4–8 days, depending upon the season and the soil type. The crop is weeded as an when required, followed by hoeing, to provide good aeration to soil.

CROP ROTATION/SEQUENCING AND INTERCROPS

In many places, sweet marjoram is essentially a short-term winter crop. Of the several possibilities of crop rotation, the raising of coriander, cumin and fnugreek are promising. These crops can be grown as monsoon crops. After their harvest, the land is rested for three months and then it can be planted with marjoram.

INSECT PESTS AND DISEASES

Marjoram is a comparatively hardy crop and no serious pest or disease has been reported on this crop in India. Among the insects, it is sometimes attacked by termites, which may be controlled by the application of Termex 20% EC. With regard to the diseases, some times leaf-rust disease is found to affect the plants particularly during cloudy weather. It can be easily controlled by spraying 0.2% Blitox at weekly intervals.

HARVESTING

Under Bangalore conditions, the crop behaves as perennial. The first harvesting is done after 90 days of planting, when the crop starts flowering. While harvesting, about 10 m of the shoot above the ground-level is left for further growth. The subsequent harvests can be carried out after 45 days of the first harvest. On an average, about 4-5 harvests are taken annually. Also, there are reports that the crop can be retained for up to seven cuttings under good management. After every harvest, a top-dressing of nitrogenous fertilizers, preferably urea, is applied. To obtain oil of export quality, the first harvesting should be done only 90 days after planting.

YIELD

Marjoram may yield about 16-18 t/ha of fresh herbage which, in turn, may yield about 35-40 kg marjoram oil on stream-distillation. An oil recovery of 0.3 to 0.4% on a fresh-weight basis may be considered satisfactory.

PRODUCTION OF ESSENTIAL OIL

The fresh herbage is steam-distilled to obtain the oil. The distillation equipment consists of a boiler, a distillation still, a condenser and a receiver. The still is made of steel. It has a perforated metal sheet at the bottom to support the herbage which is loaded into the still.

Loading and unloading can be mechanized with the help of an overhead chain-pulley block. The lid of the still can be swung aside during loading and unloading. It is important that the herbage is evenly packed inside the still, as otherwise steam channels may form during the distillation and result in poor oil-yield. The condenser, which cools the hot vapour received from the still, consists of many tubes made of copper or stainless steel and mounted inside a jacket.

The condenser is provided with an inlet and outlet for the circulation of cooling water. The hot vapours are cooled in the condenser tubes and the condensate flows out into the receiver. The oil, being lighter than water and insoluble, floats on the top in the receiver and only the water gets drained out. The oil can be drawn off separately at the end of the distillation process. The receiver is fabricated into two compartments, so that any oil escaping from the first compartment can be retained in the adjoining compartment, although this rarely happens.

Distillation is carried out at atmospheric pressure, as this will prevent any sort of burnt odour in the oil. Usually, about 4-5 hours are required for completing one distillation. The oil should be free from sediment, suspended matter and moisture before storing it in aluminum containers. The containers should be filled to the brim to exclude all air, in order to prevent deterioration of the oil during storage.

48

Thyme

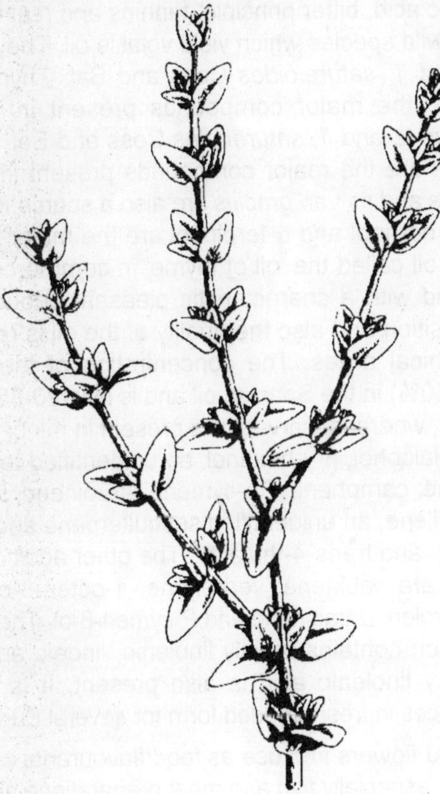

PLANT PROFILE

Family	:	*Lamiaceae; Labiatae*
English name	:	Thyme
Indian name	:	*Banajwain* (Hindi), *Thyme* (Kannada)
Species and varieties	:	*Thymus vulgaris Linn.*
		T. satureioides Coss, *T. serpyllum* L.
		T. zygus L.

Distribution : India, Asia, Australia, Canada, Europe, France, Germany, Greece, Italy, Morocco, Spain, USA

Uses : Cosmetics, Culinary purposes, Drugs, Insecticides, Perfumery

Thyme (*Thymus vulgaris* Linn.) commonly called 'Common Thyme' or 'Garden Thyme', belonging to the family *Lamiaceae; Labiatae,* is an important herb used by man since ancient times. On distillation, the herb yields the Red Thyme Oil of commerce. Apart from the oil the other constituents of thy me are triterpinoid saponins, flavones, ursolic acid (1.5% in the tops), caffeic acid, bitter principle, tannins and resins. Besides, there are several other wild species which yield volatile oil. They are *T. serpyllum* L., *T. zygus* L. and *T. satureioides* Coss and Bal. Thymol. Linalool and linalyl acetate are the major compounds present in *T. zygus* and *T. serpyllum. T. zygus* L. and *T. satureiodes* Coss and Bal. Thymol. Linalool and linalyl acetate are the major compounds present in *T. zygus* and *T. serpyllum. T. zygus* and its var. *gracitis* are also a source for genuine thyme oil, while thymol, borneol and α-terpineol are the major compounds in *T. satureioides.* The oil called the 'oil of thyme' in commerce is a colourless, yellow or red liquid with a characteristic pleasant odour, and a pungent taste. The composition and also the quality of the oil is reported to vary in different geographical areas. The concentration of the active principle (Thymol) is high (60%) in the Spanish oil and is low (20-35%) in the French and Moroccan oils, whereas, carvacrol is present in minor amounts. The oil also contains amylalcohol, β-y-hexanol, an unidentified terpene with carrot like odour, β-pinene, camphene, Po-cymene r-terpinene, linalool, l-borneol, geraniol, caryophyllene, an unidentified sesquiterpene and a sesquiterpinic alcohol, 4-terpineol and trans-4-thujanol. The other additional components present in traces are sabinene, verbenene, 1-octen-3-ol, methyl thymol verbenone, α-muurolen, α-cadinene and P-cymen-8-ol. The seeds yield 37% of a drying oil which contains mainly linolenic, lindeic and oleic acids. In addition, α-hydroxy linolenic acid is also present. It is one of the very frequently used spices in fresh or dried form for several European delicacies.

The leaves and flowers find use as food flavourants and seasoning for various food items, especially fish and meat preparations and for garnishing. Medicinally, the leaves are said to possess laxative, stomachic and tonic properties, good for the kidney and eye and are blood purifiers. The herb also has insect-repellent property. It is used in perfumery and in liquor distillery as well. The dried leaves and floral tops constituting the thyme of commerce are known as Thymi Herba in pharmacy and contain not more than 3% of stems over 1 mm in diameter and 2% of other organic matter and yields 4% acid-insoluble ash. The shoot-extracts of flowering thyme plants have antibacterial action against *Micrococcs pyogenes* var. *aureus* and *Escherichia coli.* The herb which has a pungent taste is reported to possess antiseptic, antihelmentic, expectorant, carminative, diuretic, alexiteric, emmenagogue and sedative properties; good in liver complaints, for pain in the spleen, liver or chest; useful in cold, asthma and bronchitis. It also thins the phlegm and blood.

Thyme soil has antiseptic, antispasmodic and carminative properties. It is used in mouthwashes and gargled. Formulations containing thyme oil are available for the treatment of whooping cough and bronchitis. The oil is used as a diffusible stimulant. It is mixed with olive oil and is used as a rubefacient and counter-irritant. It is also used in veterinary medicine. Thyme oil is used in soaps, perfumes and for flavouring food products such as meat, sausages, sauces and canned food. The oil is used as an intestinal antiseptic for treating hookworms and as a cure for many fungal infections of the skin. The seeds are given as a vermifuge. The infusion of the seeds is also used in skin eruptions or diseases. The seed-oil has a potential use as a superior drying oil. The plant can be grown as an ornamental edging along paths in gardens, and is also suitable for rockeries.

DISTRIBUTION AND PRODUCTION

Thyme grows wild in almost all the countries bordering the Mediterranean and also over much of Asia and in parts of Central Europe and it grows best in the hills. It is found in the western temperate Himalayas, from Kashmir to Kumaon between altitudes of 1525 m and 4000 m. Thyme is grown in Europe, Australia and North Asia. It is now cultivated in France, Germany, Spain, Italy, Greece and North Africa, Canada and the USA as well.

Among the countries producing thyme oil, Spain stands first followed by France, Morocco and the Mediterranean countries. The bulk of the world demand for thyme oil is met by Spain and Turkey.

DESCRIPTION OF THE PLANT

T. vulgaris is a low, evergreen, perennial undershrub reaching a height of 20-30 cm whereas, wild thyme (*T. serpyllum* L.) creeps on the soil surface and has broad leaves with a weaker odour. The roots are fairly robust and the stems are branched. The former has oblong-lanceolate, sessile leaves 10 mm × 3 mm in size with orange-brown, glandular dots and is coriaceous. The young leaves are slightly woolly. The flowers are small, purplish or bluish to almost white, united in spikes at the tips of the branches and have a bilabiate, tube-like calyx and a bilabiate, tubular corolla with a 3-lobed lower lip. The fruit is a nutlet, brown, 4-sectioned, smooth and is found in the remains of the calyx. The entire plant is aromatic.

SOIL

The plant prefers a light but fertile and calcareous soil for good growth and oil content. On heavy, wet soils the aroma of the leaves will be less and there are chances that the plants may soon dry up.

CLIMATE

A warm climate is best suited for this crop. It can be growth both in the hills and on the plains. Hilly regions are best suited for its cultivation. However, the plants are susceptible to frost.

SEASON

The seeds may be sown in the nursery in April. Late summer is the time for transplanting the seedlings or for planting the rooted cuttings.

LAND PREPARATION

The land is prepared well by repeated ploughing or digging and brought to a fine tilth and divided into plots of convenient size.

CULTIVATION

Propagation

Thyme can be propagated by seeds and vegetatively by the division of old plants, or by cuttings, or by the layering of side-shoots in March or April. The seeds are sown directly in rows or in well-prepared nursery beds in good soils. Fine soil is preferred for the nursery, because the seedlings are very small and remain inconspicuous for several weeks after germination.

SOWING/PLANTING

When the seeds are sown directly, they can be sown in rows 90 cm apart and, later, when the seeds germinate, the seedlings may be thinned out to 30-45 cm within the rows. While planting the seedlings or rooted cuttings or layers, they are planted 30-45 cm apart in rows, 60 cm apart. A light irrigation is provided after planting.

MANURES AND FERTILIZERS

No information is available on the use of manures and fertilizers except that a light dressing of FYM in the autumn, and an additional dressing of nitrogen in the spring can be applied. This promotes the formation of numerous leafy shoots.

IRRIGATION

No information is available on this aspect also. But, since the crop is planted late in summer, it requires frequent irrigations during the dry period.

INTERCULTURE

Interculture operations and weeding are done at regular intervals to encourage the good growth of plants. In the hills, mulching helps to avoid frost injury to the plants during the winter.

PESTS AND DISEASES

The plant is not damaged by any pests of serious nature, but wilt disease is a major problem in this crop. The disease can be controlled by improving the phytosanitation and by drenching the soil with a suitable fungicide like Blotox or Dithane M-45 at 0.3% concentration.

HARVESTING AND YIELD

The leaves and flowers which are used for culinary and medicinal purposes are harvested five months after sowing/planting. The leaves and flowers are plucked from the plants or shoots of about 15 cm are cut off from the plants, dried in the shade or in a dryer immediately after harvest and stored in airtight containers to prevent the loss of flavour. The dried leaves are curled, brownish-green in colour, usually not longer than 6-7 mm. The dried shoots may also be powdered and packed. Under favourable conditions, the yield of dry herb is around 1100-2200 kg/ha. The yield is comparatively low during the first year. The plants become woody which necessitates their replanting after three or four years. For yield is comparatively low during the first year. The plants become woody which necessitates their replanting after three or four years. For extracting the oil, the fresh herb is collected, on dry days, at the stage when it just starts flowering. At the time of collection, the lower portions of the stem, along with any yellow or brown leaves, should be rejected.

DISTILLATION OF OIL AND OIL-YIELD

The oil is distilled from the fresh flowering-tops by steam-distillation. The herb contains about 2% essential oil and the total oil recovered by distillation is about 21 kg/ha.

49

Annatto

PLANT PROFILE

Family : *Bixaceae*

English name : Arnotta plant, Annatto plant

Indian name : *Sinduri* (Sanskrit) *Sinduriya Latkan* (Hindi), *Rangmale* (Kannada) *Sappira virai*, *Uragu-manjal* (Tamil)

Species and varieties : *Bixa orellana* Linn.

Distribution : India, the Antilles, America, Brazil, Guiana, Mexico, West Indies

Uses : Chemical ink, Coating medicines, Drugs, Dyeing Food colouring, Hair oils, Polishes, Poultry feed

Annatto is a natural carotenoid obtained from *Bixa orellana* Linn., a shrub belonging to the family *Bixaceae.* In India it is called Rangmale, Latkan, Japhra or Sandri. The seeds of this plant are gaining economic importance in recent years as a highly desirable colourant. The ripe fruits of annatto, on drying, yield annatto seeds which serve as a raw material for the production of annatto colour. The seed-coat consists mostly of carotenoid dyes (about 2%) and an essential oil. Bixin (10-30%), which is the principal colouring matter present in seeds along with small amounts of 'Orellin' a water soluble yellow substance, fat, resin and a bitter stuff. Besides, Ishwarane, a tetracyclic sesquiterpene, has been isolated from the leaf-oil. In addition to Ishwarane, a few sesquiterpenes, monoterpenes, leucocynidin, ellagic acid and three new flavone bisulphates identified as 7-bisulphates of apigenin, luteolin and 8-bisulphate of hypolactin (1-OH luteofin) also occur in the leaves. The roots yield tomentosic acid. The annatto dye is non-toxic and is mainly use for colouring edible materials like butter, ghee, other milk products, chocolate and cosmetics. It neither affects the colour nor the aroma of the concentrates drinks, vienna sausages and candies. A process for colouring salmon fish has also been reported. A yellow, transparent, water-soluble ink is prepared from the dye. The dye is used as an adsorption indicator in argentometric titrations. Coloured coating materials have been made using annatto and cellulose acetate phthalate and the same is used in coating tablets, pills and granules. The addition of annatto seed-meal to poultry feed is reported to deepen the colour of the egg-yolk and also the flesh pigmentation. Annatto dye is also used in flour polishes, shoe polishes and hair oils.

ORIGIN AND DISTRIBUTION

The plant is native of tropical America and the West Indies and has been naturalized in India. It is cultivated in Brazil, Guiana, Mexico and the Antilles. In India, he annatto plant is found in Karnataka, Tamil Nadu, Andhra Pradesh, Orissa, Maharashtra, West Bengal and Assam. Since this plant is not grown on a commercial plantation-scale in India, the production and trade statistics for this commodity are not available. However, India exports annatto seeds to Russia. It is grown as a hedge-plant or a roadside tree in many places.

DESCRIPTION OF THE PLANT

Annatto is a shrub or small tree which grows to about 5 m high; the leaves are cordate, stalked, acuminate, sometimes with reddish veins; the lamina is 8-24 cm × 5-15 cm, the flowers are about 6 cm in diameter and occur in terminal, erect panicles; the sepals are 5, deciduous; and there are 5 petals.

This species occurs in two forms, one with white flowers and green capsules and the other with pink flowers and red capsules. The capsule is heart-shaped, about 5 cm long, covered with soft spines, 2-valved; the seeds are numerous, about 5 mm in diameter with a thin, pulpy, vermilion skin.

SOIL

It is a hardy tree and does not require very fertile soils for its cultivation. An average soil which has some moisture-retaining capacity is suitable for the cultivation of this crop. Any soil which has poor drainage and rocks in the subsoil should be avoided.

CLIMATE

Annatto is a tropical plant. It can be grown successfully in a warm, dry climate. It cannot withstand frost.

SEASON

The best time for raising the nursery is during the months of April and May. One-year-old, healthy seedlings can be planted in the main field at the onset of the rains.

LAND PREPARATION

The land is levelled and prepared well before planting. Later, pits of 30 cm × 30 cm × 30 cm size are dug in early March at a spacing of 4.5 m × 4.5 m. The pits are filled before the onset of the monsoon with a mixture of soil, compost and fertilizers.

CULTIVATION

Propagation

The plant can be propagated by seeds or vegetatively through mature stem-cuttings. Generally, the seedlings are raised in polythene bags containing a mixture of soil, manure and fertilizers. The seeds (1-2/bag) are sown at the centre of the polythene bag and the bags are watered regularly. The seeds germinate in 8-10 days and only one seedling is grown in each bag. The seedlings can be transplanted when they are about 20 cm tall.

PLANTING

The seedlings are planted at the centre of the pit and the pits are watered immediately after planting. At the spacing recommended above, about 500 seedlings can be planted in a 1 ha area.

AFTER-CARE

The weeds are removed around the plants in the pits as and when they appear. Light digging in the pits is also done after every weeding to encourage good growth of plants.

The plants start flowering in the first to second year after planting. To encourage good vegetative growth and for better performance of the plantation in subsequent years, the flowers are plucked off in the first two years.

PESTS AND DISEASES

The plant is very hardy in nature and is not attacked by any pests or diseases of a serious nature.

FLOWERING, FRUITING AND HARVESTING

The plants start bearing fruits after 3 years of planting and continue to give economic yields up to the age of 8 to 10 years under good management. The flowering season and also the habits are reported to differ from the hills to the plains and the forms of the species. Generally, the plants flower in the last week of August and the flowering continues p to the middle of October. In about 30 days, the flowering capsules are borne on the trees and after 90 days appear in the form of capsules. The capsules will mature and dry up in January. The dried capsules make a rattling sound. Another indication for harvesting the capsules is the formation of a crack at the stigmatic end of the capsule. The capsules should be harvested at this stage. If the capsules are allowed to burst, there is a heavy loss of seeds. After harvesting the panicles, they are packed in gunny bags which are kept closed for some days. Later, they are taken out and exposed to the sun. The seeds are separated from the dried capsules by beating them with sticks. The seeds are sun-dried, cleaned and packed in gunny bags before they are marketed.

YIELD

A 3-year-old plant will yield, on a average, ½ kg of seeds and 1 kg/ tree/year thereafter up to the 10 years of age. The seed-yield from a 1 ha plantation will be around 250 kg from a 3-year-old and 500 kg from a 4- to 10-year-old plantation.

EXTRACTION OF DYE (ANNATTO COLOUR)

Several methods have been described and patented for the extraction of crude annatto colour and bixin from the seed. One such process of extraction is by the counter-current method, using water during simultaneous mechanical friction of the seed surface. Finally, the suspension is evaporated in a vacuum and subsequently dried and ground to a fine power.

The other method of extraction involves the treatment of seeds with vegetable oil, with or without heating the mixture and also treating the seeds after swelling them in water or in steam. Another method of extraction is by boiling the seeds with sodium carbonate solution, filtering and acidifying the filtrate. Later, the dye is coagulated by boiling it with common salt, after which it is filter-pressed, washed and dried. In India, a better colour is manufactured by heating the seeds under pressure and then extracting the dye with a vegetable oil, preferably castor oil. It has been observed that the pre-treatment of seeds is not required for extraction by this method.

Bixin can be separated from the seed by boiling the seed with ethyl acetate or acetone or alcohol or chloroform. Bixin can be held in alcohol solution at a pH of 4.5 for one hour before spray-drying. The commercial cheese-colour is an alkaline solution and contains norbixin in place of bixin. It is extracted by using dilute sodium or potassium hydrochloride.

The stabilization of the annatto food colour is done by the addition of curcumin, vanillin, eugenol or vitamin-E.

50

Camphor Basil

PLANT PROFILE

Family	: *Lamiaceae; Labiatae*
English name	: Camphor Basil
Indian name	: *Karpuratulasi* (Sanskrit), *Kapurtulsi* (Hindi), *Karpura Tulasi* (Kannada), *Karpuratulasi* (Tamil)
Species and varieties	: *Ocimum kilimandscharicum* Guerke
Distribution	: India, Kenya
Uses	: Disinfectant, Gilding glass and ceramic-ware, Perfumery

Camphor basil is the camphor-rich, perennial undershrub *Ocimum kilimandscharicum* Guerke (2n=76). It belongs to the family *Lamiaceae.* The volatile oil obtained from the leaves of this plant is a valuable source of camphor. It is light-yellow in colour, and has a strong odour of camphor. The camphor content varies from 61 to 80.5% in different samples.

The oil generally contains d-camphor (70%), d-pinene (10%), d-limonene (6%), terpinolene (5%) and unidentified sesquiterpenes and sesquialcohols (9%), cineole, coriandrol and chavibetol, Eugenol is reported to be present in some samples. But linalool, safrole and methyl cinnamate are completely absent. The seeds also yield an oil (12.5%).

The camphor obtained from the leaf-oil is used is large quantities for religious purposes in India. Camphor is of considerable importance in the manufacture of celluloid and explosives, and also finds use in various pharmaceutical preparations, disinfectants, tooth-pastes, powders and ointments. It is used as a plasticizer. The oil possesses antibacterial properties also. The residuary oil left after the separation of camphor is designated as 'ocimum oil', in contrast to camphor oil obtained from *Cinnamomum camphora,* which is suitable as a cheap perfume for soaps and also disinfectants. It is also used in the application of liquid gold on glass and ceramic-ware.

ORIGIN AND DISTRIBUTION

The plant is a native of Kenya (East Africa) and was introduced into India in 1942 by the Forest Research Institute, Dehra Dun. It does not have any natural range of distribution. At present it is cultivated in Dehra Dun, Lucknow, West Bengal and Jammu and Kashmir for obtaining camphor. It is also cultivated in Sudan and few other countries. There are, however, no clear statistics regarding the cultivation of this species in the world or in India.

DESCRIPTION OF THE PLANT

The plant is a perennial, many-branched, aromatic undershrub which grows to a height of 1 to 1.5 m (4 to 6 ft). It's leaves are ovate to broadly elliptic, acute, dentate, pubescent on both the surfaces, prominently veined and about 6 cm long. The flowers occur in 4-6 flowered whorls on long villose racemes at the ends of branches and are pale purple or pinkish-white in colour. The nutlets are ovoid, oblong and black to brown in colour. When bruised, the leaves emit a strong camphor odour.

SOIL

The plant can be grown in a variety of soils. But it grows best in clayey soil. Soils which are heavy with impeded drainage are suited for the cultivation of this crop. The plant has soil-binding properties and is not grazed on by cattle.

CLIMATE

Camphor basil can be grown in the plains as well as the hills both in tropical and sub-tropical climates at altitudes up to 900 m (3000 ft). The plant can tolerate fairly high temperatures, provided it gets a sufficient moisture supply, but it cannot withstand low temperatures below 30°F. It can be grown successfully in areas where the annual rainfall is 125 cm or even less, but the rainfall should be evenly distributed or the land must have a high watertable.

SEASON

The best time for sowing the seeds in nursery beds is after the middle of March. The seedlings are transplanted into the main field at the outbreak of the monsoon or earlier, if irrigation is available.

LAND PREPARATION

The land is ploughed 3 to 4 times to bring the soil to a fine tilth. The field is then planked immediately to make the surface even and to break the clods. Well-rotted FYM or compost @ 25 t/ha hectare is incorporated into the soil before the last ploughing.

CULTIVATION

Propagation

The plant is propagated by seeds and also by stem-cuttings. The seeds can be sown directly or in nurseries. About 70-140 g of seeds are required to raise seedlings sufficient for planting 1 ha of land.

Nursery Raising

The nursery should preferably be located in a partially shaded area with adequate irrigation facilities. The soil is worked up to a depth of about 30 cm. Well-rotted FYM 92 kg/sq m) is applied to the soil, which is prepared to a fine tilth. Raised seed-beds of 3 m × 1 m × 0.15 m size are prepared. As the seeds are small, the required quantity of seeds are mixed with sand in the ratio of 1:4 and about 10 g seeds are sown in each bed and watered regularly. The seeds germinate in 10 days and the seedlings are ready for transplanting into the main field when they are 5-7 weeks old.

Vegetative Propagation

Stem-cuttings of 20 cm length are taken from full-grown plants and planted in the nursery-beds. The cuttings sprout early, in about 7-10 days and are ready for transplanting in 4-5 weeks' time. It is reported that the crop raised from stem-cuttings is ready for harvest earlier and, generally, the leaf-yield is also high.

TRANSPLANTING

The seedlings may be transplanted into the main field at a spacing of 60 cm × 30 cm. This spacing is recommended for obtaining higher yields of this species. But the spacing recommended in Jammu and Lucknow is 60 cm × 60 cm.

APPLICATION OF MANURES AND FERTILIZERS

It is reported that the application of FYM and ammonium sulphate at a 20:1 ratio increased the yield of leaves by 30% over the control using no manure. It is observed that the application of N, P and K in a 20:20:20 ratio increased the height and growth of the plants. To get a high oil content, herb and oil-yield, the fertilizer dose recommended is 120 kg N, 80 kg/ha each of P and K. Of the recommended dose of fertilizers, 50% of the N and the entire P and K is given as a basal dose; while the remaining N is applied in two split doses after the first and second cuttings.

IRRIGATION

Irrigation is provided twice a week for one month after transplantation. Later, it is given at weekly intervals, depending upon the rainfall and soil-moisture status.

WEEDING

The first weeding is done about 60 days after transplanting and the second after another 60 days. Afterwards, the plant covers the surface area and there is no problem of weeds. However, after each harvest, weeding should be done so as to avoid weed growth, if any, in the interspaces.

PESTS AND DISEASES

There are no serious insect pests or diseases reported on this crop. However, insects like leaf-rollers and mealy bug sometimes cause damage to the crop. These insects can be controlled by spraying the plants with 2 ml Methyl Parathion or Quinolphos dissolved in one litre of water.

HARVESTING AND YIELD

The first harvest can be done 4-6 months after transplanting when the plants are 60 cm in height and have just started flowering and the lower leaves begun to turn yellow. Totally, three cuttings are made in a year in the crop raised in the plains: in August-September, November-December and March-April. The plantation can be retained for 6-7 years thereafter. Whereas, in cooler locations, only two harvests are possible. While harvesting, the plants are cut by sickles at about 10 to 15 cm from the ground-level. The harvested plants are bundled and staked for heating and drying for 4 to 10 days, depending upon the weather conditions. The weathered leaves are thrashed out from the stems, thoroughly dried in the sun and stored in bags or heaped in sheds. The dried leaves can be stored for a year or so without any loss of camphor. The average yield of dried leaves from three cuttings is 5500 kg/ha. However, yields as low as 2200 kg/ha of dried leaves have also been obtained in Dehra Dun.

DISTILLATION OF OIL AND EXTRACTION OF CAMPHOR

The oil and camphor-yields vary with the locality, harvest season and also the plant-part distilled. Generally, the leaves contain the maximum amounts of oil and camphor followed by the flowers. The stem contains only small quantities of oil and camphor. It is observed that the leaves of the transplanted crop gives a higher oil-yield than the leaves harvested from the directly-sown crop. The yield obtained during the dry months and also the prior drying of leaves increases the yield of oil.

The distillation of leaves may be carried out either with direct steam generated in a separate boiler or through indirect steam, using water and steam-distillation. The recovery of camphor is carried out in stills provided with condensers, which are specially designed to avoid the risk of being blocked by camphor deposition. The leaves are then charged into the still and distilled. In this method, besides the camphor, the oil is also recovered from the distillate. The camphor is separated from the oil by chilling and centrifuging, and is then purified by sublimation. The purified crystals possess the characteristic colour and odour or the natural camphor obtained from *Cinnamomum camphora* and form a translucent mass when pressed. There are other methods for extraction of camphor in which the oil is not recovered.

The yield of distillate usually varies from 3.5 to 5%, of which 50 to 70% is camphor. In the USA, the average yield of camphor obtained is about 112 kg/ha while, in Dehra Dun, a yield of up to 90 kg/ha is obtained in the second and subsequent years thereafter.

51

Spirulina

A Wonder Gift of Nature

Spirulina is a complete, comprehensive nutritional supplement, which ensures that our everyday meal is complete. Spirulina provides all the vital nutrients in a highly bio-available form, easily digestible, as it does not have a cell wall.

Spirulina gives these required nutrients in a form, which our body can easily absorb and utilise.

Spirulina is over 60% protein content, and is the highest, most potent and digestible protein source known. Spirulina protein has an excellent aminoacid pattern comparable to reference protein like egg protein and it provides aminoacids like lysine which many cereals lack. Spirulina is a good vitamin complex containing Beta-Carotene (Provitamin A), B_1, B_3, B_6, B_{12}, E and II (Biotin) vitamins. Spirulina is the only available vegetarian source of Vitamin B_{12}. The iron in Spirulina is the best natural iron supplement as it is twice as absorbable as the form of iron found in vegetables and meats since it is bound to water soluble protein Phycocyanin. Spirulina contains Gama lnolenic acid an important phytochemical that regulates the body metabolism.

Most remarkable, Spirulina contains the highest volume of the chlorophyll, carotenoids and other plants pigments.

Spirulina is a food supplement with a blend of nutrients, has no side effects and is non-toxic in nature. Consuming Spirulina will reduce the risk of incidence of any disorder due to nutritional deficiencies. The characteristic smell of Spirulina is due to the presence of the phytonutrient Polyamines, which are responsible for maintaining the cell function.

Spirulina can be given to children those who can swallow the capsules easily. To improve the overall health 1-2 grams Spirulina i.e. 2-4 capsules can be taken with milk or buttermilk after food. Spirulina can be taken with any medicine without side effect or drug interaction.

Courtesy: Parry Nutraceuticals, Chennai

Chemical and Nutritional Composition

Major Nutrients	*Amount*
Protein	65-71%
Fat	6.7%
Crude Fibre	9.3%
Carbohydrate	16.0%
Energy (K. Cal./gm)	246
Vitamins	
Beta carotene (mg/ml)	3,20,000
Biotin	0.22 mg
Cyanocobalamin (B 12)	65.7 mg
Folic Acid	17.6 mg
B-complex	9.2 mg
Tocopherol (vit E)	0.73 Iu
Minerals (major)	
Calcium	658 mg
Phosphorus	9.77 mg
Iron	47.7 mg
Sodium	796 mg
Potassium	1.140 mg
Essential Amino Acids	
Cysine	2.99%
Cystine	0.47%
Methionine	1.38%
Phenyalanine	2.87%
Threonine	304%

Though we are self sufficient in production of food grains for four growing population, the availability of protein in terms of quality and quantity remains to be achieved. The sources of protein both of animal and plant origin, has respective host of production constraints. The per capita consumptions of pulses in India has decreased from 54 g/day to 44 g/day.

SPIRULINA AND ITS IMPORTANCE

During the last three decades, the relevance of algae and other forms of micro-organisms as source of single cell protein (SCP) has gained increasing attention. Among them, Spirulina a micro-plant placed under blue-green algae or cyanobacteria. It has been declared as super-nutritions and safe as food.

Spirulina got its name due to its spiral shape. It is the richest source of protein, vitamins, minerals and amino-acids. It also possesses abundant amount of natural pigments, blue, green, orange and yellow. Spirulina is also a typical algae discovered for the first time from Mexico and Chad lakes. The lakes Alkaline in nature contain bicarbonates, sulphates and phosphates-a staple diet of Spirulina.

Medically, this micro plant also deals a lot with Chemo-preventive therapeutic applications mainly in areas of cancer, heart ailments, diabetes, constipation, liver cirrhosis, pancreatic pains, wounds, night blindness, anaemia rheumatoid arthritis, ageing, ulcer, increased lactation and for normal well being of the human body.

In 1974, the united nations world health conference declared spirulina as the 'Best food for tomorrow'. NASA declared that 1 kg of spirulina contains as much nutrition of 1000 kg of assorted vegetables. The nutritional value of spirulina has been well documented and studied by various research institutes world over. Shri AMM Murugappa Chettiar Research Institute, Chennai, CFTRI, Mysore and Central Institute Fresh Water Aquaculture, Orissa have achieved a break-through and developed technology to grow spirulina in field conditions. In India, the algae will be used to combat malnutrition in future. Spirulina consumes just 1/10th of water consumed by soyabeans but gives twenty times more protein as it can accumulate up to 70% protein on dry weight basis. Besides, spirulina liberates tonnes and tonnes of pure oxygen into environment through its photosynthetic activity by consuming tonnes and tonnes of carbon di-oxide.

Recolina, Natoxid, *Sunova spirulina* and Multinal are its marketable brands available in India market.

In cosmetics the threshold area awaits a great future from Spirulina. It also contains green, yellow, orange and blue pigments up to 20% level. They are non-carcinogenic and easy to be incorporated in various facial mask formulations. Phycocyanin is marketed as luna m-blue in Vietnam and Taiwan for eye-lashes and facial masks. These pigments not only improve the facial value but also increased immunity and retards ageing, if taken orally.

It is a rich source of Beta-carotene almost 18 times more than carrot. Being a precursor of vitamin A and a potent antioxidant it helps in maintaining healthy eyes, skin and all tissues protects eyes from conjuctival xerosis, oral and other body parts from oncological lesions and manifestations thus averting risks of getting cancer. The National Institute of Nutrition, Hyderabad under Indian Council of Medical Research has already established the effective nutritional and long term toxicological aspects of spirulina. It is also the one and the only vegetable source of cyanocobalamin for effective erythropoiesis, simultaneously strengthening protein sheath surrounding the nerve fibres.

Presence of essential fatty acids like Alpha Gamma linoleic and linoleic acids makes it a potent cool to curb heart ailments, obesity, arthritis and for proper functioning of cell membranes, precursor of prostaglandin regulating the safety of all tissues especially those hit by hyper chloesterolic conditions.

Daily intake of spirulina at 2-5 g dose helps wound and ulcer healing. It also reduces SGPT and SGOT enzymes levels in blood thus helping in prevention of chronic liver cirrhosis. Presence of other vitamins like biotin (vit. H), tocopherol (vit. E), thiamine, riboflavin, niacin, folic acid, pyridoxic acid etc. in appreciable quantities also nourishes the human body besides Beta-carotene ad vit B12 i.e. cyanocobalamin.

Vit E prevents ageing helps in betterment of skin and hair. Thus it has become a irreplaceable ingredient in shampoos, soaps, face creams and other cosmetic ingredients.

Spirulina protein conversion efficiency ratio is very high because it is single called and its cell walls have no cellulose. After 18 hours, more than 85% of spirulina proteins are digested and assimilated.

Spirulina is a slimming agent, the alga chrystollioe, water soluble amino-acids, phenylalanine signals the brain to stop hunger pangs there by reducing the intake of food.

In India, where breast feeding is encouraged algae has a positive effect on breast milk output. Doctors prescribe spirulina tablets from the third day of delivery up to two months. It also cures hepatitis and glaucoma and reduces sugar levels in the blood. Thus there are multi-specified uses for spirulina which has got titled as "Magic Algae".

Composition: It is the world's richest source of protein "with 18 amino acids including the essential" and has the richest vegetarian value of vitamin B12. It has 30 times more Beta carotene (pro vitamin!) than in carrots and vit B1, B2, B6, C, E, H, besides calcium, phosphorus, potassium, sodium and iron, the pant contains chlorophyll, xanthophyll & phycocyanin pigments, but there is a trace of cholesterol, poly unsaturated fatty acids abound in it.

Dry spirulina powder contains 65-71% of high quality proteins (boiled eggs has only 46%, soyabean 40% chicken 20-22%, fish 15-22%, rice 7.5%, fresh cow's milk 3.9%)

Production Technology: Spirulina is a blue green algae belonging to the class Cyanophyceae, order Nostocales and family Oscillatoriaceae. It is recorded from water-logged rice fields ponds, lakes, waste water channels and brackish water pools, with alkaline and saline soil substratum being most suitable for its propagation. The algae multiplication occurs by fragmentation. The research work in India with regard to utilization has largely been carried out with two species, viz., *Spirulina platensis and Spirulina fusiformis.*

Pot Culture: Pour into a wide mouthed pot of 35 litres a simple medium of about 20 litres containing agriculture fertilizer, "Sulpha", urea, magnesium sulphate and sodium carbonate and then add spirulina (commonly *Spirulina Plantensis* or fusiforms) to it. Keep the pot out doors in the sun and stir occasionally.

The algae multiplies using sunlight and the nutrients. Harvest periodically after a week by running the medium through a fine nylon cloth. Scrape the green part and allow it to dry in the shade till it forms flakes. Villages in Tamil Nadu are growing proteins this way. Spirulina can be had from AMM Murugappa Chettair Research Centre, Tharamani, Madara; Central Marine Fisheries Research Institute, Kochi; Central Food Technology Research institute Mysore; and Central Institute of Fresh Water Aquaculture, Orissa.

52

Stevia
A Nature's gift to Diabetic Patients

Sugar forms an indispensable ingredient in the food habits of human beings. The main source of sugar has for long been cane sugar, with beet sugar contributing a small percentage. Nearly 60 per cent of centrifugal sugar comes from sugar cane and the rest from sugarbeet. Though these sugars have sweetening qualities, yet they have been found to cause obesity, gallstones, heart trouble and diabetic diseases. Hence, these sugars are not advised for consumption by diabetic patients.

A general change in the life style is that 'slim is beautiful'. However, sugar is invariable associated with fat, with these nutritional disorders and a strong desire to be slim, many affluent societies and diabetic patients societies and diabetic patients have turned to low calorie table top sweetners such as Saccharin, Aspartame, Asulfam-K etc. which are aptly called 'nutritional terrorists'. These are not only expensive but have bitter after taste. So, in the present sweet toothed society, the interest is being focussed on natural non-calorie sweetner stevia (*Stevia rebaudiana* Bertoni.).

The world of sweetners has been a change in the recent past with the introduction of stevia sugar-a sugar 250 to 300 times sweeter than table sugar and containing many positive remedial qualities and physiological properties.

Originally *Eupatorium rebaudianum,* the sweet herb of Paraguay came to the attention of Bertoni in 1889, who later found that the plant was new to science and renamed as *Stevia rebaudiana* Bertoni in 1905. Historically, the natives of Paraguay and Brazil have been using the leaves of Stevia as a sweetening essence for tea. There are more than 200 species of the stevia plant, but *Stevia rebaudiana* gave the sweetest essence.

Of great importance is the character of sweetness of Stevia leaves. Leaves of Stevia contain compounds about 250-300 times. Leaves of Stevia contain compounds about 250-300 times as table sugar. The chemicals on interest are stevioside, rebaudiside A, rebaudiside B, rebaudiside E, rebaudiside D, rebaudiside E, glucoside and steviolbioside. Among these, the principal sweet glycosides are stevioside (3 to 10% of leaf dry weight) and rebaudiside A (1 to 3% leaf dry weight) and the remaining are less concentrated. The sweetening potency (Sucrose=1) of stevioside and rebaudiside A are 250-300 and 350-400 respectively.

Stevia requires sub-humid or sub-tropical climate. In India, under Bangalore conditions it can be successfully cultivated throughout the year. It can be grown on a wide range of soils. Vegetative propagation using stem coatings is a promising propagation technique. Fertilizer requirements are minimal, but leaf yields can be increased by moderate application of nitrogen (40 kg ha^{-1}) , phosphorus (20 kg ha^{-1}) and potassium (30 kg ha^{-1}). It has good ratoons can be obtained in a year.

Stevia is a plant of very recent domestication in many countries of the world. Japan is already marketing a sweetner extracted from the leaves of Stevia. Its cultivation is standardized, it may replace the low calorie table top sweetners of the world which have prominent place in food and beverage industry. Further due to its noncaloric nature is nature's gift for the diabetic patients to enjoy sweetness.

53

Mushrooms

Mushrooms are a fleshy, spore bearing organ of fungi. Mushrooms are used as food since time immemorial and are considered for delicacy and protein nutrition. Recent investigations have proved the empirical observation of the oriental herbalists that certain mushrooms possess many useful medicinal attributes. In the recent past, a variety of medicinal preparations in the form of tablets, capsules and extracts from mushrooms have been produced and marketed. Food and agricultural organisation had recommended mushrooms as a food for people in under developed nations where malnutrition is a threat to human health. FAO has also recommended mushrooms for their medicinal values rather than for nutritional value.

MEDICINES FROM EDIBLE MUSHROOMS

Great number of edible mushrooms have medicinal properties and are used in specific diseases. At present a number of mushrooms have been reported to possess pharmacological values like antibacterial, antifungal and antiviral properties. Compounds isolated from *Falmmulina velutipes, Fimellac, Agaricus bisporus, Clitocybe. Maramius, Pleurotus, Psathryrella* and *Trichoderma* are characterised with antibacterial activity. Antibiotic effect on human pathogens like Aspergillus fumigatus is found in *Cortinarious orellanus* and *Tricholoma ustaloides.* Spread of skin pathogen *Canidida alkicans* is prevented by extracts of *Tricholoma saponaceum.* The terpenoids, illudin-M and illudin-S extracted from Clitocybe illudens are very effective against Plasmodium gallinoceum. Clitocybe illudens has antiprotozoal effect. Among the edible fungi *Valvatia gingenta*, *Chlorophyllum molybdites* and *Agaricus compestris* have antiviral activities against human diseases. Extracts of *Lentinus edodes* inhibit the growth of some viruses like influenza. In *Lentinus edodes* anti-tumour chemicals polysaccharides, basidioproteins, quinoid basis and acid proteins have been identified. Other mushrooms identified for their antitumor principle are Pleurotus sp., *Agarcius bisporus,*

Falmulina velutipus and *Agaricus bisporus* is also effective in lowering blood cholesterol. The sacred mushroom *Psilocybe maxicana* contains two chemicals viz., Psilocin and Psilocybin and are used to cure mental disorders. Two compounds viz., biotenic acid and musional are prepared from *Armilklariella mella* used cure to malformation of GABA system of brain called "Schizophrenia". *Amanita phalloides* is used against cholera and intermittent fever.

MEDICINES FROM POISONOUS MUSHROOMS

Using poisonous mushrooms as medicines in China is considered "to be a using poison as an antidote for poison". Poisonous mushroom preparations are still in use as medicines. *Amanita muscaria* commonly known as "fly agaric" is used therapeutically as a powder, tincture for swollen glands, nervous troubles and epilepsy. For heat ailments and inflammation of eyes, a lotion made of *Amanita muscaria* is used externally and internally. This mushroom is also used in homoeopathic medicines under the name ager, agarus or agaric. Muscinol and biotenic acid, the two compounds prepared from *A. muscaria* can acid, the two compounds prepared from *A. muscaria* can cure the malfunction of Gaba system of brain which is termed as schigophorenal. *Amanita phalloides* is used against cholera and intermittent fever.

MUSHROOMS IN AYURVEDIC MEDICINES

In Ayurveda, mushrooms are mentioned as body builders and energisers. They cure stomach troubles and improve sexual desire. Mushrooms boiled in milk with sugar is given for it has been reported that boiled water extract of *Nilamanga* prevents dehydration. Boiled extract in seasmum oil, applied internally, curses ear pain in children. A mixture of *Nilamanga* in butter applied externally cures body abeissions faster. Similarly, consumption of boiled milk extract of crossed *Nilamanga* is a good remedy for jaundice. These important mushrooms medicines are available in the form of extracts, powders (in capsules) and sugar coated tablets.

MUSHROOMS IN HOMOEOPATHIC MEDICINES

Fly agaric or fly mushroom (*Amantia muscaria*) is a deadly poisonous mushroom. It is used in the form of powder and tincture for curing swollen glands, nervous trembling and epilepsy. It is used externally and internally in highly diluted preparations (lotions) for heart ailments, inflammation of eyes and rheumatic arthritis. In the homoeopathic medicines it is called as agar, agric and agarus. *Armillariealla mella* is also used in the preparation of homoeopathic medicines.

MUSHROOMS IN HOME MEDICINES

Fomes ignarious and *F. fomentarious* are used for rapid coagulation of blood. *Polyporus officinals* is considered as a home medicine. It is used as drastic purge. *Armillarella mellea* is an excellent purgative. This mushroom is applied externally to stop bleeding. It is also used for chronic catarrh and diseases of lungs and breast. It is a remedy for night sweating in tuberculosis, rheumatism, gout, jaundice, dropsy and intestinal worms.

Recent researches have proved beyond doubt that mushrooms posses pharmacological activities. Even though a variety of mushrooms are well known for their edibility and nutritive values, they are yet to be exploited for medicinal use.

54

E-Mail and Postal Office Addresses related to Medicinal Plants

Mark Blumenthal
Editor,
Herbal Gram
Texas
E-mail :
herbcowboy@aol.com

Dilmani Warnasuriya
Manager-ISCITI,
Colombo
E-mail : dilmani@iti.ik

Beatriz P. del Rosario
Dy. Executive Director (R&D)
PCARRD,
Philippines
E-mail :
prosea@ultra.pcarrd.dost.gov.ph

Maria Nwosu
Botany Department
University of Nigeria
E-mail :
maynwosu@infoweb.abs.net

Anil K. Gupta
Ahmedabad
E-mail : info@nifindia.org

G. G. Parikh
Zandu
E-mail : zanduho@
giasbm01.vsnl.net.in

Sushil Kumar Agarwal
Saharanpur
E-mail :
insre@vsnl.com

A. K. Batham
Vice President (Medical)
Morepen Laboratories Ltd.,
New Delhi
E-mail :
ak.batham@morepen.com

Dr. C. K. Katiyar
DGM,
Dabur Research Foundation
E-mail :
ckkatiyar@dabur.com

Merina Benny
Manager (R&D)
Arjuna Natural Extract
Ltd.,
Alwaye
E-mail :
mail@arujunanatural.com

Sunita Garg
Editor
Natural Product Radiance
E-mail :
sunita@niscom.res.in

Gian Singh
Editor, MAPA
E-mail :
gsingh@niscom.res.in

R. Raghvendra Rao
NBRI, Lucknow
E-mail :
rr_rao@satyam.net.in

Pratap Chouhan
Jiva Ayurvedic Research
Institute
1144, Sector-9
Faridabad – 121 002
E-mail :
info@ayurvedic.org

V. P. Kapoor
NBRI
E-mail :
vpkapoor123@rediffmail.com

M. Majeed
Managing Director
SAMI Labs Ltd., Bangalore
E-mail :
mail@samilabs.com

Anil Kumar Gandhi
UDCT Matunga, Mumbai
E-mail :
anilgandhi@yahoo.com

Deccan Exhibitions Pvt. Ltd.
1170/17-B, Shivajinagar
Pune – 411 005
E-mail : fair@kisan.com
Website :
www.kisan.com

Vadamalai Consultancy Services
C2/286, 4th Main, 2 'C' Cross,
Domlur IInd Stage,
IIIrd Phase
Banglore – 560 071
E-mail :
agriculture@vsnl.net

Isra Agro Tech Systems (P) Ltd.,
S-79, 1st Floor,
GCDA Commercial Complex, P.B. No. 2710,
Marine Drive,
Cochin-682 031 (Kerala)
E-mail :
israagro@sancharnet.in
Israagro@vsnl.net

K. S. Hegde
Director
T. Stanes & Company Limited
8/23-24 Race Course Road,
Coimbatore – 641 018
E-mail :
monoram@md3vsnl.net.in,
monoram@sancharnet.in,
unitea@md2.vsnl.net.in

Vijay Kumar
Raj & Company
Behind Katuj Market,
Near Parsi Temple,
Neemuch – 458441 (M.P.)
E-mail :
rajspice@sancharnet.in

Rallis India Limited
Rallis Research Centre
21 & 22, Phase II,
Peenya Industrial Area,
Banglore – 560 058

V. R. Somvanshi
Dy. General Manager
Karnataka State Agro Corn Products Ltd.,
P.O. Box 2479, Hebbal
Banglore – 560 024

Suresh
Suresh Forestry Network
P.B. No. 15,
Chickballapur – 562 101
(Near Banglore)
E-mail :
bamboo9@rediffmail.com,
futuretrees@yahoo.co.uk

M. N. Jawahar
ED (Marketing)
SPIC Ltd.,
88, Mount Road, Guindy
Chennai – 600 032
E-mail :
mnjawahar@spic.co.in

Rohit Patre
Managing Director
Ratnagiri Impex Pvt. Ltd.
No. 4323 Promenade Raod, 2nd Cross,
Frazer Town
Bangalore – 560 005
E-mail :
ratnagiriimpex@hotmail.co.,
info@ratnagiriimpex.com

Bhaskar Rao / Mr. Jayakumar
Nandan Agro Farms#301,
Sneha Enclave,
Srinagar Colony,
Hyderabad – 500 073
E-mail: jayakumar@
nandanagrofarms.com

Mittul Shah
Neel Bio-Tech Pvt. Ltd.,
S/3 Navrang,
Swastic Cross Roads,
Navarangpura
Ahmedabad – 380 009
E-mail :
info@neelbiotech.com,
info@dewang.com

Praveen Jaipuria
Joint Managing Director
Agro Extracts Limited
Plot No. 16, Phase II,
Peenya Industrial Area,
Bangalore – 560 058
E-mail :
neemex@vsnl.com

Arun Nagarajan
Yendal Nursery Farm,
5-1-57 Main road,
Pattiveeranpatti – 624 211
E-mial : wparn@vsnl.com

Sartorius India Pvt. Ltd.,
10, 3rd Phase Peenya,
6th Main, KIADB Industrial Area, Banglore – 560 058
E-mial :
co-bang@sartorius-india.com

Jairamdass Khushiram
Plot No. 5, Sector 19-C,
Opp. Punjab National Bank, Vashi
Navi Mumbai – 400 703

M. Nagi Reddy
Managing Partner
Flowell Pump Industries
Plot No. 90, Sri Venkateshwara Coop. Industrial Estate,
Balanagar
Hyderabad – 500 037
E-mail : marketing@
flowellpumps.com

Rajeev Sodhi
S. V. Healthy Herbs India
29, Sanvid Nagar,
Kanadia Road, Indore
E-mail : healthyherbdindia
@rediffmail.com

Milan V. Mehta
Manageing Director
RYM Exports, 26, Madhu Estate, P.B. Marg,
Worli, Mumbai – 400 013
E-mail :
neemindia@yahoo.com

Mukesh K. Varshney
Breeder
Unicorn Seeds Limited
1-7-139/3, Sarojini Devi Raod
Secunderabad – 500 003
E-mail :
uniagro@hd4.vsnl.net.in

O. P. Gupta
Vedic Herbs
C-105, Indrapuri,
Raisen Road
Bhopal – 462 021
E-mail :
herbsvedic@hotmail.com

Sanjeevi M. Ramaswamy
Kosmic Ayurvedic Products
Kambakkam Road,
Varadayapalayam
Chittoor Dist.,
Andhra Pradesh
E-mail :
drji2001@yahoo.com/
drji@rediff.com

Balarama Raju. D.
Raghu Medicinal Farms
C/o Dr. Vijaya Laxmi
1-3-151/C, Rajendra Nagar
New Town,
Mahabubnagar
Andhra Pradesh-509 001

Ashok Shah
Prasad Biotech
725, G.I.D.C., (Extn)
Gundlav,
Valsad – 396 035 (Guj)
E-mail :
dracshah13@yahoo.com

Vikas Dhawan
Dhawan International
B-134, G.F. (Front),
Malviya Nagar
New Delhi-110017
E-mail :
sales@herbsnextracts.com

Fortune Bio-Tech Ltd.
6-6-125, Annam Gardens,
Kavadiguds
Secunderabad – 500 380 (A.P.)

Eugene Das
Export Manager
Zandu Exports Limited
70, Gokhale Road (South),
Dadar, Mumbai – 400 025
E-mail :
eugene.das@zandu.co.in/
Zanduusa@hotmail.com

Bharat Bhushan
Managing Director
Navayug Pharmaceuticals
48, Industrial Area,
Phase II,
Panchkula – 134 113
E-mail :
bhushan.b@mailicity.com

Anand Lakhani
Sales Officer
Gufic Biosciences Limited
Subhash Road-A,
Vile Parle (East),
Mumbai – 400 057
E-mail :
gufic@bom2.vsnl.net.in

Narayana Upadhyaya
International Inspector
Skal India
3rd Floor, Monarch Chambers,
122, Infantry Road,
Banglore – 560 001
E-mail :
skalindia@vsnl.com

Rajesh Doshi
Ayurveda Incorporation
Junagadh Road,
Manavadar – 362 630 (Guj)
E-mail :
ayurveda@ayurveda-cure.com

Rajni Kaur
Chirayu Pharmaceuticals
14, Dindayal Market,
M.L.B. Road
Gwalior – 474 009 (M.P.)
E-mail :
chirayu@chirayu.com

Rajni
Global Herbs
B-82A, Ambedkar Colony,
Chattarpur
New Delhi – 100 030
E-mail :
globalherbs@mailcity.com

Ranjit Puranik
Chief Executive Officer
Shree Dhootapapeshwar Limited
135, Nanubhai Desai Rd.,
Khetwadi
Mumbai-400 004 (India)
E-mail :
sdlho@sdlindia.com

S. Gopal Rajan
Chairman, Research
Drugs @ Pharmaceuticals (Guj) Pvt. Ltd.,
1/6, Tiger Flas,
Nava Vadaj
E-mail :
rdpl_gopal@hotmail.com

Tulsi Bhatia
Director
Shivam Enterprises Pvt. Ltd.,
Maveshno Herbal Farms Pvt. Ltd.,
B-4, Sukh Samridhi,
Tilak Nagar,
Jaipur-302004
E-main :
ma_veshno@indya.com

Dilip Trivedi
Shriji Herbal Products
Chandavarkar Road,
Subhash Sadan
Borivali (W)
Mumbai – 400 092
E-mail :
spenal@rediff.com

Vedic Lifesciences
118 Morya House,
Off New Link Road,
Andheri (W),
Mumbai – 400 053
E-mail :
vedic@ayunherbal.com

Haresh Prajapati
Sales Executive
Nagarjun Pharmaceuticals (P) Ltd.,
C-1/1114/B, Phase-IV,
GIDC.,
Naroda,
Ahmedabad – 382 230

Anurag Sharma
Chief Executive
172, Gusainpura
Jhansi – 284 002 (UP)
E-mail :
sbabl@nde.vsnl.net.in/
baidyanathayurved@hotmail.com

Pradeep Multani
Chairman cum Managing Director
36-H, Connaught Place,
New Delhi – 100 001
E-mail : multaniayurveda@hotmail.com

G. Sudesh
Managing Partner
First Step Enterprises
3-4-1005/4, Barkatpura
Bus Depot Road,
Barkatpura,
Hyderabad – 500 027
E-mail :
firststepenterprises@yahoo.com

Bawaskar Technology
16, Krishi Udhog Bhawan
1-Naveen Vajan
Katyajaval
Marketyard, Goltakadi
Pune – 38
E-mail :
agrotec@vsnl.com

55

Addresses of Eco-friendly Farming

Organic Farming

Rodale Institute Research Center
611 Siegfriedale Rd.
Kutztown, PA 19530
(610) 683-6383

Organic Crop Improvement Association (OCIA)-International
3185 Township Rd. 179
Bellefontane,
OH 43311
(513) 592-4983

Biodynamic Farming

Biodynamic Farming & Gardening Assen.
P. O. Box 550
Kimberton,
PA 19442 USA
(215) 935-7797

Michael Fields Agricultural Institute
West 2493 Country Rd.
ES
East Troy, WI 53120 USA
(414) 642-3303

Bio-Dynamic Research Institute
Main Road, Powelltown,
3797 Victoria, Australia.
Tel: +61-59-66 73 33,
Fax: +61-59-66 74 33
http://www.demeter.net/International/Betriebe/australien.htm

Institute for Biodynamic Research
Brandschneise 5, D-64295 Darmstadt,
Germany.
Tel: +49-6155 8421-0
Fax: +496155 8421-25.
http://www.ibdf.de/

Biological Farming
2617-C Edenborn Ave
Metairie, LA 70002 USA
(504) 889-2100

Biological Farming Systems Group
Wageningen University
Marijkeweg 22,
Wageningen Building nr. 527, 6709 PG
Wageningen,
The Netherlands.
Tel: +31.(0)317.478201
Fax: +31.(0)317.478213.
http://www.dpw.wageningen-ur.nl/biob/

Nature Farming

Mokichi Okada Association
c/o Pacific Culture Center
1835 Vancouver Drive
Honolulu, HI 96822

Nature Farming Research & Development Center
6495 Santa Rosa Rd.
Lompac, CA 93436
USA

56

Resources for Vermicompost

Appropriate Technology Transfer for Rural Areas (ATTRA)
Senior Technical Specialist, ATTRA, P.O. Box 3657, Fayetteville, Arkansas 72702
USA
Phone: (800) 346-9140
Fax: (501) 442-9842
E-mail : aliceb@ncatfyv.uark.edu

Beaver River Associates
P.O. Box 94
West Kingston
RI 02982 USA
Phone & Fax: (401) 782-8747

Bhawalkar Earthworm Research Institute
A/3 Kalyani
Pune, 411 0317 India
Phone: 91 212 413 714
Fax: 91 212 442 305

CSIRO, Davies Laboratory
Contact: Dr. A. V. Spain
CSIRO, Private Mail Bag
Aitkenvale, Queensland
4814 Australia
Phone: 77-719511
Fax: 77-251009

Enviro-Ganics Ecological Systems Inc.
P.O. Box 20241
Grantham Postal Statino
St. Catharines
Ontario L2M 7W7
Canada
Phone: (905) 646-8690
Fax: (905) 937-0517

Environmental Earthworm Products, Inc.
Contact: Frank Stevenson
8114 Port Said St.
Orlando
FL 32813 USA
Phone: (407) 678-6454
Fax: (407) 677-0790

The French Institute For Scientific Research For Cooperative Development (ORSTOM)
Contact: Dr. Patrick Lavelle
ORSTOM
Ceentre de Bondy
72, Route d'Aulnay
95143 Bondy Cedex
France
Phone: 33 1 48 02 55 01
Fax: 33 1 48 47 30 88

The National Agricultural Library (NAL)
10301 Baltimore Blvd.,
Beltsville, MD 20705 USA
Phone: (301) 504-5755

Oregon Soil Corporation
7810 SSW Bunker Oak Rd.,
Aloha, OR 97006, USA
Phone: (503) 629-5933.

Original Vermitech Systems, Ltd.
2338 Queen Street East
Toronto, Ontario M4E 1G9
Canada
Phone: (416) 693-1027
Fax: (416) 698-02

Vermitechnology Unlimited
P.O. Box 130
Orange Lake, FL 32681
USA
Phone: (904) 591-1111
Fax: (904) 591-4550

Hy Hunter Industries
2001 Highwater Road
Granda Hills
CA 91344 USA
Phone: (818) 363-0202
Fax: (818) 360-8562

Institute of Natural Organic Agriculture (INORA)
Contact: Professor M. R. Bhiday
100, Kalpana Apartments
Erandwan
Pune – 411 004 India
Phone: 336215

Maharashtra Agricultural Bloteks
Contact: Dr. Hemangee Jambhekar
B/9 Shivaji Housing Society
Near Sane Guruji Smark
Pune, 411 030, India
Phone: 91 212-3431983

Resource Conversion Corp.
7825 Fay Ave. Suite 380
La Jola, CA 92037 USA
Phone: (619) 551-4800
Fax: (619) 459-2794

Sound Resource Management Group
Seattle, WA 98101-1540
USA
Phone: (206) 622-9454

Archives on the Internet

Venaura Farm
7119 Old Greensboro Rd.
Chapel Hill, N. C. 27516
E-mail :
london@sunsite.unc.edugopher
www :
Gopher://
sunsit.unc.education:70/
11/.pub/acade mic/
agriculture/
sustainable_agriculture/
vermiculture

Unco Industries
7802 Old Spring Street
Racine, WI 53406
USA
Phone: (414) 886-2665

The Worm Connection
581 Camino Manzanas
Thousand Oaks
CA 91360 USA
Phone: (805) 496-2872

57

Agencies/Individuals Working on Organic Farming in India

IFOAM-India

Institute for Integrated Rural Development (IIRD)
IIRD is the Asia Regional Office for International Federation of Organic Agricultural Movements (IFOAM)
Postal address
54, Kanchan Nagar,
Nakshatrawadi,
Aurangabad – 431, 002.,
Maharashtra, India.
Tel. +91-240-2332336, 2322828
FAX +91-240-2322866
Electronic mail – General Information: Project Office (iirdind@bom4.vsnl.net.in

Vishvaneedam International
Sarvodya Centre
13 K. M. Magadi Rd.
P. O. Vishraneedam
Bangalore – 560 091

Centre for Science and Environment
41, Tughlakabad
Institutional Area
New Delhi – 110 062

Agriculture & Processed Food Product Export Development Authority (APEDA)
3rd Floor,
Ansal Chambers II,
Bhikaji Cama Place
New Delhi – 110 066

Agriculture Man and Ecology Programme
P. O. Box 7836
Bangalore – 560 078

Sana Adarsh Sewa
Samiti
Masauli
Barabanki – 225 204

Indian Institute of Forest Management
10-IIFM Colony
Kottrasultanabad
Bhopal – 462 003
M. P. (India)

Balasubramanian
Moses Compound
Sunoora Patti
Segii Patti (PO) 613 402
Dist. Tanjavore (India)

Society for Development Action
P. O. Box 16
Baripada – 757 001
Mayurbhanj
Orissa (India)

CSIR (Council of Scientific & Industrial Research)
PO Box No. 6
Palampar – 176 061
H. P. (India)

Chandrashekar Kote & Co.
M. G. Road
Chikmagalur – 577 101

Pudumjee Plant Laboratories
Jatia Chambers, 60
Dr. V. B. Gandhi Marg,
Mumbai – 400 023
India

Friends Rural Centre
Rasulia
Hoshangabad
M. P. – 461 001 (India)

Conservation Society
Nelliampathy Hills Padagiri PO
Palakkad Dist. – 678 509

Gloria Land
Aurobrindavan
Auroville – 605 101

Gram Manglam-Sultanpur
At PO Bhudasan
Via Akarund – 383 260
Ta Bayad. Dist.
Sabarkantha
Gujarat

R. M. Centre for Educational Innovation,
Indian Institute of Management,
Ahmedabad – 380 015

Gururaja, B.
E-1 Maithree Apt
6th Main, 15th Cross
Malleshiraram
Bangalore, Karnataka

Academy of Gandhian Studies
2-2-1133/4/5
New Nallakunta
Hyderabad – 500 044

Kachch Sanjivani Farm
Bidada (Mondvi)
Kutch– 370 435
Gujarat

BAIF Development Research Foundation
BAIF Bhavan,
Dr. Manibhai Desai Nagar
Warje
Pune – 411 029

Helen, S.
Justus Bhawan, Taruvai
Manavalakurichi PO
Distt. Kanayakumari
Pin 629 252
Tamil Nadu

PARD
PO Box 87
Madurai – 625 020
Tamil Nadu

Centre for Learning, Agriculture & Appropriate Technology
PO Box 57
Kodaikanal – 624 101
Tamil Nadu (India)

Caprico Enterprises
Pearl Apts – 3/47
Sidharth Nagar – 1
Goregaon (W)
Mumbai – 400 104 (India)

Gorakhpur Environmental Action Group
244 Purdilpur
M. G. College Rd.
P. O. Box 60
Gorakhpur – 273 001
(U.P.)

SEEDS
Thachankurichy (P.O.)
Gandharvakottai
Pudukkottai DT – 613 301

Annamalai Reforestation
5 Manakulavinayagar St.
Sri Ramanasramam
P. O. Tiruvanamalai
Tamil Nadu

Lok Jagriti Kendra
Madhupur – 815 353
Deoghar
Bihar

Centre of Science for Village
Dattapur,
Vardha – 442 001 (M.H.)

Society of Health, Education & Development (SHED)
The Director
PO Box No. 18
Rayagada
Orissa – 765 001

Kupvi Herbarium Workers Association
Kupvi – 171 217
Sub. The Kupvi
Distt. Simla, H. P.

Margosan Exports
P. O. Box 1122,
Bhavani Ganesh Complex,
Bejai Church Road,
Mangalore – 575 004

Prakruthi
620 Jame Jamshed Road
4th Floor, Dadar (East)
Mumbai – 400 014 (India)

Kassar Trust
Mankote
P. O. Udera
Dist. Almora
Uttaranchal

Greenpeace
J-15, Saket
New Delhi – 110 017

Tribal Area Research Centre (Amboori) College of Agriculture
Vellayani – 695 522
Thiruvananthapuram

Save the Easter Ghats Association
Y 109, Raja Street
Valaijam Battu
Chengam – 606 701 (T.N.)

Sarbik Gram Bikash Kendra
(Gandhi Mission)
PO Daspur
Dist. Midnapore, W. B.

Nazareth, Jagdish
H-3 Rushika Appartments
Near Kiran Park
Nava Wadaj
Ahmedabad – 380 013

P. S. Mani
"Ramakripa"
7/386 Tharakad
Palgat 678 001, Kerala

Padama
Prarambha
18/1 All Asker Road
Banglore – 560 052

Kumarappa Go Samvardhan Kendra
PUSAD,
Yavatmal-445 204 (M.H.)

Patel, Gunvant R.
Sarsa – 388 365, Gujarat

Gania Unnayan Committee (GUC)
At/P.O. Gania
Distt. Nayagarh
Orissa-752085

Prajapati, N. D.
Sonamukhi Nagar
Snagaria Phanta, Basni
Jodhpur – 342 004

College of Agricultural
Kerala Agricultural University
Vellayani PO
Thiruvananthapuram – 695 522, Kerala

Prakruti
123 Mahtma Gandhi Raod
Opp. Bombay University
Fort, Mumbai – 400 023

Raghavendra, K. Rao & Rao, Shylaja R.
Plot No. 13, Srinagar Colony,
Hyderabad – 500 873
Andhra Pradesh

Regional Coffee Research Station
Thandigundi
Kodaikamla Tuluk
Tamil Nadu

Centre for Ecological Sciences
Indian Institute of Science
Bangalore – 560 012

Green Foundations
839, 23rd Main, J.P. Nagar
2nd Phase, Bangalore-560 078

Reddy, L. Narayana
Srinivasapura
Via Maralenahalli
Hanabe P.O.
Doddaballapur Taluk
Karnataka – 561 203

Indian Institute of Management
Bannerghatta Road
Bangalore – 560 076

Sava, Bhaskar H.
Kalpavruksha
At & Post Deheri
Ta. Umbergaon – 396 170
Dist. Valsad (Gujarat)

Setty's Farm and Gopal T. Kalkami Vasundhara Group of Oraganic Farmers
Rattihalli – 581 116
Karnataka

College of Agriculture
Dept. of Agricultural Extension
(PO) Vellayani
Thiruvananthapuram – 695 522 Kerala

Research Foundation for Science Technology and Ecology
A-60 Hauz Khas,
New Delhi – 110 016

Central Institute of Medicinal and Aromatic Plants
Post Bag No. 1
PO Ram Sagar Misra Nagar
Lucknow – 226 016

SKAL (Certification & Exports)
3rd Floor – Monarch Chambers
122 Infancy Road,
Bangalore

Society for Human Integrety and Prosperity
9-81 Gandhinagar
Nuzvid – 521 201
Krishna Dist.
Andhra Pradesh

CAFARD (Community Action for Food & Rural Development)
Second Seven Wells Street, St. Thomas Mount
Butt Road
Chennai – 600 016
Tamil Nadu

Todiara, N. P.
Dept. of Forestry
P. O. Box 59
H. N. B. Garwhal University,
Srinagar

Bodi Bio Farms
Rajamani Cloth Centre Upstairs
Kamaraj Bazar
Bodi Nayakanur-626513
Tamil Nadu

Rural Organization on Social Elevation (Rose)
Social Awareness Centre
KANDA,
PO Kanda
Almora,
Uttaranchal – 263 63

Nu Tech Farm,
Vijay Shah
Rayan
Dist : Kutch-Mandivi
Gujarat – 370 465

58

State Medicinal Plants Board

Director
Health Services
A & N Island,
Port Blair – 744102
A & N

Chief Executive Officer
AP Medicinal Aromatic
Plant Board,
Medical, Health & Family
Welfare Dept.
205, RIVIERA Apartment,
Dwarkapuri Colony,
Panja gutta,
Hyderabad – 500082 AP.

Officer I/c of ISM & H
Cell of Directorate of
Health Services,
Naharlagun
(Itnagar
Arunachal Pardesh

Director
SFRI
Vinvihar
Itanagar Arunachal
Pradesh

Commissioner & Secreatry
Health and Family Welfare
Deptt. of
Government of Assam
Dispur (Assam)

Dy. Conservatory of Forests cum Director
Environment (and CEO,
MP Board)
Old Architect Building,
Sector-19B
Madhya Marg,
Chandigarh-160019 (UT)

Chhattisgarh State Minor Forest Produce Federation
10, Anupam Bagar,
Raipur, Chhattisgarh

Dy. Conservatory of Forests (T)
Moti Daman-396220

Managing Director
Forest Co-operation
Gandhinagar,
Gujarat

CCF (Protection) Govt. of Haryana
(Dr. Pravez Ahmed, IFS)
Van Bhawan Sector-6
Panchkula – 134109,
Chandigarh

Director (Ayurveda)
Ayurveda Bhawan
SDA Complex,
Block No. 26,
Kasumpati
Shimla-171009

Officer on Special Duty
26-SDA Complex,
Kashumpati
Shimla – 171 009

OSD/Chief Executive Officer
State Medicinal Plants
Board
3/12 AB Civil Secretariat,
Jammu/Srinagar (J&K)

Divisional Forest Officer
Forest Resource Survey
Division
Ranchi, Jharkhand

Executive Officer,
Karnataka State Medicinal
Plants Authority (KMPA)
Forest Campus, Arakere
MICO Layout
Banne Ghatta Road,
Bangalore – 560076

Managing Director
Chief Executive Officer
State Medicinal Plants
Board
The Pharmacutical Corp.
(IM) Kerala (Ltd.)
Thrissur Oushadhi
680001

Director Medicine & Health Service &
Member Secretary,
Medicinal Plants Board
Directorate of Medical &
Health Service
Kavaratti (UT of
Lakshadweep)

Commissioner,
Medicinal & Aromatic Plants,
M. P. State MFP (Trade & Dev.)
Co-operative-Federation,
Khel Parisar
Indira Nikunj,
74, Bunglow, Bhopal-1

Diector (Ayurveda)
Maharashtra State Medicinal Plants Board
2nd Floor, Pharmacy Building, R.A. Poddar
Worli, Mumbai – 400018

Secretary, Health & Family Welfare
Government of Mizoram
Aizawal
Mizoram

Programme Officer (ISM&H)
Department of Health & Family Welfare
Government of Nagaland,
Kohima

Member Secretary
Rajasthan State Medicinal Plants Board
373, Krishi Bhawan, 3rd Floor, Jaipur (Rajasthan)

Mr. A. Shekhar, IAS, Secretary (Ayu.)
Room No. 75, Main Building, Secretariat
Govt. of Rajasthan
Jaipur – 302 004

Principal CCF-cum-Secretary
(CEO & Member Secretary SMPB)
Department of Forest, Environment & Wildlife,
Govt. of Sikkim Deorali – 637 102 (Gungtok)

Commissioner,
India Systems of Medicine & Homoeopathy
Arignar Anna Government Hospital Campus
Arumbakkam,
Chennai – 600 106

Chief Executive Officer & Member Secretary
Medicinal Plants Board of Tripura
Forest Research Division
Aranya Bhawan,
Nehru Complex
P.O. Kunjaban,
Agartala – 799006

Director
Herbal Research & Development Institute
Mandal,
Gopeshwar,
Uttranchal

Secretary (IAM Branch)
State Medicinal Plants Board
Mitra Building (4th floor)
8, Lyons Range,
Kolkatta – 1 (WB)

Market Survey Cum Detailed Techno Economic Feasibility Reports

EIRI Consultants & Engineers have recently prepared the following **"Market Survey Cum Detailed Techno Economic Feasibility Reports"** which are having great future prospect. The **Detailed Project Reports** will also help you

To get Loan/Finance from Banks/Financial Institutions.

To set up your own Industry/Unit (For SSI/Medium/Large Scale Unit).

To have Detailed and Exhaustive Data on any required Items/Projects.

'ENGINEERS INDIA RESEARCH INSTITUTE' (EIRI) The Premier and Trusted Industrial Consultancy Organization from last 25 Years, offer Complete Consultancy, Liaisoning Jobs, Foreign Collaborations, Buy Back Arrangements etc. alongwith **"Market Survey Cum Detailed Techno Economic Feasibility Reports"** to the entrepreneurs as well as established Industrialists.

WHY EIRI ONLY ? Because **'EIRI'** is having (1) Well equipped data bank cum library. (2) Fully expertise team of consultants, technocrats & engineers for prepairing **"Market Survey Cum Detailed Techno Economic Feasibility Reports"** on any items in Small/ Medium/ Large Scale. (3) Record quantity of over ***32,000*** **"Market Survey Cum Detailed Techno Economic Feasibility Reports"** readily available. (4) More than thousands satisfied clients. (5) Vast experience of more than 25 years. (6) **'EIRI'** is being undertaken plants on turnkey basis and (7) Latest and detailed authentic informations Covered in each **"Market Survey Cum Detailed Techno Economic Feasibility Reports"** and many more plus points which stands **'EIRI'** on top.

BRIEF CONTENTS

BEGINING : Project Introduction, Brief History of the Product, Properties, BIS (Bureau of Indian Standard) Specifications & Requirements, Uses & Applications.

MARKET SURVEY : Present Market Position, Expected Future Demand, Installed Capacity, Actual Production & Demand, Statistics of Imports & Exports, Export Prospect, Names & Addresses of Existing Units (Present Manufacturers), List of Buyers.

MANUFACTURING PROCESS : Detailed Process of Manufacture, Selection of Process, Flow Sheet Diagram, Production Schedule.

RAW MATERIALS : List of Raw Materials, Properties, Availability of Raw Materials, Required Quantity of Raw Materials, Cost of Raw Materials, Suppliers of Raw Materials.

PLANT & MACHINERY : List of Plant & Machineries, Miscellaneous Items & Accessories, Instruments, Laboratory Equipments & Accessories, Plant Location, Electrification, Electric Load & Water Maintenance, Suppliers/Manufacturers of Plant & Machineries, Specifications of Machineries & Equipments.

PERSONNEL REQUIREMENTS : Requirement of Staff & Labour, Personnel Management, Skilled & Unskilled Labour, Manageriol Staff/Expert, Accountant etc.

LAND & BUILDING : Requirement of Land Area, Rates of the Land, Built up Area, Construction Schedule, Plant Layout, Cost of Boundry Wall etc.

FINANCIAL ASPECTS : Cost of Raw Materials, Cost of Land & Building, Cost of Plant & Machineries, Fixed Capital Investment, Working Capital, Project Cost, Capital Formation, Cost of Production, Profitability Analysis, Break Even Point (BEP), Cash Flow Statement for 5 to 10 Years, Depreciation Chart, Foreign Collaboration (if possible), Conclusion, Projected Balance sheet, Land Man Ratio.

ADDRESSES : Present Manufacturers, List of the Buyers, Plant & Equipment Suppliers/ Manufacturers, Raw Material Suppliers/Manufacturers etc.

LIST OF THE READY AVAILABLE DETAILED PROJECT REPORTS

AUTOMOBILES, MECHANICAL & METALLURGICAL

1. AGRICULTRAL EQUIPMENTS
2. AGRICULTRAL EQUIPMENTS INCLUDING THRESHERS
3. AIR BRAKE HELICAL COIL
4. AIR COOLER
5. AIR FILTERS(FOR SCOOTER CAR & EXCAVATORS ETC.)
6. ALUMINIUM & ALUMINIUM ALLOYS FROM ALUMINIUM SCRAP TO MAKE UTENSILS (INDUCTION FURNACE MELTED)
7. ALUMINIUM ALLOY WHEELS
8. ALUMINIUM ALLOYS FROM ALUMINIUM SCRAP TO MAKE UTENSILS (INDUCTION FURNACE)
9. ALUMINIUM HOT & COLD ROLLING MILL
10. ALUMINIUM BOTTLE MANUFACTURING (COLD EXTRUSION OF ALUMINIUM)
11. ALUMINIUM/COPPER CABLE LUGS
12. ALUMINIUM CANS FOR BEER PACKAGING
13. ALUMINIUM CANS FOR CAPACITORS
14. ALUMINIUM CAPS FOR INJECTION VIALS
15. ALUMINIUM EXTRUSION
16. ALUMINIUM FURNITURE & HARDWARE
17. ALUMINIUM SHEET ROLLING MILL
18. ALUMINIUM UTENSILS
19. ALUMINIUM UTENSILS & SCHOOL BOXES
20. ALUMINIUM WIRE DRAWING AND SUPER ENAMELLING FOR WINDING
21. ANODISED ALUMINIUM UTENSILS
22. ANODIZING OF ALUMINIUM
23. ANTIMONY OXIDE FROM LEAD SCRAP
24. ARC WELDING FILTER GLASS
25. ALUMINIUM FOIL CUTTING & ROLL MAKING
26. AUTO FLAPS FOR TRUCKS & BUSES
27. AUTOMOBILE WORKSHOP (GARAGE & SERVICE CENTRE)
28. AUTO GEARS
29. AUTO HORNS
30. AUTO LEAF SPRING
31. AUTO TUBES
32. AUTO PISTON RING
33. AUTO PISTON
34. BAKERY AND BISCUITS EQUIPMENTS FABRICATION
35. BALL POINT PEN REFILLS
36. BALL ROLLER & TAPER BEARING
37. BAND SAW BLADES
38. BARBED WIRE
39. BICYCLE SPOKES
40. BRAKE LINING ASBESTOES/ RESIN BASED & ASBESTOES FREE
41. BRASS ARTWARE/HOLLOW WARE CASTING (WITH THE HELP OF PHENOLIC RESIN)
42. BRASS CASTING
43. BRASS PIPES FROM BRASS SHEET WITH LONGITUDINALLY WELDING
44. BRASS WARE BY CASTING METHOD (BRASS ARTICLES VIZ. BRASS POOJA LAMPS AND OTHER CASTED)
45. BRIGHT BARS
46. BUFFING AND POLISHING INDUSTRY (JOB WORK)
47. BUTT HINGE (BRASS SHEET)
48. CARBON BRUSH HOLDER & SLIP RING
49. CO_2 WELDING WIRE ELECTRODES (COPPER/ COPPER ALLOY COATED M.S.WIRE)
50. CARBON FILM RESISTORS
51. CARBURETTORS
52. CAST STEEL PANES FOR MELTING FURNACE
53. CHEMICAL ETCHING OF STAINLESS STEEL
54. CHEMICAL RESISTANT IRON & STEEL
55. COLD FORM SECTION MILL
56. COLD ROLLED FORMING OF SECTION AND OTHER SECTIONS
57. COLD ROLLING OF MS STRIP
58. COLD TWISTED DE-FORMED RIBBED STEEL
59. COMPRESSOR (HERMETIC) FOR AIR CONDITIONERS
60. COMPRESSED NATURAL GAS (CNG KIT) FOR AUTOVEHICLE
61. CONTINUOUSLY CAST STEEL WIRE RODS (5 mm)
62. CONTINUOUS CASTING COPPER WIRE RODS
63. CONVEYOR BELTINGS
64. CONVEYOR BELT, TRANSM -ISSION BELT & V BELTS
65. COOKING RANGES
66. COPPER/BRASS SHEETS, CIRCLE & UTENSILS
67. COPPER FOIL
68. COPPER INGOTS, RODS MAKING & WIRE DRAWING
69. COPPER PRODUCTS FROM COPPER SCRAP
70. COPPER SMELTING PLANT
71. COPPER WIRE RODS FROM COPPER SCRAP
72. CORRUGATED BOX MAKING MACHINERY AND OTHER THEIR PARTS
73. CYLINDER LINER FOR AUTOMOBILES
74. DOOR LOCKS/PAD LOCKS
75. DRILL BITS & TOOL BITS
76. DRUM CLOSURES
77. ERW STEEL CONDUIT PIPE
78. EARTH MOVING EQPT.
79. ENGINE VALVES FOR AUTOMOBILES
80. FABRICATION OF HEAT EXCHANGER
81. FABRICATION OF STORAGE TANKS AND M.S. DRUM
82. FERROUS ALLOY NI-HARDY I.V CASTING
83. FERROUS Mn ALLOY CASTING BY ALUMINA THERMIC PROCESS
84. FERRO ALLOYS
85. FERRO SILICON & FERRO MANGANESE FROM DOLOMITE (SMS GRADE)
86. FIRE EXTINGUISHERS
87. FLIP-TONE CANS
88. FORGED CONECTING ROD
89. FORGING UNIT
90. FOUNTAIN PEN NIBS
91. FOUNDRY SAND
92. FUEL INJECTION SYSTEM
93. GALVANIZED M.S.STRIPS
94. GALVANIZING PLANT
95. GALVANIZED IRON WIRE
96. GAS WELDING TORCHES AND NOZZLES
97. GASKET SHEET
98. GATE GRILLS & WINDOW FRAMES
99. GENERATING SET (DIESEL)
100. HARD ANODISED ALUMINIUM
101. HOSPITAL WARES
102. HOSPITAL FURNITURES
103. HOT DIP GALVANIZING
104. HOT FORGED FASTENERS
105. HOT MIX PLANT
106. INJECTION MOULDED PLASTIC COMPOUNDS WITH TOOL ROOM
107. INJECTION MOULDED PLASTIC COMPONENTS AND METAL PIPE SPINNING UNIT
108. INVESTMENT CASTING
109. IRON/STEEL WIRE GAUGE
110. IRON TAWA
111. KNIVES (S.S.KNIVES)
112. KITCHEN SINK (S.S.)
113. L.P.G REGULATORS
114. MACHINE SCREWS & SELF TAPPING SCREWS
115. MARUTI WORKSHOP CUM SERVICE STATION
116. MAGNESIUM INGOTS & BULLETS CASTING

Above all the Detailed Project Report are available at *"ENGINEERS INDIA RESEARCH INSTITUTE"*. 4449, Nai Sarak (D), Main Road Delhi - 110 006

● Ph : 91-11-23918117, 2391 6431, 2392 0361, 31082370 ● Fax : 91-11-2391 6431

● E-Mail : eirisidi@bol.net.in

117. MANUFACTURE OF TIN CONTAINERS
118. MANUFACTURE OF STORAGE TANKS, PRESSURE VESSELS, HEAT EXCHANGERS
119. MARK II HAND PUMPS
120. MARUTI WORKSHOP CUM - SERVICE STATION
121. MECHANICAL JACKS
122. METAL CUTTING DIE DESIGN
123. METAL CUTTING OF AND GRINDING WHEELS (ABRASIVE CUTTING WHEELS)
124. METAL HOOKS & CLIPS
125. METAL SEPARATION (COPPER, TIN, LEAD) FROM SPENT WASH ACID
126. METALLIC RING JOINTS
127. METALLIC GASKET (SPIRAL WOUND)
128. MICROVEE & ABSOLUTE FILTER
129. MICROWAVE OVEN
130. MILD STEEL INGOTS
131. MINI STEEL PLANT
132. MODERN VEHICLE WORKSHOP
133. MOPED
134. M.S.HINGES
135. M.S.INGOT AND HR. STEEL STRUCTURALS
136. M.S.INGOT BY INDUCTION FURNACES
137. M.S.PIPES
138. M.S. WELDING ELECTRODE
139. MUFFLERS & SILENCERS FOR THREE WHEELERS
140. NAIL CUTTER WITH FILER & MANICURE
141. NICHROME WIRE
142. NICKEL LINED SCREENS
143. NON-FERROUS ALLOY ROLLING
144. NON-FERROUS FORGING
145. NON-FERROUS FOUNDRY
146. NON PRESSURE
147. INCANDESCENT LAMP
148. NUMBER COMBINATION LOCKS FOR LUGGAGES
149. NUTS & BOLTS
150. PAPER COATED ALUMINIUM AND COPPER WIRE
151. PETROMAX CONTAINER
152. PHOTO ETCHING OF STAINLESS STEEL PLATES
153. PIPE GALVANIZING PLANT
154. PISTON RING-AUTOMOBILE
155. PLANT PROTECTION EQUIPMENTS
156. PLATINUM LABORATORY APPARATUS
157. PRESSURE COOKER & ALUMINIUM UTENSILS
158. PRESSURE COOKER (ALUMINIUM)
159. PRESSURE DIE CASTING
160. PRINTED ALUMINIUM COLLAPSIBLE TUBES
161. PRINTED TIN CONTAINERS
162. PRINTING PRESS (CYLINDER MACHINE)
163. PUMPS FOR CHEMICAL INDUSTRY (SPECIAL)
164. RAILWAY SLEEPERS (M.S.)
165. RAZOR TWIN BLADE
166. R.C.C SPUN PIPES
167. RECONDITIONING OF M.S. DRUMS/BARRELS
168. RE-ROLLING COPPER AND BRASS SHEET AND RODS
169. RE-ROLLING MILLS
170. RESIN COATED SAND
171. RESIN CORED SOFT SOLDER WIRES
172. ROLLING MILL (BY INDUCTION FURNACE) & MANUFACTURE OF BARS, ANGLES, SQUARES, TUBES AND OTHERS
173. ROLLER BEARING & FORGING
174. ROLLING OF STAINLESS STEEL PATTA
175. RUBBER INSULATED PLIERS (HAND TOOLS)
176. RUBBING COMPOUND FOR AUTOMOBILES
177. SCIENTIFIC LABORATORY EQUIPMENTS
178. SCOOTER ASSEMBLING
179. SECONDARY LEAD EXTRAC-TION BY SCRAP BATTERY PLATES,PIPES & SHEET
180. SEAMLESS M.S. TUBES & PIPES
181. SELF TAPPING STEEL SCREW
182. SEWING NEEDLES
183. S.G. IRON & ALLOY STEEL
184. SHEET METAL PRODUCTS, (FERROUS/NON-FERROUS)
185. SHIP/MARINE CONTAINER
186. SHOCK ABSORBERS
187. SHOE EYELETS
188. SHOT AND GRITS BY AUTOMIZATION PROCESS
189. SHOVELS
190. SILICO MANGANESE ALLOYS
191. SILENCERS (MUFFLERS) EXHAUST & TAIL PIPE FOR ALL TYPES OF VEHICLES
192. SINTERED BEARING
193. SINTERED BUSHES
194. SINTERED METAL PRODUCTS
195. SOFT AND HARD FERRITES
196. SPANNERS
197. SPARK PLUGS
198. STEEL PLANT (ELECTRIC ARC FURNACE BASED- EAF)
199. SPHERIODAL GRAPHITE CAST IRON
200. SPRAY DRYER
201. STAINLESS STEEL HINGES
202. STAINLESS STEEL SHEET ROLLING TO PRODUCE STAINLESS STEEL UTENSILS
203. STAINLESS STEEL UTENSILS
204. STAPLE PINS,PAPER PIN, GEM CLIPS ETC.
205. STEEL CASTINGS
206. STEEL CHAIN
207. STEEL FOUNDRY
208. STEEL FURNITURES AND ELECTRICAL APPLIANCES
209. STEEL PLANT (MINI)
210. STEEL RODS AND COILS FROM SCRAPS
211. STEEL ROLLING MILL
212. STEEL STRIPS (COLD ROLLED) SILICON WITH GRAIN RIENTED FOR ELECTRIC USE
213. STEEL TRANSMISSION LINE TOWERS & ROLLING MILL TO PRODUCE STEEL SECTION
214. STEEL FURNITURES AND ELECTRICAL APPLIANCES
215. STEEL WIRE DRAWING AND GALVANIZING
216. STEEL WOOL
217. SUBMERGED ARC WELDED PIPES
218. SUBMERSIBLE PUMP MANUFACTURING
219. SUPER ENAMELLED COPPER WIRE
220. THREE WHEELERS
221. TIE-ROD ENDS
222. TIN CONTAINERS
223. TOOLROOM AND SHEET METAL PRODUCTS
224. TRACTOR TRAILERS
225. TRANSMISSION POWER FITTING
226. TUBULAR POLES
227. SUPER ENAMELLED COPPER WIRES
228. TUBULAR POLES FOR ELECTRICAL TRANSMISSION (BY FABRICATION PROCESS)
229. TUBULAR POLES OF M.S. & HIGH TENSILE STEEL
230. VACUUM CLEANERS
231. VACUUM FLASK (STAINLESS STEEL)
232. VALVES FOR REFRIGERA TION AND AIR-CONDITION
233. VEHICLE WELDING & PAINTING
234. VENETION BLIND
235. WASHING MACHINES (AUTOMATIC & COMPUTERISED)
236. WATER CONTROLLER (AUTOMATIC)
237. WATCH STRAPS/CHAINS/ BRACELETS/BELT BRASS & STAINLESS STEEL
238. WATER COOLERS
239. WELDED WIRE MESH
240. WELDING ELECTRODES
241. WICK STOVES
242. WIND MILL WINDOW FRAME (FERROUS & NON-FERROUS)
243. WRIST WATCH

Above all the Detailed Project Report are available at *"ENGINEERS INDIA RESEARCH INSTITUTE"*. 4449, Nai Sarak (D), Main Road Delhi - 110 006
• Ph : 91-11-23918117, 2391 6431, 2392 0361, 31082370 • Fax : 91-11-2391 6431
• E-Mail : eirisidi@bol.net.in

LIST OF FEW READILY AVAILABLE 'DETAILED PROJECT REPORTS' OUT OF 30,000 REPORTS

CHEMICALS (ORGANIC & INORGANIC)

244. ACETIC ANHYDRIDE
245. ACETIC ACID FROM ETHANOL
246. ACETYLENE BLACK
247. ACETYLENE GAS
248. ACETYLENE GAS & OXYGEN (INTEGERATED UNIT)
249. ACID SLURRY BY MANUAL PROCESS
250. ACTIVATED ALUMINA
251. ACTIVATED BLEACHING EARTH (ACTIVATED FULLERS EARTH)
252. ACTIVATED CARBON FROM CASHEWNUT SHELL
253. ACTIVATED CARBON FROM RICE HUSK
254. ACTIVATED CARBON FROM RICE HUSK, COCONUT SHELL & COCONUT POWDER
255. ACTIVATED CARBON FROM WOOD
256. ACTIVATED CARBON POWDER & GRANULES FROM COCONUT SHELL
257. ACTIVATED CARBON & SODIUM SILICATE FROM PADDY & RICE HUSK
258. ALUM FOR WATER TREATMENT
259. AEROSOL INSECTICIDES SPRAY (BAYGON, HIT, MORTEIN TYPE)
260. AGARBATTI SYNTHETIC PERFUMERY COMPOUNDS
261. ALCOHOL FROM POTATO
262. ALCOHOL FROM RICE GRAINS
263. ALCOHOL FROM RICE HUSK
264. ALCOHOL FROM MOLASSES
265. ALCOHOL, BEER, STARCH, LIQUID GLUCOSE, DEXTROSE, SORBITOL, VITAMIN-C, GERM OIL, CATTLE FEED ETC. FROM MAIZE
266. ALKYD RESIN
267. ALKYLATED PHENOL LIKE NONYL PHENOL, DODECYL PHENOL
268. ALUM (NON FERRIC)
269. ALUM (FERRIC)
260. ALUMINIUM INGOT BY BAUXITE
261. ALUMINIUM PHOSPHIDE
262. ALUMINIUM PHOSPHATE
263. AMINES & ALLIED PRODUCTS
264. AMMONIA GAS
265. AMMONIA GAS BOTTLING
266. AMMONIA LIQUOR
267. AMMONIUM CHLORIDE (PURE & TECHNICAL)
268. ANILINE
269. ARGON GAS
270. ARIEL TYPE DETERGENT POWDER
271. ANTHRAQUINONE
272. ANTIMONY TRIOXIDE
273. AZODICARBONAMIDE
274. BAKING SODA FROM ASH
275. BARIUM CARBONATE
276. BARIUM COMPOUNDS
277. BARIUM PEROXIDE
278. BARIUM-THIO-SULPHATE BANZENE
279. BARYTE POWDER
280. BEER PLANT
281. BELT PASTE (WITH BFS OIL)
282. BENZYL ACETATE, BENZYL BENZOATE, BENZYL ALCOHOL
283. BETA NAPHTHOL
284. BENTONITE POWDER
285. BENZIDINE
286. BIO GAS PLANT
287. BIO GAS FILLING IN CYLINDER
288. BI-CHROMATE OF SODIUM, POTASSIUM & AMMONIUM
289. BI-FUNCTIONAL BLACK MFGR. REACTIVE DYE (DYE FROM COTTON YARN DYEING)
290. BITUMINOUS ROAD EMULSION
291. BLACK PHENYL
292. BLACK SULPHUR
293. BLEACHING POWDER (STABLE)
294. BONE CRUSHING PLANT
295. BONE MEAL (CALCINED) ENRICHMENT WITH CALCIUM & PHOSPHORUS
296. BORIC ACID
297. B.O.N. ACID
298. BRANDY
299. BUTANOL
300. 1,4, BUTANEDIOL
301. BUTYL ACETATE
302. CAFFEIN FROM TEA WASTE
303. CALCINED LIME (DEAD BURNT DOLOMITE)
304. CALCINING OF MAGNESITE & DEAD BURNT MAGNESITE
305. CALCIUM ALUMINATE
306. CALCIUM CARBIDE
307. CALCIUM CARBONATE
308. CALCIUM CARBONATE (PRECIPITATED) FROM BY PRODUCT (LIME SLURRY & CARBON DIOXIDE)
309. CALCIUM CARBONATE (ACTIVATED & PRECIPITATED)
310. CALCIUM CHLORIDE
311. CALCIUM GLUCONATE
312. CALCIUM NITRATE
313. CALCIUM SILICATE BRICKS
314. CAMPHOR POWDER (SYNTHETIC)
315. CARBON DIOXIDE
316. CARBON BLACK FROM FERTILIZER WASTE
317. CARBOXY METHYL CELLULOSE (CMC)
318. CASEIN AND BY PRODUCTS
319. CASEIN FROM MILK
320. CATIONIC SOFTNER (STEARIC ACID BASED)
321. CAUSTIC SODA
322. CAUSTIC SODA FROM TRONA
323. CAUSTIC SODA, CHLORINE AND HYDROGEN GAS BY ELECTRO-LYSIS OF BRINE SOLUTION
324. CELLULOSE ACETATE MOULDING POWDER
325. CELLULOSE POWDER & MICRO CRYSTALLINE CELLULOSE POWDER
326. CEMENT COLOUR
327. CEMENT FROM FLY ASH & LIME
328. CEMENT TILES (GLAZED)
329. DOUBLE FIRING (HEATING)
330. CHELATED ZINC (ZN EDTA)
331. CHEMICALS FROM PRAWN HEAD
332. CHITIN & CHITOSAN FROM PRAWN SHELL WASTE
333. CHLORAL HYDRATE
334. CHLORAMPHENICOL
335. CHROMIC ACID (WITH POLLUTION CONTROL)
336. CHROMIC ACID (OXIDE) & BLUE OXIDE
337. CHLORINATED PARAFFIN WAX (CPW)
338. CHROMIC ACID
339. CEMENT PAINT & DISTEMPER
340. CITRIC ACID FROM LEMON
341. CITRIC ACID FROM MOLASSES
342. CLEANING OF COOLING SYSTEM AND BOILER
343. COAL TAR DISTILLATION
344. COBALT OCTOATE
345. COMPOST FOR MUSHROOM
346. COPPER OXYCHLORIDE
347. COPPER PHTHALOCYANINE BLUE & GREEN
348. CORRECTION FLUID
349. CYANURIC CHLORIDE
350. DEFOAMING AGENT FOR PAPER INDUSTRY
351. DE-NICKELING (ELECTROLYTIC PROCESS)
352. DETERGENT CAKE & POWDER
353. DETERGENT POWDER
354. DETERGENT CONCENTRATE (IDET 10)
355. DEXTROSE MONOHYDRATE & DEXTROSE ANHYDROUS POWDER FROM TAPIOCA STARCH
356. DI-BASIC LEAD STEARATE
357. DI CALCIUM PHOSPHATE
358. DICLOFENAL SODIUM SLOW RELEASE (SR) TABLES 100MG.

Above all the Detailed Project Report are available at *"ENGINEERS INDIA RESEARCH INSTITUTE"*. 4449, Nai Sarak (D), Main Road Delhi - 110 006

● Ph : 91-11-23918117, 2391 6431, 2392 0361, 31082370 ● Fax : 91-11-2391 6431

● E-Mail : eirisidi@bol.net.in

359. DI ETHYL OXALATE
360. DI METHYL ORTHOPHTHALATE
361. DI-METHYL PHTHALATE
362. DICLOFENAC GEL
363. DIOCTYL PHTHALATE (DOP)
364. DI PHENYL GLYCERINE
365. DI PHENYL OXIDE
366. DINITRO-CHLORO BENZENE
367. DISTILLED WATER
368. DODECYL BENZENE SULPHONATE
369. DUSTLESS CHALK
370. EDTA & ITS SALTS
371. ELECTROLESS NICKEL PLATING ON PLASTICS
372. ENDOSULFAN
373. EPOXY RESIN BASED COMPOUND
374. ETHYL ACETATE
375. EHTYL ETHER
376. ETHYL ALCOHOL (POTABLE LIQUOR)
377. ETHYL HEXANOL
378. EXTRACTION OF ESSENTIAL OILS BY SUGAR CRITICAL FLUID (CARBON DIOXIDE) METHOD FROM FLOWERS, HERBAL & SPICES
379. FERRIC ALUM
380. FERRO CHROME LIGNO SULPHONATE
381. FERRO MANGANESE
382. FERRO SILICONE
383. FERRO VANADIUM FROM VANADIUM SLUDGE
384. FERROUS SILICATE
385. FERROUS SULPHATE
386. FERTILIZER FROM ANIMAL BLOOD & LEATHER WASTE
387. FLUORESCENT TUBE LIGHT POWDER
388. FOAMED PVC COMPOUNDING & ITS PRODUCTS
389. FORMALDEHYDE
390. FRACTIONAL DISTILLATION OF D.M.O (DEMENTHOLIZED OIL)
391. FRACTIONAL DISTILLATION OF ESSENTIAL OIL & MEDICINAL PLANT EXTRACT
392. FRICTION DUST (LIQUID & POWDER) FROM CNSL
393. FRUIT FLAVOURS
394. FURFURAL FROM RICE HUSK
395. GARLIC ACID
396. GASKET SHELLAC COMPOUND
397. GEAR OIL
398. GIBBERELLIC ACID
399. GLASS PUTTY
400. GLYCERINE
401. GOSSYPOL (POLY PHENOL) FROM COTTON SEED OIL
402. GUAR GUM POWDER
403. HAIR FIXER (HAIR GEL TYPE)
404. H - ACID
405. HENNA PASTE MAKING
406. HEPTAL DEHYDE
407. HIGH CARBON FERRO CHROME
408. HYDRATED CALCIUM SILICATE BRICK
409. HYDRATED LIME FROM SEA SHELL
410. HYDROCHLORIC ACID
411. HYDRO FLUORIC ACID
412. HYDROGEN PEROXIDE (BY AUTO-OXIDATION PROCESS)
413. ICE PACKS (SOLUTIONS TYPE, WHITE GEL TYPE, VIOLET SEMI SOLID POLYMER TYPE)
414. IMPROVING DROP POINT PARAFFIN WAX FROM 45-50°C TO 75-80°C
415. INDUSTRIAL ALCOHOL
416. INTEGERATED COMPLEX OF EASTER & ALLIED PRODUCTS (D.O.P, D.B.P, ETHYL ACETATE WIRE ENAMEL & CABLE JELLY)
417. IMFL (WHISKY) & COUNTRY LIQUOR
418. IRON OXIDE FOR MAKING FERITTE
419. IRON SULPHIDE
420. JUTE BATCHING OIL
421. KESH KALA TEL (HAIR DYE LOTION) (VASMOL 33, BLACK NITE TYPE)
422. L-LYSINE MONOHYDROCHLORIDE
423. LACTIC ACID FROM WHITE SUGAR BY FERMENTATION PROCESS
424. LDPE GRANULES FROM VIRGIN (LDPE RESIN)
425. LEAD EXTRACTION FROM BATTERY SCRAP
426. LEAD OXIDE (A) LEAD MONOXIDE (B) LEAD TETRA OXIDE (C) GREYLEAD OXIDE
427. LIQUID GLUCOSE & ITS BY PRODUCTS
428. LIQUID OXYGEN BOTTLING PLANT
429. LIQUID SHOE POLISH
430. LIQUID FLOOR POLISH
431. LUBE OIL VISCOSITY IMPROVED FOR P.P.G/P.E.G.
432. LUBRICANTS ASHLESS 100% COMBUSTION
433. MAGNESIUM CARBONATE AND MAGNESIUM BICARMONATE
434. MAGNESIUM HYDROXIDE POWDER
435. MAGNESIUM SILICATE
436. MAGNESIUM SULPHATE
437. MALACHITE GREEN
438. MALEIC ANHYDRIDE
439. MANGANESE SULPHATE
440. MANUFACTURING OF CARBON MONO-OXIDE WATER GAS
441. MENTHOL BOLD CRYSTALS FROM FLAKES
442. MENTHOL CRYSTAL & MENTHA OIL
443. MERCURIC OXIDE
444. METAL PRE-TREATMENT CHEMICALS
445. METHANE GAS BY SODIUM ACETATE & SODA LIME
446. METHYL ACETYL RICINOLATE
447. METOL
448. METOL FROM HYDROQUINONE & METHYLAMINE
449. MICANITE
450. MICRO NUTRIENT MIXTURE
451. MINERAL WATER
452. MINERAL WATER AND PET BOTTILNG PLANT
453. MINERAL WATER IN BOTTLES, GLASS AND POUCHES
454. MINI CEMENT PLANT (BY ROTARY KILN PROCESS)
455. MIXED FERTILIZER
456. MOSQUITO & FLIES REPELLENT AGARBATTI (INCENSE STICKS)
457. MONO CHLORO ACETIC ACID
458. MONOCROTOPHOS (TECHNICAL)
459. MOSQUITO COIL
460. MOSQUITO COIL & MAT
461. MOSQUITO MAT
462. MOTHER TINCTURE & BIO CHEMIC MEDICINES
463. NAPHTHALENE & PHENYL (INTEGRATED UNIT)
464. NATURAL MINERAL WATER BY REVERSE OSMOSIS PROCESS
465. NICKEL PLATING BRIGHTNER (PRIMARY OR CARRIER BRIGHTNER & SECONDARY BRIGHTNER)
466. NICKEL SULPHATE
467. NICOTINE FROM TOBACCO WASTE
468. NICOTINE SULPHATE FROM TOBACCO WASTE
469. NITRO BENZENE
470. NITRO CELLULOSE SANDING SEALER/LACQUER
471. NITRO MUSK
472. NITROGEN & OXYGEN GAS PLANT
473. NON-IONIC SURFACTANT (WETTING AGENT)
474. NO-CARB PASTE
475. OCTANOL
476. ORTHO NITRO PHENOL
477. OXALIC ACID FROM MOLASSES
478. OXALIC ACID FROMRICE HUSK
479 OXALIC ACID FROM TREE BARK
470. OXALIC ACID FROM WASTE VEGETABLES
471. OXYGEN GAS PLANT
472. OXYGEN GAS PLANT (AIR SEPERATION METHOD)
473. PARA-AMINO BENZOIC ACID
474. PARA-AMINO PHENOL
475. PARA TOLUENE SULPHONIC ACID
476. PECTIN FROM RAW PAPAYA
477. PERFUME (LEMON & OTHERS)

Above all the Detailed Project Report are available at *"ENGINEERS INDIA RESEARCH INSTITUTE"*. 4449, Nai Sarak (D), Main Road Delhi - 110 006

● Ph : 91-11-23918117, 2391 6431, 2392 0361, 31082370 ● Fax : 91-11- 2391 6431

● E-Mail : eirisidi@bol.net.in

Pay Rs. 8,000/- Only

for Tailor made Report We (EIRI) are fully capable to prepare any report as per your requirements

478. PESTICIDE PREPARATION USING NEEM FRUIT & SEEDS (MARGOSA)
479. PET BOTTLES FROM PRE-FORM
480. PET PREFORM FROM RESIN FOR PET BOTTLES
481. PETROLEUM JELLY
482. PHENOL
483. PHENYL
484. PHENYL (BLACK) IN LIQUID FORM
485. PHTHALIC ANHYDRIDE
486. PHOSPHORIC ACID FROM ROCK PHOSPHATE
487. PHOSPHORUS BY CHEMICAL PROCESS
488. PHOTO EMULSION FOR ROTARY SCREEN PRINTING
489. PHTHALOCYANINE BLUE
480. PIGMENT EMULSION FOR TEXTILE
481. PIGMENT GUM
482. PLANT GROWTH REAGEN BASED CHLOROTHYL TRIMETHYL AMMONIUM CHLORIDE
483. PLANT HARMONES BASED ON 2,4-DICHLORPHENOXY ACENTIC ACID & NAPHTHALENE
484. PLASTICINE (MODELLING CLAY)
485. PLASTIC WASTE REPROCESSING
486. PLASTER OF PARIS BANDAGES
487. POLYESTER RESIN (G.P. GRADE LAMINATE GRADE, ELECTRICAL GRADE)
488. POLY VINYL ACETATE
489. POLYVINYL ACETATE EMULSION
490. POLYURETHENE FOAM
491. POTASSIUM DICHROMATE/ BICHROMATE
492. POTASSIUM IODATE
493. POTASSIUM NITRATE
494. POTASSIUM PERMAGNATE
495. POTASSIUM PER SULPHATE
496. POTASSIUM SULPHATE (FERTILIZER GRADE)
497. POTASSIUM PER OXY DI-SULPHIDE
498. POTASSIUM SILICATE
499. POTASSIUM STEARATE
500. POWER ALCOHOL
501. PVC RESIN FROM ETHYL ALCOHOL
502. PYRIDINE & ITS DERIVATIVES
503. RAPID FAST DYES (ONLY PROCESS)
504. REACTOR (CHEMICAL)
505. RECLAMATION OF USED ENGINE OIL (BY CLAY & VACUUM DISTILLATION PROCESS)
506. RECLAMATION OF SPENT BLEACHING EARTH
507. RECLAMATION OF NICKEL SPENT CATALYST FROM VANASPATI INDUSTRY
508. RECTIFIED SPIRIT FROM MOLASSES & MAHUA FLOWERS
509. RECTIFIED SPIRIT FROM RICE STRAW
510. RED OXIDE PAINT/PRIMER (ANTI CORROSIVE) BASED ORGANIC RED PIGMENTS
511. REMOVAL OF ANTIMONY FROM LEAD SCRAP
512. RESORCINOL
513. ROSIN SIZING AGENT
514. RESORCINOL
515. SALINE AND INJECTION WATER
516. SALICYLIC ACID
517. SANTONIN
518. SENNOSIDES FROM SENNO LEAF
519. SHOE POLISH
520. SILICA GEL (BLUE SELF INDICATING PROCESS)
521. SILICONE EMULSION
522. SILICONE FROM RICE HUSK
523. SILICON FROM SILICA (SEMI CONDUCTOR GRADE)
524. SILICONE RESINS
525. SILICONE SPRAYSILVER BRAZING FOIL
526. SILVER EXTRACTION FROM WASTE HYPO SOLUTION
527. SILVER NITRATE
528. SILVER PARTS FOR CERAMIC CAPACITOR SINGLE SUPER PHOSPHATE & MIXED FERTILIZER (NPK)
529. SINGLE SUPER PHOSPHATE (S.S.P) & SULPHURIC ACID
530. SODA ASH
531. SODA ASH FROM NATRON
532. SODA WATER BOTTLING PLANT (CARBONATED BEVERAGE)
533. SODIUM ALUMINATE
534. SODIUM BI-CARBONATE (BAKING SODA) FROM SODA ASH
535. SODIUM CHLORITE
536. SODIUM CHROMATE SODIUM CYCLAMATE
537. SODIUM DI-CHROMATE
538. SODIUM DI-CHROMATE & SODIUM SULPHATE AS BYE PRODUCTS
539. SODIUM HEXA META PHOSPHATE
540. SODIUM HYDROSULFITE
541. SODIUM HYPO CHLORIDE (BLEACH LIQUOR)
542. SODIUM ISO-PROPYL XANTHATE
543. SODIUM LAURYL SULPHATE
544. SODIUM LAURYL SULPHATE & SODIUM LAURYL ETHER SULPHATE
545. SODIUM NITRATE
546. SODIUM PETROLEUM SULPHONATE (EMULSIFIER)
547. SODIUM SILICATE FROM SILICA & SODA ASH
548. SODIUM SILICATE FROM (1) PADDY SILK HUSK 2) & SILICA
549. SODIUM CARBONATE & SILICA
550. SODIUM SULPHATE
551. SODIUM SULPHIDE BY BARIUM SULPHATE PROCESS
552. SODIUM SULPHIDE FROM AMMONIA & SODIUM CHLORIDE
553. SODIUM SULPHITE
554. SODIUM TRI-POLY PHOSPHATE
555. SOFTENER (CATIONIC ANIONIC & NON-IONIC)
556. SPIRIT FROM PINE APPLE
557. STANNOUS CHLORIDE
558. STEARIC ACID
559. STEARATES MANUFACTURE (CALCIUM, ZINC, ALUMINIUM, MAGNESIUM STEARATES)
560. SULPHUR FROM PYRITES & SLAG
561. SULPHUR CRYSTALS/LUMPS
562. SULPHURIC ACID
563. SULPHURIC ACID FROM DCDA PROCESS
564. SUPER PHOSPHATE (S.S.P)
565. SYNTHETIC IRON OXIDE (YELLOW)
566. SYNTHETIC RED & WELLOW IRON OXIDE FROM IRON FILLING & PICKLE LIQUOR
567. TARTARIC ACID
568. TOILET CLEANER
569. TOLUENE AND SBP FROM

Above all the Detailed Project Report are available at *"ENGINEERS INDIA RESEARCH INSTITUTE"*. 4449, Nai Sarak (D), Main Road Delhi - 110 006

● Ph : 91-11-23918117, 2391 6431, 2392 0361, 31082370 ● Fax : 91-11- 2391 6431

● E-Mail : eirisidi@bol.net.in

CRUDE NAPHTHA
570. TRIMETHYL AMMONIUM CHLORIDE
571. TRIPHENYL PHOSPHITE (T.P.P)
572. ULTRAMARINE BLUE (LIQUID)
573. UREA FORMALDEHYDE & MELAMINE FORMALDEHYDE POWDER
574. UNDECYLINIC ACID
575. VINYL ACETATE MONOMER
576. VITAMIN C
577. VITAMIN E
578. WASTE WATER TREATMENT PLANT FOR INDUSTRIAL SECTOR IN INDIA (ONLY MARKER SURVEY)
579. WIRE DRAWING LUBRICANT
580. WIRE ENAMEL
581. XANTHATES
582. YELLOW DEXTRIN
583. ZINC CHLORIDE
584. ZINC OXIDE
585. ZINC PHOSPHATING BY COLD PROCESS
586. ZINC SILICATE
587. ZINC STEARATE
588. ZINC SULPHATE
589. ZINC SULPHATE MONOHYDRATE
590. ACID BLACK
591. AURAMINE'O'
592. AZO DYES STUFF
593. DYE & DYE INTERMEDIATE
594. DYE INTERMEDIATES
595. MALACHITE GREEN
596. METHYLENE BLUE
597. PHTHALOCYANINE BLUE
598. PHTHALOCYANINE BLUE & GREEN
599. REACTIVE DYES
600. SULPHUR BLACK DYE
601. VAT DYES
602. WATER CHILLING PLANT
603. WADDING OIL (100%) FOR WADDING OF COTTON HOSIERY CLOTH IN THE DYEING PROCESS
604. WHITE OIL
605. WAX FLOOR POLISH

ELECTRICAL, ELECTONICS, COMPUTERS AND INFOTECH/IT PROJECTS

606. AIR CONDITIONING
607. ALUMINIUM ALLOY CONDUCTOR
608. ALUMINIUM CABLE
609. ALUMINIUM ELECTROYTIC CAPACITORS
610. AUDIO CASSETTE ASSEMBLING & RECORDING
611. AUDIO CASSETTES DUPLICATING RECORDING
612. AUDIO CASSETTES & AUDIO STUDIO
613. AUDIO CASSETTES PLANE & RECORDED
614. AUDIO MAGNETIC HEADS
615. AUDIO MAGNETIC TAPE
616. AUDIO/VIDEO CASSETTES
617. AUTO BULB/LAMPS
618. AUTOMATIC VOLTAGE STABILIZER
619. BATTERY PLATES
620. BACK OFFICE (Rs. 5000/-)
621. B/W TV & COMPUTER MONITOR PICTURE TUBE
622. BREAD BOARDS
623. CALL CENTRE
624. CAMERA (35 MM)
625. CAPACITORS
626. CARBON ELECTRODE USED FOR BATTERY CELL
627. CARBON POTETIOMETERS
628. CEILING FAN
629. CERAMIC INSULATOR
630. CHILDREN INFOTECH TRAINING INSTITUTE (Rs. 5000/-)
631. CHOKE AND PATTI
632. CHOKE AND STARTER
633. CHOKE USED FOR FLUORESCENT LAMPS
634. COLOUR TELEVISION
635. COLOUR AND BLACK & WHITE TELEVISION
636. COMPACT DISC
637. COMPACT DISC PLAYER (AUDIO/VIDEO)
638. COMPUTER EDUCATION INSTITUTE
639. COMPUTER ASSEMBLY
640. COMPUTER HARDWARE
641. COMPUTER KEYBOARD
642. COMPUTER PERIPHERALS
643. COMPUTER PRINTERS
644. COMPUTER RIBBON
645. COMPUTER RIBBON REINKING OR REFILLING
646. COMPUTER STATIONERY
647. COMPUTER STATIONERY &

IMPORTED HARDWARE PARTS
648. COMPUTER TERMINALS
649. COMPUTERISED WASHING MACHINE (AUTOMATIC)
650. COMPUTER SOFTWARE
651. CONDENSER FOR MOTOR USING MPP FILM
652. CONTENT DEVELOPMENT CENTRE (EOU) (Rs. 5000/-)
653. CONTROL PANEL BOARD
654. COOLING COIL FOR AIR CONDITIONERS
655. COPPER STRIP COIL FROM SCRAP
656. CORDLESS TELEPHONES
657. CYBER CAFE
658. CYBERKIOSK (Rs. 5000/-)
659. DATA PROCESSING CENTRE (Rs. 5000/-)
660. D.C. MICRO MOTORS
661. D.G.SETS
662. DISH ANTENNA AND CABLE T.V. NETWORK EQUIPMENT
663. DISTRIBUTION TRANSFORMERS & REPAIRS
664. DOMESTIC ELECTRICAL APPLIANCES- ROOM COOLER, WASHING MACHINE, WATER HEATER, ELECTRIC ROOM HEATER
665. E-SCHOOL
666. E-COMMERCE/BUSINESS
667. ELECTRIC ENERGY METER
668. ELECTRIC FANS
669. ELECTRIC HORN FOR AUTOMOBILE
670. ELECTRIC LAMP/GLS (INCANDESCENT LAMP)
671. ELECTRIC MIXER
672. ELECTRIC MOTORS UP TO 10 HP. REWINDING OF ALL TYPES OF MOTORS WATER PUMPS
673. ELECTRIC MOTOR WINDING (FOR FAN, MIXIES, ETC.)
674. ELECTRIC STEAM IRON
675. ELECTRICAL APPLIANCES
676. ELECTRICAL FIXTURES
677. ELECTRICAL STAMPING
678. ELECTROLYTIC CAPACITORS
679. ELECTROMAGNETIC RELAY
680. ELECTRONIC BALAST/CHOK
681. ELECTRICAL CHOKE
682. ELECTRONIC DIGITAL WATCHES
683. ELECTRONIC DIGITAL WEIGHING MACHINE
684. ELECTRONIC FIRE ALARM
685. ELECTRONIC GAS STOVE LIGHTERS
686. ELECTRONIC PRESSURE INDICATORS, ELECTRICALS, ELECTRONIC LIQUID LEVEL INDICATORS, ELECTRONIC TEMPERATURE INDICATOR, DIGITAL TACHOMETER
687. ELECTRONIC TELEPHONE INSTRUMENTS
688. ELECTRONIC TOYS
689. ELECTRONIC WATCHES & CLOCKS
690. FAX MACHINES
691. F.H.P MOTORS
692. FLOPPY DISKETTES
693. FLUORESCENT LAMP STARTER
694. FLUORESCENT TUBULAR

Above all the Detailed Project Report are available at *"ENGINEERS INDIA RESEARCH INSTITUTE"*. 4449, Nai Sarak (D), Main Road Delhi. - 110 006
● Ph : 91-11-23918117, 2391 6431, 2392 0361, 31082370 ● Fax : 91-11- 2391 6431
● E-Mail : eirisidi@bol.net.in

LAMPS WITH INTRODUCTION TO MERCURY VAPOUR LAMP
695. FRANCHISEE COMPUTER EDUCATION CENTRE (Rs. 5000)
696. GAS DETECTOR (L.P.G)
697. GENERATOR SET & PUMP SETS
698. GENERATOR (BATTERY OPERATED)
699. GIS SERVICE CENTRE (GEOGRAPHICAL INFORMATION SYSTEMS)
700. HARDWARE FITTING FOR TRANSMISSION LINE OVERHEAD LINE MATERIAL
701. HEADERS FOR TRANSISTOR ICS SEMI CONDUCTOR
702. H.T & L.T INSULATORS
703. H.T & M.V INDUSTRIAL CUBICAL SWITCH BOARD
704. INFORMATION MOVING DISPLAY (L.E.D TYPE)
705. INSURANCE CLAIM PROCESSING CENTRE (EOU) (Rs. 5000/-)
706. INTEGRATED CIRCUITS
707. INTERNET BASED STOCK TRADING (Rs. 5000/-)
708. INTERNET SERVICE PROVIDER (I.S.P.)
709. JELLY FILLED TELEPHONE CABLES
710. LAP TOP COMPUTERS
711. LEAD ACID BATTERIES
712. LEAD ACID BATTERY PLATES AND ASSEMBLING OF BATTERY
713. LEGAL TRANSCRIPTION & SECRETARIAL SERVICES CENTER (EOU)(Rs. 5000/-)
714. LIGHT EMITTING DIODES (L.E.D)
715. LINEAR ICS TRAINER KIT
716. LOUD SPEAKER
717. L.T TRANSFORMER REPAIRING
718. MEDICAL TRANSCRIPTION CENTRE
719. METAL FILM RESISTORS
720. METALLISED POLYPROPYLENE, POLYESTER FILM CAPACITOR
721. MICA BASE ELECTRONIC COMPONENTS
722. MICA PAPER WASTE PAPER FROM MICA WASTE
723. MICRO PROCESSORS TRAINER KITS BASED ON MICRO PROCESSORS
724. MINI COMPUTER (PERSONAL COMPUTER)
725. MINIATURE CIRCUIT BREAKER (M.C.B)
726. MINIATURE WATCH BATTERIES (BUTTON CELL)
727. MIXER/GRINDER (MIXI)
728. MONO CHROME COMPUTER MONITOR
729. MOTOR START ELECTROLYTIC CAPACITOR
730. MULTI LAYER P.C.B
731. MULTIPLE RELAY FOR LOW VOLTAGE
732. NEON INDICATOR
733. NEON SIGN MANUFACTURE
734. OPTICAL FIBRE CABLES
735. ON LINE SHOPPING MALL (Rs. 5000/-)
736. OPTO MECHANICAL & ELECTRICAL EQUIPMENTS
737. PHOTO COLOUR LAB
738. PICTURE TUBE (B/W)
739. PLAIN PAPER COPIER
740. PLASTIC FILM CAPACITORS
741. POLYESTER CAPACITORS
742. PORTABLE GENERATOR SET
743. PORTAL
744. PORTABLE TELEVISION(TV)
745. POWER CAPACITORS
746. POWER INVERTERS
747. POWER PLANT
748. POWER TRANSFORMERS UP TO 600 KVA
749. PRINTED CIRCUIT BOARD
750. PVC WIRES & CABLES
751. RE-CONDITIONING OF PICTURE TUBE
752. RESIN CAST CT & PT (1 KV)
753. SEMI CONDUCTOR DEVICE
754. SEMI CONDUCTORS FOR TRANSISTORS & DIODES
755. SETTING UP OF A VIDEO STUDIO
756. SMOKE DETECTORS
757. SOLAR CELLS
758. SOLAR MODULES
759. SOLAR PHOTO VOLTAIC SYSTEM
760. SOLDER FLUXES
761. SOLAR WATER HEATING PANELS
762. STEEL FURNITURE & ELECTRICAL APPLIANCES
763. STEREO AMPLIFIERS
764. STEREO CASSETTE RECORDERS/PLAYERS
765. STREET LIGHT FITTINGS SURGE SUPPRESSOR
766. TANTALUM CAPACITORS
767. TEFLON COATED ELECTRIC CABLE
768. TELEMEDICINE (DISTANCE HEALTH CARE) (Rs. 5000/-)
769. TELEPHONE CORD/CABLE
770. TELEPHONE (PUSH BUTTON TYPE)
771. TELEPHONE (PUSH BUTTON & CORDLESS)
772. TELEVISION (CTV & B/W)
773. TELEVISION (3-D)
774. TELEVISION DEFLECTION COMPONENTS
775. TELEVISION SIGNAL BOOSTERS
776. TELEVISION TUNERS
777. TRACTION BATTERIES
778. TRAINING INSTITUTE OF MEDICAL TRANSCRIPTION
779. TRANSFORMER FOR B/W TV
780. TRANSFORMER FOR VOLTAGE STABILIZER & E.H.T
781. TRANSMISSION POWER LINE FITTING
782. TRANSMISSION TOWER FITTING
783. TV AUDIO EQUIPMENT CABINETS & THEIR ASSEMBLING UNIT
784. UN-INTERRUPTED POWER SUPPLY (U.P.S)
785. VARIABLE FREQUENCY
786. VARIABLE VOLTAGE A.C. DRIVE
787. VIDEO CASSETTES (COMPLETE MANUFACTURING & ASSEMBLING)
788. VIDEO CASSETTES RECORDER (V.C.R)
789. VIDEO FILM STUDIO
790. VOLTAGE REGULATOR FOR AUTOMOBILES
791. VOLTAGE STABILIZERS
792. VOLTAGE STABLIZER & T.V. GAIN BOOSTER
793. WAX AND CHEMICAL COATED, BRAIDED TINSEL WIRE
794. WEBSITE DESIGN & E-MAIL REGISTERING
795. WELDING ELECTRODES
796. WIND ENERGY POWER PROJECT (10 MW)
796A WIRES (METAL)

FOOD, AGRO FOOD, PROCESSED FOOD, AGRO PLANTATION, CULTIVATION, FARMING, DAIRY/MILK, TOBACCO/PAN MASALA, BREWERY & DISTILLERY, EDIBLE OILS, EOU FOOD PRODUCTS AND ALLIED PRODUCTS

797. ALCOHOLIC BEVERAGES & VENEGAR FROM COCONUT WATER
798. ALCOHOL DRINKS FROM ETHYL ALCOHOL BY MIXING OF VARIOUS FLAVOURS
799. ANTI SCALE COMPOUND FOR ADDING INTO SUGAR JUICE BOILING
800. APPLE JUICE CONCENTRATED & DEHYDRATED FRUIT & VEGETABLES
801. ARTIFICIAL FISH MEAL FOR POULTRY FEED
802. AUTOMATIC BISCUIT PLANT
803. BABY CEREAL FOOD AND MILK POWDER
804. BACTERIA FOR CANE JUICE
805. BAKER'S YEAST
806. BAKERY INDUSTRY
807. BANANA PUREE
808. BEER & WINE
809. BEER PLANT (BREWERY)
810. BIDI
811. BIDI & CIGARETTE
812. BISCUIT PLANT

Choose & Start Your Own Industry Out of 30,000 ready Detailed Project Reports

813. BREAD (AUTOMATIC PLANT)
814. BLACK PEPPER (SPICES)
815. BREAD AND BISCUITS
816. BREEDING FARM
817. BROILER CHICKEN
819. BUTTON MUSHROOM CULTIVATION & PROCESSING
820. CANNING OF RASAGULLAS IN METAL CANS
821. CAFFEIN FROM TEA WASTE
822. CANNING OF FRUITS & VEGETABLES
823. CASEIN AND BY-PRODUCTS
824. CASHEW FRUIT JUICE FROM CASHEW FRUIT APPLE
825. CASHEWNUT KERNEL EXTRACTION FROM CASHEWNUT FRUIT
826. CASHEWNUT SHELL LIQUID & KERNEL PROCESSING
827. CASHEW FENI
828. CATECHEU (BY CHEMICAL PROCESS)
829. CATTLE FEED FROM TAPIOCA
830. CHEWING & BUBBLE GUM
831. CHICKEN/SHEEP MEAT PROCESSING
832. CHOCOLATE (MILK)
833. CIGARETTE AND BEEDIES
834. COCOA BUTTER FROM COCOA MASS
835. COCONUT PRODUCTS & BY PRODUCTS PROCESS COMPLEX
836. COLD/SOFT DRINKS
837. COLLECTION OF MILK AND MILK MAKING POWDER
838. COLLECTION OF MILK AND PACKING IN POLYTHENE POUCH (1/2 KG.1 KG. & 2 KG.)
839. CONDENSED MILK (SWEETNED)
840. CONFECTIONERY INDUSTRY (TOFFEE & CANDY, SEMI-AUTOMATIC PLANT)
841. COUNTRY LIQUOR FROM MOLASSES
842. CIGARETTE
843. DAIRY FARM AND DAIRY (MILK) PRODUCTS (PASTEURISED MILK, BUTTER, GHEE, PANEER)
844. DAIRY FARM TO PRODUCE MILK & PACKING IN POUCHES (50%) & CAN(50%)
845. DAIRY FOR MILK PROCESSING
846. DAIRY FARM (BUFALO)
847. DAL (PULSE) MILL UNIT
848. DEHYDRATION OF CARROT & GARLIC
849. DEHYDRATION & CANNING OF FRUITS & VEGETABLES
850. DEHYDRATION OF FIGS
851. DEHYDRATION OF FRUITS AND VEGETABLES
852. DEHYDRATED ONIONS AND ONION POWDER
853. DRY ICE BY BREAKING OF AIR
854. DRYING OF RED CHILLIES, HALDI, DHANIA, AND GREEN PEAS
855. EGG POWDER (40,000 EGGS PROCESSING PER DAY)
856. EXPORT OF PROCESSED FOODS AND MARINE PRODUCTS
857. FISH CANNING & POUCHING
859. FISH FARMING (PRAWN & OTHER MARINE PRODUCTS)
860. FISH MEAL
861. FLOUR MILL AND MUSTARD OIL
862. FOOD COLOUR & ORASTED GROUNDNUT GRAM PEAS, ETC IN POUCHES
863. FROG LEGS PROCESSING
864. FROZEN MEATS PROCESSING
865. FOOD FLAVOURS (WHISKY) VODKA, GRAPE, BUTTER SCOTCH)
866. FOOD PRODUCTS COMPLEX (DEHYDRATED ONIONS, GARLIC POWDER & FLAKES, CATTLE FEED, TOMATO POWDER, TOMATO PRODUCTS, CANNED FRUITS & VEGETABLES, TOMATO PURE, GROUN NUT OIL, REFIND OIL, DEHYDRATED GRAPES, BANANA POWDER & WAFFERS)
867. FRUIT JUICE, JAM, JELLIES & ALLIED PRODUCTS
868. FRUIT JUICE, PICKLES PROCESSING AND CANNING
869. FRUIT JUICE MAKING & PACKING IN PLASTIC CONTAINER/POUCHES
870. FRUIT PROCESSING (JAM & JELLIES)
871. FRUIT PULP & JUICE CONCENTRATES
872. FRUIT & VEGETABLE DRYING (FREEZE DRYING METHOD)
873. GOAT & SHEEP FARMING
874. GRAM DALL/PULSE MILL
875. GRAPE DEHYDRATION
876. HARD BOILED CANDY (TOFFEE & CANDY)
877. HERBAL CIGARETTES
878. HONEY PROCESSING & PACKAGING
879. ICE CREAM OF DIFFERENT FLAVOURS
880. ICE CREAM STABILIZER
881. ICE MAKING PLANT
882. INDIAN MADE FOREIGN LIQUOR (I.M.F.L)
883. INSTANT FOOD (IDLI MIX, DOSA MIX, GULAB JAMUN MIX)
884. INSTANT FOOD (INSTANT FOOD & FAST FOOD PARLOUR)
885. INSTANT NOODLES
886. INSTANT TEA
887. INSTANT TEA FROM BLACK TEA
888. INTEGERATED STARCH BAKING POWDER/YEAST INDUSTRY
889. IODIZED SALT
890. IODIZED SALT (ORDINARY MOISTURE-LESS/FREE FLOWING IN PLASTIC BAGS AND CONTAINERS)
891. JAM, JELLIES, FRUIT JUICE & ALLIED PRODUCTS
892. KATHA AND CUTCH
893. KHANDSARI SUGAR
894. KHANDSARI SUGAR & IMFL
895. LACTIC ACID FROM WHITE SUGAR BY FERMENTATION PROCESS
896. LACTOSE & BY PRODUCTS PROCESSING FROM MILK
897. LIQUID GLUCOSE AND ITS BYE PRODUCTS
898. MACRONI AND VERMICILLI
899. MALT EXTRACTION FROM BARLEY
900. MANGO PROCESSING (MANGO PULP, JUICE & SLICES)
901. MAYUR BRAND TYPE CHEWING TOBACCO
902. MINERAL WATER
903. MILK PRESERVATION & MARKETING TO WHOLE SELLERS (INPOUCH PACKING BY UHT TECHNOLOGY)
904. MILK PROCESSING AND PACKAGING OF MILK PRODUCTS
905. MILK PRODUCTS (CASEIN, LACTOSE, GHEE & WHEY POWDER)
906. MILK TOFFEE
907. MINI FLOUR MILL
908. MINI SUGAR PLANT
909. MISRI (PEARL SUGAR CANDIES)
910. MODERN RICE MILL
911. MURABBA
912. MUSTARD OIL EXTRACTION & REFINING
913. MUTTON TALLOW
914. NAMKEEN INDUSTRY (BHUJIA, CHANA CHUR ETC.)
915. NAMKEEN & SWEETS
916. NON-BASMATI RICE FROM PADDY
917. OLEORESIN, ESSENTIAL OIL, DYES & POWDER OF SPICES
918. OLEORESIN EXTRACTION FROM DIPTERO-CARPUT TURMINATUS AND PINUS KHASYANA
919. OLEORESIN EXTRACTION FROM CHILLI
920. PAN MASALA AND POUCH

Above all the Detailed Project Report are available at *"ENGINEERS INDIA RESEARCH INSTITUTE"*. 4449, Nai Sarak (D), Main Road Delhi - 110 006

● Ph : 91-11-23918117, 2391 6431, 2392 0361, 31082370 ● Fax : 91-11- 2391 6431

● E-Mail : eirisidi@bol.net.in

Apart from the above mentioned reports EIRI is also having other most lucrative projects (as many as 30,000). You just name it and we have that report.

MAKING
921. PAN MASALA, TOBACCO, ZARDA & KIMAM
922. PANEER FROM MILK
923. PAPPAD PLANT
924. PAPAIN FROM PAPAYA (PAPAYA LATEX)
925. PECTIN FROM MANGO PEEL PECTIN FROM APPLE POMACE
926. PHYTO TEA (HERBAL TEA)
927. PICKLES AND SAUCES
928. PICKLES MURABBA ETC. (VEG. & NON. VEG.PICKLES)
929. PIGGERY MEAT PROCESS
930. PINE-APPLE JUICE PREPARATION & PACKAGING
931. POTATO CHIPS/WAFFERS
932. POTATO POWDER
933. POUCH FILLING & PACKAGING OF EDIBLE OIL & GHEE
934. POULTRY FEED
935. PROCESSED FOODS & SPICES (EOU)
936. PROCESSED READYMADE FOOD
937. PROCESSING OF FRUITS & VEGETABLES
938. RABBIT FARMING
939. RASGULLAS MAKING & CANNING IN METAL CANS
940. READY TO EAT PROCESSED COOKED FOOD
941. READY TO EAT SNACK FOOD (CRAX, ROLL & BALL TYPE)
942. RICE & CORN FLAKES
943. ROASTED/SALTED/ MASALA,CASHEW NUTS, ALMONDS & PEANUTS
944. ROLLER FLOUR MILL
945. SALT LICKS FOR CATTLE
946. SAUSAGES FOOD CASING
947. SOFT DRINKS
948. SOFT DRINKS ESSENCES
949. SOFT DRINKS (NON CARBONATED) MANGO, LICCHI, PINEAPPLE FLAVOURS FROOTI TYPE IN TETRAPACK)
950. SOFTY ICE CREAM CONES (FULLY AUTOMATIC)
951. SOFT/COLD DRINKS (COLA, ORANGE, LEMON ETC. FLAVOURS)
952. SOYABEAN PRODUCTS
953. SOYA MILK & PANEER
954. STARCH & ALLIED PROPDUCT FROM BROKEN RICE
955. STRAWBERRY CULTIVATION & PROCESSING
956. SUGARCANE JUICE PRESERVATION
957. SUGAR CUBES FROM CANE SUGAR
988. SUGAR PLANT
989. SWEET AROMA BETEL NUT
990. SYNTHETIC TALLOW
991. TAMARIND JUICE POWDER
992. TEA & COFFEE PROCESSING & PACKAGING
993. TOFFEES, GOLIES, CANDY (HARD BOILED)
994. TOMATO PRODUCTS
994. TRADING BUSINESS OF SPICES & PAN MASALA
995. TUITY FRUITY
996. VODKA FROM POTATOES
997. WINE, BRANDY, WHISKY & CHAMPAGNE
997. WINE FROM DATES
998. YEAST FROM MOLASSES
999. ZARDA, KIMAM NO. 60,90,120,160,240,300 & 400 (TOBACCO)
1000. ZARDA-ZAFRANI (BABACHHAP TYPE)

GUMS & ADHESIVE

1001. ACRYLIC ADHESIVE
1002. ADHESIVE (FEVICOL TYPE)
1003. ADHESIVE BASED ON POLYURETHANE
1004. ADHESIVE FOR BAND AID (JOHNSON & JOHNSON TYPE)
1005. ADHESIVE INDUSTRIES (LAMINATED, STICKER,DDL & OTHER TYPES)
1006. ADHESIVE FOR GASKET (LIQUID/PASTE)
1007. GUAR GUM
1008. GUM BOTTLE (PVC)
1009. GUM FOR PASTING LABELS
1010. OFFICE PASTE
1011. RUBBER ADHESIVE
1012. SURGICAL ADHESIVE PLASTER

LEATHER & LEATHER PRODUCTS

1013. HANDMADE LEATHER
1014. LEATHER AUXILLARIES & CHEMICALS
1015. LEATHER DYES
1016. LEATHER WASHERS
1017. LEATHER BOARD FROM LEATHER WASTE
1018. LEATHER FOR UPHOLSTRY (SOFA)
1019. LEATHER GARMENTS
1020. LEATHER GOODS
1021. LEATHER SHOES
1022. LEATHER SHOE & CHAPPAL
1023. LEATHER SUITCASES, BRIEFCASES & TRAVELLING BAGS
1024. LEATHER GOODS AND GARMENTS
1025. LEATHER GARMENTS, SHOE & CHAPPAL
1026. LEATHER TANNING
1027. LEATHER TANNING & GARMENTS (EOU)
1028. SHEEP SKIN PICKLING PLANT
1029. SHOE UPPER
1030. SPORT SHOES (PLASTIC)

MISCELLANEOUS PRODUCTS

1031. AGARBATTI (INSENCE STICK)
1032. AGARBATTI (Mosquito Repellent)
1033. AGARBATI BAMBOO STICK
1034. AGARBATTI SYNTHETIC PERFUMERY COMPOUND
1035. AIR FRESHNER(ODONIL TYPE)
1036. AIR TAXI
1037. AMUSEMENT PARK
1038. ANODIC ALUMINIUM LABEL
1039. AQUACULTURE PRAWN FARMING (100% EOU)
1040. AQUA CULTURE SHRIMP FARMING (100% EOU)
1041. ARTIFICIAL FLOWERS
1042. ARTIFICIAL JEWELLERY
1043. ASBESTOS YARN
1044. ASH TRAYS FOR MARUTI VEHICLE
1045. AIR BUBBLE PACKAGING
1046. ASPHALTIC ROOFING SHEET (METAL COMPONENTS)
1047. AUTOMATIC BOOK BINDING
1048. ALKYD RESIN
1049. APPLE JUICE CONCENTRATE
1050. BALL POINT PEN FEFILLS (JOTTER TYPE)
1051. BANK BRANCH BUILDING
1052. BANQUET HALL
1053. BIO-COAL BRIQUETTES FROM AGRICULTURAL CELLULOSE WASTE
1054. BOOT CREAM/POLISH
1055. BUFFING & POLISHING COMPOUND
1056. BRASS BADGES BY ETCHING
1057. BRIQUETTED FUEL FROM AGRO WASTE
1058. BRIQUETTING OF LIGNITE COAL

Above all the Detailed Project Report are available at *"ENGINEERS INDIA RESEARCH INSTITUTE"*. 4449, Nai Sarak (D), Main Road Delhi - 110 006

● Ph : 91-11-23918117, 2391 6431, 2392 0361, 31082370 ● Fax : 91-11-2391 6431

● E-Mail : eirisidi@bol.net.in

1059. BUFFALO HORN TIP, HOOF
1060. BANQUET HALL
1061. BUTTON
1062. CALCINED PETROLEUM (C.P) COKE
1063. CANVAS SHOES
1064. CANVAS SHOES, JUNGLE BOOTS
1065. CARBON BRUSH, BRUSH HOLDER & SLIP RING
1066. CEMENT SHEETS WITH COIR FIBRE & OTHER SEGMENTS
1067. CERAMIC TILES (GLAZED) BY DOUBLE FIRING/HEATING
1068. CHILDREN RECREATION CENTRE
1069. COAL BRIQUETTES
1070. COLD STORAGE & ICE
1071. COLD STORAGE FOR FRUITS AND VEGETABLES
1072. COMPRESSOR (HERMETIC) FOR AIR CONDITIONER
1073. COSTUME JEWELLERY/ IMITATION JEWELLERY
1074. DECORATIVE LAMINATED SHEET (SUNMICA)
1075. DIAMOND CUTTING & EXPORTS
1076. DRINKING STRAW FROM PROPYLENE
1077. ENGINEERING COLLEGE
1078. ENTERTAINMENT CLUB
1079. FASHION TECHNOLOGY INSTITUTE
1080. FAST FOOD PARLOUR
1081. FAST FOOD (INSTANT FOOD & FAST FOOD PARLOUR)
1082. FIRE EXTINGUISHERS (SODA ACID TYPE)
1083. FISH NET
1084. FLORICULTURE (CUT FLOWER ROSE) WITH GREEN HOUSE
1085. FLOOR COVERING SHEET
1086. FILM STUDIO (VIDEO)
1087. FLUSH DOOR, CHIP BOARD, WOOD WOOL & OTHER INSULATING BOARDS
1088. GAS DETECTORS OF L.P.G
1089. GEMS MANUFACTURING
1090. GLASS BOTTLE BY SCRAP
1092. GOAT & SHEEP FARMING
1093. GOLD ELECTROPLATING
1094. GOLD JEWELLERY (E.O.U)
1095. GOLD PLATED SILVER JEWELLERY & CUTLERY
1096. GRANITE SLAB AND TILES
1097. GREEN HOUSE
1098. HARD CHROMIUM PLATING
1099. HEALTH CLUB AND BEAUTY PARLOUR CUM HAIR SALOON WITH SONA BATH
1100. HEALTH CLUB CUM BEAUTY PARLOUR TRAININGINSTITUTE
1101. HORN TIP,HOOVE BUTTON
1102. HOSPITAL
1103. HOSPITAL (100 BEDS)
1104. HOSPITAL (200 BEDS)
1105. ICE MAKING PLANT
1106. IMITATION AND COSTUME
1107. JEWELLERY (NECKLACE, EARRINGS EAR TOP ETC.)
1108. INITMATE SCENT CHEMICALS FROM ALL TYPES OF FLAVOUR
1109. INVESTMENT CASTING
1110. JUTE, COIR, GLASS ROPE/ SUTLI
1111. JUTE TWINE
1112. L.P.G BOTTLING PLANT
1113. L.P.G REGULATOR (DOMESTIC PURPOSE)
1114. LAMINATED PARTICLE BOARD & HARD BOARD
1115. LAMINATED SAFETY AND TOUGHENED GLASS
1116. LEASING & HIRE PURCHASE
1117. LICHEN (CHARILA)
1118. MANILA ROPES
1119. MEDICAL COLLEGE
1120. MATCH UNIT FROM WAXED PAPER
1121. MEDIUM DENSITY FIBRE BOARD
1122. MELAMINE CROCKERY
1123. MINERAL WATER
1124. MINI CEMENT PLANT
1125. MIRROR SILVER, GOLDEN, PINK, BLACK & SMOKES
1126. MODERN ADVERTISING AGENCY WITH DTP & FILM STUDIO
1127. MOTEL/SMALL HOTEL
1128. MULTI COLOUR PRINTING
1129. MULTI STOREY COMMERCIAL COMPLEX ALONGWITH RESIDENTIALAND DELUX FLATS FOR FOREIGN TOURISTS & REVOLVING RESTAURENT AT THE TOP
1130. MULTIPLE LAMINATION INDUSTRY
1131. MUSHROOM GROWING AND PROCESSING (BY DEEP FREEZING METHOD)
1132. NEWS PAPER PRINTING
1133. NICKEL LINED INDUSTRIAL SCREEN
1134. OFFSET COLOUR PRINTING PRESS (SIX COLOUR)
1135. OFFSET PRINTING PRESS
1136. P.C.C ELECTRIC POLES
1137. PHOTOGRAPHIC DEVELOPER & FIXER
1138. PVC EXTRUSION PROFILE (DOOR & WINDOWS)
1139. POP-CORN
1140. PHOTO ETCHING OF S.S.
1141. PRE STRESSED CEMENT CONCRETE PIPES
1142. PILFER PROOF CAPS
1143. PILFER PROOF CAPS AND CROWN CAP
1144. POUCH MAKING & GRAVURE PRINTING (ROTO PRINTING)
1145. POULTRY & FISH FARMING (INTEGERATED UNIT)
1146. PRINTING OF TIN SHEETS
1147. READYMADE GARMENTS
1148. RESTAURANT
1149. ROSE PLANTATION AND ROSE OIL EXTRACTION
1150. ROTOGRAVURE PRINTING
1151. SAFETY BELTS
1152. SAFETY MATCHES
1153. SHOE LACES
1154. SILK COCOON CULTIVATION (GROWING OF SILK COCOON WARM)
1155. SILK SCREEN PRINTING FORMULATIONS FOR PLASTIC, PAPER & CLOTH
1156. SPIKENARD (JATAMANSI)
1157. STENCIL COATING SOLUTION
1158. SUGAR CANDY (MISRI)
1159. SUGAR CANE PLANTATION
1160. SUGAR CANE JUICE PRESERVATION
1161. SURAT ZARI
1162. SYNTHETIC SHOES & SOLES
1163. TEA PACKAGING INDUSTRY
1164. TENNIS BALLS
1165. THREE STAR HOTEL
1166. TRAVELLING AGENCY
1167. TRAYS, TROLLEYS FOR HOSPITAL WITH SCRATCHLESS COATING
1168. WAX EXTRACTS (TANNING POWDER)
1169. WIRE ROPE SLINGS
1170. WOOD WOOL SLAB
1171. WOODEN CANE FURNITURE WITH EXPORT POTENTIAL
1172. WOODEN FURNITURE
1173. WOODEN PANEL INCLUDING KILN SEASONING
1174. WOODEN FURNITURE
1175. WATCH CASE BUFFING
1176. WATCH DIAL
1177. WRIST WATCHES
1178. WATCHES (ELECTRONIC)
1179. ZEDOARY (KACHUR)

EDIBLE OILS, ESSENTIAL OILS LURICATIING OILS, GREASES, VEGETABLE OILS, WAXES, CAMPHOR, PERFUMES & PERFUMERY COMPOUNDS AND REFINED OILS ETC.

1180. AROMATIC PERFUMERY COMPOUND
1181. AEROSOL
1182. AGARBATTI PERFUMERY COMPOUND
1183. BEES WAX MANUFACTURE
1184. CAMPHOR
1185. CARDANOL FROM,CASHEW NUT SHELL LIQUID
1186. CASTOR OIL
1187. CASTOR OIL DERIVATIVE OLEORESINS
1188. CHILLI OIL
1189. CITRONELLA OILS
1190. CLOVE OIL
1191. CONCENTRATE OF ROSE JASMINE & LILY ETC.
1192. COLOURED FLAME CANDLE

Above all the Detailed Project Report are available at *"ENGINEERS INDIA RESEARCH INSTITUTE"*. 4449, Nai Sarak (D), Main Road Delhi - 110 006

● Ph : 91-11-23918117, 2391 6431, 2392 0361, 31082370 ● Fax : 91-11-2391 6431

● E-Mail : eirisidi@bol.net.in

1193. CANDLES (SEMI-AUTOMATIC)
1194. CORN OIL (MAIZE OIL)
1195. DEHYDRATED CASTOR OIL
1196. EUGENOL FROM CINNAMON LEAF OIL
1197. EXTRACTION OF ESSENTIAL OIL (CARDAMON, JEERA, AJOWAN, GINGER OILS ETC. & PACKAGING OF GROUND SPICES)
1198. EXTRACTION OF JASMINE ESSENCE
1199. EXTRACTION OF ESSENTIAL OILS BY SUPER CRITICAL FLUID METHOD FROM FLOWERS, HERBS & SPICES
1200. EUCALYPTUS OIL
1201. EXTRACTION OF OIL FROM OIL SEED EXPANDEREXTRUSION TECHNOLOGY)
1202. FAT LIQUOR SULPHATED OIL
1203. FLAVOURS FOR FOOD
1204. GARLIC OIL & POWDER
1205. GINGER OIL, SANDALWOOD OIL AND NAGARMOTHA OIL
1206. GINGER OIL
1207. GINGER OIL & GINGER DUST
1208. INTEGERATED WAX COMPLEX
1209. IONONE FROM LEMON GRASS OIL
1210. JASMINE & LILLY FLOWER OIL
1211. LEMON GRASS OIL
1212. LIQUID PARAFFIN
1213. LUBE OIL & GREASE
1214. LUBRICATING OIL
1215. MENTHOL CRYSTALS
1216. MENTHOL OIL & CRYSTAL
1217. MICRO CRYSTALLINE WAX
1218. MUSTARD OIL (EDIBLE OIL)
1219. OIL FROM ARTEMISIA HERBS
1220. PALM OIL CRUSHING UNIT
1221. PAN MASALA
1222. PARAFFIN WAX
1223. PARAFFIN WAX FROM SLACK WAX
1224. REFINED OIL-SUN FLOWER OIL, GROUNDNUT OIL, STAFF FLOWER OIL & COTTON SEED OIL
1225. REFINED VEGETABLE OIL
1226. RECLAMATION OF USED ENGINE OIL
1227. RICE BRAN OIL (R.B.O)
1228. ROSE OIL EXTRACTION
1229. SMOKE LESS CANDLE
1230. SPICE OIL & OLEORESINS
1231. SOLVENT EXTRACTION PLANT (OIL CAKE BASED)
1232. SYNTHETIC ALMOND OIL
1233. SYNTHETIC TALLOW
1234. SYNTHETIC GHEE
1235. VEGETABLE OIL EXTRACTION & REFINING
1236. WADDING OIL (100%) FOR WADDING OF COTTON HOSIERY CLOTH IN DYEING PROCESS
1237. WAX EMULSION FOR TEXTILE
1238. WAX FLOOR POLISH

PAINT, ENAMEL, SOLVENTS, THINNERS, INKS & VARNISH

1239. ACRYLIC EMULSION PAINTS
1240. ALUMINIUM PAINT
1241. AUTOMOBILE PAINTS
1242. BALL POINT PEN REFILL INK
1243. BITUMINIOUS ROAD EMULSION
1244. BITUMEN
1245. BITUMINIOUS FELTS FOR WATER & DAMP PROOFING
1246. BITUMINIOUS ROAD EMULSION RAPID MEDIUM & SLOW SETTING
1247. BUFFING & POLISHING
1248. CEMENT PAINT FOR WHITE & GREY CEMENT

1249. DISPERSANT
1250. DRY DISTEMPER
1251. DRY DISTEMPER & CEMENT PAINT
1252. DUPLICATING INK BLACK FOR GESTNER DUPLICATOR
1255. EMULSION PAINTS (WATER BASED)
1256. HAMMERTONE PAINT
1257. INSULATING VARNISH & WIRE ENAMEL
1258. IRON OXIDE PIGMENTS
1259. INSULATING VARNISH (POLY VINYL BUTYRAL BASED, FFC GRADE)
1260. LIME COLOUR (CEMENT COLOUR)
1261. SYNTHETIC RED OXIDE FOR FLOORINGS
1262. SOLVENT & THINNERS
1263. MARKING INKS (WATER PROOF)
1264. METAL NAPHTHANATE (AS DRIER FOR PAINTS)
1265. N.C.PUTTY
1266. OFFSET PRINTING INK
1267. OIL BOUND DISTEMPER PAINT
1268. PAINT BRUSHES
1269. PAINT REMOVERS
1270. PAINT INDUSTRY
1271. PAINT & VARNISH
1272. PICTURE VARNISH
1273. POWDER COATING PAINT
1274. PRINTING INKS (OFFSET, FLEXO & ROTO GRAVURE)
1275. PRIMER PAINT & ENAMEL PAINT
1276. PUTTY & WATER PROOFING PAINT
1277. PRINTING INKS (FLEXO-GRAPHIC INK)
1278. PUTTY (METAL CASEMENT)
1279. RED OXIDE PRIMER (ANTI CORROSIVE)
1280. REFRECTORY PAINT (GRAPHITE BASED)
1281. SCREEN PRINTING INKS
1282. SILK SCREEN PRINTING INK FORMULATION FOR PLASTIC, PAPER, CLOTH
1283. STAMP & PAD INK
1284. STOVING PAINT
1285. SPIRIT SOLUBLE MALEIC RESIN
1286. TEXTURE PAINT
1287. THINNERS AND ITS ALLIED PRODUCTS
1288. TONER INK
1289. VARNISH THINNER (SOLVENT)
1290. VACUUM METALLIZING LACQUERS
1291. WOOD PRIMER

PHARMACEUTICAL, DRUGS, AYURVEDIC/HERBAL COSMETICS & MEDICINES, HOMOEOPATHIC MEDICINES, DISPOSABLE SYRINGE, DENTAL COLLEGE & FINE CHEMICALS ETC.

1292. AROMATIC PILLS
1293. ASPIRIN
1294. AYURVEDIC PAIN BALM OINTMENTS
1295. AYURVEDIC CHURAN AND TABLETS
1296. AYURVEDIC TABLETS (HAJMOLA TYPE)
1297. AYURVEDIC/HERBAL PHARMACY
1298. AYURVEDIC SHERBATS
1299. AYURVEDIC PRODUCTS
1300. BULK DRUGS (E.O.U)
1301. BLOOD BAGS
1302. CALCIUM GLUCONATE
1303. CAPSULE, TABLET & INJECTION WITH MODERN INSTRUMENTS
1304. CASHEW FENI
1305. CHLOROQUINONE PHOSPHATE (BULK DRUGS)
1306. CLINICAL THERMOMETER
1307. DENTAL CLINIC

Above all the Detailed Project Report are available at *"ENGINEERS INDIA RESEARCH INSTITUTE"*. 4449, Nai Sarak (D), Main Road Delhi - 110 006
● Ph : 91-11-23918117, 2391 6431, 2392 0361, 31082370 ● Fax : 91-11- 2391 6431
● E-Mail : eirisidi@bol.net.in

1308. DENTAL COLLEGE
1309. DENTAL GRADE EUGENOL
1310. DEXTROSE MONOHYDRATE, LIQUID GLUCOSE
1311. DEHYDRATED ONION & ONION POWDER
1312. DEXTROSE POWDER (ANHYDROUS FROM STARCH)
1314. DEXTROSE SALINE SOLUTION
1315. DISTILLERY (I.M.F.L)
1316. DISPOSABLE NEEDLES FOR SYRINGES
1317. DISPRIN
1318. DISTILLED WATER
1319. EMPTY HARD GELATINE CAPSULES
1320. FILLING & PACKING OF CAPSULES
1321. GLUCOSE - D - POWDER
1322. GLYCERINE
1323. HERBAL COSMETICS
1324. HERBAL SHAMPOO
1325. HERBAL HAIR OILS (AYURVEDIC)
1326. HOMOE & BIO-MEDICINES WITH MOTHER TINCTURE
1327. HOMOEPATHIC MEDICINES
1328. HYPODERMIC NEEDLES
1329. I.V. FLUIDS
1330. IBUPROFEN
1331. INFUSION & TRANSFUSION SETS (I.V. SET)
1332. INJECTABLE FOR PHARMACEUTICALS
1333. INJECTION AMPOULES PACKAGING BOX
1334. INTEGERATED SURGICAL COTTON
1335. ICE MAKING PLANT
1336. ICE & COLD STORAGE
1337. LACTOSE & BY PRODUCTS PROCESSING FROM MILK
1338. LICHEN (JATAMANSI CHARILA)
1339. LIQUID GLUCOSE AND ITS BY-PRODUCTS
1340. L-LYSINE MONOHYDRO CHLORIDE
1341. LIQUID GLUCOSE FROM POTATOES
1342. MEDICAL COLLEGE
1343. NICOTINE FROM TOBACCO WASTE
1344. OINTMENT-AYURVEDIC (YELLOW & WHITE)
1345. PHARMACEUTICAL AND FOOD GRADE GELATINE
1346. PHARMACEUTICAL INDUSTRY (TABLETS, CAPSULES, LIQUID, GEL, OINTMENT POWDER INJECTABLE)
1347. PHARMACEUTICAL UNIT (EOU) WITH FORMULA TIONS, INJECTABLES, ETC. PYRIDINE & DERIVATIVES
1348. SALT (IODIZED SALT)
1349. SALINE & INJECTION WATER
1350. SALINE WATER & DEXTROSE SOLUTION (I.V.FLUID IN PLASTIC BOTTLES)
1351. SORBITOL
1352. STARCH (MAIZE)
1353. SURGICAL ADHESIVE PLASTER
1354. SURGICAL BANDAGES
1355. SURGICAL GLOVES
1357. SURGICAL COTTON
1358. SURGICAL COTTON AND BANDAGE
1359. SYNTHETIC CAMPHOR POWDER
1360. TABLETS & CAPSULES
1361. TISSUE CULTURE
1362. TINCTURE FROM RECTIFIED SPIRIT
1363. TRIMETHOPIME
1364. VETERENARY MEDICINES (ONLY FORMULATIONS)
1365. VITAMIN 'C', SORBITOL' ANHYDROUS DEXTROSE, STARCH

PULP, PAPER, STRAW/GREY BOARD, KRAFT PAPER, PACKAGING, PAPER CARRY BAGE, PAPER FROM AGRO WASTE & STATIONERY ETC.

1366. AMMONIA PAPER
1367. AUTOMATIC BOOK BINDING
1368. ADHESIVE (FEVICOL TYPE)
1369. ALL PIN & GEM CLIPS
1370. CARBON PAPER
1371. CARD BOARD
1372. CARBON LESS PAPER
1373. CELLPHANE PAPER
1374. COMPUTER FORMS & SECURITY PRINTING PRESS
1375. CORRUGATED BOARD & BOX (PRINTED & LAMINATED)
1376. CORRUGATED BOARD AND BOXES FROM FROM CARD BOARDS
1377. CORRUGATED CARTONS FROM PLAIN PAPERS
1378. CORRUGATRED PACKING & MATERIAL (BULB & TUBES PACKING)
1379. DESK TOP PUBLISHING
1380. DEFOAMING AGENT FOR PAPER PLANT
1381. DRINKING STRAW PAPER
1382. D.T.P. CUM OFFSET PRESS
1383. EGG TRAYS
1384. EXERCISE NOTE BOOK, REGISTER AND PAD
1385. FLEXOGRAPHIC INK
1386. GREETING CARD BY OFFSET PRESS
1387. HAND MADE PAPER FILTER PAPER
1388. HARD BOARD
1389. INJECTION AMPOULES PACKAGING BOXES
1390. INSULATIING PAPER
1391. KRAFT PAPER
1392. KRAFT PAPER FROM BAGASSE
1393. LAMINATED PACKAGING PAPER WITH PRINTING
1394. LAMINATION & COATING ON PAPER
1395. M.G. PAPER FROM WASTE PAPER
1396. MILL PAPER FROM WASTE PAPER
1397. MILL BOARD FROM RICE & WHEAT STRAWS
1398. MILL BOARD FROM WASTE PAPER
1399. MINI PAPER PLANT FROM SISAL
1400. MINI PAPER PLANT
1401. MULTI WALL PAPER SACKS
1402. NEWS PAPER FOR CHILDREN
1403. NEWS PRINT PAPER FROM RICE STRAW BAGASSE
1404. NEWS PAPER CHILDRENS
1405. NEWS PRINT PAPER
1406. OFFSET AND TREADLE TYPE PRINTING PRESS
1407. MILL BOARD BASED ON RICE STRAW
1408. PAPER AND BOARD FROM STRAW
1409. PAPER & PAPER PRODUCTS
1410. PAPER ENVELOPES
1411. PAPER CARRY BAGS
1412. PAPER BOARD CARTON
1413. PAPER CONES FOR LOUD SPEAKERS
1414. PAPER FROM AKRA
1415. PAPER FROM BAGASSE WITH CORRUGATED BOARD & BOXES
1416. PAPER FROM BAMBOO
1417. PAPER GLASSES FOR BEVERAGES
1418. PAPER FROM RICE HUSK & WHEAT HUSK
1419. PAPER FROM TREE BARK, EUCALYPRUS WOOD
1420. PAPER PRODUCTS
1421. PAPER PLANT (WHITE WRITING & NEWS PAPER FOR PULP & WASTE PAPER)
1422. PAPER PLATES, PAPER GLASS
1423. PAPER CONES & TUBES
1425. PAPER PLANT WITH DTP & PRINTING & PUBLISHING UNIT
1426. PAPER BASED PHENOLIC SHEET
1427. PAPER CUP FOR ICE CREAM
1428. PAPER TUBES SPIRAL WINDING COMPOSIT CONTAINER
1429. PAPER LABLE FOR BEER BOTTLES
1430. PARTICLE BOARD & BLACK BOARD WITH SANDING & LAMINATION OF PARTICLE BOARD
1431. PARTICLE BOARD FROM RICE HUSK
1432. POUCH FILLING & MAKING FOR TOMATO SAUCE
1433. POUCH MAKING &

Above all the Detailed Project Report are available at *"ENGINEERS INDIA RESEARCH INSTITUTE"*. 4449, Nai Sarak (D), Main Road Delhi - 110 006
• Ph : 91-11-23918117, 2391 6431, 2392 0361, 31082370 • Fax : 91-11- 2391 6431
• E-Mail : eirisidi@bol.net.in

GRAVURE PRINTING
1434. PROCESSING OF PAPER FOR FEEDING IN COMPUTER
1435. PULP FROM BAMBOO & WOOD
1436. PAPER FILES
1437. PLAYING CARDS
1438. ROSIN SIZING AGENT (FOR PAPER PLANT)
1439. SAND PAPER
1440. SANITRY NAPKINS
1441. SILICON COATED PAPER
1442. STENCIL PAPER
1443. STRAW BOARD AND GREY BOARD
1444. STRAW BOARD & MILL BOARD
1445. STRAW BOARD AND PAPER BOARD
1446. TISSUE PAPER FACIAL
1447. TISSUE MOIST TOILETERY CLEANSING TISSUE AND RELATED PRODUCTS
1448. TISSUE PAPER ROLLS
1449. TETRA PACK FOR MILK PACKAGING, GHEE & OTHER LIQUIDS
1450. TOILET PAPER ROLLS
1451. TOILET PAPER & NAPKINS
1452. WAX COATED PRINTED PAPER
1453. WET FACE FRESHNER TISSUE
1454. WHITE WRITING & PRINTING PAPER
1455. WRITING & PRINTING PAPER (PAPER MILLS)

PLASTIC, B.O.P.P, ACRYLIC, DISPOSABLE PLASTIC PRODUCTS, PET PRODUCTS, P.V.C, H.D.P.E, P.P, L.D.P.E., P.U, A.B.S, THERMOFOARMING, MASTER BATCHES, & POLYMER AND RUBBER PRODUCTS, TYRE, TUBE, ADHESIVE, SHEET, COIR & MANY OTHERS

1456. ABS GRANULES FROM ABS SCRAPS FROM OLD T.V. CABINETS, WHITE GOODS ETC.
1457. ACRYLIC BEADS
1458. ACRYLIC COPOLYMER EMULSION
1459. ACRYLIC LATEX
1460. ACRYLIC SHEET
1461. ACRYLIC SHEET & MOULDED PRODUCTS
1462. ACRYLIC TEETH
1463. AUTO TUBES
1464. AUTO FLAPS FOR TRUCKS & BUSES
1465. AUTO TYRES & TUBES
1466. BABY BOTTLES (PLASTIC) WITH WHITESILICON RUBBER NIPPLES
1467. B.O.P.P. FILM
1468. B.O.P.P. PRESSURE SENSITIVE SELF ADHESIVE TAPE
1469. BABY NIPPLE (SILICON)
1470. BABY NIPPLE (BIG SIZE)
1471. BALLOON PLASTIC ADVERTISING
1472. BLISTER FILM PVC
1473. BLISTER PACKAGING & POUCH PAKAGING
1474. BLOW MOULDING PLASTIC CONTAINER
1475. COATING ON METALIZED POLYESTER FILM/METALISED PAPER/ ALIMINIUM FOIL
1476. COATING ON PLASTIC (ELECTROLYSIS) & GLASS
1477. COIR FOAM (RUBBERISED)
1478. COLOUR COATING ON PLASTICS
1479. COLOUR MASTER BATCHES FOR VARIOUS PLASTICS
1480. CYCLE TYRES AND TUBES
1481. DISPOSABLE PLASTIC CUPS GLASSES, ETC.
1482. DISPOSABLE PLASTIC SYRINGES & NEEDLES
1483. DISPOSABLE PLASTIC SYRINGES
1484. DOUGH MOULDING COMPOUND (D.M.C)
1485. EPOXY RESIN
1486. EXPANDED POLYESTRENE MOULDING (THERMOCOLE)
1487. F.R.P AUTO,SCOOTER ROOFS & CEILINGS
1488. F.R.P PRODUCTS (HELMET, WASHBASIN SHEETS, ROOFING SHEETS)
1489. FIBRE REINFORCED PLASTIC (HIGH PRESSURE MOULDING WITH SMC BMC AND DMC)
1490. FIELD RUBBER CONVERTED TO THE 60% LATEX RUBBER
1491. FLEXIBLE P.U. FOAM
1492. FORMALDEHYDE CROCKERY & OTHER ITEMS
1493. FORMALDEHYDE RESIN (UREA, PHENOL,MELEMINE)
1494. GASKET SHEET
1495. GUM BOTTLE (PVC)
1496. GLASS BEADS
1497. HDPE COATED PAPER SACK
1498. H.D.P.E. BAGS
1499. H.D.P.E. CONTAINERS (BLOW MOULDING)
1500. H.D.P.E. CONTAINER, POLY JARS BY INJECTION MOULDING (FOOD GRADE)
1501. H.D.P.E. JERRY CANS
1502. HDPE MANUFACTURING FROM ETHYLALCOHOL
1503. H.D.P.E PIPE AND FITTINGS
1504. H.D.P.E. PIPES
1505. H.D.P.E PRINTED BAGS
1506. H.D.P.E TWINES AND ROPES
1507. H.D.P.E. & L.D.P.E PIPES AND FITTINGS
1508. H.D.P.E/PP BOX STRAPPING
1509. H.D.P.E/PP WOVEN SACKS USING PLAIN LOOMS
1510. HOLOGRAM STICKERS-3D
1511. H.M BAG PLANT WITH PRINTING UNIT
1512. HAWAI CHAPPALS (RUBBER)
1513. I.V PLASTIC BOTTLE
1514. ICE CREAM CUP (PLASTIC)
1515. INJECTION MOULDED AUTO COMPONENTS
1516. INJECTION & BLOW MOULDED PLASTIC PRODUCTS
1517. INJECTION MOULDED PLASTIC PRODUCTS
1518. INTEGERATED COMPLEX ESTER'S & ALLIED PRODUCTS (D.O.P.D.B.P, & ETHYL ACETATE, BUYTL ACETATE, WIRE ENAMELS, JELLY CABLE COMPOUND)
1519. L.D.P.E. (LOW DENSITY POLY ETHYLENE) GRANULES FROM VIRGIN (L.D.P.E. RESIN)
1520. INTEGERATED SURGICAL RUBBER GOODS INDUSTRY
1521. INJECTION MOULDED PLASTIC BALLS
1522. L.D.P.E FROM ETHYL ALCOHOL
1523. LDPE MOULDED PRODUCTS
1524. LAMINATION OF COEXTRUSION MULTILAYER FILM IN ROLL FORM
1525. LATEX RUBBER
1526. LATEX RUBBER CONDOM
1527. MASTER BATCHES (COLOURED, P.V.C, L.D.P.E, H.D.P.E, ETC.)
1528. MELAMINE FORMALHYDE RESIN
1529. MOULDED LUGGAGE
1530. MULTI-LAYER (3 LAYER BAGS)
1531. MULTI-LAYER (3 LAYER) FILM WITH LAMINATION & PRINTING
1532. OIL SEAL
1533. PET BOTTLE/CONTAINERS
1534. PET BOTTLES FROM PRE FORM
1535. PET BOTTLE & MINERAL WATER
1536. PET PRE-FORM FROM PET RESIN
1537. PET PRE-FORM CUM PET BOTTLES
1538. PET PRE-FORM PET BOTTLES CUM MINERAL WATERS
1539. POLY CARBONATE RESIN
1540. PTFE COMPONENTS
1541. PU/PVC SOLE FOR SPORT SHOE BY IMPORTED M/C.
1542. PVC BATTERY SEPARATOR
1543. P.V.C COMPOUNDS (FRESH)
1544. P.V.C COMPOUNDS (SCRAP)
1545. P.V.C ELECTRICAL INSULATING TAPE
1546. P.V.C. EXTRUSION PROFILES
1547. P.V.C FITTINGS
1548. P.V.C FLEXIBLE FUSIBLE POWDER HEAT FUSIBLE POWDER
1549. P.V.C GRANULES (FOR

Above all the Detailed Project Report are available at *"ENGINEERS INDIA RESEARCH INSTITUTE"*. 4449, Nai Sarak (D), Main Road Delhi - 110 006
● Ph : 91-11-23918117, 2391 6431, 2392 0361, 31082370 ● Fax : 91-11-2391 6431
● E-Mail : eirisidi@bol.net.in

INSULATION & SHEETS GRADES)
1550. P.V.C GRANULES FROM PVC SCRAPS (WITH POLLUTION CONTROL)
1551. P.V.C HOSES
1552. P.V.C LEATHER CLOTH
1553. P.V.C FLEXIBLE PIPES
1554. P.V.C PIPES AND FITTINGS
1555. POLYTHENE BAGS (PRINTED)
1556. PVC PLASTICS FILM SHEET SOFT/RIGID
1557. PVC RESIN AND COMPOUND
1558. PVC RULAR
1559. PVC STABLIZERS (SINGLE PACK SYSTEM)
1560. PVC WIRE AND CABLES
1561. PAPER BASED PHENOLIC SHEET FOR ELECTRICAL
1562. PHENOL FORMALDEHYDE RESIN
1563. PHENOLIC RESIN
1564. PLASTIC BEADS FROM PLASTIC SCRAPS
1565. PLASTIC BUTTONS
1566. PLASTIC CANS
1567. PLASTIC COLLAPSIBLE TUBE
1568. PLASTIC CORRUGATED SHEET & BOXES
1569. PLASTIC FILM AND SHEETS WITH PRINTING FLEXO & ROTO/LDPE/HDPE/PP/HM/PVC
1570. PLASTIC FILTER MASTER BATCH & OTHER MASTER BATCHES FOR VARIOUS PLASTICS
1571. PLASTIC JERRY CANS
1572. PLASTIC GRANULES OR POWDER FROM PLASTIC SCRAP
1573. PLASTIC INJECTION MOULDED T.V. CABINETS
1574. PLASTIC ITEMS MANUFAC TURE FROM POWDER MELAMINE
1575. PLASTIC GOODS
1576. PLASTIC PIPES & TARPAULINES
1577. PLASTIC SHEET FROM SCRAP
1578. PLASTIC PLANT (BLOW MOULDING & INJECTION MOULDING)
1579. PLASTIC PRODUCTS (GOLD, SILVER, NICKEL)
1580. PLASTIC TOYS
1581 POLYESTER BEADING
1582. POLYESTER FILM
1583. POLYTHENE BAGS & AUTOMATIC PRINTING
1584. POLYTHENE PRINTED BAGS
1585. POLYURETHANE FOAM AND ITS PRODUCTS
1586. PROPYLENE FILM (PRINTED) & BAG MANUFACTURING
1587. PLASTIC MATS
1588. RAINBOW COLOUR ON PVC FILM & SHEET
1589. RED MUD PVC PIPES AND FITTINGS
1590. RE-RUBBERISED OF SOLID TYPE
1591. RESIN COATED SAND REXINE
1592. REXINE CLOTH & ALLIED PRODUCTS
1593. RUBBER ADHESIVE
1594. RUBBER AUTO PARTS
1595. RUBBER BELTING
1596. RUBBER MOULDING UNIT INCLUDING LINING RUBBER SHEETING
1597. RUBBER RECLAIMING
1598. RUBBER ROLLERS FOR TEXTILE MILLS & PAPER INDUSTRIES
1599. RUBBER & PLASTIC SHEETS, MATS & FLAPS
1600. RUBBER SHEET AND ALLIED HOSPITAL RUBBER GOODS
1601. RUBBERIZED PVC GASKET
1602. RUBBERISED COIR
1603. RUBBER COMPOUND FOR AUTOMOBILES
1604. SAFETY BELTS
1605. SILVER AND GOLD PLATING ON PVC AND NYLON-6
1606. SILICONE RUBBER NIPPLES/ TEATS
1607. SPECTACLE FRAMES (PLASTIC)
1608. SPUNGE RUBBER
1609. SURGICAL EXAMINATION GLOVES
1610. SYNTHETIC PEARL COATING ON POLYSTYRENE BEADS
1611. SYNTHETIC RUBBER ADHESIVE
1612. TEFLON MANUFACTURING
1613. TEFLON TAPE
1614. TEFLON TAPES & CABLES
1615. THERMOCOLE SHEET AND MOULDED PRODUCTS EXPANDED POLYESTERENE EXTRUSION PROFILES
1616. THERMOFORMED PACKAGING (BLISTER PACKAGING & POUCH PACKAGING)
1617. THERMOPLASTIC POLYURETHANE
1618. THERMOFORMED CUPS, PLATES & GLASS WITH HIPS SHEET
1619. THERMOCOLE
1620. THERMOCOLE BASED DISPOSABLE GLASS, CUPS & PLATES
1621. TOOTH BRUSHES
1622. TOY BALLOON, DECORA TIVE & INDUSTRIAL BALLOONS
1623. TREAD RUBBER
1624. TYRE RETREADING (HOT)
1625. TYRE RETREADING BY COLD PROCESS
1626. TYRE TUBES & FLAPS
1627. TYRE & TUBES
1628. UNSATURATED POLYESTER FOR REXINE
1629. V-BELT AND FAN BELT
1630. VINYL ASBESTOS AND PVC WALL PAPER
1631. VITON (FLUORO ELASTOMER)

SOAP, COSMETICS & PERFUMS

1632. ACID SLURRY, SYNTHETIC DETERGENT POWDER
1632. ACID SLURRY
1633. AGARBATTI SYNTHETIC, PERFUMERY COMPOUND
1634. AFTER SHAVE LOTION
1635. ANTISEPTIC CREAM
1636. BETA IONONE
1637, BLEACHING POWDER
1638. BLUE DETERGENT POWDER
1639. CLEANING POWDER (VIMTYPE)
1640. COLD CREAM
1641. COLOURED FLAME & PERFUMED CANDLES (RED, BLUE, GREEN FLAME)
1642. COSMETIC INDUSTRY (MODERN)
1643. COSMETIC INDUSTRY (SHAMPOO, SPRAY PERFUME, TALCUM POWDER
1644. DETERGENT POWDER (ARIEL TYPE)
1645. DETERGENT POWDER (NIRMA TYPE) FULLY AUTOMATIC PLANT
1646. DETERGENT WASHING POWDER
1647. FISH OIL SOAP
1648. GLYCERINE TRANSPARENT SOAP
1649. HAIR REMOVING CREAM
1650. HERBAL COSMETICS
1651. HERBAL SHAMPO & CREAM
1652. HERBAL/AYURVEDIC COSMETICS
1653. INCENSE POWDER, INCENSE STICKS & INCENSE CAKE
1654. OPTICAL WHITENERS
1655. ROSE OIL EXTRACTION
1656. SHAMPOOS (COCONUT OIL BASED COLD PROCESS)
1657. SHAVING CREAM
1658. SINDUR (KUMKUM)
1659. SOAP COATED PAPER
1660. SPRAY DRIED DETERGENT POWDER
1661. STAIN REMOVER
1662, TALCUM POWDER (FACE & TOILET POWDER)
1663. TOILET AND HERBAL SOAP
1664. TOOTH PASTE & POWDER
1665. WASHING DETERGENT POWDER AND WASHING SOAP
1666. WASHING POWDER LIQUID DETERGENTS, LOTION & SHAMPOO

Above all the Detailed Project Report are available at *"ENGINEERS INDIA RESEARCH INSTITUTE"*. 4449, Nai Sarak (D), Main Road Delhi - 110 006
● Ph : 91-11-23918117, 2391 6431, 2392 0361, 31082370 ● Fax : 91-11- 2391 6431
● E-Mail : eirisidi@bol.net.in

TEXTILE INDUSTRIES, READYMADE GARMENTS, COTTON, DYEING, BLEACHING, CLOTH, HOSIERY, POWER LOOM, HAND LOOM, WOOLLEN, SILK, SOCKS, SURGICAL COTTON & MANY OTHERS

1667. ANGORA RABBIT WOOL
1668. BUCKRAM
1669. CANVAS SHOES, JUNGLE BOOT, BOOT RUBBER KNEES & BOOT COMBAT
1670. CARPET FROM COTTON WASTE
1671. CERAMIC THREAD GUIDE
1672. COTTON BUDS/SWABS
1673. COTTON FROM WASTE YARN
1674. COTTON ROLLS
1675. COTTON SPIDERS FOR LOUD SPEAKERS
1676. DENIM CLOTH
1677. DENIM CLOTH (INTEGERATED UNIT WITH BLEACHING, DYEING AND PRINTING)
1678. DISPERSENT FOR TEXTILE
1679. DYEING & BLEACHING
1680. DYEING OF HANK YARN
1681. EMULSIFIER FOR WOOL BATCHING OIL
1682. EMBROIDERY ON FABRICS
1683. GARMENT DYEING, WASHING & STITCHING (JEANS, JACKETS, SKIRTS & SHIRTS)
1684. GOVES KNITTING
1685. GUNNY BAGS
1687. HDPE WOVEN SACKS
1688. HDPE TARPAULINS USING PLAIN LOOM WITH LAMINATION
1689. HDPE/PP WOVEN SACKS USING CIRCULAR LOOMS
1690. HOSIERY CLOTH (COTTON) PROCESSING (BLEACHING, DYEING, FINISHING OF CLOTH)
1691. HOSIERY INDUSTRY
1692. HOSIERY MERCERISING
1693. HOSIERY PRODUCTS LIKE VEST, BRIEF, T-SHIRTS & SOCKS
1694. JACQUARD FABRICS
1695. JUTE COIR, GRASS ROPE/ SUTLI MAKING
1696. JUTE FELT
1697. JUTE TWINES
1698. KNITTED FABRICS
1699. LAMINATED JUTE BAGS
1700. LAMINATION OF HDPE WOVEN CLOTH (JUTE,COTTON, PAPER)
1701. NYLON YARN CRIMPING, DOUBLING AND BLEACHING
1702. PIGMENT BINDER FOR TEXTILE PRINTING
1704. POLYESTER RESIN FOR WIRE ENAMEL
1705. POLYESTER RESIN
1706. POLYESTER YARN FROM WASTE POLYESTER ZIP FASTENERS
1707. POWER LOOM
1708. READYMADE GARMENTS & HOSIERY
1709. READYMADE GARMENTS MERCHANDISE
1710. READYMADE GARMENTS & COVERS
1711. READYMADE GARMENTS & EMBROIDERY OF GOWNS, SHIRTS, BLOUSES, T-SHIRTS ETC. (ONLY LADIES)
1712. READYMADE SALWAR SUIT
1713. RECOVERY OF NYLON FROM NYLON WASTE
1714. ROTARY PRINTING AND DYEING ON COTTON, SYNTHETIC TEXTILE
1715. SANITARY NAPKINS
1716. SCREEN PRINTING ON COTTON CLOTH
1717. SEWING THREAD REELS & BALLS MAKING INDUSTRIES
1718. SCREEN PRINTING ON COTTON, POLYESTER & ACRYLIC
1719. SHAWLS (WOOLLEN)
1720. SHOE LACES
1721. SILK FABRICS ON HANDLOOM
1722. SOCKS KNITTING
1723. SPINNING, DOUBLING DYEING MERCERISING & BLEACHING OF COTTON YARN
1724. SPINNING & CARDING OF WOOL INTO YARNS
1725. STARCH BOOK BINDING CLOTH
1726. SURAT JARI
1727. SURGICAL COTTON & BANDAGE
1728. SYNTHETIC TEXTILE INDUSTRY(SUITING, SHIRTING, SAREES) TERRY CLOTH
1729. T-SHIRTS
1730. TOWELS, BED SHEET COVERS
1731. TERRY TOWEL
1732. TERRY FABRICS WEAVING UNIT
1733. TEXTILE AUXILLIARIES & CHEMICALS
1734. TEXTILE BLEACHING, DYEING & FINISHING & PRINTING OF COTTON FABRICS
1735. TEXTILE (HOSIERY)
1736. TEXTILE MILL
1737. TEXTILE DYEING & PRINTING
1738. TEXTILE PRINTING (JOB WORK)
1739. TEXTILE PIGMENT PRINTING BINDER
1740. TOWEL (TERRY)
1741. VELVET CLOTH BY FLOCKING PROCESS
1742. VISCOSE STAPLE FIBRE
1743. WADDING OIL (100%) FOR WADDING OF COTTON HOSIERY CLOTH IN THE DYEING PROCESS
1744. WEAVING OF DASUTI CLOTH WITH PRINTING, DYEING, EMBROIDERY & FINISHING
1745. WASHING OF JEANS & OTHER GARMENTS
1746. WORSTED WOOLLEN YARN CLOTH
1747. ZARI GLITTER SALMA SITARA OF PLASTIC FILM

INFOTECH/IT, HOSPITALITY, HOSPITAL, COLLEGE, SCHOOL, MEDICAL, ENTERTAINMENT CLUB, WARE HOUSING & REAL ESTATE, PROJECTS

1748. AMUSEMENT PARK
1749. AMUSEMENT PARK CUM WATER PARK
1750. BANQUET HALL
1751. CALL CENTER (DOMESTIC)
1752. CALL CENTER (INTERNATIONAL)
1753. CHILDREN RECREATION CENTRE
1754. COLD STORAGE
1755. COMMUNITY HALL
1756. COMPUTER EDUCATION INSTITUTE
1757. COMPUTER SOFTWARE
1758. COLLEGE
1759. CYBER CAFE
1760. DENTAL CLINIC
1761. DENTAL COLLEGE
1762. DIAGONOSTIC CENTRE
1763. E-COMMERCE/BUSINESS
1764. E-SCHOOL (Rs. 5000/-)
1765. ENGINEERING COLLEGE
1766. ENTERTAINMENT CLUB
1767. ENTERTAINMENT CLUB, HOLIDAY RESORT, 4 STAR HOTEL, AMUSEMENT PARK CUM WATER PARK, MUSHROOM & ITS PRODUCTS, FISH FARMING, LAKE FOR BOATING, DEER PARK
1768. FASHION TECHNOLOGY INSTITUTE
1769. FAST FOOD PARLOUR
1770. FIVE STAR HOTEL
1771. FOOD PARLOUR
1772. FRANCHISE TRAINING PROGRAMME FOR IIT & ENGINEERING ENTRANCE EXAMS.
1773. GOLF COURSE
1774. HEALTH CLUB, BEAUTY PARLOUR
1775. HEALTH CLUB AND FITNESS CENTER
1776. HEALTH RESORTS
1777. HOLIDAY RESORTS
1778. HOLIDAY RESORT CUM

Above all the Detailed Project Report are available at *"ENGINEERS INDIA RESEARCH INSTITUTE"*. 4449, Nai Sarak (D), Main Road Delhi - 110 006
• Ph : 91-11-23918117, 2391 6431, 2392 0361, 31082370 • Fax : 91-11-2391 6431
• E-Mail : eirisidi@bol.net.in

ENTERTAINMENT CLUB WITH 4 STAR HOTEL
1779. HOSPITALS
1780. ICE CREAM PARLOUR
1781. INTERNET SERVICE PROVIDER (I.S.P.)
1782. MEDICAL COLLEGE
1783. MEDICAL COLLEGE, HOSPITAL & RESEARCH INSTITUTE
1784. MEDICAL TRANSCRIPTION CENTRE
1785. MENTAL RETARDATION HOSPITAL & CEREBRAL PALSY
1786. MOTEL/SMALL HOTEL
1787. MULTISTOREY COMMERCIAL COMPLEX
1788. MULTISTOREY RESIDENTIAL COMPLEX
1789. NURSERY SCHOOL
1790. NATURE CARE CENTRE
1791. NURSING HOME
1792. ONLINE SHOPPING MALL (RS. 5000/- REPORT)
1793. PORTAL
1794. REHABILITATION CENTRE FOR AGED & NEEDY PERSONS
1795. RESIDENTIAL CUM COMMERCIAL COMPLEX
1796. RESTAURANT
1797. RESTAURANT WITH PUB
1798. SCHOOL (PRIMARY)
1799. SCHOOL (HIGHER SECONDARY)
1800. THREE STAR HOTEL
1801. TOURIST CLUB
1802. TRAINING INSTITUTE FOR MEDICAL TRANSCRIPTION
1803. VIDEO FILM STUDIO
1804. WARE HOUSE
1805. WEBSITE DESIGN & E-MAIL REGISTERING

AGRO BASED INDUSTRIES

1806. COAL BRIQUETTES FROM AGROWASTE
1807. FURFURALFROM RICEHULL
1808. MUSHROOM CULTIVATION & PROCESSING (BUTTON)
1809. MUSHROOM GROWING & PROCESSING WITH AIR CONDITIONING
1810. MUSHROOM CULTIVATION & PROCESSING UNIT DEHYDRATION & PACKAGING OF OYSTER & PADDY STRAW MUSHROOMS
1811. ORGANIC MANURE
1812. PAPAYA CULTIVATION
1813. PAPAYA & TOMATO CULTIVATION
1814. PROCESSING & UTILISATION OF COCONUT
1815. PROCESSING OF SHEEP HAIR TO PRODUCE WOOL

BAKERY, CONFECTIONERY & FOOD PRODUCTS

1816. AGROLACTOR SOYA MILK
1817. APPLE FRUIT JUICE WITH CANNING BOTTLING
1818. AYURVEDIC SHARBAT
1819. BAKERY UNIT (PASTRIES, BREAD, BUNS, CAKE, TOFFEE ETC.)
1820. BAKING POWDER
1821. BANANA & ITS BY PRODUCTS
1822. BANANA POWDER
1823. BANANA WAFERS
1824. BANANA CULTIVATION
1825. BEER INDUSTRY
1826. DEHULLING OF JAUN FOR BEER
1827. BEER & WINE
1828. BEER, ALCOHOL, IMFL
1829. BESEN PLANT
1830. BISCUIT PLANT
1831. BREAD & BISCUIT PLANT
1832. BOTTLING PLANT COUNTRY LIQUOR FROM RECTIFIED SPIRIT
1833. BRANDY
1834. BREAD RUSKS
1835. CANNED FRUITS & VEGETABLES
1836. CANNING & PRESERVATION OF MEAT
1837. CANNING & PRESERVATION OF VEGETABLES
1838. CANNING OF MANGO PULP & MANGO SLICES
1839. CARBONATED BEVERAGS
1840. CASHEW FENI
1841. CASHEW NUT (DRIED & FRIED)
1842. CATTLE BREEDING
1843. CATTLE BREEDING & DAIRY FARM TO PRODUCE MILK
1844. CATTLE FEED FROM TAPIOCA
1845. CHEWING GINGER & AMLOKI
1846. CHEWING GUM
1847. CHILLI SAUCE
1848. CHILLI POWDER
1849. CHOCOLATE
1850. CIDER PLANT
1851. COCOA POWDER
1852. COCOA BUTTER & COCOA POWDER
1853. COCONUT SHELL POWDER
1854. COCONUT WATER
1855. COCONUT SWEET (WATERY)
1856. COCONUT MILK POWDER (DEHYDRATED)
1857. COCONUT PRODUCTS & BY PRODUCTS (INTEGRATED PLANT)
1858. COLD DRINK
1859. CURRY POWDER
1860. DAIRY FOR MILK PROCESSING (GHEE, BUTTER & PANEER)
1861. DAIRY PRODUCTS
1862. DAIRY PRODUCTS MILK PACKAGING IN POUCH (GHEE, BUTTER, ETC.
1863. DAIRY FARM TO PRDUCE MILK WITH PACKAGING (COW)
1864. DAIRY FARM TO PRDUCE MILK WITH PACKAGING (BUFALLOE)
1865. DAIRY FARM & MILK PRODUCTS
1866. DAL MOTH, CHANACHUR & BHUJIYA
1867. DEHYDRATION OF FRUITS & VEGETABLE
1868. DESICCATED COCONUT POWDER FROM COCONUTS
1869. DEHYDRATION & CANNINGOF FRUITS & VEGETABLES
1870. DRY FRUIT ROASTING & PACKAGING
1871. DRYING OF RED CHILLIES, HALDI, DHANIYA, PEAS & GROUND NUT
1872. EGG POWDER
1873. FISH CANNING IN TIN & POUCHES
1874. FISH DEHYRATION (DRYING OF FISH)
1875. FISH MEAL
1876. FISH PROCESSING (BEAST FREEZING PROCESSES)
1877. FLAVOURS FOR FOOD INDUSTRIES
1878. FLOUR MILL (ROLLER)
1879. FROZEN MEAT
1880. FOOD DEHYDRATION (FRUITS & VEGETABLES)
1881. FRIED & ROASTED GROUND NUT, GRAMS, PEAR ETC.
1882. FRUIT JUICE MAKING & PACKAGING IN PLASTIC CONTAINER
1883. FRUIT JUICE IN TETRA PACK (DRINKS)
1884. FRUIT JUICE, SQUASHES, SAUCE & KETCHUP, JAM, JELLY, VINEGAR ETC.
1885. GARLIC FLAKES
1886. GARLIC POWDER
1887. GHEE & BUTTER
1888. GINGER (PULVERISED)
1889. GINGER GLAZING & PRESERVATION
1890. GINGER STORAGE
1891. GINGER PROCESSING
1892. GINGER OIL & GINGER DUST
1893. GINGER POWDER (DRY) & OLEORESIN
1894. GRAPE DEHYDRATION
1895. GRAPE CULTIVATION
1896. GRAPE JUICE
1897. HONEY PROCESSING & PACKAGING
1898. ICE CREAM & ICE CANDY
1899. ICE CUBE
1900. INVERT SUGAR
1901. IDLI MIX, DOSA MIX SAMBHAR MIX, VADA MIX, GULAB JAMUN MIX
1902. INSTANT COFFEE & INSTANT TEA

Above all the Detailed Project Report are available at *"ENGINEERS INDIA RESEARCH INSTITUTE"*. 4449, Nai Sarak (D), Main Road Delhi - 110 006
• Ph : 91-11-23918117, 2391 6431, 2392 0361, 31082370 • Fax : 91-11-2391 6431
• E-Mail : eirisidi@bol.net.in

1903. INSTANT NOODLES
1904. INSTANT SOUPS
1905. IODIZED SALT FROM CRUDE SALT
1906. JAM CHUTNEY PICKLES & SQUASHES
1907. KATHA MANUFACTURING
1908. LECITHIN (SOYA BASED)
1909. LEMON & ITS PRODUCTS
1910. MACARONI MANUFACTURING
1911. MACARONI, SPAGHETTI, VERMICELLI & NOODLES
1912. MAIZE & ITS BY PRODUCTS MALTING PLANT
1913. MANGO PAPPAD (AAM PAPPAD)
1914. MANGO POWDER RIPE
1915. MANGO POWDER
1916. MANGO PROCESSING & CANNING (MANGO PULP)
1917. MEAT PROCESSING (CHICKEN MUTTON)
1918. MEAT PROCESSING (BUFFALO)
1919. MENTHOL BOLD FROM MENTHOL FLAKES
1020. MILK POWDER
1921. MILK POWDER & GHEE
1922. MILK POWDER, GHEE & SPICES
1923. MILK PRESERVATION & MARKETING TO WHOLE SELLERS
1924. MILK PRESERVATION & MARKETING TO WHOLE SELLERS (IN POUCHES)
1925. MILK TOFFEE MANUFACTURES
1926. MINERAL WATER
1927. MINERAL WATER IN POUCHES
1928. MINI FLOUR MILL ATTA MAIDA, SUJI & WHEAT BRAN
1929. MITHAI/HALWAI (SWEET & NAMKEEN)
1930. MUTTON PROCESSING
1931. PAN MASALA (MEETHA, SADA, ZARDA) MAKING & PACKING
1932. PAN MASALA AND POUCH MAKING
1933. PANEER (CHEESE)
1934. PAPAD & BARIYAN
1935. PAPAD PLANT
1936. PEPSICOLA IN POLYTUBES
1937. PETHA PACKAGING
1938. PICKLES
1939. PIGGERY/MEAT/CHICKEN PROCESSING
1940. PINE APPLE JUICE CANNING
1941. POTATO & ONION POWDER
1942. POTATO & ONION FLAKES
1943. POTATO CHIPS
1944. POTATO GRANULES
1945. POUCH FILLING FOR SAUNF SUPARI ILAICHI ETC.
1946. PRESERVATION OF RAWS MANGO JUICE
1947. PROCESSED CHEESE & MARINE PDTS.
1948. PULP FROM TARMARIND
1949. READYMATE PROCESSED FOOD
1950. RICE & CORN FLAKES
1951. RICE BASMATI (TRADING)
1952. RICE POLISHING & PACKAGING IN POUCH
1953. ROASTED/SALTED/MASALA/ CASHEW NUTS ALMONDS & PEA NUT
1954. ROLLER FLOUR MILL

INFOTECH/IT PROJECTS

1955. MEDICAL TRANSCRIPTION
1956. E-COMMERCE
1957. CYBERCAFE
1958. INTERNET SERVICE PROVIDER (ISP)
1959. COMPUTER EDUCATION CENTRE
1960. PORTAL (WEBSITE DESIGN)
1961. CALL CENTRE

TERMS AND CONDITIONS

FOR INDIA

1. Please ask for Quotations of Each *Market Survey Cum Detailed Techno Economic Feasibility Report.* Payable in advance through Draft/M.O./Cash in favour of 'ENGINEERS INDIA RESEARCH INSTITUTE', Delhi. Delivery by Regd.post within 2 Days. (Postage Free)

2. Ask for the Hi-Tech Projects Monthly magazine. Each Magazine covers many Project Profiles for selection of Industry.

FOR OVERSEAS

1. Please ask for Quotations in US $ of Each *Market Survey Cum Detailed Techno Economic Feasibility Report.* Payable in advance through Draft/M.O./Cash in favour of 'ENGINEERS INDIA RESEARCH INSTITUTE', Delhi. (Payable in India) Delivery by Regd.post within 4 Days.

2. Ask for the Hi-Tech Projects Monthly magazine. Each Magazine covers many Project Profiles for selection of Industry.

ENGINEERS INDIA RESEARCH INSTITUTE

4449, Nai Sarak (D), Main Road, Delhi - 110 006 (India)
Ph:. 91-11-23918117, 23916431, 23840361, 31082370
Fax: 91-11-23916431 E-Mail : eirisidi@bol.net.in
Website:www.startindustry.com
Also at : 4/27, Roop Nagar, Near Roop Nagar No. 1 School, Delhi - 110 007 (India) Ph:. 23840361

JUST PUBLISHED-NEW BOOKS

TECHNOLOGY OF COATINGS, RESINS, PIGMENTS & INKS INDUSTRIES

By : EIRI BOARD

ISBN. 81-86732-64-0 ★ Rs. 975/-

Introduction, Coating Properties, Polyurethane Coatings, Powder Coatings, UV Curable Powder Coatings, Polyurethane Coating, Pigments Dispersions, Colour of Pigments, Caprolactone Acrylics, Additives in Paints, Polyester- based Water- borne and Solvent-borne Coil Coatings, Zinc Dust Pigment, Alkyd Manufacturing Process using Designed Experiments, Calcium Carbonate Extenders for Powder Coating Systems, Pigments for Paints Inks and Plastics, Developments in Resins for Powder Coatings, Design of Paint Formulations on the Basis of Solubility Parameters of Resins Pigments and Solvents, Polyester Resin- A Surface Coating Agent etc.

TECHNOLOGY OF RUBBER & RUBBER GOODS INDUSTRIES

By : EIRI BOARD

ISBN. 81-86732-59-4 ★ Rs. 900/-

Natural rubber , Classification, Properties, Uses and Manufacture, Latex processing and applications, Chemical aspects of rubber technology, Physical aspects of rubber technology, Styrene Butadiene Rubber (SBR), Processing and curing of Polybutadiene and Polyisoprene, Manufacture and Processing of EPDM, Butyl and Halobutyl Rubbers, Nitrile & Polyacrylic Rubber, Neoprene (Polychloroprene) & Hypalon Rubber, Silocone Rubber, Reclaimed Rubber, Latex & Foam Rubber, Vulcanisation, Manufacturing Techniques of Rubber Products, Recycling of Wastes from Rubber & Plastic, Quality control in Rubber Industry.

CANDLE MAKING PROCESSES AND FORMULATIONS HAND BOOK

By : EIRI BOARD

ISBN. 81-86732-62-4 ★ Rs. 380/-

Introduction, Equipment & Materials, Raw Materials, How to Manufacture, Candle Making Process, Wax Melting, Moulded Candles, Surface Techniques, Novelty candles, Chemicals Colours Used, Candle Power, Waxes Used, Moulds & Machines, Selected Formulations, Coloured Candles Manufacture, Perfumed Candles, Medicated Canbles Mosquito Repellent Candles, Magic Candles , Project Profiles, Imported Machinery for Candle Making, Faults, Candle Making (Non-Drip), Candle Coating, Suppliers of Machinery, Suppliers of Raw Materials.

HAND BOOK OF SCREENPRINTING WITH PROCESSES & TECHNOLOGY

By : EIRI BOARD ★ ISBN. 81-86732-63-2 ★ Rs. 350/-

Screen Printing Methods, Screen Printing on Paper, textiles & other Printing Substrates, Screen- Process Stencils, Screen Printing Automatic Press, Choosing a printing process, Screen Printing Inks, Screen Printing Accessories, Stencils, Chemicals used and Formulations, Common Faults in Screen Printing, Printing Unit, Automatic Screen Printing Machine, Screen Printing on Different Surfaces, Inks for Screen Printing , Adhesives, Screen Printing On Glass, Colour Combination, Silk Screen Photo Stencil Preparation, Plant Economics Suppliers of Plant & Machinery & Raw Materials.

ENGINEERS INDIA RESEARCH INSTITUTE Mobile : 9811437895

4449, Nai Sarak, Main Road, Delhi - 110 006 (INDIA) Ph./Fax : 91-11- 23918117, 23916431, 23840361

JUST PUBLISHED-NEW BOOKS

START YOUR OWN EXPORT BUSINESS (HOW TO EXPORT)

By : EIRI BOARD

ISBN. 81-86732-57-8 ★ Rs. 350/-

Book covers latest methods including Rules for Successful Exporting, Brief Details for Starting Export Business, Registration of Exporters, Export of Samples, Gifts, Spares, Replacement, Repaired Goods etc., Appointing Overseas, Agents, Obtaining an Export Licence, Obtaining Export Credit Insurance, Finance Arrangement for Exports, Understanding Foreign Exchange Rates and Protection against their Adverse Movement, Procuring / Manufacturing Goods for Export and their Inspection by Government Authorities, Labelling, Packaging, Packing and Marking Goods for Export, Excise Procedure etc.

TECHNOLOGY OF PETROCHEMICALS, LUBRICANTS, GREASES & PETROLEUM REFINING

By : EIRI BOARD

ISBN. 81-86732-58-6 ★ Rs. 900/-

Refinery & petrochemicals, Hydrocarbons, Petrochemicals, Industrial organic synthesis, Lubricants, Manufacture of oils & greases, Distillation of crude petroleum, Petroleum products, Purification of petroleum products, Refining of petroleum, Testing of petroleum, Application of lubricating agents, Formulating & compounding, Reclamation of used lubricating oil, Formulating of greases, Lubricants manufacture, Various formulations of lubricants & greases, Acetic acid, Coolant, Cutting oil, Ethanol (Biofuel), Formaldehyde, Food grade grease or lubricant, Suppliers of plant & machineries, Suppliers of raw materials, List of present manufacturers.

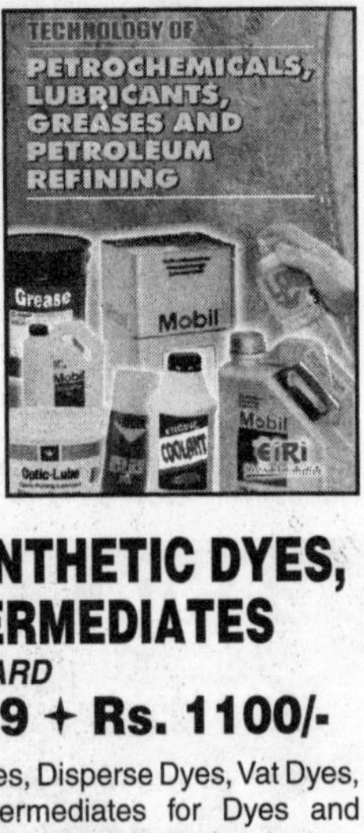

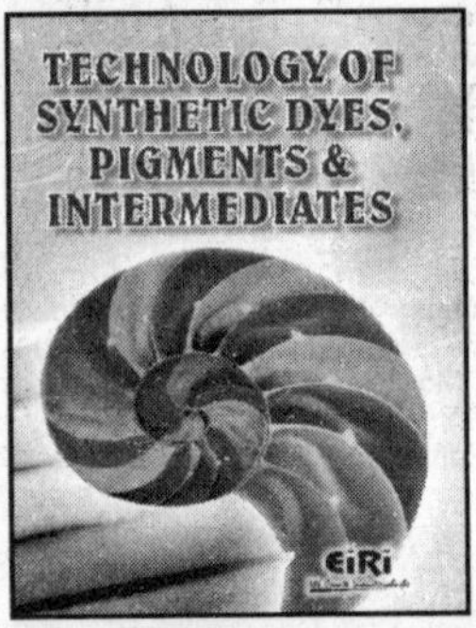

TECHNOLOGY OF SYNTHETIC DYES, PIGMENTS & INTERMEDIATES

By : EIRI BOARD

ISBN. 81-86732-51-9 ✦ Rs. 1100/-

Dyes , Azo Dyes, Acid Dyes, Basic Dyes, Disperse Dyes, Vat Dyes, Sulphur Dyes, Reactive Dyes, Intermediates for Dyes and Pigments, Fluorescent Brightners and Optical Whitening Agents, Pigments for Textiles, Paints, Pigments for Printing Inks, Plant Economics of Dye & Dye Intermediate, Suppliers of Plants, Machinery and Equipments

PRESERVATION & CANNING OF FRUITS AND VEGETABLES

By : EIRI BOARD **✦ ISBN. 81-86732-50-0 ✦ Rs. 900/-**

FOOD COLOURS, FOOD ADDITIVES, METHODS OF PRESERVATION CANNING AND BOTTLING OF FRUITS AND VEGETABLES, FRUITS AND VEGETABLES DRYING/ DEHYDRATION1AND CONCENTRATION, REEZING OF FRUITS AND VEGETABLES, FRUIT BEVERAGES, VINEGAR, JAM, JELLY AND MARMALADE, PICKLES, SAUCES/KETCHUPS & CHUTNEY, TOMATO PROCESSING, POTATO PROCESSING, PROCESSING OF MUSHROOM, MANUFACTURERS / SUPPLIERS OF PLANT, EQUIPMENTS & MACHINERIES MANUFACTURERS / SUPPLIERS OF PACKAGING MATERIALS, MANUFACTURERS/SUPPLIERS OF RAW MATERIALS

ENGINEERS INDIA RESEARCH INSTITUTE Mobile : 9811437895

4449, Nai Sarak, Main Road, Delhi - 110 006 (INDIA) Ph./Fax : 91-11- 23918117, 23916431, 23840361

JUST PUBLISHED-NEW BOOKS

HAND BOOK OF AGRO CHEMICAL INDUSTRIES (INSECTICIDES & PESTICIDES)

By : EIRI BOARD

ISBN. 81-86732-46-2 ✦ Rs. 900/-

The Book has just published and covers following Contents : Agro Chemical Industries, Pesticides, Insecticides, Fungicides, Nematicide, Rodenticides, Molluscicides, Fumigants, Acaricides, Herbicides, Plant Growth Regulators, Repellents, Attractants, Pheromones, Synergists, Synthetic Inhibitors and Proinsecticides, Toxicoligy & Safe use of Pesticides, Insecticide Act, Pesticide Formulations, Pesticide Mixtures, Modern Equipments for a Pesticide Formulation Labiratory & Pilot Plant, Aerosol Formulations, Advances in Pesticides Formulations Packaging, Aerosol Packaging Technology, Packaging In Pesticides, Emulsifier for Pesticides, Pesticide by Neem Fruits & Seed, Mosquito Coils and mats, Air Freshner (Odonil Type), Insecticide from Neem Seed & Oil, Phenyl, Recent Developments in Pesticide Formulations, Allethrin Mosquito Repellent Oil, Mosquito Repellent Agarbatti, Aerosol & Mosquito Repellent Spray (Baygon, HIT & Mortein Type), Suppliers of Plant & Machinery and Raw Materials etc..

HAND BOOK OF SPICES & PACKAGING WITH FORMULAES

By : EIRI BOARD

ISBN. 81-86732-31-4 ✦ Rs. 650/-

The Book covers new formulaes of various kinds of Spices. The major chapters of the book are Ajowan, Amchur, Aniseed, Asafoetida, Chilli, Caraway, Cardamom, Cassia, Celery Seed, Cinnamon, Clove, Coriander, Cumin Seed, Fennel, Garlic, Ginger, Pepper, Drying of Red Chilli, Dry Ginger, Onion Dehydration, Garlic Powder, Formulaes of Different Kinds of Ground Spices, Packaging of Spices, Methods of Tests, Agmark, Details of Machinery, National Standards, Importers/Exporters of Spices, Plant & Equipment Suppliers & Manufacturers of Spices

MANUFACTURE OF SNACKS FOOD, NAMKEEN, PAPPAD & POTATO PRODUCTS

By : EIRI BOARD

ISBN. 81-86732-37-3 ✦ Rs. 650/-

Extruded Snacks, Health Food Snacks, Snack Food Preservatio & Packaging, Details of Plant, Machinery & Equipments, Instant Noodles, Namkeen, Namkeen & Sweets, Potato Products. Manufacturers of Plants & Machineries of Snacks Food, Manufacturers of Machineries of Papped Plants, Manufacturers of Plant & Machineries of Namkeen, Manufacturers of Raw Materials, Suppliers of Packaging Materials. Potato, Pappad & Barian Plant, Potato Waffers, Potato Chips, Packaging of Snack Foods.

ENGINEERS INDIA RESEARCH INSTITUTE Mobile : 9811437895

4449, Nai Sarak, Main Road, Delhi - 110 006 (INDIA) Ph./Fax : 91-11- 23918117, 23916431, 23840361

JUST PUBLISHED-NEW BOOKS

HAND BOOK OF FOOD DEHYDRATION & DRYING

By : EIRI BOARD

ISBN. 81-86732-60-8 ★ Rs. 650/-

Book Covers Fruits and vegetables drying/dehydration and concentration, Types of dehydraters, Sun-drying and dehydration of fruits, Dehydration of vegetables, Dehydration of eggs, milk, butter and cheese, Dehydration of meat, fish, beef blood and gelatin, Dehydration of miscellaneous foods, Plant sanitation, Nutritive value of dried and dehydrated foods, Packaging and storage, Banana powder, Dehydration of figs by sun drying method, Desiccated coconut powder from coconuts, Dehydration of fruits and vegetables by freeze drying method, Dehydration of jack fruit, Egg powder, Egg powder, Fruit juice powder, Food dehydration, Ginger drying, Grape powder, Mustard powder, Mango kernel seed powder (starch), Milk powder, Potato powder, Potato powder (Automatic plant), Skimmed milk powder, Tomato powder, Tamarind seed powder, Turmeric powder (edible grade), Garlic powder, Dehydrated onions & onion powder, Herbal extracts (Dry), Plant & machinery suppliers, Supplier of raw materials etc.

MEAT PROCESSING & MEAT PRODUCTS HAND BOOK

By : EIRI BOARD

ISBN. 81-86732- 65-9 ★ Rs. 900/-

Book Covers Preservation of Meat, Fish and Eggs, Meat and Meat Products, Raw Materials, Nutritional Value of Some Processed Meats, Curing, Smoking, Meat Cookery and Cooked Meat Products, Cooked Meat Product Recipes, Raw Materials, Sectioned and Formed Meat Formulations, Sausages, Fermented Meat Products, Sausage Formulations, Casings, Extenders, and Additives, Use of Spices in Processed Meats, Cured and/ or Smoked Meats, Low Fat Meat Products, The Canning Process, Canned Meat Formulations, Restructured Meat Products, Methods for Tenderization of Meats, Quality Aspects of Poultry Meat and its Products, Developments in Modified Atmosphere Packaging of Meat Poultry and Fish, Broiler Chicken, Buffalo Meat Processing, Chicken Meat Processing, Chicken/ Mutton (Sheep Meat) Processing, Chicken Sausages & Chicken Hamburger, Frozen Meat, Piggery Meat Processing, Suppliers of Plant and Machineries, Suppliers of Raw Materials etc.

HAND BOOK OF MODERN BAKERY PRODUCTS

By : EIRI BOARD

 # ISBN. 81-86732-61-6 # Rs. 750/-

Baking, Biscuits, Breads & Rolls, Cakes, Cookies and Pastries, Bread Making, Cake-Making, Cookies, Pastry, Cookies, Biscuits, Cakes, Buns Pies, Icings Breads & Pizzas, Health Breads, Chicken Patties, Noodles, Fried Snack Foods: Sev, Bhujia, Bombay Mix, Fried Nuts and Dal, Packaging for biscuits, Chapati Making Unit, Details of Plant & Machinery, Bakery Machinery Suppliers, Suppliers Addresses.

HAND BOOK OF PACKAGING TECHNOLOGY

By : EIRI BOARD

 # ISBN. 81-86732-67-5 # Rs. 900/-

Packaging Materials, Rigid & Ancillary Materials and Export Packaging, Printing, Eco-Friendly Packaging, Folding Board Cartons, Corrugated Board, Multiwall Paper Sacks, Plastics, PVC in Packaging, BOPP Films, Plastic Woven Sacks, Expanded Polystyrene, Expanded Polyethylene, Flexible Packaging, Shrink & Stretch Wrapping, Glass Containers, Aluminium Foil, Adhesive Tapes, Wooden Containers, Systems Packaging, Vacuum Packaging, Strip Packaging, Aerosol Packaging, Packaging of Horticultural Crops, Packaging of Meat Fish & Poultry, Packaging of Ready to Eat Foods, Packaging of Pharmaceutical Products, Packaging of Cosmetic, Soaps & Detergents, Packaging of Hazardous Chemicals, Fertilizers & Pesticides Industry, etc.

ENGINEERS INDIA RESEARCH INSTITUTE Mobile : 9811437895

4449, Nai Sarak, Main Road, Delhi - 110 006 (INDIA) Ph./Fax : 91-11- 23918117, 23916431, 23840361

JUST PUBLISHED-NEW BOOKS

MODERN INKS FORMULAES & MANUFACTURING INDUSTRIES

By : EIRI BOARD

ISBN. 81-86732-17-9 + Rs. 325/-

The book contains Colour Matching, Raw Materials, Waxes & Additives, Typographic Inks, Formuations, Photogravure Inks Screen Process Inks, Ball Point Pen Inks, Testing of Finished Inks, Formulae, Toner Inks for Automatic Machine, Printing Inks, Screen Printing Inks, Offset Printing Inks, Stamp Pad Inks, Flexographic and Rotogravure Ink, Printing Inks (Flexographic Inks), Duplicating Ink, Ball Pen Refill Ink, Plastic Ink and Golden Silver Paste, Suppliers of Plant & Machinery, Suppliers of Raw Materials etc

HAND BOOK OF PRINTING PROCESSES TECHNOLOGIES AND INDUSTRIES

By : EIRI BOARD

ISBN. 81-86732-07-1 + Rs. 375/-

The book covers latest technology of almost all the printing technology viz; screen, offset, velvet cloth, sheetfed offset. Project profiles on various printing industries are also provided. Suppliers of machinery.

HAND BOOK OF SYNTHETIC & HERBAL COSMETICS

By : Ankur Kumar

ISBN. 81-86732-21-7 + Rs. 575/-

The Book covers Face Powder, Variations of Face Powder, Toilet Powder, Creams, Vanishing Creams, Foundation Creams, Hand Lotions, After Shaving Lotions, Deodorants, Lipsticks, Shampoos, Depilatories, Shaving Cream, Cosmetics for Nails,Tooth Powder, Tooth Paste, Mouth Washes, Facial Masks,Cosmetics for Eyes, Cosmetic for Babies, Herbal Cosmetic for the Skin, Hair Shampoos, Anti Dandruff Preparations, Hair Straighteners, Hair Dyes, Bleashes, Colourings and Dye Removers, Oral Herbal Preparations,

HAND BOOK OF REAL ESTATE PLAZAS, HOTEL, MOTEL, HOSPITAL, & COMMERCIAL COMPLEX

By : EIRI BOARD **+ Rs. 1300/-**

The Book contains most lucrative projects based on Real Estate Plazas, Hotel, Hospital. Each Project profile covers List of Plant and Machinery cost, List of basic raw materials and their estimated monthly cost., Profitability of the project, Break even point

ENGINEERS INDIA RESEARCH INSTITUTE Mobile : 9811437895

4449, Nai Sarak, Main Road, Delhi - 110 006 (INDIA) Ph./Fax : 91-11- 23918117, 23916431, 23840361

JUST PUBLISHED-NEW BOOKS

HAND BOOK OF STATIONERY, PAPER CONVERTING & PACKAGING INDUSTRIES

By : EIRI BOARD + Rs. 400/-

The Book covers Ammonia Paper, Artist Colour, Ball Pen Pen and Refill, Carbon Paper, Bopp Adhesive, Computer Stationery, Corrugated Box, Duplicating Paper, Exercise Note Book and Register, Lead Pencil, Fountain Pen, Office Paste, Paper Bags, Polythene Bags, Eraser, Sealing Wax, Tracing Paper, Wax Crayon, Xerox Paper, Sticker Making, Screen Ptg. etc.

RUBBER CHEMICALS AND PROCESSING INDUSTRIES

By : EIRI BOARD

ISBN. 81-86732-15-2 + Rs. 400/-

The book covers Technology of Rubber Chemicals and Manufacturing of Rubber Products/Goods. Various Project Profiles are given, Suppliers of Raw Materials and Machinery are also provided plus much more other details are provided.

MOULDS DESIGN AND PROCESSING HANDBOOK

By : EIRI BOARD

ISBN. 81-86732-23-3 + Rs. 495/-

Covers Classification of Moulds, Vent in The Mould, Ejection Mechanism, Production Schedule of Plastic Injection Mould, Steel for Injection Mould, Trouble Shooting Tips, Properties of Plastics, Injection Mould Design, Compression and Transfer Mould - Pot Calculations, Blow Mould Design Aspects, Standard Mould Parts, Conversion Table.

HAND BOOK OF HOSIERY READY MADE GARMENTS & TEXTILE PROJECTS WITH DIRECTORY OF TEXTILE MACHINERIES

***By : EIRI BOARD* + Rs. 1300/-**

The book covers latest project profiles on power loom, readymade garments, socks, cotton yarn dyeing, hosiery, velvet cloth, open end spinning mill & complete machinery suppliers of textiles.

ENGINEERS INDIA RESEARCH INSTITUTE Mobile : 9811437895

4449, Nai Sarak, Main Road, Delhi - 110 006 (INDIA) Ph./Fax : 91-11-23918117, 23916431, 23840361

JUST PUBLISHED-NEW BOOKS

HAND BOOK OF ICE CREAM TECHNOLOGY & FORMULAE

By : EIRI BOARD

ISBN. 81-86732-70-5 ★ Rs. 525/-

Introduction, Nutritional Value and Classification of Ice cream, Composition and Properties of Ice Cream Mixes, Raw Material used to Produce Ice Cream, Manufacturing Process, Ice Cream Freezing, Ice Cream Mix Calculations, Packaging of Ice Cream, Frozen Dairy Products and Formulations, Ice Cream Varieties, Novelties and Specials, Ices and Sherbets, Laboratory Tests, Cost and Merchandising, Project Profiles, Suppliers of Machineries etc.

HAND BOOK OF DAIRY FARMING

By : EIRI BOARD

ISBN. 81-86732-66-7 ★ Rs. 375/-

Dairy Farming, Ration for cattles, Housing for dairy animals, Livestock Management, Care for dry cows, Livestock records maintenance, Manufacturing Process, Clean milk production, Dairy cattle economics, Diseases of Animals, Milk Storage, Distribution of Milk, Suppliers of Equipments, Seeds, Drugs, etc., Packaging of Milk, Plant Economics of Dairy Farm (Buffalo) & Dairy Farm (Cow) etc.

TECHNOLOGY OF MODERN RICE MILLING & BASMATI RICE

By : EIRI BOARD ★ ISBN. 81-86732-69-1 ★ Rs. 600/-

Botany, Processing of Rice, Rice Milling, Modern Conventional Milling, Properties of Parboiled Rice, Huller Use for Milling Parboiled Rice is the Chief Obstacle, Technology of Basmati Rice Processing, Marketing of Basmati Rice, Speciality Rice, Trips and WTO, Details of Technology & Technology Providers, Directory of Basmati Rice Exporters/Importers, Important Details, Important Details, Plant Economics of Rice Puff, Rice Bran Oil, Rice Polishing & Packing, Modern Rice Mill, Basmati Rice Trading, Rice Sorting / Grading, Suppliers of Plant & Machineries, Suppliers of Packaging Materials etc.

SMALL MEDIUM AND LARGE SCALE CHEMICAL INDUSTRIES

By : EIRI BOARD ✦ ISBN. 81-86732-06-3 ✦ Rs. 375/-

Covers Various Project profiles on highly profitable chemical industries. As many as 27 Project Profiles are provided. Suppliers of Plant and Machinery are also given for the benefit of new entrepreneurs.

ENGINEERS INDIA RESEARCH INSTITUTE Mobile : 9811437895

4449, Nai Sarak, Main Road, Delhi - 110 006 (INDIA) Ph./Fax : 91-11- 23918117, 23916431, 23840361

JUST PUBLISHED-NEW BOOKS

PLASTIC PROCESSING AND PACKAGING INDUSTRIES

By : EIRI BOARD

ISBN. 81-86732-11-X # Rs. 450/-

Introduction, Plastic Processing, Injection & Blow Moulding, Compounding & Processing of PVC, PU, Project profiles and directory section. The book is covering with the 54 fully detailed chapters.

FOOD PROCESSING & AGRO BASED INDUSTRIES

By : EIRI BOARD

ISBN. 81-86732-12-8 # Rs. 450/-

Covering 31 detailed chapters including dairy, confectionery, fruit juice, chocolate, honey, chewing gum, tomato products, jams & jellies, chutney, dehydration of food, packing of food & alllied products, Project profiles on different food products.

HAND BOOK OF DAIRY FORMULATIONS PROCESSES & MILK PROCESSING INDUSTRIES

By : EIRI BOARD ★ *ISBN. 81-86732-10-1* ★ *Rs. 375/-*

Book covers Introduction, Manufacturing, Technologies, Packaging, Formulations of various Milk & Milk Based Products, Project Profiles on Dairy & Milk Products including Baby Cerial Food & Milk Powder, Casein from Milk, Confectionery Industry, Dairy Farm, Dairy Products, Flavoured Milk, Ice Cream, Milk Powder, Milk Preservation, and Suppliers of Raw Materials and Machineries with Technologies etc.

PAINT PIGMENT VARNISH & LACQUER MANUFACTURING

ISBN. 81-86732-16-0 # Rs. 450/-

The Book covers Process, Formulations, Technology, Project Profiles on various Paint, Varnish, Lacquer manufacturing industries. Suppliers of Plant, Equipments and Machinery with Raw Materials have also been incorporated.

PET PREFORM & ITS PRODUCTS MANUFACTURING

Rs. 1300/- or US$ 100/-

Processing and manufacturing technology of PETBottles, Preform and market study with Project Profiles of PET bottles, preform & others. Suppliers of Machinery & Raw Materials etc.

ENGINEERS INDIA RESEARCH INSTITUTE **Mobile : 9811437895**

4449, Nai Sarak, Main Road, Delhi - 110 006 (INDIA) Ph./Fax : 91-11- 23918117, 23916431, 23840361

JUST PUBLISHED-NEW BOOKS

HAND BOOK OF PERFUMES WITH FORMULATIONS

By : EIRI BOARD

ISBN. 81-86732-42-X + Rs. 750/-

This book covers Creating a Perfume, Flower Perfumes & Formulation, Fantasy Perfumes & their Formulation, Colognes for Men, Olfaction & Gustation, Raw Materials of Perfumes, Classification of Odours & Odourants, Packaging of Perfumes, Testing of Perfumes, Aerosol Spray, Aromatic Perfumery Compounds, Scent & Perfume, Spray Perfume, Perfumes for Soap, Detergent & Agarbatti etc. Suppliers of Raw Materials .

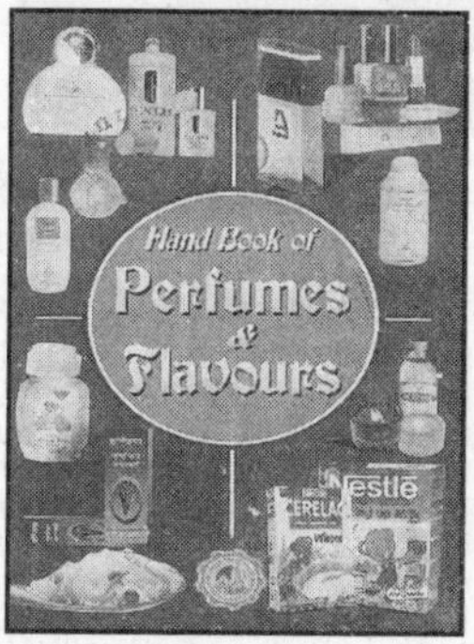

HAND BOOK OF PERFUMES & FLAVOURS

By : EIRI BOARD

ISBN. 81-86732-30-6 + Rs. 600/-

The book covers Perfume, Formulary of Perfume, Formulary of Flavour, Chemicals Specifications for Perfume & Flavour Components, Natural Odours Simulated with Aromatic Chemicals, Simulated Flower Scents, Simulated Marine Scents (Algae), Plant & Equipment Suppliers, Suppliers of Raw Materials, Manufacturer / Exporters / Suppliers of Perfumes. Project profiles has also included for the benefits of the new entrepreneurs.

AGRO BASED PLANTATION CULTIVATION & FARMING HAND BOOK

By : EIRI BOARD

ISBN. 81-86732-14-4 + Rs. 475/-

The Book Covers Goat Farm, Floriculture (Cut Flower), Tissue Culture, Tea, Banana Cultivation, Piggery Farm, Dairy Farming, Bee keeping, Mushroom Cultivation and Processing, Teak Tree Plantation and many more. Project Profiles and Suppliers of Equipments etc.

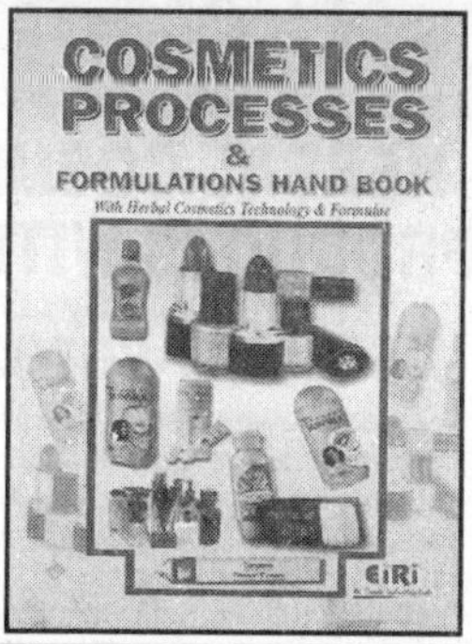

COSMETICS PROCESSES AND FORMULATIONS HAND BOOK (WITH HERBAL COSMETICS TECHNOLOGY & FORMULAE)

By : EIRI BOARD

ISBN. 81-86732-41-1 + Rs. 900/-

Raw Materials used in Cosmetics, Equipments Details, Packaging of Cosmetics, Various Herbal and other Cosmetics manufacturing Technology, Project Profiles, Suppliers of Herbs, Raw Materials and Machinery etc.

ENGINEERS INDIA RESEARCH INSTITUTE Mobile : 9811437895

4449, Nai Sarak, Main Road, Delhi - 110 006 (INDIA) Ph./Fax : 91-11- 23918117, 23916431, 23840361

JUST PUBLISHED-NEW BOOKS

HAND BOOK OF ESSENTIAL OILS MANUFACTURING & AROMATIC PLANTS

By : EIRI BOARD

ISBN. 81-86732-27-6 ✦ Rs. 450/-

Rose oil distillation method, extraction of essential oils, folk medicinal uses of indigenous aromatic plants, essential oil bearing plants status, promising aromatic plants of industrial value, fractionation of essential oil in perfumery & turpentine industry, tagetes minuta, essential oil of hyptis suaveolens poit, super critical fluid extraction technology, citronella oil, clove oil, eucalyptus oil, ginger oil, jasmine rose & lily oil, jasmine flower oil etc.

ESSENTIAL OILS PROCESSES & FORMULATIONS HAND BOOK

By : EIRI BOARD

ISBN. 81-86732-39-X ✦ Rs. 650/-

Essential Oils by Steam Distillation, Essential Oil Lemon Basill, Processing of Fresh Ginger, GC-MS studies, Essential Oil from Cinnamomum, Quality evaluation of sandalwood oil, Kewda flower distillation, Composition of essential oil from bottle brush, Essentioal Oil of Ocimum basilicum L., Composition of essential oil from flowers of Keora, Pesticidal properties of sub-critically extracted plant essential oiis, Manufacturers/Exporters/Importers & Traders of Essential oils & Aromatic Chemicals with Machinery Suppliers.

AGRO BASED HAND BOOK OF CULTIVATION, PLANTATION & FARMING

By : EIRI BOARD

ISBN. 81-86732-29-2 ✦ Rs. 500/-

The Book Covers Aonla, Chilli, Cut Flowers, Fish farming, Herbs Cultivation, Mango, Neem Cultivations, Poplar Tree Plantation, Rice Cultivation & Manufacturers of Agricultural Equipments &Implements of Agricultural Fertilizer, Seed, Chemicals etc.

HERBAL COSMETICS & BEAUTY PRODUCTS WITH FORMULATIONS

By : EIRi BOARD

ISBN. 81-86732-45-4 ✦ Rs. 750/-

The Book covers Useful Cosmetic herbs, List of Common Cosmetic Herbs their active constituents and cosmetic applications, Plant and Equipments used to produce Herbal Cosmetics, Herbal Extraction, Packaging of Herbal Cosmetics, Herbal Cosmetic Technology with their Formulations Details of Setting up a Herbal Beauty Parlour, Herbal Beauty Products manufacture etc.

ENGINEERS INDIA RESEARCH INSTITUTE **Mobile : 9811437895**

4449, Nai Sarak, Main Road, Delhi - 110 006 (INDIA) Ph./Fax : 91-11- 23918117, 23916431, 23840361

JUST PUBLISHED-NEW BOOKS

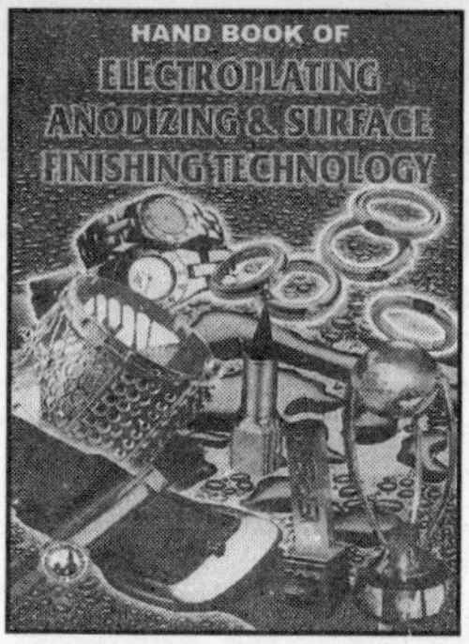

HAND BOOK OF ELECTROPLATING, ANODIZING & SURFACE FINISHING TECHNOLOGY

By : EIRI BOARD

ISBN. 81-86732-33-0 + Rs. 750/-

The book covers New & latest technology of Electroplating, Anodizing & Metal Treatments. The main chapters are principles of electroplating, technology of cleaning, pickling & dipping, electrolytic & chemical processes for the polishing of metals, nickel plating, chromium plating, hard chromium plating, copper plating, electroforming, brass plating, silver plating, gold plating, cadmium plating, zinc plating, the plating of plastics, anodic oxidation of aluminium, phosphating processes, manufacturers/suppliers of machinery & equipments, suppliers of electroplating chemicals & materials etc.

HAND BOOK OF AYURVEDIC & HERBAL MEDICINES WITH FORMULAES

By : EIRI BOARD

ISBN. 81-86732-38-1 + Rs. 750/-

Introduction, Fundamental Principles, Drugs, Cannabis in Ancient Medical Texts, Garlic in Ancient indian Medical Texts, Herbal Tonic, Hypolipidemic herbal compound, Compound for Rheumatoid Arthritis-A, Compound for Rheumatoid Arthritis-B,Compound for migraine, Antidepressive Herbs, Spermatic Tonic,Chyavanprasha Capsules, Alfalfa Tonic, Geriatric Tonic, Herbs for Benign Prostatic Hypertrophy, Herbal Vaginal Pessary, Emmenagogue Compound-A, Emmenagogue Compound-B, Tonic for non-specific Leucorrhoea-A, Tonic For Non-Specific Leucorrhoea-B, Post Parturition Tonic, Galactagogue Tonic, Formulations of ayurvedic & Herbal Medicines and Products, Ayurvedic Churns, Ayurvedic/Herbal Pharmacy, Ayurvedic Pain Balm Ointment (yellow) & pain balm ointment (white) (Zandu Type), Ayurvedic Tables, Details of Plant, Machinery & Equipments Tablet Section, Suppliers of Plant,Machinery and Equipments, Packaging Materials, Manufacturers/dealers of herbs (raw Materials) & Allied Herbal Products.

MODERN PACKAGING TECHNOLOGY FOR PROCESSED FOOD, BAKERY, SNACK FOOD, SPICES & ALLIED FOOD PRODUCTS

By : EIRI BOARD

ISBN. 81-86732-28-4 + Rs. 600/-

Book covers various latest methods of Packaging Technology which are prevailing now-a-days and the book is must for all fruits/veg. growers ,Spices mfrs., Snack food mfrs., Bakery Mfrs. & Edible oil mfrs. etc.

ENGINEERS INDIA RESEARCH INSTITUTE Mobile : 9811437895

4449, Nai Sarak, Main Road, Delhi - 110 006 (INDIA) Ph./Fax : 91-11- 23918117, 23916431, 23840361

JUST PUBLISHED-NEW BOOKS

HAND BOOK OF HERBS, MEDICINAL & AROMATIC PLANTS CULTIVATION

By : EIRI BOARD

ISBN. 81-86732-36-5 + Rs. 650/-

Book covers Aloe Vera, Ashwagandha, Babchi, Belladonna,Buckwheat, Coleus,Costus, Costus, Cowhedge, Datura, Digitalis, Discorea, Duboisa, Foxglove, Geranium, Guggal, Hop, Henna, Isabgol, Liquorice, Lemon Grass, Long Pepper, Neem, Parrot Tree, Perivinkle, Primrose, Pyrethrum, Rauvolfia, Roselle, Roselle, Rutin Bearing Eucalyptus, Rose, Senna, Steroid Bearing Solanum etc.

HAND BOOK OF SYNTHETIC DETERGENTS WITH FORMULATIONS

By : EIRI BOARD

ISBN. 81-86732-43-8 + Rs. 900/-

Group of Synthetic Detergents, Synthesis of Detergents, Manufacture of Synthetic Detergents with Formulae, Testing of Detergents and Soaps, Project Profiles, Suppliers of Machinery and Raw Materials, Acid Slurry, Sirf Excel Type Detergent, Ariel Type Detergent, Dry Mix Process, Dry Clean Unit and much more others.

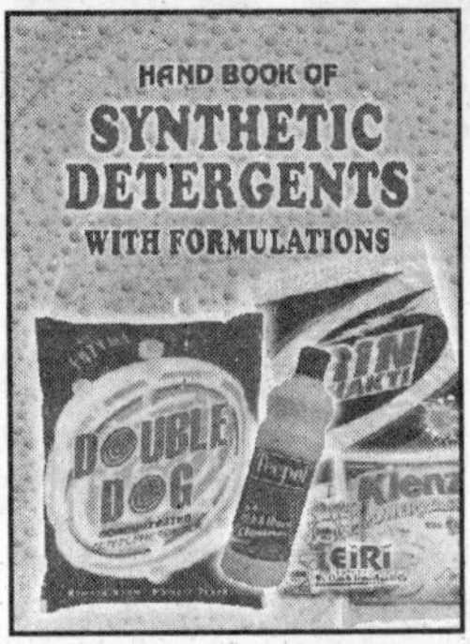

PROFITABLE SMALL SCALE MANUFACTURE OF SOAPS & DETERGENTS

By : EIRI BOARD

ISBN. 81-86732-25-X + Rs. 375/-

The Book is a unique book on soaps & detergents. All the necessary informations to produce soap & detergents have been covered including raw materials, soap manufacture on tiny scale, equipments for tiny/cottage scale soap industry, soap from non edible oil, soap from soap stock, Manufacturing of medicated soap, Shaving soap, shaving creams, synthetic detergent powder, detergent cake and powder, Enzyme detergent powder, Project Profiles on various Soap and Detergent projects, Suppliers of Plant and Machinery and raw materials etc.

TECHNOLOGY OF TEXTILES

By : EIRI BOARD

ISBN. 81-86732-58-9 + Rs. 900/-

The new edition of the book is covering latest technology including dyeing, bleaching, drying, spinning and weaving, gel spinning processes, melt spinning, denim production, properties and applications of super absorbent polymers, mechanical structures problems of staple yarn, advantage multi phase weaving, improving dye uptake of natural fibres, mill vs. powerloom fabrics, processing of lyocell fibres, antibacterial fabric, pre treatment and dyeing of fibre blends with elastane, non apparel applications of weft knitted fabrics, aquatex, making silk fabrics wrinkle free, processing technology for cotton garments, project profiles on readymade garments, necktie, hosiery, socks knitting, powerloom, cotton yarn etc., equipments suppliers, cotton fabrics suppliers etc.

ENGINEERS INDIA RESEARCH INSTITUTE Mobile : 9811437895

4449, Nai Sarak, Main Road, Delhi - 110 006 (INDIA) Ph./Fax : 91-11- 23918117, 23916431, 23840361

JUST PUBLISHED-NEW BOOKS

START YOUR OWN COLD STORAGE UNIT

By : EIRI BOARD

ISBN. 81-86732-20-9 + Rs. 375/-

The book covers Special features of Cold Storage Project, Brief about Refrigerated Cold Storage, BIS Specifications, Selection of the Location for Cold Storage, Production Details and Process, Operating Conditions, Principles of Fresh Food Storage, Refrigeration, Technical and Design Section, Refrigerated Cold Storage Design, Quotations of Different Capacity of Cold Storage Plant, Details of Plant and Machinery etc. Project Profiles of various size of cold storage units, Suppliers of Cold Storage Machinery etc.

SYNTHETIC RESINS TECHNOLOGY WITH FORMULATIONS

By : EIRI BOARD

ISBN. 81-86732-40-3 + Rs. 800/-

Book covers latest technology to manufacture various Synthetic Resins with formulae including epoxy resin, alkyd resins, acrylics, ion-exchange resin, melamine formaldehyde resin, phenol formaldehyde resin, polyester resin, polyvinyl acetate, polyvinyl alcohol, pvc resin and plastisol, silicones, urea formaldehyde resins etc. Suppliers of Machinery and Raw Materials.

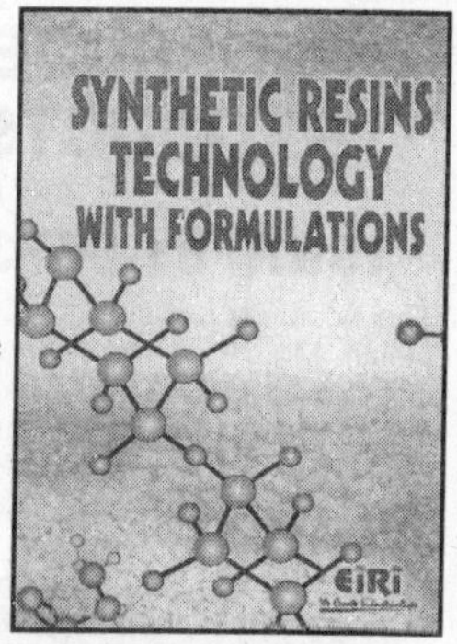

PAINT VARNISH SOLVENTS AND COATING TECHNOLOGY

By : EIRI BOARD

ISBN. 81-86732-44-6 + Rs. 750/-

Introduction, General Pigments Physical Properties, Pigments Processing, Plasticizers and Solvents, Synthetic Resins, Cellulose Ester and Ether Products, Varnishes, Pigmentation, Paints (Decorative & Building), Coatings, Industrial Paints & Coatings, Industrial Finishes, Miscellaneous Coatings and Ancillary Materials, Testing and Evaluation, Miscellaneous Formulae, Project Profiles of Aluminium Paints, Cement Paints, Acrylic Emulsion Paints, Insulating Varnish, Powder Coating & many others. Suppliers of Raw Materials, Suppliers of Plant and Machinery, Present Manufacturers, Packaging Material Addresses and many other details.

FRUITS & VEGETABLES PROCESSING HAND BOOK

By : EIRI BOARD

ISBN. 81-86732-33-2 + Rs. 650/-

Preservation principles, Canning of fruits & vegetables, Spoilage in canned foods, Fruit juices squashes & cordials, Fruit beverages, Jams & jellies, Tomato products, Pickles, Sauces & chutney, Canned fruit & vegetables, Canning of fruits, Dehydration of fruit/vegetable, Frozen foods, Fruit juices making, Frozen meat, Mango processing & canning, Pickle, Processed food, Details of machineries, Manufacturers/suppliers of plant, Equipments & machineries, Manufacturers/suppliers of packaging materials, Manufacturers/suppliers of raw materials.

ENGINEERS INDIA RESEARCH INSTITUTE Mobile : 9811437895

4449, Nai Sarak, Main Road, Delhi - 110 006 (INDIA) Ph./Fax : 91-11- 23918117, 23916431, 23840361

JUST PUBLISHED-NEW BOOKS

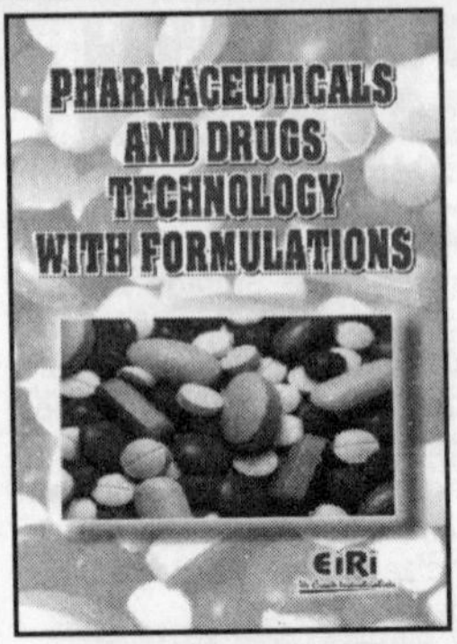

PHARMACEUTICALS AND DRUGS TECHNOLOGY WITH FORMULATIONS

By : EIRI BOARD OF CONSULTANTS & ENGINEERS

ISBN. 81-86732-52-7 + Rs. 950/-

Tablet and Capsules, Oral Preparations, External Preparations, Preparations for the Eye, Antibiotics, Formulations, Packaging, Tablets, Injectables, Liquid Orals, Capsules and Dry Syrups, Eye and Ear Preparations, Topical Preparations

MILK PROCESSING & DAIRY PRODUCTS INDUSTRIES

By : EIRI BOARD

ISBN. 81-86732-47-0 + Rs. 750/-

The Book has just published and covers following Contents : Known Indian Milk Products, Cheese, Butter, Yoghurt, Evaporated and Condensed Milks, Dried Milk/Milk Powder, Ice-Cream, Some Dried Dairy Products, Market Dahi and Pure Culture Dahi, Packaging of Milk, Packaging of Milk and Milk Products In India, Packaging Trends for Cheese and other Dairy Products, Milk-Based Soft Drink With Longer Shelf-Life, Fermented Milk Products-Flavour and Bio-technolgoy, Losses and their Possible Management In Dairy Industry, Cultured Milk Products in Human Nutrition, Freeze-Dried Starter Cultures In Fermented Dairy Products Manufacture, Dairy Products, Products Diversification In Dairy Industry, Coffee Complete, Paneer, Cheese from Buffalo Milk, Whey Protein Concentrate, Production of Yoghurt, Tea Complete, Casein from Milk, Dairy Farm, Flavoured Milk, Dairy Farm to Produce Milk, Ice Cream & Ice-Candy, Processed Cheese, Milk Powder & Ghee, Soya Milk and Paneer, Lactose and By Products Processing from Milk, Condensed Milk (Sweetened), Butter Milk, Toned Milk, Dairy Products and Milk Packaging in Pouches, Soya Milk and Tofu, Details of Machineries Used in Dairy Farms and Products, Suppliers of Plant and Machineries.

HAND BOOK OF ADHESIVES WITH THEIR FORMULAES

By : EIRI BOARD

ISBN. 81-86732-34-9 + Rs. 650/-

The Book covers Adhesive Concept and Terminology, Selecting an Adhesive, Hot Melt Adhesive, Pressure Sensitive Adhesive, Water Based Adhesive, Testing of Adhesives, Adhesive Materials, Formulations and Applications, EVA Emulsion Adhesives, Rubber Based Adhesives, Butyl and Poly Iso Butylene Rubber Adhesives, Nitrile Rubber Adhesives, SBR Adhesives, Thermoplastic Rubber Based Adhesives, Polychloroprene Adhesives, Polysulphide Sealants and Adhesives, Epoxy Resin Adhesives, Polyurethane Adhesives, Acrylic Adhesives, Cyanoacrylate Adhesives, Anaerobic Adhesives, Polyamide Adhesives, Natural Resin Based Adhesives, Dextrin Based Adhesives, Casein Glue, Soyabean Adhesives, Animal Glue, Rosin Adhesives, Other Various Adhesives, Pressure Sen. Tapes and Labels, Test Methods, Suppliers of Machinery and Raw Materials etc.

ENGINEERS INDIA RESEARCH INSTITUTE Mobile : 9811437895

4449, Nai Sarak, Main Road, Delhi - 110 006 (INDIA) Ph./Fax : 91-11- 23918117, 23916431, 23840361

JUST PUBLISHED-NEW BOOKS

TECHNOLOGY OF BUILDING MATERIALS AND CHEMICALS WITH PROCESSES

By : EIRI BOARD

ISBN. 81-86732-54-3 + Rs. 950/-

The book covers Details of Construction Chemicals, Super Plasticizers in Concrete, Mineral Admixtures, Concrete Blocks from Bricks, Extruded Clay Products, Light Weight Building Materials, Calcium Silicate Bricks, Flyash Lime Bricks, Rigid PVC Foam Sheets, Precast Hollow Core Slabs, Calcium Silicate Bricks, Blocks and Tiles, Fibreglass Reinforced Plastics Water Storage Tanks, Fibreglass Products, Ready Mixed Concrete, Timber Subsitutes, Clay-Flyash Bricks, Reinforced Flyash Brickwork, Glass Fibre Reinforced Plastics, Gypsum Plaster Boards, Precast Solid Cement Concrete Blocks, Precast Concrete Stone Masonry Blocks, Hollow or Solid Lightweight Concrete Masonry Units, Reinforced Concrete Door and Window Frames, Ferrocement Door Shutters, Precast Concrete Manhole Covers and Frames, Details of Machineries, Manufacturing of Mosaic Tiles, Mini Cement Plant, High Alumina Cement, Automatic Brick Plant, Glazed Ceramic Tiles, Polymeric Roofing Felt, Suppliers of Plant and Machinery, Suppliers of Raw Materials.

MANUFACTURE OF HOUSEHOLD SOAPS, TOILET SOAPS & OTHER SOAPS WITH FORMULATIONS

By : EIRI BOARD

ISBN. 81-86732-53-5 + Rs. 750/-

Soap base manufacture, Solid, household and toilet soaps manufacture, Raw materials for soap industry, Oils, fats and their pretreatment, Manufacture, purification of fatty acid and production of soap base, Recovery and refining of glycerine, Perfuming of soaps and detergents, Testing of soaps and detergents, Manufacturing process and formulations of various soaps, Miscellaneous formulae, Scourig bar, Detergent cake & powder, Toilet & herbal soap, Laundry soap, Liquid soap, Nerol laundry soap, Liquid shoe polish puff, Soap stone powder from raw soap stone, Complete plant Suppliers, Suppliers of fragrances, flavours, perfumes for soaps, Suppliers of soapc manufacturing chemicals, Present manufacturers etc.

स्मॉल एवं कॉटेज स्केल इण्डस्ट्रीज (लघु उद्योग)

By : EIRI BOARD

ISBN. 81-86732-55-1+ Rs. 525/-

यह पुस्तक हिन्दी भाषा में नया व्यवसाय शुरू करने वालों के लिए छापी गयी है। पुस्तक में लघु उद्योग शुरू करने से सम्बन्धित सभी जरूरी जानकारियां दी गई है। पुस्तक के कुछ संक्षिप्त विवरण इस प्रकार हैं: लघु उद्योग शुरू करने सम्बन्धी उपयोगी मार्गदर्शन एवं उन्हे मिलनेवाली सरकारी सुविधाएँ, पंजीकरण एवं अन्य कार्य, लघु उद्योग के सहायतार्थ संस्थाएं, कपड़े धोने और स्नान के साबुन, तरल तथा ठोस फिनायल, लिपस्टिक, लिपग्लॉस व लोशन, शेविगं क्रीम व लोशन्स, शैम्पू तथा हेयर वाश, हेयर आयल्स व ब्रिलियण्टाइन, काली मेहंदी, खिजाब व हेयर ब्लीच, फेस टैल्कम तथा बेबी पाउडर, टूथ पेस्ट तथा माउथ, स्याही उद्योग, फिनायल उद्योग, आतिशबाजी, रबर उद्योग, ड्राइंग-कलर निर्माण, गंधरहित डमी अगरबत्तियाँ, परम्परागत धूपबत्तियाँ, कृत्रिम सुगन्धों, पोली बैग तथा पोली पाउच, कॉरोगेटेड बोर्ड और डिब्बे, पेन, बालपेन व रिफिल, पटेटो चिप्स तथा वेफर्स, पॉपकॉर्न, डेयरी प्रोडक्ट्स, आइस कैण्डी उद्योग, दियासलाई उद्योग, रेडीमेड गारमेण्ट उद्योग, पी.वी.सी. केबल, हॉबी सेन्टर, महिला हेल्थ क्लब, ब्यूटी पार्लर, निटिंग, सुगंधित सुपारी, मशीनों व कच्चा माल के बनाने व बेचने वालों के पते। पुस्तक में सभी उद्योगों की आय व्यय योजना (प्रोजेक्ट प्रोफाइल) भी दी गई है ताकि उद्योग चुनने से पहिले ही अपनी जेब के अनुसार उद्योग चुना जा सके।

HAND BOOK OF OILS, FATS & DERIVATIVES WITH REFINING & PACKAGING TECHNOLOGY

By : EIRI BOARD

ISBN. 81-86732-56-X + Rs. 950/-

Oil Bearing Materials Derivated, Oilseeds carrying Soap making Oils, Oilseeds from Shrubs, Vegetable Oils, Oilseeds from Fruits, Oils/Fats Extraction, Fats and Oil Refining, Hydrogenation, Packaging, Fatty Acids, Glycerine, Fat Splitting, Protein Meals, Oleochemicals, Coconut Oils, Ghani Oils, Groundnut Oil, Plant Economics and Suppliers Addresses of Machinery etc.

ENGINEERS INDIA RESEARCH INSTITUTE Mobile : 9811437895

4449, Nai Sarak, Main Road, Delhi - 110 006 (INDIA) Ph./Fax : 91-11- 23918117, 23916431, 23840361

JUST PUBLISHED-NEW BOOKS

HAND BOOK OF CONFECTIONERY WITH FORMULATIONS

By : EIRI BOARD

ISBN. 81-86732-35-7 + Rs. 600/-

The book is covering Confectionery Processes & formulations, Caramels Toffees, Butterscotch Fudge, Chocolates, Supari, Nougat, Soft Nougat, Milk Toffee, Chocolate & Confectionery Spreads Chocolates Syrups, Multiple Confectionery Bars, Project Profiles, Details of Plant & Machinery,Addresses of Suppliers of Machinery, Raw Materials & Packaging Materials etc. Actual photographs of Plant and Machineries used to manufacture Confectionery items.

HAND BOOK OF BAKERY INDUSTRIES

By : EIRI BOARD

ISBN. 81-86732-8-7 + Rs. 350/-

Book covers Bakery Raw Materials, Bread Making Processes, Biscuits, Cookies & Crackers, Sponge Cakes, Pies & Puff Pastries, Sweet Yeast Dough Products, Bakery Machinery, Confectionery, Process, Packaging for Biscuits, Project Profile of Bakery, Cofectionery, Bubble Gum Plant etc., Manufacturers & Suppliers of Plant & Machineries, Manufacturers & Suppliers of Raw Materials and many other relevant details for new comers in this field.

PLASTIC COMPOUNDING MASTERBATCHES, PET AND OTHER PLASTIC PROCESSING INDUSTRIES

By : EIRI BOARD

ISBN. 81-86732-49-7 + Rs. 750/-

The book covers almost all the basic and advanced details to setup own Plastic Processing Industry. The new edition of the book is covering latest technology including Polyethylene, Extrusion, Injection Moulding, Blowmoulding, Polyester Terephthalate (PET), Rotational Moulding, Post Extrusion Process, Vacuum Metallizing, Identification of Plastic Materials, Thermosetting Plastics, Recycling, Additives for Polymers, Virgin Quality from Reprocessed, Specialty Additives and Masterbatches, PVC Compounding with Formulations, Automobile Injection Moulded Plastic Components, Colour Master Batch for various Plastics, Compact Disks, Co-Extruded Multilayer Film and Laminated Multilayer Film, Egg Trays from Plastics, Ethylene Vinyl Acetate Sheet and Sole, Polypropylene Multifilament Spinning Yarn, Plastic Films and Sheets with Printing, Plastic Granules from Fresh Resin, Plastic Injection Moulding Products, Plastic Mats, PET Bottles from Pre-form, PET Pre-form from PET Resin, PVC Pipes and Fittings, PVC Extrusion Profiles, Computer Ribbon Cartridges, HDPE/PP Woven Sacks (Bags), Semi-Conductive Compounds and Masterbatches, Plastic Sutli, Disposable Plastic Syringes, Plastic Water Storage Tanks, Thermocole Based Disposable Glass, Cups and Plates, Plastic GranulesCross Linked Polyethylene (XLPE) Compound for XLPE Cables, Suppliers of Plant, Equipments & Machineries, Suppliers of Raw Materials etc.

ENGINEERS INDIA RESEARCH INSTITUTE Mobile : 9811437895

4449, Nai Sarak, Main Road, Delhi - 110 006 (INDIA) Ph./Fax : 91-11- 23918117, 23916431, 23840361